NALOPAKHYANAM
STORY OF NALA

NALOPAKHYANAM
STORY OF NALA

MONIER-WILLIAMS

GYAN

Published by

Gyan Publishing House
5, Ansari Road
Daryaganj, New Delhi-110002
Phone: 011-47034999, 9811692060
E-mail: books@gyanbooks.com

Distribution Network
gyanbooks.com
India, USA, Canada, UK, Australia

ISBN: 978-93-7097-088-5 (HB)

First Published, 1879

2nd Impression 2025

Printed at: Gyan Press, Delhi.

NALOPAKHYANAM STORY OF NALA
Author: MONIER-WILLIAMS

STORY OF NALA.

MONIER WILLIAMS.

NALOPÁKHYÁNAM.

STORY OF NALA,

AN EPISODE OF THE MAHÁ-BHÁRATA:

THE SANSKṚIT TEXT,

WITH A COPIOUS VOCABULARY

AND

AN IMPROVED VERSION OF DEAN MILMAN'S TRANSLATION,

BY

MONIER WILLIAMS, M.A., D.C.L.,

HON. LL.D. OF THE UNIVERSITY OF CALĆUTTA,

HON. MEMBER OF THE BOMBAY ASIATIC SOCIETY,

BODEN PROFESSOR OF SANSKṚIT IN THE UNIVERSITY OF OXFORD.

M DCCC LXXIX.

PREFACE.

THE Story of Nala, as told in the following pages, is an episode of the Mahá-bhárata, one of the two great Epic poems of the Hindús, containing no less than 107,389 ślokas or stanzas. It is extracted from the sixth chapter (fifty-third section) of the third Book or Vana-parvan. Like the rest of the Mahá-bhárata, its authorship is attributed to Kṛishṇa-Dvaipáyana, who is called Vyása, because he *arranged* the Vedas [1]. It is not to be supposed, however, that the Vedas and Mahá-bhárata are really the work of the same author. The Vedas are many centuries older than the great Epic poem, and each is the composition of several authors. Probably an interval of several centuries separates the more ancient hymns of the Veda from the more modern; and a similar or perhaps greater separation may be observed between the older parts of the Mahá-bhárata and the more modern interpolations.

By ascribing this work to Vyása—who is also the reputed author of the Vedánta philosophy—it is merely implied that, at some time or other, order and sequence were given to what

---

[1] *Vivyása vedán yasmát sa tasmád vyása iti smṛitaḥ.* Mahá-bh. I. 2417. He was called *Kṛishṇa* from his dark complexion, and *Dvaipáyana* because he was brought forth by Satyavatí on an *island* in the Jumná, his father being the Ṛishi Paráśara. *Nyasto* dvípe *sa yad bálas tasmád Dvaipáyanaḥ smṛitaḥ,* line 2416.

was before a mere congeries of distinct compositions by various authors.

Part of the Mahá-bhárata is considered by some[1] to be as old as the fourth century B.C.; but all Hindú chronology is more or less conjectural; and it would be impossible to fix with certainty the date of the composition of any of the principal episodes. The Story of Nala is not part of the main plot of the poem, and probably belongs to a much earlier period of Indian history. The subject of the great Epic is the war between the Kurus or hundred sons of Dhṛita-ráshṭra and their cousins the five sons of Páṇḍu. But about this leading-thread are collected a vast number of ancient legends and traditions, under the weight of which it is often lost, if not altogether broken. In all Oriental books of fables it is common for the principal narrative to be interrupted by a series of stories within stories, loosely connected with the original theme, and often completely overlaying it. So it is with the Mahá-bhárata. The episodes form by far the greater portion of the poem, and generally intervene to break the chain of the narrative, when the incidents are most stirring and the interest is most at its height. The war between the rival princes is doubtless founded on fact; and much valuable matter has been extracted from the narrative by Professor Lassen and other Sanskritists, in elucidation of the early history of India. According to the Vishṇu-Puráṇa, Dhṛita-ráshṭra and Páṇḍu were the sons of the widow of Vićitra-vírya by his half-brother Vyása or Kṛishṇa-Dvaipáyana[2]. This Vićitra-vírya

[1] See my 'Indian Wisdom' (W. H. Allen & Co., London), p. 317.

[2] As Vićitra-vírya (Vyása's half-brother) died without children, the Hindú law, like the Mosaic, permitted Vyása to raise up offspring to his deceased brother. Satyavatí, mother of Vyása, was afterwards wife of S'ántanu.

was the son of Śántanu, who was the twenty-third in descent from Kuru, a celebrated prince of the Lunar race, himself the ninth king after Bharata, son of Dushyanta and Śakuntalá, from whom India is to this day called Bhárata-varsha. Vyása is thus reputed to be the actual grandfather of the princes whose quarrels and jealousies are narrated in the poem he is said to have arranged; and, from the genealogy, it is evident that although the sons of Dhṛita-ráshṭra are more usually called the descendants of Kuru, the sons of Páṇḍu were really descended from the same race.

The royal races of India are said to have diverged into two great lines, called Solar and Lunar. The hero of the Solar line, which commenced in Ikshváku, was Ráma-ćandra [1], whose contests with the barbarous tribes of the south of India is described in the Rámáyaṇa, the more ancient of the two great Epics. The Kurus and Páṇḍavas, as equally descendants of Kuru, belonged to the Lunar line, and probably represented different branches of one tribe of Sanskṛit-speaking immigrants, who arrived in India at different times. According to the Mahá-bhárata, Páṇḍu, the father of the five Páṇḍavas, after yielding the succession to his blind brother Dhṛita-ráshṭra, retired to the mountains and died. His five boys were then adopted by Dhṛita-ráshṭra and educated with his own large family of a hundred sons. After escaping many dangers from the malevolence of their cousins, they were ultimately permitted to share with them in the sovereignty. Yudhishṭhira, the eldest of the Páṇḍavas, and his four brothers ruled at Indra-prastha (the modern Delhi), and Duryodhana with his ninety-nine brothers (usually

[1] This Ráma, who is the most celebrated incarnation of Vishṇu, must not be confounded with the two inferior Rámas, Paraśu-Ráma and Bala-Ráma. See my Sanskṛit Dictionary (published at the Clarendon Press) under *Ráma*.

called the Kurus) were sovereigns at the neighbouring town of Hastiná-pura. The Páṇḍavas, whose disposition was as amiable as that of the Kurus was malevolent, seem to have been very successful in subduing the districts contiguous to their own; and, notwithstanding the animosity of their neighbouring cousins, to have attained considerable prosperity. A great misfortune, however, overtakes them. Tempted to amuse themselves with dice, and yielding to a weakness which has ever been a fashionable failing amongst the Hindús, Yudhishṭhira loses all his possessions, at a game of hazard, to his cousin Duryodhana: and, retiring with his brethren into exile, lives for twelve years in the forest (vana). It is to console them under their affliction that the sage Vṛihadaśva relates to king Yudhishṭhira the Story of Nala, who, himself a virtuous monarch, lost his kingdom also through his passion for dice; but after suffering great hardships again recovered it.

The following short summary of the Story of Nala may be useful as an introduction to the study of the poem.

Nala, who is described as 'gifted with choicest virtues,' and is especially noted for his skill in driving, has only one fault, the inherent love of gambling[1]. He was king of Nishadha, a country in central India, in the S. E. division, whence his other name of Naishadha. In a neighbouring country, called Vidarbha (the modern Berár), reigned Bhíma, whose only daughter, Damayantí, was so beautiful that her fame reached the ears of Nala. His interest in her being excited, was fanned into a flame by the following incident:—

Walking in his garden one day, and seeing some swans

[1] The epithet *aksha-priya*, 'fond of dice,' is applied to Nala in enumerating his good qualities (verse 3), and Kali, therefore, only assailed him in his weak point. See, however, the vocabulary under *aksha-priya*.

disporting themselves near him, the fancy takes him to catch one out of sport. The bird, addressing him in human language, promises, if he will release it, to fly to Damayantí and praise Nala in her presence. This plan being agreed upon and carried into effect, Damayantí becomes duly inspired with a passion for Nala. Bhíma, her father, seeing his daughter pining in secret, determines to celebrate her Svayaṃvara, that is, to proclaim the public choice of a husband by Damayantí, according to the custom of that age. All the princes of India, including Nala, flock to Vidarbha, as suitors for the hand of Damayantí. The gods also, hearing of her beauty, resolve to be present; and, meeting Nala on their road to the Svayaṃvara, commission him to plead their cause with Damayantí. He confesses himself enamoured also, and entreats to be excused; but being adjured sternly, promises to deliver their message, and is introduced by them unseen into the palace. There he has an interview with Damayantí, who, slighting the message of the gods, confesses her love to Nala, and her intention to choose him and him only. Accordingly, at the Svayaṃvara, in spite of the artifice of the deities who assume Nala's shape, she detects her lover by his shadow, (the gods having none,) and selects him. It appears that at the time of the Svayaṃvara, Kali, an evil genius, the fourth Age of the world or Vice personified, had set out for Vidarbha with the intention of making Damayantí his consort; but, hearing of the completion of the marriage-ceremony, he resolves out of jealousy to work the ruin of Nala. For twelve years he watches his opportunity, and at last, detecting Nala in some trifling neglect of his ablutions, enters and acquires power over his body. Infatuating his victim, he instigates him to play at dice with his brother Pushkara. The game goes on for many months; and Nala, after losing his kingdom and all his possessions, is driven with Damayantí into exile. In the forest, Nala, still infatuated by Kali, deserts Damayantí; who, wandering alone, and escaping many perils, at last finds a refuge at the court of the king of Ćedi. Meanwhile, Nala, passing through the forest, rescues a serpent from a flaming bush. This serpent turns out to be Karkoṭaka, one of the principal Nágas (see vocabulary under नाग) or semi-divine beings inhabiting the regions under the earth. In return for the service rendered by Nala, Karkoṭaka promises to deliver Nala from the power of Kali. He accordingly metamorphoses Nala into a dwarfish charioteer, but gives him a magic garment, by assuming which he can at any time regain his proper form. Nala, now transformed to the short-armed Váhuka, enters the service of Ṛituparṇa, king of Ayodhyá, a monarch celebrated for his skill in dice. Meanwhile, king Bhíma, searching the world for his lost daughter, discovers her at length at Ćedi, and sends for her thence to his own capital. There, pining for the lost Nala, she devises a plan to recover him. Suspecting that he is living, disguised as Váhuka, with Ṛituparṇa, king of Ayodhyá, she causes the latter to be told that king Bhíma would celebrate on the morrow a second Svayaṃvara for his daughter Damayantí. Ṛituparṇa determines to be present, but can only be so by the help of his charioteer Váhuka, whose skill in horsemanship enables him to drive from Ayodhyá to Vidarbha in one day. On the road Nala, disguised as Váhuka, agrees to impart to Ṛituparṇa his knowledge of horsemanship in return for that monarch's skill in dice. They make the exchange, and, arriving at Ayodhyá, Nala re-assumes his own form and is restored to his wife. Returning with her to Nishadhá, he seeks Pushkara, renews the game, and wins back his kingdom. Then, with noble generosity, he forgives Pushkara, and enters on a long and happy reign with his consort Damayantí.

That this Story of Nala, however comparatively modern the version in the Mahá-bhárata, is of great antiquity, may be proved by internal evidence. The prominence given to the deities Indra, Agni, Varuṇa, and Yama, and the absence of all allusion to the great Hindú Triad, connect the narrative more with the Vedic than the Epic and Puránic periods[1]. If Nala was of the Solar race, as represented by Kálidása, he must have been the fourth from the great Ráma, son of Daśa-ratha, the genealogy, according to the Raghu-vanśa, running thus:—Raghu, Aja, Daśa-ratha, Ráma, Kuśa, Atithi, Nishadha, Nala, Nabhas. But if he belonged to the Lunar dynasty, reigning at Nishadha, when Ṛituparṇa of the Solar race reigned at Ayodhyá, then we must assign him a much earlier date, and place him fourteen reigns before Ráma.

The story, no doubt, rests on a foundation of fact, and, on account of its age, is a favourite subject with Hindú poets. It not only appears as an episode to the Mahá-bhárata, but forms the subject of two other celebrated poems, one called the Nalodaya, attributed to the great Kálidása, the author of Śakuntalá; and the other called the Naishadha, written by Śrí Harsha. It is also introduced by Somadeva Bhaṭṭa into his collection of stories called Kathá-sarit-ságara, and told there with variations. It is, moreover, the subject-matter of a very curious composition, half prose, half verse, called Ćampú,

[1] According to Professor Brockhaus, the personification of Kali as the demon of the fourth Age, and not of the dice, shews that the modern arranger of the story did not understand this old Vedic term, and is another proof of the earlier existence of the Nala. The word Tretá (which denotes the second Age of the world) is also used for a throw of dice. See the second Act of the Mṛiććhakaṭi.

by an author named Tri-vikrama, and of a well-known work in Tamil, called the Nala-Rájá, and again of another in Telugu, by the poet Rághava, written about A. D. 1650; these latter poems being independent compositions, and not mere translations from the Sanskṛit.

It is a noteworthy circumstance in the history of Indian literature, that the later Hindú poets, with much exuberance of fancy, displayed little originality in their conceptions. Whether they thought it a sacred duty to follow in the beaten track, or whether their inventive faculties were feeble, it rarely enters into their heads to devise a new story for themselves. They content themselves with the regular stock materials, and exercise their ingenuity either in diluting them or serving them up in a concentrated form, with here and there a few embellishments or additions of their own. The two Epic poems are their grand repertories. These gigantic compositions, like vast national banks with inexhaustible resources, are drawn upon freely by every poet. The history of Ráma, which is narrated at full length in the Rámáyaṇa, is condensed into moderate dimensions by Kálidása in his Raghu-vanśa, reduced to a mere table of contents by Bhaṭṭi in his grammatical poem, and represented with dramatic richness of detail by Bhava-bhúti in his well-known play, the Uttara-Ráma-ćaritra. Then we have a celebrated poet Mágha, writing his epic on a story taken from the seventh chapter of the second Book or Sabhá-parva of the Mahábhárata (the destruction of Śiśupála, king of Ćedi, by Kṛishṇa); and the poet Bháravi, the author of another well-known Epic called Kirátárjuníya (or the contest of Arjuna with Śiva as a mountaineer), selecting his subject from the fourth chapter of the third Book or Vana-parva of the same great poem. One advantage of this is, that if we have not a variety of subjects, we have at least a diversity of styles. The same subject could not be treated by every author in the same way. We have, therefore, specimens of every shade of composition between the most tedious diffuseness and the most laconic curtness,—the most turgid ornament and the most severe simplicity. In no other language but the ductile, flexible, and infinitely copious Sanskṛit could such opposite extremes be possible. The very same idea which by one author is expressed with a brevity unapproachable in English, is by another expanded and beaten out till the substance of the original metal almost disappears. In the one case we have every needless word rejected, and the meaning so obscured, that sentences have to be interpreted like oracles, and every line of text to be illustrated by pages of commentary; in the other, huge compounds are introduced, epithets heaped on epithets, metaphors on metaphors, till the mind of the venturesome reader is hopelessly bewildered. This is what has happened to the Story of Nala. Presented to us in the plainest manner in the Mahá-bhárata, it is condensed in the Nalodaya with a compression and concentration absolutely painful; in the Naishadha it is diluted by prolix descriptions or overdone with rich imagery; in Somadeva's Kathá-sarit-ságara it is again exhibited in its simple form; whilst in Tri-vikrama's Ćampú it is buried under a dead weight of long words, ponderous compounds, and inflated periods.

The main features of the present edition of the Mahá-bhárata version of the Nala will be patent at once.

In the first place, it presents, as far as possible, a pure and accurate text. Excellent MSS. of the Mahá-bhárata, belonging to the India Office and Bodleian Libraries, have been at my command, and the text of the following pages is the result of a careful collation of these with the various printed editions already before the public.

With regard to the vocabulary appended to this work, I have only to say that I have spared no pains to make it more complete than that of the first edition, and to bring it into harmony with the fourth edition of my Sanskṛit Grammar, also published by the Delegates of the Clarendon Press. The amount of labour entailed by a glossary of this kind is only to be appreciated by those who have themselves undergone it. I believe this to be the only vocabulary in which each word, as it stands in the text, whatever be its form, either of case or tense, or whatever the change in that form resulting from the rules of euphony, occupies its proper alphabetical place. Those who have had experience in teaching will understand the value of this aid to students just beginning to read a language abounding in intricate combinations and perplexing euphonic changes. There cannot be a greater mistake than to suppose that the amount of assistance required in a Sanskṛit vocabulary is to be measured by that given in Greek or Latin glossaries. We have in Sanskṛit two peculiarities. One is the constant use of long compound words; the other is the habit of joining words together by a strict system of euphony, which, though not carried to the same extreme in all printed books, must always be a source of perplexity. The learner has to make repeated references to his vocabulary, and every facility should be accorded to him. I have known pupils, who have worked their way steadily through the grammar, puzzle themselves hopelessly over the following three words in the first story of the Hitopadeśa, *visarpan tán taṇḍulakaṇán*, because, in accordance with euphonic laws, these words are printed in the text thus,—*visarpanstánstaṇḍulakaṇán* (विसर्प-

स्तांस्तण्डुलकणान्), while the original words, in their unchanged form, are exhibited in the glossary. If the words were divided, the difficulty would not be insurmountable: but not finding विसर्पंस्, the student concludes that he has mistaken the division. Referring again to the vocabulary, he finds वि and सर्पं, and taking these for his first words goes entirely wrong. Now according to my method, as before explained, the words would be separated in the text thus, —*visarpans táns taṇḍulakaṇán;* and they would moreover be so exhibited in their proper places in the glossary, an explication of the euphonic changes being added. In all cases where separation is undesirable, as when two vowels blend into one, or when a final *i* or *u* has been changed to *y* or *v*, the whole combination is given, and the division of the words indicated.

I believe the present vocabulary will be found to contain every word in the text. If each separate article is not always as full of details as might be expected, it should be borne in mind that the perfection of a special work of this kind consists in its not being burdened with more words and meanings than are wanted for the one book which it elucidates. Moreover, the grammar is intended to go hand in hand with the vocabulary, and a complete explanation of a difficulty is often to be sought in the rules to which constant reference is made.

With regard to the metrical translation which accompanies this edition of the Nala, the late Dean Milman, shortly before his death, kindly adopted many of my suggestions for the improvement of his original version, so as to adapt it more closely to the text. Its continued use has revealed the need of further slight alterations, which I have been obliged to make on my own responsibility.

The metre of the Sanskṛit text never varies from the regular śloka measure called Anushṭubh, an account of which, with a table of all the most common varieties of metre, is given at the end of the fourth edition of my Sanskṛit Grammar, published at the Clarendon Press. It consists of sixteen syllables to the half-line or thirty-two to each verse of two lines.

The first line of the poem serves as a model for the whole, and with the exception of the six syllables, whose quantities are here marked by the usual prosodial marks (⏑ – – || ⏑ – ⏑), the poet is allowed the option of either long or short:

ásíd rájá nălō nāma || vírasenasŭtō bălí.

Occasionally the 6th and 7th syllables are short instead of long.

M. W.

Oxford, June 1879.

॥ नलोपाख्यानम् ॥

STORY OF NALA.

॥ नलोपाख्यानम् ॥

वृहदश्व उवाच ।

आसीद् राजा नलो नाम वीरसेनसुतो बली ।
उपपन्नो गुणैर् इष्टै रूपवान् अश्वकोविदः ॥१॥
अतिष्ठद् मनुजेन्द्राणां मूर्ध्नि देवपतिर् इव ।
उपर्युपरि सर्वेषाम् आदित्य इव तेजसा ॥२॥
ब्रह्मण्यो वेदविच् छूरो निषधेषु महीपतिः ।
अक्षप्रियः सत्यवादी महान् अक्षौहिणीपतिः ॥३॥
ईप्सितो वरनारीणाम् उदारः संयतेन्द्रियः ।
रक्षिता धन्विनां श्रेष्ठः साक्षाद् इव मनुः स्वयं ॥४॥
तथैवासीद् विदर्भेषु भीमो भीमपराक्रमः ।
शूरः सर्वगुणैर् युक्तः प्रजाकामः स चाप्रजः ॥५॥
स प्रजार्थे परं यत्नम् अकरोत् सुसमाहितः ।
तम् अभ्यगच्छद् ब्रह्मर्षिर् दमनो नाम भारत ॥६॥
तं स भीमः प्रजाकामस् तोषयामास धर्मवित् ।
महिष्या सह राजेन्द्र सत्कारेण सुवर्चसं ॥७॥
तस्मै प्रसन्नो दमनः सभार्याय वरं ददौ ।
कन्यारत्नं कुमारांश्च त्रीन् उदारान् महायशाः ॥८॥
दमयन्तीं दमं दान्तं दमनञ्च सुवर्चसं ।
उपपन्नान् गुणैः सर्वैर् भीमान् भीमपराक्रमान् ॥९॥

STORY OF NALA.

VṚIHADAŚVA spake:

LIVED of yore, a Rája, Nala, Vírasena's mighty son,
Gifted he with choicest virtues, beauteous, skilled in taming steeds:
Head of all the kings of mortals, like the monarch of the gods,
Over, over all exalted, in his splendour like the sun:
Holy, deep-read in the Vedas, in Nishadha lord of earth;
Loving dice, of truth unblemished, chieftain of a mighty host;
The admired of noble women, generous, with each sense subdued;
Guardian of the state; of archers best, a present Manu he.
So there dwelt in high Vidarbha, Bhíma, terrible in strength,
With all virtues blest, but childless, long for children had he pined.
Many an holy act, on offspring still intent, had he performed.
To his court there came a Bráhman, Damana the seer was named.
Him the child-desiring Bhíma, in all duties skilled, received,
Feasted with his royal consort, in his hospitable hall.
Pleased on him the grateful Daman, and his queen a boon bestowed,
One sweet girl, the pearl of maidens, and three fair and noble sons.
Damayantí, Dama, Dánta, and illustrious Damana,
Richly gifted with all virtues, mighty, fearful in their might.

दमयन्ती तु रूपेण तेजसा यशसा श्रिया।
सौभाग्येन च लोकेषु यशः प्राप सुमध्यमा ॥१०॥
अथ तां वयसि प्राप्ते दासीनां समलंकृतं।
शतं शतं सखीनाञ्च पर्युपासच् छचीम् इव ॥११॥
तत्र स्म राजते भैमी सर्वाभरणभूषिता।
सखीमध्येऽनवद्याङ्गी विद्युत् सौदामिनी यथा ॥१२॥
अतीव रूपसम्पन्ना श्रीर् इवायतलोचना।
न देवेषु न यक्षेषु तादृग् रूपवती क्वचित् ॥१३॥
मानुषेष्वपि चान्येषु दृष्टपूर्वाथवा श्रुता।
चित्तप्रमाथिनी बाला देवानाम् अपि सुन्दरी ॥१४॥
नलश्च नरशार्दूलो लोकेष्वप्रतिमो भुवि।
कन्दर्प इव रूपेण मूर्तिमान् अभवत् स्वयं ॥१५॥
तस्याः समीपे तु नलं प्रशशंसुः कुतूहलात्।
नैषधस्य समीपे तु दमयन्तीं पुनः पुनः ॥१६॥
तयोर् अदृष्टकामोऽभूत् शृण्वतोः सततं गुणान्।
अन्योन्यं प्रति कौन्तेय स व्यवर्धत हृच्छयः ॥१७॥
अशक्नुवन् नलः कामं तदा धारयितुं हृदा।
अन्तःपुरसमीपस्थे वन आस्ते रहो गतः ॥१८॥
स ददर्श ततो हंसान् जातरूपपरिष्कृतान्।
वने विचरतां तेषाम् एकं जग्राह पक्षिणं ॥१९॥
ततोऽन्तरीक्षगो वाचं व्याजहार नलं तदा।
हन्तव्योऽस्मि न ते राजन् करिष्यामि तव प्रियं ॥२०॥
दमयन्तीसकाशे त्वां कथयिष्यामि नैषध।
यथा त्वदन्यं पुरुषं न सा मंस्यति कर्हिचित् ॥२१॥
एवम् उक्तस् ततो हंसम् उत्ससर्ज महीपतिः।
ते तु हंसाः समुत्पत्य विदर्भान् अगमंस् ततः ॥२२॥

Damayantí with her beauty, with her brilliance, brightness, grace,
Through the worlds unrivalled glory won the slender-waisted maid.
Her, arrived at bloom of beauty, sat a hundred slaves around,
And a hundred virgin handmaids, as around great Indra's queen.
In her court shone Bhíma's daughter, decked with every ornament,
'Mid her handmaids, like the lightning, shone she with her faultless form;
Like the long-eyed queen of beauty, without rival, without peer.
Never 'mid the gods immortal, never 'mid the Yaksha race,
Nor 'mong men was maid so lovely, ever heard of, ever seen,
As the soul-disturbing maiden, that disturbed the souls of gods.
Nala too, 'mong kings the tiger, peerless among earthly men,
Like Kandarpa in his beauty, like that bright-embodied god.
All around Vidarbha's princess, praised they Nala in their joy;
Ever praised they Damayantí, round Nishadha's noble king.
Hearing so each other's virtues, all unseen they 'gan to love.
Thus of each, O son of Kunti, the deep silent passion grew.

Nala, in his heart impatient, longer that deep love to bear,
To the grove, in secret, wandered, by the palace' inmost court.
There the swans he saw disporting, with their wings bedropped with gold:
Through the grove thus lightly moving one of these bright birds he caught.
But the bird, in human language, thus the wondering king addressed:
'Slay me not, O gentle monarch! I will do thee service true;
So in Damayantí's presence will I praise Nishadha's king,
Never after shall the maiden think of mortal man but thee.'

Thus addressed, at once the monarch let the bright-winged bird depart.
Flew away the swans rejoicing, to Vidarbha straight they flew;

विदर्भनगरीं गत्वा दमयन्त्यास् तदान्तिके ।
निपेतुस् ते गरुत्मन्तः सा ददर्श च तान् गणान् ॥२३॥
सा तान् अद्भुतरूपान् वै दृष्ट्वा सखीगणावृता ।
हृष्टा ग्रहीतुं खगमांस् त्वरमाणोपचक्रमे ॥२४॥
अथ हंसा विससृपुः सर्वतः प्रमदावने ।
एकैकशस् तदा कन्यास् तान् हंसान् समुपाद्रवन् ॥२५॥
दमयन्ती तु यं हंसं समुपाधावद् अन्तिके ।
स मानुषीं गिरं कृत्वा दमयन्तीम् अथाब्रवीत् ॥२६॥
दमयन्ति नलो नाम निषधेषु महीपतिः ।
अश्विनोः सदृशो रूपे न समास् तस्य मानुषाः ॥२७॥
तस्य वै यदि भार्या त्वं भवेथा वरवर्णिनि ।
सफलं ते भवेज् जन्म रूपं चेदं सुमध्यमे ॥२८॥
वयं हि देवगन्धर्वमानुषोरगराक्षसान् ।
दृष्टवन्तो न चास्माभिर् दृष्टपूर्वस् तथाविधः ॥२९॥
त्वञ्चापि रत्नं नारीणां नरेषु च नलो वरः ।
विशिष्टाया विशिष्टेन सङ्गमो गुणवान् भवेत् ॥३०॥
एवम् उक्ता तु हंसेन दमयन्ती विशाम्पते ।
अब्रवीत् तत्र तं हंसं त्वमप्येवं नले वद ॥३१॥
तथेत्युक्त्वाण्डजः कन्यां विदर्भस्य विशाम्पते ।
पुनर् आगम्य निषधान् नले सर्वं न्यवेदयत् ॥३२॥

॥ इति नलोपाख्याने प्रथमः सर्गः ॥१॥

To Vidarbha's stately city: there by Damayantí's feet,
Down with drooping plumes they settled, and she gazed upon the flock,
Wondering at their forms so graceful, where amid her maids she sat.
Sportively began the damsels all around to chase the birds;
Scattering flew the swans before them, all about the lovely grove.
Lightly ran the nimble maidens, every one her bird pursued;
But the swan that through the forest gentle Damayantí chased,
Suddenly, in human language, spake to Damayantí thus:—

'Damayantí, in Nishadha Nala dwells, the noble king;
Like the Aśvinas in beauty, peerless among men is he.
O incomparable princess, to this hero wert thou wed,
Noble birth and perfect beauty not unworthy fruit had borne.
Gods, Gandharvas, men, the Serpents, and the Rákshasas we've seen;
All we've seen—of noble Nala never have we seen the peer.
Pearl art thou among all women, Nala is the pride of men.
If the peerless wed the peerless, blessed must the union be.'

When the bird thus strangely speaking gentle Damayantí heard,
Answered thus the wondering maiden, 'Thus to Nala, speak thou too.'
'Be it so,' replied the egg-born to Vidarbha's beauteous maid.
Home then flew he to Nishadha, and to Nala told it all.

End of Book I.

बृहदश्व उवाच ।

दमयन्ती तु तच् छ्रुत्वा वचो हंसस्य भारत ।
ततः प्रभृति न स्वस्था नलं प्रति बभूव सा ॥१॥
ततश् चिन्तापरा दीना विवर्णवदना कृशा ।
बभूव दमयन्ती तु निःश्वासपरमा तदा ॥२॥
ऊर्ध्वदृष्टिर् ध्यानपरा बभूवोन्मत्तदर्शना ।
पाण्डुवर्णा क्षणेनाथ हृच्छयाविष्टचेतना ॥३॥
न शय्यासनभोगेषु रतिं विन्दति कर्हिचित् ।
न नक्तं न दिवा शेते हा हेति रुदती पुनः ॥४॥
ताम् अस्वस्थां तदाकारां सख्यस् ता जज्ञुर् इङ्गितैः ।
ततो विदर्भपतये दमयन्त्याः सखीजनः ॥५॥
न्यवेदयत् ताम् अस्वस्थां दमयन्तीं नरेश्वरे ।
तच् छ्रुत्वा नृपतिर् भीमो दमयन्तीसखीगणात् ॥६॥
चिन्तयामास तत् कार्यं सुमहत् स्वां सुतां प्रति ।
किम् इयं दुहिता मेऽद्य नातिस्वस्थेव लक्ष्यते ॥७॥
स समीक्ष्य महीपालः स्वां सुतां प्राप्तयौवनां ।
अपश्यद् आत्मना कार्यं दमयन्त्याः स्वयंवरं ॥८॥
स सन्निमन्त्रयामास महीपालान् विशाम्पतिः ।
अनुभूयताम् अयं वीराः स्वयंवर इति प्रभो ॥९॥
श्रुत्वा तु पार्थिवाः सर्वे दमयन्त्याः स्वयंवरं ।
अभिजग्मुस् ततो भीमं राजानो भीमशासनात् ॥१०॥
हस्त्यश्वरथघोषेण पूरयन्तो वसुन्धरां ।
विचित्रमाल्याभरणैर् बलैर् दृश्यैः स्वलंकृतैः ॥११॥

Vṛihadaśva spake:

Damayantí, ever after she the swan's sweet speech had heard,
With herself she dwelt no longer, all herself with Nala dwelt.
Lost in thought she sat dejected, pale her melancholy cheek,
Damayantí sat and yielded all her soul to sighs of grief.
Upward gazing, meditative, with a wild distracted look,
Wan was all her soft complexion, and with passion heart-possessed,
Nor in sleep nor gentle converse, nor in banquets found she joy;
Night nor day she could not slumber, Woe! oh woe! she wept and said.
Her no longer her own mistress, from her looks, her gesture, knew
Damayantí's virgin handmaids, to Vidarbha's monarch they
Told how pined his gentle daughter for the sovereign of men.
This from Damayantí's maidens when the royal Bhíma heard,
In his mind he gravely pondered for his child what best were done.
'Wherefore is my gentle daughter from herself in mind estranged?'
When the lord of earth his daughter saw in blooming youth mature,
Knew he for the Svayaṃvara Damayantí's time was come.
Straight the lord of many peasants summoned all the chiefs of earth,
'Come ye to the Svayaṃvara all ye heroes of the world!'
Damayantí's Svayaṃvara, soon as heard the kings of men,
All obeyed king Bhíma's summons, all to Bhíma's court drew near;
Elephants, and steeds, and chariots, swarmed along the sounding land;
All with rich and various garlands, with his stately army each,

तेषां भीमो महाबाहुः पार्थिवानां महात्मनां ।
यथार्हम् अकरोत् पूजां तेऽवसंस् तत्र पूजिताः ॥१२॥
एतस्मिन् एव काले तु सुराणाम् ऋषिसत्तमौ ।
अटमानौ महात्मानाव् इन्द्रलोकम् इतो गतौ ॥१३॥
नारदः पर्वतश्चैव महाप्राज्ञौ महाव्रतौ ।
देवराजस्य भवनं विविशाते सुपूजितौ ॥१४॥
ताव् अर्चयित्वा मघवा ततः कुशलम् अव्ययं ।
पप्रच्छानामयं चापि तयोः सर्वगतं विभुः ॥१५॥

नारद उवाच ।

आवयोः कुशलं देव सर्वत्र गतम् ईश्वर ।
लोके च मघवन् कृत्स्ने नृपाः कुशलिनो विभो ॥१६॥

वृहदश्व उवाच ।

नारदस्य वचः श्रुत्वा पप्रच्छ बलवृत्रहा ।
धर्मज्ञाः पृथिवीपालास् त्यक्तजीवितयोधिनः ॥१७॥
शस्त्रेण निधनं काले ये गच्छन्त्यपराङ्मुखाः ।
अयं लोकोऽक्षयस् तेषां यथैव मम कामधुक् ॥१८॥
क्व नु ते क्षत्रियाः शूरा न हि पश्यामि तान् अहं ।
आगच्छतो महीपालान् दयितान् अतिथीन् मम ॥१९॥
एवम् उक्तस्तु शक्रेण नारदः प्रत्यभाषत ।

नारद उवाच ।

शृणु मे मघवन् येन न दृश्यन्ते महीक्षितः ॥२०॥
विदर्भराज्ञो दुहिता दमयन्तीति विश्रुता ।
रूपेण समतिक्रान्ता पृथिव्यां सर्वयोषितः ॥२१॥
तस्याः स्वयंवरः शक्र भविता नचिराद् इव ।
तत्र गच्छन्ति राजानो राजपुत्राश्च सर्वशः ॥२२॥

All the lofty-minded Rájas, Bhíma with the arm of strength,
As beseemed, received with honour, on their thrones of state they sat.

At this very hour the wisest of the sages, the divine,
Moving in their might ascended up from earth to Indra's world,
Great in holiness and wisdom, Nárada and Parvata,
Honoured entered they the palace of the monarch of the gods.
Them salutes the cloud-compeller, of their everlasting weal—
Of their weal the worlds pervading, courteous asks the immortal lord.

Nárada spake:

Well it fares with us, Immortal, in our weal the world partakes;
In the world, O cloud-compeller, well it fares with all her kings.

Vṛihadaśva spake:

He that Bali slew and Vṛitra asked of Nárada again,
'All earth's just and righteous rulers, reckless of their lives in fight,
Who the shaft's descending death-blow meet with unaverted eye,
Theirs this everlasting kingdom, even as Kámadhuk is mine.
Where are they, the Kshatriya heroes? wherefore see I not approach
All the earth's majestic guardians, all mine ever-honoured guests?'
Thus addressed by holy S'akra, Nárada replied and said:

Nárada spake:

Hear me now, O cloud-compeller, why earth's kings appear not here.
Of Vidarbha's king the daughter Damayantí, the renowned—
Through the earth the loveliest women in her beauty she transcends—
Soon she holds her Svayaṃvara, soon her lord the maid will choose.
Thither all the kings are hastening, thither all the sons of kings.

तां रत्नभूतां लोकस्य प्रार्थयन्तो महीक्षितः ।
काङ्क्षन्ति स्म विशेषेण बलवृत्रनिषूदन ॥२३॥
एतस्मिन् कथ्यमाने तु लोकपालाश्च साग्निकाः ।
आजग्मुर् देवराजस्य समीपम् अमरोत्तमाः ॥२४॥
ततस् ते शुश्रुवुः सर्वे नारदस्य वचो महत् ।
श्रुत्वैव चाब्रुवन् हृष्टा गच्छामो वयम् अप्युत ॥२५॥
ततः सर्वे महाराज सगणाः सहवाहनाः ।
विदर्भान् अभिजग्मुस् ते यतः सर्वे महीक्षितः ॥२६॥
नलोऽपि राजा कौन्तेय श्रुत्वा राज्ञां समागमं ।
अभ्यगच्छद् अदीनात्मा दमयन्तीम् अनुव्रतः ॥२७॥
अथ देवाः पथि नलं ददृशुर् भूतले स्थितं ।
साक्षाद् इव स्थितं मूर्त्या मन्मथं रूपसम्पदा ॥२८॥
तं दृष्ट्वा लोकपालास् ते भ्राजमानं यथा रविं ।
तस्थुर् विगतसङ्कल्पा विस्मिता रूपसम्पदा ॥२९॥
ततोऽन्तरीक्षे विष्टभ्य विमानानि दिवौकसः ।
अब्रुवन् नैषधं राजन् अवतीर्य नभस्तलात् ॥३०॥
भो भो नैषध राजेन्द्र नल सत्यव्रतो भवान् ।
अस्माकं कुरु साहाय्यं दूतो भव नरोत्तम ॥३१॥

॥ इति नलोपाख्याने द्वितीयः सर्गः ॥२॥

Suitors for her hand the Rájas, her of all the world the pearl,
O thou mighty giant-slayer! one and all approach to woo.
As he spake, the world-protectors with the god of fire drew near;
Of the immortals all, the highest stood before the king of gods.
As they all stood silent hearing Nárada's majestic speech,
All exclaimed in sudden rapture, 'Thither we likewise will go;'
All the immortals on the instant, with their chariots, with their hosts,
Hastened down towards Vidarbha, where the lords of earth were met.
Nala, too, no sooner heard he of that concourse of the kings,
Set he forth, with soul all sanguine, full of Damayantí's love.
Saw the gods, king Nala standing on the surface of the earth;
Standing in transcendent beauty, equal to the god of love.
Him beheld the world's high guardians, in his radiance like the sun;
Each arrested stood and silent, at his peerless form amazed.
All their chariots the celestials in the midway air have checked,
Through the blue air then descending, they Nishadha's king address:
'Ho! what, ho! Nishadha's monarch, Nala, king, for truth renowned;
Do our bidding, bear our message, O, most excellent of men!'

End of Book II.

बृहदश्व उवाच ।

तेभ्यः प्रतिज्ञाय नलः करिष्य इति भारत ।
अथैतान् परिपप्रच्छ कृताञ्जलिर् उपस्थितः ॥१॥
के वै भवन्तः कश्चासौ यस्याहं दूत ईप्सितः ।
किञ्च तद् वो मया कार्यं कथयध्वं यथातथं ॥२॥
एवम् उक्ते नैषधेन मघवान् अभ्यभाषत ।
अमरान् वै निबोधास्मान् दमयन्त्यर्थम् आगतान् ॥३॥
अहम् इन्द्रोऽयम् अग्निश्च तथैवायम् अपाम्पतिः ।
शरीरान्तकरो नृणां यमोऽयम् अपि पार्थिव ॥४॥
त्वं वै समागतान् अस्मान् दमयन्त्यै निवेदय ।
लोकपाला महेन्द्राद्याः सभां यान्ति दिदृक्षवः ॥५॥
प्राप्तुम् इच्छन्ति देवास् त्वां शक्रोऽग्निर् वरुणो यमः ।
तेषाम् अन्यतमं देवं पतित्वे वरयस्व ह ॥६॥
एवम् उक्तः स शक्रेण नलः प्राञ्जलिर् अब्रवीत् ।
एकार्थसमुपेतं मां न प्रेषयितुम् अर्हथ ॥७॥
कथं तु जातसङ्कल्पः स्त्रियम् उत्सहते पुमान् ।
परार्थम् ईदृशं वक्तुं तत् क्षमन्तु महेश्वराः ॥८॥

देवा ऊचुः ।

करिष्य इति संश्रुत्य पूर्वम् अस्मासु नैषध ।
न करिष्यसि कस्मात् त्वं व्रज नैषध माचिरं ॥९॥

बृहदश्व उवाच ।

एवम् उक्तः स देवैस् तैर् नैषधः पुनर् अब्रवीत् ।
सुरक्षितानि वेश्मानि प्रवेष्टुं कथम् उत्सहे ॥१०॥

Vṛihadaśva spake:

Nala made his solemn promise, 'All your bidding will I do;'
Then with folded hands adoring humbly of their will enquired.
'Who are ye? to whom must Nala as your welcome herald go?
What is my commanded service? tell me, mighty gods, the truth.'
Spake the sovereign of Nishadha, Indra answered thus and said:—
'Know us, the Immortals, hither come for Damayantí's love.
Indra I, and yòn is Agni, and the king of waters there—
Slayer he of mortal bodies, Yama, too, is here, O king!
Thou, O Nala, of our coming must to Damayantí tell:
Thee to see, the world's dread guardians, Indra and the rest came down,
Indra, Agni, Varun, Yama, each to seek thine hand are come.
One of these celestial beings choose, O maiden, for thy lord.'
Nala, thus addressed by Indra, with his folded hands replied:
'Thus, with one accord commanding, on this mission send not me.
How can man, himself enamoured, for another plead his cause?
Spare me then, ye gods, in mercy, this unwelcome service, spare.'

The Gods spake:

'I will do your bidding freely,' thus thou'st said, Nishadha's king;
Wilt thou now belie thy promise? Nala, go, nor more delay.

Vṛihadaśva spake:

By the gods adjured so sternly, thus rejoined Nishadha's king:—
'Strictly guarded is yon palace, how may I find entrance there?'

प्रवेक्ष्यसीति तं शक्रः पुनर् एवाभ्यभाषत ।
स जगाम तथेत्युक्त्वा दमयन्त्या निवेशनं ॥११॥
ददर्श तत्र वैदर्भीं सखीगणसमावृतां ।
देदीप्यमानां वपुषा श्रिया च वरवर्णिनीं ॥१२॥
अतीव सुकुमाराङ्गीं तनुमध्यां सुलोचनां ।
आक्षिपन्तीम् इव प्रभां शशिनः स्वेन तेजसा ॥१३॥
तस्य दृष्ट्वैव ववृधे कामस् तां चारुहासिनीं ।
सत्यं चिकीर्षमाणस्तु धारयामास हृच्छयं ॥१४॥
ततस् ता नैषधं दृष्ट्वा सम्भ्रान्ताः परमाङ्गनाः ।
आसनेभ्यः समुत्पेतुस् तेजसा तस्य धर्षिताः ॥१५॥
प्रशशंसुश्च सुप्रीता नलं ता विस्मयान्विताः ।
न चैनम् अभ्यभाषन्त मनोभिस् त्वभ्यपूजयन् ॥१६॥
अहो रूपम् अहो कान्तिर् अहो धैर्यं महात्मनः ।
कोऽयं देवोऽथवा यक्षो गन्धर्वो वा भविष्यति ॥१७॥
न तास् तं शक्नुवन्ति स्म व्याहर्तुम् अपि किञ्चन ।
तेजसा धर्षितास् तस्य लज्जावत्यो वराङ्गनाः ॥१८॥
अथैनं स्मयमानं तु स्मितपूर्वाभिभाषिणी ।
दमयन्ती नलं वीरम् अभ्यभाषत विस्मिता ॥१९॥
कस् त्वं सर्वानवद्याङ्ग मम हृच्छयवर्धन ।
प्राप्तोऽस्यमरवद् वीर ज्ञातुम् इच्छामि तेऽनघ ॥२०॥
कथम् आगमनं चेह कथं चासि न लक्षितः ।
सुरक्षितं हि मे वेश्म राजा चैवोग्रशासनः ॥२१॥
एवम् उक्तस्तु वैदर्भ्या नलस् तां प्रत्युवाच ह ।

नल उवाच ।

नलं मां विद्धि कल्याणि देवदूतम् इहागतं ॥२२॥
देवास् त्वां प्राप्तुम् इच्छन्ति शक्रोऽग्निर् वरुणो यमः ।

'Thou shalt enter;' thus did Indra to the unwilling king reply.
In the bower of Damayantí, as they spake, king Nala stood.
There he saw Vidarbha's maiden, girt with all her virgin bands;
In her glowing beauty shining, all excelling in her form;
Every limb in smooth proportion, slender waist and lovely eyes;
E'en the moon's soft gleam disdaining in her own o'erpowering light.
As he gazed, his love grew warmer to the softly smiling maid,
Yet to keep his truth, his duty, all his passion he suppressed.
Then Nishadha's king beholding, all those maids with beauteous limbs
From their seats sprang up in wonder, at his matchless form amazed.
In their rapture to king Nala, all admiring, homage paid;
Yet, not venturing to accost him, in their secret souls adored.
'Oh the beauty! oh the splendour! oh the mighty hero's strength!
Who is he? or god, or Yaksha, or Gandharba may he be?'
Not one single word to utter, dared that fair-limbed maiden band;
All struck dumb before his beauty, in their bashful silence stood.
Smiling, first, upon the monarch, as on her he gently smiled,
Damayantí, in her wonder, to the hero Nala spake:—
'Who art thou of form so beauteous, thou that wakenest all my love?
Cam'st thou here like an immortal? I would know thee, sinless chief.
How hast entered in our palace? how hast entered all unseen?
Watchful are our chamber-wardens, stern the mandate of the king.'
By the maiden of Vidarbha Nala thus addressed, replied:—

Nala spake:

Know, O loveliest, I am Nala, here the messenger of gods,
Gods desirous to possess thee; one of these, the lord of heaven,

तेषाम् अन्यतमं देवं पतिं वरय शोभने ॥२३॥
तेषाम् एव प्रभावेन प्रविष्टोऽहम् अलक्षितः ।
प्रविशन्तं न मां कश्चिद् अपश्यन् नाप्यवारयत् ॥२४॥
एतदर्थम् अहं भद्रे प्रेषितः सुरसत्तमैः ।
एतच् छ्रुत्वा शुभे बुद्धिं प्रकुरुष्व यथेच्छसि ॥२५॥

॥ इति नलोपाख्याने तृतीयः सर्गः ॥३॥

बृहदश्व उवाच ।

सा नमस्कृत्य देवेभ्यः प्रहस्य नलम् अब्रवीत् ।
प्रणयस्व यथाश्रद्धं राजन् किं करवाणि ते ॥१॥
अहं चैव हि यच् चान्यन् ममास्ति वसु किञ्चन ।
तत् सर्वं तव विश्रब्धं कुरु प्रणयम् ईश्वर ॥२॥
हंसानां वचनं यत् तु तन् मां दहति पार्थिव ।
त्वत्कृते हि मया वीर राजानः सन्निपातिताः ॥३॥
यदि त्वं भजमानां मां प्रत्याख्यास्यसि मानद ।
विषम् अग्निं जलं रज्जुम् आस्थास्ये तव कारणात् ॥४॥
एवम् उक्तस् तु वैदर्भ्या नलस् तां प्रत्युवाच ह ।
तिष्ठत्सु लोकपालेषु कथं मानुषम् इच्छसि ॥५॥
येषाम् अहं लोककृताम् ईश्वराणां महात्मनां ।
न पादरजसा तुल्यो मनस् ते तेषु वर्ततां ॥६॥
विप्रियं ह्याचरन् मर्त्यो देवानां मृत्युम् ऋच्छति ।
त्राहि माम् अनवद्याङ्गि वरयस्व सुरोत्तमान् ॥७॥

Indra, Agni, Varun, Yama, choose thou, princess, for thy lord.
Through their power, their power almighty, I have entered here unseen;
As I entered in thy chamber none hath seen, and none might stay.
This, the object of my mission, fairest, from the highest gods,
Thou hast heard me, noble princess; even as thou wilt, decide.

End of Book III.

Vṛihadaśva spake:

To the gods performed her homage, smiled she, and to Nala spake:—
'Pledge to me thy faith, O Rája; how that faith may I requite?
I myself, and whatsoever in the world I have, is thine—
In full trust is thine—O grant me in thy turn thy love, O king!
'Tis the swan's enamouring language that hath kindled all my soul.
Only for thy sake, O hero, are the assembled Rájas met.
But if thou mine homage scornest, scornest me, all honoured king,
Poison for thy sake, fire, water, the vile noose will I endure.'
So, when spake Vidarbha's maiden, Nala answered thus, and said:—
'With the world's dread guardians present wilt thou mortal husband choose?
We with them, the world's creators, with these mighty lords compared,
Lowlier than the dust they tread on, raise to them thy loftier mind.
Man the gods displeasing, hastens to inevitable death—
Fair-limbed! from that fate preserve me, choose the all-excelling gods.

विरजांसि च वासांसि दिव्याश् चित्राः स्रजस् तथा ।
भूषणानि च मुख्यानि देवान् प्राप्य तु भुंक्ष्व वै ॥८॥
य इमां पृथिवीं कृत्स्नां सङ्क्षिप्य ग्रसते पुनः ।
हुताशम् ईशं देवानां का तं न वरयेत् पतिं ॥९॥
यस्य दण्डभयात् सर्वे भूतग्रामाः समागताः ।
धर्मम् एवानुरुध्यन्ति का तं न वरयेत् पतिं ॥१०॥
धर्मात्मानं महात्मानं दैत्यदानवमर्दनं ।
महेन्द्रं सर्वदेवानां का तं न वरयेत् पतिं ॥११॥
क्रियताम् अविशङ्केन मनसा यदि मन्यसे ।
वरुणं लोकपालानां सुहृद्वाक्यम् इदं शृणु ॥१२॥
नैषधेनैवमुक्ता सा दमयन्ती वचोऽब्रवीत् ।
समाप्लुताभ्यां नेत्राभ्यां शोकजेनाथ वारिणा ॥१३॥
देवेभ्योऽहं नमस्कृत्य सर्वेभ्यः पृथिवीपते ।
वृणे त्वाम् एव भर्तारं सत्यम् एतद् ब्रवीमि ते ॥१४॥
ताम् उवाच ततो राजा वेपमानां कृताञ्जलिं ।
दौत्येनागत्य कल्याणि कथं स्वार्थम् इहोत्सहे ॥१५॥
कथं ह्यहं प्रतिश्रुत्य देवतानां विशेषतः ।
परार्थे यत्नम् आरभ्य कथं स्वार्थम् इहोत्सहे ॥१६॥
एष धर्मो यदि स्वार्थो ममापि भविता ततः ।
एवं स्वार्थं करिष्यामि तथा भद्रे विधीयतां ॥१७॥
ततो वाष्पाकुलां वाचं दमयन्ती शुचिस्मिता ।
प्रत्याहरन्ती शनकैर् नलं राजानम् अब्रवीत् ॥१८॥
उपायोऽयं मया दृष्टो निरपायो नरेश्वर ।
येन दोषो न भविता तव राजन् कथञ्चन ॥१९॥
त्वञ्चैव हि नरश्रेष्ठ देवाश् चेन्द्रपुरोगमाः ।
आयान्तु सहिताः सर्वे मम यत्र स्वयंवरः ॥२०॥

Robes by earthly dust unsullied, crowns of amaranthine flowers,
Every bright celestial glory, wedded to the gods, enjoy.
He, who all the world compressing, with devouring might consumes,
Sovereign of the gods, Hutáśa, where is she who would not wed?
He, in awe of whose dread sceptre all the assembled hosts of men
Cultivate eternal justice, where is she who would not wed?
Him the all-righteous, lofty-minded, slayer of the infernal host,
Of all gods, the mighty monarch, who is she that would not wed?
Nor let trembling doubt arrest thee, in thy mind if thou couldst choose
Varuṇa, amongst earth's guardians; hear the language of a friend.'

To the sovereign of Nishadha Damayantí spake, and said,
And her eyes grew dim with moisture flowing from her inward grief:—
'To the gods, to all, my homage, king of earth, I humbly pay;
Yet thee only, thee, my husband, may I choose, Be this my vow!'
Answered he the trembling maiden, as with folded hands she stood,
'Bound upon this solemn mission, mine own cause how dare I urge?
Plighted by a sacred promise to the everlasting gods;
Thus engaged to plead for others, for myself I may not plead.
This my duty; yet hereafter come I on my own behalf,
Then I'll plead mine own cause boldly, weigh it, beauteous, in thy thought.'
Damayantí smiled serenely, and with tear-impeded speech,
Uttered brokenly and slowly, thus to royal Nala spake:—
'Yet I see a way of refuge, 'tis a blameless way, O king;
Whence no sin to thee, O Rája, may by any chance arise.
Thou, O noblest of all mortals, and the gods by Indra led,
Come and enter in together, where the Svayaṃvara meets;

ततोऽहं लोकपालानां सन्निधौ त्वां नरेश्वर।
वरयिष्ये नरव्याघ्र नैवं दोषो भविष्यति ॥२१॥
एवम् उक्तस्तु वैदर्भ्या नलो राजा विशाम्पते।
आजगाम पुनस् तत्र यत्र देवाः समागताः ॥२२॥
तम् अपश्यंस् तथायान्तं लोकपाला महेश्वराः।
दृष्ट्वा चैनं ततोऽपृच्छन् वृत्तान्तं सर्वम् एव तं ॥२३॥
कच्चिद् दृष्टा त्वया राजन् दमयन्ती शुचिस्मिता।
किम् अब्रवीच्च नः सर्वान् वद भूमिपतेऽनघ ॥२४॥

नल उवाच।

भवद्भिर् अहम् आदिष्टो दमयन्त्या निवेशनं।
प्रविष्टः सुमहाकक्षं दण्डिभिः स्थविरैर् वृतं ॥२५॥
प्रविशन्तञ्च मां तत्र न कश्चिद् दृष्टवान् नरः।
ऋते तां पार्थिवसुतां भवताम् एव तेजसा ॥२६॥
सख्यश्च चास्या मया दृष्टास् ताभिश्च चाप्युपलक्षितः।
विस्मिताश्चाभवन् सर्वा दृष्ट्वा मां विबुधेश्वराः ॥२७॥
वर्ण्यमानेषु च मया भवत्सु रुचिरानना।
माम् एव गतसङ्कल्पा वृणीते सा सुरोत्तमाः ॥२८॥
अब्रवीच्चैव मां बाला आयान्तु सहिताः सुराः।
त्वया सह नरव्याघ्र मम यत्र स्वयंवरः ॥२९॥
तेषाम् अहं सन्निधौ त्वां वरयिष्यामि नैषध।
एवं तव महाबाहो दोषो न भवितेति ह ॥३०॥
एतावद् एव विबुधा यथावृत्तम् उदाहृतं।
मया शेषे प्रमाणं तु भवन्तस् त्रिदशेश्वराः ॥३१॥

॥ इति नलोपाख्याने चतुर्थः सर्गः ॥४॥

Then will I, before the presence of the guardians of the world,
Name thee, lord of men! my husband, nor to thee may blame accrue.'

By the maiden of Vidarbha, royal Nala thus addressed,
Back again returned, where waited eager, the expecting gods.
Him, the mighty lords, earth's guardians, ere he yet drew near, beheld,
Him they saw, and bade him instant all his tidings to unfold—
'Was she seen of thee, O monarch, Damayantí with soft smile?
Spake she of us all? what said she? tell, O blameless lord of earth.'

Nala spake:

To the bower of Damayantí, on your solemn mission sent,
Entered I the lofty portal, by the aged warders watched;
Mortal eye might not behold me, there as swift I entered in;
None save that fair Rája's daughter, through your all-prevailing power.
And her virgin handmaids saw I, and by them in turn was seen;
And they all in mute amazement gazed upon me as I stood.
I described your godlike presence, but the maid with beauteous face
Chooses me, bereft of reason, O most excellent of gods!
Thus she spake, that maiden princess, 'Let the gods together come,
Come with thee, O king of mortals, where the Svayaṃvara meets;
There will I, before their presence, choose thee, Rája, for my lord.
So to thee, O strong-armed warrior, may no blame, no fault ensue.'
Thus it was, even as I tell you word for word did it befall;
As for what remains, the judgment rests with you, of gods the chief!

End of Book IV.

बृहदश्व उवाच ।

अथ काले शुभे प्राप्ते तिथौ पुण्ये क्षणे तथा ।
आजुहाव महीपालान् भीमो राजा स्वयंवरे ॥१॥
तच् छ्रुत्वा पृथिवीपालाः सर्वे हृच्छयपीडिताः ।
त्वरिताः समुपाजग्मुर् दमयन्तीम् अभीप्सवः ॥२॥
कनकस्तम्भरुचिरं तोरणेन विराजितं ।
विविशुस् ते नृपा रङ्गं महासिंहा इवाचलं ॥३॥
तत्रासनेषु विविधेष्वासीनाः पृथिवीक्षितः ।
सुरभिस्रग्धराः सर्वे प्रमृष्टमणिकुण्डलाः ॥४॥
तत्र स्म पीना दृश्यन्ते बाहवः परिघोपमाः ।
आकारवर्णसुश्लक्ष्णाः पञ्चशीर्षा इवोरगाः ॥५॥
सुकेशान्तानि चारूणि सुनासाक्षिभ्रुवाणि च ।
मुखानि राज्ञां शोभन्ते नक्षत्राणि यथा दिवि ॥६॥
तां राजसमितिं पुण्यां नागैर् भोगवतीम् इव ।
सम्पूर्णां पुरुषव्याघ्रैर् व्याघ्रैर् गिरिगुहाम् इव ॥७॥
दमयन्ती ततो रङ्गं प्रविवेश शुभानना ।
मुष्णन्ती प्रभया राज्ञां चक्षूंषि च मनांसि च ॥८॥
तस्या गात्रेषु पतिता तेषां दृष्टिर् महात्मनां ।
तत्र तत्रैव सक्ताभून् न चचाल च पश्यतां ॥९॥
ततः सङ्कीर्त्यमानेषु राज्ञां नामसु भारत ।
ददर्श भैमी पुरुषान् पञ्च तुल्याकृतीन् अथ ॥१०॥
तान् समीक्ष्य ततः सर्वान् निर्विशेषाकृतीन् स्थितान् ।
सन्देहाद् अथ वैदर्भी नाभ्यजानान् नलं नृपं ॥११॥

Vṛihadaśva spake:

Came the day of happy omen, moonday meet, and moment apt;
Bhíma to the Svayaṃvara summoned all the lords of earth.
One and all, upon the instant, rose th' enamoured lords of earth,
Suitors all to Damayantí in their loving haste they came.
They, the court with golden columns rich, and glittering portal arch,
Like the lions on the mountains entered they the hall of state.
There the lords of earth were seated, each upon his several throne;
All their fragrant garlands wearing, all with pendant ear-gems rich.
Arms were seen robust and vigorous as the ponderous battle mace,
Some like the five-headed serpents, delicate in shape and hue:
With bright locks profuse and flowing, fine-formed nose, and eye and brow,
Shone the faces of the Rájas like the radiant stars in heaven.
As with serpents, Bhogavatí, the wide hall was full of kings;
As the mountain-caves with tigers, with the tiger-warriors full.
Damayantí in her beauty entered on that stately scene,
With her dazzling light entrancing every eye and every soul.
O'er her lovely person gliding all the eyes of those proud kings;
There were fixed, there moveless rested, as they gazed upon the maid.
Then as they proclaimed the Rájas, (by his name was each proclaimed,)
In dismay saw Bhíma's daughter, five in garb, in form the same.
On those forms, all undistinguished each from each, she stood and gazed.
In her doubt Vidarbha's princess Nala's form might not discern,

यं यं हि ददृशे तेषां तं तं मेने नलं नृपं ।
सा चिन्तयन्ती बुद्ध्याथ तर्कयामास भाविनी ।
कथं हि देवान् जानीयां कथं विद्यां नलं नृपं ॥१२॥
एवं सञ्चिन्तयन्ती सा वैदर्भी भृशदुःखिता ।
श्रुतानि देवलिङ्गानि तर्कयामास भारत ॥१३॥
देवानां यानि लिङ्गानि स्थविरेभ्यः श्रुतानि मे ।
तानीह तिष्ठतां भूमाव् एकस्यापि न लक्षये ॥१४॥
सा विनिश्चित्य बहुधा विचार्य च पुनः पुनः ।
शरणं प्रति देवानां प्राप्तकालम् अमन्यत ॥१५॥
वाचा च मनसा चैव नमस्कारं प्रयुज्य सा ।
देवेभ्यः प्राञ्जलिर् भूत्वा वेपमानेदम् अब्रवीत् ॥१६॥
हंसानां वचनं श्रुत्वा यथा मे नैषधो वृतः ।
पतित्वे तेन सत्येन देवास् तं प्रदिशन्तु मे ॥१७॥
मनसा वचसा चैव यथा नाभिचराम्यहं ।
तेन सत्येन विबुधास् तम् एव प्रदिशन्तु मे ॥१८॥
यथा देवैः स मे भर्ता विहितो निषधाधिपः ।
तेन सत्येन मे देवास् तम् एव प्रदिशन्तु मे ॥१९॥
यथेदं व्रतम् आरब्धं नलस्याराधने मया ।
तेन सत्येन मे देवास् तम् एव प्रदिशन्तु मे ॥२०॥
स्वञ्चैव रूपं कुर्वन्तु लोकपाला महेश्वराः ।
यथाहम् अभिजानीयां पुण्यश्लोकं नराधिपं ॥२१॥
निशम्य दमयन्त्यास् तत् करुणं परिदेवितं ।
निश्चयं परमं तथ्यम् अनुरागञ्च नैषधे ॥२२॥
मनोविशुद्धिं बुद्धिञ्च भक्तिं रागञ्च नैषधे ।
यथोक्तं चक्रिरे देवाः सामर्थ्यं लिङ्गधारणे ॥२३॥
सापश्यद् विबुधान् सर्वान् अस्वेदान् स्तब्धलोचनान् ।

Whichsoe'er the form she gazed on, him her Nala, him she thought.
She within her secret spirit deeply pondering, stood and thought:
'How shall I the gods distinguish? royal Nala how discern?'
Pondering thus Vidarbha's maiden in the anguish of her heart—
Th' attributes of the immortals sought, as heard of yore, to see.
'Th' attributes of each celestial, that our aged sires describe,
As on earth they stand before me, not of one may I discern.'
Long she pondered in her silence, and again, again she thought.
To the gods, her only refuge, turned she at this trying hour.
With her voice and with her spirit she her humble homage paid.
Folding both her hands and trembling to the gods the maiden spake:
'As when heard the swan's sweet language chose I then Nishadha's king,
By this truth I here adjure ye, oh, ye gods, reveal my lord!
As in word or thought I swerve not from my faith, all-knowing powers!
By this truth I here adjure ye, oh, ye gods, reveal my lord!
As the gods themselves have destined for my lord Nishadha's king;
By this truth I here adjure ye, oh, ye gods, my lord reveal!
As my vow, so pledged to Nala, holily must be maintained,
By this truth I here adjure ye, oh, ye gods my lord reveal!
Each the form divine assume ye, earth's protectors, mighty lords;
So shall I discern my Nala, I shall know the king of men.'

As they heard sad Damayantí uttering thus her piteous prayer,
At her high resolve they wonder, steadfast truth and fervent love,
Holiness of soul, and wisdom, to her lord her constant faith.
As she prayed, the gods obedient stood with attributes revealed:
With unmoistened skins the Immortals saw she, and with moveless eyes;

हृषितस्रग्रजोहीनान् स्थितान् अस्पृशतः क्षितिं ॥२४॥
छायाद्वितीयो म्लानस्रग् रजःस्वेदसमन्वितः ।
भूमिष्ठो नैषधश्चैव निमेषेण च सूचितः ॥२५॥
सा समीक्ष्य तु तान् देवान् पुण्यश्लोकञ्च भारत ।
नैषधं वरयामास भैमी धर्मेण पाण्डव ॥२६॥
विलज्जमाना वस्त्रान्ते जग्राहायतलोचना ।
स्कन्धदेशेऽसृजत् तस्य स्रजं परमशोभनां ॥२७॥
वरयामास चैवैनं पतित्वे वरवर्णिनी ।
ततो हा हेति सहसा मुक्तः शब्दो नराधिपैः ॥२८॥
देवैर् महर्षिभिस् तत्र साधु साध्विति भारत ।
विस्मितैर् ईरितः शब्दः प्रशंसद्भिर् नलं नृपं ॥२९॥
दमयन्तीं तु कौरव्य वीरसेनसुतो नृपः ।
आश्वासयद् वरारोहां प्रहृष्टेनान्तरात्मना ॥३०॥
यत् त्वं भजसि कल्याणि पुमांसं देवसन्निधौ ।
तस्मान् मां विद्धि भर्तारम् एवं ते वचने रतं ॥३१॥
यावच्च मे धरिष्यन्ति प्राणा देहे शुचिस्मिते ।
तावत् त्वयि भविष्यामि सत्यम् एतद् ब्रवीमि ते ॥३२॥
दमयन्तीं तथा वाग्भिर् अभिनन्द्य कृताञ्जलिः ।
तौ परस्परतः प्रीतौ दृष्ट्वा त्वग्निपुरोगमान् ।
तान् एव शरणं देवान् जग्मतुर् मनसा तदा ॥३३॥
वृते तु नैषधे भैम्या लोकपाला महौजसः ।
प्रहृष्टमनसः सर्वे नलायाष्टौ वरान् ददुः ॥३४॥
प्रत्यक्षदर्शनं यज्ञे गतिञ्चानुत्तमां शुभां ।
नैषधाय ददौ शक्रः प्रीयमाणः शचीपतिः ॥३५॥
अग्निर् आत्मभवं प्रादाद् यत्र वाञ्छति नैषधः ।
लोकान् आत्मप्रभांश्चैव ददौ तस्मै हुताशनः ॥३६॥

Fresh their dust-unsullied garlands hovered they, nor touched the earth.
By his shadow doubled, dust-soiled, garland-drooping, moist with sweat,
On the earth Nishadha's monarch stood confessed, with twinkling eyes;
On the gods an instant gazed she, then upon the king of men;
And of right king Bhíma's daughter named Nishadha's king her lord.
Modestly the large-eyed maiden lifted up his garment's hem,
Round his shoulders threw she lightly the bright zone of radiant flowers.
So she chose him for her husband, Nala, that high-hearted maid.
Then 'alas! alas!' burst wildly, from that conclave of the kings,
And 'well done, well done,' as loudly, from the gods and sages broke.
All in their extatic wonder glorified Nishadha's king.
Then to royal Damayantí, Vírasena's kingly son,
To that slender-waisted damsel spake he comfort in his joy;
'Since thou'st own'd me for thine husband, in the presence of the gods,
For thy faithful consort know me, aye delighting in thy words.
While this spirit fills this body, maiden with the smile serene!
Thine am I, so long thine only, this the solemn truth I vow.'
Thus he gladdened Damayantí with the assurance of his faith.
Then, rejoicing in each other, that blest pair, upon the gods
Led by Agni, gazed in homage, on their great protectors gazed.

Chosen thus Nishadha's monarch, the bright guardians of the world,
In their gladness all on Nala eight transcendant gifts bestowed;
To discern the visible godhead in the sacrifice, a gait
Firm and noble, S'ačí's husband, Indra to king Nala gave.
Agni gave his own bright presence whensoe'er the monarch called.
All the worlds instinct with splendour through his power Hutáśa gave.

यमस्त्वन्नरसं प्रादाद् धर्मे च परमां स्थितिं ।
अपाम्पतिर् अपाम्भावं यत्र वाञ्छति नैषधः ॥३७॥
स्रजश्चोत्तमगन्धाढ्याः सर्वे च मिथुनं ददुः ।
वरान् एवं प्रदायास्य देवास् ते त्रिदिवं गताः ॥३८॥
पार्थिवाश्चानुभूयास्य विवाहं विस्मयान्विताः ।
दमयन्त्याश्च मुदिताः प्रतिजग्मुर् यथागतं ॥३९॥
गतेषु पार्थिवेन्द्रेषु भीमः प्रीतो महामनाः ।
विवाहं कारयामास दमयन्त्या नलस्य च ॥४०॥
उष्य तत्र यथाकामं नैषधो द्विपदां वरः ।
भीमेन समनुज्ञातो जगाम नगरं स्वकं ॥४१॥
अवाप्य नारीरत्नं तु पुण्यश्लोकोऽपि पार्थिवः ।
रेमे सह तया राजन् शच्येव बलवृत्रहा ॥४२॥
अतीव मुदितो राजा भ्राजमानोऽंशुमान् इव ।
अरञ्जयत् प्रजा वीरो धर्मेण परिपालयन् ॥४३॥
ईजे चाप्यश्वमेधेन ययातिर् इव नाहुषः ।
अन्यैश्च बहुभिर् धीमान् क्रतुभिश्चाप्तदक्षिणैः ॥४४॥
पुनश्च रमणीयेषु वनेषूपवनेषु च ।
दमयन्त्या सह नलो विजहारामरोपमः ॥४५॥
जनयामास च नलो दमयन्त्या महामनाः ।
इन्द्रसेनं सुतञ्चापि इन्द्रसेनाञ्च कन्यकां ॥४६॥
एवं स यजमानश्च विहरंश्च नराधिपः ।
ररक्ष वसुसम्पूर्णां वसुधां वसुधाधिपः ॥४७॥

॥ इति नलोपाख्याने पञ्चमः सर्गः ॥५॥

Subtle taste in food gave Yama, and in virtue eminence;
Varun gave obedient water to be present at his call;
Garlands too of matchless fragrance; each his double blessing gave.
Thus bestowed their gracious favours, to the heavens the gods returned;
And the Rájas, who with wonder Nala's marriage saw confirmed
With the gentle Damayantí, as they came, in joy returned.
Thus the kings of earth departed; Bhíma in his joy and pride,
Solemnized the stately bridals of the maiden and the king.
Fitting time when there he'd sojourned, best of men, Nishadha's king;
Courteous parting with king Bhíma to his native city went.
Having gained the pearl of women the majestic lord of earth
Lived in bliss, as with his S'ací, he that those old giants slew.
In his joy the elated monarch, shining radiant as the sun,
Ruled the subjects of his kingdom with a just and equal sway.
Of the horse the famous offering, like Náhusha's mighty son,
Every sacrifice performed he, with rich gifts to holy men.
And full oft in flowering gardens, and delicious shady groves,
Like a god, the royal Nala took with Damayantí joy.
So begat from Damayantí, Nala, of heroic soul,
Indrasená one fair daughter, Indrasen one beauteous son.
Thus in sacrifice and pleasance took his joy the king of men,
So the earth with riches teeming ruled the sovereign of the earth.

End of Book V.

बृहदश्व उवाच।

वृते तु नैषधे भैम्या लोकपाला महौजसः।
यान्तो ददृशुर् आयान्तं द्वापरं कलिना सह ॥१॥
अथाब्रवीत् कलिं शक्रः सम्प्रेक्ष्य बलवृत्रहा।
द्वापरेण सहायेन कले ब्रूहि क्व यास्यसि ॥२॥
ततोऽब्रवीत् कलिः शक्रं दमयन्त्याः स्वयंवरं।
गत्वा हि वरयिष्ये तां मनो हि मम तां गतं ॥३॥
तम् अब्रवीत् प्रहस्येन्द्रो निवृत्तः स स्वयंवरः।
वृतस् तया नलो राजा पतिर् अस्मत्समीपतः ॥४॥
एवम् उक्तस्तु शक्रेण कलिः क्रोधसमन्वितः।
देवान् आमन्त्र्य तान् सर्वान् उवाचेदं वचस् तदा ॥५॥
देवानां मानुषं मध्ये यत् सा पतिम् अविन्दत।
तत्र तस्या भवेन् न्याय्यं विपुलं दण्डधारणं ॥६॥
एवम् उक्ते तु कलिना प्रत्यूचुस् ते दिवौकसः।
अस्माभिः समनुज्ञाते दमयन्त्या नलो वृतः ॥७॥
का च सर्वगुणोपेतं नाश्रयेत नलं नृपं।
यो वेद धर्मान् अखिलान् यथावच् चरितव्रतः ॥८॥
योऽधीते चतुरो वेदान् सर्वान् आख्यानपञ्चमान्।
नित्यं तृप्ता गृहे यस्य देवा यज्ञेषु धर्मतः ॥९॥
अहिंसानिरतो यश्च सत्यवादी दृढव्रतः।
यस्मिन् सत्यं धृतिर् दानं तपः शौचं दमः शमः ॥१०॥
ध्रुवाणि पुरुषव्याघ्रे लोकपालसमे नृपे।
एवंरूपं नलं यो वै कामयेच् छपितुं कले ॥११॥

Vṛihadaśva spake:

Nala chosen by Bhíma's daughter, the bright guardians of the world,
As they parted thence, with Kali, Dvápara approaching saw.
Kali as he saw, did Indra, did the giant-killer say,
'Here, with Dvápara attended, whither, Kali, dost thou go?'
Kali spake, 'The Svayaṃvara we of Damayantí seek;
Her I go to make my consort, into her mine heart hath passed.'
'Closed and ended is that bridal,' Indra answered with a smile,
'Nala she hath chosen for husband, in the presence of us all.'
Thus addressed by Indra, Kali, in the transport of his wrath,
All the heavenly gods saluting, thus his malediction spake,
'Since before the Immortals' presence she a mortal spouse did choose,
Of her impious crime most justly, heavy be the penal doom.'
Kali hardly thus had spoken than the heaven-born gods replied:
'With our full and liberal sanction Damayantí chose her lord.
Who to Nala, with all virtue rich endowed, would not incline?
He that rightly knows each duty, he who ever rightly acts,
He who reads the whole four Vedas, the Puráṇas too the fifth,
In whose palace with pure offerings ever are the gods adored,
Gentle to all living creatures, true in word and strict in vow;
Good and constant he, and generous, holy, temperate, patient, pure;
His are all these virtues ever, equal to the earth-guarding gods.
Thus endowed, the noble Nala, he, O Kali, that would curse,

आत्मानं स शपेन् मूढो हन्याद् आत्मानम् आत्मना।
एवङ्गुणं नलं यो वै कामयेच् छपितुं कले ॥१२॥
कृच्छ्रे स नरके मज्जेद् अगाधे विपुले हृदे।
एवम् उक्त्वा कलिं देवा द्वापरश्च दिवं ययुः ॥१३॥
ततो गतेषु देवेषु कलिर् द्वापरम् अब्रवीत्।
संहर्तुं नोत्सहे कोपं नले वत्स्यामि द्वापर ॥१४॥
भ्रंशयिष्यामि तं राज्यान् न भैम्या सह रंस्यते।
त्वमप्यक्षान् समाविश्य साहाय्यं कर्तुम् अर्हसि ॥१५॥

॥ इति नलोपाख्याने षष्ठः सर्गः ॥६॥

बृहदश्व उवाच।

एवं स समयं कृत्वा द्वापरेण कलिः सह।
आजगाम ततस् तत्र यत्र राजा स नैषधः ॥१॥
स नित्यम् अन्तरप्रेप्सुर् निषधेष्ववसच् चिरं।
अथास्य द्वादशे वर्षे ददर्श कलिर् अन्तरं ॥२॥
कृत्वा मूत्रम् उपस्पृश्य सन्ध्याम् अन्वास्त नैषधः।
अकृत्वा पादयोः शौचं तत्रैनं कलिर् आविशत् ॥३॥
स समाविश्य च नलं समीपं पुष्करस्य च।
गत्वा पुष्करम् आहेदम् एहि दीव्य नलेन वै ॥४॥
अक्षद्यूते नलं जेता भवान् हि सहितो मया।
निषधान् प्रतिपद्यस्व जित्वा राज्यं नलं नृपं ॥५॥
एवम् उक्तस्तु कलिना पुष्करो नलम् अभ्ययात्।
कलिश्चैव वृषो भूत्वा गवां पुष्करम् अभ्यगात् ॥६॥
आसाद्य तु नलं वीरं पुष्करः परवीरहा।

On the fool recoil his curses, only fatal to himself.
Nala, gifted with such virtues, he, O Kali, who would curse—
Be he plunged in hell's dark torments, in the deep and vasty lake.'
Thus the gods to Kali speaking to their native heavens arose.
Soon as they had parted, Kali thus to Dvápara began:
'I my wrath can curb no longer, I henceforth in Nala dwell;
From his kingdom will I cast him, from his bliss with his sweet bride.
Thou within the dice embodied, Dvápara, my cause assist.'

End of Book VI.

Vṛihadaśva spake:

Bound by that malignant treaty, Kali with his dark ally,
Haunted they the stately palace, where Nishadha's monarch ruled;
Watching still the fatal instant, in Nishadha long they dwelt.
Twelve long years had passed ere Kali saw that fatal instant come.
Nala after act uncleanly holy water having sipped,
Went to prayer, with feet unwashen;—Kali seized the fatal hour.
Into Nala straight he entered, and possessed his inmost soul.
Pushkara in haste he summoned—'Come, with Nala play at dice,
Ever in the gainful hazard, by my subtle aid thou'lt win,
Even the kingdom of Nishadha, even from Nala all his realm.'
Pushkara by Kali summoned, to his brother Nala came,
In the chief of dice embodied, Kali Pushkara stood near.
Pushkara the hero-slayer to king Nala standing near:

दीव्यावेत्यब्रवीद् भ्राता वृषेणेति मुहुर् मुहुः ॥७॥
न चक्षमे ततो राजा समाह्वानं महामनाः ।
वैदर्भ्याः प्रेक्षमाणायाः पणकालम् अमन्यत ॥८॥
हिरण्यस्य सुवर्णस्य यानयुग्यस्य वाससां ।
आविष्टः कलिना द्यूते जीयते स्म नलस् तदा ॥९॥
तम् अक्षमदसम्मत्तं सुहृदां न तु कश्चन ।
निवारणेऽभवच् छक्तो दीव्यमानम् अरिन्दमं ॥१०॥
ततः पौरजनाः सर्वे मन्त्रिभिः सह भारत ।
राजानं द्रष्टुम् आगच्छन् निवारयितुम् आतुरं ॥११॥
ततः सूत उपागम्य दमयन्त्यै न्यवेदयत् ।
एष पौरजनो देवि द्वारि तिष्ठति कार्यवान् ॥१२॥
निवेद्यतां नैषधाय सर्वाः प्रकृतयः स्थिताः ।
अमृष्यमाणा व्यसनं राज्ञो धर्मार्थदर्शिनः ॥१३॥
ततः सा वाष्पकलया वाचा दुःखेन कर्षिता ।
उवाच नैषधं भैमी शोकोपहतचेतना ॥१४॥
राजन् पौरजनो द्वारि त्वां दिदृक्षुर् अवस्थितः ।
मन्त्रिभिः सहितः सर्वै राजभक्तिपुरस्कृतः ।
तं द्रष्टुम् अर्हसीत्येवं पुनः पुनर् अभाषत ॥१५॥
तां तथा रुचिरापाङ्गीं विलपन्तीं तथाविधां ।
आविष्टः कलिना राजा नाभ्यभाषत किञ्चन ॥१६॥
ततस् ते मन्त्रिणः सर्वे ते चैव पुरवासिनः ।
नायम् अस्तीति दुःखार्ता व्रीडिता जग्मुर् आलयान् ॥१७॥
तथा तद् अभवद् द्यूतम् पुष्करस्य नलस्य च ।
युधिष्ठिर बहून् मासान् पुण्यश्लोकस्त्वजीयत ॥१८॥

॥ इति नलोपाख्याने सप्तमः सर्गः ॥७॥

'Play we with the dice, my brother,' thus again his brother said.
Long the lofty-minded Rája that bold challenge might not brook,
In Vidarbha's princess' presence deemed he now the time for play.
For his wealth, his golden treasures, for his chariots, for his robes,
Then possessed by Kali, Nala in the game was worsted still.
He with love of gaming maddened, of his faithful friends not one
Might arrest the desperate frenzy of the conqueror of his foes.
Came the citizens assembling, with the counsellors of state,
To behold the king approached they to restrain his dread disease.
Then the charioteer advancing thus to Damayantí spake:
'All the city, noble princess, stands assembled at the gate,
Say thou to Nishadha's monarch, "All his subjects here are met;
Ill they brook this dire misfortune in their justice-loving king."'
Then, her voice half-choked with anguish, spake the sorrow-stricken queen,
Spirit-broken, Bhíma's daughter to Nishadha's sovereign spake,
'Rája, lo! the assembled city at the gate their king to see:
With the counsellors of wisdom, by their loyal duty led.
Deign thou, monarch, to admit them,' thus again, again she said.
To the queen with beauteous eyelids uttering thus her sad lament,
Still possessed by wicked Kali, answered not the king a word.
Then those counsellors of wisdom, and those loyal citizens,
''Tis not he,' exclaimed in sorrow, and in shame and grief went home.
Thus of Pushkara and Nala still went on that fatal play;
Many a weary month it lasted, and still lost the king of men.

End of Book VII.

वृहदश्व उवाच ।

दमयन्ती ततो दृष्ट्वा पुण्यश्लोकं नराधिपं ।
उन्मत्तवद् अनुन्मत्ता देवने गतचेतसं ॥१॥
भयशोकसमाविष्टा राजन् भीमसुता ततः ।
चिन्तयामास तत् कार्यं सुमहत् पार्थिवं प्रति ॥२॥
सा शङ्कमाना तत्पापं चिकीर्षन्ती च तत्प्रियं ।
नलञ्च हृतसर्वस्वम् उपलभ्येदम् अब्रवीत् ॥३॥
वृहत्सेनाम् अतियशां तां धात्रीं परिचारिकां ।
हितां सर्वार्थकुशलाम् अनुरक्तां सुभाषितां ॥४॥
वृहत्सेने व्रजामात्यान् आनाय्य नलशासनात् ।
आचक्ष्व यद् धृतं द्रव्यम् अवशिष्टञ्च यद् वसु ॥५॥
ततस् ते मन्त्रिणः सर्वे विज्ञाय नलशासनं ।
अपि नो भागधेयं स्याद् इत्युक्त्वा नलम् आव्रजन् ॥६॥
तास्तु सर्वाः प्रकृतयो द्वितीयं समुपस्थिताः ।
न्यवेदयद् भीमसुता न च स प्रत्यनन्दत ॥७॥
वाक्यम् अप्रतिनन्दन्तं भर्तारम् अभिवीक्ष्य सा ।
दमयन्ती पुनर् वेश्म व्रीडिता प्रविवेश ह ॥८॥
निशम्य सततं चाक्षान् पुण्यश्लोकपराङ्मुखान् ।
नलञ्च हृतसर्वस्वं धात्रीं पुनर् उवाच ह ॥९॥
वृहत्सेने पुनर् गच्छ वार्ष्णेयं नलशासनात् ।
सूतम् आनय कल्याणि महत् कार्यम् उपस्थितं ॥१०॥
वृहत्सेना तु तच् छ्रुत्वा दमयन्त्या प्रभाषितं ।

VṚIHADAŚVA spake:

DAMAYANTÍ then beholding Puṇyaśloka, king of men,
Undistracted, him distracted with the maddening love of play.
In her dread and in her sorrow thus did Bhíma's daughter speak;
Pondering on the weighty business that concerned the king of men;
Trembling at his guilty frenzy, yet to please him still intent.
Nala, 'reft of all his treasures, when the noble woman saw,
Thus addressed she Vṛihatsená, her old faithful slave and nurse,
Friendly, in all business dextrous, most devoted, wise in speech:
'Vṛihatsená, go, the council as at Nala's call convene,
Say what he hath lost of treasure, and what treasure yet remains.'
Then did all that reverend council, Nala's summons as they heard,
'Our own fate is now in peril,' speaking thus, approach the king.
And a second time his subjects all assembling, crowded near,
And the queen announced their presence; of her words he took no heed.
All her words thus disregarded, when king Bhíma's daughter found,
To the palace Damayantí to conceal her shame returned.
When the dice she heard for ever adverse to the king of men,
And of all bereft, her Nala, to the nurse again she spake:
'Go again, my Vṛihatsená, in the name of Nala, go,
To the charioteer, Várshṇeya, great the deed must now be done.'
Vṛihatsená on the instant Damayantí's words she heard,

वार्ष्णेयम् आनयामास पुरुषैर् आप्तकारिभिः ॥११॥
वार्ष्णेयं तु ततो भैमी सान्त्वयन् श्लक्ष्णया गिरा ।
उवाच देशकालज्ञा प्राप्तकालम् अनिन्दिता ॥१२॥
जानीषे त्वं यथा राजा सम्यग्वृत्तः सदा त्वयि ।
तस्य त्वं विषमस्थस्य साहाय्यं कर्तुम् अर्हसि ॥१३॥
यथा यथा हि नृपतिः पुष्करेणेव जीयते ।
तथा तथास्य वै द्यूते रागो भूयोऽभिवर्धते ॥१४॥
यथा च पुष्करस्याक्षाः पतन्ति वशवर्तिनः ।
तथा विपर्ययश्चापि नलस्याक्षेषु दृश्यते ॥१५॥
सुहृत्स्वजनवाक्यानि यथावन्न शृणोति च ।
ममापि च तथा वाक्यं नाभिनन्दति मोहितः ॥१६॥
नूनं मन्ये न दोषोऽस्ति नैषधस्य महात्मनः ।
यत्तु मे वचनं राजा नाभिनन्दति मोहितः ॥१७॥
शरणं त्वां प्रपन्नाऽस्मि सारथे कुरु मद्वचः ।
न हि मे शुध्यते भावः कदाचिद् विनशेद् अपि ॥१८॥
नलस्य दयितान् अश्वान् योजयित्वा मनोजवान् ।
इदम् आरोप्य मिथुनं कुण्डिनं यातुम् अर्हसि ॥१९॥
मम ज्ञातिषु निक्षिप्य दारकौ स्यन्दनं तथा ।
अश्वांश चेमान् यथाकामं वस वान्यत्र गच्छ वा ॥२०॥
दमयन्त्यास्तु तद् वाक्यं वार्ष्णेयो नलसारथिः ।
न्यवेदयद् अशेषेण नलामात्येषु मुख्यशः ॥२१॥
तैः समेत्य विनिश्चित्य सोऽनुज्ञातो महीपते ।
ययौ मिथुनम् आरोप्य विदर्भास् तेन वाहिना ॥२२॥
हयांस् तत्र विनिक्षिप्य सूतो रथवरं च तं ।
इन्द्रसेनाञ्च तां कन्याम् इन्द्रसेनञ्च बालकं ॥२३॥
आमन्त्र्य भीमं राजानम् आर्तः शोचन् नलं नृपं ।

Caused the charioteer be summoned by her messengers of trust.
Bhíma's daughter to Várshṇeya, winning with her gentle voice,
Spake, the time, the place well choosing for the deed, nor spake in vain:
'Well thou know'st the full reliance that in thee the king hath placed,
In his fatal hour of peril wilt not thou stand forth to aid?
As by Pushkara is worsted, ever more and more the king,
More and more the fatal frenzy maddens in his heart for play.
As to Pushkara obedient ever fall the lucky dice,
Thus those dice to royal Nala still with adverse fortune fall.
Nor the voice of friend or kindred, as beseems him, will he hear;
E'en to me he will not listen, in the madness of his heart.
Of the lofty-minded Nala well I know 'tis not the sin,
That my words this senseless monarch in his frenzy will not hear.
Charioteer, to thee my refuge come I, do thou my behest;
I am not o'er calm in spirit, haply he may perish thus.
Yoke the much-loved steeds of Nala, fleet of foot, as thought, are they,
In the chariot place our children, to Kuṇḍina's city go.
Leave the children with my kindred, and the chariot and the steeds;
Then or dwell there at thy pleasure, or depart where'er thou wilt.'
When the speech of Damayantí heard king Nala's charioteer,
He, the chief of Nala's council, thus in full divan addressed,
Weighed within their solemn conclave, and their full assent obtained,
With the children in the chariot to Vidarbha straight he drove.
There he rendered up the horses with the chariot, there he left
That young maiden Indrasená, Indrásen, that noble boy.
To king Bhíma paid his homage, sad, for Nala's fall distressed,

अटमानस् ततोऽयोध्यां जगाम नगरीं तदा ॥२४॥
ऋतुपर्णं स राजानम् उपतस्थे सुदुःखितः ।
भृतिञ्चोपययौ तस्य सारथ्येन महीपतेः ॥२५॥

॥ इति नलोपाख्याने अष्टमः सर्गः ॥८॥

बृहदश्व उवाच ।

ततस् तु याते वार्ष्णेये पुण्यश्लोकस्य दीव्यतः ।
पुष्करेण हृतं राज्यं यच्चान्यद् वसु किञ्चन ॥१॥
हृतराज्यं नलं राजन् प्रहसन् पुष्करोऽब्रवीत् ।
द्यूतं प्रवर्ततां भूयः प्रतिपाणोऽस्ति कस् तव ॥२॥
शिष्टा ते दमयन्त्येका सर्वम् अन्यज् जितं मया ।
दमयन्त्याः पणः साधु वर्ततां यदि मन्यसे ॥३॥
पुष्करेणैवम् उक्तस्य पुण्यश्लोकस्य मन्युना ।
व्यदीर्यतेव हृदयं न चैनं किञ्चिद् अब्रवीत् ॥४॥
ततः पुष्करम् आलोक्य नलः परममन्युमान् ।
उत्सृज्य सर्वगात्रेभ्यो भूषणानि महायशाः ॥५॥
एकवासा ह्यसंवीतः सुहृच्छोकविवर्धनः ।
निश्चक्राम ततो राजा त्यक्त्वा सुविपुलां श्रियं ॥६॥
दमयन्त्येकवस्त्राऽथ गच्छन्तं पृष्ठतोऽन्वगात् ।
स तया बाह्यतः सार्धं त्रिरात्रं नैषधोऽवसत् ॥७॥
पुष्करस्तु महाराज घोषयामास वै पुरे ।
नले यः सम्यग् आतिष्ठेत् स गच्छेद् बध्यतां मम ॥८॥

Thence departing, to Ayodhyá, took the charioteer his way.
In his grief to Ṛituparṇa, that illustrious king, he came,
As his charioteer, the service entered of the lord of earth.

End of Book VIII.

Vṛihadaśva spake:

Scarce Várshṇeya had departed, still the king of men played on,
Till to Pushkara his kingdom, all that he possessed, was lost.
Nala then, despoiled of kingdom, smiling Pushkara bespake:
'Throw we yet another hazard, Nala, where is now thy stake?
There remains but Damayantí, all thou hast beside, is mine.
Throw we now for Damayantí, come, once more the hazard try.'
Thus, as Pushkara addressed him, Puṇyaśloka's inmost heart
By his grief was rent asunder, not a single word he spake.
And on Pushkara, king Nala in his silent anguish gazed.
All his ornaments of splendour from his person stripped he off,
With a single vest, scarce covered, 'mid the sorrow of his friends,
Slowly wandered forth the monarch fallen from such an height of bliss.
Damayantí with one garment slowly followed him behind.
Three long nights Nishadha's monarch there without the gates had dwelt.
Proclamation through the city then did Pushkara bid make,
'Whosoe'er befriendeth Nala shall to instant death be doomed.'

पुष्करस्य तु वाक्येन तस्य विद्वेषणेन च ।
पौरा न तस्य सत्कारं कृतवन्तो युधिष्ठिर ॥९॥
स तथा नगराभ्यासे सत्कारार्हो न सत्कृतः ।
चिरात्रम् उषितो राजा जलमात्रेण वर्तयन् ॥१०॥
पीड्यमानः क्षुधा तत्र फलमूलानि कर्षयन् ।
प्रातिष्ठत ततो राजा दमयन्ती तम् अन्वगात् ॥११॥
क्षुधया पीड्यमानस्तु नलो बहुतिथेऽहनि ।
अपश्यच् छकुनान् कांश्चिद् धिरण्यसदृशच्छदान् ॥१२॥
स चिन्तयामास तदा निषधाधिपतिर् बली ।
अस्ति भक्ष्यो ममाद्यायं वसु चेदं भविष्यति ॥१३॥
ततस् तान् परिधानेन वाससा स समावृणोत् ।
तस्य तद् वस्त्रम् आदाय सर्वे जग्मुर् विहायसा ॥१४॥
उत्पतन्तः खगा वाक्यम् एतद् आहुस् ततो नलं ।
दृष्ट्वा दिग्वाससं भूमौ स्थितं दीनम् अधोमुखं ॥१५॥
वयम् अक्षाः सुदुर्बुद्धे तव वासो जिहीर्षवः ।
आगता न हि नः प्रीतिः सवाससि गते त्वयि ॥१६॥
तान् समीक्ष्य गतान् अक्षान् आत्मानञ्च विवाससं ।
पुण्यश्लोकस् तदा राजन् दमयन्तीम् अथाब्रवीत् ॥१७॥
येषां प्रकोपाद् ऐश्वर्यात् प्रच्युतोऽहम् अनिन्दिते ।
प्राणयात्रां न विन्दे च दुःखितः क्षुधयान्वितः ॥१८॥
येषां कृते न सत्कारम् अकुर्वन् मयि नैषधाः ।
त इमे शकुना भूत्वा वासोऽप्यपहरन्ति मे ॥१९॥
वैषम्यं परमं प्राप्तो दुःखितो गतचेतनः ।
भर्ता तेऽहं निबोधेदं वचनं हितम् आत्मनः ॥२०॥
एते गच्छन्ति बहवः पन्थानो दक्षिणापथं ।
अवन्तीम् ऋक्षवन्तञ्च समतिक्रम्य पर्वतं ॥२१॥

Thus, as Pushkara gave order, in the terror of his power,
Might the citizens no longer hospitably serve the king.
Near the walls, of kind reception worthiest, but by none received,
Three nights longer staid the monarch, water was his only drink.
He in unfastidious hunger plucked the fruits, the roots of earth.
Then went forth again the outcast; Damayantí followed slow.
In the agony of famine Nala, after many days,
Saw some birds around him settling with their golden tinctured wings.
Then the monarch of Nishadha thought within his secret heart,
These to-day my welcome banquet, and my treasure these will be.
Over them his single garment spreading light he wrapped them round.
Up that single garment bearing to the air they sprang away;
And the birds above him hovering thus in human accents spake,
Naked as they saw him standing on the earth, and sad, and lone:—
'Lo, we are the dice, to spoil thee thus descended, foolish king!
While thou hadst a single garment all our joy was incomplete.'
When the dice he saw departing, and himself without his robe,
Mournfully did Puṇyaśloka thus to Damayantí speak:
'They, O blameless, by whose anger from my kingdom I am driven,
Life-sustaining food unable in my misery to find—
They, through whom Nishadha's people, may not house their outcast king—
They, the forms of birds assuming, my one robe have borne away.
In the dark extreme of misery, sad and frantic as I am,
Hear me, princess, hear and profit by thy husband's best advice.
Hence are many roads diverging to the region of the south,
Passing by Avantí's city, and the height of Ṛikshaván;

एष विन्ध्यो महाशैलः पयोष्णी च समुद्रगा ।
आश्रमाश्च महर्षीणां बहुमूलफलान्विताः ॥२२॥
एष पन्था विदर्भाणाम् असौ गच्छति कोशलान् ।
अतःपरञ्च देशोऽयं दक्षिणे दक्षिणापथः ॥२३॥
एतद् वाक्यं नलो राजा दमयन्तीं समाहितः ।
उवाचासकृद् आर्तो हि भैमीम् उद्दिश्य भारत ॥२४॥
ततः सा वाष्पकलया वाचा दुःखेन कर्षिता ।
उवाच दमयन्ती तं नैषधं करुणं वचः ॥२५॥
उद्वेजते मे हृदयं सीदन्त्यङ्गानि सर्वशः ।
तव पार्थिव सङ्कल्पं चिन्तयन्त्याः पुनः पुनः ॥२६॥
हृतराज्यं हृतद्रव्यं विवस्त्रं क्षुत्तृषान्वितं ।
कथम् उत्सृज्य गच्छेयम् अहं त्वां निर्जने वने ॥२७॥
श्रान्तस्य ते क्षुधार्तस्य चिन्तयानस्य तत् सुखं ।
वने घोरे महाराज नाशयिष्याम्यहं क्लमं ॥२८॥
न च भार्यासमं किञ्चिद् विद्यते भिषजां मतं ।
औषधं सर्वदुःखेषु सत्यम् एतद् ब्रवीमि ते ॥२९॥

नल उवाच ।

एवम् एतद् यथात्थ त्वं दमयन्ति सुमध्यमे ।
नास्ति भार्यासमं मित्रं नरस्यार्तस्य भेषजं ॥३०॥
न चाहं त्यक्तुकामस् त्वां किमर्थं भीरु शङ्कसे ।
त्यजेयम् अहम् आत्मानं न चैवं त्वाम् अनिन्दिते ॥३१॥

दमयन्त्युवाच ।

यदि मां त्वं महाराज न विहातुम् इहेच्छसि ।
तत् किमर्थं विदर्भाणां पन्थाः समुपदिश्यते ॥३२॥
अवैमि चाहं नृपते न तु मां त्यक्तुम् अर्हसि ।

Vindhya here, the mighty mountain, and Payoshṇí's seaward stream;
And the lone retreats of hermits, richly stored with roots and fruits.
This will lead thee to Vidarbha, this to Kośala away,
Far beyond the region stretches southward to the southward clime.'
In these words to Damayantí did the royal Nala speak,
More than once to Bhíma's daughter anxious pointing out the way.
She, with voice half-choked with sorrow, with her weight of woe oppressed,
These sad words did Damayantí to Nishadha's monarch speak:—
'My afflicted heart is breaking, and my sinking members fail,
When, O king, thy desperate counsel once I think of, once again.
Robbed of kingdom, robbed of riches, naked, thirst and hunger-worn;
How shall I depart and leave thee in the wood by man untrod?
When thou sad and famine-stricken thinkest of thy former bliss,
In the wild wood, oh, my husband, I thy weariness will soothe!
Like a wife, in every sorrow, this the wise physicians own,
Healing herb is none or balsam, Nala, 'tis the truth I speak.'

Nala spake:

Slender-waisted Damayantí, true, indeed, is all thou'st said;
Like a wife no friendly medicine to afflicted man is given.
Fear not that I thee abandon, Wherefore, timid, dread'st thou this?
Oh, myself might I abandon, and not thee, thou unreproached!

Damayantí spake:

If indeed, oh mighty monarch, thou wilt ne'er abandon me,
Wherefore then towards Vidarbha dost thou point me out the way?
Well, I know thee, noble Nala, to desert me far too true,

चेतसा त्वपकृष्टेन मां त्यजेथा महीपते ॥३३॥
पन्थानं हि ममाभीक्ष्णम् आख्यासि च नरोत्तम।
अतोनिमित्तं शोकं मे वर्धयस्यमरोपम ॥३४॥
यदि चायम् अभिप्रायस् तव ज्ञातीन् व्रजेद् इति।
सहिताव् एव गच्छावो विदर्भान् यदि मन्यसे ॥३५॥
विदर्भराजस् तत्र त्वां पूजयिष्यति मानद।
तेन त्वं पूजितो राजन् सुखं वत्स्यसि नो गृहे ॥३६॥

॥ इति नलोपाख्याने नवमः सर्गः ॥९॥

नल उवाच।

यथा राज्यं तव पितुस् तथा मम न संशयः।
न तु तत्र गमिष्यामि विषमस्थः कथञ्चन ॥१॥
कथं समृद्धो गत्वाऽहं तव हर्षविवर्धनः।
परिच्युतो गमिष्यामि तव शोकविवर्धनः ॥२॥

वृहदश्व उवाच।

इति ब्रुवन् नलो राजा दमयन्तीं पुनः पुनः।
सान्त्वयामास कल्याणीं वाससोऽर्धेन संवृतां ॥३॥
ताव् एकवस्त्रसंवीताव् अटमानाव् इतस्ततः।
क्षुत्पिपासापरिश्रान्तौ सभां काञ्चिद् उपेयतुः ॥४॥
तां सभाम् उपसम्प्राप्य तदा स निषधाधिपः।
वैदर्भ्या सहितो राजा निषसाद महीतले ॥५॥
स वै विवस्त्रो विकटो मलिनः पांशुगुण्ठितः।

Only with a soul distracted would'st thou leave me, lord of earth.
Yet, again, the way thou pointest, yet, again, thou best of men,
Thus my sorrow still enhancing, oh, thou like the immortal gods!
If this be thy better counsel, 'to her kindred let her go,'
Be it so, and both together, to Vidarbha set we forth.
Thee Vidarbha's king will honour, honour'd in his turn by thee;
Held in high respect and happy in our mansion thou shalt dwell.

End of Book IX.

Nala spake:

Mighty is thy father's kingdom, once was mine as mighty too;
Never will I there seek refuge in my base extremity.
There I once appeared in glory, to the exalting of thy pride;
Shall I now appear in misery, to the increasing of thy shame?

Vṛihadaśva spake:

Nala thus to Damayantí spake again, and yet again,
Comforting the noble lady, scant in half a garment clad.
Both together by one garment covered, roamed they here and there;
Wearied out by thirst and famine, to a cabin they drew near.
When they reached that lowly cabin then did great Nishadha's king
With the princess of Vidarbha on the hard earth seat them down;
Naked, with no mat to rest on, wet with mire and stained with dust.

दमयन्त्या सह श्रान्तः सुष्वाप धरणीतले ॥६॥
दमयन्त्यपि कल्याणी निद्रयाऽपहृता ततः ।
सहसा दुःखम् आसाद्य सुकुमारी तपस्विनी ॥७॥
सुप्तायां दमयन्त्यां तु नलो राजा विशाम्पते ।
शोकोन्मथितचित्तात्मा न स्म शेते यथा पुरा ॥८॥
स तद् राज्यापहरणं सुहृत्त्यागञ्च सर्वशः ।
वने च तं परिध्वंसं प्रेक्ष्य चिन्ताम् उपेयिवान् ॥९॥
किं नु मे स्याद् इदं कृत्वा किं नु मे स्याद् अकुर्वतः ।
किं नु मे मरणं श्रेयः परित्यागो जनस्य वा ॥१०॥
माम् इयं ह्यनुरक्तेव दुःखं प्राप्नोति मत्कृते ।
मद्विहीना त्वियं गच्छेत् कदाचित् स्वजनं प्रति ॥११॥
मयि निःसंशयं दुःखम् इयम् प्राप्स्यत्यनुव्रता ।
उत्सर्गे संशयः स्यात्तु विन्देतापि सुखं क्वचित् ॥१२॥
स विनिश्चित्य बहुधा विचार्य च पुनः पुनः ।
उत्सर्गं मन्यते श्रेयो दमयन्त्या नराधिपः ॥१३॥
न चैषा तेजसा शक्या कैश्चिद् धर्षयितुं पथि ।
यशस्विनी महाभागा मद्भक्तेयं पतिव्रता ॥१४॥
एवं तस्य तदा बुद्धिर् दमयन्त्यां न्यवर्तत ।
कलिना दुष्टभावेन दमयन्त्या विसर्जने ॥१५॥
सोऽवस्त्रताम् आत्मनश्च तस्याश्चाप्येकवस्त्रतां ।
चिन्तयित्वाऽध्यगाद् राजा वस्त्रार्धस्यावकर्तनं ॥१६॥
कथं वासो विकर्तेयं न च बुध्येत मे प्रिया ।
विचिन्त्यैवं नलो राजा सभां पर्यचरत् तदा ॥१७॥
परिधावन्न् अथ नल इतश्चेतश्च भारत ।
आससाद सभोद्देशे विकोषं खड्गम् उत्तमं ॥१८॥
तेनार्धं वाससश् छित्त्वा निवस्य च परन्तपः ।

Weary then with Damayantí on the earth he fell asleep.
Sank the lovely Damayantí by his side with sleep opprest,
She thus plunged in sudden misery, she the tender, the devout.
But while on the cold earth slumbered Damayantí, all distraught
Nala in his mind by sorrow might no longer calmly sleep;
For the losing of his kingdom, the desertion of his friends,
And his weary forest-wanderings, painful on his thought arose.
'If I do it, what may follow? what if I refuse to do?
Were my instant death the better, or to abandon her I love?
But to me too deep devoted suffers she distress and shame;
Reft of me she home may wander to her royal father's house.
Faithful wandering ever with me certain sorrow will she bear,
But if separated from me chance of solace may be hers.'
Long within his heart he pondered, and again, again weighed o'er.
Best he thought it Damayantí to desert, that wretched king.
From her virtue none dare harm her in the lonely forest way,
Her the fortunate, the noble, my devoted wedded wife.
Thus his mind on Damayantí dwelt in its perverted thought,
Wrought by Kali's evil influence to desert his lovely wife.
Of himself without a garment, and of her with only one
As he thought, approached he near her to divide that single robe.
'How shall I divide the garment by my loved one unperceived?'
Pondering this within his spirit round the cabin Nala went.
In that narrow cabin's circuit Nala wandered here and there,
Till he found without a scabbard, shining, a well-tempered sword.
Then when half that only garment he had severed, and put on,

सुप्ताम् उत्सृज्य वैदर्भीं प्राद्रवद् गतचेतनः ॥१९॥
ततो निवृत्तहृदयः पुनर् आगम्य तां सभां ।
दमयन्तीं तदा दृष्ट्वा रुरोद निषधाधिपः ॥२०॥
यां न वायुर् न चादित्यः पुरा पश्यति मे प्रियां ।
सेयमद्य सभामध्ये शेते भूमाव् अनाथवत् ॥२१॥
इयं वस्त्रावकर्तेन संवीता चारुहासिनी ।
उन्मत्तेव वरारोहा कथं बुद्ध्वा भविष्यति ॥२२॥
कथम् एका सती भैमी मया विरहिता शुभा ।
चरिष्यति वने घोरे मृगव्यालनिषेविते ॥२३॥
आदित्या वसवो रुद्रा अश्विनौ समरुद्गणौ ।
रक्षन्तु त्वां महाभागे धर्मेणासि समावृता ॥२४॥
एवमुक्त्वा प्रियां भार्यां रूपेणाप्रतिमां भुवि ।
कलिनापहृतज्ञानो नलः प्रातिष्ठद् उद्यतः ॥२५॥
गत्वा गत्वा नलो राजा पुनर् एति सभां मुहुः ।
आकृष्यमाणः कलिना सौहृदेनावकृष्यते ॥२६॥
द्विधेव हृदयं तस्य दुःखितस्याभवत् तदा ।
दोलेव मुहुर् आयाति याति चैव सभां प्रति ॥२७॥
अवकृष्टस्तु कलिना मोहितः प्राद्रवन् नलः ।
सुप्ताम् उत्सृज्य तां भार्यां विलप्य करुणं बहु ॥२८॥
नष्टात्मा कलिना स्पृष्टस् तत् तद् विगणयन् नृपः ।
जगामैकां वने शून्ये भार्याम् उत्सृज्य दुःखितः ॥२९॥

॥ इति नलोपाख्याने दशमः सर्गः ॥१०॥

In her sleep Vidarbha's princess, with bewildered mind he fled.
Yet, his cruel heart relenting, to the cabin turns he back;
On the slumbering Damayantí gazing, sadly wept the king:
'Thou, that sun nor wind hath ever roughly visited, my love!
On the hard earth in a cabin sleepest with thy guardian gone.
Thus attired in half a garment she that aye so sweetly smiled,
Like to one distracted, beauteous, how at length will she awake?
How will't fare with Bhíma's daughter, lone, abandoned by her lord,
Wandering in the savage forest, where wild beasts and serpents dwell?
May the suns and winds of heaven, may the genii of the woods,
Noblest, may they all protect thee, thine own virtue thy best guard.'
To his wife of peerless beauty on the earth, 'twas thus he spoke.
Then of sense bereft by Kali Nala hastily set forth;
And departing, still departing he returned again, again;
Dragged away by that bad demon, ever by his love drawn back.
Nala, thus his heart divided into two conflicting parts,
Like a swing goes backward, forward, from the cabin, to and fro.
Torn away at length by Kali flies afar the frantic king,
Leaving there his wife in slumber, making miserable moans.
Reft of sense, possessed by Kali, thinking still on her he left,
Passed he in the lonely forest, leaving his deserted wife.

End of Book X.

बृहदश्व उवाच ।

अपक्रान्ते नले राजन् दमयन्ती गतक्लमा ।
अबुध्यत वरारोहा सन्त्रस्ता विजने वने ॥१॥
अपश्यमाना भर्तारं शोकदुःखसमन्विता ।
प्राक्रोशद् उच्चैः सन्त्रस्ता महाराजेति नैषधं ॥२॥
हा नाथ हा महाराज हा स्वामिन् किं जहासि मां ।
हा हताऽस्मि विनष्टाऽस्मि भीताऽस्मि विजने वने ॥३॥
ननु नाम महाराज धर्मज्ञः सत्यवाग् असि ।
कथम् उक्त्वा तथा सत्यं सुप्ताम् उत्सृज्य मां गतः ॥४॥
कथम् उत्सृज्य गन्तासि दक्षां भार्याम् अनुव्रतां ।
विशेषतोऽनपकृते परेणापकृते सति ॥५॥
शक्यसे ता गिरः सम्यक्कर्तुं मयि नरेश्वर ।
यास् तेषां लोकपालानां सन्निधौ कथिताः पुरा ॥६॥
नाकाले विहितो मृत्युर् मर्त्यानां पुरुषर्षभ ।
यत्र कान्ता त्वयोत्सृष्टा मुहूर्तमपि जीवति ॥७॥
पर्याप्तः परिहासोऽयम् एतावान् पुरुषर्षभ ।
भीताऽहम् अतिदुर्धर्ष दर्शयात्मानम् ईश्वर ॥८॥
दृश्यसे दृश्यसे राजन्न् एष दृष्टोऽसि नैषध ।
आवार्य गुल्मैर् आत्मानं किं मां न प्रतिभाषसे ॥९॥
नृशंसं वत राजेन्द्र यन् माम् एवङ्गताम् इह ।
विलपन्तीं समागम्य नाश्वासयसि पार्थिव ॥१०॥
न शोचाम्यहम् आत्मानं न चान्यदपि किञ्चन ।
कथं नु भवितास्येक इति त्वां नृप रोदिमि ॥११॥

Vṛihadaśva spake:

Scarce, O king, had Nala parted, Damayantí now refreshed,
Wakened up, the slender-waisted, timorous in the desert wood.
When she did not see her husband, overpowered with grief and pain,
Loud she shriek'd in her first anguish, 'Where art thou, Nishadha's king?
Mighty king! my soul-protector; O my lord! desert'st thou me?
Oh, I'm lost! undone for ever, helpless in the wild wood left;
Faithful once to every duty wert thou not, and true in word?
Art thou faithful to thy promise to desert me thus in sleep?
Could'st thou then depart, forsaking thy devoted, constant wife?
Her in sooth that never wronged thee, wronged indeed, but not by her.
Keep'st thou thus thy solemn promise, oh, unfaithful lord of men,
There, when all the gods were present, plighted to thy wedded wife?
Death is but decreed to mortals at its own appointed time;
Hence one moment, thus deserted, one brief moment do I live.—
But thou'st had thy sport—enough then, now desist, O king of men,
Mock not thou a trembling woman, show thee to me, O my lord!
Yes, I see thee, there I see thee hidden as thou think'st from sight,
In the bushes why conceal thee? answer me, why speak'st thou not?
O ungentle prince of monarchs! to this piteous plight reduced,
Wherefore wilt thou not approach me to console me in my woe?
For myself I will not sorrow, nor for aught to me befalls.
Thou art all alone, my husband, I will only mourn for thee.

कथं नु राजंस् तृषितः क्षुधितः श्रमकर्षितः ।
सायाह्ने वृक्षमूलेषु माम् अपश्यन् भविष्यसि ॥१२॥
ततः सा तीव्रशोकार्ता प्रदीप्तेव च मन्युना ।
इतश्चेतश्च रुदती पर्यधावत दुःखिता ॥१३॥
मुहुर् उत्पतते बाला मुहुः पतति विह्वला ।
मुहुर् आलीयते भीता मुहुः क्रोशति रोदिति ॥१४॥
अतीव शोकसन्तप्ता मुहुर् निःश्वस्य दुःखिता ।
उवाच भैमी निःश्वस्य रुदत्यथ पतिव्रता ॥१५॥
यस्याभिशापाद् दुःखार्तो दुःखं विन्दति नैषधः ।
तस्य भूतस्य नो दुःखाद् दुःखम् अभ्यधिकं भवेत् ॥१६॥
अपापचेतसं पापो य एवं कृतवान् नलं ।
तस्माद् दुःखतरं प्राप्य जीवत्वसुखजीविकां ॥१७॥
एवं तु विलपन्ती सा राज्ञो भार्या महात्मनः ।
अन्वेषमाणा भर्तारं वने श्वापदसेविते ॥१८॥
उन्मत्तवद् भीमसुता विलपन्ती ततस्ततः ।
हा हा राजन् इति मुहुर् इतश्चेतश्च धावति ॥१९॥
तां क्रन्दमानाम् अत्यर्थं कुररीम् इव वाशती ।
करुणं बहु शोचन्तीं विलपन्तीं मुहुर् मुहुः ॥२०॥
सहसाभ्यागतां भैमीम् अभ्यासपरिवर्तिनीं ।
जग्राहाजगरो ग्राहो महाकायः क्षुधान्वितः ॥२१॥
सा ग्रस्यमाना ग्राहेण शोकेन च परिप्लुता ।
नात्मानं शोचति तथा यथा शोचति नैषधं ॥२२॥
हा नाथ माम् इह वने ग्रस्यमानाम् अनाथवत् ।
ग्राहेणानेन विजने किमर्थं नानुधावसि ॥२३॥
कथं भविष्यसि पुनर् माम् अनुस्मृत्य नैषध ।
शापान् मुक्तः पुनर् लब्ध्वा बुद्धिं चेतो धनानि च ॥२४॥

How will't fare with thee, my Nala, thirsting, famished, faint with toil?
Nor beholding me await thee underneath the trees at eve.'
Then, in all her depth of anguish, with her trouble as on fire,
Hither, thither, went she weeping, all around she went and wailed.
Now springs up the desolate princess, now falls down in prostrate grief;
Now she pines in silent sorrow, now she shrieks and wails aloud.
So consumed with inward misery, ever sighing more and more,
Spake at length king Bhíma's daughter, spake the still devoted wife:
'He, by whose dire imprecation Nala this dread suffering bears,
May he far surpass in suffering all that Nala suffers now.
May the evil one, to evil, who the blameless Nala drives,
Smitten by a curse as fatal, live a dark unblessed life.'
Thus her absent lord lamenting that high-minded Rája's queen,
Everywhere her lord went seeking in the satyr-haunted wood.
Like a maniac, Bhíma's daughter, wandered wailing here and there;
And 'alas! alas! my husband,' everywhere her cry was heard.
Her beyond all measure wailing like the osprey screaming shrill,
Miserably still deploring, still renewing her lament.
Suddenly king Bhíma's daughter, as she wandered near his lair,
Seized a huge gigantic serpent in his raging famine fierce.
In the grasp of that fierce serpent, round about with terror girt,
Not herself she pities only, pities she Nishadha's king.
'O my guardian, thus unguarded in this savage forest seized,
Seized by this terrific serpent, wherefore art not thou at hand?
How will't be, when thou rememberest once again thy faithful wife,
From this dreadful curse delivered, mind, and sense, and wealth returned?

श्रान्तस्य ते क्षुधार्तस्य परिग्लानस्य नैषध ।
कः श्रमं राजशार्दूल नाशयिष्यति तेऽनघ ॥२५॥
ततः कश्चिन् मृगव्याधो विचरन् गहने वने ।
आक्रन्दमानां संश्रुत्य जवेनाभिससार ह ॥२६॥
तां तु दृष्ट्वा तथा ग्रस्ताम् उरगेणायतेक्षणां ।
त्वरमाणो मृगव्याधः समभिक्रम्य वेगतः ॥२७॥
मुखतः पाटयामास शस्त्रेण निशितेन च ।
निर्विचेष्टं भुजङ्गं तं विशस्य मृगजीवनः ॥२८॥
मोक्षयित्वा स तां व्याधः प्रक्षाल्य सलिलेन च ।
समाश्वास्य कृताहाराम् अथ पप्रच्छ भारत ॥२९॥
कस्य त्वं मृगशावाक्षि कथञ्चाभ्यागता वनं ।
कथञ्चेदं महत् कृच्छ्रं प्राप्तवत्यसि भाविनि ॥३०॥
दमयन्ती तथा तेन पृच्छ्यमाना विशाम्पते ।
सर्वम् एतद् यथावृत्तम् आचचक्षेऽस्य भारत ॥३१॥
ताम् अर्धवस्त्रसंवीतां पीनश्रोणिपयोधरां ।
सुकुमारानवद्याङ्गीं पूर्णचन्द्रनिभाननां ॥३२॥
अरालपक्ष्मनयनां तथा मधुरभाषिणीं ।
लक्षयित्वा मृगव्याधः कामस्य वशम् ईयिवान् ॥३३॥
ताम् एवं श्लक्ष्णया वाचा लुब्धको मृदुपूर्वया ।
सान्त्वयामास कामार्तस् तद् अबुध्यत भाविनी ॥३४॥
दमयन्त्यपि तं दुष्टम् उपलभ्य पतिव्रता ।
तीव्ररोषसमाविष्टा प्रजज्वालेव मन्युना ॥३५॥
स तु पापमतिः क्षुद्रः प्रधर्षयितुम् आतुरः ।
दुर्धर्षां तर्कयामास दीप्ताम् अग्निशिखाम् इव ॥३६॥
दमयन्ती तु दुःखार्ता पतिराज्यविनाकृता ।
अतीतवाक्पथे काले शशापैनं रुषान्विता ॥३७॥

When thou'rt weary, when thou'rt hungry, when thou'rt fainting with fatigue,
Who will soothe, O blameless Nala, all thy weariness, thy woe?'

Then a huntsman, as he wandered in the forest jungle thick,
As he heard her thus bewailing, in his utmost haste drew near.
By the serpent that long-eyed one firmly grasped when he beheld,
Instant did the nimble huntsman, rapidly as he came on,
Strike that unresisting serpent with a sharp and mortal shaft:
In the mouth he pierced that serpent, skill'd in slaughter of the chase.
Her released he from her peril washed he then with water pure,
And with sylvan food refreshed her, and with soothing words address'd:
'Who art thou that roam'st the forest with the eyes of the gazelle;
How to this extreme of misery, noble lady, hast thou fallen?'
Damayantí, by the huntsman, thus in soothing tone addressed,
All the story of her misery told him, as it all befell;
Her, scant-clothed in half a garment, with soft-swelling limbs and breast,
Form of youthful faultless beauty, and her fair and moonlike face,
And her eyes with brows dark arching, and her softly-melting speech,
Saw long time that wild-beast hunter, kindled all his heart with love.
Then with winning voice that huntsman, bland beginning his discourse,
Fain with amorous speech would soothe her; she his dark intent perceived.
Damayantí, chaste and faithful, soon as she his meaning knew,
In the transport of her anger, her indignant soul took fire,
In his wicked thought the dastard her yet powerless to subdue,
On the unsubdued stood gazing, as like some bright flame she shone.
Damayantí, in her sorrow, of her realm, her lord bereft,
Deemed the time gone by for parley, uttered loud her curse of wrath,—

यथाऽहं नैषधाद् अन्यं मनसापि न चिन्तये ।
तथायं पततां क्षुद्रः परासुर् मृगजीवनः ॥३८॥
उक्तमात्रे तु वचने तथा स मृगजीवनः ।
व्यसुः पपात मेदिन्याम् अग्निदग्ध इव द्रुमः ॥३९॥

॥ इति नलोपाख्यान एकादशः सर्गः ॥११॥

बृहदश्व उवाच ।

सा निहत्य मृगव्याधं प्रतस्थे कमलेक्षणा ।
वनं प्रतिभयं शून्यं झिल्लिकागणनादितं ॥१॥
सिंहद्वीपिरुरुव्याघ्रमहिषर्क्षगणैर् युतं ।
नानापक्षिगणाकीर्णं म्लेच्छतस्करसेवितं ॥२॥
शालवेणुधवाश्वत्थतिन्दुकेङ्गुदकिंशुकैः ।
अर्जुनारिष्टसञ्छन्नं स्यन्दनैश्च सशाल्मलैः ॥३॥
जम्ब्वाम्रलोध्रखदिरसालवेत्रसमाकुलं ।
पद्मकामलकप्लक्षकदम्बोडुम्बरावृतं ॥४॥
वदरीविल्वसञ्छन्नं न्यग्रोधैश्च समाकुलं ।
प्रियालतालखर्जूरहरीतकविभीतकैः ॥५॥
नानाधातुशतैर् नद्धान् विविधान् अपि चाचलान् ।
निकुञ्जान् परिसङ्घुष्टान् दरीश्चाद्भुतदर्शनाः ॥६॥
नदीः सरांसि वापीश्च विविधांश्च मृगद्विजान् ।
सा बहून् भीमरूपांश्च पिशाचोरगराक्षसान् ॥७॥
पल्वलानि तडागानि गिरिकूटानि सर्वशः ।
सरितो निर्झरांश्चैव ददर्शाद्भुतदर्शनान् ॥८॥

'As my pure and constant spirit swerves not from Nishadha's lord,
Instant so may this base hunter lifeless fall upon the earth.'
Scarce that single word was uttered, suddenly that hunter bold
Down upon the earth fell lifeless, like a lightning-blasted tree.

End of Book XI.

Vṛihadaśva spake:

Slain that savage wild-beast hunter, onward went the lotus-eyed,
Through the dread and desert forest ringing with the cricket's song;
Full of lions, pards, and tigers, stags, and buffalos, and bears,
Where all kinds of birds were flocking, and wild men and robbers dwelt.
Thick with Śáls, bamboos, Aśvatthas, Dhavas, and the Ebon dark,
Oily In-guds, Kinśuks, Arjuns, Ním trees, Syandans, Śálmalas;
Full with Rose-apples and Mangoes, Lodh trees, Catechus and Canes,
Blushing Lotuses, Kadambas, and the tree with massy leaves;
Close o'erspread with Jujubes, Bel trees, tangled with the holy Fig,
Palms, Priyálas, Dates, Harítas, trees of every form and name.
Pregnant with rich mines of metal many a mountain it enclosed,
Many a shady resonant arbour, many a deep and wondrous glen;
Many a lake, and pool, and river, birds and beasts of every shape.
She, in forms terrific round her, serpents, elves, and giants saw:
Pools, and tanks of lucid water, and the shaggy tops of hills,
Flowing streams and headlong torrents saw, and wondered at the sight.

यूथशो ददृशे चात्र विदर्भाधिपनन्दिनी ।
महिषांश्च वराहांश्च ऋक्षांश्च वनपन्नगान् ॥ ९॥
तेजसा यशसा लक्ष्म्या स्थित्या च परया युता ।
वैदर्भी विचरत्येका नलम् अन्वेषती तदा ॥ १०॥
नाबिभ्यत् सा नृपसुता भैमी तत्राथ कस्यचित् ।
दारुणाम् अटवीं प्राप्य भर्तृव्यसनपीडिता ॥ ११॥
विदर्भतनया राजन् विललाप सुदुःखिता ।
भर्तृशोकपरीताङ्गी शिलातलम् अथाश्रिता ॥ १२॥

दमयन्त्युवाच ।

व्यूढोरस्क महाबाहो नैषधानां जनाधिप ।
क्व नु राजन् गतोऽसीह त्यक्त्वा मां विजने वने ॥ १३॥
अश्वमेधादिभिर् वीर क्रतुभिर् भूरिदक्षिणैः ।
कथम् इष्ट्वा नरव्याघ्र मयि मिथ्या प्रवर्तसे ॥ १४॥
यत् त्वयोक्तं नरश्रेष्ठ मत्समक्षं महाद्युते ।
स्मर्तुम् अर्हसि कल्याण वचनं पार्थिवर्षभ ॥ १५॥
यच्चोक्तं विहगैर् हंसैः समीपे तव भूमिप ।
मत्समक्षं यदुक्तञ्च तदवेक्षितुम् अर्हसि ॥ १६॥
चत्वार एकतो वेदाः साङ्गोपाङ्गाः सविस्तराः ।
स्वधीता मनुजव्याघ्र सत्यम् एकं किलैकतः ॥ १७॥
तस्माद् अर्हसि शत्रुघ्न सत्यं कर्तुं नरेश्वर ।
उक्तवान् असि यद् वीर मत्सकाशे पुरा वचः ॥ १८॥
हा वीर ननु नामाहम् इष्टा किल तवानघ ।
अस्याम् अटव्यां घोरायां किं मां न प्रतिभाषसे ॥ १९॥
भक्षयत्येष मां रौद्रो व्यात्तास्यो दारुणाकृतिः ।
अरण्यराट् क्षुधाविष्टः किं मां न त्रातुम् अर्हसि ॥ २०॥

And the princess of Vidarbha gazed where, in their countless herds,
Buffalos and boars were feeding, bears, and serpents of the wood.
Safe in virtue, bright in beauty, glorious, and of high resolve,
Now alone, Vidarbha's daughter wandering, her lost Nala sought.
Yet no fear king Bhíma's daughter for herself might deign to feel,
Travelling the dreary forest, only for her lord distressed;
Him she mourned, that noble princess, him in bitterest anguish wailed,
Every limb with sorrow trembling stood she on a beetling rock;

Damayantí spake:

Monarch, with broad chest capacious, monarch, with the sinewy arm,
Me in this dread forest leaving, whither hast thou fled away?
Thou the holy Aśvamedha, thou each costliest sacrifice
Hast performed, to me, me only, in thy holy faith thou'st failed.
That which thou, O best of husbands, in mine hearing hast declared,
Thy most solemn vow remember, call to mind thy plighted faith.
Of the swift-winged swans the language uttered, monarch, by thy side,
That thyself, before my presence, didst renew, bethink thee well.
Thou the Vedas, thou the Angas, with the Upángas oft has read,
Of each heaven-descended volume one and simple is the truth.
Therefore, of thy foes the slayer! reverence thou the sacred truth
Of thy solemn plighted promise, in my presence sworn so oft.
Am not I the loved so dearly, purely, sinlessly beloved?
In this dark and awful forest wherefore dost thou not reply?
Here with monstrous jaws wide yawning, with his fierce and horrid form,
Gapes the forest-king to slay me, and thou art not here to save.

न मे त्वदन्या काचिद्धि प्रियाऽस्तीत्यब्रवीः सदा ।
ताम् ऋतां कुरु कल्याण पुरोक्तां भारतीं नृप ॥२१॥
उन्मत्तां विलपन्तीं मां भार्याम् इष्टां नराधिप ।
ईप्सिताम् ईप्सितो नाथ किं मां न प्रतिभाषसे ॥२२॥
कृशां दीनां विवर्णाञ्च मलिनां वसुधाधिप ।
वस्त्रार्धप्रावृताम् एकां विलपन्तीम् अनाथवत् ॥२३॥
यूथभ्रष्टाम् इवैकां मां हरिणीं पृथुलोचन ।
न मानयसि माम् आर्य रुदतीम् अरिकर्षण ॥२४॥
महाराज महारण्ये अहम् एकाकिनी सती ।
दमयन्त्यभिभाषे त्वां किं मां न प्रतिभाषसे ॥२५॥
कुलशीलोपसम्पन्न चारुसर्वाङ्गशोभन ।
नाद्य त्वां प्रतिपश्यामि गिराव् अस्मिन् नरोत्तम ॥२६॥
वने चास्मिन् महाघोरे सिंहव्याघ्रनिषेविते ।
शयानम् उपविष्टं वा स्थितं वा निषधाधिप ॥२७॥
प्रस्थितं वा नरश्रेष्ठ मम शोकविवर्धन ।
कं नु पृच्छामि दुःखार्ता त्वदर्थे शोककर्षिता ॥२८॥
कच्चिद् दृष्टस् त्वयाऽरण्ये सङ्गत्येह नलो नृपः ।
को नु मे वाऽथ प्रष्टव्यो वनेऽस्मिन् प्रस्थितं नलं ॥२९॥
अभिरूपं महात्मानं परव्यूहविनाशनं ।
यम् अन्वेषसि राजानं नलं पद्मनिभेक्षणं ॥३०॥
अयं स इति कस्याद्य श्रोष्यामि मधुरां गिरं ।
अरण्यराड् अयं श्रीमांश् चतुर्दंष्ट्रो महाहनुः ॥३१॥
शार्दूलोऽभिमुखोऽभ्येति व्रजाम्येनम् अशङ्किता ।
भवान् मृगाणाम् अधिपस् त्वम् अस्मिन् कानने प्रभुः ॥३२॥
विदर्भराजतनयां दमयन्तीति विद्धि मां ।
निषधाधिपतेर् भार्यां नलस्यामित्रघातिनः ॥३३॥

None but I, thou'st said, for ever, none but I to thee am dear!
Make this oft-repeated language, make this oft-sworn promise true.
To thy queen bereft of reason, to thy weeping wife beloved,
Why repliest thou not—her only thou desir'st—she only thee?
Meagre, miserable, pallid, tainted with the dust and mire,
Scantly clad in half a garment, lone, with no protector near;
Large-eyed! like a hind that wanders separate from the wonted herd,
Thou regard'st me not, thus weeping, oh thou tamer of thy foes!
Mighty king, alone yet virtuous, in the vast and trackless wood,
Damayantí, I address thee, wherefore answerest not my voice?
Nobly born, and nobly minded, beautiful in every limb,
Do I not e'en now behold thee, in this mountain, first of men!
In this lion-haunted forest, in this tiger-howling wood,
Lying down or seated, standing, or in majesty and might
Moving, do I not behold thee, the enhancer of my woe?
Whom shall I address, afflicted, wasted by my grief for thee?
'Hast thou haply seen my Nala in the solitary wild?'
Who will answer me enquiring for my lost one in the wood,
Beautiful and royal-minded, conqueror of a host of foes?
'Him thou seek'st with eyes of lotus, Nala, sovereign of men—
Lo, he's here!' whose voice of music may I hear thus sweetly speak?
Lo, with fourfold tusks before me, and with wide and gaping jaws,
Stands the forest-king, the tiger, I approach him without fear.
Of the beasts art thou the monarch, all this forest thy domain;
Of Vidarbha's king the daughter, Damayantí know thou me,
Consort of Nishadha's sovereign, Nala, slayer of his foes—

पतिम् अन्वेषतीम् एकां कृपणां शोककर्षितां ।
आश्वासय मृगेन्द्रेह यदि दृष्टस् त्वया नलः ॥३४॥
अथवारण्यनृपते नलं यदि न शंससि ।
मां खादय मृगश्रेष्ठ दुःखाद् अस्माद् विमोचय ॥३५॥
श्रुत्वाऽरण्ये विलपितं ममैष मृगराट् स्वयं ।
यात्येतां मृष्टसलिलाम् आपगां सागरङ्गमां ॥३६॥
इमं शिलोच्चयं पुण्यं शृङ्गैर् बहुभिर् उच्छ्रितैः ।
विराजद्भिर् दिविस्पृग्भिर् नैकवर्णैर् मनोहरैः ॥३७॥
नानाधातुसमाकीर्णं विविधोपलभूषितं ।
अस्यारण्यस्य महतः केतुभूतम् इवोत्थितं ॥३८॥
सिंहशार्दूलमातङ्गवराहर्क्षमृगायुतं ।
पतत्त्रिभिर् बहुविधैः समन्ताद् अनुनादितं ॥३९॥
किंशुकाशोकवकुलपुन्नागैर् उपशोभितं ।
कर्णिकारधवप्लक्षैः सुपुष्पैर् उपशोभितं ॥४०॥
सरिद्भिः सविहङ्गाभिः शिखरैश्च समाकुलं ।
गिरिराजम् इमं तावत् पृच्छामि नृपतिं प्रति ॥४१॥
भगवन्न् अचलश्रेष्ठ दिव्यदर्शन विश्रुत ।
शरण्य बहुकल्याण नमस् तेऽस्तु महीधर ॥४२॥
प्रणमे त्वाभिगम्याहं राजपुत्रीं निबोध मां ।
राज्ञः स्नुषां राजभार्यां दमयन्तीति विश्रुतां ॥४३॥
राजा विदर्भाधिपतिः पिता मम महारथः ।
भीमो नाम क्षितिपतिश् चातुर्वर्ण्यस्य रक्षिता ॥४४॥
राजसूयाश्वमेधानां क्रतूनां दक्षिणावतां ।
आहर्ता पार्थिवश्रेष्ठः पृथुचार्वञ्चितेक्षणः ॥४५॥
ब्रह्मण्यः साधुवृत्तश्च सत्यवाग् अनसूयकः ।
शीलवान् वीर्यसम्पन्नः पृथुश्रीर् धर्मविच् छुचिः ॥४६॥

Seeking here my exile husband, lonely, wretched, sorrow-driven,
Thou, O king of beasts, console me, if my Nala thou hast seen;
Or, O lord of all the forest, Nala if thou canst not show,
Best of savage beasts, devour me, from this misery set me free.
Hearing thus my lamentation, now does that fell king of beasts
Go towards the crystal river, flowing downward to the sea.—
Turn I to this holy mountain, crowned with many a lofty peak,
In its soul-exalting splendour, rising, many-hued, to heaven;
Full within of precious metals, rich with many a glowing gem,
Rising o'er this spreading forest like a banner broad and high,
Ranged by elephants and lions, tigers, boars, and bears, and stags;
Sweetly sounding all around me with the songs of many birds;
All the trees of richest foliage, all the trees of stateliest height,
All the flowers and golden fruitage on its crested summits wave,
Down its peaks in many a streamlet dip the water-birds their wings:
This, the monarch of all mountains, ask I of the king of men;
O all-honoured Prince of Mountains, with thy heaven-ward soaring peaks,
Refuge of the lost, most noble, thee, O Mountain, I salute;
I salute thee, lowly bowing, I, the daughter of a king;
Of a king the royal consort, of a king's son I the bride.
Of Vidarbha the great sovereign, mighty hero is my sire,
Named the lord of earth, king Bhíma, of each caste the guardian he;
Of the holy Aśvamedha, of the regal sacrifice,
He the offerer, best of monarchs, known by large and lustrous eyes.
Pious, and of life unblemished, true in word, of generous speech,
Affable, courageous, prosperous, skilled in every duty, pure.

सम्यग्गोप्ता विदर्भाणां निर्जितारिगणः प्रभुः ।
तस्य मां विद्धि तनयां भगवंस् त्वाम् उपस्थितां ॥४७॥
निषधेषु महाराजः श्वशुरो मे नरोत्तमः ।
गृहीतनामा विख्यातो वीरसेन इति स्म ह ॥४८॥
तस्य राज्ञः सुतो वीरः श्रीमान् सत्यपराक्रमः ।
क्रमप्राप्तं पितुः स्वं यो राज्यं समनुशास्ति ह ॥४९॥
नलो नामारिहा श्यामः पुण्यश्लोक इति श्रुतः ।
ब्रह्मण्यो वेदविद् वाग्मी पुण्यकृत् सोमपोऽग्निमान् ॥५०॥
यष्टा दाता च योद्धा च सम्यक्चैव प्रशासिता ।
तस्य माम् अचलश्रेष्ठ विद्धि भार्याम् इहागतां ॥५१॥
त्यक्तश्रियं भर्तृहीनाम् अनाथां व्यसनान्वितां ।
अन्वेषमाणां भर्तारं तं वै नरवरोत्तमं ॥५२॥
खम् उल्लिखद्भिर् एतैर् हि त्वया शृङ्गशतैर् नृपः ।
कच्चिद् दृष्टोऽचलश्रेष्ठ वनेऽस्मिन् दारुणे नलः ॥५३॥
गजेन्द्रविक्रमो धीमान् दीर्घबाहुर् अमर्षणः ।
विक्रान्तः सत्यवाग् वीरो भर्ता मम महायशाः ॥५४॥
निषधानाम् अधिपतिः कच्चिद् दृष्टस् त्वया नलः ।
किं मां विलपन्तीम् एकां पर्वतश्रेष्ठ विह्वलां ॥५५॥
गिरा नाश्वासयस्यद्य स्वां सुताम् इव दुःखितां ।
वीर विक्रान्त धर्मज्ञ सत्यसन्ध महीपते ॥५६॥
यद्यस्यस्मिन् वने राजन् दर्शयात्मानम् आत्मना ।
कदा सुस्निग्धगम्भीरां जीमूतस्वनसन्निभां ॥५७॥
श्रोष्यामि नैषधस्याहं वाचं ताम् अमृतोपमां ।
वैदर्भीत्येव विस्पष्टां शुभां राज्ञो महात्मनः ॥५८॥
आम्नायसारिणीम् ऋद्धां मम शोकविनाशिनीं ।
भीताम् आश्वासयत मां नृपते धर्मवत्सल ॥५९॥

Of Vidarbha the protector, conqueror of a host of foes;
Know me of that king the daughter lowly thus approaching thee.
In Nishadha, mighty Mountain! dwelt the father of my lord,
High the name he won, the illustrious Vírasena was he called.
Of this king the son, the hero, prosperous and truly brave,
He who rules his father's kingdom by hereditary right,
Slayer of his foes, dark Nala, Puṇyaśloka is he called;
Holy, Veda-read, and eloquent, Soma-quaffing, fire-adoring,
Sacrificer, liberal giver, warrior, in all points a king,—
Of this monarch, best of mountains! know, the wife before thee stands,
Fallen from bliss, bereft of husband, unprotected, sorrow-doomed,
Seeking everywhere her husband, him the best of noblest men.
Best of mountains, heaven-upsoaring, with thy hundred stately peaks,
Hast thou seen the kingly Nala in this dark and awful wood?
Like the elephant in courage, wise, impetuous, with long arms,
Valiant, and of truth unquestioned, my heroic, glorious lord;
Hast thou seen Nishadha's sovereign, mighty Nala hast thou seen?
Why repliest thou not, O Mountain, sorrowing, lonely, and distressed,
With thy voice why not console me as thine own afflicted child?

Hero, mighty, strong in duty, true of promise, lord of earth!
If thou art within the forest show thee in thy proper form.
When so eloquently deep-toned, like the sound of some dark cloud,
Shall I hear thy voice, oh Nala! sweet as the Amṛita draught,
Saying, 'daughter of Vidarbha!' with distinct, with blessed sound,
Musical as holy Veda, rich, and soothing all my pain;
Thus console me, trembling, fainting, thou, oh virtue-loving king!

इति सा तं गिरिश्रेष्ठम् उक्त्वा पार्थिवनन्दिनी ।
दमयन्ती ततो भूयो जगाम दिशम् उत्तरां ॥ ६० ॥
सा गत्वा त्रीन् अहोरात्रान् ददर्श परमाङ्गना ।
तापसारण्यम् अतुलं दिव्यकाननदर्शनं ॥ ६१ ॥
वशिष्ठभृग्वत्रिसमैस् तापसैर् उपशोभितं ।
नियतैः संयताहारैर् दमशौचसमन्वितैः ॥ ६२ ॥
अब्भक्षैर् वायुभक्षैश्च पर्णाहारैस् तथैव च ।
जितेन्द्रियैर् महाभागैः स्वर्गमार्गदिदृक्षुभिः ॥ ६३ ॥
वल्कलाजिनसंवीतैर् मुनिभिः संयतेन्द्रियैः ।
तापसाध्युषितं रम्यं ददर्शाश्रममण्डलं ॥ ६४ ॥
नानामृगगणैर् जुष्टं शाखामृगगणायुतं ।
तापसैः समुपेतञ्च सा दृष्ट्वैव समाश्वसत् ॥ ६५ ॥
सुभ्रूः सुकेशी सुश्रोणी सुकुचा सुद्विजानना ।
वर्चस्विनी सुप्रतिष्ठा स्वसितायतलोचना ॥ ६६ ॥
सा विवेशाश्रमपदं वीरसेनसुतप्रिया ।
योषिद्रत्नं महाभागा दमयन्ती तपस्विनी ॥ ६७ ॥
साऽभिवाद्य तपोवृद्धान् विनयावनता स्थिता ।
स्वागतं त इति प्रोक्ता तैः सर्वैस् तापसैश्च सा ॥ ६८ ॥
पूजां चास्या यथान्यायं कृत्वा तत्र तपोधनाः ।
आस्यताम् इत्यथोचुस् ते ब्रूहि किं करवामहै ॥ ६९ ॥
तान् उवाच वरारोहा कच्चिद् भगवताम् इह ।
तपस्यग्निषु धर्मेषु मृगपक्षिषु चानघाः ॥ ७० ॥
कुशलं वो महाभागाः स्वधर्माचरणेषु च ।
तैर् उक्ता कुशलं भद्रे सर्वत्रेति यशस्विनि ॥ ७१ ॥
ब्रूहि सर्वानवद्याङ्गि का त्वं किञ्च चिकीर्षसि ।
दृष्ट्वैव ते परं रूपं द्युतिञ्च परमाम् इह ॥ ७२ ॥

To the holiest of mountains spake the daughter of the king.
Damayantí then set forward toward the region of the north.
Three days long, three nights she wandered, then that noble woman saw
The unrivalled wood of hermits like to a celestial grove.
To Vaśishṭha, Bhṛigu, Atri, equal was that sacred crew;
Self-denying, strict in diet, temperate, and undefiled;
Water-drinking, air-inhaling, and the leaves their simple food;
Mortified, for ever blessed, seeking the right way to heaven;
Bark for vests and skins for raiment wore those hermits, sense-subdued.
She beheld the pleasant circle of those hermits' lonely cells;
Round them flocks of beasts were grazing, wantoned there the monkey-tribes.
When she saw those holy dwellings all her courage was revived.
Lovely-browed, and lovely-tressed, lovely-bosom'd, lovely-lipp'd,
In her brightness, in her glory, with her large dark beauteous eyes,
Entered she those hermit-dwellings, wife of Vírasena's son;
Pearl of women, ever blessed, Damayantí the devout.
She those holy men saluting stood with modest form half-bent.
'Hail, and welcome!' thus those hermits instant with one voice exclaimed.
And those sacred men no sooner had the fitting homage paid,
'Take thy seat,' they said, 'oh lady! and command what we must do.'
Thus replied the slender-waisted, 'Blessed are ye, holy men;
In your sacred fires, your worship blameless, with your beasts and birds.
Doth the grace of heaven attend you in your duties, in your deeds?'
Answered they, 'The grace of heaven ever blesses all our deeds.
But say thou, of form so beauteous, who thou art, and what thou would'st?
As thy noble form we gaze on, on thy brightness as we gaze,

विस्मयो नः समुत्पन्नः समाश्वसिहि मा शुचः ।
अस्यारण्यस्य देवी त्वम् उताहोऽस्य महीभृतः ॥७३॥
अस्याश्च नद्याः कल्याणि वद सत्यम् अनिन्दिते ।
साऽब्रवीत् तान् ऋषीन् नाहम् अरण्यस्यास्य देवता ॥७४॥
न चाप्यस्य गिरेर् विप्रा नैव नद्याश्च देवता ।
मानुषीं मां विजानीत यूयं सर्वे तपोधनाः ॥७५॥
विस्तरेणाभिधास्यामि तन् मे शृणुत सर्वशः ।
विदर्भेषु महीपालो भीमो नाम महीपतिः ॥७६॥
तस्य मां तनयां सर्वे जानीत द्विजसत्तमाः ।
निषधाधिपतिर् धीमान् नलो नाम महायशाः ॥७७॥
वीरः सङ्ग्रामजिद् विद्वान् मम भर्ता विशाम्पतिः ।
देवताभ्यर्चनपरो द्विजातिजनवत्सलः ॥७८॥
गोप्ता निषधवंशस्य महातेजा महाबलः ।
सत्यवाग् अस्त्रवित् प्राज्ञः सत्यसन्धोऽरिमर्दनः ॥७९॥
ब्रह्मण्यो दैवतपरः श्रीमान् परपुरञ्जयः ।
नलो नाम नृपश्रेष्ठो देवराजसमद्युतिः ॥८०॥
मम भर्ता विशालाक्षः पूर्णेन्दुवदनोऽरिहा ।
आहर्ता क्रतुमुख्यानां वेदवेदाङ्गपारगः ॥८१॥
सपत्नानां मृधे हन्ता रविसोमसमप्रभः ।
स कैश्चिन् निकृतिप्रज्ञैर् अनार्यैर् अकृतात्मभिः ॥८२॥
आहूय पृथिवीपालः सत्यधर्मपरायणः ।
देवने कुशलैर् जिह्मैर् जितो राज्यं वसूनि च ॥८३॥
तस्य माम् अवगच्छध्वं भार्यां राजर्षभस्य वै ।
दमयन्तीति विख्यातां भर्तुर् दर्शनलालसां ॥८४॥
सा वनानि गिरींश्चैव सरांसि सरितस् तथा ।
पल्वलानि च सर्वाणि तथाऽरण्यानि सर्वशः ॥८५॥

In amaze we stand and wonder, cheer thee up, and mourn no more.
Of the wood art thou the goddess, or the mountain-goddess thou;
Or the goddess of the river? Blessed Spirit, speak the truth.'
'Nor the sylvan goddess am I,' to the Wise she thus replied;
'Neither of the mountain, Bráhmans, nor the river-nymph am I.
Know me but a mortal being, O, ye rich in holiness!
All my tale at length I'll tell you, if meet audience ye will give.
In Vidarbha mighty guardian Bhíma dwells, the lord of earth;
Of that noble king the daughter, best of twice-born, know ye me.
And the monarch of Nishadha, Nala wise and great in fame;
Brave in battle, conqueror, prudent is my lord, the peasants' king;
To the gods devout in worship, friendly to the Bráhman race,
Of Nishadha's race the guardian, great in glory, great in might,
True in word, in weapons skilful, wise and slayer of his foes;
Pious, heaven-devoted, prosperous, conqueror of hostile towns;
Nala named, the best of sovereigns, splendid as the king of gods.
Know that large-eyed chief, my husband, like the full-orbed moon his face,
Giver he of costly offerings, deep in holy volumes read;
Slayer of his foes in battle, glorious as the sun and moon.
He by some most evil-minded, unrespected, wicked men,
After many a challenge yielding, he the virtue-loving king,
By these clever gamesters, fraudful, was bereft of realm and wealth.
Know ye me the hapless consort of that noble king of kings,
Damayantí, so they name me, yearning for my husband's sight.
I through forests, over mountains, stagnant marsh and river broad,
Lake with wide pellucid surface, through the long and trackless wood,

अन्वेषमाणा भर्तारं नलं रणविशारदं।
महात्मानं कृतास्त्रञ्च विचरामीह दुःखिता ॥८६॥
कच्चिद् भगवतां रम्यं तपोवनम् इदं नृपः।
भवेत् प्राप्तो नलो नाम निषधानां जनाधिपः ॥८७॥
यत्कृतेऽहम् इदं दुर्गं प्रपन्ना भृशदारुणं।
वनं प्रतिभयं घोरं शार्दूलमृगसेवितं ॥८८॥
यदि कैश्चिद् अहोरात्रैर् न द्रक्ष्यामि नलं नृपं।
आत्मानं श्रेयसा योक्ष्ये देहस्यास्य विमोचनात् ॥८९॥
को नु मे जीवितेनार्थस् तम् ऋते पुरुषर्षभं।
कथं भविष्याम्यद्याहं भर्तृशोकाभिपीडिता ॥९०॥
तथा विलपन्तीम् एकाम् अरण्ये भीमनन्दिनीं।
दमयन्तीम् अथोचुस् ते तापसाः सत्यदर्शिनः ॥९१॥
उदर्कस् तव कल्याणि कल्याणो भविता शुभे।
वयं पश्यामस् तपसा क्षिप्रं द्रक्ष्यसि नैषधं ॥९२॥
निषधानाम् अधिपतिं नलं रिपुनिपातिनं।
भैमि धर्मभृतां श्रेष्ठं द्रक्ष्यसे विगतज्वरं ॥९३॥
विमुक्तं सर्वपापेभ्यः सर्वरत्नसमन्वितं।
तद् एव नगरं भूयः प्रशासतम् अरिन्दमं ॥९४॥
द्विषतां भयकर्तारं सुहृदां शोकनाशनं।
पतिं द्रक्ष्यसि कल्याणि कल्याणाभिजनं नृपं ॥९५॥
एवम् उक्त्वा नलस्येष्टां महिषीं पार्थिवात्मजां।
तापसाऽन्तर्हिताः सर्वे साग्निहोत्राश्रमास् तदा ॥९६॥
सा दृष्ट्वा महद् आश्चर्यं विस्मिता ह्यभवत् तदा।
दमयन्त्यनवद्याङ्गी वीरसेननृपस्नुषा ॥९७॥
किं नु स्वप्नो मया दृष्टः कोऽयं विधिर् इहाभवत्।
क्व नु ते तापसाः सर्वे क्व तद् आश्रममण्डलं ॥९८॥

Ever seeking for my husband Nala, skilful in the fight.
Mighty in the use of weapons, wander, desolate and sad.
Tell me, to this pleasant sojourn, sacred to these holy men,
Hath he come, the royal Nala? hath Nishadha's monarch come?
For whose sake through ways all trackless, terrible, have I set forth,
In this drear, appalling forest, where the deer and tiger range,
If I see not noble Nala ere few days, few nights are o'er,
I to heavenly bliss will join me, from this mortal frame set free.
Reft of him, my princely husband, what have I to do with life?
How endure existence longer, for my husband thus distressed?'
To the lady thus complaining, lonely in the savage wood,
Answered thus those holy hermits, spake the gifted seers the truth:—
'There will be a time hereafter, beautiful, the time will come,
Through devotion now we see him, and thou too wilt see him soon;
That good monarch of Nishadha, Nala, slayer of his foes;
That dispenser of strict justice, Bhíma's daughter! free from grief,
From all sin released, thou'lt see him glittering in his royal gems,
Governing again that city, o'er his enemies supreme.
To his foemen causing terror, to his friends allaying grief,
Thou, oh noble, shalt thy husband see, that king of noble race!'
To the much-loved wife of Nala, to the princess speaking thus,
Vanished then those holy hermits, with their sacred fires, their cells.
As she gazed upon the wonder, wrapt in mute amaze she stood;
Damayantí, fair-limbed princess, wife of Vírasena's son:
'Have I only seen a vision, what hath been this wondrous chance?
Where are all those holy hermits, where the circle of their cells?

क्व सा पुण्यजला रम्या नदी द्विजनिषेविता ।
क्व नु ते ह नगा हृद्याः फलपुष्पोपशोभिताः ॥९९॥
ध्यात्वा चिरं भीमसुता दमयन्ती शुचिस्मिता ।
भर्तृशोकपरा दीना विवर्णवदनाऽभवत् ॥१००॥
सा गत्वाथापरां भूमिं वाष्पसन्दिग्धया गिरा ।
विललापाश्रुपूर्णाक्षी दृष्ट्वाऽशोकतरुं ततः ॥१०१॥
उपगम्य तरुश्रेष्ठम् अशोकं पुष्पितं वने ।
पल्लवापीडितं हृद्यं विहङ्गैर् अनुनादितं ॥१०२॥
अहोवतायम् अगमः श्रीमान् अस्मिन् वनान्तरे ।
आपीडैर् बहुभिर् भाति श्रीमान् पर्वतराड् इव ॥१०३॥
विशोकां कुरु मां क्षिप्रम् अशोक प्रियदर्शन ।
वीतशोक भयाबाधं कच्चित् त्वं दृष्टवान् नृपं ॥१०४॥
नलं नामारिमर्दनं दमयन्त्याः प्रियं पतिं ।
निषधानाम् अधिपतिं दृष्टवान् असि मे प्रियं ॥१०५॥
एकवस्त्रार्धसंवीतं सुकुमारतनुत्वचं ।
व्यसनेनार्दितं वीरम् अरण्यम् इदम् आगतं ॥१०६॥
यथा विशोका गच्छेयम् अशोकनग तत् कुरु ।
सत्यनामा भवाशोक अशोकः शोकनाशनः ॥१०७॥
एवं साऽशोकवृक्षं तम् आर्ता वै परिगम्य ह ।
जगाम दारुणतरं देशं भैमी वराङ्गना ॥१०८॥
सा ददर्श नगान् नैकान् नैकाश्च सरितस् तथा ।
नैकांश्च पर्वतान् रम्यान् नैकांश्च मृगपक्षिणः ॥१०९॥
कन्दरांश्च नितम्बांश्च नदीश्चाद्भुतदर्शनाः ।
ददर्श सा भीमसुता पतिम् अन्वेषती तदा ॥११०॥
गत्वा प्रकृष्टम् अध्वानं दमयन्ती शुचिस्मिता ।
ददर्शाथ महासार्थं हस्त्यश्वरथसङ्कुलं ॥१११॥

Where that pure and pleasant river, haunted by the dipping birds?
Where those trees with grateful umbrage, with their pendant fruits and flowers?'
Long within her heart she pondered, Damayantí with sweet smile,
For her lord, to grief abandoned, miserable, pale of hue;
To another region passed she, there with voice by weeping choked
Mourns she, till with eyes o'erflowing an Aśoka tree she saw.
Best of trees, the Aśoka blooming, in the forest she approached,
Gemmed all o'er with glowing fruitage, vocal with the songs of birds.

'Ah, behold, amid the forest flourishes this happy tree,
With its leafy garlands radiant as the joyous mountain-king.
O thou tree with pleasant aspect from my sorrow set me free!
Vítaśoka, hast thou seen him, hast the fearless Rája seen,
Nala, of his foes the slayer, Damayantí's lord beloved?
Hast thou seen Nishadha's monarch, hast thou seen mine only love,
Clad in half a single garment, delicate and soft of skin?
Hast thou seen th' afflicted hero wandering in this forest lone?
That I may depart ungrieving, fair Aśoka, answer me.
Truly be thou named Aśoka, as the extinguisher of grief.'
Thus in her o'erpowering anguish moved she round the Aśoka tree.
Then she went her way in sadness to a region still more dread.
Many a tree she stood and gazed on, many a river passed she o'er;
Passed she many a pleasant mountain, many a wild deer, many a bird;
Many a hill and many a cavern, many a bright and wondrous stream,
Saw king Bhíma's wandering daughter as she sought her husband lost.

Long she roamed her weary journey, Damayantí with sweet smile;
Lo, a caravan of merchants, elephants, and steeds, and cars,

उत्तरन्तं नदीं रम्यां प्रसन्नसलिलां शुभां ।
सुशान्ततोयां विस्तीर्णां हृदिनीं वेतसैर् वृतां ॥११२॥
प्रोद्घुष्टां क्रौञ्चकुररैश् चक्रवाकोपकूजितां ।
कूर्मग्राहझषाकीर्णां पुलिनद्वीपशोभितां ॥११३॥
सा दृष्ट्वैव महासार्थं नलपत्नी यशस्विनी ।
उपसर्प्य वरारोहा जनमध्यं विवेश ह ॥११४॥
उन्मत्तरूपा शोकार्ता तथा वस्त्रार्धसंवृता ।
कृशा विवर्णा मलिना पांशुध्वस्तशिरोरुहा ॥११५॥
तां दृष्ट्वा तत्र मनुजाः केचिद् भीताः प्रदुद्रुवुः ।
केचिच् चिन्तापरास् तस्थुः केचित् तत्र प्रचुक्रुशुः ॥११६॥
प्रहसन्ति स्म तां केचिद् अभ्यसूयन्ति चापरे ।
अकुर्वत दयां केचित् पप्रच्छुश्चापि भारत ॥११७॥
काऽसि कस्यासि कल्याणि किं वा मृगयसे वने ।
त्वां दृष्ट्वा व्यथिताः स्मेह कच्चित् त्वम् असि मानुषी ॥११८॥
वद सत्यं वनस्यास्य पर्वतस्याथवा दिशः ।
देवता त्वं हि कल्याणि त्वां वयं शरणं गताः ॥११९॥
यक्षी वा राक्षसी वा त्वम् उताहोऽसि सुराङ्गना ।
सर्वथा कुरु नः स्वस्ति रक्ष चास्मान् अनिन्दिते ॥१२०॥
यथाऽयं सर्वथा सार्थः क्षेमी शीघ्रम् इतो व्रजेत् ।
तथा विधत्स्व कल्याणि यथा श्रेयो हि नो भवेत् ॥१२१॥
तथोक्ता तेन सार्थेन दमयन्ती नृपात्मजा ।
प्रत्युवाच ततः साध्वी भर्तृव्यसनपीडिता ॥१२२॥
सार्थवाहञ्च सार्थञ्च जना ये तत्र केचन ।
युवस्थविरबालाश्च सार्थस्य च पुरोगमाः ॥१२३॥
मानुषीं मां विजानीत मनुजाधिपतेः सुतां ।
नृपस्नुषां राजभार्यां भर्तृदर्शनलालसां ॥१२४॥

Passing o'er a pleasant river, with its waters cool and clear.
'Twas a still stream broad and waveless, girt about with spreading canes;
There the curlew, there the osprey, there the red-geese clamouring stood;
Swarmed the turtles, fish and serpents, there rose many a shoal and isle.

When she saw that numerous concourse, Nala's once all-glorious wife,
Entered she, the slender-waisted, in the midst of all the host;
Maniac-like in form and feature, and in half a garment clad,
Thin and pallid, travel-tainted, matted all her locks with dust.
As they all beheld her standing some in terror fled away;
Some stood still in speechless wonder, others raised their voice and cried;
Mocked her some with cruel tauntings, others spake reproachful words;
Others looked on her with pity, and enquired her state, her name.
'Who art thou? whose daughter, Lady, in the forest seek'st thou aught?
At thy sight we stand confounded, art thou of our mortal race?
Of this wood art thou the goddess? of this mountain? of that plain?
Who art thou, O noble lady, thee, our refuge, we adore.
Art thou sylvan nymph or genius, or celestial nymph divine?
Every way regard our welfare, and protect us, undespised:
So our caravan in safety may pursue its onward way,
So ordain it, O illustrious! that good fortune wait on all.'
Thus addressed by that assemblage, Dámayantí, kingly-born,
Answered thus with gentle language, grieving for her husband lost.
Of that caravan the leader, and the whole assembled host,
Youths and boys, and grey-haired elders, and the guides, thus answered she:
'Know me, like yourselves, a mortal, daughter of a king of men,
Of another king the consort seeking for my royal lord;

विदर्भराड् मम पिता भर्ता राजा च नैषधः ।
नलो नाम महाभागस् तम् मार्गाम्यपराजितं ॥१२५॥
यदि जानीथ नृपतिं क्षिप्रं शंसत मे प्रियं ।
नलं पुरुषशार्दूलम् अमित्रगणसूदनं ॥१२६॥
ताम् उवाचानवद्याङ्गीं सार्थस्य महतः प्रभुः ।
सार्थवाहः शुचिर् नाम शृणु कल्याणि मद्वचः ॥१२७॥
अहं सार्थस्य नेता वै सार्थवाहः शुचिस्मिते ।
मनुष्यं नलनामानं न पश्यामि यशस्विनि ॥१२८॥
कुञ्जरद्वीपिमहिषशार्दूलर्क्षमृगान् अपि ।
पश्याम्यस्मिन् वने कृत्स्ने ह्यमनुष्यनिषेविते ॥१२९॥
ऋते त्वां मानुषीं मर्त्ये न पश्यामि महावने ।
तथा नो यक्षराड् अद्य मणिभद्रः प्रसीदतु ॥१३०॥
साऽब्रवीद् वणिजः सर्वान् सार्थवाहञ्च तं ततः ।
क्व नु यास्यति सार्थोऽयम् एतद् आख्यातुम् अर्हसि ॥१३१॥

सार्थवाह उवाच ।

सार्थोऽयं चेदिराजस्य सुबाहोः सत्यदर्शिनः ।
क्षिप्रं जनपदं गन्ता लाभाय मनुजात्मजे ॥१३२॥

॥ इति नलोपाख्याने द्वादशः सर्गः ॥१२॥

Know, Vidarbha's king, my father, and Nishadha's king, my lord,
Nala, is his name, the glorious, him, th' unconquered, do I seek.
Know ye aught of that good monarch, tell me, quick, of my beloved,
Of the tiger hero, Nala, slayer of a host of foes.'

Of the caravan the captain thus the lovely-limbed addressed,
S'ući was his name, the merchant: 'Hear, illustrious queen, my speech;
Of this caravan the captain I, O Lady with sweet smile,
Him that bears the name of Nala nowhere have these eyes beheld.
Elephants, and pards, and tigers, lynxes, buffalos, and bears,
See I in this trackless forest, uninhabited by men;
Save thyself, of human feature, nought of human form, I've seen.
So may he, the king of Yakshas, Maṇibhadra, guard us well.'
To the merchants all she answered, to the leader of the host:
'Tell me whither do ye travel? whither bound your caravan?'

The Captain of the Caravan spake:

'To the realm of Ćedi's sovereign, truth-discerning Subáhu,
Soon this caravan will enter, travelling in search of gain.'

End of Book XII.

वृहदश्व उवाच ।

सा तच् छ्रुत्वानवद्याङ्गी सार्थवाहवचस् तदा ।
जगाम सह तेनैव सार्थेन पतिलालसा ॥१॥
अथ काले बहुतिथे वने महति दारुणे ।
तडागं सर्वतोभद्रं पद्मसौगन्धिकं महत् ॥२॥
ददृशुर् बणिजो रम्यं प्रभूतयवसेन्धनं ।
बहुपुष्पफलोपेतं नानापक्षिनिषेवितं ॥३॥
निर्मलस्वादुसलिलं मनोहारि सुशीतलं ।
सुपरिश्रान्तवाहास् ते निवेशाय मनो दधुः ॥४॥
सम्मते सार्थवाहस्य विविशुर् वनम् उत्तमं ।
उवास सार्थः स महान् वेलाम् आसाद्य पश्चिमां ॥५॥
अथार्धरात्रसमये निःशब्दस्तिमिते तदा ।
सुप्ते सार्थे परिश्रान्ते हस्तियूथम् उपागमत् ॥६॥
पानीयार्थं गिरिनदीं मदप्रस्रवणाविलां ।
अथापश्यत सार्थं तं सार्थजान् सुबहून् गजान् ॥७॥
ते तान् ग्राम्यगजान् दृष्ट्वा सर्वे वनगजास् तदा ।
समाद्रवन्त वेगेन जिघांसन्तो मदोत्कटाः ॥८॥
तेषाम् आपततां वेगः करिणां दुःसहोऽभवत् ।
नगाग्राद् इव शीर्णानां शृङ्गाणां पततां क्षितौ ॥९॥
स्यन्दताम् अपि नागानां मार्गा नष्टा वनोद्भवैः ।
मार्गं संरुध्य संसुप्तं पद्मिन्याः सार्थम् उत्तमं ॥१०॥
ते तं ममर्दुः सहसा चेष्टमानं महीतले ।
हाहाकारम् प्रमुञ्चन्तः सार्थिकाः शरणार्थिनः ॥११॥

Vṛihadaśva spake:

This the lovely princess hearing from the captain of the band,
With the caravan set forward, seeking still her royal lord.
Long their journey through the forest, through the dark and awful glens.
Then a lake of loveliest beauty, fragrant with the lotus flowers,
Saw those merchants, wide and pleasant, with fresh grass and fuel rich;
Flowers and fruits bedecked its borders where the birds melodious sang:
In its clear delicious waters, soul-enchanting, icy cool,
With their beasts all overwearied, thought they then to plunge and bathe.
At the signal of the captain entered all that pleasant grove.
At the close of day arriving there encamped they for the night.

When the midnight came, all noiseless came in silence deep and still,
Weary slept the band of merchants, lo, a herd of elephants,
Oozing moisture from their temples, came to drink the troubled stream.
When that caravan they gazed on, with their slumbering beasts at rest,
The tame elephants they scented, those wild forest-elephants;
Forward rush they fleet and furious, mad to slay, and wild with heat;
Irresistible the onset of the rushing ponderous brutes,
As the peaks from some high mountain down the valley thundering roll.
Strewn was all the way before them with the boughs, the trunks of trees;
On they rushed to where the travellers slumbered by the lotus-lake.
Trampled down and vainly struggling, helpless on the earth they lay.
'Woe, oh, woe!' shrieked out the merchants, wildly some began to fly,

वनगुल्मांश्च धावन्तो निद्रान्धा बहवोऽभवन् ।
केचिद् दन्तैः करैः केचित् केचित् पद्भ्यां हता गजैः ॥१२॥
निहतोष्ट्राश्च बहुलाः पदातिजनसङ्कुलाः ।
भयाद् आधावमानाश्च परस्परहतास् तदा ॥१३॥
घोरान् नादान् विमुञ्चन्तो निपेतुर् धरणीतले ।
वृक्षेष्वारुह्य संरब्धाः पतिता विषमेषु च ॥१४॥
एवम् प्रकारैर् बहुभिर् दैवेनाक्रम्य हस्तिभिः ।
राजन् विनिहतं सर्वं समृद्धं सार्थमण्डलं ॥१५॥
आरावः सुमहांश्चासीत् त्रैलोक्यभयकारकः ।
एषोऽग्निर् उत्थितः कष्टस् त्रायध्वं धावताधुना ॥१६॥
रत्नराशिर् विशीर्णोऽयं गृह्णीध्वं किं प्रधावथ ।
सामान्यम् एतद् द्रविणं न मिथ्यावचनं मम ॥१७॥
एवम् एवाभिभाषन्तो विद्रवन्ति भयात् तदा ।
पुनर् एवाभिधास्यामि चिन्तयध्वं सकातराः ॥१८॥
तस्मिंस् तथा वर्तमाने दारुणे जनसङ्क्षये ।
दमयन्ती च बुबुधे भयसन्त्रस्तमानसा ॥१९॥
अपश्यद् वैशसं तत्र सर्वलोकभयङ्करं ।
अदृष्टपूर्वं तद् दृष्ट्वा बाला पद्मनिभेक्षणा ॥२०॥
संसक्तवदनाश्वासा उत्तस्थौ भयविह्वला ।
ये तु तत्र विनिर्मुक्ताः सार्थात् केचिद् अविक्षताः ॥२१॥
तेऽब्रुवन् सहिताः सर्वे कस्येदं कर्मणः फलं ।
नूनं न पूजितोऽस्माभिर् मणिभद्रो महायशाः ॥२२॥
तथा यक्षाधिपः श्रीमान् न वै वैश्रवणः प्रभुः ।
न पूजा विघ्नकर्तॄणाम् अथवा प्रथमं कृता ॥२३॥
शकुनानां फलं वाऽथ विपरीतम् इदं ध्रुवं ।
ग्रहा न विपरीतास्तु किम् अन्यद् इदम् आगतं ॥२४॥

In the forest-thickets plunging; some stood gasping, blind with sleep;
And the elephants down beat them with their tusks, their trunks, their feet.
Many saw their camels dying, mingled with the men on foot,
And in frantic tumult rushing wildly struck each other down;
Many miserably shrieking cast them down upon the earth,
Many climbed the trees in terror, on the rough ground stumbled some.
Thus in various wise and fatal, by the elephants assailed,
Lay that caravan so wealthy, scattered all abroad or slain.
Such, so fearful was the tumult, the three worlds seemed all appalled:
''Tis a fire amid the encampment, save ye, fly ye, for your lives.
Lo, your precious pearls ye scatter, take them up, why fly so fast?
Save them, 'tis a common venture, fear ye not that I deceive.'
Thus t' each other shrieked the merchants as in fear they scattered round.
'Yet again I call upon you, cowards! think ye what ye do.'
All around this frantic carnage raging through the prostrate host,
Damayantí, soon awakened, with her heart all full of dread;
There she saw a hideous slaughter, the whole world might well appal.
To such sights all unfamiliar gazed the queen with lotus-eyes,
Pressing in her breath with terror slowly rose she on her feet.
And the few that scaped the carnage, few that scaped without a wound,
All at once exclaimed together: 'Of whose deeds is this the doom?
Hath not mighty Maṇibhadra adoration meet received?
And Vaiśravaṇa the holy, of the Yakshas lord and king,
Have not all that might impede us, ere we journied, been addressed?
Was it doomed, that all good omens by this chance should be belied?
Were no planets haply adverse? how hath fate, like this, befall'n!'

अपरे त्वब्रुवन् दीना ज्ञातिद्रव्यविनाकृताः ।
याऽसावद्य महासार्थे नारी ह्युन्मत्तदर्शना ॥२५॥
प्रविष्टा विकृताकारा कृत्वा रूपम् अमानुषं ।
तयेयं विहिता पूर्वं माया परमदारुणा ॥२६॥
राक्षसी वा ध्रुवं यक्षी पिशाची वा भयङ्करी ।
तस्याः सर्वम् इदं पापं नात्र कार्या विचारणा ॥२७॥
यदि पश्येम तां पापां सार्थघ्नीं नैकदुःखदां ।
लोष्टभिः पांशुभिश्चैव तृणैः काष्ठैश्च मुष्टिभिः ॥२८॥
अवश्यमेव हन्याम सार्थस्य किल कृत्यकां ।
दमयन्ती तु तच् छ्रुत्वा वाक्यं तेषां सुदारुणं ॥२९॥
ह्रीता भीता च संविग्ना प्राद्रवद् यत्र काननं ।
आशङ्कमाना तत् पापम् आत्मानं पर्यदेवयत् ॥३०॥
अहो ममोपरि विधेः संरम्भो दारुणो महान् ।
नानुबध्नाति कुशलं कस्येदं कर्मणः फलं ॥३१॥
न स्मराम्यशुभं किञ्चित् कृतं कस्यचिद् अण्वपि ।
कर्मणा मनसा वाचा कस्येदं कर्मणः फलं ॥३२॥
नूनं जन्मान्तरकृतं पापम् आपतितं महत् ।
अपश्चिमाम् इमां कष्टाम् आपदं प्राप्तवत्यहं ॥३३॥
भर्तृराज्यापहरणं स्वजनाच्च पराजयः ।
भर्त्रा सह वियोगश्च तनयाभ्याञ्च विच्युतिः ॥३४॥
निर्नाथता वने वासो बहुव्यालनिषेविते ।
अथापरेद्युः सम्प्राप्ते हतशिष्टा जनास् तदा ॥३५॥
देशात् तस्माद् विनिष्क्रम्य शोचन्ते वैशसं कृतं ।
भ्रातरं पितरं पुत्रं सखायञ्च नराधिप ॥३६॥
अशोचत् तत्र वैदर्भी किं नु मे दुष्कृतं कृतं ।
योऽपि मे निर्जनेऽरण्ये सम्प्राप्तोऽयं जनार्णवः ॥३७॥

Others answered in their misery, reft of kindred and of wealth,
'Who is that ill-omened woman, that with maniac-staring eyes,
Joined our host, mis-shaped in aspect, and with scarcely human form?
Surely all this wicked witchcraft by her evil power is wrought;
Witch or sorceress she, or demon, fatal cause of all our fears,
Hers is all the guilt, the misery, who such damning proof may doubt?
Could we but behold that false one, murderess, bane of all our host,
With the clods, the dust, the bamboos, with our staves, or with our fists,
We would slay her on the instant, of our caravan the fate.'
But no sooner Damayantí their appalling words had heard,
In her shame and in her terror to the forest shade she fled.
And that guilt imputed dreading thus her fate began to wail:
'Woe is me, still o'er me hovers the terrific wrath of fate;
No good fortune e'er attends me, of what guilt is this the doom?
Not a sin can I remember, not the least to living man.
Or in deed, or thought, or language, of what guilt is this the doom?
In some former life committed expiate I now the sin;
To this infinite misfortune hence by penal justice doomed.
Lost my husband, lost my kingdom, from my kindred separate;
Separate from noble Nala, from my children far away,
Widowed of my rightful guardian, in the serpent-haunted wood.'
Of that caravan at morning then the sad surviving few,
Setting forth from that dread region, o'er that hideous carnage grieve;
Each a brother mourns, or father, or a son, or dearest friend.
Still Vidarbha's princess uttered: 'What the sin that I have done?
Scarcely in this desert forest had I met this host of men,

स हतो हस्तियूथेन मन्दभाग्याद् ममैव तत् ।
प्राप्तव्यं सुचिरं दुःखं नूनम् अद्यापि वै मया ॥ ३८ ॥
नाप्राप्तकालो म्रियते श्रुतं वृद्धानुशासनं ।
यद् नाहम् अद्य मृदिता हस्तियूथेन दुःखिता ॥ ३९ ॥
न ह्यदैवं कृतं किञ्चिन् नराणाम् इह विद्यते ।
न च मे बालभावेऽपि किञ्चित् पापकृतं कृतं ॥ ४० ॥
कर्मणा मनसा वाचा यद् इदं दुःखम् आगतं ।
मन्ये स्वयंवरकृते लोकपालाः समागताः ॥ ४१ ॥
प्रत्याख्याता मया तत्र नलस्यार्थाय देवताः ।
नूनं तेषां प्रभावेन वियोगं प्राप्तवत्यहम् ॥ ४२ ॥
एवमादीनि दुःखार्ता सा विलप्य वराङ्गना ।
प्रलापानि तदा तानि दमयन्ती पतिव्रता ॥ ४३ ॥
हतशेषैः सह तदा ब्राह्मणैर् वेदपारगैः ।
अगच्छद् राजशार्दूल चन्द्रलेखेव शारदी ॥ ४४ ॥
गच्छन्ती सा चिराद् बाला पुरम् आसादयद् महत् ।
सायाह्ने चेदिराजस्य सुबाहोः सत्यदर्शिनः ॥ ४५ ॥
अथ वस्त्रार्धसंवीता प्रविवेश पुरोत्तमं ।
तां विह्वलां कृशां दीनां मुक्तकेशीम् अमार्जितां ॥ ४६ ॥
उन्मत्ताम् इव गच्छन्तीं ददृशुः पुरवासिनः ।
प्रविशन्तीं तु तां दृष्ट्वा चेदिराजपुरीं तदा ॥ ४७ ॥
अनुजग्मुस् तत्र बाला ग्रामिपुत्राः कुतूहलात् ।
सा तैः परिवृताऽगच्छत् समीपं राजवेश्मनः ॥ ४८ ॥
तां प्रासादगताऽपश्यद् राजमाता जनैर् वृतां ।
धात्रीम् उवाच गच्छैनाम् आनयेह ममान्तिकं ॥ ४९ ॥
जनेन क्लिश्यते बाला दुःखिता शरणार्थिनी ।
तादृग् रूपञ्च पश्यामि विद्योतयति मे गृहं ॥ ५० ॥

By the elephants they perish, this is through my luckless fate;
A still lengthening life of sorrow I henceforth must sadly lead.
Ere his destined day none dieth, this of aged seers the lore;
Therefore am not I too trampled by this herd of furious beasts.
Every deed of living mortal by o'er-ruling fate is done.
Yet no sin have I committed, in my blameless infancy,
To deserve this dire disaster, or in word, or deed, or thought.
For the choosing of my husband are the guardians of the world,
Angry are the gods? rejected for the noble Nala's sake,
From my lord this long divorcement through their power do I endure.'
Thus the noblest of all women to bewail her fate began,
The deserted Damayantí, with these sad and bitter words.
With some Veda-reading Bráhmans that survived that scattered host,
Then she went her way in sadness, like the young autumnal moon.
Wandering long, a mighty city that afflicted queen drew near:
'Twas the king of Ćedi's city, truth-discerning Subáhu.
Scantly clad in half a garment entered she that stately town.
Her disturbed, emaciate, wretched, with dishevelled hair, unwashed,
Like a maniac, onward-moving, saw that city's wondering throng.
Gazing on her as she entered to the monarch's royal seat;
All the city boys her footsteps followed in their curious play;
Circled round by these she wandered near the royal palace-gate.
From the lofty palace-terrace her the mother of the king
Saw, and thus her nurse addressed she, 'Go, and lead that wanderer in!
Sad she roves, without a refuge, troubled by those gazing men.
Yet in form so bright, irradiate, is our palace where she moves;

उन्मत्तवेशा कल्याणी श्रीर् इवायतलोचना ।
सा जनं वारयित्वा तं प्रासादतलम् उत्तमं ॥५१॥
आरोप्य विस्मिता राजन् दमयन्तीम् अपृच्छत ।
एवमप्यसुखाविष्टा बिभर्षि परमं वपुः ॥५२॥
भासि विद्युद् इवाभ्रेषु शंस मे काऽसि कस्य वा ।
न हि ते मानुषं रूपं भूषणैर् अपि वर्जितं ॥५३॥
असहाया नरेभ्यश्च नोद्विजस्यमरप्रभे ।
तच् छ्रुत्वा वचनं तस्या भैमी वचनम् अब्रवीत् ॥५४॥
मानुषीं मां विजानीहि भर्तारं समनुव्रतां ।
सैरन्ध्रीं जातिसम्पन्नां भुजिष्यां कामवासिनीं ॥५५॥
फलमूलाशनाम् एकां यत्रसायम्प्रतिश्रयां ।
असङ्ख्येयगुणो भर्ता माञ्च नित्यम् अनुव्रतः ॥५६॥
भक्ताऽहम् अपि तं वीरं छायेवानुगता पथि ।
तस्य दैवात् प्रसङ्गोऽभूद् अतिमात्रं स्म देवने ॥५७॥
द्यूते स निर्जितश्चैव वनम् एक उपेयिवान् ।
तम् एकवसनं वीरम् उन्मत्तम् इव विह्वलं ॥५८॥
आश्वासयन्ती भर्तारम् अहमप्यगमं वनं ।
स कदाचिद् वने वीरः कस्मिंश्चित् कारणान्तरे ॥५९॥
क्षुत्परीतस्तु विमनास् तदप्येकं व्यसर्जयत् ।
तम् एकवसना नग्नम् उन्मत्तवद् अचेतसं ॥६०॥
अनुव्रजन्ती बहुला न स्वपामि निशास् तदा ।
ततो बहुतिथे काले सुप्ताम् उत्सृज्य मां क्वचित् ॥६१॥
वाससोऽर्धं परिच्छिद्य त्यक्तवान् माम् अनागसं ।
तं मार्गमाणा भर्तारं दह्यमाना दिवानिशं ॥६२॥
साऽहं कमलगर्भाभम् अपश्यन्ती हृदि प्रियं ।
न विन्दाम्यमरप्रख्यं प्रियं प्राणेश्वरं प्रभुं ॥६३॥

Though so maniac-like, half-clothed, like Heaven's long-eyed queen she seems.'
Then the nurse those men dispersing, quickly to the palace-top
Made her mount, and in amazement her the mother-queen addressed:
'Thus though bowed and worn with sorrow such a shining form thou wear'st,
As through murky clouds the lightning; tell me who thou art and whose:
For thy form is more than human, of all ornament despoiled:
Men thou fear'st not, unattended, in celestial beauty safe.'

Hearing thus her gentle language Bhíma's daughter made reply:
'Know me like thyself a mortal, a distressed, devoted wife;
Of illustrious race a handmaid, making where I will mine home;
On the roots and wild-fruits feeding, lonely, at the fall of eve.
Gifted with unnumber'd virtues is my true, my faithful lord,
And I still the hero followed, like his shadow on the way.
'Twas his fate, with desp'rate fondness, to pursue the love of play,
And in play subdued and ruined entered he yon lonely wood.
Him, arrayed in but one garment, like a madman wandering wild,
To console my noble husband I too entered the deep wood.
He within that dreary forest from some accidental cause,
Wild with hunger, reft of reason, that one single robe he lost.
I with but one robe, him naked, frantic, and with mind diseased,
Following through the boundless forest, many a night I had not slept.
Then, when I had sunk to slumber, me the blameless leaving there,
Half my garment having severed, he his sinless consort fled.
Seeking him, my outcast husband, day and night am I consumed:
Him I see not, ever shining, like the lotus-cup, beloved;
Find him not, most like th' immortals, lord of all, my life, my soul.'

ताम् अश्रुपरिपूर्णाक्षीं विलपन्तीं तथा बहु ।
राजमाताऽब्रवीद् आर्तां भैमीम् आर्ततरा स्वयं ॥६४॥
वसस्व मयि कल्याणि प्रीतिर् मे परमा त्वयि ।
मृगयिष्यन्ति ते भद्रे भर्तारं पुरुषा मम ॥६५॥
अपि वा स्वयम् आगच्छेत् परिधावन् इतस्ततः ।
इहैव वसती भद्रे भर्तारम् उपलप्स्यसे ॥६६॥
राजमातुर् वचः श्रुत्वा दमयन्ती वचोऽब्रवीत् ।
समयेनोत्सहे वस्तुं त्वयि वीरप्रजायिनि ॥६७॥
उच्छिष्टं नैव भुञ्जीयां न कुर्यां पादधावनं ।
न चाहं पुरुषान् अन्यान् प्रभाषेयं कथञ्चन ॥६८॥
प्रार्थयेद् यदि मां कश्चिद् दण्ड्यस् ते स पुमान् भवेत् ।
बध्यश्च तेऽसकृन् मन्द इति मे व्रतम् आहितं ॥६९॥
भर्तुर् अन्वेषणार्थन्तु पश्येयं ब्राह्मणान् अहं ।
यद्य् एवम् इह कर्तव्यं वत्स्याम्यहमसंशयं ॥७०॥
अतोऽन्यथा न मे वासो वर्तते हृदये क्वचित् ।
तां प्रहृष्टेन मनसा राजमातेदमब्रवीत् ॥७१॥
सर्वम् एतत् करिष्यामि दिष्ट्या ते व्रतम् ईदृशं ।
एवम् उक्त्वा ततो भैमीं राजमाता विशाम्पते ॥७२॥
उवाचेदं दुहितरं सुनन्दां नाम भारत ।
सैरन्ध्रीम् अभिजानीष्व सुनन्दे देवरूपिणीं ॥७३॥
वयसा तुल्यतां प्राप्ता सखी तव भवत्वियं ।
एतया सह मोदस्व निरुद्विग्नमनाः सदा ॥७४॥
ततः परमसंहृष्टा सुनन्दा गृहम् आगमत् ।
दमयन्तीम् उपादाय सखीभिः परिवारिता ॥७५॥

॥ इति नलोपाख्याने त्रयोदशः सर्गः ॥१३॥

Even as thus, with eyes o'erflowing, uttered she her sad lament,
Sad herself, sad Bhíma's daughter did the mother-queen address:
'Dwell with me, then, noble Lady, deep the joy in thee I feel,
And the servants of my household shall thy royal husband seek.
Haply hither he may wander as he roams about the world;
Dwelling here in peace and honour thou thy husband wilt rejoin.'
To the king of Ćedi's mother Damayantí made reply:
'On these terms will I live with thee, mother of heroic sons—
That I eat not broken victuals, wash not feet with menial hand;
Nor with stranger men have converse, in my chaste, secluded state.
If that any man demand me, be he punished; if again,
Death-doomed be the wretch on th' instant, this the vow that I have sworn.
Only, if they seek my husband, holy Bráhmans will I see.
Be my terms by thee accepted, gladly will I sojourn here,
But on other terms no sojourn will this heart resolved admit.'
Then to her with joyful spirit spake the mother of the king:
'As thou wilt shall all be ordered, be thou blest, since such thy vow.'
Speaking thus to Bhíma's daughter did the royal mother then
In these words address her daughter, young Sunandá was her name:
'See this handmaid, my Sunandá, gifted with a form divine;
She in age thy lovely compeer, be she to thee as a friend;
Joined with her in sweet communion, take thy pleasure without fear.'
Young Sunandá, all rejoicing, to her own abode went back,
Taking with her Damayantí, circled with her virgin peers.

End of Book XIII.

वृहदश्व उवाच।

उत्सृज्य दमयन्तीं तु नलो राजा विशाम्पते।
ददर्श दावं दह्यन्तं महान्तं गहने वने ॥१॥
तत्र शुश्राव शब्दं वै मध्ये भूतस्य कस्यचित्।
अभिधाव नलेत्युच्चैः पुण्यश्लोकेति चासकृत् ॥२॥
मा भैर् इति नलश्चोक्त्वा मध्यम् अग्नेः प्रविश्य तं।
ददर्श नागराजानं शयानं कुण्डलीकृतं ॥३॥
स नागः प्राञ्जलिर् भूत्वा वेपमानो नलं तदा।
उवाच मां विद्धि राजन् नागं कर्कोटकं नृप ॥४॥
मया प्रलब्धो महर्षिर् नारदः स महातपाः।
तेन मन्युपरीतेन शप्तोऽस्मि मनुजाधिप ॥५॥
तिष्ठ त्वं स्थावर इव यावद् एव नलः क्वचित्।
इतो नेता हि तत्र त्वं शापाद् मोक्ष्यसि मत्कृतात् ॥६॥
तस्य शापाद् न शक्तोऽस्मि पदाद् विचलितुं पदं।
उपदेक्ष्यामि ते श्रेयस् त्रातुम् अर्हति मां भवान् ॥७॥
सखा च ते भविष्यामि मत्समो नास्ति पन्नगः।
लघुश्च ते भविष्यामि शीघ्रम् आदाय गच्छ मां ॥८॥
एवम् उक्त्वा स नागेन्द्रो बभूवाङ्गुष्ठमात्रकः।
तं गृहीत्वा नलः प्रायाद् देशं दावविवर्जितं ॥९॥
आकाशदेशम् आसाद्य विमुक्तं कृष्णवर्त्मना।
उत्स्रष्टुकामं तं नागः पुनः कर्कोटकोऽब्रवीत् ॥१०॥
पदानि गणयन् गच्छ स्वानि नैषध कानिचित्।
तत्र तेऽहं महाबाहो श्रेयो धास्यामि यत् परं ॥११॥

Vṛihadaśva spake:

Damayantí when deserting royal Nala fled, ere long
Blazing in the forest jungle he a mighty fire beheld;
Thence, as of a living being, from the midst a voice he heard:
'Hasten, Nala!' oft and loudly, 'Puṇyaśloka, haste,' it cried.
'Fear thou not,' king Nala answered, plunging in the ruddy flame;
There he saw the King of Serpents lying, coiled into a ring.
There with folded hands the Serpent trembling, thus to Nala spake:
'Me, Karkoṭaka, the Serpent know, thou sovereign of men;
Nárada, the famous hermit, I deceived, the holy sage;
He in righteous indignation smote me with this awful curse:
Stay thou there as one unmoving till king Nala passing by
Lead thee hence; save only Nala, none can free thee from this curse.
Through this potent execration I no step have power to move;
I the way to bliss will show thee, if thou sav'st me from this fate.
I will show thee noble friendship, Serpent none is like to me;
Lightly shall I weigh, uplift me in thy hand, with speed, O king.'
Thus when spake the King of Serpents to a finger's size he shrank;
Him when Nala lightly lifted to the unburning space he passed.
To the air all cool and temperate brought him, by the flame unreached.
As he fain on th' earth would place him, thus Karkoṭaka began:
'Move thou now, O king, and slowly, as thou movest, count thy steps.
Then the best of all good fortune will I give thee, mighty armed!'

ततः सङ्ख्यातुम् आरब्धम् अदशद् दशमे पदे ।
तस्य दष्टस्य तद्रूपं क्षिप्रम् अन्तरधीयत ॥ १२॥
स दृष्ट्वा विस्मितस् तस्थाव् आत्मानं विकृतं नलः ।
स्वरूपधारिणं नागं ददर्श च महीपतिः ॥ १३॥
ततः कर्कोटको नागः सान्त्वयन् नलम् अब्रवीत् ।
मया तेऽन्तर्हितं रूपं न त्वां विद्युर् जना इति ॥ १४॥
यत्कृते चासि निकृतो दुःखेन महता नल ।
विषेण स मदीयेन त्वयि दुःखं निवत्स्यति ॥ १५॥
विषेण संवृतैर् गात्रैर् यावत् त्वां न विमोक्ष्यति ।
तावत् त्वयि महाराज दुःखं वै स निवत्स्यति ॥ १६॥
अनागा येन निकृतस् त्वम् अनर्हो जनाधिप ।
क्रोधाद् असूययित्वा तं रक्षा मे भवतः कृता ॥ १७॥
न ते भयं नरव्याघ्र दंष्ट्रिभ्यः शत्रुतोऽपि वा ।
ब्रह्मर्षिभ्यश्च भविता मत्प्रसादाद् नराधिप ॥ १८॥
राजन् विषनिमित्ता च न ते पीडा भविष्यति ।
सङ्ग्रामेषु च राजेन्द्र शश्वज् जयम् अवाप्स्यसि ॥ १९॥
गच्छ राजन् इतः सूतो वाहुकोऽहम् इति ब्रुवन् ।
समीपम् ऋतुपर्णस्य स हि वेदाक्षनैपुणं ॥ २०॥
अयोध्यां नगरीं रम्याम् अद्य वै निषधेश्वर ।
स तेऽक्षहृदयं दाता राजाश्वहृदयेन वै ॥ २१॥
इक्ष्वाकुकुलजः श्रीमान् मित्रञ्चैव भविष्यति ।
भविष्यसि यदाऽक्षज्ञः श्रेयसा योक्ष्यसे तदा ॥ २२॥
समेष्यसि च दारैस् त्वं मास्म शोके मनः कृथाः ।
राज्येन तनयाभ्याञ्च सत्यम् एतद् ब्रवीमि ते ॥ २३॥
स्वरूपञ्च यदा द्रष्टुम् इच्छेथास् त्वं नराधिप ।
संस्मर्तव्यस् तदा तेऽहं वासश्चेदं निवासयेः ॥ २४॥

Ere the tenth step he had counted, him the sudden Serpent bit:
As he bit him, on the instant all his kingly form was changed.
There he stood and gazed in wonder, Nala, on his altered form.
In his proper shape the Serpent saw the sovereign of men.
Then Karkoṭaka the Serpent thus to Nala comfort spake:
'Through my power thy form is altered, lest thou should'st be known of men.
He through whom thou'rt thus afflicted, Nala, with intensest grief,
Through my poison, shall in anguish ever dwell within thy soul.
All his body steeped in poison till he free thee from thy woe,
Shall he dwell within thee prison'd in the ecstacy of pain.
So from him, by whom, thou blameless! sufferest such unworthy wrong,
By the curse I lay upon him thy deliverance shall be wrought.
Fear not thou the tusked wild boar, foeman fear not thou, O king,
Neither Bráhman fear, nor Sages, safe through my prevailing power.
King, this salutary poison gives to thee nor grief nor pain;
In the battle, chief of Rájas, victory is ever thine.
Go thou forth, thyself thus naming, 'Váhuka, the charioteer,'
To the royal Ṛituparṇa, in the dice all-skilful he;
To Ayodhyá's pleasant city, sovereign of Nishadha! go;
He his skill in dice will give thee for thy skill in taming steeds:
Of Ikshváku's noble lineage he will be thy best of friends.
Thou the skill in dice possessing soon wilt rise again to bliss;
With thy consort reunited yield not up thy soul to grief.
Thou thy kingdom, thou thy children wilt regain, the truth I speak.
When again thou would'st behold thee in thy proper form, O king,
Summon me to thy remembrance, and this garment put thou on:

अनेन वाससाच्छन्नः स्वरूपं प्रतिपत्स्यसे ।
इत्युक्त्वा प्रददौ तस्मै दिव्यं वासोयुगं तदा ॥२५॥
एवं नलञ्च सन्दिश्य वासो दत्त्वा च कौरव ।
नागराजस् ततो राजंस् तत्रैवान्तरधीयत ॥२६॥

॥ इति नलोपाख्याने चतुर्दशः सर्गः ॥१४॥

बृहदश्व उवाच ।

तस्मिन्न् अन्तर्हिते नागे प्रययौ नैषधो नलः ।
ऋतुपर्णस्य नगरं प्राविशद् दशमेऽहनि ॥१॥
स राजानम् उपातिष्ठद् वाहुकोऽहम् इति ब्रुवन् ।
अश्वानां वाहने युक्तः पृथिव्यां नास्ति मत्समः ॥२॥
अर्थकृच्छ्रेषु चैवाहं प्रष्टव्यो नैपुणेषु च ।
अन्नसंस्कारम् अपि च जानाम्यन्यैर् विशेषतः ॥३॥
यानि शिल्पानि लोकेऽस्मिन् यच्चैवान्यत् सुदुष्करं ।
सर्वं यतिष्ये तत् कर्तुम् ऋतुपर्ण भरस्व मां ॥४॥

ऋतुपर्ण उवाच ।

वस वाहुक भद्रं ते सर्वम् एतत् करिष्यसि ।
शीघ्रयाने सदा बुद्धिर् ध्रियते मे विशेषतः ॥५॥
स त्वम् आतिष्ठ योगं तं येन शीघ्रा हया मम ।
भवेयुर् अश्वाध्यक्षोऽसि वेतनं ते शतं शताः ॥६॥
त्वाम् उपस्थास्यतश्चैव नित्यं वार्ष्णेयजीवलौ ।
एताभ्यां रंस्यसे सार्धं वस वै मयि वाहुक ॥७॥
एवम् उक्तो नलस् तेन न्यवसत् तत्र पूजितः ।
ऋतुपर्णस्य नगरे सहवार्ष्णेयजीवलः ॥८॥

In this garment clad resum'st thou instantly thy proper form.'
Saying thus, of vests celestial gave he to the king a pair.
And king Nala, thus instructed, gifted with these magic robes,
Instantly the King of Serpents vanished from his sight away.

End of Book XIV.

Vṛihadaśva spake:

Vanished thus the King of Serpents set Nishadha's Rája forth,
Ṛituparṇa's royal city on the tenth day entered he.
Straight before the royal presence, 'Váhuka am I,' he said,
'In the skill of taming horses on the earth is not my peer;
Use me, where the arduous counsel, where thou want'st the dexterous hand;
In the art of dressing viands I am skilful above all.
Whatsoe'er the art, whatever be most difficult to do,
I will strive to execute it, take me to thy service, king.'

Ṛituparṇa spake:

'Váhuka, I bid thee welcome, all this service shalt thou do,
On my horses' rapid motion deeply is my mind engaged.
Take thou then on thee the office, that my steeds be fleet of foot,
Of my horse be thou the master, hundred hundreds is thy pay:
Ever shalt thou have for comrades Várshṇeya and Jívala:
With these two pursue thy pleasure, Váhuka, abide with me.'
Thus addressed, did Nala, honoured by king Ṛituparṇa long,
With Várshṇeya in that city and with Jívala abide:

स वै तत्रावसद् राजा वैदर्भीम् अनुचिन्तयन् ।
सायं सायं सदा चेमं श्लोकम् एकं जगाद ह ॥९॥
क्व नु सा क्षुत्पिपासार्ता श्रान्ता शेते तपस्विनी ।
स्मरन्ती तस्य मन्दस्य कं वा साऽद्योपतिष्ठति ॥१०॥
एवं ब्रुवन्तं राजानं निशायां जीवलोऽब्रवीत् ॥११॥
काम् इमां शोचसे नित्यं श्रोतुम् इच्छामि बाहुक ।
आयुष्मन् कस्य वा नारी याम् एवम् अनुशोचसि ॥१२॥
तम् उवाच नलो राजा मन्दप्रज्ञस्य कस्यचित् ।
आसीद् बहुमता नारी तस्यादृढतरं वचः ॥१३॥
स वै केनचिद् अर्थेन तया मन्दो व्ययुज्यत ।
विप्रयुक्तः स मन्दात्मा भ्रमत्यसुखपीडितः ॥१४॥
दह्यमानः स शोकेन दिवारात्रम् अतन्द्रितः ।
निशाकाले स्मरंस् तस्याः श्लोकम् एकं स्म गायति ॥१५॥
स विभ्रमन् महीं सर्वां क्वचिद् आसाद्य किञ्चन ।
वसत्यनर्हस् तद्दुःखं भूय एवानुसंस्मरन् ॥१६॥
सा तु तं पुरुषं नारी कृच्छ्रेऽप्यनुगता वने ।
त्यक्ता तेनाल्पपुण्येन दुष्करं यदि जीवति ॥१७॥
एका बालाऽनभिज्ञा च मार्गाणाम् अतथोचिता ।
क्षुत्पिपासापरीताङ्गी दुष्करं यदि जीवति ॥१८॥
श्वापदाचरिते नित्यं वने महति दारुणे ।
त्यक्ता तेनाल्पभाग्येन मन्दप्रज्ञेन मारिष ॥१९॥
इत्येवं नैषधो राजा दमयन्तीम् अनुस्मरन् ।
अज्ञातवासं न्यवसद् राज्ञस् तस्य निवेशने ॥२०॥

॥ इति नलोपाख्याने पञ्चदशः सर्गः ॥१५॥

There abode he, sadly thinking of Vidarbha's daughter still.
In the evening, every evening uttered he this single verse;
'Where is she, by thirst and hunger worn, and weary, pious still,
Thinking of her unwise husband, in whose presence is she now?'
Thus the Rája, ever speaking, Jívala one night addressed;
'Who is she, for whom thou grievest? Váhuka, I fain would hear.
Who may be the lady's husband? tell me—length of days be thine!'
Answered thus the royal Nala, 'To a man of sense bereft,
Once belonged a peerless lady, most infirm of word was he;
From some cause from her dissevered went that frantic man away,
In his foolish soul thus parted wanders he, by sorrow racked;
Day and night, and still for ever by his parching grief consumed:
Nightly brooding o'er his sorrows sings he this sad single verse.
O'er the whole wide earth a wanderer, chance-alighting in some place,
Dwells that woful man, unworthy, ever wakeful with his grief.
Him that noble lady following, in the forest lone and dread,
Lives, of that bad man forsaken, hard it is to say, she lives!
Lone, and young, the ways unknowing, undeserving of such fate,
Pines she there with thirst and hunger, hard it is to say, she lives.
In that vast and awful forest, haunted by fierce beasts of prey,
Jívala, she roams forsaken by that hapless senseless lord.'
Thus remembering Damayantí did Nishadha's king unknown
Long within that dwelling sojourn, in the palace of the king.

End of Book XV.

बृहदश्व उवाच ।

हृतराज्ये नले भीमः सभार्ये प्रेष्यतां गते ।
द्विजान् प्रस्थापयामास नलदर्शनकाङ्क्षया ॥१॥
सन्दिदेश च तान् भीमो वसु दत्त्वा च पुष्कलं ।
मृगयध्वं नलं यूयं दमयन्तीञ्च मे सुतां ॥२॥
अस्मिन् कर्मणि सम्पन्ने विज्ञाते निषधाधिपे ।
गवां सहस्रं दास्यामि यो वस् ताव् आनयिष्यति ॥३॥
अग्रहारांश्च दास्यामि ग्रामं नगरसम्मितं ।
न चेच् छक्याव् इहानेतुं दमयन्ती नलोऽपि वा ॥४॥
ज्ञातमात्रेऽपि दास्यामि गवां दश शतं धनं ।
इत्युक्तास् ते ययुर् हृष्टा ब्राह्मणाः सर्वतो दिशं ॥५॥
पुरराष्ट्राणि चिन्वन्तो नैषधं सह भार्यया ।
नैव क्वापि प्रपश्यन्ति नलं वा भीमपुत्रिकां ॥६॥
ततश् चेदिपुरीं रम्यां सुदेवो नाम वै द्विजः ।
विचिन्वानोऽथ वैदर्भीम् अपश्यद् राजवेश्मनि ॥७॥
पुण्याहवाचने राज्ञः सुनन्दासहितां स्थितां ।
मन्दं प्रख्यायमानेन रूपेणाप्रतिमेन तां ।
निबद्धां धूमजालेन प्रभाम् इव विभावसोः ॥८॥
तां समीक्ष्य विशालाक्षीम् अधिकं मलिनां कृशां ।
तर्कयामास भैमीति कारणैर् उपपादयन् ॥९॥

सुदेव उवाच ।

यथेयं मे पुरा दृष्टा तथारूपेयम् अङ्गना ।
कृतार्थोऽस्म्यद्य दृष्ट्वेमां लोककान्ताम् इव श्रियं ॥१०॥

Vṛihadaśva spake:

Nala thus bereft of kingdom with his wife to slavery sunk,
Forth king Bhíma sent the Bráhmans, Nala through the world to seek.
Thus the royal Bhíma charged them, with abundant wealth supplied:—
'Go ye now and seek king Nala, Damayantí seek, my child:
And, achieved this weighty business, found Nishadha's royal lord,
Which of you shall hither bring them shall a thousand kine receive;
And a royal grant for maintenance of a village like a town.
If nor hither Damayantí nor king Nala may be brought,
Know ye where they are, rich guerdon still we give, ten hundred kine.'
Thus addressed, the joyful Bráhmans went to every clime of earth,
Through the cities, through the kingdoms, seeking Nala and his queen:
Nala, or king Bhíma's daughter, in no place might they behold.
Then a Bráhman, named Sudeva, came to pleasant Ćedi-pur;
There within the kingly palace he Vidarbha's daughter saw,
Standing with the fair Sunandá, on a royal holiday.
With her beauty once so peerless worthy now of little praise,
Like the sun-light feebly shining through the dimness of a cloud.
Gazing on the large-eyed princess, dull in look, and wasted still,
Lo, he thought, king Bhíma's daughter, pondering thus within his mind.—

Sudeva spake:

E'en as once I wont to see her, such is yonder woman's form,
I my work have done, beholding, like the goddess world-adored,

पूर्णचन्द्रनिभां श्यामां चारुवृत्तपयोधरां ।
कुर्वन्तीं प्रभया देवीं सर्वा वितिमिरा दिशः ॥११॥
चारुपद्मविशालाक्षीं मन्मथस्य रतीम् इव ।
इष्टां समस्तलोकस्य पूर्णचन्द्रप्रभाम् इव ॥१२॥
विदर्भसरसस् तस्माद् दैवदोषाद् इवोद्धृतां ।
मलपङ्कानुलिप्ताङ्गीं मृणालीम् इव चोद्धृतां ॥१३॥
पौर्णमासीम् इव निशां राहुग्रस्तनिशाकरां ।
पतिशोकाकुलां दीनां शुष्कस्रोतां नदीम् इव ॥१४॥
विध्वस्तपर्णकमलां वित्रासितविहङ्गमां ।
हस्तिहस्तपरामृष्टां व्याकुलाम् इव पद्मिनीं ॥१५॥
सुकुमारीं सुजाताङ्गीं रत्नगर्भगृहोचितां ।
दह्यमानाम् इवार्केण मृणालीम् इव चोद्धृतां ॥१६॥
रूपौदार्यगुणोपेतां मण्डनार्हाम् अमण्डितां ।
चन्द्रलेखाम् इव नवां व्योम्नि नीलाभ्रसंवृतां ॥१७॥
कामभोगैः प्रियैर् हीनां हीनां बन्धुजनेन च ।
देहं धारयतीं दीनां भर्तृदर्शनकाङ्क्षया ॥१८॥
भर्ता नाम परं नार्या भूषणं भूषणैर् विना ।
एषा हि रहिता तेन शोभमाना न शोभते ॥१९॥
दुष्करं कुरुते ऽत्यन्तं हीनो यद् अनया नलः ।
धारयत्यात्मनो देहं न शोकेनावसीदति ॥२०॥
इमाम् असितकेशान्तां शतपत्रायतेक्षणां ।
सुखार्हां दुःखितां दृष्ट्वा ममापि व्यथते मनः ॥२१॥
कदा नु खलु दुःखस्य पारं यास्यति वै शुभा ।
भर्तुः समागमात् साध्वी रोहिणी शशिनो यथा ॥२२॥
अस्या नूनम् पुनर्लाभाद् नैषधः प्रीतिम् एष्यति ।
राजा राज्यपरिभ्रष्टः पुनर् लब्ध्वा च मेदिनीं ॥२३॥

Like the full moon, darkly beauteous, with her fair and swelling breasts,
Her, the queen, that with her brightness makes each clime devoid of gloom,
With her lotus-eyes expanding, like Manmatha's queen divine;
Like the moonlight in its fulness, the desire of all the world;
From Vidarbha's pleasant waters her by cruel fate plucked up,
Like a lotus-flower uprooted, with the mire and dirt around;
Like the pallid night, when Ráhu swallows up the darkened moon;
For her husband wan with sorrow, like a gentle stream dried up;
Like a pool, where droops the lotus, whence the affrighted birds have fled,
By the elephant's proboscis, in its quiet depths disturbed;
Tender, soft-limbed, in a palace fit, of precious stones, to dwell;
Like the lotus-stem, uprooted, parched and withered by the sun;
Fair as generous, of adornment worthy, yet all unadorned,
Like the young moon's slender crescent in the heavens by dark clouds veiled;
Widowed now of all love's pleasures, of her noble kin despoiled,
Wretched, bearing life, her husband in her hope again to see.
To the unadorned, a husband is the chiefest ornament;
Of her husband if forsaken she in splendour is not bright.
Difficult must be the trial; does king Nala, reft of her,
Still retain his wretched body, nor with sorrow pine away?
Her with her dark flowing tresses, with her long and lotus-eyes,
Worthy of all joy, thus joyless, as I see, my soul is wrung.
To the furthest shore of sorrow when will pass this beauteous queen?
To her husband reunited, as the moon's bride to the moon?
Her recovering shall king Nala to his happiness return,
King, albeit despoiled of kingdom, he his realm shall reassume;

तुल्यशीलवयोयुक्तां तुल्याभिजनसंवृतां ।
नैषधोऽर्हति वैदर्भीं तञ्चेयमसितेक्षणा ॥२४॥
युक्तं तस्याप्रमेयस्य वीर्यसत्त्ववतो मया ।
समाश्वासयितुं भार्यां पतिदर्शनलालसां ॥२५॥
अहम् आश्वासयाम्येनां पूर्णचन्द्रनिभाननां ।
अदृष्टपूर्वां दुःखस्य दुःखार्तां ध्यानतत्परां ॥२६॥

वृहदश्व उवाच ।

एवं विमृश्य विविधैः कारणैर् लक्षणैश्च तां ।
उपागम्य ततो भैमीं सुदेवो ब्राह्मणोऽब्रवीत् ॥२७॥
अहं सुदेवो वैदर्भि भ्रातुस् ते दयितः सखा ।
भीमस्य वचनाद् राज्ञस् त्वाम् अन्वेष्टुम् इहागतः ॥२८॥
कुशली ते पिता राज्ञि जननी भ्रातरश्च ते ।
आयुष्मन्तौ कुशलिनौ तचस्थौ दारकौ च तौ ॥२९॥
त्वत्कृते बन्धुवर्गाश्च गतसत्त्वा इवासते ।
अन्वेष्टारो ब्राह्मणाश्च भ्रमन्ति शतशो महीं ॥३०॥
अभिज्ञाय सुदेवं तं दमयन्ती युधिष्ठिर ।
पर्यपृच्छत तान् सर्वान् क्रमेण सुहृदः स्वकान् ॥३१॥
रुरोद च भृशं राजन् वैदर्भी शोककर्षिता ।
दृष्ट्वा सुदेवं सहसा भ्रातुर् इष्टं द्विजोत्तमं ॥३२॥
ततो रुदन्तीं तां दृष्ट्वा सुनन्दा शोककर्षितां ।
सुदेवेन सहैकान्ते कथयन्तीञ्च भारत ॥३३॥
जनित्र्याः कथयामास सैरन्ध्री रोदितीति वै ।
ब्राह्मणेन समागम्य तां वेत्थ यदि मन्यसे ॥३४॥
अथ चेदिपतेर् माता राज्ञश्चान्तःपुरात् तदा ।
जगाम यत्र सा बाला ब्राह्मणेन सहाभवत् ॥३५॥

In their age and virtues equal, equal in their noble race,
He alone of her is worthy, worthy she alone of him.
Me beseems it of that peerless, of that brave and prudent king,
To console the loyal consort, pining for her husband's sight.
Her will I address with comfort, with her moonlike glowing face;
Her with woe once unacquainted, woful now and lost in thought.

Vṛihadaśva spake:

Thus when he had gazed and noted all her marks, her features well,
To the daughter of king Bhíma thus the sage Sudeva spake:
'I am named Sudeva, lady, I, thy brother's chosen friend,
By king Bhíma's royal mandate hither come in search of thee.
Well thy sire, thy royal mother, well thy noble brethren fare,
And well fare those little infants, well and happy are they both.
For thy sake thy countless kindred sit as though of sense bereft:
Seeking thee a hundred Bráhmans now are wandering o'er the earth.'
She no sooner knew Sudeva, Damayantí, of her kin,
Many a question asked in order, and of every friend beloved.
And the daughter of Vidarbha freely wept, so sudden thus
On Sudeva, best of Bráhmans, gazing, on her brother's friend.
Her beheld the young Sunandá weeping, wasted with distress,
As she thus her secret converse with the wise Sudeva held.
Thus she spake unto her mother, 'Lo, how fast our handmaid weeps,
Questioning the holy Bráhman, who she is, thou soon may'st know.'
Forth the king of Ćedi's mother from the inner chamber went,
And she passed where with the Bráhman that mysterious woman stood.

ततः सुदेवम् आनाय्य राजमाता विशाम्पते ।
पप्रच्छ भार्या कस्येयं सुता वा कस्य भाविनी ॥३६॥
कथञ्च भ्रष्टा ज्ञातिभ्यो भर्तुर् वा वामलोचना ।
त्वया च विदिता विप्र कथम् एवङ्गता सती ॥३७॥
एतद् इच्छाम्यहं श्रोतुं त्वत्तः सर्वम् अशेषतः ।
तत्त्वेन हि ममाचक्ष्व पृच्छन्त्या देवरूपिणीं ॥३८॥
एवम् उक्तस् तया राजन् सुदेवो द्विजसत्तमः ।
सुखोपविष्ट आचष्टे दमयन्त्या यथातथं ॥३९॥

॥ इति नलोपाख्याने षोडशः सर्गः ॥१६॥

सुदेव उवाच ।

विदर्भराजो धर्मात्मा भीमो नाम महाद्युतिः ।
सुतेयं तस्य कल्याणी दमयन्तीति विश्रुता ॥१॥
राजा तु नैषधो नाम वीरसेनसुतो नलः ।
भार्येयं तस्य कल्याणी पुण्यश्लोकस्य धीमतः ॥२॥
स द्यूते निर्जितो भ्रात्रा हृतराज्यो महीपतिः ।
दमयन्त्या गतः सार्धं न प्राज्ञायत कर्हिचित् ॥३॥
ते वयं दमयन्त्यर्थे चरामः पृथिवीम् इमां ।
सेयम् आसादिता बाला तव पुत्रनिवेशने ॥४॥
अस्या रूपेण सदृशी मानुषी न हि विद्यते ।
अस्या ह्येष भ्रुवोर् मध्ये सहजः पिप्लुर् उत्तमः ॥५॥
श्यामायाः पद्मसङ्काशो लक्षितोऽन्तर्हितो मया ।
मलेन संवृतो ह्यस्याश छन्नोऽभ्रेणेव चन्द्रमाः ॥६॥

Them the mother-queen Sudeva bade before her presence stand;
And she asked, 'Whose wife, whose daughter may this noble stranger be?
From her kindred how dissevered, from her husband, the soft-eyed?
Is she known to thee, O Bráhman, how to this sad state reduced?
This I fain would hear, and clearly, all her strange and wondrous tale.
Tell me all that hath befallen to this heaven-formed, plainly tell.'
Best of Bráhmans, thus Sudeva, by the mother-queen addressed,
All the truth of Damayantí, sitting at his ease, declared.

End of Book XVI.

Sudeva spake:

'In Vidarbha the just monarch, Bhíma, in his glory dwells.
Of that king is she the daughter, Damayantí is her name;
And the Rája of Nishadha, Nala, Vírasena's son,
Of that king is she the consort, Puṇyaśloka named, the Wise.
Him in play his brother worsted, spoiled of realm the king of earth.
He set forth with Damayantí, whither is unknown of men.
For the sake of Damayantí wander we about the earth;
Till I found yon noble woman in the palace of your son.
Like to her of mortal women is there none, her beauty's peer;
In the midst, between her eyebrows, from her birth a lovely mole
Dark was seen, and like a lotus that hath vanished from my sight,
Covered over with defilement, like the moon behind a cloud.

चिह्नभूतो विभूत्यर्थम् अयं धात्रा विनिर्मितः ।
प्रतिपत्कलुषस्येन्दोर् लेखा नातिविराजते ॥७॥
न चास्या नश्यते रूपं वपुर्मलसमाचितं ।
असंस्कृतम् अपि व्यक्तं भाति काञ्चनसन्निभं ॥८॥
अनेन वपुषा बाला पिप्लुनाऽनेन सूचिता ।
लक्षितेयं मया देवी निभृतोऽग्निर् इवोष्मणा ॥९॥

वृहदश्व उवाच ।

तच् छ्रुत्वा वचनं तस्य सुदेवस्य विशाम्पते ।
सुनन्दा शोधयामास पिप्लुप्रच्छादनं मलं ॥१०॥
स मलेनापकृष्टेन पिप्लुस् तस्या व्यरोचत ।
दमयन्त्यास् तदा व्यभ्रे नभसीव निशाकरः ॥११॥
पिप्लुं दृष्ट्वा सुनन्दा च राजमाता च भारत ।
रुदन्त्यौ तां परिष्वज्य मुहूर्तम् इव तस्थतुः ॥१२॥
उत्सृज्य वाष्पं शनकै राजमातेदम् अब्रवीत् ।
भगिन्या दुहिता मेऽसि पिप्लुनाऽनेन सूचिता ॥१३॥
अहञ्च तव माता च राज्ञस् तस्य महात्मनः ।
सुते दशार्णाधिपतेः सुदाम्नश् चारुदर्शने ॥१४॥
भीमस्य राज्ञः सा दत्ता वीरबाहोर् अहं पुनः ।
त्वं तु जाता मया दृष्टा दशार्णेषु पितुर् गृहे ॥१५॥
यथैव ते पितुर् गेहं तथैव मम भाविनि ।
यथैव च ममैश्वर्यं दमयन्ति तथा तव ॥१६॥
तां प्रहृष्टेन मनसा दमयन्ती विशाम्पते ।
प्रणम्य मातुर् भगिनीम् इदं वचनम् अब्रवीत् ॥१७॥
अज्ञायमानापि सती सुखम् अस्म्युषिता त्वयि ।
सर्वकामैः सुविहिता रक्ष्यमाणा सदा त्वया ॥१८॥

This soft mole by Brahmá fashioned, sign of his creative power,
As at change the moon's thin crescent only dim and faintly gleams.
Yet her beauty is not faded; though her form be soiled with dust,
Unadorned, it shines more nobly, like the native unwrought gold.
With that beauteous form yon woman, gifted with that lovely mole,
Instant knew I for the Princess, as the heat betrays the fire.'

Vṛihadaśva spake:

To Sudeva as she listened uttering thus his strange discourse:
'All the dust that mole concealing young Sunandá washed away.
By the obscuring dust unclouded shining out that mole appeared;
On the brow of Damayantí, like the unclouded moon in heaven.'
Gazing on that mole, Sunandá, and the mother of the king,
Wept as fondly they embraced her, and an instant silent stood.
Then her tears awhile suppressing, thus the royal mother spake:
'Thou art mine own sister's daughter, by that beauteous mole made known;
I, oh beauteous, and thy mother, of that lofty-minded king,
Are the daughters, king Sudáman, he that in Daśárṇa reigns;
She was wedded to king Bhíma, and to Vírabáhu I.
In my father's home, Daśárṇa once I saw thee, newly-born.
As to me thy father's lineage is akin, so mine to thee;
Whatsoe'er my power commandeth, Damayantí, all is thine.'

To the queen did Damayantí, in the gladness of her heart,
Having bowed in courteous homage to her mother's sister, speak:
'While unknown I might continue, gladly dwelt I here with thee;
Every want supplied on th' instant, guarded by thy gentle care.

सुखात् सुखतरो वासो भविष्यति न संशयः ।
चिरविप्रोषितां मातर् माम् अनुज्ञातुम् अर्हसि ॥१९॥
दारकौ च हि मे नीतौ वसतस् तत्र बालकौ ।
पित्रा विहीनौ शोकार्तौ मया चैव कथं नु तौ ॥२०॥
यदि चापि प्रियं किञ्चिद् मयि कर्तुम् इहेच्छसि ।
विदर्भान् यातुम् इच्छामि शीघ्रं मे यानम् आदिश ॥२१॥
बाढम् इत्येव ताम् उक्त्वा हृष्टा मातृष्वसा नृप ।
गुप्तां बलेन महता पुत्रस्यानुमते ततः ॥२२॥
प्रास्थापयद् राजमाता श्रीमतीं नरवाहिना ।
यानेन भरतश्रेष्ठ ह्यन्नपानपरिच्छदां ॥२३॥
ततः सा नचिराद् एव विदर्भान् अगमत् पुनः ।
तां तु बन्धुजनः सर्वः प्रहृष्टः समपूजयत् ॥२४॥
सर्वान् कुशलिनो दृष्ट्वा बान्धवान् दारकौ च तौ ।
मातरम् पितरञ्चोभौ सर्वञ्चैव सखीजनं ॥२५॥
देवताः पूजयामास ब्राह्मणांश्च यशस्विनी ।
परेण विधिना देवी दमयन्ती विशाम्पते ॥२६॥
अतर्पयत् सुदेवञ्च गोसहस्रेण पार्थिवः ।
प्रीतो दृष्ट्वैव तनयां ग्रामेण द्रविणेन च ॥२७॥
सा व्युष्टा रजनीं तत्र पितुर् वेश्मनि भाविनी ।
विश्रान्ता मातरं राजन् इदं वचनम् अब्रवीत् ॥२८॥
मां चेद् इच्छसि जीवन्तीं मातः सत्यम् ब्रवीमि ते ।
नरवीरस्य चैतस्य नलस्यानयने यत ॥२९॥
दमयन्त्या तथोक्ता तु सा देवी भृशदुःखिता ।
बाष्पेणापिहिता राजन् नोत्तरं किञ्चिद् अब्रवीत् ॥३०॥
तदवस्थां तु तां दृष्ट्वा सर्वम् अन्तःपुरं तदा ।
हाहाभूतम् अतीवासीद् भृशञ्च प्ररुरोद ह ॥३१॥

Yet than even this pleasant dwelling, a more pleasant may there be;
Long a banished woman, mother! give me leave from hence to part,
Thither where my infant children dwell, my tender little ones,
Orphaned of their sire, in sorrow orphaned, ah, how long of me!
If thou yet wilt grant a favour, o'er all other favours dear,
To Vidarbha would I journey, quick the palanquin command.'
'Be it so,' her mother's sister, joyful, instant made reply.
Guarded by a mighty army, with th' approval of her son,
Sent the queen, that happy lady, in a palanquin, by men
Borne aloft, and well provided with all raiment, drink, and food.

Thus the princess to Vidarbha after brief delay returned.
Her her whole assembled kindred welcomed home with pride and joy,
All in health she found her kinsmen, and that lovely infant pair,
With her mother, with her father, and her troop of female friends.
To the gods she paid her worship, to the Bráhmans in her joy;
So the queenly Damayantí all in noblest guise performed.
And her royal sire Sudeva, with the thousand kine made glad,
Joyous to behold his daughter, with a village and much wealth.
There, when in her father's palace she the quiet night had passed,
In these words the noble lady to her mother 'gan to speak:
'If in life thou would'st preserve me, mother, hear the truth I speak;
Home to bring the hero Nala be it now thy chiefest toil.'

Thus addressed by Damayantí, very sorrowful the queen
Clouded all her face with weeping, not a word in answer spake.
But the princess, thus afflicted, when the female train beheld,
'Woe! oh woe!' they shrieked together, all in pitying sadness wept.

ततो भीमं महाराजं भार्या वचनम् अब्रवीत् ।
दमयन्ती तव सुता भर्तारम् अनुशोचति ॥ ३२ ॥
अपकृष्य च लज्जां सा स्वयम् उक्तवती नृप ।
प्रयतन्तु तव प्रेष्याः पुण्यश्लोकस्य मार्गणे ॥ ३३ ॥
तया प्रदेशितो राजा ब्राह्मणान् वशवर्तिनः ।
प्रास्थापयद् दिशः सर्वा यतध्वं नलमार्गणे ॥ ३४ ॥
ततो विदर्भाधिपतेर् नियोगाद् ब्राह्मणास् तदा ।
दमयन्तीम् अथो दृत्वा प्रस्थिताः स्मेत्यथाब्रुवन् ॥ ३५ ॥
अथ तान् अब्रवीद् भैमी सर्वराष्ट्रेष्विदं वचः ।
ब्रूयास्त जनसंसत्सु तत्र तत्र पुनः पुनः ॥ ३६ ॥
क्व नु त्वं कितव छित्त्वा वस्त्रार्धं प्रस्थितो मम ।
उत्सृज्य विपिने सुप्ताम् अनुरक्तां प्रियां प्रिय ॥ ३७ ॥
सा वै यथा समादिष्टा तथास्ते त्वत्प्रतीक्षिणी ।
दह्यमाना भृशं बाला वस्त्रार्धेनाभिसंवृता ॥ ३८ ॥
तस्या रुदन्त्याः सततं तेन शोकेन पार्थिव ।
प्रसादं कुरु वै वीर प्रतिवाक्यं वदस्व च ॥ ३९ ॥
एवम् अन्यच्च वक्तव्यं कृपां कुर्याद् यथा मयि ।
वायुना धूयमानो हि वनं दहति पावकः ॥ ४० ॥
भर्तव्या रक्षणीया च पत्नी हि पतिना सदा ।
तन् नष्टम् उभयं कस्माद् धर्मज्ञस्य सतस् तव ॥ ४१ ॥
ख्यातः प्राज्ञः कुलीनश्च सानुक्रोशो भवान् सदा ।
संवृत्तो निरनुक्रोशः शङ्के मद्भाग्यसङ्क्षयात् ॥ ४२ ॥
तत् कुरुष्व नरव्याघ्र दयां मयि नरेश्वर ।
आनृशंस्यं परो धर्मस् त्वत्त एव मया श्रुतः ॥ ४३ ॥
एवं ब्रुवाणान् यदि वः प्रतिब्रूयाद् धि कश्चन ।
स नरः सर्वथा ज्ञेयः कश्चासौ क्व च वर्तते ॥ ४४ ॥

To the mighty Rája Bhíma did the queen that speech relate.
'Damayantí, lo, thy daughter for her husband sits and mourns;
Breaking through all bashful silence, thus, oh king, to me she spake:
"Be it now thy servants' business to find out the king of men."'
Urged by her the king his Bráhmans, to his will obedient all,
Sent around to every region, 'Be your care the king to find.'
Then those Bráhmans at the mandate of Vidarbha's royal lord,
First drew near to Damayantí, 'Lo, now set we forth,' they said.
Then to them spake Bhíma's daughter, 'In all realms be this your speech,
Wheresoever men assemble, this repeat again, again:
Whither went'st thou then, oh gamester! half my garment severing off,
Leaving in the forest sleeping, all forsaken, thy beloved?
Even as thou commandedst, sits she, sadly waiting thy return.
Parched with sorrow sits that woman, in her scant half-garment glad.
Oh to her thus ever weeping in the extreme of her distress,
Grant thy pity, noble hero, answer to her earnest prayer!
Be this also said, to move him to compassionate my state,
For by wind within the forest fanned, intensely burns the fire.
Ever by her consort guarded and sustained the wife should be.
Why hast thou forgot both duties, thou in every duty skilled?
Thou wert ever called the generous, thou the pitiful, the wise.
Art thou now estranged from pity through my sad injurious fate?
Prince of men, O grant thy pity, grant it, lord of men, to me;
"Mercy is the chief of duties," oft from thine own lips I've heard.
Thus as ye are ever speaking should there any one reply,
Mark him well, lest he be Nala, who he is, and where he dwells.

यश्चैवं वचनं श्रुत्वा ब्रूयात् प्रतिवचो नरः ।
तद् आदाय वचस् तस्य ममावेद्यं द्विजोत्तमाः ॥४५॥
यथा च वो न जानीयाद् ब्रुवतो मम शासनात् ।
पुनरागमनञ्चैव तथा कार्यम् अतन्द्रितैः ॥४६॥
यदिवाऽसौ समृद्धः स्याद् यदिवाऽप्यधनो भवेत् ।
यदिवाऽप्यर्थकामः स्याज् ज्ञेयं तस्य चिकीर्षितं ॥४७॥
एवम् उक्तास् त्वगच्छंस् ते ब्राह्मणाः सर्वतो दिशः ।
नलं मृगयितुं राजंस् तदा व्यसनिनं तथा ॥४८॥
ते पुराणि सराष्ट्राणि ग्रामान् घोषांस् तथाश्रमान् ।
अन्वेषन्तो नलं राजन् नाधिजग्मुर् द्विजातयः ॥४९॥
तच्च वाक्यं तथा सर्वे तत्र तत्र विशाम्पते ।
श्रावयाञ्चक्रिरे विप्रा दमयन्त्या यथेरितं ॥५०॥

॥ इति नलोपाख्याने सप्तदशः सर्गः ॥१७॥

बृहदश्व उवाच ।

अथ दीर्घस्य कालस्य पर्णादो नाम वै द्विजः ।
प्रत्येत्य नगरं भैमीम् इदं वचनम् अब्रवीत् ॥१॥
नैषधं मृगयानेन दमयन्ति मया नलं ।
अयोध्यां नगरीं गत्वा भाङ्गासुरिर् उपस्थितः ॥२॥
श्रावितश्च मया वाक्यं त्वदीयं स महामते ।
ऋतुपर्णो महाभागो यथोक्तं वरवर्णिनि ॥३॥
तच् छ्रुत्वा नाब्रवीत् किञ्चिद् ऋतुपर्णो नराधिपः ।
न च पारिषदः कश्चिद् भाष्यमाणो मयासकृत् ॥४॥

He who to this speech hath listened, and hath thus his answer made,
Be his words, O best of Bráhmans, treasured and brought home to me,
Lest he haply should discover that by my command ye speak,
That again ye may approach him, do ye this without delay.
Whether he be of the wealthy, whether of the poor he be;
Be he covetous of riches, learn ye all he would desire.'
Thus addressed, went forth the Bráhmans to the realms on every side,
Seeking out the royal Nala in his dark concealed distress.
They through kingdoms, cities, hamlets, pastoral dwellings, hermits' cells,
Nala everywhere went seeking, yet those Bráhmans found him not.
All in every part went speaking in the language they were taught;
In the words of Damayantí spake they in the ears of men.

End of Book XVII.

Vṛihadaśva spake:

Long the time that passed, a Bráhman, wise Parṇáda was his name,
Home returning to the city, thus to Bhíma's daughter spake:
'Damayantí! royal Nala as I sought, Nishadha's king,
Came I to Ayodhyá's city; there Bháṅgásuri approached,
Stood before me, eager listening to the words thou bad'st us speak,
He, the prosperous Ṛituparṇa, thy own words, O lady fair.
Thus as spake I, answered nothing Ṛituparṇa, king of men;
Nor of all that full assemblage, more than once addressed by me.

अनुज्ञातं तु मां राज्ञा विजने कश्चिद् अब्रवीत् ।
ऋतुपर्णस्य पुरुषो बाहुको नाम नामतः ॥५॥
सूतस् तस्य नरेन्द्रस्य विरूपो ह्रस्वबाहुकः ।
शीघ्रयानेषु कुशलो मिष्टकर्ता च भोजने ॥६॥
स विनिःश्वस्य बहुशो रुदित्वा च पुनः पुनः ।
कुशलञ्चैव मां पृष्ट्वा पश्चाद् इदम् अभाषत ॥७॥
वैषम्यम् अपि सम्प्राप्ता गोपायन्ति कुलस्त्रियः ।
आत्मानम् आत्मना सत्यो जितस्वर्गा न संशयः ॥८॥
रहिता भर्तृभिश्चैव न क्रुध्यन्ति कदाचन ।
प्राणांश्च चारित्रकवचान् धारयन्ति वरस्त्रियः ॥९॥
विषमस्थेन मूढेन परिभ्रष्टसुखेन च ।
यत् सा तेन परित्यक्ता तत्र न क्रोद्धुम् अर्हति ॥१०॥
प्राणयात्रां परिप्रेप्सोः शकुनैर् हृतवाससः ।
आधिभिर् दह्यमानस्य श्यामा न क्रोद्धुम् अर्हति ॥११॥
सत्कृताऽसत्कृता वाऽपि पतिं दृष्ट्वा तथागतं ।
भ्रष्टराज्यं श्रिया हीनं क्षुधितं व्यसनाप्लुतं ॥१२॥
तस्य तद् वचनं श्रुत्वा त्वरितोऽहम् इहागतः ।
श्रुत्वा प्रमाणं भवती राज्ञश्चैव निवेदय ॥१३॥
एतच् छ्रुत्वाऽश्रुपूर्णाक्षी पर्णादस्य विशाम्पते ।
दमयन्ती रहोऽभ्येत्य मातरं प्रत्यभाषत ॥१४॥
अयम् अर्थो न संवेद्यो भीमे मातः कथञ्चन ।
त्वत्सन्निधौ नियोक्ष्येऽहं सुदेवं द्विजसत्तमं ॥१५॥
यथा न नृपतिर् भीमः प्रतिपद्येत मे मतिं ।
तथा त्वया प्रयत्तव्यं मम चेत् प्रियम् इच्छसि ॥१६॥
यथा चाहं समानीता सुदेवेनाशु बान्धवान् ।
तेनैव मङ्गलेनाशु सुदेवो यातु माचिरं ॥१७॥

By the king dismissed, when sate I in a solitary place,
One of Ṛituparṇa's household, Váhuka his name, drew near,
Charioteer of that great Rája, with short arms and all deformed,
Skilled to drive the rapid chariot, skilled the viands to prepare.
He, when much he'd groaned in anguish, and had wept again, again,
First his courteous salutation made, then spake in words like these:
"Even in the extreme of misery noble women still preserve
Over their ownselves the mastery, by their virtues winning heaven;
Of their faithless lords abandoned, anger feel not even then.
In the breastplate of their virtue noble women live unharmed.
By the wretched, by the senseless, by the lost to every joy,
She by such a lord forsaken yet to anger will not yield.
Against him his sustenance seeking, of his robe by birds despoiled,
Him consumed with utmost misery, still no wrath the dark-hued feels;
Treated well, or ill-entreated, when her husband she beholds,
Spoiled of bliss, bereft of kingdom, famine-wasted, worn with woe."
Having heard the stranger's language, hither hasted I to come.
Thou hast heard, be thine the judgment, to the king relate thou all.'
To Parṇáda having listened, with her eyes o'erflowed with tears,
Secretly went Damayantí, and her mother thus addressed:
'Let not what I speak, to Bhíma, O my mother, be made known—
In thy presence to Sudeva, best of Bráhmans, I would speak.
Let not this my secret counsel to king Bhíma be disclosed;
This the object we must compass if thy daughter thou wouldst please,
As myself was to my kindred swiftly by Sudeva brought,
With the same good fortune swiftly may Sudeva part from hence

समानेतुं नलं मातर् अयोध्यां नगरीम् इतः ।
विश्रान्तं तु ततः पश्चात् पर्णादं द्विजसत्तमं ॥१८॥
अर्चयामास वैदर्भी धनेनातीव भाविनी ।
नले चेहागते विप्र भूयो दास्यामि ते वसु ॥१९॥
त्वया हि मे बहु कृतं यथा नान्यः करिष्यति ।
यद् भर्त्राऽहं समेष्यामि शीघ्रम् एव द्विजोत्तम ॥२०॥
एवम् उक्तोऽथाश्वास्य ताम् आशीर्वादैः समङ्गलैः ।
गृहान् उपययौ चापि कृतार्थः सुमहामनाः ॥२१॥
ततः सुदेवम् आभाष्य दमयन्ती युधिष्ठिर ।
अब्रवीत् सन्निधौ मातुर् दुःखशोकसमन्विता ॥२२॥
गत्वा सुदेव नगरीम् अयोध्यावासिनं नृपं ।
ऋतुपर्णं वचो ब्रूहि सम्पतन्न् इव कामगः ॥२३॥
आस्थास्यति पुनर् भैमी दमयन्ती स्वयंवरं ।
तत्र गच्छन्ति राजानो राजपुत्राश्च सर्वशः ॥२४॥
तथा च गणितः कालः श्वोभूते स भविष्यति ।
यदि सम्भावनीयस् ते गच्छ शीघ्रम् अरिन्दम ॥२५॥
सूर्योदये द्वितीयं सा भर्तारं वरयिष्यति ।
न हि स ज्ञायते वीरो नलो जीवति वा न वा ॥२६॥
एवं तया यथोक्तो वै गत्वा राजानम् अब्रवीत् ।
ऋतुपर्णं महाराज सुदेवो ब्राह्मणस् तदा ॥२७॥

॥ इति नलोपाख्याने अष्टादशः सर्गः ॥१८॥

To Ayodhyá's city, mother, home to bring my royal lord.'

Resting from his toil, Parṇáda, of the Bráhman race the best,
Did the daughter of Vidarbha honour, and with wealth reward.
'Bráhman! home if come my Nala, richer guerdon will I give;
Much hast thou achieved, and wisely, so as none but thou has done.
That again with my lost husband, noblest Bráhman, I may meet.'
Thus addressed, his grateful homage and his benedictions paid,
Having thus achieved his mission, home the wise Parṇáda went.

Then accosting good Sudeva, Damayantí thus began,
And before her mother's presence in her pain and grief she spake:
'Go, Sudeva, to the city, where Ayodhyá's Rája dwells,
Speak thou thus to Ṛituparṇa, (thither coming as by chance):—
"Once again her Svayaṃvara does king Bhíma's daughter hold,
Damayantí, thither hasten all the kings and sons of kings.
Closely now the time is reckoned when to-morrow's dawn appears;
If that thou would'st win the princess, speed thou, tamer of thy foes.
When the sun is in his rising she a second lord will choose:
Whether lives or is not living, royal Nala, no one knows."'
Thus, as he received his mission, hastening to the king, he spake,
To the royal Ṛituparṇa spake Sudeva, in these words.

End of Book XVIII.

वृहदश्व उवाच ।

श्रुत्वा वचः सुदेवस्य ऋतुपर्णो नराधिपः ।
सान्त्वयन् श्लक्ष्णया वाचा वाहुकं प्रत्यभाषत ॥१॥
विदर्भां यातुम् इच्छामि दमयन्त्याः स्वयंवरं ।
एकाह्ना हयतत्त्वज्ञ मन्यसे यदि वाहुक ॥२॥
एवम् उक्तस्य कौन्तेय तेन राज्ञा नलस्य ह ।
व्यदीर्यत मनो दुःखात् प्रदध्यौ च महामनाः ॥३॥
दमयन्ती वदेद् एतत् कुर्याद् दुःखेन मोहिता ।
अस्मदर्थे भवेद् वाऽयम् उपायश् चिन्तितो महान् ॥४॥
नृशंसं वत वैदर्भी कर्तुकामा तपस्विनी ।
मया क्षुद्रेण निकृता कृपणा पापबुद्धिना ॥५॥
स्त्रीस्वभावश् चलो लोके मम दोषश्च दारुणः ।
स्याद् एवम् अपि कुर्यात् सा विवासाद् गतसौहृदा ॥६॥
मम शोकेन संविग्ना नैराश्यात् तनुमध्यमा ।
नैवं सा कर्हिचित् कुर्यात् सापत्या च विशेषतः ॥७॥
यद् अत्र सत्यं वाऽसत्यं गत्वा वेत्स्यामि निश्चयं ।
ऋतुपर्णस्य वै कामम् आत्मार्थं च करोम्यहं ॥८॥
इति निश्चित्य मनसा वाहुको दीनमानसः ।
कृताञ्जलिर् उवाचेदम् ऋतुपर्णं नराधिपं ॥९॥
प्रतिजानामि ते वाक्यं गमिष्यामि नराधिप ।
एकाह्ना पुरुषव्याघ्र विदर्भनगरीं नृप ॥१०॥
ततः परीक्षाम् अश्वानां चक्रे राजन् स वाहुकः ।
अश्वशालाम् उपागम्य भाङ्गासुरिर्नृपाज्ञया ॥११॥

Vṛihadaśva spake:

Hearing thus Sudeva's language, Ṛituparṇa, king of men,
With a gentle voice and blandly, thus to Váhuka began:
'Where the princess Damayantí doth her Svayaṃvara hold,
Skilled in horses! to Vidarbha, in one day I fain would go.'
In these words the unknown Nala by his royal lord addressed,
All his heart was torn with anguish, thus the lofty-minded thought—
'Can she speak thus, Damayantí, thus with sorrow frantic act?
Is't a stratagem thus subtly for my sake devised and plann'd?
To desire this deed unholy is that holy princess driven,
Wrong'd by me, her basest husband, miserable, mind-estranged!
Fickle is the heart of woman, grievous too is my offence!
Hence she thus might act ignobly in her exile, reft of friends,
Soul-disturbed by my great sorrow, in the excess of her despair.
No! she could not thus have acted, she with noble offspring blest.
Where the truth, and where the falsehood, setting forth, I best shall judge,
I the will of Ṛituparṇa, for my own sake, will obey.'
Thus within his mind revolving, Váhuka, his wretched mind,
With his folded hands addressed he Ṛituparṇa, king of men:
'I thy mandate will accomplish, I will go, O king of men,
In a single day, O Rája, to Vidarbha's royal town.'
Váhuka of all the coursers did a close inspection make,
Entering in the royal stable by Bhángásuri's command.

स त्वर्यमाणो बहुश ऋतुपर्णेन वाहुकः ।
अश्वान् जिज्ञासमानो वै विचार्य च पुनः पुनः ॥१२॥
अध्यगच्छत् कृशान् अश्वान् समर्थान् अध्वनि क्षमान् ।
तेजोबलसमायुक्तान् कुलशीलसमन्वितान् ॥१३॥
वर्जिताँल् लक्षणैर् हीनैः पृथुप्रोथान् महाहनून् ।
शुद्धान् दशभिर् आवर्तैः सिन्धुजान् वातरंहसः ॥१४॥
दृष्ट्वा तान् अब्रवीद् राजा किञ्चित् कोपसमन्वितः ।
किम् इदं प्रार्थितं कर्तुं प्रलब्धव्या न ते वयं ॥१५॥
कथम् अल्पबलप्राणा वक्ष्यन्तीमे हया मम ।
महदध्वानम् अपि च गन्तव्यं कथम् ईदृशैः ॥१६॥

वाहुक उवाच ।

एको ललाटे द्वौ मूर्ध्नि द्वौ द्वौ पार्श्वोपपार्श्वयोः ।
द्वौ द्वौ वक्षसि विज्ञेयौ प्रयाणे चैक एव तु ॥१७॥
एते हया गमिष्यन्ति विदर्भान् नात्र संशयः ।
यान् अन्यान् मन्यसे राजन् ब्रूहि तान् योजयामि ते ॥१८॥

ऋतुपर्ण उवाच ।

त्वम् एव हयतत्त्वज्ञः कुशलो ह्यसि वाहुक ।
यान् मन्यसे समर्थांस् त्वं क्षिप्रं तान् एव योजय ॥१९॥

वृहदश्व उवाच ।

ततः सदश्वांश् चतुरः कुलशीलसमन्वितान् ।
योजयामास कुशलो जवयुक्तान् रथे नलः ॥२०॥
ततो युक्तं रथं राजा समारोहत् त्वरान्वितः ।
अथ पर्यपतन् भूमौ जानुभिस् ते हयोत्तमाः ॥२१॥

Ever urged by Ṛituparṇa, Váhuka, in horses skilled,
Long within himself debating which the fleetest steeds to choose,
He approached four slender coursers, fit and powerful for the road,
Blending mighty strength with fleetness, high in courage and in blood;
Free from all the well-known vices, broad of nostril, large of jaw;
With the ten good marks distinguished, bred in Sindhu, fleet as wind.
As he gazed upon those coursers spoke the king, almost in wrath:
'Is then thus fulfilled our mandate? think not to deceive us so.
How will these my coursers bear us, slight in strength and slightly breathed?
How can such a way be travelled, and so long, by steeds like these?'—

Váhuka spake:

'Two on th' head, one on the forehead, two and two on either flank—
Two, behold, the chest discloses, and upon the crupper one—
These the horses to Vidarbha that will bear us, doubt not thou;
Yet, if others thou preferest, speak, and I will yoke them straight.'

Ṛituparṇa spake:

'In the knowledge thou of horses, Váhuka, hast matchless skill;
Whichso'er thou think'st the fittest harness thou without delay.'

Vṛihadaśva spake:

Then those four excelling horses, nobly bred, of courage high,
In their harness to the chariot did the skilful Nala yoke.—
To the chariot yoked as mounted in his eager haste the king,
To the earth those best of horses bowed their knees and stooped them down.

ततो नरवरः श्रीमान् नलो राजा विशाम्पते ।
सान्त्वयामास तान् अश्वांस् तेजोबलसमन्वितान् ॥२२॥
रश्मिभिश्च समुद्यम्य नलो यातुम् इयेष सः ।
सूतम् आरोप्य वार्ष्णेयं जवम् आस्थाय वै परं ॥२३॥
ते चोद्यमाना विधिवद् वाहुकेन हयोत्तमाः ।
समुत्पेतुर् अथाकाशं रथिनं मोहयन्न् इव ॥२४॥
तथा तु दृष्ट्वा तान् अश्वान् वहतो वातरंहसः ।
अयोध्याधिपतिः श्रीमान् विस्मयं परमं ययौ ॥२५॥
रथघोषं तु तं श्रुत्वा हयसङ्ग्रहणञ्च तत् ।
वार्ष्णेयश् चिन्तयामास वाहुकस्य हयज्ञतां ॥२६॥
किं नु स्याद् मातलिर् अयं देवराजस्य सारथिः ।
तथा तल्लक्षणं वीरे वाहुके दृश्यते महत् ॥२७॥
शालिहोत्रोऽथ किं नु स्याद् धयानां कुलतत्त्ववित् ।
मानुषं समनुप्राप्तो वपुः परमशोभनं ॥२८॥
उताहो स्विद् भवेद् राजा नलः परपुरञ्जयः ।
सोऽयं नृपतिर् आयात इत्येव समचिन्तयत् ॥२९॥
अथवा यां नलो वेद विद्यां ताम् एव वाहुकः ।
तुल्यं हि लक्षये ज्ञानं वाहुकस्य नलस्य च ॥३०॥
अपिचेदं वयस् तुल्यं वाहुकस्य नलस्य च ।
नायं नलो महावीर्यस् तद्विद्यश्च भविष्यति ॥३१॥
प्रच्छन्ना हि महात्मानश् चरन्ति पृथिवीम् इमां ।
दैवेन विधिना युक्ताः प्रच्छन्नाश्चापि रूपतः ॥३२॥
भवेत्तु मतिभेदो मे गात्रवैरूप्यतां प्रति ।
प्रमाणात् परिहीनस्तु भवेद् इति मतिर् मम ॥३३॥
वयःप्रमाणं तत् तुल्यं रूपेण तु विपर्ययः ।
नलं सर्वगुणैर् युक्तं मन्ये वाहुकम् अन्ततः ॥३४॥

Then the noblest of all heroes, Nala, with a soothing voice,
Spake unto those horses, gifted both with fleetness and with strength.
Up the reins when he had gathered he the charioteer bade mount
First, Várshṇeya, skilled in driving, at full speed then set he forth.

Urged by Váhuka, those coursers, to the utmost of their speed,
All at once in th' air sprung upward, as the driver to unseat.
Then, as he beheld those horses bearing him as fleet as wind,
Did the monarch of Ayodhyá in his silent wonder sit.
When the rattling of the chariot, when the guiding of the reins,
When of Váhuka the science saw he, thus Várshṇeya thought:
'Is it Mátali, the chariot of the king of heaven that drives?
Lo, in Váhuka each virtue of that godlike charioteer!
Is it S'álihotra, skilful in the breed, the strength of steeds,
That hath ta'en a human body, thus all-glorious to behold?
Is't, or can it be, king Nala, conqueror of his foemen's realms?
Is the lord of men before us?' thus within himself he thought.
'If the skill possessed by Nala, Váhuka possesseth too,
Lo, of Váhuka the knowledge and of Nala equal seems;
And of Váhuka and Nala thus alike the age should be.
If 'tis not the noble Nala it is one of equal skill.
Mighty ones, disguised, are wandering in the precincts of this earth.
They, divine by inborn nature, but in earthly forms concealed.
His deformity of body that my judgment still confounds;
Yet that proof alone is wanting, what shall then my judgment be?
In their age they still are equal, though unlike that form misshaped,
Nala gifted with all virtues, Váhuka I needs must deem.'

एवं विचार्य बहुशो वार्ष्णेयः पर्यचिन्तयत् ।
हृदयेन महाराज पुण्यश्लोकस्य सारथिः ॥३५॥
ऋतुपर्णस्तु राजेन्द्रो वाहुकस्य हयज्ञतां ।
चिन्तयन् मुमुदे राजा सहवार्ष्णेयसारथिः ॥३६॥
ऐकाग्र्यञ्च तथोत्साहं हयसङ्ग्रहणे च तत् ।
परं यत्नञ्च सम्प्रेक्ष्य परां मुदम् अवाप ह ॥३७॥

॥ इति नलोपाख्याने नवदशः सर्गः ॥१९॥

वृहदश्व उवाच ।

स नदीः पर्वतांश्चैव वनानि च सरांसि च ।
अचिरेणातिचक्राम खेचरः खे चरन् इव ॥१॥
तथा प्रयाते तु रथे तदा भाङ्गासुरिर् नृपः ।
उत्तरीयम् अधोऽपश्यद् भ्रष्टं परपुरञ्जयः ॥२॥
ततः स त्वरमाणस्तु पटे निपतिते तदा ।
ग्रहीष्यामीति तं राजा नलम् आह महामनाः ॥३॥
निगृह्णीष्व महाबुद्धे हयान् एतान् महाजवान् ।
वार्ष्णेयो यावद् एतं मे पटम् आनयताम् इह ॥४॥
नलस् तं प्रत्युवाचाथ दूरे भ्रष्टः पटस् तव ।
योजनं समतिक्रान्तो नाहर्तुं शक्यते पुनः ॥५॥
एवम् उक्तो नलेनाथ तदा भाङ्गासुरिर् नृपः ।
आससाद वने राजन् फलवन्तं विभीतकं ॥६॥
तं दृष्ट्वा वाहुकं राजा त्वरमाणोऽभ्यभाषत ।
ममापि सूत पश्य त्वं सङ्ख्याने परमं बलं ॥७॥

Thus the charioteer Várshṇeya sate debating in his mind;
Much, and much again he pondered, in the silence of his thought.
But the royal Ṛituparṇa, Váhuka's surpassing skill,
With the charioteer Várshṇeya, sat admiring, and rejoiced.
In the guiding of the coursers his attentive hand be watchẹd,
Wondered at his skill consummate, in consummate joy himself.

End of Book XIX.

Vṛihadaśva spake:

Over rivers, over mountains, through the forests, over lakes,
Fleetly passed they, rapid gliding, like a bird along the air.
As the chariot swiftly travelled, lo, Bhángásuri the king
Saw his upper garment fallen from the lofty chariot-seat;
Though in urgent haste, no sooner he his fallen mantle saw
Than the king exclaimed to Nala, 'Pause, and let us take it up:
Check, an instant, mighty-minded! check thy fiery-footed steeds,
While Várshṇeya, swift dismounting, bears me back my fallen robe.'
Nala answered, 'Far behind us doth thy fallen garment lie;
Five miles, lo, it lies behind us, turn we not, to gain it, back.'
Answered thus by noble Nala, then Bhángásuri the king
Bowed with fruit, within the forest, saw a tall Vibhítak-tree:
Gazing on that tree, the Rája spake to Váhuka in haste,
'Now, O charioteer, in numbers thou shalt see my passing skill.

सर्वः सर्वं न जानाति सर्वज्ञो नास्ति कश्चन ।
नैकत्र परिनिष्ठाऽस्ति ज्ञानस्य पुरुषे क्वचित् ॥८॥
वृक्षेऽस्मिन् यानि पर्णानि फलान्यपि च वाहुक ।
पतितान्यपि यान्यत्र तत्रैकम् अधिकं शतं ॥९॥
एकम् अत्राधिकं पत्रं फलम् एकञ्च वाहुक ।
पञ्चकोट्योऽथ पत्राणां द्वयोर् अपि च शाखयोः ॥१०॥
प्रचिनुह्यस्य शाखे द्वे याश्चाप्यन्याः प्रशाखिकाः ।
आभ्यां फलसहस्रे द्वे पञ्चोनं शतम् एव च ॥११॥
ततो रथम् अवस्थाप्य राजानं वाहुकोऽब्रवीत् ।
परोक्षम् इव मे राजन् कत्थसे शत्रुकर्षण ॥१२॥
प्रत्यक्षम् एतत् कर्तास्मि शातयित्वा विभीतकं ।
अथात्र गणिते राजन् विद्यते न परोक्षता ॥१३॥
प्रत्यक्षं ते महाराज शातयिष्ये विभीतकं ।
अहं हि नाभिजानामि भवेद् एवं न वेति च ॥१४॥
सङ्ख्यास्यामि फलान्यस्य पश्यतस् ते जनाधिप ।
मुहूर्तम् अपि वार्ष्णेयो रश्मीन् यच्छतु वाजिनां ॥१५॥
तम् अब्रवीन् नृपः सूतं नायं कालो विलम्बितुं ।
वाहुकस् त्वब्रवीद् एनं परं यत्नं समास्थितः ॥१६॥
प्रतीक्षस्व मुहूर्तं त्वम् अथवा त्वरते भवान् ।
एष याति शिवः पन्था याहि वार्ष्णेयसारथिः ॥१७॥
अब्रवीद् ऋतुपर्णस्तु सान्त्वयन् कुरुनन्दन ।
त्वम् इव यन्ता नान्योऽस्ति पृथिव्याम् अपि वाहुक ॥१८॥
त्वत्कृते यातुम् इच्छामि विदर्भान् हयकोविद ।
शरणं त्वां प्रपन्नोऽस्मि न विघ्नं कर्तुम् अर्हसि ॥१९॥
कामञ्च ते करिष्यामि यन् मां वक्ष्यसि वाहुक ।
विदर्भान् यदि यात्वाद्य सूर्यं दर्शयितासि मे ॥२०॥

Each one knows not every science, none there is who all things knows:
Perfect skill in every knowledge in one mind there may not be.
Of the leaves on yonder fruit-tree, Váhuka, and of the fruits,
Would'st thou know how many are fallen? one above a hundred, there.
One leaf here above a hundred, and one fruit, O Váhuka!
And of leaves are five ten millions hanging on those branches two.
Those two branches if thou gather, and the twigs that on them grow,
On those two are fruits two thousand and a hundred, less by five.'
Then, when he had check'd the chariot, answered Váhuka the king,
'What thou speakest, to mine eyesight all invisible appears;
Visible I'll make it, cleaving yonder tall Vibhítak-tree;
Then, when I have strictly numbered, I mistrust mine eyes no more.
In thy presence, mighty monarch, I will sever yonder branch;
Whether it may be, or may not, this not done, I cannot know;
I will number, thou beholding, all its fruits, O king of men,
But an instant let Várshṇeya hold the bridles of the steeds.'
To the charioteer the Rája answered, 'Time is none to stay.'
Váhuka replied, all eager his own purpose to fulfil,
'Either stay thou here an instant, or go onward in thy speed,
With the charioteer Várshṇeya go, for straight the road before.'
Answered him king Ṛituparṇa with a bland and soothing voice:
'Charioteer! on earth thine equal, Váhuka, there may not be;
By thy guidance, skilled in horses! to Vidarbha I would go:
I in thee have placed reliance, interrupt not then our course:
Willingly will I obey thee, Váhuka, in what thou ask'st,
If this day we reach Vidarbha ere the sun hath sunk in night.'

अथाब्रवीद् वाहुकस् तं सङ्ख्याय च विभीतकं।
ततो विदर्भान् यास्यामि कुरुष्वैवं वचो मम ॥२१॥
अकाम इव तं राजा गणयस्वेत्युवाच ह।
एकदेशञ्च शाखायाः समादिष्टं मयाऽनघ ॥२२॥
गणयस्वास्य तत्त्वज्ञ ततस् त्वं प्रीतिम् आवह।
सोऽवतीर्य रथात् तूर्णं शातयामास तं द्रुमं ॥२३॥
ततः स विस्मयाविष्टो राजानम् इदम् अब्रवीत्।
गणयित्वा यथोक्तानि तावन्त्येव फलानि च ॥२४॥
अत्यद्भुतम् इदं राजन् दृष्टवान् अस्मि ते बलं।
श्रोतुम् इच्छामि तां विद्यां ययैतज् ज्ञायते नृप ॥२५॥
तम् उवाच ततो राजा त्वरितो गमने नृपः।
विद्ध्यक्षहृदयज्ञं मां सङ्ख्याने च विशारदं ॥२६॥
वाहुकस् तम् उवाचाथ देहि विद्याम् इमां मम।
मत्तोऽपि चाश्वहृदयं गृहाण पुरुषर्षभ ॥२७॥
ऋतुपर्णस् ततो राजा वाहुकं कार्यगौरवात्।
हयज्ञानस्य लोभाच्च तथेत्येवाब्रवीद् वचः ॥२८॥
यथोक्तं त्वं गृहाणेदम् अक्षाणां हृदयं परं।
निक्षेपो मेऽश्वहृदयं त्वयि तिष्ठति वाहुक ॥२९॥
एवम् उक्त्वा ददौ विद्याम् ऋतुपर्णो नलाय वै।
तस्याक्षहृदयज्ञस्य शरीराद् निःसृतः कलिः।
कर्कोटकविषं तीक्ष्णं मुखात् सततम् उद्वमन् ॥३०॥
कलेस् तस्य तदार्तस्य शापाग्निः स विनिःसृतः।
स तेन कर्षितो राजा दीर्घकालम् अनात्मवान् ॥३१॥
ततो विषविमुक्तात्मा स्वं रूपम् अकरोत् कलिः।
तं शप्तुम् ऐच्छत् कुपितो निषधाधिपतिर् नलः ॥३२॥
तम् उवाच कलिर् भीतो वेपमानः कृताञ्जलिः।

Váhuka replied, 'No sooner have I numbered yonder fruits,
To Vidarbha will I hasten, grant me then my prayer, O king.'
Then the Rája, all reluctant, 'Stay then, and begin to count;
Of one branch one part, O blameless, that one designated part,
Man of truth, begin to number, and make glad thine inmost soul.'
From the chariot quick alighting Nala tore the branch away.
Then, his soul possess'd with wonder, to the Rája thus he said;
'Having counted, as thou saidest, even so many fruits there are,
Marvellous thy power, O monarch, by mine eyes beheld and proved,
Of that wonder-working science fain the secret would I hear.'
Then the Rája spake in answer, eager to pursue his way,
'I of dice possess the science, and in numbers thus am skilled.'
Váhuka replied, 'That science if to me thou wilt impart,
In return, O king, receive thou my surpassing skill in steeds.'
Then the Rája Ṛituparṇa, by his pressing need induced,
Eager for that skill in horses, 'Be it so,' thus 'gan to say;
'Well, O Váhuka, thou speakest, thou my skill in dice receive,
And of steeds thy wondrous knowledge be to me a meet return.'
Ṛituparṇa all his science, saying this, to Nala gave.
Soon as he in dice grew skilful, Kali from his body passed,
All Karkoṭaka's foul poison vomiting from out his mouth.
Straight from forth his tortured body issued Kali's fiery curse.
Nala, wasted by that conflict, came not instant to himself.
But, released from that dread venom, Kali his own form resumed:
And Nishadha's monarch, Nala, fain would curse him in his ire.
Him addressed th' affrighted Kali, trembling, and with folded hands:

कोपं संयच्छ नृपते कीर्तिं दास्यामि ते परां ॥३३॥
इन्द्रसेनस्य जननी कुपिता माऽशपत् पुरा ।
यदा त्वया परित्यक्ता ततोऽहं भृशपीडितः ॥३४॥
अवसं त्वयि राजेन्द्र सुदुःखम् अपराजित ।
विषेण नागराजस्य दह्यमानो दिवानिशं ॥३५॥
शरणं त्वां प्रपन्नोऽस्मि शृणु चेदं वचो मम ।
ये च त्वां मनुजा लोके कीर्तयिष्यन्त्यतन्द्रिताः ॥३६॥
मत्प्रसूतं भयं तेषां न कदाचिद् भविष्यति ।
भयार्तं शरणं यातं यदि मां त्वं न शप्स्यसे ॥३७॥
एवम् उक्तो नलो राजा न्ययच्छत् कोपम् आत्मनः ।
ततो भीतः कलिः क्षिप्रं प्रविवेश विभीतकं ॥३८॥
कलिस् त्वन्येन नादृश्यत् कथयन् नैषधेन वै ।
ततो गतज्वरो राजा नैषधः परवीरहा ॥३९॥
सम्प्रणष्टे कलौ राजन् सङ्ख्याय च फलान्युत ।
मुदा परमया युक्तस् तेजसाऽथ परेण च ॥४०॥
रथम् आरुह्य तेजस्वी प्रययौ जवनैर् हयैः ।
विभीतकश्चाप्रशस्तः संवृत्तः कलिसंश्रयात् ॥४१॥
हयोत्तमान् उत्पततो द्विजान् इव पुनः पुनः ।
नलः सञ्चोदयामास प्रहृष्टेनान्तरात्मना ॥४२॥
विदर्भाभिमुखो राजा प्रययौ स महायशाः ।
नले तु समतिक्रान्ते कलिर् अप्यगमद् गृहं ॥४३॥
ततो गतज्वरो राजा नलोऽभूत् पृथिवीपतिः ।
विमुक्तः कलिना राजन् रूपमात्रवियोजितः ॥४४॥

॥ इति नलोपाख्याने विंशतितमः सर्गः ॥२०॥

'Lord of men, restrain thine anger, I will give thee matchless fame;
Indrasena's wrathful mother laid on me her fatal curse,
When by thee she was deserted, since that time, O king of men,
I have dwelt in thee in anguish, in the ecstacy of pain.
By the King of Serpents' poison I have burned by day, by night:
To thy mercy now for refuge flee I, hear my speech, O king:
Wheresoe'er men, unforgetful, through the world shall laud thy name,
Shall the awful dread of Kali never in their soul abide.
If thou wilt not curse me, trembling, and to thee for refuge fled.'
Thus addressed, the royal Nala all his rising wrath suppressed,
And the fearful Kali entered in the cloven Vibhítak-tree:
To no eyes but those of Nala visible, had Kali spoken.
Then the monarch of Nishadha, from his inward fever freed,
When away had vanished Kali, when the fruits he had numbered all,
Triumphing in joy unwonted, blazing in his splendour forth,
Proudly mounting on the chariot, onward urged the rapid steeds.
But that tree by Kali entered since that time stands aye accursed.
Those fleet horses, forward flying, like to birds, again, again,
All his soul elate with transport, Nala swifter, swifter drove;
With his face towards Vidarbha rode the Rája in his pride:
And when forward Nala journeyed, Kali to his home returned.
So released from all his sufferings Nala went, the king of men,
Dispossessed by Kali, wanting only now his proper form.

End of Book XX.

बृहदश्व उवाच ।

ततो विदर्भान् सम्प्राप्तं सायाह्ने सत्यविक्रमं ।
ऋतुपर्णं जना राज्ञे भीमाय प्रत्यवेदयन् ॥ १ ॥
स भीमवचनाद् राजा कुण्डिनं प्राविशत् पुरं ।
नादयन् रथघोषेण सर्वाः सविदिशो दिशः ॥ २ ॥
ततस् तं रथनिर्घोषं नलाश्वास् तत्र शुश्रुवुः ।
श्रुत्वा तु समाहृष्यन्त पुरेव नलसन्निधौ ॥ ३ ॥
दमयन्ती तु शुश्राव रथघोषं नलस्य तं ।
यथा मेघस्य नदतो गम्भीरं जलदागमे ॥ ४ ॥
परं विस्मयम् आपन्ना श्रुत्वा नादम् महास्वनं ।
नलेन सङ्गृहीतेषु पुरेव नलवाजिषु ॥ ५ ॥
सदृशं हयनिर्घोषं मेने भैमी तथा हयाः ।
प्रासादस्थाश्च शिखिनः शालास्थाश्चैव वारणाः ।
हयाश्च शुश्रुवुस् तस्य रथघोषं महीपतेः ॥ ६ ॥
ते श्रुत्वा रथनिर्घोषं वारणाः शिखिनस् तथा ।
प्रणेदुर् उन्मुखा राजन् मेघनाद इवोत्सुकाः ॥ ७ ॥

दमयन्त्युवाच ।

यथाऽसौ रथनिर्घोषः पूरयन्न् इव मेदिनीं ।
ममाह्लादयते चेतो नल एष महीपतिः ॥ ८ ॥
अद्य चन्द्राभवक्त्रं तं न पश्यामि नलं यदि ।
असङ्ख्येयगुणं वीरं विनंक्ष्यामि न संशयः ॥ ९ ॥
यदि चैतस्य वीरस्य बाह्वोर् नाद्याहम् अन्तरं ।
प्रविशामि सुखस्पर्शं न भविष्याम्यसंशयं ॥ १० ॥

Vṛihadaśva spake:

With the evening in Vidarbha, men at watch, as they drew near,
Mighty Ṛituparṇa's coming, to king Bhíma did proclaim.
Then that king, by Bhíma's mandate, entered in Kuṇḍina's walls,
All the region round him echoing with the thunders of his car.
But the echoing of that chariot when king Nala's horses heard,
In their joy they neighed and trampled, even as Nala's self were there.
Damayantí, too, the rushing of king Nala's chariot heard,
As a cloud that hoarsely thunders at the coming of the rains.
All her heart was thrilled with wonder at that old familiar sound.
On they seemed to come, as Nala drove of yore his trampling steeds:
Like it seemed to Bhíma's daughter, and e'en so to Nala's steeds.
On the palace-roofs the peacocks, th' elephants within their stalls,
And the horses heard the rolling of the mighty monarch's car.
Elephants and peacocks hearing the fleet chariot rattling on,
Up they raised their necks and clamoured, as at sound of coming rain.

Damayantí spake:

'How the rolling of yon chariot, filling, as it seems, the earth,
Thrills my soul with unknown transport! it is Nala, king of men.
If this day I see not Nala with his glowing moonlike face,
Him, the king with countless virtues, I shall perish without doubt.
If this day within th' embraces of that hero's clasping arms,
I his gentle pressure feel not, without doubt I shall not live.

T

यदि मां मेघनिर्घोषो नोपगच्छति नैषधः ।
अद्य चामीकरप्रख्यं प्रवेक्ष्यामि हुताशनं ॥११॥
यदि मां सिंहविक्रान्तो मत्तवारणविक्रमः ।
नाभिगच्छति राजेन्द्रो विनंक्ष्यामि न संशयः ॥१२॥
न स्मराम्यनृतं किञ्चिन् न स्मराम्यपकारतां ।
न च पर्युषितं वाक्यं स्वैरेष्वपि कदाचन ॥१३॥
प्रभुः क्षमावान् वीरश्च दाता चाभ्यधिको नृपैः ।
रहोऽनीचानुवर्ती च क्लीववद् मम नैषधः ॥१४॥
गुणांस् तस्य स्मरन्त्या मे तत्पराया दिवानिशं ।
हृदयं दीर्यत इदं शोकात् प्रियविनाकृतं ॥१५॥
एवं विलपमाना सा नष्टसञ्ज्ञेव भारत ।
आरुरोह महद् वेश्म पुण्यश्लोकदिदृक्षया ॥१६॥
ततो मध्यमकक्षायां ददर्श रथम् आस्थितं ।
ऋतुपर्णं महीपालं सहवार्ष्णेयवाहुकं ॥१७॥
ततोऽवतीर्य वार्ष्णेयो वाहुकश्च रथोत्तमात् ।
हयांस् तान् अवमुच्याथ स्थापयामास वै रथं ॥१८॥
सोऽवतीर्य रथोपस्थाद् ऋतुपर्णो नराधिपः ।
उपतस्थे महाराजं भीमं भीमपराक्रमं ॥१९॥
तं भीमः प्रतिजग्राह पूजया परया ततः ।
अकस्मात् सहसा प्राप्तं स्त्रीमन्त्वं न स्म विन्दति ॥२०॥
किं कार्यं स्वागतं तेऽस्तु राज्ञा पृष्टः स भारत ।
नाभिजज्ञे स नृपतिर् दुहित्रर्थे समागतं ॥२१॥
ऋतुपर्णोऽपि राजा स धीमान् सत्यपराक्रमः ।
राजानं राजपुत्रं वा न स्म पश्यति कञ्चन ॥२२॥
नैव स्वयंवरकथां न च विप्रसमागमं ।
ततो विगणयन् राजा मनसा कोशलाधिपः ॥२३॥

If Nishadha's monarch comes not, with the sound of thunder-cloud,
I this day the fire will enter, burning like the hue of gold.
In his might like the strong lion, like the raging elephant,
Comes he not, the prince of princes, I shall perish without doubt.
Not a falsehood I remember, I remember no offence;
Not an idle word remember, in his noble converse free.
Lofty, patient, like a hero, liberal beyond all kings,
Nought ignoble, as the base-born, even in private, may he do.
As I think upon his virtues, as I think by day, by night,
All this heart is rent with anguish, widowed of its own beloved.'

Thus lamenting, she ascended, as with frenzied mind possessed,
To the lofty mansion's summit to behold the king of men.
In the middle court high seated in the car, the lord of earth,
Ṛituparṇa with Várshṇeya and with Váhuka she saw,
When Várshṇeya from that chariot, and when Váhuka came down,
He let loose those noble coursers, and he stopped the glowing car.
From that chariot-seat descended Ṛituparṇa, king of men,
To the noble monarch Bhíma he drew near, for strength renowned.
Him received with highest honour Bhíma, for without due cause
Deemed not he the Rája's visit, nor divined his daughter's plot;
'Wherefore com'st thou? hail and welcome!' thus that gracious king enquires;
For his daughter's sake he knew not that the lord of men had come.
But the Rája Ṛituparṇa, great in wisdom as in might,
When nor king within the palace, nor king's son he could behold,
Nor of Svayaṃvara heard he, nor assembled Bráhmans saw,
Thus within his mind deep pondering spoke of Kośala the lord;

आगतोऽस्मीत्युवाचैनं भवन्तम् अभिवादकः ।
राजापि च स्मयन् भीमो मनसा समचिन्तयत् ॥२४॥
अधिकं योजनशतं तस्यागमनकारणं ।
ग्रामान् बहून् अतिक्रम्य नाध्यगच्छद् यथातथं ॥२५॥
अल्पकार्यं विनिर्दिष्टं तस्यागमनकारणं ।
पश्चाद् उदर्के ज्ञास्यामि कारणं यद् भविष्यति ॥२६॥
नैतद् एवं स नृपतिस् तं सत्कृत्य व्यसर्जयत् ।
विश्राम्यताम् इत्युवाच क्लान्तोऽसीति पुनः पुनः ॥२७॥
स सत्कृतः प्रहृष्टात्मा प्रीतः प्रीतेन पार्थिवः ।
राजप्रेष्यैर् अनुगतो दिष्टं वेश्म समाविशत् ॥२८॥
ऋतुपर्णे गते राजन् वार्ष्णेयसहिते नृपे ।
वाहुको रथम् आदाय रथशालाम् उपागमत् ॥२९॥
स मोचयित्वा तान् अश्वान् उपचर्य च शास्त्रतः ।
स्वयं चैतान् समाश्वास्य रथोपस्थ उपाविशत् ॥३०॥
दमयन्ती तु शोकार्ता दृष्ट्वा भाङ्गासुरिं नृपं ।
सूतपुत्रञ्च वार्ष्णेयं वाहुकञ्च तथाविधं ॥३१॥
चिन्तयामास वैदर्भी कस्यैष रथनिस्वनः ।
नलस्येव महान् आसीन् न च पश्यामि नैषधं ॥३२॥
वार्ष्णेयेन भवेन् नूनं विद्या सैवोपशिक्षिता ।
तेनाद्य रथनिर्घोषो नलस्येव महान् अभूत् ॥३३॥
आहोस्विद् ऋतुपर्णोऽपि यथा राजा नलस् तथा ।
तथाऽयं रथनिर्घोषो नैषधस्येव लक्ष्यते ॥३४॥
एवं सा तर्कयित्वा तु दमयन्ती विशाम्पते ।
दूतीं प्रस्थापयामास नैषधान्वेषणे शुभा ॥३५॥

॥ इति नलोपाख्याने एकविंशतितमः सर्गः ॥२१॥

'Hither, O majestic Bhíma, to salute thee am I come.'
But king Bhíma smiled in secret, as he thought within his mind
On the object of this journey of a hundred Yojanas.
'Passing through so many cities for this cause he set not forth;
For this cause of little moment to our court he hath not come,
'Tis not so;—perchance hereafter I may know his journey's aim.'
After royal entertainment then the king his guest dismissed:
'Take then thy repose,' thus said he, 'weary of thy journey, rest.'
He refreshed, with courteous homage of that courteous king took leave,
Ushered by the royal servants to th' appointed chamber went:
There retired king Ṛituparṇa, with Várshṇeya in his suite.
Váhuka, meantime, the chariot to the chariot-house had led,
There the coursers he unharnessed, skilfully he dressed them there,
And with gentle words caressed them, on the chariot-seat sat down.

But the woful Damayantí, when Bhángásuri she'd seen,
And the charioteer Várshṇeya, and the seeming Váhuka,
Thought within Vidarbha's princess, 'Whose was that fleet chariot's sound?
Such it seems as noble Nala's, yet no Nala do I see.
Hath the charioteer Várshṇeya Nala's noble science learned?
Therefore did the thundering chariot sound as driven by Nala's self?
Or may royal Ṛituparṇa like the skilful Nala drive?
Therefore did the rolling chariot seem as of Nishadha's king?'
Thus when Damayantí pondered in the silence of her soul,
She, the beauteous, sent her handmaid to that king her messenger.

End of Book XXI.

दमयन्त्युवाच ।

गच्छ केशिनि जानीहि क एष रथवाहकः ।
उपविष्टो रथोपस्थे विकृतो ह्रस्वबाहुकः ॥१॥
अभ्येत्य कुशलं भद्रे मृदुपूर्वं समाहिता ।
पृच्छेथाः पुरुषं ह्येनं यथातत्त्वम् अनिन्दिते ॥२॥
अत्र मे महती शङ्का भवेद् एष नलो नृपः ।
यथा च मनसस् तुष्टिर् हृदयस्य च निर्वृतिः ॥३॥
ब्रूयाश्चैनं कथान्ते त्वं पर्णादवचनं यथा ।
प्रतिवाक्यञ्च सुश्रोणि बुध्येथास् त्वम् अनिन्दिते ॥४॥

बृहदश्व उवाच ।

ततः समाहिता गत्वा दूती बाहुकम् अब्रवीत् ।
दमयन्त्यपि कल्याणी प्रासादस्था ह्युपैक्षत ॥५॥

केशिन्युवाच ।

स्वागतं ते मनुष्येन्द्र कुशलं ते ब्रवीम्यहं ।
दमयन्त्या वचः साधु निबोध पुरुषर्षभ ॥६॥
कदा वै प्रस्थिता यूयं किमर्थम् इह चागताः ।
तत् त्वम् ब्रूहि यथान्यायं वैदर्भी श्रोतुम् इच्छति ॥७॥

बाहुक उवाच ।

श्रुतः स्वयंवरो राज्ञा कौशलेन महात्मना ।
द्वितीयो दमयन्त्या वै भविता श्व इति द्विजात् ॥८॥

Damayantí spake:

'Speed thee, Keśiní, enquire thou who is yonder charioteer,
On the chariot-seat reposing, all deformed, with arms so short?
Blessed maid, approach, and courteous open thou thy bland discourse:
Undespis'd! ask thou thy question, and the truth let him reply.
Much and sorely do I doubt me, whether Nala it may be,
As my bosom's rapture augurs, as the gladness of my heart.
Speak thou, ere thou close the converse, even as good Parṇáda spake,
And his answer, slender-waisted, undespis'd! remember thou.'

Vṛihadaśva spake:

Then to Váhuka departing went that zealous messenger,
On the lofty palace-terrace Damayantí sat and gazed.

Keśiní spake:

'Happy omen mark thy coming, I salute thee, king of men:
Of the princess Damayantí hear, O lord of men, the speech:
"From what region came ye hither? with what purpose are ye come?"
Answer thou, as may beseem you, so Vidarbha's princess wills.'

Váhuka spake:

'Soon a second Svayamvara, heard the king of Kośala,
Damayantí holds: to-morrow will it be, the Bráhman said:

श्रुत्वैतत् प्रस्थितो राजा शतयोजनयायिभिः ।
हयैर् वातजवैर् मुख्यैर् अहम् अस्य च सारथिः ॥९॥

केशिन्युवाच ।

अथ योऽसौ तृतीयो वः स कुतः कस्य वा पुनः ।
त्वञ्च कस्य कथञ्चेदं त्वयि कर्म समाहितं ॥१०॥

वाहुक उवाच ।

पुण्यश्लोकस्य वै सूतो वार्ष्णेय इति विश्रुतः ।
स नले प्रद्रुते भद्रे भाङ्गासुरिम् उपस्थितः ॥११॥
अहम् अप्यश्वकुशलः सूतत्वे च प्रतिष्ठितः ।
ऋतुपर्णेन सारथ्ये भोजने च वृतः स्वयं ॥१२॥

केशिन्युवाच ।

अथ जानाति वार्ष्णेयः क्व नु राजा नलो गतः ।
कथञ्च त्वयि चैतेन कथितं स्यात् तु वाहुक ॥१३॥

वाहुक उवाच ।

इहैव पुत्रौ निक्षिप्य नलस्याशुभकर्मणः ।
गतस् ततो यथाकामं नैष जानाति नैषधं ॥१४॥
न चान्यः पुरुषः कश्चिन् नलं वेत्ति यशस्विनि ।
गूढश् चरति लोकेऽस्मिन् नष्टरूपो महीपतिः ॥१५॥
आत्मैव तु नलं वेत्ति या चास्य तदनन्तरा ।
न हि वै स्वानि लिङ्गानि नलः शंसति कर्हिचित् ॥१६॥

केशिन्युवाच ।

योऽसाव् अयोध्यां प्रथमं गतवान् ब्राह्मणस् तदा ।
इमानि नारीवाक्यानि कथयानः पुनः पुनः ॥१७॥

Hearing this, with fleetest coursers, that a hundred Yojans speed,
Set he forth, the wind less rapid, and his charioteer am I.'

Keśiní spake:

'Who the third that journeys with you? who is he, and what his race?
Of what race art thou? this office wherefore dost thou undertake?'

Váhuka spake:

''Tis the far-renowned Várshṇeya, Puṇyaśloka's charioteer:
He, when Nala fled, fair lady! to Bhángásuri retired.
Skilful I in taming horses, and a famous charioteer.
Ṛituparṇa's chosen driver, dresser of his food am I.'

Keśiní spake:

'Knows the charioteer Várshṇeya whither royal Nala went?
Of his fortune hath he told thee? Váhuka, what hath he said?'

Váhuka spake:

'He of the unhappy Nala safe the children borne away,
Wheresoe'er he would departed, of king Nala knows he nought:
Nothing of Nishadha's Rája, fair one! living man doth know.
Through the world, concealed, he wanders, having lost his proper form.
Only Nala's self of Nala knows, and his own inward soul,
Of himself to living mortal Nala will no sign betray.'

Keśiní spake:

'He that to Ayodhyá's city went, the holy Bráhman first,
Of his faithful wife these sayings uttered once and once again:

क्व नु त्वं कितव छित्त्वा वस्त्रार्धं प्रस्थितो मम।
उत्सृज्य विपिने सुप्ताम् अनुरक्तां प्रियां प्रिय ॥१८॥
सा वै यथा समादिष्टा तथास्ते त्वत्प्रतीक्षिणी।
दह्यमाना दिवारात्रं वस्त्रार्धेनाभिसंवृता ॥१९॥
तस्या रुदन्त्याः सततं तेन दुःखेन पार्थिव।
प्रसादं कुरु वै वीर प्रतिवाक्यं वदस्व च ॥२०॥
तस्यास् तत् प्रियम् आख्यानं प्रवदस्व महामते।
तद् एव वाक्यं वैदर्भी श्रोतुम् इच्छत्यनिन्दिता ॥२१॥
एतच् छ्रुत्वा प्रतिवचस् तस्य दत्तं त्वया किल।
यत् पुरा तत् पुनस् त्वत्तो वैदर्भी श्रोतुम् इच्छति ॥२२॥

वृहदश्व उवाच।

एवम् उक्तस्य केशिन्या नलस्य कुरुनन्दन।
हृदयं व्यथितञ्चासीद् अश्रुपूर्णे च लोचने ॥२३॥
स निगृह्यात्मनो दुःखं दह्यमानो महीपतिः।
वाष्पसन्दिग्धया वाचा पुनर् एवेदम् अब्रवीत् ॥२४॥

वाहुक उवाच।

वैषम्यमपि सम्प्राप्ता गोपायन्ति कुलस्त्रियः।
आत्मानम् आत्मना सत्यो जितस्वर्गा न संशयः ॥२५॥
रहिता भर्तृभिश्चापि न क्रुध्यन्ति कदाचन।
प्राणांश् चारित्रकवचान् धारयन्ति वरस्त्रियः ॥२६॥
विषमस्थेन मूढेन परिभ्रष्टसुखेन च।
यत् सा तेन परित्यक्ता तत्र न क्रोद्धुम् अर्हति ॥२७॥
प्राणयात्रां परिप्रेप्सोः शकुनैर् हृतवाससः।
आधिभिर् दह्यमानस्य श्यामा न क्रोद्धुम् अर्हति ॥२८॥

"Whither went'st thou then, O gamester, half my garment severing off;
Leaving in the forest sleeping, all forsaken, thy belov'd?
Even as thou commanded'st, sits she, sadly waiting thy return,
Day and night, consumed with sorrow, in her scant half-garment clad.
Oh! to her for ever weeping, in the extreme of her distress,
Grant thy pity, noble hero, answer to her earnest prayer."
Speak again the words thou uttered'st, words of comfort to her soul,
The renowned Vidarbha's princess fain that speech would hear again,
When the Bráhman thus had spoken, what thou answered'st back to him,
That again Vidarbha's princess in the self-same words would hear.'

Vṛihadaśva spake:

Of king Nala, in such language by fair Keśiní addressed,
All the heart was wrung with sorrow, and the eyes o'erflowed with tears.
But his anguish still suppressing, inly though consumed, the king,
With a voice half-choked with weeping, thus repeated his reply.

Váhuka spake:

'Even in the extreme of misery, noble women still preserve
Over their ownselves the mastery, by their virtues winning heaven;
By their faithless lords abandoned, anger feel they not, e'en then;
In the breastplate of their virtue, noble women live unharmed.
By the wretched, by the senseless, by the lost to every joy,
She by such a lord forsaken to resentment will not yield.
Against him, his sustenance seeking, of his robe by birds despoiled,
Him consumed with utmost misery, still no wrath the fair one feels;

सत्कृताऽसत्कृता वाऽपि पतिं दृष्ट्वा तथागतं।
भ्रष्टराज्यं श्रिया हीनं क्षुधितं व्यसनाप्लुतं ॥२९॥
एवं ब्रुवाणस् तद् वाक्यं नलः परमदुःखितः।
न वाष्पम् अशकत् सोढुं प्ररुरोदाथ भारत ॥३०॥
ततः सा केशिनी गत्वा दमयन्त्यै न्यवेदयत्।
तत् सर्वं कथितञ्चैव विकारञ्चैव तस्य तं ॥३१॥

॥ इति नलोपाख्याने द्वाविंशतितमः सर्गः ॥२२॥

वृहदश्व उवाच।

दमयन्ती तु तच् छ्रुत्वा भृशं शोकपरायणा।
शङ्कमाना नलं तं वै केशिनीम् इदम् अब्रवीत् ॥१॥
गच्छ केशिनि भूयस् त्वं परीक्षां कुरु वाहुके।
अब्रुवाणा समीपस्था चरितान्यस्य लक्षय ॥२॥
यदा च किञ्चित् कुर्यात् स कारणं तत्र भाविनि।
तत्र सञ्चेष्टमानस्य लक्षयन्ती विचेष्टितं ॥३॥
न चास्य प्रतिबन्धेन देयोऽग्निर् अपि केशिनि।
याचते न जलं देयं सर्वथा त्वरमाणया ॥४॥
एतत् सर्वं समीक्ष्य त्वं चरितं मे निवेदय।
निमित्तं यत् त्वया दृष्टं वाहुके दैवमानुषं।
यच्चान्यदपि पश्येथास् तच्चाख्येयं त्वया मम ॥५॥
दमयन्त्यैवम् उक्ता सा जगामाथ च केशिनी।
निशम्याथ हयज्ञस्य लिङ्गानि पुनर् आगमत् ॥६॥
सा तत् सर्वं यथावृत्तं दमयन्त्यै न्यवेदयत्।
निमित्तं यत् तया दृष्टं वाहुके दिव्यमानुषं ॥७॥

Treated well, or ill-entreated, when her husband thus she sees
Spoiled of bliss, bereft of kingdom, famine-wasted, worn with woe.'
In these words as spake king Nala in the anguish of his heart,
Could he not refrain from weeping, his unwilling tears burst forth.
Then fair Keśiní departing, told to Damayantí all,
All that Váhuka had spoken, all th' emotion he betrayed.

End of Book XXII.

Vṛihadaśva spake:

Hearing this, fair Damayantí, all abandoned to her grief,
Thinking still that he was Nala, spake to Keśiní again:
'Go, O Keśiní, examine Váhuka and all his acts,
Silent take thy stand beside him, and observe whate'er he does;
And when any act soever, virtuous maiden! he may do,
Closely watching all his movements, mark the bearing of the man.
Nor, fair Keśiní, be given him fire his labours to assist:
Neither be there given him water, in thy haste, at his demand:
All, when thou hast well observed him, every act to me repeat,
Every act, divine or mortal, that in Váhuka appears;
And whatever else thou seest, be it straightway told to me.'
Thus addressed by Damayantí Keśiní again set forth;
Of the tamer of the horses every act observed, came back;
Every act as she had seen it she to Damayantí told:
Each divine or mortal wonder that in Váhuka appeared.

केशिन्युवाच ।

दृढं शुच्युपचारोऽसौ न मया मानुषः क्वचित् ।
दृष्टपूर्वः श्रुतो वापि दमयन्ति तथाविधः ॥ ८ ॥
ह्रस्वम् आसाद्य सञ्चारं नासौ विनमते क्वचित् ।
तं तु दृष्ट्वा यथासङ्गम् उत्सर्पति यथासुखं ॥ ९ ॥
ऋतुपर्णस्य चार्थाय भोजनीयम् अनेकशः ।
प्रेषितं तत्र राज्ञा तु मांसं बहु च पाशवं ॥ १० ॥
तस्य प्रक्षालनार्थाय कुम्भास् तत्रोपकल्पिताः ।
ते तेनावेक्षिताः कुम्भाः पूर्णा एवाभवंस् ततः ॥ ११ ॥
ततः प्रक्षालनं कृत्वा समधिश्रित्य वाहुकः ।
तृणमुष्टिं समादाय सवितुस् तं समादधत् ॥ १२ ॥
अथ प्रज्वलितस् तत्र सहसा हव्यवाहनः ।
तद् अद्भुततमं दृष्ट्वा विस्मिताऽहम् इहागता ॥ १३ ॥
अन्यच्च तस्मिन् सुमहद् आश्चर्यं लक्षितं मया ।
यद् अग्निम् अपि संस्पृश्य नैवासौ दह्यते शुभे ॥ १४ ॥
छन्देन चोदकं तस्य वहत्यावर्जितं द्रुतं ।
अतीव चान्यत् सुमहद् आश्चर्यं दृष्टवत्यहं ॥ १५ ॥
यत् स पुष्पाण्युपादाय हस्ताभ्यां ममृदे शनैः ।
मृद्यमानानि पाणिभ्यां तेन पुष्पाणि तान्यथ ॥ १६ ॥
भूय एव सुगन्धीनि हृषितानि भवन्ति हि ।
एतान्यद्भुतलिङ्गानि दृष्ट्वाऽहं द्रुतम् आगता ॥ १७ ॥

वृहदश्व उवाच ।

दमयन्ती तु तच् छ्रुत्वा पुण्यश्लोकस्य चेष्टितं ।
अमन्यत नलं प्राप्तं कर्मचेष्टाभिसूचितं ॥ १८ ॥
सा शङ्कमाना भर्तारं नलं वाहुकरूपिणं ।

Keśiní spake:

'Very holy is he, never mortal man in all my life
Have I seen, or have I heard of, Damayantí, like to him.
He drew near the lowly entrance, bowed not down his stately head;
On the instant, as it saw him, up th' expanding portal rose.
For the use of Ṛituparṇa much and various viands came;
Sent, as meet, by royal Bhíma, and abundant animal food.
These to cleanse, with meet ablution, were capacious vessels set;
As he looked on them, the vessels stood, upon the instant, full.
Then, the meet ablutions over, Váhuka went forth and took
Of the withered grass a handful, held it upward to the sun:
On the instant, brightly blazing, shone the all-consuming fire.
Much I marvelled at the wonder, and amazed am hither come;
Lo, a second greater marvel sudden burst upon my sight!
He that blazing fire stood handling, yet unharmed, unburned remained.
At his will flows forth the water, and as quickly sinks again.
And another greater wonder, lady, did I there behold:
He the flowers which he had taken gently moulded in his hands,
In his hands the flowers, so moulded, as with freshening life endued,
Blossomed out with richer fragrance, stood erect upon their stems:
All these marvels having noted, swiftly came I back to thee.'

Vṛihadaśva spake:

Damayantí when these wonders of the king of men she heard,
Thought yet more king Nala present, by his acts and mien revealed.
She her royal lord suspecting in the form of Váhuka,

केशिनीं श्लक्ष्णया वाचा रुदती पुनर् अब्रवीत् ॥१९॥
पुनर् गच्छ प्रमत्तस्य वाहुकस्योपसंस्कृतं ।
महानसाच् छ्रुतं मांसं समादायैहि भाविनि ॥२०॥
सा गत्वा वाहुकस्याग्रे तन् मांसम् अपकृष्य च ।
अत्युष्णम् एव त्वरिता तत्क्षणात् प्रियकारिणी ।
दमयन्त्यै ततः प्रादात् केशिनी कुरुनन्दन ॥२१॥
सोचिता नलसिद्धस्य मांसस्य बहुशः पुरा ।
प्राश्य मत्वा नलं सूतं प्राक्रोशद् भृशदुःखिता ॥२२॥
वैक्लव्यं परमं गत्वा प्रक्षाल्य च मुखं ततः ।
मिथुनं प्रेषयामास केशिन्या सह भारत ॥२३॥
इन्द्रसेनां सह भ्रात्रा समभिज्ञाय वाहुकः ।
अभिद्रुत्य ततो राजा परिष्वज्याङ्कम् आनयत् ॥२४॥
वाहुकस् तु समासाद्य सुतौ सुरसुतोपमौ ।
भृशं दुःखपरीतात्मा सुस्वरं प्ररुरोद ह ॥२५॥
नैषधो दर्शयित्वा तु विकारम् असकृत् तदा ।
उत्सृज्य सहसा पुत्रौ केशिनीम् इदम् अब्रवीत् ॥२६॥
इदं सुसदृशं भद्रे मिथुनं मम पुत्रयोः ।
अतो दृष्ट्वैव सहसा वाष्पम् उत्सृष्टवान् अहं ॥२७॥
बहुशः सम्पतन्तीं त्वां जनः शङ्केत दोषतः ।
वयञ्च देशातिथयो गच्छ भद्रे यथासुखं ॥२८॥

॥ इति नलोपाख्याने त्रयोविंशतितमः सर्गः ॥२३॥

With a gentle voice and weeping spake to Keśiní again:
'Go, again, and whilst he heeds not, meat by Váhuka prepared
From the kitchen softly taking hither Keśiní return.'
She to Váhuka approaching, unperceived stole soft away
Of the well-cooked meat a morsel, warm she bore it in her haste,
And to Damayantí gave it, Keśiní, without delay.
Of the food prepared by Nala oft the flavour had she tried;
Tasting it she shrieked in anguish, 'Nala is yon charioteer.'
Stirred by vehement emotion, of her mouth ablution made:
She her pair of infant children sent with Keśiní to him.
Soon as he young Indrasená with her little brother saw,
Up he sprang, his arms wound round them, to his bosom folding both.
When he gazed upon the children, like the children of the gods,
All his heart o'erflowed with pity, and aloud his tears broke forth.
Yet Nishadha's lord perceiving she his strong emotion marked,
From his hold released the children, and to Keśiní spake thus:
'Oh! so like mine own twin children was yon lovely infant pair,
Seeing them thus unexpected have I broken out in tears.
If so oft thou comest hither men some evil will suspect,
We within this land are strangers, beauteous maiden, part in peace.'

End of Book XXIII.

वृहदश्व उवाच ।

सर्वं विकारं दृष्ट्वा तु पुण्यश्लोकस्य धीमतः ।
आगत्य केशिनी क्षिप्रं दमयन्त्यै न्यवेदयत् ॥१॥
दमयन्ती ततो भूयः प्रेषयामास केशिनीं ।
मातुः सकाशं दुःखार्ता नलदर्शनकाङ्क्षया ॥२॥
परीक्षितो मे बहुशो वाहुको नलशङ्कया ।
रूपे मे संशयस् त्वेकः स्वयम् इच्छामि वेदितुं ॥३॥
स वा प्रवेश्यतां मातर् मां वानुज्ञातुम् अर्हसि ।
विदितं वाऽथ वाऽज्ञातं पितुर् मे संविधीयतां ॥४॥
एवम् उक्ता तु वैदर्भ्या सा देवी भीमम् अब्रवीत् ।
दुहितुस् तम् अभिप्रायम् अन्वजानात् स पार्थिवः ॥५॥
सा वै पित्राभ्यनुज्ञाता मात्रा च भरतर्षभ ।
नलं प्रवेशयामास यत्र तस्याः प्रतिश्रयः ॥६॥
तां स्म दृष्ट्वैव सहसा दमयन्तीं नलो नृपः ।
आविष्टः शोकदुःखाभ्यां बभूवाश्रुपरिप्लुतः ॥७॥
तं तु दृष्ट्वा तथायुक्तं दमयन्ती नलं तदा ।
तीव्रशोकसमाविष्टा बभूव वरवर्णिनी ॥८॥
ततः काषायवसना जटिला मलपङ्किनी ।
दमयन्ती महाराज वाहुकं वाक्यम् अब्रवीत् ॥९॥
पूर्वं दृष्टस् त्वया कश्चिद् धर्मज्ञो नाम वाहुक ।
सुप्ताम् उत्सृज्य विपिने गतो यः पुरुषः स्त्रियं ॥१०॥
अनागसं प्रियां भार्यां विजने श्रममोहितां ।
अपहाय तु को गच्छेत् पुण्यश्लोकम् ऋते नलं ॥११॥

Vṛihadaśva spake:

Seeing the profound emotion of that wisest king of men,
Keśiní in haste returning told to Damayantí all.
Then again did Damayantí give to Keśiní command,
To approach her royal mother, in her haste her lord to see.
'Váhuka we've watched most closely, Nala we suspect him still;
Only from his form we doubt him, this myself would fain behold.
Cause him enter here, my mother, or permit me him to seek;
Known or unknown to my father let it be decided now.'
By that handmaid thus accosted, then the queen to Bhíma told
All his daughter's secret counsel, and the Rája gave assent.
Instant from her sire the princess from her mother leave obtained,
Bade them make king Nala enter in the chamber where she dwelt.
Sudden as he gazed upon her, upon Damayantí gazed,
Nala, he was seized with anguish, and with tears his eyes o'erflowed.
And when Damayantí gazed on Nala thus approaching near,
With an agonizing sorrow was the noble lady seized.
Clad, then, in a scarlet mantle, hair-dishevelled, mire-defiled,
Unto Váhuka this language Damayantí thus addressed:
'Váhuka beheld'st thou ever an upright and noble man
Who departed and abandoned in the wood his sleeping wife?
The beloved wife and blameless, in the wild wood worn with grief,
Who was he who thus forsook her? who but Nala, king of men?

किं नु तस्य मया बाल्याद् अपराद्धं महीपतेः ।
यो माम् उत्सृज्य विपिने गतवान् निद्रया हृतां ॥१२॥
साक्षाद् देवान् अपहाय वृतो यः स मया पुरा ।
अनुव्रतां साभिकामां पुत्रिणीं त्यक्तवान् कथं ॥१३॥
अग्नौ पाणिं गृहीत्वा तु देवानाम् अग्रतस् तथा ।
भविष्यामीति सत्यं तु प्रतिश्रुत्य क्व तद् गतं ॥१४॥
दमयन्त्या ब्रुवन्त्यास् तु सर्वम् एतद् अरिन्दम ।
शोकजं वारि नेत्राभ्याम् असुखं प्रास्रवद् बहु ॥१५॥
अतीव कृष्णसाराभ्यां रक्तान्ताभ्यां जलं तु तत् ।
परिस्रवद् नलो दृष्ट्वा शोकार्ताम् इदम् अब्रवीत् ॥१६॥
मम राज्यं प्रणष्टं यद् नाहं तत् कृतवान् स्वयं ।
कलिना तत् कृतं भीरु यच्च त्वाम् अहम् अत्यजं ॥१७॥
त्वया तु पापः कृच्छ्रेण शापेनाभिहतः पुरा ।
वनस्थया दुःखितया शोचन्त्या मां दिवानिशं ॥१८॥
स मच्छरीरे त्वच्छापाद् दह्यमानोऽवसत् कलिः ।
त्वच्छापदग्धः सततं सोऽग्नाव् अग्निर् इवाहितः ॥१९॥
मम च व्यवसायेन तपसा चैव निर्जितः ।
दुःखस्यान्तेन चानेन भवितव्यं हि नौ शुभे ॥२०॥
विमुच्य मां गतः पापस् ततोऽहम् इह चागतः ।
त्वदर्थं विपुलश्रोणि न हि मेऽन्यत् प्रयोजनं ॥२१॥
कथं तु नारी भर्तारम् अनुरक्तम् अनुव्रतं ।
उत्सृज्य वरयेद् अन्यं यथा त्वं भीरु कर्हिचित् ॥२२॥
दूताश् चरन्ति पृथिवीं कृत्स्नां नृपतिशासनात् ।
भैमी किल स्म भर्तारं द्वितीयं वरयिष्यति ॥२३॥
स्वैरवृत्ता यथाकामम् अनुरूपम् इवात्मनः ।
श्रुत्वैव चैतत् त्वरितो भाङ्गासुरिर् उपस्थितः ॥२४॥

To the lord of earth, from folly, what offence can I have given
That he fled, within the forest leaving me by sleep oppressed?
Openly, the gods rejected, was he chosen by me, my lord:
Could he leave the true, the loving, her that hath his children borne!
By the nuptial fire, in presence of the gods, he clasped my hand,
"I will be," this truth he plighted, where is now that promise gone?'

While all this in broken accents sadly Damayantí spake,
From her eyes the drops of sorrow flowed in copious torrents down.
Those dark eyes, with vermeil corners, thus with trembling moisture dewed,
When king Nala saw and gazed on, to the sorrowful he spake:
'Gaming that I lost my kingdom, 'twas not mine own guilty deed,
That was wrought by Kali, timid! hence it was I thee forsook.
Therefore smitten was the miscreant by thy scathing curse long since
In the wild wood as thou wanderedst, grieving day and night for me,
He then dwelt within my body, burning with that powerful curse,
Ever burning, fiercer, hotter, as when fire is heaped on fire.
He by my religious patience, my devotion, now subdued,
Lo! the end of all our sorrows, beautiful! is now at hand.
I, the evil one departed, hither have made haste to come;
For thy sake, O round-limbed! only; other business have I none.
Yet, O how may high-born woman from her vowed, her plighted lord
Swerving, choose another husband, even as thou, O trembler, would'st?
Over all the earth the heralds travel by the king's command,
"Now the daughter of king Bhíma will a second husband choose,
Free from every tie, as wills she, as her fancy may beseem,"
Hearing this, came hither speeding king Bhángásuri in haste.'

दमयन्ती तु तच् छ्रुत्वा नलस्य परिदेवितं ।
प्राञ्जलिर् वेपमाना च भीता च नलम् अब्रवीत् ॥ २५ ॥
न माम् अर्हसि कल्याण दोषेण परिशङ्कितुं ।
मया हि देवान् उत्सृज्य वृतस् त्वं निषधाधिप ॥ २६ ॥
तवाधिगमनार्थं तु सर्वतो ब्राह्मणा गताः ।
वाक्यानि मम गाथाभिर् गायमाना दिशो दश ॥ २७ ॥
ततस् त्वां ब्राह्मणो विद्वान् पर्णादो नाम पार्थिव ।
अभ्यगच्छत् कोशलायाम् ऋतुपर्णनिवेशने ॥ २८ ॥
तेन वाक्ये कृते सम्यक् प्रतिवाक्ये तथाहृते ।
उपायोऽयं मया दृष्टो नैषधानयने तव ॥ २९ ॥
त्वाम् ऋते न हि लोकेऽन्य एकाह्ना पृथिवीपते ।
समर्थो योजनशतं गन्तुम् अश्वैर् नराधिप ॥ ३० ॥
स्पृशेयं तेन सत्येन पादाव् एतौ महीपते ।
यथा नासत्कृतं किञ्चिद् मनसापि चराम्यहं ॥ ३१ ॥
अयं चरति लोकेऽस्मिन् भूतसाक्षी सदागतिः ।
एष मे मुञ्चतु प्राणान् यदि पापं चराम्यहं ॥ ३२ ॥
तथा चरति तिग्मांशुः परेण भुवनं सदा ।
स मुञ्चतु मम प्राणान् यदि पापं चराम्यहं ॥ ३३ ॥
चन्द्रमाः सर्वभूतानाम् अन्तश्चरति साक्षिवत् ।
स मुञ्चतु मम प्राणान् यदि पापं चराम्यहं ॥ ३४ ॥
एते देवास् त्रयः कृत्स्नं त्रैलोक्यं धारयन्ति वै ।
विब्रुवन्तु यथासत्यम् एते वाऽद्य त्यजन्तु मां ॥ ३५ ॥
एवम् उक्तस् तया वायुर् अन्तरीक्षाद् अभाषत ।
नैषा कृतवती पापं नल सत्यं ब्रवीमि ते ॥ ३६ ॥
राजन् शीलनिधिः स्फीतो दमयन्त्या सुरक्षितः ।
साक्षिणो रक्षिणश् चास्या वयं त्रीन् परिवत्सरान् ॥ ३७ ॥

Damayantí, when from Nala heard she this his grievous charge,
With her folded hands, and trembling, thus to Nala made reply:
'Do not me, O noble-minded, of such shameless guilt suspect,
Thou, when I the gods rejected, Nala, wert my chosen lord.
Only thee to find, the Bráhmans went to the ten regions forth,
Chaunting to their holy measures, but the words that I had taught.
Then that Bráhman wise, Parṇáda, such the name he bears, O king,
Thee in Kośalá, the palace of king Ṛituparṇa, found.
There to thee my words addressed he, answer there from thee received.
I this subtle wile imagined, king of men, to bring thee here.
Since, beside thyself, no mortal in the world, within the day,
Could drive on the fleetest coursers for a hundred Yojanas.
To attest this truth, O monarch! I would touch thy sacred feet;
Even in heart have I committed never evil thought 'gainst thee.
He through all the world that wanders, witness the all-seeing wind,
Let him now of life bereave me, if in this 'gainst thee I've sinned:
And the sun that moveth ever over all the world, on high,
Let him now of life bereave me, if in this 'gainst thee I've sinned.
Witness, too, the moon that permeates every being's inmost thought;
Let this god of life bereave me, if herein 'gainst thee I've sinned.
These three gods are they that govern the three worlds, so let them speak;
This my sacred truth attest they, or this day abandon me.'

Thus adjured, a solemn witness, spake the wind from out the air;
'She hath done or thought no evil, Nala, 'tis the truth we speak:
King, the treasure of her virtue in its fulness hath she kept,
Her we have watched and guarded ever closely for three livelong years.

उपायो विहितश् चायं त्वदर्थम् अतुलोऽनया ।
न ह्येकाह्ना शतं गन्ता त्वाम् ऋतेऽन्यः पुमान् इह ॥३८॥
उपपन्ना त्वया भैमी त्वञ्च भैम्या महीपते ।
नात्र शङ्का त्वया कार्या सङ्गच्छ सह भार्यया ॥३९॥
तथा ब्रुवति वायौ तु पुष्पवृष्टिः पपात ह ।
देवदुन्दुभयो नेदुर् ववौ च पवनः शिवः ॥४०॥
तद् अद्भुततमं दृष्ट्वा नलो राजाऽथ भारत ।
दमयन्त्यां विशङ्कां तां व्यपाकर्षद् अरिन्दम ॥४१॥
ततस् तद् वस्त्रम् अरजः प्रावृणोद् वसुधाधिपः ।
संस्मृत्य नागराजं तं ततो लेभे स्वकं वपुः ॥४२॥
स्वरूपिणं तु भर्तारं दृष्ट्वा भीमसुता तदा ।
प्राक्रोशद् उच्चैर् आलिङ्ग्य पुण्यश्लोकम् अनिन्दिता ॥४३॥
भैमीम् अपि नलो राजा भ्राजमानो यथा पुरा ।
सस्वजे स्वसुतौ चापि यथावत् प्रत्यनन्दत ॥४४॥
ततः स्वोरसि विन्यस्य वक्त्रं तस्य शुभानना ।
परीता तेन दुःखेन निशश्वासायतेक्षणा ॥४५॥
तथैव मलदिग्धाङ्गीं परिष्वज्य शुचिस्मितां ।
सुचिरं पुरुषव्याघ्रस् तस्थौ शोकपरिप्लुतः ॥४६॥
ततः सर्वं यथावृत्तं दमयन्त्या नलस्य च ।
भीमायाकथयत् प्रीत्या वैदर्भीजननी नृप ॥४७॥
ततोऽब्रवीद् महाराजः कृतशौचम् अहं नलं ।
दमयन्त्या सहोपेतं कल्यं द्रष्टा सुखोषितं ॥४८॥

वृहदश्व उवाच ।

ततस् तौ सहितौ रात्रिं कथयन्तौ पुरातनं ।
वने विचरितं सर्वम् ऊषतुर् मुदितौ नृप ॥४९॥

This unrivalled scheme she plotted only for thy absent sake;
In one day a hundred Yojans who beside thyself may drive?
Thou hast met with Bhíma's daughter, Bhíma's daughter meets with thee,
Cast away all jealous scruple, to thy bosom take thy wife.'

Even as thus the wind was speaking, flowers fell showering all around:
And the gods sweet music sounded on the zephyr floating light.
As on this surpassing wonder royal Nala stood and gazed,
Of the blameless Damayantí melted all his jealous doubts.
Then by dust all undefiled he the heavenly vest put on,
Thought upon the King of Serpents, and his proper form resumed.
In his own proud form her husband Bhíma's royal daughter saw;
Loud she shrieked, the undespised, and embraced the king of men.
Bhíma's daughter, too, king Nala, shining glorious as of old,
Clasped unto his heart, and fondled gently that sweet infant pair.
Then her face upon his bosom, as the lovely princess laid,
In her calm and gentle sorrow, softly sighed the long-eyed queen.
He, that form still mire-defiled, as he clasped with smile serene,
Long the king of men stood silent, in the ecstacy of woe.
All the tale of Damayantí, and of Nala all the tale,
To king Bhíma, in her transport, told Vidarbha's mother-queen.
Then replied that mighty monarch, 'Nala, his ablutions done,
Thus re-joined to Damayantí I to-morrow will behold.'

Vṛihadaśva spake:

They the night in joy together passed relating, each to each,
All their wanderings in the forest, and each wild adventure strange.

गृहे भीमस्य नृपतेः परस्परसुखैषिणौ ।
वसेतां हृष्टसङ्कल्पौ वैदर्भी च नलश्च ह ॥५०॥
स चतुर्थे ततो वर्षे सङ्गम्य सह भार्यया ।
सर्वकामैः सुसिद्धार्थो लब्धवान् परमां मुदं ॥५१॥
दमयन्त्यपि भर्तारम् आसाद्याप्यायिता भृशं ।
अर्धसञ्जातशस्येव तोयं प्राप्य वसुन्धरा ॥५२॥
सैवं समेत्य व्यपनीय तन्द्रां शान्तज्वरा हर्षविवृद्धसत्त्वा ।
रराज भैमी समवाप्तकामा शीतांशुना रात्रिर् इवोदितेन ॥५३॥

॥ इति नलोपाख्याने चतुर्विंशतितमः सर्गः ॥२४॥

बृहदश्व उवाच ।

अथ तां व्युषितो रात्रिं नलो राजा स्वलङ्कृतः ।
वैदर्भ्या सहितः काले ददर्श वसुधाधिपं ॥१॥
ततोऽभिवादयामास प्रयतः श्वशुरं नलः ।
ततोऽनु दमयन्ती च ववन्दे पितरं शुभा ॥२॥
तं भीमः प्रतिजग्राह पुत्त्रवत् परया मुदा ।
यथार्हं पूजयित्वा च समाश्वासयत प्रभुः ।
नलेन सहितां तत्र दमयन्तीं पतिव्रतां ॥३॥
ताम् अर्हणां नलो राजा प्रतिगृह्य यथाविधि ।
परिचर्यां स्वकां तस्मै यथावत् प्रत्यवेदयत् ॥४॥
ततो बभूव नगरे सुमहान् हर्षजः स्वनः ।
जनस्य सम्प्रहृष्टस्य नलं दृष्ट्वा तथागतं ॥५॥

In king Bhíma's royal palace, studying each the other's bliss,
With glad hearts Vidarbha's princess and the kingly Nala dwelt.
In his fourth year of divorcement, reunited to his wife,
Richly fraught with every blessing, at the height of joy he stood.
Damayantí too re-wedded, still increasing in her bliss,
Like as the glad earth to water opens its half-budding fruits,
She of weariness unconscious, soothed each grief, and full each joy,
Every wish fulfilled, shone brightly as the night when high the moon.

End of Book XXIV.

Vṛihadaśva spake:

When that night was passed and over, Nala, that high-gifted king,
Wedded to Vidarbha's daughter, in fit hour her sire beheld.
Humbly Nala paid his homage to the father of his queen,
Reverently did Damayantí pay her homage to her sire.
Him received the royal Bhíma, as his son, with highest joy,
Honoured, as became him, nobly: then consoled that monarch wise
Damayantí, to king Nala reconciled, the faithful wife.
Royal Nala all these honours, as his homage meet, received:
And in fitting terms, devotion to the royal Bhíma paid.
Mighty then through all the city ran the wakening sound of joy;
All in every street exulting at king Nala's safe return.

अशोभयन्त नगरं पताकाध्वजमालिनं ।
सिक्ताः सुमृष्टपुष्पाढ्या राजमार्गाः स्वलङ्कृताः ॥६॥
द्वारि द्वारि च पौराणां पुष्पभङ्गः प्रकल्पितः ।
अर्चितानि च सर्वाणि देवतायतनानि च ॥७॥
ऋतुपर्णोऽपि शुश्राव वाहुकच्छद्मिनं नलं ।
दमयन्त्या समायुक्तं जहृषे च नराधिपः ॥८॥
तम् आनाय्य नलो राजा क्षमयामास पार्थिवं ।
स च तं क्षमयामास हेतुभिर् बुद्धिसम्मितैः ॥९॥
स सत्कृतो महीपालो नैषधं विस्मिताननः ।
दिष्ट्या समेतो दारैः स्वैर् भवान् इत्यभ्यनन्दत ॥१०॥
कच्चित्तु नापराधं ते कृतवान् अस्मि नैषध ।
अज्ञातवासं वसतो मद्गृहे वसुधाधिप ॥११॥
यदि वा बुद्धिपूर्वाणि यद्यबुद्ध्यापि कानिचित् ।
मया कृतान्यकार्याणि तानि त्वं क्षन्तुम् अर्हसि ॥१२॥

नल उवाच ।

न मेऽपराधं कृतवांस् त्वं स्वल्पम् अपि पार्थिव ।
कृतेऽपि च न मे कोपः क्षन्तव्यं हि मया तव ॥१३॥
पूर्वं ह्यपि सखा मेऽसि सम्बन्धी च जनाधिप ।
अत ऊर्ध्वं तु भूयस् त्वम् प्रीतिम् आहर्तुम् अर्हसि ॥१४॥
सर्वकामैः सुविहितैः सुखम् अस्म्युषितस् त्वयि ।
न तथा स्वगृहे राजन् यथा तव गृहे सदा ॥१५॥
इदञ्चैव हयज्ञानं त्वदीयं मयि तिष्ठति ।
तद् उपाकर्तुम् इच्छामि मन्यसे यदि पार्थिव ॥१६॥
एवम् उक्त्वा ददौ विद्याम् ऋतुपर्णाय नैषधः ।
स च तां प्रतिजग्राह विधिदृष्टेन कर्मणा ॥१७॥

All the city with their banners and with garlands decked they forth.
All the royal streets well watered, and with stainless flowers were strewn;
And from door to door the garlands of festooning flowers were hung;
And of all the gods the altars were with fitting rites adorned.
Ṛituparṇa heard of Nala in the guise of Váhuka,
Now re-wed to Damayantí, and the king of men rejoiced.
To the king, before his presence, Nala courteous made excuse,
In his turn Ayodhyá's monarch in like courteous language spake.
He, received thus hospitably, wondering to Nishadha's king,
'Bliss be with thee, reunited to thy queen:' 'twas thus he said.
'Have I aught offensive ever done to thee, or said, O king,
Whilst unknown within my palace thou wert dwelling, king of men?
If designed or undesigning any single act I've done
I might wish undone, thy pardon grant me, I beseech thee, king.'

Nala spake:

'Not or deed or word discourteous, not the slightest hast thou done;
Hadst thou, I might not resent it, freely would I pardon all.
Thou of old, my friend, my kinsman wert, O sovereign of men,
From this time henceforth thy friendship still on me thou must bestow.
Every wish anticipated, pleasantly I dwelt with thee;
Not in mine own palace dwelt I ever, as, O king, in thine.
My surpassing skill in horses, all is thine that I possess;
That on thee bestow I gladly, if, O king, it seem thee good.'

Nala thus to Ṛituparṇa gave his subtle skill in steeds,
Gladly he received the present, with each regulation meet.

गृहीत्वा चाश्वहृदयं राजन् भाङ्गासुरिर् नृपः।
निषधाधिपतेश्चापि दत्त्वाऽक्षहृदयं नृपः।
सूतम् अन्यम् उपादाय ययौ स्वपुरम् एव ह ॥१८॥
ऋतुपर्णे गते राजन् नलो राजा विशाम्पते।
नगरे कुण्डिने कालं नातिदीर्घम् इवावसत् ॥१९॥

॥ इति नलोपाख्याने पञ्चविंशतितमः सर्गः ॥२५॥

बृहदश्व उवाच।

स मासम् उष्य कौन्तेय भीमम् आमन्त्र्य नैषधः।
पुराद् अल्पपरीवारो जगाम निषधान् प्रति ॥१॥
रथेनैकेन शुभ्रेण दन्तिभिः परिषोडशैः।
पञ्चाशद्भिर् हयैश्चैव षट्शतैश्च पदातिभिः ॥२॥
स कम्पयन्न् इव महीं त्वरमाणो महीपतिः।
प्रविवेश सुसंरब्धस् तरसैव महामनाः ॥३॥
ततः पुष्करम् आसाद्य वीरसेनसुतो नलः।
उवाच दीव्याव पुनर् बहु वित्तं मयार्जितं ॥४॥
दमयन्ती च यच्चान्यद् मम किञ्चन विद्यते।
एष वै मम सन्यासस् तव राज्यं तु पुष्कर ॥५॥
पुनः प्रवर्ततां द्यूतम् इति मे निश्चिता मतिः।
पणेनैकेन भद्रं ते प्राणयोश्च पणावहे ॥६॥
जित्वा परस्वम् आहृत्य राज्यं वा यदिवा वसु।
प्रतिपाणः प्रदातव्यः परमो धर्म उच्यते ॥७॥

Gifted with that precious knowledge, then Bhángásuri the king,
When in dice his skill mysterious to king Nala he had given,
Home returned to his own city with another charioteer.
Ṛituparṇa thus departed, Nala, then, O king of men
In the city of Kuṇḍina sojourned for no length of time.

End of Book XXV.

Vṛihadaśva spake:

There a month when he had sojourned, of king Bhíma taking leave,
Guarded he by few attendants to Nishadha took his way.
With a single splendid chariot, and with elephants sixteen,
And with fifty armed horsemen, and six hundred men on foot;
Making, as 'twere, earth to tremble, hastening onward, did the king
Enter awful in his anger, and terrific in his speed.
Then the son of Vírasena to king Pushkara drew near;
'Play we once again,' then said he, 'much the wealth I have acquired:
All I have, even Damayantí, every treasure I possess,
Set I now upon the hazard, Pushkara, thy kingdom thou:
In the game once more contend we, 'tis my settled purpose this,
Brother, at a single hazard, play we boldly for our lives.
From another he who treasures, he who mighty realm hath won,
'Tis esteemed a bounden duty to play back the counter game.

न चेद् वाञ्छसि द्यूतं त्वं युद्धद्यूतं प्रवर्ततां ।
द्वैरथेनास्तु वै शान्तिस् तव वा मम वा नृप ॥ ८॥
वंशभोज्यम् इदं राज्यम् अर्थितव्यं यथातथा ।
येन केनाप्युपायेन वृद्धानाम् इति शासनं ॥ ९॥
द्वयोर् एकतरे बुद्धिः क्रियताम् अद्य पुष्कर ।
कैतवेनाक्षवत्यां वा युद्धे वा नाम्यतां धनुः ॥ १०॥
नैषधेनैवम् उक्तस्तु पुष्करः प्रहसन्न् इव ।
ध्रुवम् आत्मजयं मत्वा प्रत्याह पृथिवीपतिं ॥ ११॥
दिष्ट्या त्वयाऽर्जितं वित्तं प्रतिपणाय नैषध ।
दिष्ट्या च दुष्करं कर्म दमयन्त्याः क्षयं गतं ॥ १२॥
दिष्ट्या च ध्रियसे राजन् सदारोऽद्य महाभुज ।
धनेनानेन वै भैमी जितेन समलङ्कृता ॥ १३॥
माम् उपस्थास्यति व्यक्तं दिवि शक्रम् इवाप्सराः ।
नित्यशो हि स्मरामि त्वां प्रतीक्षेऽपि च नैषध ॥ १४॥
देवनेन मम प्रीतिर् न भवत्यसुहृद्गणैः ।
जित्वा त्वद्य वरारोहां दमयन्तीम् अनिन्दितां ॥ १५॥
कृतकृत्यो भविष्यामि सा हि मे नित्यशो हृदि ।
श्रुत्वा तु तस्य ता वाचो बद्धबद्धप्रलापिनः ॥ १६॥
इयेष स शिरश् छेत्तुं खड्गेन कुपितो नलः ।
स्मयंस्तु रोषताम्राक्षस् तम् उवाच ततो नलः ॥ १७॥
पणावः किं व्याहरसे जितो न व्याहरिष्यसि ।
ततः प्रावर्तत द्यूतं पुष्करस्य नलस्य च ॥ १८॥
एकपाणेन वीरेण नलेन स पराजितः ।
स रत्नकोषनिचयैः प्राणेन पणितोऽपि च ॥ १९॥
जित्वा च पुष्करं राजा प्रहसन्न् इदम् अब्रवीत् ।
मम सर्वम् इदं राज्यम् अव्यग्रं हतकण्टकं ॥ २०॥

If thou shrinkest from the hazard, be our game the strife of arms,
Meet we in the single combat all our difference to decide.
An hereditary kingdom may by any means be sought,
Be re-won by any venture, this the maxim of the seers.
Of two courses set before thee, Pushkara, the option make,
Or in play to stand the hazard, or in combat stretch the bow.'
By Nishadha's lord thus challenged, Pushkara, with smile suppressed,
As secure of easy victory, answered to the lord of earth:
'Oh what joy! abundant treasures thou hast won, again to play.
Oh what joy! of Damayantí, now the hard-won prize is mine.
Oh what joy! again thou livest with thy consort, mighty-armed!
With the wealth I win bedeckëd soon shall Bhíma's daughter stand,
By my side, as by great Indra stands the Apsará in heaven.
Still on thee hath dwelt my memory, still I've waited, king, for thee;
In the play I find no rapture but 'gainst kinsman like thyself.
When this day the round-limbed princess Damayantí, undespised,
I shall win, I rest contented, still within mine heart she dwells.'

Hearing his contemptuous language franticly thus pouring forth,
With his sword th' indignant Nala fain had severed off his head.
But with haughty smile, with anger glaring in his blood-red eyes,
'Play we now, nor talk thus idly, conquered, thou'lt no longer talk.'
Then of Pushkara the gaming and of Nala straight began;
In a single throw by Nala was the perilous venture gained;
Pushkara, his gold, his jewels, at one hazard all was won!
Pushkara in play thus conquered, with a smile the king rejoined:
'Mine again is all this kingdom, undisturbed, its foes o'ercome.

वैदर्भी न त्वया शक्या राजापसद वीक्षितुं ।
तस्यास् त्वं सपरीवारो मूढ दासत्वम् आगतः ॥२१॥
न त्वया तत् कृतं कर्म येनाहं विजितः पुरा ।
कलिना तत् कृतं कर्म त्वं च मूढ न बुध्यसे ॥२२॥
नाहं परकृतं दोषं त्वय्याधास्ये कथञ्चन ।
यथासुखं वै जीव त्वं प्राणान् अवसृजामि ते ॥२३॥
तथैव सर्वसम्भारं स्वम् अंशं वितरामि ते ।
तथैव च मम प्रीतिस् त्वयि वीर न संशयः ॥२४॥
सौहार्दं चापि मे त्वत्तो न कदाचित् प्रहास्यति ।
पुष्कर त्वं हि मे भ्राता सञ्जीव शरदः शतं ॥२५॥
एवं नलः सान्त्वयित्वा भ्रातरं सत्यविक्रमः ।
स्वपुरं प्रेषयामास परिष्वज्य पुनः पुनः ॥२६॥
सान्त्वितो नैषधेनैवं पुष्करः प्रत्युवाच ह ।
पुण्यश्लोकं तदा राजन् अभिवाद्य कृताञ्जलिः ॥२७॥
कीर्तिर् अस्तु तवाक्षय्या जीव वर्षायुतं सुखी ।
यो मे वितरसि प्राणान् अधिष्ठानञ्च पार्थिव ॥२८॥
स तथा सत्कृतो राज्ञा मासम् उष्य तदा नृपः ।
प्रययौ स्वपुरं हृष्टः पुष्करः स्वजनावृतः ॥२९॥
महत्या सेनया सार्धं विनीतैः परिचारकैः ।
भ्राजमान इवादित्यो वपुषा भरतर्षभ ॥३०॥
प्रस्थाप्य पुष्करं राजा वित्तवन्तम् अनामयं ।
प्रविवेश पुरीं श्रीमान् अत्यर्थम् उपशोभितां ।
प्रविश्य सान्त्वयामास पौरांश्च निषधाधिपः ॥३१॥
पौरजानपदाश्चापि सम्प्रहृष्टतनूरुहाः ।
ऊचुः प्राञ्जलयः सर्वे सामात्यप्रमुखा जनाः ॥३२॥
अद्य स्म निर्वृता राजन् पुरे जनपदेऽपि च ।

Fallen king! Vidarbha's daughter by thine eyes may ne'er be seen.
Foolish king! thou'rt now her bondsman, thou and thine to slavery sunk.
Not thyself achieved the conquest that subdued me heretofore;
'Twas achieved by mightier Kali, that thou didst not, fool, perceive.
Yet my wrath, by him enkindled, will I not 'gainst thee direct;
Live thou henceforth at thy pleasure, freely I thy life bestow,
And of thine estate and substance give I thee thy fitting share.
Such my pleasure, in thy welfare, hero, do I take delight,
And mine unabated friendship never shall from thee depart.
Pushkara, thou art my brother, may'st thou live a hundred years!'

Nala thus consoled his brother, in his conscious power and strength;
Sent him home to his own city, once embracing, once again.
Pushkara, thus finding comfort, answered to Nishadha's lord,
Answered he to Puṇyaśloka, bowing low with folded hands:
'Everlasting be thy glory! may'st thou live ten thousand years!
That my life to me thou grantest, and a city for mine home!'

Hospitably entertainëd, there a month when he had dwelt,
Cheered in spirit to his city, Pushkara, with all his kin,
With a well-appointed army, of attendant slaves a host,
Shining like the sun, departed, in his full meridian orb.

Pushkara thus crowned with riches, thus unharmed, when he dismissed,
Entered then his royal city, with surpassing pomp, the king.
As he entered, to his subjects Nala spake the words of peace,
From the city, from the country, all, with hair erect with joy,
Came, with folded hands addressed him, and the counsellors of state.
'Happy are we now, O monarch, in the city, in the fields,

उपासितुं पुनः प्राप्ता देवा इव शतक्रतुं ॥३३॥
प्रशान्ते तु पुरे हृष्टे सम्प्रवृत्ते महोत्सवे ।
महत्या सेनया राजा दमयन्तीम् उपानयत् ॥३४॥
दमयन्तीम् अपि पिता सत्कृत्य परवीरहा ।
प्रास्थापयद् अमेयात्मा भीमो भीमपराक्रमः ॥३५॥
आगतायां तु वैदर्भ्यां सपुत्रायां नलो नृपः ।
वर्तयामास मुदितो देवराड् इव नन्दने ॥३६॥
ततः प्रकाशतां यातो जम्बुद्वीपे स राजसु ।
पुनः शशास तद् राज्यं प्रत्याहृत्य महायशाः ।
ईजे च विविधैर् यज्ञैर् विधिवच् चाप्तदक्षिणैः ॥३७॥

॥ इति नलोपाख्यानं समाप्तम् ॥

Setting forth to do thee homage, as to Indra all the gods.'

Then at peace the tranquil city, the first festal gladness o'er,
With a mighty host escorted, Damayantí brought he home.
Damayantí rich in treasures, in her father's blessings rich,
Glad dismissed the mighty-minded Bhíma, fearful in his strength.
With the daughter of Vidarbha, with his children in his joy,
Nala lived, as lives the sovereign of the gods in Nandana.
Re-ascended thus to glory, he, among the kings of earth,
Ruled his realm in Jambudvípa, thus re-won, with highest fame;
And all holy rites performed he with devout munificence.

End of the Story of Nala.

A

VOCABULARY

(SANSKRIT AND ENGLISH)

OF ALL THE WORDS

WHICH OCCUR IN THE FOREGOING PAGES.

AN EXPLANATION

OF THE

ABBREVIATIONS USED IN THE FOLLOWING VOCABULARY.

---

abl. — ablative case.
acc. — accusative case.
adj. — adjective.
adv. — adverb or adverbial.
agt. — noun of agency.
anom. — anomalous.
aor. — aorist.
átm. — átmane-pada.

BAH. OR REL. COMP. — BAHU-VRÍHI OR RELATIVE COMPOUND.

caus. — causal.
cl. — class of nouns or verbs.
comp. — compound.
conj. — conjugation of verbs.
cr. — crude base.

dat. — dative case.
des. — desiderative.
du. — dual.
DVAN. OR AGG. COMP. — DVANDVA OR AGGREGATIVE COMPOUND.

f. — feminine.
freq. — frequentative.
fut. — future.
fut. pass. p. — future passive participle.

gen. — genitive case.

imp. — imperative.
impf. — imperfect.
ind. — indeclinable.
inf. — infinitive.
ins. — instrumental case.
interrog. — interrogative.

KARM. OR DES. COMP. — KARMA-DHÁRAYA OR DESCRIPTIVE COMPOUND.

lit. — literally.
loc. — locative case.

m. — masculine.
m. f. — masculine and feminine.
m. f. n. — masculine, feminine, and neuter.
m. n. — masculine and neuter.

n. — neuter.
nom. — nominative case.

p. — participle.
par. — parasmai-pada.
pass. — passive.
past act. p. — past active participle.
past ind. p. — past indeclinable participle.
past p. p. — past passive participle.
pl. — plural.
pot. — potential.
prep. — preposition.
pres. — present.
pres. p. — present participle.
pron. — pronoun.

q. v. — quod vide.

rt — root.

sin. — singular.
superl. — superlative.

TAT. OR DEP. COMP. — TAT-PURUSHA OR DEPENDENT COMPOUND.

v. — verb.
voc. — vocative case.

VOCABULARY,

SANSKRIT AND ENGLISH.

Observe—In the following vocabulary a final *m* is sometimes expressed by म् although represented by anusvára (ं) in the text.

The numbers refer to the numbers of the rules in the Sanskṛit Grammar by Monier Williams, published for the University of Oxford by Macmillan & Co., 4th edition.

अ.

अ *ind.,—a negative or privative particle, prefixed to words beginning with consonants,*—no, not. *Often equivalent to the English prefixes* in, un. *In composition* अ *becomes* अन् *before a vowel.*

अंशं *acc. sin. of* अंश *m.* a share.

अंशुमान् *nom. sin. of* अंशुमत् *m.* the sun, 5*th cl.* 140.

अकथयत् he or she told; 3*d sin. impf. of rt* कथ् 10*th cl.*

अकरोत् he made, he performed, he did, he assumed; 3*d sin. impf. of rt* कृ 8*th cl.* 682, to make, to do.

अकस्मात् *ind.* without cause, without a wherefore; (*from* अ not, *and* कस्मात् *abl. sin. of* किं who? what?) 715.

अकाम *for* अकामस् *nom. sin. m. of* अकाम *m. f. n.* reluctant, unwilling, one who does anything against his will; (*from* अ not, *and* काम.)

अकार्याणि *nom. pl. of* अकार्य *n.* that which ought not to be done, improper action.

अकाले out of time; *loc. sin. of* अकाल *m.* improper time; (*from* अ not, 726, *and* काल.)

अकीर्त्तिं *acc. sin. of* अकीर्त्ति *f.* disgrace, dishonour.

अकीर्त्तिकरं *nom. sin. n.* not conducive to glory; (अ not, कीर्त्ति fame, कर causing.)

अकीर्त्तिर् *for* अकीर्त्तिस् *nom. sin.* disgrace.

अकुर्वत they made; 3*d pl. impf. átm. of rt* कृ 8*th cl.* 683.

अकुर्वतः *gen. sin. m. of* अकुर्वत् *m. f. n.* not doing; (*from* अ not, 726, *and* कुर्वत् *pres. p. par. of rt* कृ 524, 682.)

अकुर्वन् they made, they were making; 3*d pl. impf. of rt* कृ 8*th cl.* 682.

अकृतात्मभिः *ins. pl. of* अकृतात्मन् *m. f. n.* having an unformed or ungoverned mind, having unsubdued senses; (Bah. or Rel. comp. अकृत *cr.* unformed, uncultivated, unimproved, 726, *and* आत्मन् soul, 147.)

अकृत्वा without having performed; (*comp. of* अ not, 726, *and* कृत्वा *past ind. p. of rt* कृ 682.)

अक्लेद्यो *for* अक्लेद्यस् *nom. sin. m. of* अक्लेद्य *m. f. n.* not to be moistened, incapable of receiving moisture.

अक्षज्ञः *nom. sin. m.* skilled in dice; (*comp.*

of अक्ष *cr.* dice, *and* ज्ञ *m. f. n.* knowing, *see* 580.)

अक्षद्यूते TAT. OR DEP. COMP. 740 *or* 743; अक्ष *cr.* dice, द्यूते *loc. sin. of* द्यूत *n.* a game.

अक्षनैपुणं *acc. sin. n.* skill in dice; (*comp. of* अक्ष *cr.* dice, *and* नैपुण *n.* skill.)

अक्षप्रियः TAT. OR DEP. COMP. 743; अक्ष *cr.* a die, dice, प्रियः *nom. sin. m. of* प्रिय *m. f. n.* fond of, 1*st cl.* 103. Gaming with dice has been common in India from the earliest times. In Hindú poetry princes and heroes are constantly found indulging in it; but it is deemed a great vice notwithstanding, and the epithet अक्षप्रिय seems out of place in Book I. 3, where Nala's virtues are enumerated. अङ्कप्रियः 'fond of numbers' or 'arithmetic' would be a better reading, and one more in unison with the narrative in Book XX. All the MSS. and printed editions, however, read अक्षप्रियः

अक्षमदसम्मत्तं TAT. OR DEP. COMP. 745; अक्ष *cr.* dice, मद fury, passion for, सम्मत्तं *acc. sin. m. of* सम्मत्त *m. f. n.* mad, maddened; *past p. p. of rt* मद् 539.

अक्षयस् *nom. sin. of* अक्षय *m. f. n.* imperishable, eternal; (*from* अ not, *and* क्षय.)

अक्षय्या *nom. sin. f. of* अक्षय्य *m. f. n.* undecaying; (*from* अ not, *and* क्षय्य.)

अक्षवत्यां *loc. sin. of* अक्षवती *f.* playing with dice, 106.

अक्षहृदयं *acc. sin. n.* knowledge of dice, skill in dice; (TAT. OR DEP. COMP. अक्ष *cr.* dice, *and* हृदय *n.* heart, core, innermost part, profound knowledge.)

अक्षहृदयज्ञं TAT. OR DEP. COMP. 745; अक्ष *cr.* dice, हृदय *cr.* knowledge, ज्ञम् *acc. sin. m. of* ज्ञ *m. f. n.* acquainted with, 580.

अक्षहृदयज्ञस्य *gen. sin. See preceding.*

अक्षाः *nom. pl. of* अक्ष *m.* a die, dice, 1*st cl.* 103.

अक्षाणां *gen. pl. of* अक्ष *m.* a die, dice.

अक्षान् *acc. pl. of* अक्ष *m.* a die.

अक्षेषु *loc. pl. of* अक्ष *m.* a die.

अक्षौहिणीपतिः TAT. OR DEP. COMP. 743; अक्षौहिणी *cr.* a complete army, consisting of ten अनीकिनी, or 109,350 foot, 65,610 horse, 21,870 chariots, 21,870 elephants, पतिः *for* पतिस् *nom. sin. of* पति *m.* a lord.

अखिलान् *acc. pl. m. of* अखिल *m. f. n.* all, entire.

अगच्छंस् *for* अगच्छन् they went; 3*d pl. impf. of rt* गम् 1*st cl.* 602.

अगच्छत् he or she proceeded onwards; 3*d sin. impf. of rt* गम् 1*st cl.* 602.

अगच्छद्. *See preceding.*

अगमं I went; 1*st sin. aor. of rt* गम् 602.

अगमः *nom. sin. m.* a tree.

अगमंस् *for* अगमन् they went; 3*d pl. aor. of rt* गम् 602, 436.

अगमत् he or she went; 3*d sin. aor. of rt* गम्.

अगमद् he went; 3*d sin. aor. of rt* गम् 602.

अगाधे *loc. sin. n. of* अगाध *m. f. n.* deep, unfathomable, bottomless, 1*st cl.* 187.

अग्नाव् *for* अग्नौ (37), *q. v.*

अग्निं *acc. sin. of* अग्नि *m.* fire, the god of fire, 2*d cl.* Fire is still an important object of veneration with the Hindús, as with the ancient Persians.

अग्निदग्ध TAT. OR DEP. COMP. 740; अग्नि *cr.* fire, दग्ध *nom. sin. m. of* दग्ध *m. f. n.* burnt; *past p. p. of rt* दह् 539.

अग्निम् *acc. sin. of* अग्नि *m.* fire, 2*d cl.*

अग्निपुरोगमान् having Agni for their leader, BAH. OR REL. COMP. 761; अग्नि *cr.* Agni, the god of fire, पुरोगमान् *acc. pl. of* पुरोगम *m.* a leader, 1*st cl.* 103.

अग्निमान् *nom. sin. of* अग्निमत् *m.* one who maintains or worships a consecrated fire.

अग्निर् *for* अग्निस् *nom. sin. of* अग्नि *m.* fire, 2*d cl.* 110.

अग्निश् *for* अग्निस् *nom. sin. of* अग्नि *m.* fire.

अग्निशिखाम् TAT. OR DEP. COMP. 743;

अग्नि *cr.* fire, *and* शिखाम् *acc. sin. of* शिखा *f.* a flame.

अग्निषु *loc. pl. of* अग्नि *m.* fire, a sacred fire, 2*d cl.* 110.

अग्नेः *gen. sin. of* अग्नि *m.* fire, 2*d cl.* 110.

अग्नौ *loc. sin. of* अग्नि *m.* fire, ('on the fire,' Book XXIV. 14.)

अग्रतस् *ind.* in the presence of, before, 731; (अग्र *with affix* तस् 719.)

अग्रहारांश् *for* अग्रहारान् *acc. pl. of* अग्रहार *m.* a grant of land (made to Bráhmans), a village inhabited by Bráhmans.

अग्रे *ind.* into the presence of, before, in front of, 731.

अङ्कम् *acc. sin. of* अङ्क *m.* the lap, the part above the hip where a child is carried.

अङ्गना *nom. sin. f.* a woman.

अङ्गानि *nom. pl. of* अङ्ग *n.* a limb, 1*st cl.* 104.

अङ्गुष्ठमात्रकः *nom. sin. m.* of the size of a thumb; (*comp. of* अङ्गुष्ठ *cr.* a thumb, *and* मात्रक of the measure of or size.)

अचलम् *acc. sin. of* अचल *m.* a mountain, 1*st cl.* 103.

अचलश्रेष्ठ *voc. sin.* O chief of mountains, TAT. OR DEP. COMP. 743; अचल *cr.* a mountain, श्रेष्ठ *voc. sin. of* श्रेष्ठ *m. f. n.* best, 743. *b*, 194.

अचलान् *acc. pl. of* अचल *m.* a mountain.

अचलो *nom. sin. m. of* अचल *m. f. n.* immovable, fixed.

अचिन्त्यो *nom. sin. m. of* अचिन्त्य *m. f. n.* incomprehensible, inconceivable.

अचिराद् *for* अचिरात् (45) *ind.* in a short time, shortly, 715, 726.

अचिरेण *ind.* in a short time, rapidly, 714.

अचेतनम् *acc. sin. m. of* अचेतन *m. f. n.* senseless, out of one's senses, unconscious; (*comp. of* अ not, 726, *and* चेतन sense.)

अचेतसं *acc. sin. m. of* अचेतस् *m. f. n.* devoid of reason, out of one's mind; (*comp. of* अ not, 726, *and* चेतस् mind, 164.)

अच्छेद्यो *nom. sin. m. of* अच्छेद्य *m. f. n.* indivisible; (अ not, छेद्य to be cut.)

अजं *acc. sin. m. or n.* unborn. *See* अजो.

अजगरो *nom. sin. of* अजगर *m.* the boa, a large serpent (that can swallow a goat).

अजम् *acc. sin. m.* unborn. *See* अजो.

अजीयत he was conquered, he was beaten; 3*d sin. impf. of rt* जि *in pass.* 590, 463.

अजो *nom. sin. m.* unborn; (अ not, ज born, 580.)

अज्ञातं *nom. sin. n. of* अज्ञात *m. f. n.* unknown; (*comp. of* अ not, 726, *and* ज्ञात known, *past p. p. of rt* ज्ञा 532.)

अज्ञातवासं *ind.* without having (his) habitation known; (*comp. of* अ not, 726, ज्ञात *cr.* known, वासं *acc. sin. of* वास *m.* habitation, *used adverbially.*)

अज्ञायमाना *nom. sin. f.* not being known; (*from* अ not, 726, *and* ज्ञायमान *pres. p. of* ज्ञा *in pass.*)

अटमानस् *nom. sin. m. of* अटमान *m. f. n.* wandering, *pres. p. átm. of rt* अट् 526.

अटमानाव् *for* अटमानौ *nom. du. of* अटमान *m. f. n.* wandering about. *See next.*

अटमानौ wandering, moving about; *nom. du. m. of* अटमान *m. f. n., pres. p. átm. of rt* अट् 526.

अटवीम् *acc. sin. of* अटवी *f.* a forest, 1*st cl.* 106.

अटव्यां *loc. sin. of* अटवी *f.* a forest, 1*st cl.* 106.

अणु *acc. sin. n. of* अणु *m. f. n.* minute, little, infinitesimal.

अण्डजः *for* अण्डजस् *nom. sin. of* अण्डज *m.* a bird, (*lit.* egg-born, *from* अण्ड an egg, *and* ज born, 580. *b*,) 1*st cl.* 103.

अण्वपि *for* अणु अपि *by* 34.

अतःपरं *ind.* beyond this, hereafter, henceforward; अतस् (*see* 719) *for* अस्मात्, *and* परं beyond, 731.

अतयोचिता *nom. sin. f.* not deserving such (a fate), not meriting such treatment; अ

not, 726, तथा so, उचिता *nom. sin. f. of* उचित *m. f. n.* deserving, worthy.

अतन्द्रितः *for* अतन्द्रितस् *ind.* unweariedly, incessantly, 719.

अतन्द्रिताः *nom. pl. m. of* अतन्द्रित *m. f. n.* unwearied, active, eager.

अतन्द्रितैः *ins. pl. m. of* अतन्द्रित *m. f. n.* not slothful, unwearied, active.

अतर्पयत् he made glad, he satisfied; *3d sin. impf. of rt* तृप् *in caus.* 481.

अति *prep.* over, beyond, very, beyond measure.

अतिक्रम्य having passed through or by; *past ind. p. of rt* क्रम् *with* अति, 559.

अतिचक्राम he passed over or passed through; *3d sin. perf. of rt* क्रम् *with* अति, 364.

अतिचरामि I transgress, I sin against; *1st sin. pres. of* चर् *with* अति, *1st cl.* 261.

अतिथि *m.* a guest, *2d cl.* 110.

अतिथीन् *acc. pl. of* अतिथि, *q. v.*

अतिदीर्घं *acc. sin. m. of* अतिदीर्घ *m. f. n.* very long; नातिदीर्घं कालं no very long time, not a very long while, 821.

अतिदुर्धर्ष *voc. sin. m.* O thou who art too difficult of approach; (*from* अति 726. *a, and* दुर्धर्ष *m. f. n., 1st cl.* 103.)

अतिमात्रं *ind.* beyond measure, excessively.

अतियशां *acc. sin. f. of* अतियश *m. f. n.* very illustrious, bearing a high name or character; (*comp. of* अति very, 726. *a, and* यशस् *m.* glory, *see* 769. *b.*) *Observe*—अतियश *is used irregularly for* अतियशस्, *just as* शुष्कस्रोत *for* शुष्कस्रोतस् *in* Book XVI. 4.

अतिरिच्यते it is more important, it exceeds, it is worse than; *3d sin. pres. of* रिच् *in pass. with* अति (*governing abl.*)

अतिविराजते he or it shines very much; *3d sin. pres. átm. of rt* राज् *with* अति *and* वि, *1st cl.* 261.

अतिष्ठत् he stood; *3d sin. impf. of rt* स्था to stand, to exist, to be, *1st cl.* 269, 587.

अतिस्वस्था *nom. sin. f. of* अतिस्वस्थ *m.* very well, in very good health, very sound (in body or mind); (*comp. of* अति very, 726. *a,* स्व own self, स्थ staying, being.)

अतीतवाक्पथे Bah. or Rel. comp. 761; अतीत *cr.* passed, वाक्पथे *loc. sin. m. of* वाक्पथ suitable for speaking, (*lit.* the path of speech, *from* वाच् 176, *and* पथ *m.* road, path.)

अतीव *ind.* excessively, very, very much.

अतीवासीद् *for* अतीव आसीत् *by* 31.

अतुलं *acc. sin. n. of* अतुल *m. f. n.* unrivalled, incomparable.

अतुलो *for* अतुलस् *nom. sin. of* अतुल *m. f. n.* unequalled, incomparable.

अतो *for* अतस् *ind.* hence. *Sometimes used for* अस्मात् from this, than this.

अतोनिमित्तं *ind.* on this account, for this reason; (*from* अतो *for* अतस् 719, *and* निमित्त cause, reason.)

अत्यजं I deserted; *1st sin. impf. of rt* त्यज् *1st cl.* 596.

अत्यद्भुतम् *acc. sin. n. of* अत्यद्भुत *m. f. n.* very surprising, very wonderful; (*comp. of* अति very, 726. *a, and* अद्भुत surprising.)

अत्यन्तं *ind.* exceedingly, beyond measure.

अत्यर्थं *ind.* beyond measure, excessively.

अत्युष्णाम् *acc. sin. n. of* अत्युष्ण *m. f. n.* quite hot, very hot; (*comp. of* अति 726. *a, and* उष्ण.)

अत्र *ind.* here, in this place.

अथ *ind.* then, now, afterwards.

अथवा *ind.* or, or whether; but; moreover.

अथवारण्यनृपते *for* अथवा अरण्यनृपते *by* 31.

अथापरेद्युः *for* अथ अपरेद्युः *by* 31.

अथापश्यत् *for* अथ अपश्यत् *by* 31.

अथाब्रवीत् *for* अथ अब्रवीत् *by* 31.

अथार्धरात्रसमये *for* अथ अर्धरात्रसमये *by* 31.

अथाश्वास्य *for* अथ आश्वास्य *by* 31.

अथास्य *for* अथ अस्य *by* 31.

अथैनं *for* अथ एनं *by* 33.

अथो *ind., same as* अथ.

अधोचुस् *for* अध ऊचुस् *by* 32.

अदशद् he bit; 3*d sin. impf. of rt* दंश् to bite, 1*st cl.* 270. *d.*

अदस् *pron.* he, this, that, 225.

अदाह्यो *nom. sin. m. of* अदाह्य *m. f. n.* incombustible, not to be consumed by fire.

अदीनात्मा BAH. OR REL. COMP. 766; अदीन *cr.* not depressed, not sorrowful, elated, आत्मा *nom. sin. of* आत्मन् *m.* soul, spirit, 6*th cl.* 146.

अदृढतरं *nom. sin. n. of* अदृढतर *m. f. n.* very irresolute, very undecided.

अदृश्यः *nom. sin. m. of* अदृश्य *m. f. n.* invisible, not to be seen; (*comp. of* अ not, 726, *and* दृश्य to be seen.)

अदृश्यत् he was seen; 3*d sin. impf. of* दृश् *in pass., with parasmai-pada termination; —an anomaly occasionally occurring in the Mahá-bhárata. See* 461. *c. note.*

अदृष्टकामो TAT. OR DEP. COMP. 743; अदृष्ट *cr.* not seen, कामो *nom. sin. of* काम *m.* love, passion, 1*st cl.* 103.

अदृष्टपूर्वं *acc. sin. n.* never seen before. *See next.*

अदृष्टपूर्वां *acc. sin. f. of* अदृष्टपूर्व *m. f. n.* who has never before seen or experienced; (*comp. of* अ not, 726, दृष्ट *cr.* seen, पूर्व before.)

अदैवं *nom. sin. n. of* अदैव *m. f. n.* without fate, without destiny, undestined; (*comp. of* अ not, 726, *and* दैव, *q. v.*)

अद्भुततमं *acc. sin. n. of* अद्भुततम *m. f. n.* most wonderful, marvellous or prodigious; (*superl. of* अद्भुत, *see* 191.)

अद्भुतदर्शनाः BAH. OR REL. COMP.; *acc. pl. f. of* अद्भुतदर्शन *m. f. n.* wondrous to behold, of wondrous aspect; (*from* अद्भुत *cr.* wonderful, *and* दर्शन *n.* sight, aspect, 1*st cl.* 108.)

अद्भुतदर्शनान् *acc. pl. m. See last.*

अद्भुतरूपान् BAH. OR REL. COMP. 766; अद्भुत *cr.* surprising, wonderful, रूपान् *acc. pl. m. of* रूप *n.* shape, form, figure, 1*st cl.* 108.

अद्भुतलिङ्गानि KARM. OR DES. COMP. 755; अद्भुत *cr.* astonishing, surprising, लिङ्गानि *acc. pl. of* लिङ्ग *n.* a mark, a sign.

अद्य *ind.* to-day, now.

अद्यापि *ind.* even now, still, henceforth.

अधनो *nom. sin. m. of* अधन *m. f. n.* poor; (*comp. of* अ not, *and* धन wealth.)

अधर्मकृच्छ्रे KARM. OR DES. COMP. 755; अधर्म *cr.* unrighteous, evil, कृच्छ्रे *loc. sin. of* कृच्छ्र *n.* calamity, trouble.

अधर्मो *nom. sin. m.* unrighteousness, lawlessness, abandonment of duty.

अधि *prep.* over, above, upon.

अधिकं *nom. or acc. sin. n. of* अधिक *m. f. n.* more. *See next.*

अधिकः *nom. sin. m. of* अधिक *m. f. n.* more, excessive, greater, in addition, over.

अधिकम् *ind.* excessively, very much, more, 713.

अधिगमनार्थं *ind.* for the sake of finding; (*comp. of* अधिगमन obtaining, finding, *and* अर्थं, *see* 791.)

अधिजग्मुर् they found, they obtained; 3*d pl. perf. of rt* गम् *with* अधि, 376.

अधिपतिः *nom. sin. m.* ruler, sovereign, lord.

अधिपस् *nom. sin. of* अधिप *m.* a sovereign.

अधिष्ठानं *acc. sin. of* अधिष्ठान *n.* an abode, place of residence.

अधीते he reads; 3*d sin. pres. átm. of rt* इ to go, *with* अधि over, 2*d cl.* 311.

अधुना *ind.* now.

अधो *for* अधस् (64) *ind.* down, 731.

अधोमुखम् *acc. sin. m. of* अधोमुख *m. f. n.* downcast, (*lit.* having the face cast down; *from* अधस् down, *and* मुख the face, 64.)

अध्यगच्छत् he approached, he found; 3*d sin. impf. of rt* गम् *with* अधि, 602.

अध्यगच्छद् he came to. *See last.*

अध्यगाद् he approached, he addressed himself to, he undertook; *3d sin. aor. of rt* **इ** *or* **गा** *with* **अधि**; *see* 645.

अध्वनि *loc. sin. of* **अध्वन्** *m.* a road, 147.

अध्वानं *acc. sin. of* **अध्वन्** *m.* a road, *6th cl.* 147.

अनघ O sinless one, O blameless one, *voc. sin. m. of* **अनघ**; (*comp. of* **अन्** *for* **अ** not, 726, *and* **अघ** *n.* sin.)

अनघाः O blameless men, *voc. pl. m. of* **अनघ** *m. f. n.* *See last.*

अनपकृते *loc. sin. m. of* **अनपकृत** *m. f. n.* uninjured; (*from* **अ** not, 726, *and* **अपकृत** *past p. p. of rt* **कृ** *with* **अप**.)

अनभिज्ञा *nom. sin. f. of* **अनभिज्ञ** not acquainted with, not knowing.

अनया by her, *ins. sin. f.*; (*from nom.* **इयं** she, 224.)

अनयोस् of these two, *gen. du. m. of* **इदं**, (*nom.* **अयं** 224.)

अनर्हस् *nom. sin. m.* unworthy. *See next.*

अनर्हो *nom. sin. m. of* **अनर्ह** *m. f. n.* unworthy, undeserving; (*comp. of* **अन्** 726, *and* **अर्ह** worthy.)

अनवद्याङ्गि O thou with faultless limbs, *voc. sin.* *See next.*

अनवद्याङ्गी Bah. or Rel. comp. 766; **अनवद्य** *cr.* faultless, not to be found fault with, **अङ्गी** *nom. f. from* **अङ्ग** *n.* a limb or the bodily frame, *1st cl.* 108.

अनसूयकः *nom. sin. of* **अनसूयक** *m. f. n.* unenvious; (*comp. of* **अन्** 726, *and* **असूयक** envious.)

अनागसं *acc. sin. f. of* **अनागस्** *m. f. n.* without blame, sinless, innocent, *7th cl.* 164. *a*; (*comp. of* **अन्** 726, *and* **आगस्** sin.)

अनागा *for* **अनागास्** *nom. sin. m. of* **अनागस्** *m. f. n.* blameless, *7th cl.* 164. *a*; (*comp. of* **अन्** 726, *and* **आगस्** *n.* sin.)

अनात्मवान् *nom. sin. m. of* **अनात्मवत्** *m. f. n.* not one's self, not self-possessed, not in one's right mind; (*comp. of* **अन्** 726, **आत्म** 146, *and affix* **वत्** 140.)

अनाथवत् *ind.* like one without a protector, like one unprotected or deprived of her lord; (*comp. of* **अ** not, 726, **नाथ** a protector or lord, *and affix* **वत्** 724.)

अनाथां *acc. sin. f. of* **अनाथ** *m. f. n.* without a lord or protector; (*comp. of* **अ** not, 726, *and* **नाथ** a lord.)

अनामयं *acc. sin. of* **अनामय** *n.* health, *1st cl.* 104; (*comp. of* **अन्** not, 726, *and* **आमय** disease.)

अनामयम् *acc. sin. of* **अनामय** *m. f. n.* unharmed, safe, in good health; (*from* **अन्** not, 726, *and* **आमय** sickness.)

अनार्यैर् *ins. pl. of* **अनार्य** *m. f. n.* unworthy, vile.

अनाशिनो *gen. sin. m. of* **अनाशिन्** *m. f. n.* imperishable, indestructible.

अनित्यास् *nom. pl. m. of* **अनित्य** *m. f. n.* not eternal, transient, temporary.

अनिन्दिता *nom. sin. f. of* **अनिन्दित** *m. f. n.* unblamed, innocent, irreproachable; (*comp. of* **अ** not, 726, *and* **निन्दित** *past p. p. of rt* **निन्द्** 538.)

अनिन्दिताम् *acc. sin. f.* *See* **अनिन्दिता**.

अनिन्दिते O blameless one, *voc. sin. f.* *See* **अनिन्दिता**.

अनीचानुवर्ती *nom. sin. m.* not following low (practices), not acting in a mean manner; (*comp. of* **अ** not, 726, **नीच** *cr.* low, **अनुवर्तिन्** *m. f. n.* following, 159.)

अनु *prep.* after, 730. *d.* (*In* Book XXV. 2. **अनु** *governs* **ततो**, *which is equivalent to* **तस्मात्** after that, 719.)

अनुगता *nom. sin. f. of* **अनुगत** *m. f. n.* followed, following, gone after; *past p. p. of rt* **गम्** (545) *with* **अनु**; *see also* 896.

अनुगतो *nom. sin. m. of* **अनुगत** *m. f. n.* followed, attended by. *See last.*

अनुचिन्तयन् *nom. sin. m. of* **अनुचिन्तयत्**

m. f. n. thinking of; *pres. p. par. of rt* चिन्त् *with* अनु, 641, 524.

अनुजग्मुस् they followed after, they went after; *3d pl. perf. of rt* गम् *with* अनु, 602.

अनुज्ञातं *acc. sin. m. of* अनुज्ञात *m. f. n.* permitted (to depart), dismissed; *past p. p. of rt* ज्ञा *with* अनु.

अनुज्ञातो *nom. sin. of* अनुज्ञात *m. f. n. See last.*

अनुज्ञातुम् to permit (to depart); *inf. of rt* ज्ञा *with* अनु, 459.

अनुत्तमां *acc. sin. f. of* अनुत्तम *m. f. n.* most excellent.

अनुधावसि thou runnest after, thou comest hastily after (or to the rescue); *2d sin. pres. of rt* धाव् *with* अनु, *1st cl.*

अनुनादितम् *acc. sin. m. of* अनुनादित *m. f. n.* made to echo or ring, made to resound; *past p. p. of rt* नद् *in caus. with* अनु, 549.

अनुन्मत्ता *nom. sin. f. of* अनुन्मत्त *m. f. n.* not mad; (*comp. of* अन् not, 726, *and* उन्मत्त mad.)

अनुपश्यामि I foresee or see what is to come; *1st sin. pres. of rt* दृश् *with* अनु.

अनुबध्नाति he or it follows or attends upon; *3d sin. pres. of rt* बन्ध् *with* अनु, *9th cl.* 692.

अनुभूय having perceived, having understood; *past ind. p. of rt* भू *with* अनु, 559.

अनुभूयतां let it be enjoyed, let it be tried; *3d sin. imp. of* भू *in pass. with* अनु. In Book II. 9, where this word occurs, the verse is too long by one foot: but violations of metre as well as of grammar are not uncommon in the Mahá-bhárata.

अनुमते *loc. sin. of* अनुमत *n.* consent; 'with the consent of.'

अनुरक्तम् *acc. sin. m.* attached. *See next.*

अनुरक्ता *nom. sin. f. of* अनुरक्त *m. f. n.* devotedly attached, affectionate; *past p. p. of rt* रञ्ज् *with* अनु, 539.

अनुरक्तां *acc. sin. f. of* अनुरक्त *m. f. n. See last.*

अनुरागं *acc. sin. of* अनुराग *m.* affection, love, ardent attachment, *1st cl.* 103.

अनुरुध्यन्ति they cultivate, they addict themselves to; *3d pl. pres. par. of rt* रुध् *4th cl. with* अनु, 272.

अनुरूपम् *acc. sin. m. of* अनुरूप *m. f. n.* conformable, suitable, agreeable to.

अनुव्रजन्ती *nom. sin. f. of* अनुव्रजत् *m. f. n.* following, going after; *pres. p. par. of rt* व्रज् *with* अनु, 524.

अनुव्रतः *nom. sin. of* अनुव्रत *m. f. n.* devoted to, ardently attached to (as a husband to a wife; *from* अनु after, *and* व्रत *n.* a vow).

अनुव्रतम् *acc. sin. m. of* अनुव्रत. *See last.*

अनुव्रता *nom. sin. f. of* अनुव्रत *m. f. n. See last.*

अनुव्रतां *acc. sin. of* अनुव्रता *f.* a devoted, faithful wife.

अनुव्रताम् *acc. sin. f. of* अनुव्रत *m. f. n.* devotedly attached.

अनुशुश्रुम we have heard (traditionally or from sacred writ, श्रुति); *1st pl. perf. of rt* श्रु *with* अनु, 369.

अनुशोचति he or she bewails or grieves for; *3d sin. pres. of rt* शुच् *with* अनु, *1st cl.* 261, 594. *e.*

अनुशोचन्ति they grieve for. *See last.*

अनुशोचसि thou bewailest. *See last.*

अनुशोचितुम् to mourn for or after, to grieve for; *inf. of rt* शुच् *with* अनु.

अनुसंस्मरन् *nom. sin. m. of* अनुसंस्मरत् *m. f. n.* calling to mind, remembering; *pres. p. of rt* स्मृ *with* अनु *and* सम्, 524.

अनुस्मरन् *nom. sin. m. of* अनुस्मरत् *m. f. n.* calling to mind, remembering; *pres. p. of rt* स्मृ *with* अनु, 524.

अनुस्मृत्य calling to mind, remembering; *past ind. p. of rt* स्मृ *with* अनु, 560.

अनृतं *acc. sin. of* अनृत *n.* falsehood, untruth.

अनेकशः *for* अनेकशस् *ind.* in large quantities or numbers, in abundance, not in units; (*from* अनेक, *affix* शस्, 725.)

अनेन *ins. sin. n. of* इदं this, 224.

अन्तःपुरं *nom. sin. n.* the inner or female apartments, the harem.

अन्तःपुरसमीपस्थे TAT. OR DEP. COMP. 745; अन्तःपुर *cr.* the private apartments of a palace, समीप *cr.* neighbourhood, स्थे *loc. sin. n. of* स्थ *m. f. n.* situated, being; *agt. of rt* स्था to stand, *see* 580. *b.*

अन्तःपुरात् *abl. sin. of* अन्तःपुर *n.* *See last.*

अन्ततः *for* अन्ततस् *ind.* lastly, finally, 719.

अन्तरं *acc. sin. of* अन्तर *n.* an opportune moment, an occasion; *also*, the middle, the midst, intermediate space; 1*st cl.* 104.

अन्तरधीयत he or it disappeared or was changed, he vanished; 3*d sin. impf. of rt* धा *in pass. with* अन्तर्; *see* 465.

अन्तरप्रेप्सुर् TAT. OR DEP. COMP. 739; अन्तर *cr.* opportune moment, occasion, प्रेप्सुर् *nom. sin. of* प्रेप्सु *m. f. n.* anxious to obtain, desirous of obtaining; *des. adj. from rt* आप् *with* प्र; *see* 503, 82. VII, 824.

अन्तरात्मना *ins. sin. of* अन्तरात्मन् *m.* the soul, *lit.* the inner soul or spirit; (*from* अन्तर् *and* आत्मन् 6*th cl.* 146.)

अन्तरिक्षे *loc. sin. of* अन्तरिक्ष *n.* the sky, air, atmosphere, heaven, 1*st cl.* 104.

अन्तरीक्षगो *nom. sin. of* अन्तरीक्षग *m.* a bird, *lit.* sky-goer, 1*st cl.* 103; (*comp. of* अन्तरीक्ष *cr.* sky, *and* ग goer, *agt. of rt* गम् 580. *b.*)

अन्तरीक्षाद् *abl. sin. of* अन्तरीक्ष *n.* the sky, the heaven.

अन्तर्हितं *nom. sin. n. of* अन्तर्हित *m. f. n.* made to disappear, made to change, vanished; *past p. p. of rt* धा to hold, *with* अन्तर्, 533. *a.*

अन्तर्हिताः *nom. pl. m.* vanished. *See last.*

अन्तर्हिते *loc. sin. m.* *See last.*

अन्तर्हितो *nom. sin. m.* disappeared.

अन्तवन्त *nom. pl. m. of* अन्तवत् *m. f. n.* possessed of an end, finite, 140.

अन्तश् *for* अन्तर् (71. *b*) *ind.* within, between.

अन्तस् *nom. sin. of* अन्त *m.* the end.

अन्तिक *n.* presence, vicinity, 1*st cl.* 103.

अन्तिकम् *ind.* near; *governing the genitive case.*

अन्तिके near, close up to, into the presence of; *loc. sin. of* अन्तिक, *q. v.*

अन्तेन *ins. sin. of* अन्त *m.* end.

अन्नपानपरिच्छदाम् BAH. OR REL. COMP.; अन्न *cr.* food, पान *cr.* drink, beverage, परिच्छदाम् *acc. sin. f. from* परिच्छद *m.* dress, clothes, apparel, useful articles.

अन्नरसम् TAT. OR DEP. COMP. 743; अन्न *cr.* food, रसम् *acc. sin. of* रस *m.* taste, 1*st cl.* 103.

अन्नसंस्कारम् TAT. OR DEP. COMP. 743; अन्न *cr.* food, viands, संस्कारम् *acc. sin. of* संस्कार *m.* preparation. (Perfection in the art of dressing viands was one of the gifts bestowed by the gods on Nala at his marriage.)

अन्य *m. f. n.* other, another, the other, 236.

अन्यं *acc. sin. m. of* अन्य, *q. v.*

अन्यः *nom. sin. m. of* अन्य, *q. v.*

अन्यच् *for* अन्यत् *nom. sin. n.* other, another, 48.

अन्यज् *for* अन्यत् *nom. sin. n.* other, another, 48.

अन्यत् *nom. sin. n. of* अन्य other, another.

अन्यतमं *acc. sin. of* अन्यतम one or the other; (अन्यतम *is* one of many, *as opposed to* अन्यतर one of two, 236.)

अन्यत्र *ind.* elsewhere, in another place, 720.

अन्यथा *ind.* otherwise, 721.

अन्यद् *nom. or acc. sin. n. of* अन्य other, another.

अन्यन् *for* अन्यत् other, *nom. sin. n. of* अन्य other, another.

अन्यम् *acc. sin. m. of* अन्य *m. f. n.* other, another.

अन्या *nom. sin. f.* another woman, 236.

अन्याः *nom. pl. f. of* अन्य other, another.

अन्यान् *acc. pl. m. of* अन्य other, another.

अन्यानि *acc. pl. n. of* अन्य *m. f. n.* other, another.

अन्येन *ins. sin. m. of* अन्य other, another.

अन्येषु *loc. pl. of* अन्य other, another.

अन्यैर् *ins. pl. of* अन्य other, another.

अन्यैश् *ins. pl. m. of* अन्य other, another.

अन्यैस् *ins. pl. of* अन्य other, another.

अन्योन्यम् *acc. sin. of* अन्योन्य *m. f. n.* one another, 1*st cl.* 103.

अन्वगात् he or she followed; 3*d sin. aor. of rt* गा *with* अनु.

अन्वजानात् he consented, he permitted; 3*d sin. impf. of rt* ज्ञा *with* अनु, 9*th cl.* 688.

अन्वयात् he or she followed; 3*d sin. aor. of rt* इ to go, *with* अनु, *see* 645, 438. *e.*

अन्वास्त he performed; 3*d sin. impf. of rt* आस् *with* अनु, 2*d cl.* 317.

अन्वितः *nom. sin. of* अन्वित *m. f. n.* possessed of, labouring under, afflicted with.

अन्वेषणार्थं *ind.* for the sake of seeking after, *see* 760. *d*, 791.

अन्वेषती *nom. sin. f. of* अन्वेषत् *m. f. n.* seeking, looking for; *pres. p. par. of rt* एष् *with* अनु, 524.

अन्वेषतीम् *acc. sin. f.* *See last.*

अन्वेषन्तौ *nom. pl. m. of* अन्वेषत्. *See* अन्वेषती.

अन्वेषमाणा *nom. sin. f. of* अन्वेषमाण *m. f. n.* looking after, seeking for; *pres. p. átm. of rt* एष् *with* अनु, 1*st cl.* 526.

अन्वेषमाणाम् *acc. sin. f.* *See last.*

अन्वेषसि thou seekest, thou searchest for; 2*d sin. pres. of rt* एष् *with* अनु, 1*st cl.* 261.

अन्वेष्टारौ *nom. pl. m. of* अन्वेष्टृ *m. f. n.* a seeker, seeking for; *agt. of rt* इष् *with* अनु, 581.

अन्वेष्टुम् to seek for; *inf. of rt* इष् *with* अनु, 459.

अप *prep.* off, away, from.

अपकारताम् *acc. sin. of* अपकारता *f.* offence, wrong, injuriousness.

अपकृते *loc. sin. m. of* अपकृत *m. f. n.* injured; *past p. p. of rt* कृ *with* अप.

अपकृष्टेन *ins. sin. m. or n. of* अपकृष्ट *m. f. n.* abstracted, rubbed off, removed, distracted; *past p. p. of rt* कृष् *with* अप, 539.

अपकृष्य having taken away, having removed, having abstracted; *past ind. p. of rt* कृष् *with* अप, 559; अपकृष्य लज्जां having discarded shame.

अपक्रान्ते *loc. sin. of* अपक्रान्त *m. f. n.* departed, gone away; *past p. p. of rt* क्रम् *with* अप, 546.

अपरां *acc. sin. f. of* अपर other, another.

अपराङ्मुखाः with unaverted faces; *nom. pl. m. of* अपराङ्मुख *m. f. n.*; (*comp. of* अ not, *and* पराङ्मुख having the face पराच् turned away, 176. *b*, 43. *a.*)

अपराजित *voc. sin.* O unconquered one.

अपराजितम् *acc. sin. m. of* अपराजित *m. f. n.* unconquered, 726.

अपराणि *acc. sin. n. of* अपर *m. f. n.* other.

अपराद्धम् *nom. sin. n. of* अपराद्ध *m. f. n.* one who has given offence or has been guilty of a fault, offended against, (*governing a genitive at* Book XXIV. 12.)

अपराधं *acc. sin. of* अपराध *m.* fault, offence.

अपरिहार्ये *loc. sin. m. of* अपरिहार्य *m. f. n.* unavoidable, not to be shunned.

अपरे others, *nom. pl. m. of* अपर *m. f. n.* other, another, 238. *a.*

अपरेद्युः *for* अपरेद्युस् (63) *ind.* the following

day, the next day. In Book XIII. 35 this word is used as a substantive in the locative case.

अपश्चिमाम् *acc. sin. f. of* **अपश्चिम** having no termination, having no end; (*comp. of* **अ** 726, *and* **पश्चिम** behind, latter.)

अपश्यंस् *for* **अपश्यन्** they saw; 3*d pl. impf. of rt* **दृश्** 1*st cl.* 604, 53.

अपश्यच् *for* **अपश्यत्** he saw; 3*d sin. impf. of rt* **दृश्** 1*st cl.* 604, 48..

अपश्यत he or it saw; 3*d sin. impf. átm. of rt* **दृश्** 1*st cl.* 604.

अपश्यद् he or she saw; 3*d sin. impf. from rt* **दृश्** 1*st cl.* 604.

अपश्यन् *for* **अपश्यत्** he saw; 3*d sin. impf. of rt* **दृश्** 1*st cl.* 270, 604.

अपश्यन् *nom. sin. m. of* **अपश्यत्** *m. f. n.* not seeing; (*from* **अ** not, 726, *and* **पश्यत्** *pres. p. of rt* **दृश्** 524, 604.)

अपश्यन्ती *nom. sin. f. of* **अपश्यत्** *m. f. n.* not seeing; (*comp. of* **अ** not, 726, *and* **पश्यत्** *pres. p. of rt* **दृश्** 604, 524.)

अपश्यमाना *nom. sin. f.* not beholding; (*from* **अ** not, 726, *and* **पश्यमान** *m. f. n. pres. p. átm. of rt* **दृश्** 604, 526.)

अपहरन्ति they carry off; 3*d pl. pres. of rt* **हृ** *with* **अप**, 593.

अपहाय having abandoned or discarded; *past ind. p. of rt* **हा** *with* **अप**, 559.

अपहृतज्ञानो Bah. or Rel. comp. 766; **अपहृत** *cr.* robbed of, bereft of, **ज्ञानो** *nom. sin. m. from* **ज्ञान** *n.* sense, wisdom, *see* 108.

अपहृता *nom. sin. f. of* **अपहृत** *m. f. n.* carried away, carried off; *past p. p. of rt* **हृ** *with* **अप**, 532.

अपापचेतसम् Bah. or Rel. comp. 766; **अपाप** *cr.* sinless, blameless, **चेतसम्** *acc. sin. m. from* **चेतस्** *n.* mind, soul, 7*th cl.* 164. *a.*

अपाम् *gen. pl. of* **अप्** *f.* water, *see* 178. *b.*

अपाम्पतिः *nom. sin. m.* Varuṇa. *See next.*

अपाम्पतिर् the lord of waters, *i. e.* Varuṇa, Tat. or Dep. comp. 743. *c;* **अपाम्** *gen. pl. of* **अप्** water, 178. *b*, **पतिर्** *nom. sin. of* **पति** *m.* lord, 2*d cl.* 121.

अपावृतं *acc. sin. n. of* **अपावृत** *m. f. n.* opened.

अपि *ind.* even, also, though, although, assuredly.

अपिहिता *nom. sin. f. of* **अपिहित** *m. f. n.* (*also written* **पिहित**) covered, filled with; **वाष्पेण अपिहिता** bathed in tears, suffused with tears. **अपि** *is here a preposition before* **हित** *the pass. p. of rt* **धा** 533. *a.*

अपृच्छत् he or she asked; 3*d sin. impf. See next.*

अपृच्छन् they asked; 3*d pl. impf. of rt* **प्रच्छ्** 6*th cl.* 631.

अप्यश्वकुशलः *for* **अपि अश्वकुशलः**.

अप्रजः *nom. sin. m. of* **अप्रज** *m. f. n.* childless.

अप्रतिनन्दन्तम् not regarding, not heeding or welcoming; *acc. sin. m. of* **अप्रतिनन्दत्** *pres. p. of rt* **नन्द्** *with* **प्रति** *and prefix* **अ** (726), 524, 141.

अप्रतिमां *acc. sin. f. of* **अप्रतिम** *m. f. n.* incomparable, peerless, unequalled.

अप्रतिमेन *ins. sin. n. of* **अप्रतिम** *m. f. n. See last.*

अप्रतिमो *nom. sin. m. of* **अप्रतिम** *m. f. n.* unequalled, incomparable, without a peer, 1*st cl.* 103.

अप्रतीकारम् *acc. sin. m.* not retaliating, not defending (myself), unresisting; (**अ** not, **प्रतीकार** retaliation.)

अप्रमेयस्य *gen. sin. m. of* **अप्रमेय** *m. f. n.* immeasurable, infinite, incomparable, 726.

अप्रशस्तः *nom. sin. of* **अप्रशस्त** *m. f. n.* not good, worthless, accursed.

अप्राप्तकालो one whose time has not arrived, Bah. or Rel. comp. 767; **अप्राप्त** *cr.* not reached, **कालो** *nom. sin. m. of* **काल** time.

अप्सराः *nom. sin. of* अप्सरस् *f.* a celestial nymph of Svarga or Indra's heaven (163. *a*). The Apsarasas were the nymphs of Indra's heaven, produced at the churning of the ocean (see note under अमृतोपमां at p. 189). Their birth is thus described in the Rámáyaṇa:

'Then from the agitated deep upsprung
The legion of Apsarasas, so named,
That to the watery element they owed
Their being. Myriads were they born, and all
In vesture heavenly clad and heavenly gems.'

Wilson, Preface to Vikramorvaśí, p. 13.

अबध्यो *nom. sin. m. of* अबध्य *m. f. n.* not to be killed.

अबिभ्यत् he or she feared; 3*d sin. impf. irreg. for* अबिभेत् *of rt* भी 3*d cl.* 666, *see also* 859.

अबुद्धा unintentionally, unwittingly; *ins. sin. of* अबुद्धि *f.* absence of design; (*from* अ not, 726, *and* बुद्धि design, 112.)

अबुध्यत he or she perceived, she awoke; 3*d sin. impf. of rt* बुध् 4*th cl.* 614.

अब्भक्षैर् *for* अब्भक्षैस् *ins. pl. of* अब्भक्ष *m. f. n.* feeding on water; (*comp. of* अप् *cr.* water, 43, *and* भक्षैर् *ins. pl. of* भक्ष eating.)

अब्रवीः *for* अब्रवीस् thou saidest. *See* अब्रवीत्.

अब्रवीच् *for* अब्रवीत् *by* 48, *q. v.*

अब्रवीत् he or she spoke to, addressed; 3*d sin. impf. of rt* ब्रू 2*d cl.* 314, 649.

अब्रवीन् *for* अब्रवीत्, *q. v.*

अब्रुवन् they said, they addressed; 3*d pl. impf. of rt* ब्रू 314, 649.

अब्रुवाणा *nom. sin. f.* not speaking; (*from* अ not, 726, *and* ब्रुवाण, *q. v.*)

अभवंस् *for* अभवन् *by* 53.

अभवच् *for* अभवत्. *See next.*

अभवत् he was, it was; 3*d sin. impf. of rt* भू 1*st cl.* 585.

अभवद् *for* अभवत्, *q. v.*

अभवन् they were; 3*d pl. impf. of rt* भू 585.

अभावो *nom. sin. m.* non-existence.

अभाषत he or she said, he spoke; 3*d sin. impf. átm. of rt* भाष् 1*st cl.* 261.

अभि *prep.* to, towards, over, upon.

अभिगच्छति he goes towards, he returns to; 3*d sin. pres.* *See* अभिजग्मुस्.

अभिगम्य having approached; *past ind. p. of rt* गम् *with* अभि, 559, 602.

अभिचरामि I transgress, I sin against; 1*st sin. pres. of rt* चर् *with* अभि.

अभिजग्मुस् they approached, they went towards, they went; 3*d pl. perf. of rt* गम् *with prep.* अभि, 602, 376.

अभिजज्ञे he knew, he was aware; 3*d sin. perf. átm. of rt* ज्ञा *with* अभि, 688.

अभिजानामि I know; 1*st sin. pres. of rt* ज्ञा *with* अभि, 9*th cl.* 688.

अभिजानीयाम् I may recognise; 1*st sin. pot. See last.*

अभिजानीष्व understand thou, know thou; 2*d sin. imp. átm.* *See last.*

अभिज्ञाय having recognised; *past ind. p.*

अभिद्रुत्य having ran towards; *past ind. p. of rt* द्रु *with* अभि, 560.

अभिधाव hasten thou here, *lit.* run thou towards; 2*d sin. imp. of rt* धाव् *with* अभि, 1*st cl.* 261.

अभिधास्यामि I will address, I will speak to; I will relate; 1*st sin.* 2*d fut. of rt* धा *with* अभि, 664.

अभिनन्दति he attends to, he heeds; 3*d sin. pres. of rt* नन्द् *with* अभि, 1*st cl.* 261.

अभिनन्द्य having gladdened; *past ind. p. of rt* नन्द् *in caus. with* अभि, 566.

अभिप्रायं *acc. sin. of* अभिप्राय *m.* wish, intention.

अभिप्रायस् *nom. sin.* intention. *See last.*

अभिभवति he or it prevails over, he or it overcomes; 3*d sin. pres. of rt* भू *with* अभि.

अभिभाषन्तो *nom. pl. m. of* अभिभाषत् *m. f. n.* speaking to, calling to; *pres. p. par. of rt* भाष् *with* अभि, 524.

अभिभाषिणी *nom. sin. f.* addressing, 1*st cl.* 105; *agt. from* भाष् *with* अभि, 582. *a.*

अभिभाषे I address; 1*st sin. pres. átm. of rt* भाष् *with* अभि, 1*st cl.* 261.

अभिमुखो *nom. sin. m. of* अभिमुख *m. f. n.* facing, opposite, in front, before one's face.

अभिरूपम् *acc. sin. m. of* अभिरूप *m. f. n.* beautiful.

अभिवर्धते increases; 3*d sin. pres. átm. of rt* वृध् *with* अभि, 1*st cl.* 261.

अभिवादकः *nom. sin. m.* a saluter, one who offers salutation.

अभिवादयामास he saluted; 3*d sin. perf. of rt* वद् *in caus. with* अभि, 490.

अभिवाद्य having saluted; *past ind. p. of rt* वद् *in caus. with* अभि, 566.

अभिवीक्ष्य having seen, having observed; *past ind. p. of rt* ईक्ष् *with* अभि *and* वि, 559.

अभिव्यक्तं *ind.* plainly, manifestly, 713.

अभिशापाद् *abl. sin. of* अभिशाप *m.* curse, imprecation, anathema, 1*st cl.* 103.

अभिसंवृता *nom. sin. f. of* अभिसंवृत *m. f. n.* covered, clothed; *past p. p. of rt* वृ *with* अभि *and* सं.

अभिससार he came up, (he came to her assistance;) 3*d sin. perf. of rt* सृ *with* अभि, 364.

अभिहतः *nom. sin. m. of* अभिहत *m. f. n.* smitten, stricken; *past p. p. of rt* हन् *with* अभि, 545.

अभीक्ष्णम् *ind.* repeatedly, again and again.

अभीप्सवः *nom. pl. of* अभीप्सु *m. f. n.* desirous of obtaining, 3*d cl.* 110; *formed from des. of rt* आप्, *see* 503, 82. VII.

अभूद् he, she or it was, there was, there arose; 3*d sin. aor. of rt* भू 585.

अभ्यगच्छत् he approached, he went to; 3*d sin. impf. of rt* गम् *with* अभि, 602.

अभ्यगच्छद् *for* अभ्यगच्छत् he proceeded to.

अभ्यगात् he approached; 3*d sin. aor. of rt* गा *or of rt* इ *with* अभि, *see* 438. *e.*

अभ्यजानात् he or she recognised; 3*d sin. impf. of rt* ज्ञा *with* अभि, 9*th cl.* 360, 688.

अभ्यधिकं *acc. sin. n. of* अभ्यधिक *m. f. n.* greater, superior. *See next.*

अभ्यधिको *nom. sin. m. of* अभ्यधिक *m. f. n.* greater, superior, (*governing abl. at* Book XI. 16, *and ins. at* Book XXI. 14.)

अभ्यनन्दत he saluted, he congratulated; 3*d sin. impf. átm. of rt* नन्द् *with* अभि, 1*st cl.* 261.

अभ्यनुज्ञाता *nom. sin. f. of* अभ्यनुज्ञात *m. f. n.* permitted; *past p. p. of rt* ज्ञा *with* अनु *and* अभि.

अभ्यपूजयन् they worshipped; 3*d pl. impf. of rt* पूज् *with* अभि, 10*th cl.* 283.

अभ्यभाषत he addressed, he spoke to, he replied; 3*d sin. impf. átm. of rt* भाष् *with* अभि, 1*st cl.* 261.

अभ्यभाषन्त they addressed; 3*d pl. impf. átm. See last.*

अभ्ययात् he went to; 3*d sin. impf. of rt* या *with* अभि (34), 2*d cl.* 644.

अभ्यसूयन्ति they abuse, they speak angrily or contemptuously; 3*d pl. pres. of* असूय *with* अभि, *nominal verb from* असूया detraction; *see* 519. *a.*

अभ्यागता *nom. sin. f. of* अभ्यागत *m. f. n.* come to; *past p. p. of rt* गम् *with* आ *and* अभि, 545.

अभ्यागताम् *acc. sin. f. of* अभ्यागत *m. f. n.* approached, arrived; *past p. p. of rt* गम् *with* आ *and* अभि, 545.

अभ्यासपरिवर्तिनीम् *acc. sin. f.* wandering about or near; (*from* अभ्यास *cr.* near, *and* परिवर्तिनीम् *from* परिवर्तिन् *m. f. n.* going round.)

अभ्येति approaches, comes towards; 3*d sin. pres. of rt* इ *with* अभि, 2*d cl.* 645.

अभ्येत्य having approached, having come to; *past ind. p. of rt* इ *with* आ *and* अभि, 560.

अभ्रेण *ins. sin. of* अभ्र *n.* a cloud.

अभ्रेषु *loc. pl. of* अभ्र *n.* a cloud.

अमण्डिताम् *acc. sin. f. of* **अमण्डित** *m. f. n.* unadorned.

अमनुष्यनिषेविते TAT. OR DEP. COMP. 740; **अ** not, 726, **मनुष्य** *cr.* men, **निषेविते** *loc. sin. n. of* **निषेवित** *m. f. n.* inhabited.

अमन्यत he or she thought; 3*d sin. impf. átm. of rt* **मन्** 617.

अमरप्रख्यम् *acc. sin. m.* like an immortal; (*comp. of* **अमर** *cr.* immortal, *and* **प्रख्य** *m. f. n.* like, 777.)

अमरप्रभे O beautiful as an immortal, ANOM. COMP. 777; **अमर** *cr.* immortal, **प्रभे** *voc. sin. of* **प्रभा** *f.* beauty, lustre, 1*st cl.* 105.

अमरवद् *for* **अमरवत्** like an immortal; (*comp. of* **अमर** immortal, *and affix* **वत्** 724.)

अमरान् *acc. pl. of* **अमर** *m. f. n.* immortal, 1*st cl.* 103.

अमरोत्तमाः TAT. OR DEP. COMP. 743. *b*; **अमर** *cr.* immortal, **उत्तमाः** *nom. pl. m. of* **उत्तम** best, 1*st cl.* 103; **अमर + उत्तम = अमरोत्तम** *by* 32.

अमरोपम *voc. sin. m.* O thou like the immortals; (*from* **अमर** *cr.* immortal, *and* **उपम** like, 777.)

अमरोपमः *nom. sin. m. See last.*

अमर्षणः *nom. sin. m. of* **अमर्षण** *m. f. n.* impetuous, impatient, intolerant.

अमात्यान् *acc. pl. of* **अमात्य** *m.* a minister, 1*st cl.* 103.

अमानुषम् *acc. sin. m. or n. of* **अमानुष** *m. f. n.* not human; (*comp. of* **अ** not, 726, *and* **मानुष**, *q. v.*)

अमार्जिताम् *acc. sin. f. of* **अमार्जित** *m. f. n.* uncleansed, unwashed; (*comp. of* **अ** not, 726, *and* **मार्जित** *past p. p. of rt* **मृज्** *or* **मार्ज्** 549.)

अमित्रगणसूदनम् TAT. OR DEP. COMP. 745; **अमित्र** *cr.* an enemy, **गण** *cr.* a host, **सूदनम्** *acc. sin. m. of* **सूदन** *m.* a destroyer, 582. *c.*

अमित्रघातिनः TAT. OR DEP. COMP. 743; **अमित्र** *cr.* an enemy, **घातिनः** *gen. sin. m. of* **घातिन्** *m. f. n.* a slayer, killer, 6*th cl.* 159.

अमृतत्वाय *dat. sin. of* **अमृतत्व** *n.* immortality.

अमृतोपमां ANOM. COMP. 777; **अमृत** *cr.* the beverage or food of immortality, nectar or ambrosia, **उपमां** *acc. sin. f. of* **उपम** *m. f. n.* like. The following is the account of the production of the **अमृत** in the Vishṇu Puráṇa (p. 74, &c.): 'The gods (Suras) discomfited by the Daityas fled to Vishṇu for refuge. He addressed them, and said, "I will restore your strength. Let all the gods, associated with the Asuras (or Daityas, see note under **दैत्य**, &c.), cast medicinal herbs into the sea of milk, and then taking the mountain Maṇḍara for the churning-stick, the serpent Vásuki for the rope, churn the ocean for ambrosia. To secure the aid of the Daityas you must make peace with them, and promise them an equal portion." The gods, after collecting the herbs and casting them into the sea, took the mountain Maṇḍara for the staff, the serpent Vásuki for the cord, and commenced churning for the amṛita. The gods were stationed at the tail of the serpent and the Daityas at the head. In the midst of the sea, Vishṇu himself, in the form of a tortoise, served as a pivot for the mountain as it whirled round. From the ocean thus churned came forth Dhanvantari (the physician of the gods) robed in white, bearing in his hand the cup of amṛita. The gods quaffed the nectar, and receiving new vigour defeated the Daityas. The nectar and ambrosia thus produced was preserved in the moon. Accumulated there it is distilled by the lunar rays, and serves the gods and pitris (progenitors) for food.'

अमृष्यमाणा *for* **अमृष्यमाणास्** *nom. pl. of* **अमृष्यमाण** *m. f. n.* not enduring, not bearing or tolerating; *pres. p. átm. of rt* मृष् *4th cl.* 526. *a.*

अमेयात्मा Bah. or Rel. comp. 766; अमेय *cr.* immeasurable, immense, आत्मा *nom. sin. of* आत्मन् *m.* mind, soul, 146.

अयं this, he; *nom. sin. of* इदं, *q. v.*

अयं स Here he (is)! 224, 220. स *for* सस् 67.

अयोध्यां *acc. sin. of* अयोध्या *f.* the city Ayodhyá (*i. e.* the Invincible), the modern Oude. This city is celebrated in all Hindú poetry as the ancient capital of Ráma-ćandra, founded by Ikshváku, the first king of the solar dynasty. In the Rámáyaṇa (Book I. Chap. V) it is thus described: 'On the banks of the Sarayú is a large country called Kośala, gay and happy, abounding with cattle, corn, and wealth. In that country was a famous city called Ayodhyá, built formerly by Manu, the lord of men. A great city, twelve yojanas in extent, the houses of which stood in triple and long-extended rows. It was rich, and perpetually adorned with new improvements. The streets were well-disposed and well-watered. It was filled with merchants of various descriptions, and adorned with abundance of jewels; crowded with houses, beautified with gardens and groves of mango-trees, surrounded by a deep and impregnable moat, and completely furnished with arms.' In the S'akuntalá (Act VI) Ayodhyá is called Sáketaka.

अयोध्याधिपतिः *nom. sin. m.* the sovereign of Ayodhyá; (*comp. of* अयोध्या *and* अधिपति, *q. v.*, 743.)

अयोध्यावासिनं *acc. sin. m.* inhabiting Ayodhyá; (*comp. of* अयोध्या *and* वासिन् dwelling in, inhabitant, 582. *a.*)

अरजः *acc. sin. n. of* अरजस् *m. f. n.* free from dust, clean, pure, 164. *a*; (*from* अ 726, *and* रजस् dust.)

अरञ्जयत् he conciliated (the affections of); *3d sin. impf. of rt* रञ्ज् *in caus.* 479.

अरण्यं *nom. or acc. sin. of* अरण्य *n.* a forest, a wood.

अरण्यनृपते Tat. or Dep. comp. 743; अरण्य *cr.* forest, नृपते *voc. sin. of* नृपति *m.* a king, *2d cl.* 110.

अरण्यराट् Tat. or Dep. comp. 743; अरण्य *cr.* forest, राट् *nom. sin. of* राज् *m.* a king, *see* 176. *e.*

अरण्यस्य *gen. sin. of* अरण्य *n.* a forest.

अरण्यस्यास्य *for* अरण्यस्य अस्य *by* 31.

अरण्यानि *acc. pl. of* अरण्य *n.* a forest.

अरण्ये *loc. sin. of* अरण्य *n.* a forest, a wood.

अरालपक्ष्मनयनां Complex comp. 771; अराल *cr.* curved, पक्ष्म *cr.* eye-lash, नयनां *acc. sin. f. from* नयन *n.* the eye; *see* 108.

अरिकर्षण O thou tamer of thy enemies, Tat. or Dep. comp. 743; अरि *cr.* an enemy, कर्षण *voc. sin. of* कर्षण *m.* harasser, annoyer, *1st cl.* 103.

अरिन्दम *voc. sin. m.* *See next.*

अरिन्दमं *acc. sin. of* अरिन्दम *m.* the conqueror of (his) foes; *see* 580. *a*, 739. *c.*

अरिमर्दनं Tat. or Dep. comp. 743; अरि *cr.* an enemy, मर्दनं *acc. sin. of* मर्दन *m.* a destroyer, a crusher, *agt. of rt* मृद् 582. *c.*

अरिमर्दनः *nom. sin. m.* *See last.*

अरिसूदन *voc. sin. m.* O destroyer of (thy) foes; (अरि an enemy, सूदन destroying.)

अरिहा *nom. sin. m.* slayer of (his) foes; (*comp. of* अरि *cr.* an enemy, *and* हा *nom. sin. of* हन् a killer, *6th cl.* 157.)

अर्केण *ins. sin. of* अर्क *m.* the sun, *1st cl.* 103.

अर्चयामास he or she honoured; *3d sin. perf. of rt* अर्च् *10th cl.* 283.

अर्चयित्वा having honoured; *past ind. p. of rt* अर्च् *10th cl.* 558.

अर्चितानि *nom. pl. n. of* अर्चित *m. f. n.* honoured; *past p. p. of rt* अर्च् 538.

अर्जितम् *nom. sin. n. of* अर्जित *m. f. n.* acquired, earned; *past p. p. of rt* अर्ज् 538.

अर्जुनारिष्टसञ्छन्नं COMPLEX COMP. 771; अर्जुन the Arjuna, a kind of tree (Pentaptera Arjuna), अरिष्ट the Arishṭa or Ním-tree, सञ्छन्नं *acc. sin. n. of* सञ्छन्न *m. f. n.* covered, shrouded; *past p. p. of rt* छद् *with* सं, 540.

अर्थं *ind.* for the sake of, *see* अर्थे.

अर्थकामः *nom. sin. m.* desirous of riches; (*comp. of* अर्थ wealth, *and* काम wishing for.)

अर्थकामांस् *for* अर्थकामान् (53), *acc. pl. m. See last.*

अर्थकृच्छ्रेषु *loc. pl. n.* in difficult matters; (*comp. of* अर्थ *cr.* thing, matter, *and* कृच्छ्र *n.* difficulty.)

अर्थस् *nom. sin. m.* use, profit, advantage.

अर्थाय *ind.* for the sake of, for the use of. *The dative case is here used adverbially; but* अर्थं *and* अर्थे *are more common, see* 731, 917.

अर्थितव्यं *nom. sin. n. of* अर्थितव्य *m. f. n.* to be sought; *fut. pass. p. of rt* अर्थ 569.

अर्थे *loc. sin. of* अर्थ *m.* thing, matter.

अर्थे *ind.* for the sake of, (*governing genitive case or preceded by crude.*)

अर्थेन *ins. sin. of* अर्थ *m.* matter, thing.

अर्थो *for* अर्थस् *nom. sin. m.* matter, thing.

अर्दितं *acc. sin. m. of* अर्दित *m. f. n.* afflicted; *past p. p. of rt* अर्द् 538.

अर्धं *nom. or acc. sin. of* अर्ध *n.* half.

अर्धरात्रसमये TAT. OR DEP. COMP. 743; अर्धरात्र *cr.* midnight, *lit.* half-night, *see* 778, समये *loc. sin. of* समय *m.* time.

अर्धवस्त्रसंवीताम् COMPLEX COMP. 771; अर्ध *cr.* half, वस्त्र *cr.* garment, संवीताम् *acc. sin. f. of* संवीत *m. f. n.* clothed, enveloped; *past p. p. of* व्ये *with* सं, 535.

अर्धसञ्जातशस्या BAH. OR REL. COMP. 767; अर्ध *cr.* half, सञ्जात produced, grown, शस्या *nom. sin. f. from* शस्य *n.* corn, fruit, 108.

अर्धेन *ins. sin. of* अर्ध *n.* half, 1*st cl.* 104.

अर्हणां *acc. sin. of* अर्हणा *f.* honour.

अर्हति he is worthy of, he deserves, he or she deigns (*Lat.* dignus) or condescends; 3*d sin. pres. of rt* अर्ह् 1*st cl. In* Book XIV. 7. भवान् अर्हति *must be translated,* let your honour deign.

अर्हथ deign ye, be ye willing; 2*d pl. pres. of rt* अर्ह्.

अर्हसि do thou deign; 2*d sin. pres.* 608, 870.

अर्हसीत्येव *for* अर्हसि इति एव *by* 31. *a*, 34.

अर्हा *for* अर्हास् *nom. pl. of* अर्ह worthy, right, proper.

अलक्षितः *nom. sin. m. of* अलक्षित *m. f. n.* unobserved, unseen, unperceived; (*comp. of* अ not, 726, *and* लक्षित, *q. v.*)

अल्पकार्यं *nom. sin. n.* a small matter; (*from* अल्प small, *and* कार्य, *q. v.*)

अल्पपरीवारो BAH. OR REL. COMP. 766; अल्प *cr.* small, परीवारो *nom. sin. m. of* परीवार *m.* retinue, train.

अल्पपुण्येन BAH. OR REL. COMP. 761; अल्प *cr.* small, पुण्येन *ins. sin. m. from* पुण्य *n.* virtue, religious merit.

अल्पबलप्राणा *for* अल्पबलप्राणास् COMPLEX COMP. 771; अल्प *cr.* little, बल *cr.* strength, प्राणास् *nom. pl. m. of* प्राण *m.* breath.

अल्पभाग्येन BAH. OR REL. COMP. 761; अल्प *cr.* little, भाग्येन *ins. sin. m. from* भाग्य *n.* fortune, luck, 108.

अव *prep.* down, off, away, from.

अवकर्तनम् *acc. sin. of* अवकर्तन *n.* cutting off.

अवकृष्टस् *nom. sin. m. of* अवकृष्ट *m. f. n.* dragged, drawn along, dragged down; *past p. p. of rt* कृष् *with* अव, 539.

अवकृष्यते he is drawn back or dragged down; 3*d sin. pres. pass. of rt* कृष् *with* अव, 463.

अवगच्छध्वं know ye; 2*d pl. imp. átm. of rt* गम् *with* अव, 1*st cl.* 602.

अवतीर्य having descended, having alighted; *past ind. p. of rt* तॄ *with* अव, 561.

अवन्तीम् *acc. sin. of* अवन्ती *f.* Avantí, name of a city, the modern Oujein; *also called* Ujjayiní, Vis'álá, and Pushpa-karandiní. This city is noticed in the Megha-dúta, verses 28 and 31:

> 'Behold the city whose immortal fame
> Glows in Avantí's or Visálá's name.'

अवमुच्य having unloosed, having unharnessed; *past ind. p. of rt* मुच् *with* अव.

अवशिष्टं *nom. sin. n. of* अवशिष्ट *m. f. n.* left; *past p. p. of rt* शिष् *with* अव, 672.

अवश्यम् *ind.* certainly.

अवसं I dwelt; *1st sin. impf. of rt* वस् *1st cl.* 607.

अवसंस् *for* अवसन् (53), *3d pl. impf.* they dwelt. *See* अवसत्.

अवसक्ता *nom. sin. f. of* अवसक्त *m. f. n.* fixed; *past p. p. of rt* सञ्ज् to adhere, *with* अव, 597. *a.*

अवसच् *for* अवसत् *by* 48, *q. v.*

अवसत् he dwelt; *3d sin. impf. of rt* वस् *1st cl.* 607.

अवसद् *for* अवसत् he dwelt; *3d sin. impf. of rt* वस्.

अवसीदति he or she pines away, wastes away or sinks; *3d sin. pres. of rt* सद् *with* अव, *1st cl.* 270, 599. *a.*

अवसृजामि I concede, I grant, I bestow; *1st sin. pres. of rt* सृज् *with* अव, 625.

अवस्त्रतां *acc. sin. of* अवस्त्रता *f.* state of being without a garment, nakedness; (*from* अ not, 726, *and* वस्त्रता *abstract noun,* 80. XXIII.)

अवस्थातुं to stand; *inf. of rt* स्था *with* अव.

अवस्थाप्य having stopped, having made to stand still; *past ind. p. of rt* स्था *in caus. with* अव, 483, 559.

अवस्थितः *nom. sin. of* अवस्थित *m. f. n.* standing, arrayed, drawn up in array; *past p. p. of rt* स्था *with* अव, 533, 896. *a.*

अवस्थिता *for* अवस्थितास् *nom. pl. m. See* अवस्थितः.

अवस्थिताः *nom. pl. m. See* अवस्थितः.

अवस्थितान् *acc. pl. m. See* अवस्थितः.

अवाप he obtained; *3d sin. perf. of rt* आप् *with* अव, 364. *a.*

अवाप्य having obtained; *past ind. p. of rt* आप् *with* अव.

अवाप्स्यसि thou wilt obtain; *2d sin. 2d fut. of rt* आप् *with* अव, 681.

अवारयत् he prevented; *3d sin. impf. of rt* वृ *in caus.* 481.

अविक्षताः *nom. pl. m. of* अविक्षत *m. f. n.* uninjured, unhurt; (*comp. of* अ not, 726, *and* विक्षत hurt, injured; *past p. p. of rt* क्षण् *with* वि, 684, 685, 545.)

अविनाशिनं *acc. sin. m. of* अविनाशिन् indestructible.

अविन्दत he or she obtained, he or she found; *3d sin. impf. átm. of rt* विन्द् *or* विद् *6th cl.* 281.

अविशङ्केन without doubting, without hesitation; *ins. sin. of* अविशङ्क, *used adverbially,* (अ *prefixed to* विशङ्क 726.)

अवेक्षिताः *nom. pl. m. of* अवेक्षित *m. f. n.* seen, looked upon; *past p. p. of rt* ईक्ष् *with* अव, 538.

अवेक्षितुम् to consider; *inf. of rt* ईक्ष् *with* अव, 459.

अवेक्ष्य having considered, having regarded; *past ind. p. of rt* ईक्ष् *with* अव.

अवैमि I know, I trow; *1st sin. pres. of rt* इ *with* अव, 311. *a.*

अव्यक्तो *nom. sin. m. of* अव्यक्त *m. f. n.* imperceptible, unperceived.

अव्यग्रं *nom. sin. n. of* अव्यग्र *m. f. n.* undisturbed.

अव्ययं *acc. sin. n. of* अव्यय *m. f. n.* imperishable, eternal, everlasting; (*comp. of* अ not, 726, *and* व्यय decay.)

अव्ययस्य *gen. sin. of* अव्यय *m. f. n.* imperishable, immutable, eternal.

अव्ययां *acc. sin. f. of* अव्यय imperishable.

अशकत् he was able; *3d sin. aor. of rt* शक् 679.

अशक्नुवन् not being able; (*comp. of* **अ** not, *and* **शक्नुवन्** *nom. sin. m. of* **शक्नुवत्** *pres. p. of rt* **शक्** *5th cl.* 679, 524.)

अशङ्किता *nom. sin. f. of* **अशङ्कित** *m. f. n.* fearless.

अशपत् he cursed; 3*d sin. impf. of rt* **शप्** 1*st cl.* 261.

अशस्त्रं *acc. sin. m. of* **अशस्त्र** unarmed, disarmed; (**अ** not, **शस्त्र** weapon.)

अशुभं *acc. sin. of* **अशुभ** *n.* sin, evil, wickedness; (*comp. of* **अ** 726, *and* **शुभ** good.)

अशुभकर्मणः Bah. or Rel. comp. 761; **अशुभ** *cr.* not good, evil, unhappy, **कर्मणः** *gen. sin. m. from* **कर्मन्** *n.* 152.

अशेषतः *for* **अशेषतस्** *ind.* without reserve, fully; (**अ** not, 726, **शेष** remainder, *and* **तस्** *affix,* 719.)

अशेषेण *ind.* entirely, wholly, without reserve; (*comp. of* **अ** not, 726, *and* **शेष** remainder, *see* 714.)

अशोक *voc. sin.* O Aśoka. This tree (supposed to be named Aśoka from *a* 'not' and *śoka* 'sorrow') is one of the most beautiful of Indian trees. Sir W. Jones observes, that 'the vegetable world scarcely exhibits a richer sight than an Aśoka-tree in full bloom. It is about as high as an ordinary cherry-tree. The flowers are very large, and beautifully diversified with tints of orange-scarlet, of pale yellow, and of bright orange, which form a variety of shades according to the age of the blossom.' The Aśoka is sacred to Śiva, and is planted near his temples. It grows abundantly in Ceylon. In Hindú poetry despairing lovers very commonly address objects of nature, clouds, elephants, and birds, on the subject of their lost or absent mistresses. See the Megha-dúta, the 4th Act of the Vikramorvaśí, and the 9th Act of the Málati Mádhava.

अशोकं *acc. sin. of* **अशोक** *m.* the Aśoka-tree.

अशोकः *nom. sin. m.* the Aśoka-tree.

अशोकतरुं *acc. sin. of* **अशोकतरु** *m.* an Aśoka-tree. *See note under* **अशोक.**

अशोकनग *voc. sin. m.* O Aśoka-tree; (*comp. of* **अशोक** *cr. and* **नग** *m.* a tree.)

अशोकवृक्षं *acc. sin. m.* the Aśoka-tree; (*comp. of* **अशोक** *and* **वृक्ष** *m.* a tree.)

अशोचत् he or she grieved; 3*d sin. impf. of rt* **शुच्** 1*st cl.* 261.

अशोच्यान् *acc. pl. m. of* **अशोच्य** *m. f. n.* not to be mourned; (**अ** not, *and* **शोच्य.**)

अशोभयन्त they adorned; 3*d pl. impf. átm. of rt* **शुभ्** *in caus.* 481.

अशोष्य *for* **अशोष्यस्** *nom. sin. m. of* **अशोष्य** *m. f. n.* not to be dried.

अश्रुपरिपूर्णाक्षीं Complex comp. 771; **अश्रु** *cr.* tears, **परिपूर्ण** *cr.* filled, **अक्षीं** *acc. sin. f. from* **अक्ष** *m.* the eye, *see* 778.

अश्रुपरिप्लुतः Tat. or Dep. comp. 740; **अश्रु** *cr.* tears, **परिप्लुतः** *nom. sin. m.* bathed, overflowed.

अश्रुपूर्णाक्षी Bah. or Rel. comp. 767; **अश्रु** *cr.* tears, **पूर्ण** *cr.* filled with, **अक्षी** *nom. sin. f. from* **अक्ष** *for* **अक्षि** *n.* the eye, 778.

अश्रुपूर्णे Tat. or Dep. comp. 740; **अश्रु** *cr.* tears, **पूर्णे** *nom. du. n. of* **पूर्ण** *m. f. n.* full, filled with.

अश्वकुशलः *nom. sin. m.* skilled in horses; (*from* **अश्व** a horse, *and* **कुशल** *m. f. n.* skilful.)

अश्वकोविदः *for* **अश्वकोविदस्** Tat. or Dep. comp. 744; **अश्व** *cr.* a horse, **कोविदः** *nom. of* **कोविद** *m. f. n.* skilled.

अश्वमेधादिभिर् Bah. or Rel. comp. 764; **अश्वमेध** *cr.* the Aśva-medha or horse-sacrifice, *see below,* **आदिभिर्** *ins. pl. of* **आदि** beginning with, et cetera.

अश्वमेधेन *ins. sin. of* **अश्वमेध** *m.* the Aśva-medha or horse-sacrifice. This sacrifice is described in the Puráṇas as one of the highest order, insomuch that if it be performed a hundred times it elevates the sacrificer to the throne of Svarga, and thereby effects the deposal of Indra himself. In the Ṛig-veda, however, the object of this rite seems to be nothing more than the acquiring of wealth and posterity; and even in the Rámáyaṇa it is merely performed by king Daśaratha as the means of obtaining a son. From the Ṛig-veda it appears that the horse was immolated, and afterwards cut up into fragments, part of which were eaten by the assisting priests, and part offered as burnt-offering to the gods. The rite as described in the Puráṇas has been introduced by Southey into 'the Curse of Keháma.'

अश्वशालाम् *acc. sin. f.* a stable; (*comp. of* **अश्व** *cr.* a horse, *and* **शाला** *f.* a house.)

अश्वहृदयं *nom. and acc. sin. n.* knowledge of horses.

अश्वहृदयेन *ins. sin. n.* (in exchange) with or for skill in horses; (*comp. of* **अश्व** *cr.* horses, *and* **हृदय** *n.* knowledge, skill.)

अश्वांश्चेमान् *for* **अश्वान् च इमान्** *by* 53, 32.

अश्वांस् *for* **अश्वान्**, *q. v.*

अश्वाध्यक्षो TAT. OR DEP. COMP. 743; **अश्व** *cr.* horses. **अध्यक्षो** *nom. sin. m.* a master, superintendent, overseer, inspector.

अश्वान् *acc. pl. of* **अश्व** *m.* a horse, 1*st cl.* 103.

अश्वानां *gen. pl. of* **अश्व** *m.* a horse, 103.

अश्विनोः *gen. du. of* **अश्विन्** *declined in du.* the twin sons of the Sun by his wife Saññjñá, who was transformed to a mare (**अश्विनी**). They are endowed with perpetual youth and beauty, and are the physicians of the gods. Professor Wilson (Introduction to the Ṛig-veda, p. xxxv) says, 'Demigods who are more frequently than any other, except the Maruts, the object of laudation in the Veda, are the two Aśvins, the sons of the Sun according to later mythology, but of whose origin we have no such legend in the Veda. They are said, in one place, to have the sea (Sindhu) for their mother, but this is explained to intimate their identity, as affirmed by some authorities, with the sun and moon, which rise apparently out of the ocean. They are called Dasras—destroyers either of foes or diseases, for they are the physicians of the gods. They are also called Násatyas—in whom there is no untruth. They are represented as ever young, handsome, travelling in a three-wheeled and triangular car drawn by asses, and as mixing themselves up with a variety of human transactions, bestowing benefits upon their worshippers, enabling them to foil their enemies, assisting them in their need, and extricating them from difficulty and danger. Their business seems to be more on earth than in heaven, and they belong by their exploits more to heroic than to celestial mythology. They are, however, connected in various passages with the radiance of the sun, and are said to be precursors of dawn, at which season they ought to be worshipped with libations of Soma-juice.'

अश्विनौ *nom. du. m. See last.*

अश्वैर् *ins. pl. of* **अश्व** *m.* a horse.

अष्टमः *nom. sin. of* **अष्टम** *m. f. n.* eighth, 209.

अष्टादशः *nom. sin. m.* eighteenth, 210.

अष्टौ *acc. of* **अष्टन्** eight, *see* 205.

असंवीतः imperfectly covered, scarcely covered; (**अ** not, 726, *and* **संवीत** *m. f. n.* covered; *past p. p. of rt* **व्ये** 535.)

असंशयं *ind.* without doubt.

असंस्कृतम् *nom. sin. n. of* **असंस्कृत** *m. f. n.* unadorned.

असकृद् *for* **असकृत्** *ind.* more than once, repeatedly, (*lit.* not once.)

असकृन् *for* **असकृत्** *ind.* more than once.

असंख्येयगुणं *acc. sin. m. See next.*

असंख्येयगुणो Bah. or Rel. comp. 761; असंख्येय cr. innumerable, unnumbered, गुणो nom. sin. m. virtue, good quality.

असतो gen. sin. of असत् m. f. n. not existing; pres. p. of rt अस् with अ prefixed.

असत्कृतं acc. sin. n. evil, evil action; (comp. of अ not, 726, सत् good, and कृत done.)

असत्कृता nom. sin. f. of असत्कृत m. f. n. not well-treated, not hospitably entertained; (comp. of अ not, 726, and सत्कृत, q. v.)

असत्यं acc. sin. of असत्य n. falsehood, untruth.

असपत्नम् acc. sin. n. without a rival, without an adversary; (अ not, सपत्न a rival.)

असहाया nom. sin. f. of असहाय m. f. n. unattended, without a companion; (comp. of अ 726, and सहाय a companion.)

असावद्य for असौ अद्य by 37.

असि thou art; 2d sin. pres. of rt अस् 584.

असितकेशान्तां Bah. or Rel. comp. 761; असित cr. black, केशान्तां acc. sin. f. from केशान्त m. (lit. the end of the hair), the hair, the locks, 108.

असितेक्षणा Bah. or Rel. comp. 761; असित cr. black, ईक्षणा nom. sin. f. from ईक्षण n. the eye, 108.

असीह for असि इह by 31.

असुखं nom. sin. n. of असुख m. f. n. painful.

असुखजीविकाम् Karm. or Des. comp. 755; असुख cr. joyless, जीविकाम् acc. sin. of जीविका f. life.

असुखपीडितः Tat. or Dep. comp. 740; असुख cr. sorrow, grief, 726, पीडितः nom. sin. m. afflicted, pained.

असुखाविष्टा Tat. or Dep. comp. 740; असुख cr. grief, pain, unhappiness, आविष्टा nom. sin. f. of आविष्ट m. f. n. affected by, afflicted with.

असुहृद्गणैः ins. pl. with parties of people (who are) not friends; (comp. of अ not, 726, सुहृद् a friend, and गण m. a company.)

असूययित्वा having scorned, having cursed; past ind. p. of the nominal verb असूय् 521, 558.

असृजत् he or she let fall or let drop; 3d sin. impf. of rt सृज् 6th cl. 625.

असौ he or she; nom. sin. of अदस् 225.

अस्ति he, she or it is; 3d sin. pres. of rt अस् 2d cl. 584.

अस्तीति for अस्ति इति by 31. a.

अस्तु let it be; 3d sin. imp. of rt अस् 584.

अस्त्रवित् nom. sin. m. skilled in weapons; (comp. of अस्त्र a weapon, and वित् nom. sin. m. of विद् one who knows, knowing, 5th cl. 138, 743.)

अस्पृशतः not touching; acc. pl. m. of अस्पृशत् m. f. n.; (comp. of अ not, 726, and स्पृशत् pres. p. par. of rt स्पृश् 524.)

अस्मत्समीपतः for अस्मत्समीपतस् Adv. comp. 791; अस्मत् cr. us, 218, समीपतस् ind. near, 719. b.

अस्मदर्थे ind. on my account, for my sake; (comp. of अस्मद् 218, and अर्थे 760. d, 791.)

अस्माकं of us; gen. pl. of अस्मत्.

अस्मान् us; acc. pl. of अस्मत्.

अस्मान् from this, for अस्मात् abl. sin. of इदं this.

अस्माभिः for अस्माभिस् by us; ins. pl. of अस्मत्.

अस्माभिर् for अस्माभिस् by us. See last.

अस्मासु in us, for us, to us; loc. pl. of अस्मत्.

अस्मि I am; 1st sin. pres. of rt अस् 2d cl. 584.

अस्मिन् in this; loc. sin. of इदं this.

अस्म्यद्य for अस्मि अद्य by 34.

अस्म्युषितस् for अस्मि उषितस् by 34.

अस्म्युषिता for अस्मि उषिता by 34.

अस्य gen. sin. m. from nom. अयं this (इदं).

अस्यमरवद् for असि अमरवद् by 34.

अस्या for अस्यास् of her; gen. sin. f. from nom. इयं she (इदं).

अस्याम् loc. sin. f. See last.

अस्यारण्यस्य *for* **अस्य अरण्यस्य** *by* 31.

अस्याश् *gen. sin. f. from nom.* **इयं** she (**इदं**).

अस्वर्ग्यम् *nom. sin. n.* not conducive to heaven, unheavenly; (**अ** not, **स्वर्ग्य**.)

अस्वस्थां *acc. sin. f. of* **अस्वस्थ** *m. f. n.* not well, not herself, (*lit.* not staying in herself, *a, sva, stha; see* 580. *b.*)

अस्वेदान् *acc. pl. m. of* **अस्वेद** *m. f. n.* not perspiring, without perspiration; (*comp. of* **अ** not, 726, *and* **स्वेद** perspiration.)

अहं I; *nom. sin. of* **मत्** *or* **अस्मत्** 218.

अहत्वा not having slain; *past ind. p. of rt* **हन्**, *see* 558. *c.*

अहनि *loc. sin. of* **अहन्** *n.* a day, *6th cl.* 156.

अहिंसानिरतो TAT. OR DEP. COMP. 744; **अहिंसा** *cr.* harmlessness, doing no injury to living creatures, kindness, gentleness, **निरतो** *nom. sin. m. of* **निरत** *m. f. n.* engaged in, devoted to; *past p. p. of rt* **रम्** *with* **नि**, 545.

अहिताः *nom. pl. m. of* **अहित** *m. f. n.* unfriendly, hostile.

अहो *interj.* Oh! Ah! Alas! 732.

अहोरात्रान् days and nights, *acc. pl. of* **अहोरात्र** *m.; (comp. of* **अहर्** *for* **अहन्** a day, 778, *and* **रात्र** *m. for* **रात्रि** *f.* a night, 778.)

अहोरात्रैर् *ins. pl.; see last. The instrumental case is generally used with reference to any particular division of time, being then equivalent to the English* in, 820.

अहोवत् *ind.* Alas! Oh! Ah!

अहोवतायम् *for* **अहोवत अयम्** *by* 31.

अहोस्विद् *ind.* a particle implying doubt.

आ.

आ *prep.* to, at, as far as, until. *When prefixed to a noun in the sense of* up to, as far as, until, *it generally governs the ablative case. When prefixed to verbs which denote* giving *or* going, *it reverses the action: thus* **दा** *is* to give, *but* **आदा** to take; **गम्** *is* to go, *but* **आगम्** to come.

आकारवन्तः *nom. pl. of* **आकारवत्** *m. f. n.* well-formed, shapely.

आकारवर्णसुश्लक्ष्णाः COMPLEX COMP. 771; **आकार** *cr.* form, shape, **वर्ण** *cr.* colour, hue, **सुश्लक्ष्णाः** *nom. pl. of* **सुश्लक्ष्ण** *m. f. n.* very smooth or delicate.

आकाशं *acc. sin. of* **आकाश** *m.* the sky, the air, the atmosphere.

आकाशदेशम् TAT. OR DEP. COMP. 743; **आकाश** *cr.* the air, **देशम्** *acc. sin. m.* region.

आकृष्यमाणः *nom. sin. m. of* **आकृष्यमाण** *m. f. n.* being dragged away; *pres. p. pass. of rt* **कृष्** *with* **आ**, 528.

आक्रन्दमानां *acc. sin. f. of* **आक्रन्दमान** *m. f. n.* crying out, calling to; *pres. p. átm. of rt* **क्रन्द्** *with* **आ**.

आक्रम्य attacking, having assaulted or invaded; *past ind. p. of rt* **क्रम्** *with* **आ**, 559.

आक्षिपन्तीम् bringing into contempt, casting a slight upon, *acc. sin. of* **आक्षिपन्ती** *f.; (from* **आक्षिपत्** *pres. p. of rt* **क्षिप्** *with* **आ**, 141. *b*, 525. *b*, 635.)

आख्यातुम् to tell; *inf. of rt* **ख्या** *with* **आ**, 459, 437. *b.*

आख्यानं *acc. sin. of* **आख्यान** *n.* a tale, a story, words uttered.

आख्यानपञ्चमान् having the Purāṇas as the fifth, BAH. OR REL. COMP. 761; **आख्यान** *cr.* a story, the mythological stories of the Purāṇas, written long subsequently to the Vedas, **पञ्चमान्** *acc. pl. of* **पञ्चम** *m. f. n.* fifth, 209.

आख्यासि thou tellest, thou dost point out; *2d sin. pres. of rt* **ख्या** *with* **आ**, *2d cl.* 437. *b.*

आख्येयं *nom. sin. n. of* **आख्येय** *m. f. n.* to be told; *fut. pass. p. of rt* **ख्या** *with* **आ**, 571. *a.*

आगच्छतो *acc. pl. m. of* **आगच्छत्** *m. f. n.*

coming, approaching; *pres. p. par. of rt* गम् *with prep.* आ; 524, 602.

आगच्छन् they came; *3d pl. impf. of rt* गम् to go, *with* आ, 602, 783. *i.*

आगच्छेत् he may come; *3d sin. pot. of rt* गम् to go, *with* आ, 602.

आगतं *acc. sin. m. n. or nom. sin. n. of* आगत *m. f. n.* happened, arrived; *past p. p. of rt* गम् *with* आ, 545.

आगतः *nom. sin. m. of* आगत *m. f. n.* come.

आगता *nom. sin. f. or for* आगतास् *nom. pl. m. of* आगत *m. f. n.* come.

आगतान् *acc. pl. m. of* आगत *m. f. n.* come.

आगताम् *acc. sin. f. of* आगत *m. f. n.* come, arrived, present; *past p. p. of rt* गम् to go, *with* आ, 545.

आगतायां *loc. sin. f. of* आगत *m. f. n.* come.

आगते *loc. sin. m. or n. of* आगत *m. f. n.* come.

आगत्य having come; *past ind. p. of rt* गम् to go, *with* आ, 564. *b.*

आगमत् he or she came; *3d sin. aor. of rt* गम् to go, *with* आ, 602.

आगमनं *nom. sin. of* आगमन *n.* coming, 1st *cl.* 104.

आगमनकारणं TAT. OR DEP. COMP. 743; आगमन *cr.* coming, कारणं *acc. sin. n.* cause.

आगम्य having come to, having met; *past ind. p. of rt* गम् to go, *with prep.* आ, 564. *b*, 602, 783. *i.*

आचक्ष्व tell thou, relate thou, describe thou; *2d sin. imp. átm. of rt* चक्ष् *with* आ, *2d cl.* 320.

आचचक्षे he or she told; *3d sin. perf. átm. of rt* चक्ष् *with* आ, 320, 364.

आचरन् *nom. sin. m. of* आचरत् *m. f. n.* performing; *pres. p. par. of rt* चर् *with* आ, 524.

आचष्टे he relates, he describes; *3d sin. pres. of rt* चक्ष् *with* आ, *2d cl.* 320.

आचार्याः *nom. pl. of* आचार्य *m.* a preceptor.

आचार्यान् *acc. pl. of* आचार्य *m.* a preceptor.

आच्छन्नः *nom. sin. m.* clothed, clad; *past p. p. of rt* छद् to cover, *with* आ, 540.

आजगाम he came; *3d sin. perf. of rt* गम् *with* आ, 602.

आजग्मुर् they came; *3d pl. perf. of rt* गम् 602, 376.

आजुहाव he invited; *3d sin. perf. of rt* ह्वे to call, *with* आ, 373. *e.*

आततायिनः *acc. pl. of* आततायिन् *m.* a traitor, a malignant man, an evil-doer.

आतिष्ठ undertake thou, practise thou; *2d sin. imp. of rt* स्था *with* आ, *1st cl.* 587.

आतिष्ठद् he set out; *3d sin. impf. of rt* स्था *with* आ, *1st cl.* 261.

आतिष्ठेत् he may act; *3d sin. pot. of rt* स्था *with* आ, *1st cl.* 587.

आतुरः *nom. sin. of* आतुर *m. f. n.* weak, incapable, unable, *used with an infinitive. Also*, sick, diseased.

आतुरम् *acc. sin. m. of* आतुर *m. f. n.* sick.

आत्थ thou hast said; *2d sin. perf. of defective root* अह्, *see* 384. *b.*

आत्मजयम् *acc. sin. m.* his own victory; (*comp. of* आत्म 232, *and* जय victory.)

आत्मन् *m. f.* self, himself, herself, myself, &c., 146, 232.

आत्मनः *gen. sin. of* आत्मन् self, *q. v.*

आत्मनश् of himself, *gen. sin. See last.*

आत्मना *ins. sin. of* आत्मन् self, *q. v.*

आत्मनो *gen. sin. of* आत्मन् *m.* self, *q. v.*

आत्मप्रभांश् *for* आत्मप्रभान् self-luminous, self-glorious; आत्म *cr.* self, प्रभान् *acc. pl. m. from* प्रभा *f.* light, glory, *1st cl.* 108.

आत्मभवम् *acc. sin.* his own essence; (*comp. of* आत्म own, 232, भवम् *acc. sin. of* भव *m.* being, existence.)

आत्मा *nom. sin. m. of* आत्मन् *m.* self, 146. (*In* Book XXII. 16 he himself.)

आत्मानम् *acc. sin. of* आत्मन् *m.* self, 146.

आत्मार्थे for (my) own sake; (*comp. of* आत्म *for* आत्मन् 57, 146, *and* अर्थे 791.)

आदाय having taken, having received; *past ind. p. of rt* दा to give, *with* आ, 559, 783. *i.*

आदित्य *for* आदित्यस् *nom. sin. of* आदित्य *m.* the sun, 1*st cl.* 103.

आदित्यः *for* आदित्यस् *nom. sin. of* आदित्य *m.* the sun, 1*st cl.* 103.

आदित्या *for* आदित्यास् *nom. pl. of* आदित्य *m.* an Áditya, a deity of a particular class, being a form of the Sun. There are twelve Ádityas, who are supposed to be the offspring of Kaśyapa and Aditi his wife. They are merely emblems of the Sun in each month of the year. Their names, according to some, are, सूर्यः, वरुणः, वेदाङ्गः, भानुः, इन्द्रः, रविः, गभस्तिः, यमः, स्वर्णरेताः, दिवाकरः, मित्रः, विष्णुः. According to the Vishṇu Puráṇa (p. 122, Wilson) they are, विष्णु, शक्र, आर्यमन्, धृति, त्वष्टृ, पूषन्, विवस्वत्, सवितृ, मित्र, वरुण, अंशु, भग. Most of these are names or epithets of the Sun itself.

आदित्यो *nom. sin. of* आदित्य *m.* the sun.

आदिश command thou, order thou; 2*d sin. imp. of rt* दिश् *with* आ, 6*th cl.* 583.

आदिष्टो *nom. sin. m. of* आदिष्ट *m.f.n.* commissioned, commanded; *past p. p. of rt* दिश् to point out, *with* आ, 539, 583.

आधावमानाश् *nom. pl. m. of* आधावमान *m.f.n.* running, rushing onwards or at; *pres. p. átm. of rt* धाव् *with* आ, 526.

आधास्ये I will lay, I will place, I will attribute; 1*st sin. 2d fut. átm. of rt* धा *with* आ, 664.

आधिपत्यं *acc. sin. n.* sovereignty.

आधिभिर् *ins. pl. of* आधि *m.* anxiety, agony, pain.

आनय bring thou, fetch thou; 2*d sin. imp. of rt* नी *with* आ, 1*st cl.* 590. *a.*

आनयत् he brought, he took; 3*d sin. impf. of rt* नी *with* आ.

आनयताम् let him bring back; 3*d sin. imp. átm. of rt* नी *with* आ, 1*st cl.* 590. *a.*

आनयने *loc. sin. of* आनयन *n.* bringing, bringing back.

आनयिष्यति he shall bring back; 3*d sin.* 2*d fut. of rt* नी *with* आ. *The more usual form is* आनेष्यति; *see* 394. *a*, 590. *a.*

आनयेह *for* आनय इह *by* 32.

आनाययामास he or she caused to be brought; 3*d sin. perf. of rt* नी *in caus. with* आ, 385. *a*, 590. *a.*

आनाय्य having caused to be brought, having caused to be introduced, having brought together, having convened; *past ind. p. of rt* नी *in caus. with* आ, 566. *a*, 482.

आनृशंस्यम् *nom. sin. n.* mercy, absence of cruelty; *abstract noun from* अनृशंस not cruel, not given to injury; *see* 726, 80. LXXVII.

आनेतुं to bring, to be brought; *inf.* (*act. and pass.*) *of rt* नी *with* आ, *see* 869.

आपगां *acc. sin. of* आपगा *f.* a river, 1*st cl.* 105.

आपततां *gen. pl. of* आपतत् *m.f.n.* rushing onwards; *pres. p. par. of rt* पत् *with* आ, 524.

आपतितम् *nom. sin. n. of* आपतित *m.f.n.* fallen upon, happened; *past p. p. of rt* पत् *with* आ, 538.

आपदम् *acc. sin. of* आपद् *f.* calamity, 84. IV.

आपन्ना *nom. sin. f. of* आपन्न *m.f.n.* unfortunate, afflicted; obtained, acquired.

आपीडैर् *ins. pl. of* आपीड *m.* a wreath, a garland.

आपो *nom. pl. of* अप् *f.* water, (*always declined in the plural, see* 178. *b.*)

आप्तकारिभिः *ins. pl. m. of* आप्तकारिन् *m.f.n.* trusty, confidential, 6*th cl.* 159.

आप्तदक्षिणैः Bah. or Rel. comp. 766, having proper gifts, or furnished with gifts (to Bráhmans); आप्त *cr.* fit, suitable, obtained, furnished, दक्षिणैः *ins. pl. m. from* दक्षिणा *f.* a gift to a Bráhman at a sacrifice, 1*st cl.* 108.

आप्नोति he or she obtains, he or she incurs or will incur; *3d sin. pres. of rt* आप् *5th cl.* 681.

आप्यायिता *nom. sin. f. of* आप्यायित *m. f. n.* satisfied, comforted, refreshed; *past p. p. of rt* प्यै *in caus.* 549.

आभाष्य having addressed or spoken to; *past ind. p. of rt* भाष् *with* आ.

आभ्याम् *dat. du. of* इदं this, 224.

आमन्त्र्य having saluted, having bid farewell to; *past ind. p. of rt* मन्त्र् *with* आ, 559.

आम्नायसारिणीं having the essence of the Veda, or flowing (musically) like the Veda, BAH. OR REL. COMP. 761; आम्नाय *cr.* the Veda, सारिणीं *acc. sin. f. of* सारिन् possessed of the essence (*sára*), *6th cl.* 159; or flowing, *agt. of rt* सृ 582. *a.*

आयतलोचना BAH. OR REL. COMP. 761; आयत *cr.* long, लोचना *nom. sin. f. from* लोचन *n.* the eye, 108.

आयतेक्षणा BAH. OR REL. COMP. 766; आयत *cr.* long, *and* ईक्षणा *nom. sin. f. from* ईक्षण *n.* an eye.

आयतेक्षणाम् *acc. sin. f.* See *last.*

आयात *for* आयातस् *nom. sin. m. of* आयात *m. f. n.* come; *past p. p. of rt* या to go, *with* आ, 532, 644.

आयाति he comes; *3d sin. pres. of rt* या to go, *with* आ, *2d cl.*

आयान्तं *acc. sin. m. of* आयात् coming; *pres. p. of rt* या *with* आ, 644, 524.

आयान्तु let them come; *3d pl. imp. of rt* या *with* आ, 644.

आयुक्तं *acc. sin. m. of* आयुक्त *m. f. n.* united, joined, obtained; *past p. p. of rt* युज् *with* आ, 539.

आयुष्मन् O long-lived one, *voc. sin. of* आयुष्मत् *5th cl.* 140. *See next.*

आयुष्मन्तौ *nom. du. m. of* आयुष्मत् *m. f. n.* possessed of (long) life; a respectful mode of addressing kings and princes.

आरब्धं *nom. or acc. sin. n. or acc. sin. m. of* आरब्ध *m. f. n.* begun, undertaken; *past p. p. of rt* रभ् *with* आ, 601. *a*, 539.

आरभ्य having commenced or undertaken; *past ind. p. of rt* रभ् *with* आ, 559.

आराधने *loc. sin. of* आराधन *n.* the act of winning over or gaining, propitiating, honouring.

आरावः *nom. sin. m.* noise, tumult, cry.

आरुरोह he or she ascended; *3d sin. perf. of rt* रुह् *with* आ, 364.

आरुह्य having ascended; *past ind. p. of rt* रुह् *with* आ, 559.

आरोप्य having made to ascend, having caused to mount, having placed upon; *ind. past p. of rt* रुह् *in caus. with* आ, 566, 488.

आर्तः *nom. sin. of* आर्त *m. f. n.* grieved, pained; *past p. p. of rt* अर्द् *with* आ, *see* 542.

आर्ततरा *nom. sin. f. of* आर्ततर *m. f. n.* more afflicted, more sad; *see* 191.

आर्तस्य *gen. sin. m. of* आर्त *m. f. n.* afflicted, tormented.

आर्ता *nom. sin. f. of* आर्त *m. f. n.* afflicted, 542. *See* आर्तः.

आर्ताम् *acc. sin. f. See* आर्तः.

आर्तो *nom. sin. m.* afflicted. *See* आर्तः.

आर्य *voc. sin.* O honourable man, O Sir.

आलयान् *acc. pl. of* आलय *m.* a house, a dwelling, *1st cl.* 103.

आलिङ्ग्य having embraced; *past ind. p. of rt* लिङ्ग् *with* आ, 559.

आलीयते he or she faints away; *3d sin. pres. átm. of rt* ली *with* आ, *4th cl.* 272.

आलोक्य having looked at; *ind. past p. of rt* लोक् *with* आ, 559.

आवयोः of us two; *gen. du. of* मत् *or* अस्मत्, *q. q. v. v.*

आवर्जितं *nom. sin. n. of* आवर्जित *m. f. n.* inclined, poured down, made to flow downwards; *past p. p. of rt* वृज् *with* आ, 538.

आवर्तैः *ins. pl. of* आवर्त *m.* a curl, a lock of hair that curls backwards in a horse, a peculiar mark. Ávartas are locks, curls or twists of hair in certain forms on different parts of the body. In Book XIX. 14 they are apparently, forehead 1, head 2, chest 2, ribs 2, flanks 2, crupper 1. In the poem of Mágha, chap. v. 4, we have the adjective Ávartinaḥ applied to horses, on which the commentator observes, 'Ávartinaḥ signifies horses having the ten ávartas or marks of excellence; they are, two on the breast, two on the head, one on the forehead, two on the hollows of the ribs, two on the hollows of the flanks, and one on the crupper (*prapáta*); these are called the ten ávartas.' Ávarta means an eddy or whirlpool, and is applied to the twists of hair on a horse resembling a whirlpool.

आवह convey thou (to thyself), take thou; *2d sin. imp. of rt* **वह्** *with* **आ**, *1st cl.* 261.

आवार्य having concealed; *past ind. p. of rt* **वृ** *in caus. with* **आ**, 675, 481.

आविशत् he entered; *3d sin. impf. of rt* **विश्** *with* **आ**, *6th cl.* 278.

आविष्टः *nom. sin. m. of* **आविष्ट** *m. f. n.* entered, affected by; *past p. p. of rt* **विश्** *with* **आ**, 556.

आविष्टम् *acc. sin. m. of* **आविष्ट** *m. f. n.* affected by, filled with.

आविष्टो *nom. sin. m. of* **आविष्ट** *m. f. n.* affected by.

आवेद्यं *nom. sin. n. of* **आवेद्य** *m. f. n.* to be told, to be announced; *fut. pass. p. of rt* **विद्** *in caus. with* **आ**, 571; *governing the genitive case by* 859. *a.*

आव्रजन् they went to, they approached; *3d pl. impf. of rt* **व्रज्** to go, *with* **आ**, *1st cl.* 261.

आशङ्कमाना *nom. sin. f. of* **आशङ्कमान** *m. f. n.* fearing, apprehending; *pres. p. átm. of rt* **शङ्क्** *with* **आ**, 526.

आशीर्वादैः *ins. pl. of* **आशीर्वाद** *m.* a blessing, benediction.

आशु *ind.* quickly, 717. *e.*

आश्चर्यं *nom. or acc. sin. n.* a wonder, prodigy.

आश्रमपदं *acc. sin. of* **आश्रमपद** *n.* a hermitage, *1st cl.* 104.

आश्रममण्डलं TAT. OR DEP. COMP. 743; **आश्रम** *cr.* a hermit's cell, a hermitage, **मण्डलम्** *nom. or acc. sin. of* **मण्डल** *n.* a circle.

आश्रमान् *acc. pl. of* **आश्रम** *m.* a hermitage.

आश्रमाश् *nom. pl. of* **आश्रम** *m.* a hermitage, an anchorite's retreat, *1st cl.* 103.

आश्रयेत् he would incline to. *See next.*

आश्रयेद् he or it might attach itself or have recourse to; *3d sin. pot. of rt* **श्रि** to serve, *with* **आ**, *1st cl.*

आश्रिता *nom. sin. f. of* **आश्रित** *m. f. n.* having resorted to, standing upon; *past p. p. of rt* **श्रि** *with* **आ**, *see* 896. *a.*

आश्वासय comfort thou, console thou; *2d sin. imp. of rt* **श्वस्** *in caus. with* **आ**.

आश्वासयत encourage ye, comfort ye; *2d pl. imp. of rt* **श्वस्** *in caus. with* **आ**, 481. *In* Book XII. 59, *the plural seems used out of respect, or, as the Scholiast observes, from confusion and agitation of mind.*

आश्वासयद् *for* **आश्वासयत्** he consoled, he comforted, he caused to breathe; *3d sin. impf. of rt* **श्वस्** *in caus. with* **आ**, 481.

आश्वासयन्ती *nom. sin. f. of* **आश्वासयत्** *m. f. n.* comforting, consoling; *pres. p. See last.*

आश्वासयसि thou consolest; *2d sin. pres.*

आश्वासयामि I (will) console; *1st sin. pres.*

आश्वास्य having consoled, having cheered; *past ind. p. of rt* **श्वस्** *in caus. with* **आ**.

आसं I was; *1st sin. impf. of rt* **अस्** 584.

आसते they sit, they remain; *3d pl. pres. of rt* **आस्** *2d cl.* 317, 292.

आसनेभ्यः *abl. pl. of* **आसन** *n.* a seat, *1st cl.* 104.

आसनेषु *loc. pl. of* **आसन** *n.* a seat, *1st cl.* 104.

आससाद he approached, he came to, he found; *3d sin. perf. of rt* **सद्** *with* **आ**, 375. *a*, 559. *a.*

आसादयद् *for* **आसादयत्** he or she approached or arrived at; *3d sin. impf. of rt* **सद्** *with* **आ**, *10th cl.* 283.

आसादिता *nom. sin. f. of* आसादित *m. f. n.* met with, found.

आसाद्य having arrived at, having reached, having gone near to, having met with, having found, having experienced; *past ind. p. of rt* सद् *in caus. with* आ, 599. *a*, 566.

आसीद् *for* आसीत् he or it was, there was; 3*d sin. impf. of rt* अस् 584.

आसीन् *for* आसीत्. *See last.*

आसीनाः *nom. pl. m. of* आसीन *m. f. n.* sitting, seated; *pres. p. átm. of rt* आस् 526. *a.*

आस्ते he or she sits; 3*d sin. pres. átm. of rt* आस् 2*d cl.* 317.

आस्थाय having recourse to, having made use of; *past ind. p. See next.*

आस्थास्यति he or she will perform, will engage in, will observe; 3*d sin.* 2*d fut. of rt* स्था *with* आ, 587.

आस्थास्ये I shall have recourse to, I will make use of; 1*st sin.* 2*d fut. átm. of rt* स्था *with* आ, 587.

आस्थितम् *acc. sin. m. of* आस्थित *m. f. n.* standing on; *past p. p. of rt* स्था *with* आ, 533, 896. *a.*

आस्यताम् let it be sat down; 3*d sin. pres. of rt* आस् *in pass.* 463.

आह he said; 3*d sin. perf. of defective root* अह्, *see* 384. *b.*

आहर्ता *nom. sin. of* आहर्तृ *m.* an offerer, one who offers or performs a sacrifice; *agt. of rt* हृ *with* आ, 4*th cl.* 127.

आहर्तुं to bring, to take away, to cause, to be taken up, to be picked up; *inf. of rt* हृ *with* आ. (N.B. *The root* शक् *in pass. gives a pass. sense to the infinitive.*)

आहवे *loc. sin. of* आहव *m.* battle, war.

आहितः *nom. sin. m. of* आहित. *See last.*

आहितम् *nom. sin. n. of* आहित *m. f. n.* placed, deposited, made, undertaken; *past p. p. of rt* धा *with* आ, 533.

आहुस् they spoke, they said; 3*d pl. perf. of defective root* अह्, *see* 384. *b.*

आहूय having challenged; *past ind. p. of rt* ह्वे to call, *with* आ, 562. *a.*

आहृते *loc. sin. n. of* आहृत *m. f. n.* brought; *past p. p. of rt* हृ *with* आ.

आहृत्य having taken away; *past ind. p. of rt* हृ *with* आ, 560.

आहेदं *for* आह इदं *by* 32.

आहोस्विद् *for* आहोस्वित् *ind.* a particle implying doubt.

आह्लादयते he or it rejoices; 3*d sin. pres. átm. of rt* ह्लाद् *in caus. with* आ, 481.

आह्वानम् *acc. sin. of* आह्वान *n.* a challenge, (*lit.* calling to,) 1*st cl.* 104.

इ.

इक्ष्वाकुकुलजः *nom. sin. m.* born in the family of Ikshváku; (*comp. of* इक्ष्वाकु *cr.* Ikshváku, the first prince of the Solar dynasty, कुल *cr.* family, *and* ज *m. f. n.* born, *see* 580. *b.*

इङ्गितैः *ins. pl. of* इङ्गित *n.* a gesture, hint.

इच्छति he or she wishes; 3*d sin. pres. of rt* इष् 6*th cl.* 637.

इच्छन्ति they desire, they wish; 3*d pl. pres.*

इच्छसि thou wishest; 2*d sin. pres. See next.*

इच्छामि I wish, I desire; 1*st sin. pres. of rt* इष् 6*th cl.* 637.

इच्छेयास् thou mayest wish; 2*d sin. pot. of rt* इष् 6*th cl.* 637.

इतः hence, from hence. *See* इतस्.

इतश्चेतश्च *ind.* hither and thither, here and there, *for* इतस् च इतस् च *by* 62 *and* 32.

इतस् *ind.* from hence, hence, here, hither, 719.

इतस्ततः *ind.* hither and thither, here and there; (*comp. of* इतस् *and* ततस्.)

इति *ind.* so, thus, to this effect, so saying, 717. *e*, 927.

इतो *for* इतस् *ind.* from hence.

इत्यथोचुस् *for* इति अथ ऊचुस् *by* 34 *and* 32.

इदं *nom. or acc. sin. n. of* इदं *m. f. n.* this.

इन्दोर् *gen. sin. of* इन्दु *m.* the moon.

इन्द्रपुरोगमाः preceded or led on by Indra, having Indra as their leader; इन्द्र *cr.* Indra, पुरोगमाः *nom. pl. of* पुरोगम *m.* a leader, 761. *See next.*

इन्द्रलोकम् TAT. OR DEP. COMP. 743; इन्द्र *cr.* Indra, लोकम् *acc. sin. of* लोक *m.* the world, 1*st cl.* 103. The god Indra takes a very important position in each of the three periods of Hindú mythology. In the Vedic period he is the great Being who inhabits the firmament, guides the winds and clouds, dispenses rain, and hurls the thunderbolt. In the Epic period he is a principal deity, taking precedence of Agni, Varuṇa, and Yama. In the Puránic period he is still a chief deity, only inferior in rank to the great Triad, Brahmá, Vishṇu, and S'iva. His heaven is called Svarga or Indraloka; his pleasure-garden or elysium नन्दन; his city (sometimes placed on Mount Meru, the Olympus of the Greeks) अमरावती; his palace वैजयन्त; his horse उच्चैःश्रवस्; his charioteer मातलि; his thunderbolt वज्र; his elephant ऐरावत; his bow (the rainbow) शक्रधनुस्.

इन्द्रसेनं *acc. sin. of* इन्द्रसेन *m.* Indrasena, son of Nala and Damayantí, 1*st cl.* 103.

इन्द्रसेनस्य *gen. sin. See last.*

इन्द्रसेनां *acc. sin. of* इन्द्रसेना *f.* Indrasená, daughter of Nala and Damayantí, 1*st cl.* 105.

इन्द्रियाणां *gen. pl. of* इन्द्रिय *n.* an organ of sense.

इन्द्रो *for* इन्द्रस् *nom. sin. of* इन्द्र *m.* Indra, the god of the atmosphere.

इमं this; *acc. sin. m. of* इदं, (*nom.* अयं.)

इमां this; *acc. sin. f. of* इदं, (*nom.* इयं.)

इमानि these; *acc. pl. n. of* इदं.

इमे these; *nom. pl. m. of* इदं, (*nom.* अयं.)

इयम् she; *nom. sin. f. of* इदं 224.

इयेष he desired, he wished; 3*d sin. perf. of rt* इष् 367.

इव *ind.* like, as, as if, as it were.

इवाचलम् *for* इव अचलम् *by* 31.

इवाभ्रेषु *for* इव अभ्रेषु *by* 31.

इवार्केण *for* इव अर्केण *by* 31.

इवासते *for* इव आसते *by* 31.

इवैकाम् *for* इव एकाम् *by* 33.

इवोत्थितम् *for* इव उत्थितम् *by* 32.

इवोद्धृताम् *for* इव उद्धृताम् *by* 32.

इवोरगाः *for* इव उरगाः *by* 32.

इषुभिः *ins. pl. of* इषु *m.* an arrow.

इष्ट *m. f. n.* desired, wished, desirable, excellent, choice; *past p. p. of rt* इष् 539.

इष्टं *acc. sin. m. of* इष्ट *m. f. n.* desired, beloved. *See last.*

इष्टा *nom. sin. f. of* इष्ट *m. f. n.* beloved.

इष्टां *acc. sin. f. of* इष्ट beloved, *q. v.*

इष्टै *for* इष्टैस् *ins. pl. of* इष्ट, *q. v.;* ais *to* air, *and* r *dropped by* 65. *a.*

इष्ट्वा having sacrificed; *past ind. p. of* यज् 556, 597.

इह *ind.* here, 717. *g.*

इहागतः *nom. sin. m.* come or arrived hither; (*from* इह, *q. v., and* आगत come.)

इहागतम् *for* इह आगतम्. *See above.*

इहागताम् *for* इह आगताम्. *See above.*

इहानेतुं *for* इह आनेतुं *by* 31.

इहाभवत् *for* इह अभवत् *by* 31.

इहेच्छसि *for* इह इच्छसि *by* 32.

इहैव *for* इह एव *by* 33.

इहोत्सहे *for* इह उत्सहे *by* 32.

ई.

ईक्षणाम् *acc. sin. f. from* ईक्षण *n.* an eye.

ईजे he sacrificed; 3*d sin. perf. átm. of rt* यज्, *see* 375. *e.*

ईदृश *for* ईदृशस् *m. f. n.* such as this, such-like, 234.

ईदृशम् *nom. or acc. sin. n. of* ईदृश *m. f. n.* such, such as this, *see* 234.

ईदृशैः *ins. pl. m. of* ईदृश *m. f. n.* such-like.

ईप्सितः *nom. sin. of* ईप्सित *m. f. n.* desired, wished for; *past p. p. of rt* आप् to obtain, *in des. form*, 550, 503.

ईप्सिताम् *acc. sin. f. of* ईप्सित. *See last.*

ईप्सितो *nom. sin. m.* desired, admired. *See last.*

ईयिवान् he went; *nom. sin. m. of* ईयिवस् *participle of perf. of rt* इ 554, 645.

ईरितः *nom. sin. m. of* ईरित *m. f. n.* sent forth, uttered; *past p. p. of rt* ईर् 538.

ईरितम् *nom. sin. n.* said, uttered. *See last.*

ईशं *acc. sin. of* ईश *m.* a lord.

ईश्वर *voc. sin. of* ईश्वर *m.* a lord, a master, 1st *cl.* 103.

ईश्वराणाम् *gen. pl. of* ईश्वर, *q. v.*

उ.

उक्त *m. f. n.* addressed, spoken, spoken to; *past p. p. of rt* वच् 543, 650.

उक्तं *nom. sin. n. of* उक्त spoken, spoken to.

उक्तमात्रे on merely being uttered, immediately on being uttered; उक्त *cr.* uttered, spoken, मात्रे *loc. sin. of* मात्र *n.* mere; *see* 919 *and* 840.

उक्तवती she spoke, *nom. sin. f. of* उक्तवत् *m. f. n.* who has spoken; *past. act. p. of rt* वच् 553.

उक्तवान् *nom. sin. of* उक्तवत् *m. f. n. See last.*

उक्तस् *nom. sin. m.* spoken to, addressed. *See last.*

उक्तस्य *gen. sin. of* उक्त addressed.

उक्ता *nom. sin. f. of* उक्त. *See last.*

उक्ताः *for* उक्तास् *nom. pl. m.* addressed.

उक्तास् *nom. pl. m.* addressed.

उक्ते on being addressed, on being spoken to; *loc. sin.*

उक्तो *nom. sin. m.* addressed.

उक्त्वा having said, having spoken; *ind. p. of rt* वच् 556, 650.

उग्रशासनः strict in his orders, Bah. or Rel. comp. 766; उग्र *cr.* severe, शासनः *nom. sin. m. from* शासन *n.* an order, command, 1st *cl.* 108.

उचिता *nom. sin. f. of* उचित *m. f. n.* accustomed, usual, well-known, (*governing the genitive case at* Book XXIII. 22.)

उच्चैः *for* उच्चैस् *ind.* loudly, in a loud voice, 714.

उच्चैर् *for* उच्चैस् *ind.* loud, loudly. *See last.*

उच्छिष्टं *acc. sin. n.* that which is left, the leavings (of food); *from rt* शिष् *with* उत्.

उच्छोषणम् *acc. sin. n. of* उच्छोषण *m. f. n.* that which dries or parches up; (उत् शुष् *in caus.*)

उच्छ्रितैः *ins. pl. of* उच्छ्रित *m. f. n.* lofty, high, 1st *cl.* 103.

उच्यते it is called; 3*d sin. pres. of rt* वच् *in pass.*

उत् *prep.* up, above, upwards, on, upon.

उत *ind.* an expletive, a redundant particle.

उताहो *interrog. p.* or whether?

उताहोस्विद् *ind.* or whether, (a particle of doubt or deliberation.)

उत्तमं *acc. sin. m. or n. of* उत्तम *m. f. n.* excellent.

उत्तमः *nom. sin. m. of* उत्तम excellent, fine.

उत्तमगन्धाढ्याः possessing abundantly the most delicate scent or delicious fragrance, Complex comp., *see* 772. *a*; उत्तम *cr.* best, गन्ध *cr.* fragrance, आढ्याः *nom. pl. f. of* आढ्य *m. f. n.* abounding in, rich, possessing abundantly.

उत्तरं *acc. sin. of* उत्तर *n.* an answer.

उत्तरन्तं *acc. sin. m. of* उत्तरत् *m. f. n.* crossing over, passing, going over; *pres. p. of rt* तॄ to cross, *with* उत्.

उत्तराम् *acc. sin. f. of* उत्तर *m. f. n.* northern, northerly.

उत्तरीयम् *acc. sin. of* उत्तरीय *n.* an upper garment.

उत्तस्थौ he or she stood up; 3*d sin. perf. of rt* स्था *with* उत्, 587, 783. *j.*

उत्तिष्ठ rise thou up, arise thou; *2d sin. imp. of rt* **स्था** *with* **उत्**.

उत्थितः *nom. sin. m.* arisen; *past p. p. of rt* **स्था** *with* **उत्**, 533, 783. *j.*

उत्थितम् *acc. sin. m. of* **उत्थित** *m. f. n.* rising or towering over. *See last.*

उत्पतते she springs up; *3d sin. pres. átm. of rt* **पत्** *with* **उत्**, *1st cl.* 261.

उत्पततो *acc. pl. m. of* **उत्पतत्** *m. f. n.* flying upwards, flying onwards. *See next.*

उत्पतन्तः *nom. pl. m. of* **उत्पतत्** *m. f. n.* flying upwards; *pres. p. of rt* **पत्** *with* **उत्**, 524.

उत्सर्गे *loc. sin. of* **उत्सर्ग** *m.* abandonment, *1st cl.* 103.

उत्सर्पति he or it rises up or becomes elongated; *3d sin. pres. of rt* **सृप्** *with* **उत्**, *1st cl.* 261.

उत्ससर्ज he released, he let go; *3d sin. perf. of rt* **सृज्** *with prep.* **उत्**, 625.

उत्सहते he is able, he endures, he bears up; *3d sin. pres. See next.*

उत्सहे I am able, I shall be able, I can endure, (*equivalent in* Book IV. 15, 16, *to* can I dare (to plead)?) *1st sin. pres. átm. of rt* **सह्** *with* **उत्**, 611. *a.*

उत्साद्यन्ते they are subverted, they are destroyed; *3d pl. pres. of rt* **सद्** *in pass. with* **उत्**.

उत्सुकाः *nom. pl. m. of* **उत्सुक** *m. f. n.* eager for, anxiously expecting, (*governing the locative case in* Book XXI. 7.)

उत्सृज्य having abandoned, having cast off, having released, having let go, having shed; *past ind. p. of rt* **सृज्** *with* **उत्**, 559.

उत्सृष्टवान् *nom. sin. m. of* **उत्सृष्टवत्** *m. f. n.* who has let fall, who has shed (as tears); *past act. p. of rt* **सृज्** *with* **उत्**.

उत्सृष्टा *nom. sin. f. of* **उत्सृष्ट** *m. f. n.* left, abandoned, cast off, let go.

उत्स्रष्टुकामं *acc. sin. m.* wishing to let go, wishing to put down; (*comp. of* **उत्स्रष्टु** *for* **उत्स्रष्टुम्** *inf. of rt* **सृज्** *with* **उत्**, 625, *and* **काम**, *see* 871.)

उदकं *nom. sin. of* **उदक** *n.* water.

उदर्कस् *nom. sin. m.* future time, *1st cl.* 103.

उदर्के *loc. sin. of* **उदर्क** *m.* future, future time.

उदारः *for* **उदारस्** *nom. sin. m. of* **उदार** *m. f. n.* noble, generous, *1st cl.* 103.

उदारान् *acc. pl. See last.*

उदाहृतम् *nom. sin. n. of* **उदाहृत** *m. f. n.* related, declared; *past p. p. of rt* **हृ** *with* **आ** *and* **उत्**, 532, 593.

उदितेन *ins. sin. m. of* **उदित** *m. f. n.* risen; *past p. p. of rt* **इ** *with* **उत्**, 532.

उद्दिश्य *ind.* pointing at, with reference to, *see* 924.

उद्धृताम् *acc. sin. f. of* **उद्धृत** *m. f. n.* torn up, uprooted; *past p. p. of rt* **हृ** *with* **उत्**, 50, 783. *j.*

उद्यतः *nom. sin. of* **उद्यत** *m. f. n.* eager, in earnest, prepared.

उद्यताः *nom. pl. of* **उद्यत** *m. f. n.* prepared, ready.

उद्वमन् *nom. sin. m. of* **उद्वमत्** *m. f. n.* vomiting up; *pres. p. of rt* **वम्** *with* **उत्**, 524.

उद्विजसि thou fearest; *2d sin. pres. of rt* **विज्** *with* **उत्**, *6th cl.* 278. *This verb governs the ablative case, see* 855.

उद्वेजते trembles; *3d sin. pres. átm. of rt* **विज्** *with* **उत्**, *1st cl. This rt is generally in the 6th cl.; see last.*

उद्वेपते trembles, is agitated; *3d sin. pres. átm. of rt* **वेप्** *with* **उद्**, *1st cl.* 261.

उन्मत्तं *acc. sin. m. of* **उन्मत्त** *m. f. n.* mad.

उन्मत्तदर्शना BAH. OR REL. COMP. 767; **उन्मत्त** *cr.* mad, maniac-like, **दर्शना** *nom. sin. f. from* **दर्शन** *n.* aspect, 108.

उन्मत्तरूपा BAH. OR REL. COMP. 766; **उन्मत्त** *cr.* a maniac, **रूपा** *nom. sin. f. from* **रूप** *n.* form, 108.

उन्मत्तवद् *ind.* like one mad, as if mad, like a maniac; (*comp. of* **उन्मत्त** mad, *and affix* **वत्**, *see* 724.)

उन्मत्तवेशा Bah. or Rel. comp. 767; उन्मत्त cr. mad, a maniac, वेशा *nom. sin. f. from* वेश *m.* a dress, garb, 108.

उन्मत्ता *nom. sin. f. of* उन्मत्त *m. f. n.* mad.

उन्मत्तां *acc. sin. f. of* उन्मत्त *m. f. n.* mad.

उन्मत्तेव *for* उन्मत्ता इव *by* 32.

उन्मुखा *for* उन्मुखास् *nom. pl. m. of* उन्मुख *m. f. n.* looking upwards, raising their faces upwards.

उप *prep.* to, towards, near, with.

उपकल्पिताः *nom. pl. m. of* उपकल्पित *m. f. n.* prepared, made ready; *past p. p. of rt* क्लृप् *with* उप, 538.

उपगच्छति he comes to, he returns to; *3d sin. pres. of rt* गम् *with* उप, 602.

उपगम्य having approached, having gone up to or near; *past ind. p. of rt* गम् *with* उप, 602, 559.

उपचक्रमे he or she endeavoured or attempted; *3d sin. perf. átm. of rt* क्रम् *with* उप, 364.

उपचर्य having groomed or tended (the horses); *past ind. p. of rt* चर् *with* उप, 559.

उपतस्थे he approached, he went to; *3d sin. perf. átm. of rt* स्था *with* उप, 373.

उपतिष्ठति he or she goes near, or she stays with; *3d sin. pres. of rt* स्था *with* उप, 587.

उपदेक्ष्यामि I will instruct or shew; *1st sin. 2d fut. of rt* दिश् *with* उप, 411, 583.

उपपद्यते it is becoming, it is fitting; *3d sin. pres. átm. of rt* पद् *with* उप, *4th cl.*

उपपन्नं obtained, offered; *acc. sin. n. See* उपपन्नो.

उपपन्ना *nom. sin. f. of* उपपन्न *m. f. n.* obtained, gained.

उपपन्नान् *acc. pl. m. See next and last.*

उपपन्नो endowed with, *nom. sin. m. of* उपपन्न *m. f. n.; past p. p. of* पद् *with* उप, 540.

उपपादयन् inferring, proving, establishing; *pres. p. of rt* पद् *in caus. with* उप, 525.

उपययौ he went, he went near, he returned, he entered upon, he undertook; *3d sin. perf. of rt* या *with* उप, 644.

उपरतं *acc. sin. m. of* उपरत *m. f. n.* withdrawn or retired from.

उपरि *ind.* above, over, upon, towards, 917.

उपलक्षितः *nom. sin. of* उपलक्षित *m. f. n.* seen, observed; *past p. p. of rt* लक्ष् *with* उप, 538.

उपलप्स्यसे thou wilt obtain, thou wilt recover; *2d sin. 2d fut. átm. of rt* लभ् *with* उप, 601.

उपलभ्य having comprehended, having observed, having perceived; *past ind. p. of rt* लभ् *with* उप, 559.

उपलभ्येदं *for* उपलभ्य इदं *by* 32.

उपवनेषु *loc. pl. of* उपवन *n.* a grove, *1st cl.* 104.

उपविष्टं *acc. sin. m. of* उपविष्ट *m. f. n.* sitting down, seated; *past p. p. of rt* विश् *with* उप.

उपविष्टो *nom. sin. of* उपविष्ट *m. f. n.* seated.

उपशिक्षिता *nom. sin. f. of* उपशिक्षित *m. f. n.* learned, studied; *past p. p. of rt* शिक्ष् *with* उप, 538.

उपशोभितं *acc. sin. m. or n.* adorned. *See next.*

उपशोभितां *acc. sin. f. of* उपशोभित *m. f. n.* adorned, beautified; *past p. p. of rt* शुभ् *with* उप, 538.

उपसंस्कृतम् *acc. sin. n. of* उपसंस्कृत *m. f. n.* cooked, dressed; *past p. p. of rt* कृ *with* सं *and* उप, 783. *s.*

उपसम्प्राप्य having arrived at; *past ind. p. of rt* आप् *with* सम् *and* उप, 559.

उपसर्प्य having approached, *for* उपसृप्य; *past ind. p. of rt* सृप् *with* उप, 564.

उपस्थास्यतश् they two shall stay with, they two shall attend upon; *3d du. 2d fut. of rt* स्था *with* उप, 587.

उपस्थास्यति he or she shall stand near; *3d sin. 2d fut. of rt* स्था *with* उप, 587.

उपस्थितः *nom. sin. m. of* उपस्थित *m. f. n.* arrived, approached, standing or remaining near; *past p. p. of rt* स्था *with* उप, 533.

उपस्थितम् *nom. sin. n. of* उपस्थित. *See last.*

उपस्थितां *acc. sin. f.* See उपस्थितः.

उपस्पृश्य having sipped water; *past ind. p. of rt* स्पृश् *with* उप. The verb उपस्पृश् means properly 'to touch,' and is applied to sipping water as part of the ceremony of purification. In the Mitákshara, on the subject of personal purification, the direction is द्विजो नित्यम् उपस्पृशेत् 'let the twice-born man (after evacuations) always perform the *upasparśa;*' i.e. says the commentator, आचमेत् 'let him sip water.' According to Professor Wilson the sense of the passage in Book VII. 4 is 'that Nala sat down to evening prayer (as Manu directs, "he who repeats it sitting at evening twilight &c.") after performing his purifications and sipping water, but without having washed his feet; such ablution being necessary, not because they had been soiled, but because such an act is also part of the rite of purification.'

उपाकर्तुं to bestow, to make over; *inf. of rt* कृ *with* उप *and* आ, 459.

उपागमत् he or it approached; *3d sin. aor. of rt* गम् *with* उप, 602.

उपागम्य having approached, having gone near or towards; *past ind. p. of rt* गम् *with* उप *and* आ, 602, 559.

उपातिष्ठद् he went to, he approached; *3d sin. impf. of rt* स्था *with* उप, 587.

उपादाय taking, having taken; *past ind. p. of rt* दा *with* उप *and* आ, 559, 783. *i.*

उपानयत् he brought, he brought nigh; *3d sin. impf. of rt* नी *with* उप, 590. *a.*

उपायश् *nom. sin. m.* a stratagem, plan.

उपायेन *ins. sin. of* उपाय *m.* a contrivance, plan, device, means.

उपायो *for* उपायस् *nom. sin. of* उपाय *m.* a plan, contrivance, remedy, *1st cl.* 103.

उपाविशत् he sat down; *3d sin. impf. of rt* विश् *with* उप, *6th cl.* 278.

उपासितुम् to wait upon, to do homage; *inf. of rt* आस् to sit, *with* उप near, 459.

उपेतं *acc. sin. m. of* उपेत *m. f. n.* come near to, united, endowed with.

उपेयतुः they two arrived at, they two came to; *3d du. perf. of rt* इ *with* उप.

उपेयिवान् he had recourse to, he went to; *nom. sin. m. of* उपेयिवस् *m. f. n. participle of perf. of rt* इ *with* उप, *see* 554, 645.

उपैक्षत he or she overlooked, he or she looked on; *3d sin. impf. átm. of rt* ईक्ष् *with* उप, *1st cl.* 605.

उभयं *nom. sin. n. of* उभय *m. f. n.* both, 238. कस्माद् उभयं नष्टं तव why have both (the circumstances before mentioned) been forgotten by you? *i.e.* the abandoning of your wife in the forest, and the leaving her unsupported.

उभयोर् *gen. du. f. of* उभय *m. f. n.* both.

उभौ *acc. du. m. of* उभ *m. f. n.* both.

उरगाः *nom. pl. of* उरग *m.* a snake, a serpent, *1st cl.* 103.

उरगेण *ins. sin. of* उरग *m.* a serpent, a snake.

उरगेणायतेक्षणाम् *for* उरगेण आयतेक्षणाम्.

उल्लिखद्भिर् *ins. pl. n. of* उल्लिखत् *m. f. n.* soaring upwards, *lit.* making lines or marks on high; *pres. p. par. of rt* लिख् *with* उत्, 524.

उवाच he spoke, he said; *3d sin. perf. of rt* वच् 375. *c,* 650.

उवाचाथ *for* उवाच अथ.

उवाचानवद्याङ्गीं *for* उवाच अनवद्याङ्गीं *by* 31.

उवाचासकृद् *for* उवाच असकृद्.

उवाचेदं *for* उवाच इदं *by* 32.

उवास he, she or it lodged or dwelt or encamped; *3d sin. perf. of rt* वस् 375. *c,* 607.

उषितस् *nom. sin. m. of* उषित *m. f. n.* resided. *See next.*

उषिता *nom. sin. f. of* उषित *m. f. n.* dwelt; *past p. p. of rt* वस् 543, 607; उषिता अस्मि I have dwelt, *see* 895.

उषितौ *nom. sin. of* उषित *m. f. n.* dwelt. (*In* Book IX. 10 he abided, *see* 896.)

उष्मणा *ins. sin. of* उष्मन् *m.* heat, *6th cl.* 147.

उष्य having resided, having dwelt; *past ind. p. of rt* वस्, *see* 565 *and* 556 *note.*

ऊ.

ऊचुः they said; *3d pl. perf. of rt* वच्. *See* उवाच.

ऊचुस् they said; *3d pl. perf. See last.*

ऊर्ध्वं *ind.* after; (अत ऊर्ध्वं after this, from this time forward, henceforth, *see* 917, 719.)

ऊर्ध्वदृष्टिर् Bah. or Rel. comp. 766; ऊर्ध्व *cr.* upwards, दृष्टिर् *nom. sin. f. of* दृष्टि *f.* a look, *2d cl.* 112.

ऊषतुर् they two passed the night, (*lit.* they two lodged;) *3d du. perf. of rt* वस् 375. c.

ऋ.

ऋक्षवन्तं *acc. sin. of* ऋक्षवत् *m.* Ṛikshavat, name of a mountain, *lit.* bear-having; (*from* ऋक्ष a bear, *and* वत्, *affix,* of possession.) The mountain of bears is part of the Vindhya chain, separating Malwa from Khandesh and Berár.

ऋक्षांश् *for* ऋक्षान् *acc. pl. of* ऋक्ष *m.* a bear, *1st cl.* 103.

ऋच्छति goes to; *3d sin. pres. of rt* ऋ (*substituting* ऋच्छ्), *1st cl.* 261.

ऋतां *acc. sin. f. of* ऋत *m. f. n.* true, *1st cl.* 187.

ऋतुपर्ण *voc. sin. m.* O Ṛituparṇa. *See next.*

ऋतुपर्णं *acc. sin. of* ऋतुपर्ण *m.* Ṛituparṇa, name of a king of Ayodhyá.

ऋतुपर्णनिवेशने Tat. or Dep. comp. 743; ऋतुपर्ण Ṛituparṇa, निवेशने *loc. sin. of* निवेशन *n.* dwelling, abode.

ऋतुपर्णस्य *gen. sin. of* ऋतुपर्ण *m.* Ṛituparṇa.

ऋतुपर्णाय *dat. sin. of* ऋतुपर्ण *m.* Ṛituparṇa.

ऋतुपर्णे *loc. sin. of* ऋतुपर्ण *m.* Ṛituparṇa.

ऋतुपर्णेन *ins. sin. of* ऋतुपर्ण *m.* Ṛituparṇa,

ऋतुपर्णो *nom. sin. m.* Ṛituparṇa, name of a king.

ऋते *ind.* except, besides, without; *governing accusative case,* 731.

ऋद्धं *acc. sin. n. of* ऋद्ध *m. f. n.* prosperous, thriving, rich.

ऋद्धां *acc. sin. f. of* ऋद्ध *m. f. n.* rich. (*In* Book XII. 59 applied to the sound of Nala's voice.)

ऋषिसत्तमौ Tat. or Dep. comp. 743; ऋषि *cr.* a sage, सत्तमौ *nom. du. m. of* सत्तम *m. f. n.* best, most excellent, *superl. of* सत् good, 191.

ऋषीन् *acc. pl. of* ऋषि *m.* a sage, a saint, a holy man.

ए.

एक *cr. m. f. n.* one, 200, 239.

एक *for* एकस् *nom. sin. of* एक *m. f. n.* one.

एकं *nom. sin. n. or acc. sin. m. of* एक one, 200.

एकः *for* एकस् one. *See* एक.

एकतः *for* एकतस् *ind.* on one side, on one part.

एकतरे *loc. sin. n. of* एकतर *m. f. n.* one of two, 236.

एकतो *for* एकतस् *ind.* in one manner, on one side, 719.

एकत्र *ind.* in one, in one place, together.

एकदेशं *acc. sin. of* एकदेश *m.* one part.

एकपाणेन *ins. sin. m.* in one game, in a single wager or stake; (*comp. of* एक one, *and* पाण stake.)

एकवसनं *acc. sin. m.* having only one garment; (*comp. of* एक *cr.* one, *and* वसन a garment, 761.)

एकवसना *nom. sin. f.* having only one robe. *See last*

एकवस्त्रताम् *acc. sin. of* एकवस्त्रता *f.* state of having a single garment; (*from* एक *cr.* one, *and* वस्त्रता *abstract noun,* 80. XXIII.)

एकवस्त्रसंवीताव् *for* एकवस्त्रसंवीतौ Complex comp. 771; एक *cr.* one, वस्त्र *cr.* garment, संवीताव् *nom. du. of* संवीत *m. f. n.* clothed.

एकवस्त्रा BAH. OR REL. COMP. 761; एक *cr.* one, वस्त्रा *nom. sin. f. from* वस्त्र *n.* a garment, vest, 1*st cl.* 108.

एकवस्त्रार्धसंवीतं clothed in half a single garment, COMPLEX COMP. 771; एक *cr.* one, वस्त्र *cr.* vestment, अर्ध *cr.* a half, संवीतं *acc. sin. m.* clothed.

एकवासा *for* एकवासास् (66. *a*) *nom. sin. m.* wearing a single garment, BAH. OR REL. COMP. 766; एक *cr.* single, वासा *nom. sin. m. from* वासस् *n.* a vest, *see* 164. *a.*

एकविंशतितमः *nom. sin. m.* twenty-first, 211.

एकस्य *gen. sin. m. of* एक *m. f. n.* one, 200.

एकस्यापि *for* एकस्य अपि *by* 31.

एका *nom. sin. f. of* एक *m. f. n.* one, alone.

एकां *acc. sin. f. of* एक *m. f. n.* single, alone, solitary.

एकाकिनी *nom. sin. f. of* एकाकिन् *m. f. n.* alone, solitary, 6*th cl.* 159.

एकादशः *nom. sin. m.* eleventh, *see* 210.

एकान्ते *ind.* in private, secretly, 716.

एकार्थसमुपेतं COMPLEX COMP. 771; एक *cr.* one, one and the same, अर्थ *cr.* object, समुपेतं *acc. sin. of* समुपेत *m. f. n.* come, arrived, 1*st cl.* 103; *past p. p. of rt* इ *with* उप *and* सम्.

एकाह्ना *ins. sin. n.* in one day; (*comp. of* एक one, *and* अहन् *n.* a day, *see* 156.)

एकेन *ins. sin. m. or n. of* एक one, alone.

एकैकशस् *ind.* one by one, singly.

एको *nom. sin. m. of* एक *m. f. n.* one.

एतज् *for* एतत् this; *nom. sin. n.*

एतत् *m. f. n.* this; *nom. or acc. sin. n.*

एतद् *for* एतत् this; *acc. sin. n.*

एतदर्थम् on this account, for this cause; (*comp. of* एतद् *and* अर्थं 760. *d.*)

एतया with her; *ins. sin. f. of* एतत् 223.

एतस्मिन् in this, at this; *loc. sin. of* एतत् this, 223.

एतस्मिन्न् *for* एतस्मिन् in this, at this (52).

एतां this; *acc. sin. f. of* एतत्.

एतान् them, these; *acc. pl. m. of* एतत्, *q.v.*

एतानि these; *acc. pl. n. of* एतत्, *q. v.*

एताभ्यां with these two; *ins. du. of* एतत् 223.

एतावत् *ind.* so far, to such an extent, 234, 713. *a.*

एतावद् *nom. sin. n. of* एतावत् *m. f. n.* thus much, so much, 234.

एतावान् *nom. sin. m. of* एतावत् *m. f. n.* thus much, so much.

एति he goes; 3*d sin. pres. of rt* इ 2*d cl.*

एते these; *nom. pl. m. of* एतत्, *q. v.*

एतेन by him; *ins. sin. m. or n. of* एतत्, *q. v.*

एतौ these two; *acc. du. m. of* एतत्.

एनं him; *acc. sin. m. of* एतत् 223.

एनां her; *acc. sin. f. from nom.* एषा. *See* एतत् 223.

एनाम् her; *acc. sin. f. See last.*

एव *ind.* also, even, indeed, very, in like manner.

एवं *ind.* thus, so, in this manner, 717. *c.*

एवंरूपं *acc. sin. m. of* एवंरूप *m. f. n.* of such a form, of such a kind as this; (*comp. of* एवं *ind.* such, *and* रूप *n.* form, 1*st cl.* 103.)

एवङ्गता *nom. sin. f. of* एवङ्गत *m. f. n.* in such a state, fallen into such a condition; (*comp. of* एवं so, *and* गत, *q. v.*)

एवङ्गताम् *acc. sin. f. of* एवंगत *m. f. n.* in such a state, in such a condition as this.

एवङ्गुणं having such good qualities, possessing such virtues; (*comp. of* एवं *ind.* so, *and* गुण *m.* a quality, a virtue.)

एवमप्यसुखाविष्टा *for* एवम् अपि असुखाविष्टा.

एवमादीनि *acc. pl. n.* such-like, *lit.* beginning thus; *see* 764.

एवाभिधास्यामि *for* एव अभिधास्यामि *by* 31.

एवाभिभाषन्तो *for* एव अभिभाषन्तो *by* 31.

एवाभ्यभाषत *for* एव अभ्यभाषत.

एष *for* एषस् he, this; *nom. sin. m. of* एतत्, *q. v.*

एषां of them, of these; *gen. pl. of* एतत्, *q. v.*

एषो *for* एषस् he, this; *nom. sin. m.*

एष्यति he will go to; 3*d sin.* 2*d fut. of rt* इ 645.

एहि come; *2d sin. imp. of rt* इ *with* आ, *see* 311. *a.*

ऐ.

ऐकाग्र्यं *acc. sin. n.* attention, close attention to one object.

ऐच्छत् he wished, he desired; *3d sin. impf. of rt* इष् 637.

ऐश्वर्यं *nom. sin. n.* supremacy, kingdom, dominion.

ऐश्वर्यात् *abl. sin. of* ऐश्वर्य *n.* kingdom, 1*st cl.* 104.

औ.

औषधं *nom. sin. of* औषध *n.* a medicine.

क.

कं whom? *acc. sin. m. of* किं.

कः who? *nom. sin. m. of* किं.

कच्चित् *interrog.* whether? *See next.*

कच्चिद् *for* कच्चित् *ind. an interrogative particle, equivalent to Latin* an, whether? 717. *b.*

कञ्चन *acc. sin. m. of* कश्चन *m. f. n.* any, 229.

कतरन् *for* कतरत् (47) *nom. sin. n.* which of two things? whether of the twain? 236.

कत्थसे thou boastest; *2d sin. pres. átm. of rt* कत्थ् 1*st cl.* 261.

कथं *ind.* how? in what manner?

कथञ्चन *ind.* any how, by any means, 230.

कथयध्वं tell, say, relate; *2d pl. imp. átm. of rt* कथ् 286. *a*, 643.

कथयन् *nom. sin. m. of* कथयत् *m. f. n.* talking, speaking; *pres. p. of rt* कथ् 10*th cl.* 524.

कथयन्तीं *acc. sin. f. of* कथयत् *m. f. n.* speaking, talking. *See last.*

कथयन्तौ *nom. du. m. of* कथयत् *m. f. n.* relating.

कथयानः *nom. sin. m. of* कथयान *m. f. n.* telling, speaking; *pres. p. átm. of rt* कथ्, *see* 527.

कथयामास he or she said or told; *3d sin. 2d pret. of rt* कथ् 10 *cl.* 643.

कथयिष्यन्ति they will relate; *3d pl. 2d fut. of rt* कथ् 10*th cl.*

कथयिष्यामि I will speak of, I will tell of; 1*st sin. 2d fut. of rt* कथ्.

कथयेद् he can tell, he may tell; *3d sin. pot. of rt* कथ्.

कथान्ते TAT. OR DEP. COMP. 743; कथा *cr.* conversation, अन्ते *loc. sin. of* अन्त *m. n.* end.

कथितं *nom. sin. n. of* कथित *m. f. n.* told, related; *past p. p. of rt* कथ् 538.

कथिता *nom. sin. f. of* कथित. *See last.*

कथ्यमाने being said; *loc. sin. n. of* कथ्यमान *pres. p. pass. of rt* कथ्.

कदा *ind.* when?

कदाचन *ind.* at some time or other, ever.

कदाचिद् *for* कदाचित् *ind.* at some time or other, perchance, 230.

कदाचिन् *for* कदाचित्. *See last.*

कनकस्तम्भरुचिरं TAT. OR DEP. COMP. 745; कनक *cr.* gold, स्तम्भ column, रुचिरं *acc. sin. m. of* रुचिर shining, beautiful, 1*st cl.* 103.

कन्दरांश् *for* कन्दरान् (53) *acc. pl. of* कन्दर *m.* a ravine, a glen.

कन्दर्प *for* कन्दर्पस् *nom. sin. of* कन्दर्प the god of love or Hindú cupid. He is also called Káma and Kámadeva, Manmatha or heart-agitator, Manasija or heart-born, Ananga or the bodiless. He was the son of Vishṇu or Kṛishṇa by Lakshmí, who is then called Máyá or Rukminí. According to another account, he was produced in the heart of Brahmá. He is usually represented as a handsome youth, sometimes riding on a parrot and attended by nymphs, one of whom bears his banner, which consists of a fish (*makara*). Endeavouring to influence S'iva with love for his wife Párvatí, he discharged an arrow at him, but S'iva, enraged, reduced him to ashes by a beam of fire darted from his central eye. Hence his name, Ananga. His bow is made of flowers, with a string formed of bees and five arrows, each tipped with the blossom of a flower which is devoted to a separate sense.

कन्यकाम् *acc. sin. of* **कन्यका** *f.* a girl, *1st cl.* 105.

कन्या *f.* a maiden, a girl, *1st cl.* 105.

कन्यां *acc. sin. of* **कन्या** *f.* a maiden, a daughter.

कन्यारत्नं *acc. sin. of* **कन्यारत्न** *n.* a jewel of a damsel, a lovely girl; (*comp. of* **कन्या** *cr.* a maiden, *and* **रत्न** *n.* a gem.)

कन्यास् *nom. pl. of* **कन्या** *f.* a maiden, *q. v.*

कमलगर्भाभम् *acc. sin. m.* bright as the lotus-cup; (*comp. of* **कमल** *cr.* lotus, **गर्भ** *cr.* cup, *and* **आभ** *m. f. n. from* **आभा** *f.* light, beauty, 775. *a.*)

कमलेक्षणा BAH. OR REL. COMP. 766; **कमल** *cr.* lotus, **ईक्षणा** *nom. sin. f. from* **ईक्षण** *n.* an eye, *see* 108.

कम्पयन् *for* **कम्पयन्** (52) *nom. sin. m. of* **कम्पयत्** *m. f. n.* shaking, causing to tremble; *pres. p. of* **कम्प्** *in caus.* 527.

करवाणि I must do, I can do; *1st sin. imp. of rt* **कृ** 682; **किं करवाणि** what can I do? (*properly*, let me do?) *see* 796.

करवामहै we must do, let us do; *1st pl. imp. átm. of rt* **कृ** 683.

करिणां *gen. pl. of* **करिन्** *m.* an elephant, *6th cl.* 159.

करिष्य *for* **करिष्ये** I will do, I will perform; *1st sin. 2d fut. átm. of rt* **कृ** 683.

करिष्यति he will do, he will perform; *3d sin. 2d fut. par. of rt* **कृ**.

करिष्यसि thou wilt do; *2d sin. 2d fut. of rt* **कृ**.

करिष्यामि I will do, I will perform; *3d sin. 2d fut. of rt* **कृ**.

करुणम् *ind.* piteously, 713.

करुणम् *acc. sin. n. of* **करुण** *m. f. n.* piteous, *1st cl.* 187.

करैः *ins. pl. of* **कर** *m.* an elephant's trunk.

करोमि I perform, I (will) do; *1st sin. pres. of rt* **कृ** 682; (*present with future signification* 873.)

कर्कोटकं *acc. sin. of* **कर्कोटक** *m.* Karkoṭaka, the name of a Nága or serpent.

कर्कोटकविषं TAT. OR DEP. COMP. 743; **कर्कोटक** *cr.* Karkoṭaka, **विषं** *acc. sin. of* **विष** *n.* poison.

कर्कोटको *nom. sin. m. See* **कर्कोटकं**.

कर्णिकारधवप्लक्षैः DVAN. OR AGG. COMP. 748; **कर्णिकार** *cr.* the Karṇikára-tree, **धव** *cr.* the Dhava-tree, Grislea tomentosa, **प्लक्षैः** *ins. pl. of* **प्लक्ष** *m.* the Plaksha, a kind of fig-tree.

कर्तव्यं *nom. sin. n. of* **कर्तव्य** *m. f. n.* to be done; *fut. pass. p. of rt* **कृ** 569.

कर्तास्मि I will make; *1st sin. 1st fut. of rt* **कृ** 682.

कर्तुं to make, to do, to perform; *inf. of rt* **कृ** 459, 682.

कर्तुकामा *nom. sin. f. of* **कर्तुकाम** *m. f. n.* desirous or willing to do; (*comp. of* **कर्तु** *for* **कर्तुम्** *inf. of rt* **कृ** *and* **काम**, *see* 871.)

कर्तुम् to do, to be done; *inf. of rt* **कृ** 459.

कर्म *nom. sin. of* **कर्मन्** *n.* action, business, 152.

कर्मचेष्टाभिसूचितम् COMPLEX COMP. 771; **कर्म** *cr.* action, **चेष्टा** *cr.* gesture, **अभिसूचितम्** *acc. sin. m.* indicated, denoted.

कर्मणः *gen. sin. of* **कर्मन्** *n.* a deed.

कर्मणा *ins. sin. of* **कर्मन्** *n.* an act, action.

कर्मणि *loc. sin. of* **कर्मन्** *n.* an action.

कर्षयन् *nom. sin. m. of* **कर्षयत्** *m. f. n.* pulling, picking, gathering; *pres. p. of rt* **कृष्** *in caus.* 525.

कर्षिता *nom. sin. f. of* **कर्षित** *m. f. n.* distracted; *past p. p. of rt* **कृष्** 538.

कर्षितो *nom. sin. m. of* **कर्षित** *m. f. n.* tormented, harassed.

कर्हिचित् *ind.* ever, at any time; **न कर्हिचित्** never, at no time, 718.

कलिं *acc. sin. of* **कलि** *m.* Kali. *See next.*

कलिः *nom. sin. m.* Kali, the 4th Age of the world personified as a deity or evil genius.

कलिना *ins. sin. of* **कलि** *m.* Kali.

कलिनापहृतज्ञानो *for* **कलिना अपहृतज्ञानो** *by* 31.

कलिर् *for* **कलिस्** *nom. sin. m.* Kali.

कलिसंश्रयात् TAT. OR DEP. COMP. 743; **कलि** *cr.* Kali, **संश्रयात्** *abl. sin. of* **संश्रय** *m.* entrance, the act of betaking one's self to.

कले O Kali; *voc. sin. of* **कलि** *m.* Kali, 2*d cl.* 110.

कलेस् *gen. sin. of* **कलि** *m.* Kali.

कलौ *loc. sin. of* **कलि** *m.* Kali.

कल्पते he is fitted for; 3*d sin. pres. átm. of rt* **क्लृप्**, (*governing dative case, see* 853. *a.*)

कल्यं *nom. or acc. sin. n.* to-morrow.

कल्याण O illustrious one; *voc. sin. of* **कल्याण** *m. f. n.* good, noble, illustrious, 1*st cl.* 103.

कल्याणाभिजनं *acc. sin.* of noble family, BAH. OR REL. COMP. 766; **कल्याण** *cr.* noble, **अभिजनं** *acc. sin. of* **अभिजन** *m.* family.

कल्याणि O excellent lady, O good lady, O noble lady, O happy fair one; *voc. sin. of* **कल्याणी** *f. of* **कल्याण** good.

कल्याणी *nom. sin. f.* illustrious lady. *See next.*

कल्याणीं *acc. sin. f. of* **कल्याणी** *f. of* **कल्याण** *m. f. n.* good, noble, generous, 1*st cl.* 106.

कल्याणो *nom. sin. m.* noble. *See* **कल्याण**.

कश् *for* **कस्** who? *nom. sin. m. of* **किं**, *q. v.*

कश्चन *nom. sin. m. of* **किञ्चन** any one, *see* 229.

कश्चासौ *for* **कस् च असौ** *by* 62 *and* 31.

कश्चिद् any one, some one, *for* **कश्चित्** *nom. sin. m. of* **किञ्चित्**.

कश्चिन् *for* **कश्चित्** (47) some one, a certain.

कश्मलम् *nom. sin. n.* dejection of mind, depression of spirits, lowness, weakness.

कष्टस् *nom. sin. m. of* **कष्ट** *m. f. n.* bad, destructive.

कष्टाम् *acc. sin. f. of* **कष्ट** *m. f. n.* evil, bad.

कस् *nom. sin. m.* who?

कस्मात् why? wherefore? *abl. sin. m. or n. of* **किं** 227.

कस्माद् *for* **कस्मात्** why?

कस्मिंश्चित् *loc. sin. m. or n. of* **किञ्चित्** some, any, certain.

कस्य of whom? *gen. sin. of* **किम्**.

कस्यचित् *gen. sin. m. or n. of* **किञ्चित्** some, any, a certain one, 228.

कस्यचिद् *for* **कस्यचित्**, *q. v.*

कस्याद्य *for* **कस्य अद्य** *by* 31.

कस्यासि *for* **कस्य असि** *by* 31.

कस्येदं *for* **कस्य इदं** *by* 32.

का who? what? *nom. sin. f. of* **किं** 227.

कांश्चिद् *acc. pl. m. of* **किञ्चित्** some, *see* 228.

काङ्क्षन्ति they desire; 3*d pl. pres. par. of rt* **काङ्क्ष्** 1*st cl.* 261.

काङ्क्षितं *nom. sin. n. of* **काङ्क्षित** *m. f. n.* desired.

काङ्क्षे I desire, I seek; 1*st sin. pres. átm. of rt* **कांक्ष्**.

काचिद् *nom. sin. f.* any woman, *see* 228.

काचिद्धि *for* **काचिद् हि** *by* 50.

काञ्चनसन्निभम् ANOM. COMP. 777; **काञ्चन** *cr.* gold, *and* **सन्निभम्** *nom. sin. n. of* **सन्निभ** *m. f. n.* like.

काञ्चिद् *for* **काञ्चित्** *acc. sin. f. of* **किञ्चित्** some, any, a certain, 228.

काननम् *nom. sin. n.* a wood, forest, grove.

कानने *loc. sin. of* **कानन** *n.* a forest, 1*st cl.* 104.

कानिचित् *nom. or acc. pl. n. of* **किञ्चित्** any, some, 228.

कान्ता *nom. sin. f.* beloved, loved one.

कान्तिर् *for* **कान्तिस्** *nom. sin. of* **कान्ति** *f.* beauty, brilliancy, 2*d cl.* 112.

काम् *acc. sin. f. of* **किम्** whom? *see* 227.

काम *m.* love, the god of love (*see note under* **कन्दर्प**), 1*st cl.* 103.

कामं *acc. sin. of* **काम** *m.* love.

कामं *ind.* willingly.

कामगः *nom. sin. m.* one who comes accidentally or unexpectedly, a casual visitor, one who travels about without any specific purpose; (*from* काम pleasure, *and* ग who goes.)

कामधुक् *nom. sin. of* कामदुह् *f.* the cow of plenty, *8th cl.* 182; (*comp. of* काम desire, *and* दुह् who milks.) The cow of plenty was a fabulous cow (granting all desires) produced at the churning of the ocean by the Suras and Asuras, after the deluge, for the recovery or production of fourteen sacred things; see note under अमृतोपमां.

कामभोगैः TAT. OR DEP. COMP. 743; काम *cr.* love, भोगैः *ins. pl. of* भोग *m.* enjoyment.

कामयेच् *for* कामयेत् he or she may desire; *3d sin. pot. of rt* कम् *10th cl.* 283.

कामवासिनीम् *acc. sin. f.* dwelling where one wishes; (*comp. of* काम wish, desire, *and* वासिन् *m. f. n.* a dweller.)

कामस् *nom. sin. of* काम *m.* love.

कामस्य *gen. sin. of* काम *m.* love, *1st cl.* 103.

कामार्तस् TAT. OR DEP. COMP. 740; काम *cr.* love, *and* आर्त *m. f. n.* pained, afflicted, sick, *see* 542.

कारणं *acc. sin. of* कारण *n.* cause, action.

कारणात् on account of, by reason of; *abl. sin. of* कारण *n.* cause; *used adverbially.*

कारणान्तरे *loc. sin. n.* on the occasion of a cause; (*comp. of* कारण *cr.* a cause, *and* अन्तर occasion.)

कारणैर् *ins. pl. of* कारण *n.* a reason, cause.

कारयामास he caused to be done, he performed; *3d sin. perf. of* कृ *in caus.* 385. *a.*

कार्य *m. f. n.* to be done, to be performed; *fut. pass. p. of rt* कृ 682, 571. *c.*

कार्य *n.* an affair, business, matter, *1st cl.* 104.

कार्यं *nom. sin. n. of* कार्य *m. f. n.* to be done.

कार्यं *acc. sin. of* कार्य *n.* matter, business.

कार्यगौरवात् TAT. OR DEP. COMP. 743; कार्य *cr.* business, affair, गौरवात् *abl. sin. of* गौरव *n.* importance, urgency, weightiness.

कार्यवान् having business (to transact); *nom. sin. m. of* कार्यवत् *m. f. n., 5th cl.* 140.

कार्या *nom. sin. f. of* कार्य *m. f. n.* to be made, to be done; *fut. pass. p. of rt* कृ 571.

काल *m.* time, *1st cl.* 103.

कालं *acc. sin. of* काल *m.* time.

कालः *nom. sin. of* काल *m.* time.

कालस्य *gen. sin. of* काल *m.* time; दीर्घस्य कालस्य after a long time.

काले *loc. sin. of* काल *m.* time, opportunity, *1st cl.* 103, *see* 840.

कालो *nom. sin. of* काल *m.* time.

काषायवसना BAH. OR REL. COMP. 761; काषाय *cr.* dark brown, red, reddish, वसना *nom. sin. f. from* वसन *n.* a garment, 108.

काष्ठैश् *ins. pl. of* काष्ठ *n.* wood, a stick, *1st cl.* 104.

कासि *for* का असि *by* 31.

किं *pron.* what? who? which? 227.

किंशुकाशोकवकुलपुन्नागैर् DVAN. OR AGG. COMP. 748; किंशुक *cr.* the Kinśuka-tree (Butea frondosa); अशोक *cr.* the Aśoka-tree (Jonesia Aśoka); वकुल the Vakul-tree (Mimusops Elengi); पुन्नागैर् *ins. pl. of* पुन्नाग the Punnága-tree (Rottleria tinctoria).

किञ्चन *nom. or acc. sin. n.* anything, something, some place, *see* 229.

किञ्चित् *pron. n.* something, anything, any, 228.

किञ्चिद् *for* किञ्चित् *nom. sin. n.* any.

किञ्चिन् *for* किञ्चित् (47) any, some.

कितव *voc. sin. m.* O mischievous fellow, O you rogue; (*often an expression of endearment or coquetry.*)

किनु *ind.* how much less! what? *a particle of interrogation.*

किमर्थं *ind.* on what account? why? 791.

किल *ind.* indeed, truly, that is to say.

किलैकतः *for* किल + एकतः *by* 33.

कीर्तयिष्यन्ति they shall celebrate; 3*d pl.* 2*d fut. of rt* कृत् 10*th cl.* 287.

कीर्तिं *acc. sin. of* कीर्ति *f.* glory, fame.

कीर्तिर् *for* कीर्तिस् *nom. sin. f.* glory, renown.

कुञ्जरद्वीपिमहिषशार्दूलर्क्षमृगान् DVAN. OR AGG. COMP. 748; कुञ्जर *cr.* an elephant, द्वीपि *for* द्वीपिन् (57) a panther, महिष *cr.* a buffalo, शार्दूल *cr.* a tiger, ऋक्ष *cr.* a bear (32), मृगान् *acc. pl. of* मृग *m.* a deer, 1*st cl.* 103.

कुण्डलीकृतम् *acc. sin. m.* coiled into a ring; (*comp. of* कुण्डल a collar, a ring, *and* कृत, *see* 788.)

कुण्डिनं *acc. sin. of* कुण्डिन *n.* Kuṇḍina, a city in Berar, also called Vidarbha, the capital of Bhíma, father-in-law of Nala.

कुण्डिने *loc. sin. n. See last.*

कुतस् *ind.* wherefore? why?

कुतूहलात् *abl. sin. of* कुतूहल *n.* eagerness, joy, pleasure, fun, curiosity, 1*st cl.* 103.

कुपिता *nom. sin. f. of* कुपित *m. f. n.* enraged.

कुपितो *nom. sin. m. of* कुपित *m. f. n.* enraged, angry.

कुमारांश् *for* कुमारान् *acc. pl. of* कुमार *m.* a boy, youth, young man, 1*st cl.* 103.

कुमारांश्च *for* कुमारान् च *by* 53.

कुम्भाः *for* कुम्भास् *nom. pl. See next.*

कुम्भास् *nom. pl. of* कुम्भ *m.* a water-jar.

कुररीम् *acc. sin. of* कुररी *f.* an osprey.

कुरु *m.* name of a prince of the lunar race, sovereign of the North-West of India and the country about Delhi. He was ancestor of both Páṇḍu and Dhṛitaráshṭra. The patronymic derived from his name is applied to the sons of either, but more usually to those of the latter.

कुरु do thou, perform thou, make thou, give thou; 2*d sin. imp. of rt* कृ 682.

कुरुते he does; 3*d sin. pres. átm. of rt* कृ 683.

कुरुनन्दन *voc. sin. m.* O son of Kuru; (*comp. of* कुरु *q. v., and* नन्दन *q. v.*)

कुरुष्व make thou, perform thou; 2*d sin. imp. átm. of rt* कृ 683.

कुर्यात् he may do; 3*d sin. pot. of rt* कृ 682.

कुर्याद् he may perform, he may make, he or she may act; 3*d sin. pot. of rt* कृ 682.

कुर्याम् I may do; 1*st sin. pot. of rt* कृ 682.

कुर्वन्तीम् *acc. sin. f. of* कुर्वत् *m. f. n.* making; *pres. p. par. of rt* कृ 524.

कुर्वन्तु let them make, let them assume; 3*d pl. imp. of rt* कृ 682.

कुलं *acc. sin. n.* a family.

कुलघ्नानां *gen. pl. of* कुलघ्न *m.* a destroyer of a family or tribe; (*comp. of* कुल a family, *and* घ्न a destroyer.)

कुलतत्त्ववित् COMPLEX COMP. 770; कुल family, race, तत्त्व nature, true state, वित् *nom. sin. of* विद् *m.* one who knows, 138.

कुलधर्माः *nom. pl.* the laws or duties of a tribe. *See next.*

कुलधर्माश् *nom. pl. m.* the laws of tribe, the usages of tribe; (कुल a family or tribe, धर्म law, TAT. OR DEP. COMP.)

कुलशीलसमन्वितान् COMPLEX COMP. 771; कुल family, breeding, शील *cr.* good temper or disposition, समन्वितान् *acc. pl. m.* endowed or endued with.

कुलशीलोपसम्पन्न COMPLEX COMP. 771; कुल *cr.* family, high birth, शील *cr.* good disposition, उपसम्पन्न *voc. sin. of* उपसम्पन्न *m. f. n.* endowed with.

कुलस्त्रिय *for* कुलस्त्रियस् *nom. pl. f.* the women of the family. *See next.*

कुलस्त्रियः *nom. pl. f.* noble women; (*comp. of* कुल a family, a noble family, *and* स्त्री a woman, 123. *b.*)

कुलस्य *gen. sin. of* कुल *n.* a family.

कुलीनश् *nom. sin. m. of* कुलीन *m. f. n.* noble, well-born.

कुशलं *nom. or acc. sin. n.* well-being, health, prosperity, good fortune, welfare, freedom from calamity, 1*st cl.* 104. *Used in salutation:* Is it well? It is well. Hail!

कुशलस् *nom. sin. m. of* कुशल *m. f. n.* well, in good health.

कुशलिनो *for* कुशलिनस् *nom. or acc. pl. m. of* कुशलिन् *m. f. n.* well, healthy, prosperous, in good health, *6th cl.* 159.

कुशलिनौ *nom. du. m. of* कुशलिन् *m. f. n.* well, in good health, *6th cl.* 159.

कुशली *nom. sin. m. of* कुशलिन् *m. f. n.* well, in good health.

कुशलैर् *ins. pl. m. of* कुशल *m. f. n.* clever, skilful, adept.

कुशलो *nom. sin. m. of* कुशल *m. f. n.* clever, skilful.

कूर्मग्राहझषाकीर्णां COMPLEX COMP. 771; कूर्म *cr.* turtles, ग्राह alligators, झष *cr.* fish, आकीर्णां *acc. sin. f. of* आकीर्ण *m. f. n.* filled with, crowded, thronged.

कृच्छ्रम् *acc. sin. of* कृच्छ्र *n.* calamity, trouble.

कृच्छ्रे *loc. sin. m. or n. of* कृच्छ्र *m. f. n.* difficult, difficult to be passed, painful.

कृच्छ्रेण *ins. sin. m. or n. of* कृच्छ्र painful, tormenting.

कृतं *nom. or acc. sin. n. of* कृत *m. f. n.* done, performed.

कृतकृत्यो *nom. sin. m.* one who has accomplished his object; (*comp. of* कृत done, *and* कृत्य *n.* that which is to be done, 767.)

कृतनिश्चयः *nom. sin. m.* one who has made a resolution, determined, resolved; (कृत, निश्चय determination.)

कृतवती *nom. sin. f. of* कृतवत् who has done. *See next.*

कृतवन्तो they performed; *nom. pl. m. of* कृतवत्. *See next.*

कृतवांस् *for* कृतवान्, *q. v.*

कृतवान् *nom. sin. m. of* कृतवत् *m. f. n.* who has done, who has made, who has caused; *past act. p. of rt* कृ 553, 897.

कृतशौचम् BAH. OR REL. COMP. 767; कृत *cr.* performed, शौचम् *acc. sin. m. from* शौच *n.* purification, ablution.

कृता *nom. sin. f. of* कृत *m. f. n.* made; *past p. p. of rt* कृ 532.

कृताञ्जलिं *acc. sin. f.* *See* कृताञ्जलिर्.

कृताञ्जलिः *nom. sin. m.* *See next.*

कृताञ्जलिर् *for* कृताञ्जलिस् BAH. OR REL. COMP. 767; कृत *cr.* having made, अञ्जलिर् *nom. sin. of* अञ्जलि *m.* reverential salutation with joined palms, *2d cl.* 110.

कृतानि *nom. pl. n. of* कृत done. *See* कृता.

कृतार्थः *nom. sin. m. of* कृतार्थ *m. f. n.* *See last.*

कृतार्थो *nom. sin. m. of* कृतार्थ *m. f. n.* successful, having accomplished an object; (*comp. of* कृत effected, *and* अर्थ object, 767.)

कृतास्त्रं *acc. sin. m. of* कृतास्त्र *m. f. n.* skilled in (the use of) weapons; (*comp. of* कृत formed, *and* अस्त्र *n.* a weapon.)

कृताहाराम् BAH. OR REL. COMP. 761; कृत *cr.* made, taken, आहाराम् *acc. sin. f. from* आहार *m.* a meal, food, 108.

कृते *loc. sin. n.* being made, on its being done.

कृते *ind.* by reason of, on account of, 731.

कृत्यकाम् *acc. sin. of* कृत्यका *f.* a woman who is the fatal cause of injury or destruction, the fatal destroyer, the bane.

कृत्वा having made, having done, having settled, having considered; *past ind. p. of rt* कृ 682.

कृत्स्न *m. f. n.* whole, entire, all, *1st cl.* 187.

कृत्स्नं *acc. sin. m. or n. of* कृत्स्न *m. f. n.* entire, whole.

कृत्स्नां *acc. sin. f. of* कृत्स्न *m. f. n.* entire, whole.

कृत्स्ने *loc. sin. m. or n. of* कृत्स्न *m. f. n.* entire.

कृथाः *for* अकृथाः *2d sin. aor. átm. of rt* कृ to do, to make, to place, 683. मा मनः कृथाः do not place thy mind, *see* 861. *a*, 889.

कृपणा *nom. sin. f. of* कृपण *m. f. n.* miserable, wretched, poor, mean.

कृपणां *acc. sin. f. of* कृपण *m. f. n.* wretched.

कृपया *ins. sin. of* कृपा *f.* compassion.

कृपयाविष्टम् *for* कृपया आविष्टम् *by* 31.

कृपां *acc. sin. of* कृपा *f.* pity, compassion.

कृश *m. f. n.* thin, emaciated, 1*st cl.* 187.

कृशा *nom. sin. f. of* कृश *m. f. n.* thin, emaciated, lean.

कृशां *acc. sin. f. of* कृश *m. f. n.* thin, emaciated.

कृशान् *acc. pl. of* कृश *m. f. n.* slender, thin.

कृष्णवर्त्मना *ins. sin. of* कृष्णवर्त्मन् *m.* fire, 6*th cl.* 147; (*lit.* having or making a black path, *from* कृष्ण black, *and* वर्त्मन् path.)

कृष्णसाराभ्यां *abl. du. n. of* कृष्णसार *m. f. n.* black in the centre, spotted with black, having dark pupils; (*from* कृष्ण black, *and* सार essence.)

के who? *nom. pl. of* किं, *q. v.*

केचन *nom. pl. of* किञ्चित् some, *see* 228.

केचिच् *for* केचित् *nom. pl. m.* some.

केचिद् *for* केचित् *nom. pl. m. of* किञ्चित् some, 228.

केतुभूतम् *acc. sin. n.* being or become a banner; (*comp. of* केतु *m.* a banner, *and* भूत *m. f. n.* become, *past p. p. of rt* भू 532, 585.)

केनचिद् by some, by some one, 228.

केशिनि *voc. sin. of* केशिनी *f.* Keśiní.

केशिनी *nom. sin. f.* Keśiní, name of a maidservant or female attendant.

केशिनीं *acc. sin. f.* Keśiní. (Fine-haired.)

केशिन्या *ins. sin. f.* by Keśiní. *See* केशिनी.

कैतवेन *ins. sin. of* कैतव *n.* gambling, gaming.

कैश्चिद् *for* कैश्चित् *ins. pl. m. of* किञ्चित् some.

कैश्चिन् *for* कैश्चित् *ins. pl.* by some; (*from* किञ्चित्.)

कोट्यो *nom. pl. of* कोटि *f.* a krore or ten millions, 199. *b.*

कोपः *nom. sin. m.* anger.

कोपं *acc. sin. of* कोप *m.* anger, 1*st cl.* 103.

कोपम् *acc. sin. of* कोप *m.* anger.

कोपसमन्वितः TAT. OR DEP. COMP. 740; कोप *cr.* anger, समन्वितः *nom. sin. m.* affected by.

कोशलाधिपः TAT. OR DEP. COMP. 743; कोशल *cr.* Kośala, अधिपः *nom. sin. m.* king, sovereign.

कोशलान् *acc. pl. of* कोशल *m. pl.* Kośala, the name of a country or its inhabitants. *In the sin. it is also fem. See next.*

कोशलायाम् *loc. sin. of* कोशला *f.* a country described in the Rámáyaṇa (V. 5) as the district round Ayodhyá or Oude. According to some it is also the name of a town. In the Brahmáṇḍa-puráṇa Kośala is mentioned as beyond the Vindhya mountains.

कौन्तेय *voc. sin. of* कौन्तेय son of Kuntí, a name of Yudhishṭhira, (to whom Vṛihadaśva relates the story of Nala,) or of either of the three elder Páṇḍava princes, who were the reputed sons of Páṇḍu by Kuntí; (*from* कुन्ती patronymic, 80. XIV.)

कौमारं *nom. sin. n.* childhood, youth.

कौरव *voc. sin. m.* O descendant of Kuru.

कौरव्य *voc. sin. of* कौरव्य *m.* descendant of Kuru, 1*st cl.* 103.

कौशलेन *ins. sin. of* कौशल *m.* king of Kośala.

क्रतुभिर् *for* क्रतुभिस् *ins. pl. of* क्रतु *m.* a sacrifice.

क्रतुभिश् *ins. pl. of* क्रतु *m.* a sacrifice, 3*d cl.* 111.

क्रतुमुख्यानां *gen. pl.* of the principal sacrifices; (*comp. of* क्रतु *m.* a sacrifice, *and* मुख्यानां *gen. pl. of* मुख्य chief.)

क्रतूनां *gen. pl. of* क्रतु *m.* a sacrifice, 3*d cl.* 111.

क्रन्दमानाम् *acc. sin. f. of* क्रन्दमान *m. f. n.* weeping, wailing, crying aloud for help; *pres. p. átm. of rt* क्रन्द् 526.

क्रमप्राप्तं TAT. OR DEP. COMP. 740, received by succession or hereditary descent; क्रम *cr.* succession, प्राप्तम् *acc. sin. of* प्राप्त *m. f. n.* received, obtained; *past p. p. of rt* आप् *with* प्र, 539.

क्रमेण *ind.* in order, successively, 714.

क्रियताम् let it be done, let it be set, let it be placed; 3*d sin. imp. of* कृ *in pass.* 701.

क्रुध्यन्ति they are angry; *3d pl. pres. of rt* क्रुध् *4th cl.* 272.

क्रोद्धुम् to be angry; *inf. of rt* क्रुध् *4th cl.* 459.

क्रोधसमन्वितः Tat. or Dep. comp. 740; क्रोध *cr.* anger, समन्वितः *nom. sin. of* समन्वित *m. f. n.* filled with.

क्रोधाद् *abl. sin. of* क्रोध *m.* anger.

क्रोशति she screams; *3d sin. pres. of rt* क्रुश् *1st cl.* 261.

क्रौञ्चकुररैश् Dvan. or Agg. comp. 748; क्रौञ्च *cr.* herons, कुररैश् *ins. pl. of* कुरर *m.* an osprey.

क्लमं *acc. sin. of* क्लम *m.* weariness, *1st cl.* 103.

क्लान्तो *nom. sin. m. of* क्लान्त *m. f. n.* wearied, fatigued.

क्लिश्यते he or she is annoyed or distressed, he or she is tormented or harassed; *3d sin. pres. of* क्लिश् *in pass.* 463.

क्लीववद् *for* क्लीववत् like a base man, like a weak-minded, effeminate person; (*from* क्लीव an impotent man, *and* वत् 724.)

क्लैव्यं *acc. sin. of* क्लैव्य *n.* weakness.

क्व *ind.* where? 717. *g.*

क्वचित् *ind.* anywhere, somewhere, in some place or other, 717. *g*, 230.

क्वचिद् *ind.* somewhere, anywhere.

क्वापि *ind.* anywhere, 230.

क्षण *m.* a moment, an instant.

क्षणे *loc. sin. of* क्षण *m.* a moment, *1st cl.* 103.

क्षणेन instantly, presently, soon, in a short time; *ins. sin. of* क्षण, *used adverbially*, 714.

क्षणेनाथ *for* क्षणेन अथ *by* 31. *See the words.*

क्षत्रियस्य *gen. sin. of* क्षत्रिय *m.* a Kshatriya, a man of the second or military caste. *See next.*

क्षत्रियाः *for* क्षत्रियास् *nom. pl. of* क्षत्रिय *m.* a soldier, a man of the second or military caste. *See note under* विशाम्पते. Kshatriyas or warriors slain in battle are transported to Indra's heaven by the Apsarasas or nymphs of Svarga. Thus in Manu VII. 89 it is said, 'Those rulers of the earth who, desirous of defending each other, exert their utmost strength in battle, without ever averting their faces, ascend after death directly to heaven.' In Book II. 19 of the Nala, Indra means to say, 'Why are no warriors slain now-a-days, that I see none arriving in heaven to honour as my guests?'

क्षन्तव्यं *nom. sin. n. of* क्षन्तव्य *m. f. n.* to be pardoned; *fut. pass. p. of rt* क्षम् 569.

क्षन्तुम् to pardon, to excuse; *inf. of rt* क्षम् 459.

क्षमन्तु let them pardon, let them excuse; *3d pl. pres. of rt* क्षम् *1st cl.* 261.

क्षमयामास he asked to be pardoned, he excused himself; *3d sin. perf. of rt* क्षम् *in caus.* 490, 487. *a.*

क्षमान् *acc. pl. of* क्षम *m. f. n.* capable, powerful.

क्षमावान् *nom. sin. of* क्षमावत् *m. f. n.* patient.

क्षयं *acc. sin. of* क्षय *m.* end, termination.

क्षितिपतिश् *for* क्षितिपतिस् Tat. or Dep. comp. 743; क्षिति *cr.* the earth, पतिश् *nom. sin. of* पति *m.* a lord, 121.

क्षितिम् *acc. sin. of* क्षिति *f.* the earth, *2d cl.* 112.

क्षितौ *loc. sin. of* क्षिति *f.* the earth, the ground, *2d cl.* 112.

क्षिप्रं *ind.* quickly, soon, 713.

क्षुत्तृषान्वितम् Complex comp. 771; क्षुत् *for* क्षुध् *cr.* hunger (42), तृषा *cr.* thirst, अन्वितम् *acc. sin. m. of* अन्वित *m. f. n.* possessed of, afflicted with, distressed by.

क्षुत्परीतस् Tat. or Dep. comp. 740; क्षुत् *for* क्षुध् *cr.* hunger (42), परीतस् *nom. sin. m. of* परीत affected by, filled with.

क्षुत्पिपासापरिश्रान्तौ Complex comp. 771; क्षुत् *cr. for* क्षुध् (42) hunger, पिपासा *cr.* thirst, परिश्रान्तौ *nom. du. of* परिश्रान्त *m. f. n.* worn, wearied; *past p. p. of rt* श्रम् 546.

क्षुत्पिपासापरीताङ्गी Complex comp. 771; क्षुत् *for* क्षुध् *cr.* hunger, पिपासा *f.* thirst, परीत *cr.* affected, अङ्गी *nom. sin. f. from* अङ्ग *n.* the body.

क्षुत्पिपासार्ता *nom. sin. f.* afflicted with hunger and thirst; (*comp. of* क्षुत् *for* क्षुध् *cr.* 42, hunger, पिपासा *cr.* thirst, आर्ता *nom. sin. f.* pained, afflicted, 542.)

क्षुद्रं *acc. sin. n.* mean, little, low. *See next.*

क्षुद्रः *nom. sin. of* क्षुद्र *m. f. n.* vile.

क्षुद्रेण *ins. sin. of* क्षुद्र *m. f. n.* base, vile.

क्षुधया *ins. sin. of* क्षुधा *f.* hunger, 1*st cl.* 105.

क्षुधयान्वित *for* क्षुधया अन्वित *by* 31.

क्षुधा *ins. sin. of* क्षुध् *f.* hunger, 8*th cl.* 177.

क्षुधान्वितः *nom. sin. m.* famished with hunger; (*from* क्षुधा *cr.* hunger, *and* अन्वित *m. f. n.* possessed.)

क्षुधार्तस्य *gen. sin. m. of* क्षुधार्त *m. f. n.* hungry; (*from* क्षुधा *cr.* hunger, *and* आर्त pained, 542.)

क्षुधाविष्टः Tat. or Dep. comp. 740; क्षुधा *cr.* hunger, आविष्टः *nom. sin. of* आविष्ट *m. f. n.* affected by.

क्षुधितं *acc. sin. m. of* क्षुधित *m. f. n.* hungry.

क्षुधितः *nom. sin. m. of* क्षुधित *m. f. n.* hungry.

क्षेमतरं *nom. sin. n. of* क्षेमतर *m. f. n.* better, happier.

क्षेमी *nom. sin. m. of* क्षेमिन् *m. f. n.* safe, well, prosperous.

ख.

खगमांस् *for* खगमान् *acc. pl. of* खगम *m.* a bird, (*lit.* sky-goer,) 1*st cl.* 103.

खगा *for* खगास् *nom. pl. of* खग *m.* a bird, 1*st cl.* 103.

खड्गम् *acc. sin. of* खड्ग *m.* a sword, 1*st cl.* 103.

खड्गेन *ins. sin. of* खड्ग *m.* a sword, cimeter.

खम् *acc. sin. of* ख *n.* the sky, heaven, 1*st cl.* 104.

खलु *ind.* indeed.

खादय devour thou, eat thou; 2*d sin. imp. of rt* खाद् 10*th cl.* 283.

खे *loc. sin. of* ख *n.* the sky, heaven.

खेचरः *nom. sin. m.* a bird; (*from* खे *loc. sin. of* ख the sky, *and* चर going.)

ख्यातः *nom. sin. m. of* ख्यात *m. f. n.* called, styled, celebrated; *past p. p. of rt* ख्या 532.

ग.

ग (*at the end of compounds*) going; *agent from rt* गम्.

गच्छ go thou; 2*d sin. imp. of rt* गम् 1*st cl.* 602.

गच्छति he or she goes; 3*d sin. pres. of rt* गम् 1*st cl.*

गच्छन्तम् *acc. sin. m. of* गच्छत् *m. f. n.* going; *pres. p. par. of rt* गम् 524.

गच्छन्ति they go; 3*d pl. pres. of rt* गम् 1*st cl.* 602, 270.

गच्छन्ती *nom. sin. f. of* गच्छत् *m. f. n.* going, proceeding on; *pres. p. par. of rt* गम् 524.

गच्छन्तीम् *acc. sin. f.* going. *See last.*

गच्छन्त्यपराङ्मुखाः *for* गच्छन्ति अपराङ्मुखाः *by* 34.

गच्छामो we (will) go; 1*st pl. pres.* (*with fut. signification* 873) *of rt* गम् 270, 602.

गच्छावो *for* गच्छावस् we two (will) go; 1*st du. pres. of rt* गम् 1*st cl.* 602.

गच्छेत् he or she may or should go; 3*d sin. pot. of rt* गम् 1*st cl.* 602.

गच्छेद् he may or should go, let him go. *See last.*

गच्छेयं I may go, I can go; 1*st sin. pot. of rt* गम् 1*st cl.* 602.

गच्छैनाम् *for* गच्छ एनाम् *by* 33.

गजान् *acc. pl. of* गज *m.* an elephant, 1*st cl.* 103.

गजेन्द्रविक्रमो Bah. or Rel. comp. 761; गजेन्द्र *cr.* the prince of elephants, विक्रमो *nom. sin. of* विक्रम *m.* valour.

गजैः *ins. pl. of* गज *m.* an elephant.

गण *m.* a troop, a flock, a number.

गणयन् *nom. sin. of* गणयत् *m. f. n.* counting; *pres. p. par. of rt* गण् 10*th cl.* 524.

गणयस्व count thou; 2*d sin. imp. átm. of rt* गण् 10*th cl.* 283.

गणयस्यास्य *for* **गणयस्य अस्य** *by* 31.

गणयित्वा having reckoned; *past ind. p. of rt* **गण्** 558.

गणान् *acc. pl. of* **गण** *m.* a troop, a flock, a number.

गणितः *nom. sin. m. of* **गणित** *m. f. n.* calculated, reckoned; *past p. p. of rt* **गण्** 538.

गणिते *loc. sin. n. of* **गणित** *m. f. n.* reckoned, numbered, counted; *past p. p. of rt* **गण्** 538.

गत gone, departed; he went; *past p. p. of rt* **गम्** to go, 545, 896.

गतः *for* **गतस्** *nom. sin. See last.*

गतक्लमा Bah. or Rel. comp. 766; **गत** *cr.* gone, removed, **क्लमा** *nom. sin. f. from* **क्लम** *m.* fatigue, weariness.

गतचेतनः Bah. or Rel. comp. 766; **गत** *cr.* gone, deprived of, **चेतनः** *nom. sin. m. from* **चेतना** *f.* sense, mind, 1*st cl.* 108.

गतचेतसम् Bah. or Rel. comp. 766; **गत** *cr.* gone, **चेतसम्** *acc. sin. m. from* **चेतस्** *n.* the mind, senses, consciousness, 7*th cl.* 163.

गतज्वरो Bah. or Rel. comp. 767; **गत** *cr.* gone, freed from, **ज्वरो** *nom. sin. of* **ज्वर** *m.* fever, trouble, affliction.

गतवान् *nom. sin. m. of* **गतवत्** *m. f. n.* who went, who has gone; *past act. p. of rt* **गम्** 553, 897.

गतसङ्कल्पा Bah. or Rel. comp. 767; **गत** *cr.* gone to, fixed on, **सङ्कल्पा** *nom. sin. f. from* **सङ्कल्प** *m.* thought, affection. **मां गतसङ्कल्पा** with thoughts or affections fixed on me. *So in* S'akuntalá (Act III), **तद्गतेन अभिलाषेण**.

गतसत्त्वा *for* **गतसत्त्वास्** Bah. or Rel. comp. 767; **गत** *cr.* gone, **सत्त्वा** *nom. pl. of* **सत्त्व** *m. from* **सत्त्व** *n.* strength, spirit, 108.

गतसौहृदा Bah. or Rel. comp. 767; **गत** *cr.* gone, **सौहृदा** *nom. sin. f. from* **सौहृद** *n.* friendship, 108, (bereft of friends.)

गताः *nom. pl. m. of* **गत** *m. f. n.* gone, (they went, going to, 896;) *past p. p. of rt* **गम्** 545.

गतासून् *acc. pl. m. of* **गतासु** *m. f. n.* dead, expired; (**गत** gone, **असु** breath.)

गतिं *acc. sin. of* **गति** *f.* gait, bearing, 2*d cl.* 112.

गते *loc. sin. m. of* **गत** *m. f. n.* gone.

गतेषु being gone, having gone; *loc. pl. of* **गत** *m. f. n.* gone.

गतो *nom. sin. m.* gone, departed. *See* **गत**.

गतौ *nom. du. m. of* **गत** gone, departed.

गत्वा having gone; *past ind. p. of rt* **गम्** 602, 556.

गत्वाथापराम् *for* **गत्वा अथ अपराम्** *by* 31.

गन्तव्यं *nom. sin. n. of* **गन्तव्य** *m. f. n.* to be travelled, to be gone; *fut. pass. p. of rt* **गम्** 569.

गन्ता he or it will go, he will travel; 3*d sin.* 1*st fut. of rt* **गम्**.

गन्तासि thou wilt go; 2*d sin.* 1*st fut. of rt* **गम्** 602.

गन्तुम् to go; *inf. of rt* **गम्** 459.

गन्धर्वो *nom. sin. of* **गन्धर्व** *m.* a Gandharva or celestial musician. These are demigods or angels who inhabit Indra's heaven, and form the orchestra at the banquets of the gods. They are described as witnesses of the actions of men, and are sixty millions in number.

गमः *for* **अगमः** 2*d sin. aor. of rt* **गम्**, *used with* **मा** *or* **मास्म** *for the imperative; as,* **मास्म गमः** do not go, 889.

गमने *loc. sin. of* **गमन** *n.* going, advancing.

गमिष्यन्ति they will go. *See next.*

गमिष्यामि I shall or will go; 1*st sin.* 2*d fut. of rt* **गम्** 602.

गम्भीरं *ind.* deeply, 713.

गरीयो *nom. sin. n. of* **गरीयस्** *m. f. n.* more heavy, heavier, worse, worst, 194, 167.

गरुत्मन्तः *for* **गरुत्मन्तस्** *nom. pl. m. of* **गरुत्मत्** a bird, (*lit.* possessed of wings,) 5*th cl.* 140.

गवां *gen. pl. of* **गो** *f.* a cow, an ox, 133. Used in Nala VII. 6 as the name given to the ordinary dice, as distinguished from the **वृष** or principal die.

गहने *loc. sin. m. or n. of* गहन *m. f. n.* dense, thick, impenetrable.

गात्रवैरूप्यताम् Tat. or Dep. comp. 743; गात्र *cr.* limbs, body, वैरूप्यताम् *acc. sin. f.* deformity.

गात्राणि *nom. pl. of* गात्र *n.* a limb, a member.

गात्रेषु *loc. pl. of* गात्र *n.* a limb.

गात्रैर् *ins. pl. of* गात्र *n.* a limb.

गाथाभिर् *for* गाथाभिस् *ins. pl. of* गाथा *f.* a song, a chant.

गायति he sings, he repeats; *3d sin. pres. of rt* गै *1st cl.* 268.

गायमाना *for* गायमानास् *nom. pl. of* गायमान *m. f. n.* singing; *pres. p. átm. of rt* गै *1st cl.* 595. *a*, 524.

गिरं *acc. sin. of* गिर् *f.* speech, voice, *8th cl.* 180.

गिरः *acc. pl. of* गिर् *f.* speech, word, *8th cl.* 180.

गिरम् *acc. sin. of* गिर् *f.* speech, *8th cl.* 180.

गिरा *ins. sin. of* गिर् *f.* voice, speech, *8th cl.* 180.

गिराव् *for* गिरौ *loc. sin. of* गिरि *m.* a mountain, *2d cl.* 110.

गिरिकूटानि Tat. or Dep. comp. 743; गिरि *cr.* a mountain, कूटानि *nom. pl. of* कूट *n.* a peak, a summit, *1st cl.* 104.

गिरिगुहाम् Tat. or Dep. comp. 743; गिरि *cr.* a mountain, गुहाम् *acc. sin. of* गुहा *f.* a cave, a cavern.

गिरिनदीम् Tat. or Dep. comp. 743; गिरि *cr.* a mountain, नदीम् *acc. sin. of* नदी *f.* a river.

गिरिराजम् Tat. or Dep. comp. 743; गिरि *cr.* a mountain, राजम् *acc. sin. for* राजानं *from* राजन् *m.* a king, 151. *a.*

गिरिश्रेष्ठम् Tat. or Dep. comp. 743. *b*; गिरि *cr.* a mountain, श्रेष्ठम् *acc. sin. m. of* श्रेष्ठ *m. f. n.* best.

गिरींश् *for* गिरीन् (53) *acc. pl. of* गिरि.

गिरेर् *gen. sin. of* गिरि *m.* a mountain, *2d cl.* 110.

गुण *m.* quality, virtue, excellence, *1st cl.* 103.

गुणवान् *nom. sin. m. of* गुणवत् *m. f. n.* excellent, good, possessed of advantages or excellencies (*guṇa*), *5th cl.* 140.

गुणांस् *for* गुणान् *acc. pl. of* गुण *m.* quality, virtue, merit, excellence.

गुणान् *acc. pl. of* गुण *m.* quality, virtue.

गुणैः *for* गुणैस् *ins. pl. of* गुण quality, virtue.

गुणैर् *for* गुणैस् *ins. pl. of* गुण quality, virtue.

गुप्ताम् *acc. sin. f. of* गुप्त *m. f. n.* guarded; *past p. p. of rt* गुप् 556.

गुरून् *acc. pl. m. of* गुरु *m. f. n.* venerable, dearly valued.

गुल्मैर् *ins. pl. of* गुल्म *m.* a bush, a shrub, *1st cl.* 103.

गूढश् *nom. sin. of* गूढ *m. f. n.* hidden, concealed; *past p. p. of rt* गुह् 539.

गृहम् *acc. sin. of* गृह *n.* a house.

गृहाण take thou, receive thou; *2d sin. imp. of rt* ग्रह् *9th cl.* 699.

गृहान् *acc. pl. of* गृह *m.* a house, a wife. (*When* गृह *is used in the plural, it signifies generally* home, *and is always masculine.*)

गृहीतनामा *nom. sin.* one who has gained a name, Bah. or Rel. comp. 766; गृहीत *cr.* taken, received, नामा *nom. sin. m. from* नामन् *n.* a name, *6th cl.* 154.

गृहीत्वा having taken, having taken up, having raised; *past ind. p. of rt* ग्रह् 699.

गृहे *loc. sin. of* गृह *n.* a house, *1st cl.* 104.

गृह्णाति he takes; *3d sin. pres. of* ग्रह् *9th cl.* 699.

गृह्णीध्वं take ye; *2d pl. imp. átm. of rt* ग्रह् *9th cl.* 699.

गेहं *nom. sin. n.* a house.

गोपायन्ति they guard, they protect; *3d pl. pres. of rt* गुप् *1st cl.* 271.

गोप्ता *nom. sin. m. of* गोप्तृ *m.* a protector, guardian, *4th cl.* 127.

गोसहस्रेण *ins. sin. n.* with a thousand kine; (*comp. of* गो a cow, ox, *and* सहस्र a thousand, 206.)

ग्रसते he devours, he consumes; *3d sin. pres. átm. of rt* ग्रस् *1st cl.* 261.

ग्रस्ताम् *acc. sin. f. of* **ग्रस्त** *m. f. n.* seized; *past p. p. of rt* **ग्रस्** 539.

ग्रस्यमाना *nom. sin. f. of* **ग्रस्यमान** *m. f. n.* being seized; *pres. p. pass. of rt* **ग्रस्** 528.

ग्रस्यमानाम् *acc. sin. f. See last.*

ग्रहा *for* **ग्रहास्** *nom. pl. of* **ग्रह** *m.* a planet.

ग्रहीतुं to catch, to take; *inf. mood of rt* **ग्रह्** 699, 459.

ग्रहीष्यामि I will take, I will take up; *1st sin. 2d fut. of rt* **ग्रह्** 399. *a.*

ग्रामं *acc. sin. of* **ग्राम** *m.* a village.

ग्रामान् *acc. pl. of* **ग्राम** *m.* a village.

ग्रामिपुत्राः TAT. OR DEP. COMP. 743; **ग्रामि** *for* **ग्रामिन्** (57) *cr.* a villager, **पुत्राः** *nom. pl. of* **पुत्र** *m.* a son, a boy.

ग्रामेण *ins. sin. of* **ग्राम** *m.* a village.

ग्राम्यगजान् KARM. OR DES. COMP. 755; **ग्राम्य** *cr.* tame, *lit.* village-born, **गजान्** *acc. pl. of* **गज** *m.* an elephant.

ग्राहेण *ins. sin. of* **ग्राह** *m.* a serpent.

ग्राहेणानेन *for* **ग्राहेण अनेन** *by* 31.

ग्राहो *nom. sin. of* **ग्राह** *m.* a serpent.

घ.

घातयति he or it kills; *3d sin. pres. of rt* **हन्** *in caus., see* 488.

घोरं *acc. sin. n. of* **घोर** *m. f. n.* frightful, awful, *1st cl.* 187.

घोरान् *acc. pl. m. of* **घोर** *m. f. n.* terrible, *1st cl.* 187.

घोरायां *loc. sin. f. of* **घोर** *m. f. n.* terrible, dreadful, *1st cl.* 187.

घोरे *loc. sin. m. or n. of* **घोर** *m. f. n.* terrible, *1st cl.* 104.

घोषयामास he proclaimed; *3d sin. perf. of rt* **घुष्** *10th cl.* 385. *a.*

घोषांस् *for* **घोषान्** *acc. pl. of* **घोष** *m.* a station of herdsmen.

घ्नतो *acc. pl. m. of* **घ्नत्** *m. f. n.* striking, killing; *pres. p. of rt* **हन्** 524.

च.

च *ind.* and, also, both, 727.

चक्रवाकोपकूजिताम् TAT. OR DEP. COMP. 740; **चक्रवाक** *cr.* the Ćakraváka or Brahmany duck, **उपकूजिताम्** *acc. sin. f. of* **उपकूजित** *m. f. n.* made resonant with cooing or the cry (of the Ćakraváka).

चक्रिरे they made, they showed; *3d pl. perf. átm. of rt* **कृ** 683.

चक्रे he made; *3d sin. perf. átm. of rt* **कृ** 683.

चक्षमे he endured, he bore; *3d sin. perf. átm. of rt* **क्षम्** 364.

चक्षूंषि *acc. pl. of* **चक्षुस्** *n.* the eye, *7th cl.* 165.

चचाल he, she or it moved; *3d sin. perf. of rt* **चल्** to move, 364.

चतुरः *acc. pl. m. of* **चतुर्** four, 203.

चतुरो *acc. pl. m. of* **चतुर्** four, *see* 203.

चतुर्थः *nom. sin. of* **चतुर्थ** *m. f. n.* fourth, 209.

चतुर्थे *loc. sin. of* **चतुर्थ** *m. f. n.* fourth, 209.

चतुर्दशः *nom. sin. m.* fourteenth, 210.

चतुर्दंष्ट्रो having four tusks; (*comp. of* **चतुर्** four, *and* **दंष्ट्रो** *nom. sin. m. from* **दंष्ट्रा** *f.* a tusk, 108.

चतुर्विंशतितमः *nom. sin. m.* twenty-fourth, 211.

चत्वार *for* **चत्वारस्** *nom. pl. of* **चतुर्** four, *see* 203.

चन्द्रमाः *nom. sin. of* **चन्द्रमस्** *m.* the moon, *7th cl.* 163.

चन्द्रलेखा *nom. sin. f.* digit of the moon. *See next.*

चन्द्रलेखाम् *acc. sin. f. of* **चन्द्रलेखा** *f.* a crescent or digit of the moon; (*comp. of* **चन्द्र** the moon, *and* **लेखा** a line, streak.)

चन्द्रलेखेव *for* **चन्द्रलेखा इव** *by* 32.

चन्द्राभवक्त्रं BAH. OR REL. COMP. 761; **चन्द्र** *cr.* the moon, **आभ** *cr.* like, **वक्त्रं** *acc. sin. m. from* **वक्त्र** *n.* the face, 108.

चरति he roams, he wanders, he or it moves; *3d sin. pres. of rt* **चर्** *1st cl.*

चरन्ति they wander about, they go; *3d pl. pres. of rt* चर् *1st cl.* 261.

चरन् *nom. sin. m. of* चरत् *m. f. n.* going, moving; *pres. p. of rt* चर् 524.

चरामः we wander over; *1st pl. pres. of rt* चर् *1st cl.* 261.

चरामि I commit, I act; *1st sin. pres. of rt* चर्.

चरितम् *acc. sin. of* चरित *n.* act, action.

चरितव्रतः BAH. OR REL. COMP. 766; चरित *cr.* performed, practised, व्रत *nom. sin. m. from* व्रत *m. n.* a vow, an act of devotion.

चरितानि *acc. pl. of* चरित *n.* an act, action.

चरिष्यति he or she will wander; *3d sin. 2d fut. of rt* चर् *1st cl.* 261.

चलो *nom. sin. m. of* चल *m. f. n.* fickle, changeable, moveable.

चाक्षान् *for* च अक्षान्, *q. q. v. v.*

चाचलान् *for* च अचलान्, *q. q. v. v.*

चातुर्वर्ण्यस्य *gen. sin. of* चातुर्वर्ण्य *n.* the four castes, *1st cl.* 104. *See note under* विश्राम्यते.

चादित्यः *for* च आदित्यः *by* 31.

चाद्भुतदर्शना: *for* च अद्भुतदर्शना: *by* 31.

चानघाः *for* च अनघाः *by* 31.

चानुत्तमां *for* च अनुत्तमां *by* 31.

चानुभूयास्य *for* च अनुभूय अस्य *by* 31.

चानेन *for* च अनेन *by* 31.

चान्यद् *for* च अन्यद् *by* 31.

चान्यन् *for* च अन्यन् *by* 31.

चापरे *for* च अपरे *by* 31.

चापि *for* च अपि *by* 31.

चाप्रदक्षिणैः *for* च आप्रदक्षिणैः *by* 31.

चाप्यश्वमेधेन *for* च अपि अश्वमेधेन *by* 31 *and* 34.

चाप्यस्य *for* च अपि अस्य *by* 31, 34.

चाप्युपलक्षितः *for* च अपि उपलक्षितः 31, 34.

चाग्रजः *for* च अग्रजः *by* 31.

चाभवन् *for* च अभवन् *by* 31.

चाभ्यागता *for* च अभ्यागता *by* 31.

चामीकरप्रख्यम् *acc. sin. m.* like gold; (*comp. of* चामीकर gold, *and* प्रख्य like.)

चारित्रकवचान् BAH. OR REL. COMP. 761; चारित्र *cr.* virtuous conduct, कवचान् *acc. pl. from* कवच *m.* armour, mail (cased in the armour of chastity.)

चारुदर्शने *voc. sin. f.* O thou of lovely aspect; (*from* चारु beautiful, *and* दर्शन sight.)

चारुपद्मविशालाक्षीम् COMPLEX COMP. 771; चारु *cr.* beautiful, पद्म *cr.* a lotus, विशाल *cr.* large, अक्षीं *acc. sin. of* अक्षी *f. from* अक्ष *m.* (*in comp.*) an eye, 778.

चारुवृत्तपयोधराम् COMPLEX COMP. 771; चारु *cr.* beautiful, वृत्त *cr.* round, पयोधराम् *acc. sin. f. from* पयोधर *m.* a woman's breast, 108.

चारुसर्वाङ्गशोभन O thou who art fair and beautiful in every limb, COMPLEX COMP. 771; चारु *cr.* fair, handsome, सर्व *cr.* all, every, अङ्ग *cr.* limb, शोभन *voc. sin. m. of* शोभन *m. f. n.* beautiful.

चारुहासिनी sweetly smiling; *nom. sin. f. See next.*

चारुहासिनीम् sweetly smiling, KARM. OR DES. COMP. 755; चारु *cr.* sweet, sweetly, हासिनीं *acc. sin. of* हासिनी *f.* smiling, *1st cl.* 106; (*from* हासिन् *agt. of rt* हस् 582. *a.*)

चारूणि *nom. pl. n. of* चारु *m. f. n.* beautiful, *3d cl.* 114.

चासकृत् *for* च असकृत् *by* 31.

चासि *for* च असि *by* 31.

चासीत् *for* च आसीत् *by* 31.

चास्मान् *for* च अस्मान् *by* 31.

चास्माभिर् *for* च अस्माभिर् *by* 31.

चास्मिन् *for* च अस्मिन् *by* 31.

चास्या *for* च अस्यास् *by* 31.

चाहम् *for* च अहम् *by* 31.

चिकीर्षन्ती *nom. sin. f. of* चिकीर्षत् *m. f. n.* desirous of doing, wishing to perform; *pres. p. of rt* कृ *in des.* 502, 525.

चिकीर्षमाणस् *nom. sin. m. of* चिकीर्षमाण *m. f. n.* anxious to perform, wishing to do; *pres. p. átm. of rt* कृ *in des.* 502, 528.

चिकीर्षसि thou dost desire to do; *2d sin. pres. of rt* कृ *in des.* 502.

चिकीर्षितम् *nom. sin. n.* design, intention, (what is wished to be done;) *see* 502, 550.

चित्तप्रमाथिनी TAT. OR DEP. COMP. 739; चित्त *cr.* heart, soul, mind, प्रमाथिनी *nom. sin. f. of* प्रमाथिन् *m. f. n.* agitating, afflicting; (*agt. from rt* मन्थ् 693. *a, with* प्र;) *6th cl.* 159.

चित्राः *acc. pl. f. of* चित्र *m. f. n.* variegated, *1st cl.* 105, 187.

चिन्तयध्वं think ye; *2d pl. imp. átm. of rt* चिन्त् *10th cl.* 641.

चिन्तयन् *nom. sin. m. of* चिन्तयत् *m. f. n.* thinking on; *pres. p. of rt* चिन्त् *10th cl.* 641.

चिन्तयन्ती thinking, reflecting; *nom. sin. f. of* चिन्तयत्.

चिन्तयन्त्याः *gen. sin. f. of* चिन्तयत् *m. f. n.* thinking of.

चिन्तयानस्य *gen. sin. m. of* चिन्तयान *m. f. n.* thinking of; *pres. p. átm. of rt* चिन्त् *10th cl.* 527.

चिन्तयामास he or she thought on, pondered on, considered; *3d sin. perf. of rt* चिन्त् *10th cl.* 385. *a.*

चिन्तयित्वा having thought on, having considered; *ind. past p. of rt* चिन्त् *10th cl.* 558.

चिन्तये I think on; *1st sin. pres. átm. of rt* चिन्त् *10th cl.* 641.

चिन्तापरा lost in thought, TAT. OR DEP. COMP. 744; चिन्ता *cr.* thought, परा *nom. sin. f. of* पर *m. f. n.* principally engaged in, *1st cl.* 187.

चिन्तापरास् *nom. pl. m.* thoughtful. *See last.*

चिन्ताम् *acc. sin. of* चिन्ता *f.* thought, anxiety.

चिन्तितो *nom. sin. m. of* चिन्तित *m. f. n.* thought of, contrived, devised; *past p. p. of rt* चिन्त् 538.

चिन्वन्तो *nom. pl. m. of* चिन्वत् *m. f. n.* seeking for, searching through; *pres. p. of rt* चि *5th conj.* 524.

चिरम् *ind.* for a long time, for a long while.

चिरविप्रोषिताम् *acc. sin. f.* long banished, long absent; (*comp. of* चिर long, *and* विप्रोषित dwelling away.)

चिराद् *for* चिरात् *ind.* after a long time, for a long while.

चिह्नभूतो *nom. sin. m. of* चिह्नभूत *m. f. n.* become a mark, (Book XVII. 7,) formed into a mark.

चेत् *ind.* if.

चेतसा *ins. sin. of* चेतस् *n.* the mind, the heart.

चेतो *acc. sin. of* चेतस् *n.* mind, heart, *7th cl.* 164.

चेदं *for* च इदं *by* 32.

चेदिपतेर् TAT. OR DEP. COMP. 743; चेदि *cr.* Ćedi, पतेर् *gen. sin. of* पति *m.* a lord, 121. Ćedi is the name of a country, perhaps the same as the modern Ćandail. It is often named in the marriage of Rukmiṇí, extracted from the Harivanśa by M. Langlois, Monumens de l'Inde, p. 96.

चेदिपुरीं *acc. sin. of* चेदिपुरी *f.* Ćedi-pur, *i. e.* the city of Ćedi; (*comp. of* चेदि *and* पुरी a city.)

चेदिराजपुरीं TAT. OR DEP. COMP. 745; चेदि *cr.* Ćedi, राज *cr.* king, पुरीं *acc. sin. of* पुरी *f.* a city.

चेदिराजस्य *gen. sin. m.* of the king of Ćedi; (*comp. of* चेदि *cr.* Ćedi, *and* राजस्य *gen. for* राज्ञः 151.)

चेन्द्रपुरोगमाः *for* च इन्द्रपुरोगमाः *by* 32.

चेष्टमानम् *acc. sin. of* चेष्टमान *m. f. n.* struggling; *pres. p. átm. of rt* चेष्ट् *1st cl.* 526.

चेह *for* च इह *by* 32.

चेहागते *for* च इह आगते *by* 32 *and* 31.

चैतस्य *for* च एतस्य *by* 33.

चैनं *for* च एनं *by* 33.

चैव *for* च एव *by* 33.

चैवाहम् *for* च एव अहम् *by* 33, 31.

चैवोग्रशासनः *for* च एव उग्रशासनः *by* 33 *and* 32.

चैषा *for* च एषा *by* 33.

चोक्तं *for* च उक्तं *by* 32.

चोन्नमगन्धाढ्याः *for* च उन्नमगन्धाढ्याः *by* 32.

चोद्यमाना *for* चोद्यमानास् *nom. pl. m. of* चोद्यमान *m. f. n.* being urged; *pres. p. of rt* चुद् *in caus. pass.* 496.

च्छित्त्वा *for* छित्त्वा *by* 48. *b.*

छ.

छकुनान् *for* शकुनान् (*by* 49) *acc. pl. of* शकुन *m.* a bird, 1*st cl.* 103.

छक्तो *for* शक्तो able, *q. v.*

छचीम् *for* शचीम् *acc. sin. of* शची *f.* the wife of Indra, 1*st cl.* 106.

छन्देन *ins. sin. of* छन्द *n.* will, wish.

छन्नः *nom. sin. m.* covered, clothed, clad; *past p. p. of rt* छद् 540.

छपितुं *for* शपितुं (49) to curse; *inf. of rt* शप् 459.

छाया *nom. sin. f.* a shadow.

छायाद्वितीयो ANOM. COMP., *see* 777. *b;* छाया *cr.* shadow, द्वितीयो *nom. sin. m. of* द्वितीय *m. f. n.* accompanied by, (*lit.* doubled, made two.)

छायेवानुगता *for* छाया इव अनुगता *by* 32, 31.

छित्त्वा having cut, having cut off; *past ind. p. of rt* छिद् 556.

छिन्दन्ति they cut, they cleave; 3*d pl. pres. of rt* छिद् 7*th cl.*

छुचिः *for* शुचिः (49) *nom. sin. m. of* शुचि *m. f. n.* pure.

छूरो *for* शूरो (49) *nom. sin.* a hero, *q. v.*

छृतम् *for* शृतं (49) *acc. sin. n. of* शृत *m. f. n.* cooked, boiled; *past p. p. of rt* श्रा 532.

छेत्तुं to cut, to cut off; *inf. of rt* छिद् 459.

छोकम् *for* शोकम् sorrow, *q. v.*

छ्रुत्वा having heard; *ind. p. of rt* श्रु 556, 676.

छ्रुत्वानवद्याङ्गी *for* छ्रुत्वा अनवद्याङ्गी *by* 31.

छ्रेयः *for* श्रेयः (49) *nom. sin. n.* better.

छ्रेयो *for* श्रेयो (49) *nom. sin. n.* better.

ज.

ज (*at the end of compounds*) *denotes* arising, born, produced; (*agt. of rt* जन् to be born.)

जगाद he uttered, he recited; 3*d sin. perf. of rt* गद् 364.

जगाम he or she went; 3*d sin. perf. of rt* गम् 376, 602.

जगामैकां *for* जगाम एकां *by* 33.

जग्मतुर् they two went, they both had recourse; 3*d du. perf. of rt* गम्, *see* 376.

जग्मुर् they went; 3*d pl. perf. of rt* गम् 376.

जग्राह he or she took hold of, he seized, he caught; 3*d sin. perf. of rt* ग्रह् 9*th cl.* 699.

जग्राहाजगरो *for* जग्राह अजगरो *by* 31.

जग्राहायतलोचना *for* जग्राह आयतलोचना *by* 31.

जज्ञुर् they perceived, they observed, they knew; 3*d pl. perf. from rt* ज्ञा 688, 373.

जटिला *nom. sin. f. of* जटिल *m. f. n.* having clotted or entangled hair.

जनं *acc. sin. of* जन *m.* a man, people.

जननी *nom. sin. f.* a mother, a parent.

जनपदं *acc. sin. of* जनपद *m.* an inhabited country.

जनपदे *loc. sin. of* जनपद *m.* the country (as distinct from the town).

जनमध्यं TAT. OR DEP. COMP. 743; जन *cr.* men, मध्यं *acc. sin. of* मध्य *n.* the midst.

जनयामास he begat; 3*d sin. perf. of rt* जन् *in caus.* 385. *a.*

जनसंसत्सु TAT. OR DEP. COMP. 743; जन *cr.* men, संसत्सु *loc. pl. of* संसद् *f.* an assembly, 138.

जनसङ्क्षये TAT. OR DEP. COMP. 743; जन *cr.* men, सङ्क्षये *loc. sin. of* सङ्क्षय *m.* destruction.

जनस्य *gen. sin. of* जन *m.* a person, a human being, people.

जना *for* जनास् *nom. pl. of* जन *m.* a man, 1*st cl.* 103.

जनाधिप *voc. sin. m.* O lord of men.

जनाधिपः *nom. sin. m.* a sovereign, (*lit.* lord of men; *comp. of* जन *cr.* a man, *and* अधिप *m.* a lord.)

जनाधिपाः *nom. pl. m. See last.*

जनार्णवः *nom. sin. m.* host of men, (*lit.* sea of men; *from* जन *cr.* men, *and* अर्णव *m.* the ocean.)

जनास् *nom. pl. of* जन *m.* a man, people.

जनित्र्याः *gen. sin. of* जनित्री *f.* a mother, 106; *see* 859. *a.*

जनेन *ins. sin. of* जन *m.* a man, people.

जनैर् *ins. pl. of* जन *m.* a man, a person.

जन्म *nom. sin. of* जन्मन् *n.* birth, *6th cl.* 153.

जन्मान्तरकृतम् *nom. sin. n.* committed in another birth; (*comp. of* जन्म *cr.* birth, अन्तर *cr.* another, 777. *b, and* कृत, *q.v.*)

जम्बुद्वीपे *loc. sin. of* जम्बुद्वीप *m.* Jambudvípa, the central division of the world. India is so called in the Puráṇas.

जम्ब्वाम्रलोध्रखदिरसालवेत्रसमाकुलं COMPLEX COMP. 771; जम्बु *cr.* the Jambu or rose-apple (34), आम्र *cr.* the Mango-tree, लोध्र *cr.* the Lodhra or Lodh, a kind of tree (Symplocos racemosa), the bark of which is used in dyeing, खदिर the Khadira or Catechu-tree, the exudation of which is used in medicine, साल *cr.* the Sál-tree, वेत्र *cr.* a cane, a ratan, समाकुलम् *acc. sin. n. of* समाकुल *m. f. n.* crowded.

जयम् *acc. sin. of* जय *m.* victory.

जयेम we may conquer; *1st pl. pot. of rt* जि *1st cl.*

जयेयुः they may conquer; *3d pl. pot. of rt* जि *1st cl.*

जरा *nom. sin. f.* old age.

जलं *nom. or acc. sin. of* जल *n.* water, *1st cl.* 104.

जलदागमे TAT. OR DEP. COMP. 743; जलद *cr.* a cloud (water-giver), आगमे *loc. sin. of* आगम *m.* approach, arrival.

जलमात्रेण by mere water, on mere water; (*from* जल *cr.* water, *and* मात्रेण *ins. sin. of* मात्र, *see* 919.)

जवं *acc. sin. of* जव *m.* speed, velocity.

जवनैर् *ins. pl. m. of* जवन *m. f. n.* fleet, swift.

जवयुक्तान् *acc. pl. m.* fleet, swift, (*lit.* possessed of fleetness; *from* जव *cr.* velocity, *and* युक्त possessed of.)

जवेन *ins. sin. of* जव *m.* rapidity, speed.

जवेनाभिससार *for* जवेन अभिससार *by* 31.

जहासि thou dost desert; *2d sin. pres. of rt* हा *3d cl.* 665.

जहृषे he rejoiced; *3d sin. perf. átm. of rt* हृष् 364.

जातरूपपरिष्कृतान् TAT. OR DEP. COMP. 740; जातरूप *cr.* gold, परिष्कृतान् *acc. pl. m. of* परिष्कृत *m. f. n.* adorned; *past p. p. of* कृ *with* परि, 783. *o*, 532.

जातसङ्कल्पः BAH. OR REL. COMP. 767; जात *cr.* arisen, experienced, felt, सङ्कल्पः *nom. sin. of* सङ्कल्प *m.* thought, desire, love, *1st cl.* 103.

जातस्य *gen. sin. n. of* जात *m. f. n.* born.

जाता *nom. sin. f. of* जात *m. f. n.* born.

जातिधर्माः *nom. pl. m.* the laws of caste, the usages of caste; (जाति caste, धर्म law, usage, TAT. OR DEP. COMP.)

जातिसम्पन्नाम् *acc. sin. f.* of noble race, endowed with (high) birth; (*comp. of* जाति *cr.* race, *and* सम्पन्न accomplished, endowed with.)

जातु *ind.* ever; न जातु never.

जानाति he knows; *3d sin. pres. of rt* ज्ञा *9th cl.* 688.

जानामि I know, I understand; *1st sin. pres. of rt* ज्ञा.

जानाम्यन्यैर् *for* जानामि अन्यैर् *by* 34.

जानीत know ye; *2d pl. imp. of rt* ज्ञा.

जानीथ ye know; *2d pl. pres. of rt* ज्ञा.

जानीयां may I recognise; *1st sin. pot. of rt* ज्ञा *9th cl.* 688.

जानीयाद् he may know, he may recognise; *3d sin. pot. of rt* ज्ञा *9th cl.* 688.

जानीषे thou knowest; *2d sin. pres. átm. of rt* ज्ञा *9th cl.* 688.

जानीहि ascertain thou; *2d sin. imp. of rt* ज्ञा.

जानुभिस् *ins. pl. of* जानु *n.* the knee.

जायते he, she or it is produced or born; *3d sin. pres. of rt* जन् *4th cl.*

जिघांसन्तो *nom. pl. m. of* जिघांसत् *m. f. n.* desirous of killing; *pres. p. par. of rt* हन् *in des.* 503, 525.

जिज्ञासमानो *nom. sin. m.* desirous of knowing, testing or proving; *pres. p. átm. of rt* ज्ञा *in des.* 500. *b*, 528.

जितम् *nom. sin. n. of* जित *m. f. n.* conquered; *past p. p. of rt* जि 532.

जितस्वर्गा *for* जितस्वर्गास् BAH. OR REL. COMP. 767; जित *cr.* conquered, won, gained, स्वर्गास् *nom. pl. f. from* स्वर्ग *m.* heaven, 108.

जितेन *ins. sin. of* जित *m. f. n.* conquered.

जितेन्द्रियैर् BAH. OR REL. COMP. 767; जित *cr.* conquered, subdued, इन्द्रियैर् *ins. pl. m. from* इन्द्रिय *n.* an organ of sense.

जितो *nom. sin. m. of* जित *m. f. n.* conquered, beaten. *In* Book XII. 83 जित *is followed by an accusative: thus,* जितो राज्यं वसूनि च deprived (in play) of his kingdom and his wealth.

जित्वा having conquered, having won; *past ind. p. of rt* जि 556. *With double accusative; as,* जित्वा राज्यं नलं having won the kingdom from Nala.

जिहीर्षवः *nom. pl. m. of* जिहीर्षु *m. f. n.* wishing to seize, desirous of taking; *des. adj. from rt* हृ 502, 593, 82. VII.

जिह्मैर् *for* जिह्मैस् *ins. pl. m. of* जिह्म *m. f. n.* dishonest, vicious, (*lit.* crooked,) *1st cl.* 103.

जीमूतस्वनसन्निभाम् like the sound of a cloud, ANOM. COMP. 777; जीमूत *cr.* a cloud, स्वन *cr.* sound, सन्निभाम् *acc. sin. f. of* सन्निभ *m. f. n.* like, resembling.

जीयते he is conquered, he is beaten; *3d sin. pres. pass. of rt* जि 590, 463.

जीर्णानि *acc. pl. n. of* जीर्ण *m. f. n.* old, worn out.

जीव live thou; *2d sin. imp. of rt* जीव् *1st cl.* 603.

जीवति he or she lives; *3d sin. pres. of rt* जीव् *1st cl.* 603.

जीवतु let him live; *3d sin. pres. of rt* जीव् *1st cl.* 603.

जीवत्वसुखजीविकाम् *for* जीवतु असुखजीविकाम् *by* 34.

जीवन्तीं *acc. sin. f. of* जीवत् *m. f. n.* living; *pres. p. of rt* जीव् 524.

जीवितेन *ins. sin. of* जीवित *n.* life, *1st cl.* 104.

जीवितेनार्थस् *for* जीवितेन अर्थस् *by* 31.

जुष्टं *acc. sin. n. of* जुष्ट *m. f. n.* frequented by, resorted to.

जेता he will conquer; *3d sin. 1st fut. of rt* जि 590.

ज्ञ (*at the end of compounds*) *denotes* knowing, acquainted with; (*agt. of rt* ज्ञा.)

ज्ञातमात्रे *loc. sin. n.* on its being ascertained merely (where they are); *comp. of* ज्ञात *cr.* known, *and* मात्र merely, *see* 919.

ज्ञातिद्रव्यविनाकृताः COMPLEX COMP. 771; ज्ञाति *cr.* kindred, द्रव्य *cr.* substance, wealth, विनाकृताः *nom. pl. m.* deprived of.

ज्ञातिभ्यो *abl. pl. of* ज्ञाति *m.* a relation, *2d cl.* 110.

ज्ञातिषु *loc. pl. of* ज्ञाति *m.* a kinsman, a relative, *2d cl.* 110; *see* 861.

ज्ञातीन् *acc. pl. of* ज्ञाति *m.* a kinsman, a relative, *2d cl.* 110.

ज्ञातुम् to know, to ascertain; *inf. mood of rt* ज्ञा 459, 688.

ज्ञानं *acc. sin. of* ज्ञान *n.* knowledge.

ज्ञानस्य *gen. sin. of* ज्ञान *n.* knowledge.

ज्ञायते he or it is known; *3d sin. pres. of rt* ज्ञा *in pass.* 463.

ज्ञास्यामि I will ascertain, I will know; *1st sin. 2d fut. of rt* **ज्ञा** 688.

ज्ञेयः *nom. sin. m. of* **ज्ञेय** *m. f. n.* to be known; *fut. pass. p. of rt* **ज्ञा** 571. *a.*

ज्ञेयम् *nom. sin. n. of* **ज्ञेय** *m. f. n.* to be known, to be ascertained; *fut. pass. p. of rt* **ज्ञा**.

झ.

झिल्लिकागणनादितं TAT. OR DEP. COMP. 745; **झिल्लिका** *cr.* a cricket, **गण** *cr.* a multitude, swarm, **नादितम्** sounding, resounding, resonant; *past p. p. of rt* **नद्** *in caus.* 566.

त.

त *for* **ते** *dat. sin. of* **त्वत्** thee, *or nom. pl. m. of* **तत्** he, that, 36.

त इमे *for* **ते इमे** (36) they themselves, the very same, 220. *a.*

तच् *for* **तत्**, *q. v.*

तच् छ्रुत्वा *for* **तत् श्रुत्वा** *by* 49. *See the words.*

तडागं *acc. sin. of* **तडाग** *n.* a pool, a lake.

तडागानि *acc. pl. of* **तडाग** *n.* a tank, *1st cl.* 104.

तत् *pron. m. f. n.* he, she, it, that, 220.

तत् that; *acc. sin. n. of* **तत्**. *See last.*

तत् *ind.* therefore, 713. *a.*

ततः *for* **ततस्**, *q. v.*

ततः प्रभृति *ind.* from that time forward, thenceforward.

ततश् *for* **ततस्**, *q. v.*

ततस् *ind.* then, afterwards, thence.

ततस्ततः *ind.* hither and thither; *compare* **इतस्ततः**.

ततो *for* **ततस्** thence, afterwards.

ततो *for* **तस्मात्** *ind.* than this, than that.

तत्क्षणात् *ind.* at that very moment, at the very instant; (*from* **तत्** 220, *and* **क्षण** moment, 715.)

तत्त्वं *acc. sin. of* **तत्त्व** *n.* truth, exact state.

तत्त्वज्ञ *voc. sin. m.* O truth-knower; (*comp. of* **तत्त्व** divine truth, *and* **ज्ञ** a knower, 580.)

तत्त्वेन truthfully; *ins. sin. of* **तत्त्व** *n.* truth, 714.

तत्पराया *for* **तत्परायास्** *gen. sin. f. of* **तत्पर** *m. f. n.* devoted, devotedly attached.

तत्पापं TAT. OR DEP. COMP. 743; **तत्** *cr.* he (of him), **पापं** *acc. sin. of* **पाप** *n.* sin, crime, *1st cl.* 104.

तत्प्रियं TAT. OR DEP. COMP. 743; **तत्** *cr.* he (of him, to him), **प्रियं** *acc. sin. of* **प्रिय** *n.* a kindness, a favour.

तत्र *ind.* there, in that place, 720.

तत्रस्थौ *nom. du. m. of* **तत्रस्थ** *m. f. n.* abiding there; (*comp. of* **तत्र** there, 720, *and* **स्थ** standing, dwelling, 580.)

तत्राथ *for* **तत्र अथ** *by* 31.

तत्रावसन्नाभूत् *for* **तत्र + अवसन्ना + अभूत्** *by* 31 *and* 47.

तत्रावसद् *for* **तत्र अवसद्** *by* 31.

तत्रासनेषु *for* **तत्र आसनेषु** *by* 31.

तत्रैनं *for* **तत्र एनं** *by* 33.

तत्रैव *for* **तत्र एव** *by* 33.

तथा *ind.* thus, so, likewise, in like manner, 913.

तथागतं *acc. sin. m. of* **तथागत** *m. f. n.* in such a condition; (*comp. of* **तथा** so, *and* **गत** gone.)

तथापि *ind.* nevertheless, still,

तथायम् *for* **तथा अयम्** *by* 31.

तथायान्तं *for* **तथा आयान्तं** *by* 31.

तथारण्यानि *for* **तथा अरण्यानि** *by* 31.

तथारूपा *nom. sin. f. of* **तथारूप** *m. f. n.* of such a form; (*comp. of* **तथा** such, so, *and* **रूप**, *q. v.*)

तथारूपेयम् *for* **तथारूपा इयम्** *by* 32.

तथाविधं *acc. sin. m. or n. or ind.* in such a manner, of such a kind, 713.

तथाविधः *nom. sin. m. of* **तथाविध** *m. f. n.* of such a sort or kind.

तथाविधां *acc. sin. f. of* **तथाविध** *m. f. n.* in such a state or plight.

तथेत्युक्ता *for* **तथा इति उक्ता** *by* 32 *and* 34.

तथैव *ind.* even so, just so, so also, in like manner.

तथैवासीद् *for* **तथा एव आसीत्** *by* 33 *and* 31.

तथोक्ता *for* **तथा उक्ता** *by* 32.

तथोत्साहं *acc. sin. m.* making such great effort; (*from* **तथा** so, *and* **उत्साह** effort.)

तथ्यम् *acc. sin. of* **तथ्य** *n.* truth, 1*st cl.* 104.

तद् *for* **तत्** that, therefore; *nom. n. of* **तत्**, *q. v.*

तदनन्तरा *nom. sin. f. of* **तदनन्तर** *m. f. n.* next to him, nearest to him; (*comp. of* **तद्** 220, *and* **अनन्तर** without interval.)

तदवस्थां *acc. sin. f. of* **तदवस्थ** *m. f. n.* in that condition; (*comp. of* **तद्** 220, *and* **अवस्था** state.)

तदा *ind.* then, 722.

तदाकारां having that appearance or aspect, Bah. or Rel. comp. 761; **तद्** *cr.* that, **आकारां** *acc. sin. f. from* **आकार** *m.* form, appearance, 1*st cl.* 103.

तदार्तस्य *for* **तदा आर्तस्य** *by* 31.

तद्दुःखम् *acc. sin. n.* that grief, or grief for her, or her grief; (*comp. of* **तद्** *for* **तत्** 220, *and* **दुःख** grief, *q. v.*)

तद्रूपं *nom. sin. n.* the form itself; (*comp. of* **तत्** 220, *and* **रूप** *n.* form.)

तद्विद्यश् Bah. or Rel. comp. 762; **तद्** he, 220, **विद्यश्** *nom. sin. m. from* **विद्या** *f.* knowledge, 108, (possessing his knowledge.)

तन् *for* **तत्** (47) *nom. sin. n.* that.

तनयां *acc. sin. of* **तनया** *f.* a daughter.

तनयाभ्यां by or from (my) two children; *ins. or abl. du. of* **तनय** *m.* a child, 1*st cl.* 103. (The two children alluded to in Book XIII. 34 are Indrasena and Indrasená, who had been sent by Damayantí to her father at Vidarbha.)

तनुमध्यमा Bah. or Rel. comp. 766; **तनु** *cr.* slender, graceful, **मध्यमा** *nom. sin. f. from* **मध्यम** *m.* the waist, middle.

तनुमध्यां Bah. or Rel. comp. 766; **तनु** *cr.* slender, **मध्यां** *acc. sin. f. from* **मध्य** *n.* waist, 1*st cl.* 108.

तन्द्रीं *acc. sin. of* **तन्द्री** *f.* weariness, fatigue.

तपः *nom. sin. of* **तपस्** *n.* penance, self-mortification, 7*th cl.* 164.

तपसा *ins. sin. of* **तपस्** *n.* penance, devotion.

तपसि *loc. sin. of* **तपस्** *n.* devotion.

तपस्यग्निषु *for* **तपसि अग्निषु** *by* 34.

तपस्विनी *nom. sin. f. of* **तपस्विन्** *m. f. n.* devout, pious; poor, wretched, miserable, 159.

तपोधनाः *nom. or voc. pl. m.* rich in devotion; (*comp. of* **तपस्** devotion, penance, 64, *and* **धन** *n.* wealth.)

तपोवनम् *acc. sin. n.* penance-grove, sacred wood; (*comp. of* **तपस्** penance, 64, *and* **वन** *n.* a wood.)

तपोवृद्धान् *acc. pl. m.* grown old in devotion; (*comp. of* **तपस्** devotion, penance, 64, *and* **वृद्ध** grown, increased.)

तम् him; *acc. sin. m. of* **तत्** *m. f. n.* he, she, it, 220.

तया by her, with her; *ins. sin. f. of* **तत्**.

तयेयं *for* **तया इयं** *by* 32.

तयोः *for* **तयोस्** of those two; *gen. du. of* **तत्**.

तयोर् *for* **तयोस्** of those two; *gen. du. of* **तत्**.

तरसा *ins. sin. of* **तरस्** *n.* speed, velocity.

तरुश्रेष्ठं *acc. sin. of* **तरुश्रेष्ठ** *m.* the best of trees, *see* 743. *b.*

तर्कयामास he or she considered, he suspected, he conjectured; 3*d sin. perf. of rt* **तर्क्** 10*th cl.* 385. *a.*

तर्कयित्वा having considered, having reflected; *past ind. p. of rt* **तर्क्** 10*th cl.* 558.

तल्लक्षणं *nom. sin. n.* the mark of him; (*comp. of* **तल्** *for* **तत्** 48, 220, *and* **लक्षण** a mark, 743.)

तव of thee; *gen. sin. of* **त्वत्**, *q. v.*

तवानघ *for* **तव अनघ** *by* 31.

तस्थतुः they two stood; 3*d du. perf. of rt* **स्था** 587.

तस्थुः they stood; 3*d pl. perf. of rt* **स्था**.

तस्थुर् *for* **तस्थुस्** they stood; 3*d pl. perf. of rt* **स्था** 373.

तस्थौ he stood; 3*d sin. perf. of rt* **स्था** 373, 587.

तस्माद् from that, than that, therefore, on that account; *abl. sin. of* **तत्**, *see* 829.

तस्मान् *for* तस्मात् (47) therefore.

तस्मिंस् *for* तस्मिन् (53) in that; *loc. sin. m. or n.*

तस्मिन्न् *for* तस्मिन् (52) in that; *loc. sin.*

तस्मै to him; *dat. sin. m. of* तत् *m. f. n.* he, she, it, 220.

तस्य of him; *gen. sin. of* तत्, *q. v.*

तस्या *for* तस्यास् of her; *gen. sin. f. of* तत्.

तस्याः of her; *gen. sin. f. of* तत् *m. f. n.* he, she, it, 220.

तस्यादृढतरं *for* तस्य अदृढतरं *by* 31.

तस्याप्रमेयस्य *for* तस्य अप्रमेयस्य *by* 31.

तस्याश् of her; *gen. sin. f.*

तस्यास् of her; *gen. sin. f.*

ता *for* तास् (66. *a*) they; *nom. or acc. pl. f. of* तत्, *q. v.*

तां her; *acc. sin. f. of* तत् *m. f. n.* he, she, it, 220.

तांस् *for* तान् them, those, *by* 53.

तादृग् *nom. sin. f. or n. of* तादृश् *m. f. n.* such, such-like, such as that, 234, 181.

तान् them, those; *acc. pl. m. of* तत् 220.

तानि those; *acc. pl. n. of* तत् he, she, it, 220.

तानीह *for* तानि इह *by* 31.

तापसा *for* तापसास् *nom. pl. of* तापस *m.* a hermit, a devotee. *In* Book XII. 96 तापसाऽन्तर्हिताः *is an irregularity, see* तापसान्तर्हिताः.

तापसाः *nom. pl. of* तापस *m.* a hermit.

तापसाध्युषितं TAT. OR DEP. COMP. 740; तापस *cr.* a hermit, अध्युषितं *acc. sin. n. of* अध्युषित *m. f. n.* inhabited; *past p. p. of rt* वस् *with* अधि, 607, 543.

तापसान्तर्हिताः *is a violation of the usual rule of Sandhi*, 66. *a. By that rule the two words should be separated*, तापसा (*for* तापसास् *nom. pl.*) अन्तर्हिताः.

तापसारण्यम् TAT. OR DEP. COMP. 743; तापस *cr.* a hermit, an ascetic, अरण्यम् *acc. sin. n.* a wood, a forest, *1st cl.* 104.

तापसैः *ins. pl. of* तापस *m.* a devotee.

तापसैर् *for* तापसैस् *ins. pl. of* तापस *m.* an ascetic.

तापसैश् *ins. pl. of* तापस *m.* a hermit.

ताभिश् *for* ताभिस् by them; *ins. pl. f. of* तत्.

ताव् *for* तौ (37) those two; *acc. du. m. of* तत् 220.

तावत् *ind.* so long.

तावन्ति *nom. pl. n. of* तावत् *m. f. n.* so many, 234.

तास् they; *nom. pl. f. of* तत् he, she, it, 220.

तिग्मांशुः *nom. sin. m.* the sun; (*from* तिग्म hot, *and* अंशु a ray, 766.)

तिथौ *loc. sin. of* तिथि *m. f.* a lunar day. The month is divided into thirty tithis or lunar days, which are personified as nymphs. In the laws of Manu are various directions concerning fortunate and unfortunate days of the month; thus IV. 114, 'The dark lunar day or day of new moon (अमावास्या) destroys the spiritual teacher, the fourteenth destroys the learner, the eighth and the day of the full moon destroys all remembrance of scripture, for which reason he must avoid reading on those lunar days.' Hence the Hindús are careful to wait for an auspicious day before commencing any action of importance.

तिष्ठ stay thou, remain thou; *2d sin. imp. of rt* स्था 587.

तिष्ठताम् *gen. pl. m. of* तिष्ठत् *m. f. n.* standing; *pres. p. of rt* स्था *1st cl.* 269, 587, 524.

तिष्ठति he stands, he or it remains; *3d sin. pres. of rt* स्था *1st cl.* 587.

तिष्ठत्सु *loc. pl. m. of* तिष्ठत् *m. f. n.* being present; *pres. p. par. of rt* स्था 524, 587.

तीक्ष्णम् *acc. sin. n. of* तीक्ष्ण *m. f. n.* sharp, noxious, virulent.

तीव्ररोषसमाविष्टा COMPLEX COMP. 771; तीव्र *cr.* fierce, रोष *cr.* anger, समाविष्टा *nom. sin. f. of* समाविष्ट *m. f. n.* possessed by, affected by, filled with.

तीव्रशोकसमाविष्टा COMPLEX COMP. 771; **तीव्र** *cr.* severe, excessive, **शोक** *cr.* sorrow, **समाविष्टा** *nom. sin. f.* filled with, penetrated by.

तीव्रशोकार्ता COMPLEX COMP. 771; **तीव्र** *cr.* excessive, poignant, **शोक** *cr.* grief, **आर्ता** *nom. sin. f. of* **आर्त** *m. f. n.* afflicted, 542.

तु *ind.* but, 728. *a.*

तुल्यं *nom. or acc. sin. n. of* **तुल्य** *m. f. n.* equal.

तुल्यताम् *acc. sin. of* **तुल्यता** *f.* equality.

तुल्यशीलवयोयुक्तां COMPLEX COMP. 771; **तुल्य** *cr.* equal, **शील** *cr.* good disposition, **वयो** *cr. for* **वयस्** age, 64, **युक्तां** *acc. sin. f. of* **युक्त** *m.* possessed of.

तुल्याकृतीन् BAH. OR REL. COMP. 766; **तुल्य** *cr.* similar, **आकृतीन्** *acc. pl. m. from* **आकृति** *f.* form, *2d cl.* 119.

तुल्याभिजनसंवृताम् COMPLEX COMP. 771; **तुल्य** *cr.* equal, **अभिजन** birth, family, rank, **संवृताम्** *acc. sin. f. of* **संवृत** *m. f. n.* surrounded by, possessed of.

तुल्यो *nom. sin. of* **तुल्य** *m. f. n.* equal, *1st cl.* 187; *see* 826.

तुष्टिर् *for* **तुष्टिस्** *nom. sin. f.* satisfaction, pleasure.

तूर्णं *ind.* quickly.

तूष्णीं *ind.* silent, silently.

तृणमुष्टिं TAT. OR DEP. COMP. 743; **तृण** *cr.* grass, hay, **मुष्टिं** *acc. sin. of* **मुष्टि** *f.* a handful.

तृणैः *ins. pl. of* **तृण** *n.* grass, any gramineous plant. *In* Nala XIII. 28 *it may mean* a bamboo, reed, &c.

तृतीयः *nom. sin. of* **तृतीय** *m. f. n.* third, 208.

तृतीयो *for* **तृतीयस्** *nom. sin. m.* third.

तृप्ता *nom. pl. m. of* **तृप्त** *m. f. n.* satisfied; *past p. p. of rt* **तृप्** 539.

तृषितः *nom. sin. m. of* **तृषित** *m. f. n.* thirsty.

ते they, those; *nom. pl. m. of* **तत्**, *q. v.*

ते of thee, by thee, from thee, to thee; *gen. sin. or dat. sin. of* **त्वत्** *or* **युष्मत्**, *q. v.*

तेजसा *ins. sin. of* **तेजस्** *n.* glory, splendour, beauty, might, power, dignity, spirit, virtue, *7th cl.* 164.

तेजस्वी *nom. sin. m. of* **तेजस्विन्** *m. f. n.* glorious, illustrious, 159.

तेजोबलसमन्वितान् COMPLEX COMP. 771; **तेजो** *cr. for* **तेजस्** spirit, **बल** *cr.* strength, **समन्वितान्** *acc. pl. m.* endowed with.

तेजोबलसमायुक्तान् COMPLEX COMP. 771; **तेजो** *for* **तेजस्** (64) *cr.* spirit, fire, **बल** *cr.* strength, **समायुक्तान्** *acc. pl. m.* endowed with, possessing.

तेन by him, by that; *ins. sin. m. or n. of* **तत्**.

तेनार्थे *for* **तेन अर्थे** *by* 31.

तेनैव *for* **तेन एव** *by* 33.

तेभ्यः *for* **तेभ्यस्** to them; *dat. pl. of* **तत्**, *q. v.*

तेषां of them, of those; *gen. pl. m. of* **तत्**, *q. v.*

तेषु in them; *loc. pl. m. of* **तत्**, *q. v.*

तैर् *for* **तैस्** by them, by those; *ins. pl. m. or n. of* **तत्**.

तोयम् *acc. sin. of* **तोय** *n.* water.

तोरणेन *ins. sin. of* **तोरण** *m. n.* an arch, an arched gateway, *1st cl.* 103.

तोषयामास he pleased, gratified; *3d sin. perf. of rt* **तुष्** to be pleased, *in caus.* 490.

तौ those two; *nom. du. m. of* **तत्**, *q. v.*

त्यक्तजीवितयोधिनः COMPLEX COMP. 771; **त्यक्त** *cr.* abandoned, sacrificed, **जीवित** *cr.* life, **योधिनः** *nom. pl. of* **योधिन्** *m.* a fighter, (*agt. from rt* **युध्** 582. *a,*) *6th cl.* 159.

त्यक्तवान् who has abandoned, (he left, he deserted;) *nom. sin. m. of* **त्यक्तवत्** *past act. p. of rt* **त्यज्** 553, 897.

त्यक्तश्रियम् *acc. sin. f.*, BAH. OR REL. COMP. 767; **त्यक्त** *cr.* abandoned, deserted, **श्रियं** *acc. sin. of* **श्री** *f.* fortune, 123.

त्यक्ता *nom. sin. f. of* **त्यक्त** *m. f. n.* abandoned, deserted; *past p. p. of rt* **त्यज्** 539.

त्यक्तुं to abandon; *inf. of rt* **त्यज्**.

त्यक्तुकामस् *nom. sin. m.* wishing to abandon, desirous of leaving; *see* 871.

त्यक्त्वा having abandoned, having deserted, having quitted; *past ind. p. of rt* **त्यज्** 556, 596.

त्यजन्तु let them abandon; *3d pl. imp. of rt* **त्यज्**.

त्यजेथाः thou wouldest abandon; *2d sin. pot. átm. of rt* त्यज्.

त्यजेयं I may abandon; *1st sin. pot. of rt* त्यज्.

त्रयः *nom. pl. of* त्रि three, *see* 202.

त्रयोदशः *nom. sin. m.* thirteenth, 210.

त्रयोविंशतितमः *nom. sin.* twenty-third, 211.

त्रातुम् to rescue, to save; *inf. of rt* त्रै 268, 459.

त्रायध्वं save yourselves; *2d pl. imp. átm. of rt* त्रै *1st cl.* 268.

त्राहि preserve thou, rescue thou; *2d sin. imp. 1st cl.* 267. *Irregular for* त्रायस्व.

त्रिदशेश्वराः O lords of the immortals, TAT. OR DEP. COMP. 743; त्रिदश *cr.* a god, an immortal, ईश्वराः *voc. pl. of* ईश्वर *m.* a lord, *1st cl.* 103.

त्रिदिवं *acc. sin. of* त्रिदिव *m. n.* heaven, *1st cl.* 104.

त्रिरात्रं for three nights, DVI. OR COL. COMP. 759.

त्रीन् *acc. pl. m. of* त्रि *m. f. n.* three, 202.

त्रैलोक्यं *acc. sin. of* त्रैलोक्य *n.* the three worlds collectively, *i. e.* heaven, earth, and the lower regions.

त्रैलोक्यभयकारकः TAT. OR DEP. COMP. 745; त्रैलोक्य *cr.* the three worlds, or heaven, earth, and the lower regions, भय *cr.* fear, कारकः *nom. sin. m.* a causer, maker.

त्रैलोक्यराज्यस्य *gen. sin.* of the sovereignty of the three worlds; (त्रैलोक्य the three worlds or triple realm, राज्य kingdom; TAT. OR DEP. COMP. 743.)

त्वं thou, you; *nom. sin. of* त्वत् *or* युष्मत् 219.

त्वक् *nom. sin. of* त्वच् *f.* the skin.

त्वच्छापदग्धः TAT. OR DEP. COMP. 745; त्वच् *for* त्वत् *cr.* thy, 49, 219, छाप *for* शाप *cr.* (49) curse, दग्धः *nom. sin. m.* burnt, consumed; *past p. p. of rt* दह् 539.

त्वच्छापाद् *abl. sin.* through thy curse; (*from* त्वत् 219, *and* शाप curse, 49, 743.)

त्वच्चापि *for* त्वम् च अपि *by* 60 *and* 31.

त्वत् *pron. used as cr.* thou, you; *also abl. sin.* from you, than you, 219.

त्वत्कृते *ind.* on thy account, by means of thee, through thee; (*comp. of* त्वत् thou, 219, *and* कृते 731, 917.)

त्वत्त *for* त्वत्तस् from thee, *see* 719.

त्वत्तः *for* त्वत्तस् from thee; (त्वत् 219, *with affix* तस् 719.)

त्वत्तो *for* त्वत्तस् from thee, *for* त्वत्; (*affix* तस् 719.)

त्वत्प्रतीक्षिणी *nom. sin. f.* waiting for thee; (*comp. of* त्वत् 219, *and* प्रतीक्षिन् *m. f. n.* expecting, looking for, 159.)

त्वत्सन्निधौ TAT. OR DEP. COMP. 743; त्वत् *cr.* thee, सन्निधौ *loc. sin. of* सन्निधि *f.* presence, proximity.

त्वद् than thee; *abl. sin.* 219, 829.

त्वदन्यं *acc. sin. m.* other than thee.

त्वदर्थम् *ind.* on thy account; (*comp. of* त्वद् *for* त्वत् 219, *and* अर्थे 791.)

त्वदर्थे *ind.* on thy account, respecting thee, about thee; (*comp. of* त्वद् *for* त्वत् 219, *and* अर्थे 791.)

त्वदीयम् *nom. sin. n. of* त्वदीय *m. f. n.* thine, thy, 231.

त्वन्येन *for* तु अन्येन *by* 34.

त्वब्रुवन् *for* तु अब्रुवन् *by* 34.

त्वभ्यपूजयन् *for* तु अभ्यपूजयन् *by* 34.

त्वम् thou, you; *nom. sin. of* त्वत् *or* युष्मत् 219.

त्वमप्येवं *for* त्वम् अपि एवं *by* 34.

त्वया by thee; *ins. sin. of* त्वत् *or* युष्मत् 219.

त्वयाधर्मकृच्छ्रे *for* त्वया अधर्मकृच्छ्रे *by* 31.

त्वयारण्ये *for* त्वया अरण्ये *by* 31.

त्वयि in thee; (Book XIII. 67, with thee, at thy house;) *loc. sin. of* त्वत् *or* युष्मत्.

त्वयोक्तं *for* त्वया उक्तं *by* 32.

त्वयोत्सृष्टा *for* त्वया उत्सृष्टा *by* 32.

त्वरते he hastens on; *3d sin. pres. átm. of rt* त्वर् *1st cl.* 261.

त्वरमाणया *ins. sin. f. of* त्वरमाण *m. f. n.* hastening. (By thee, in thy haste.)

त्वरमाणस् *nom. sin. m. of* त्वरमाण *m. f. n.* hastening; *pres. p. átm. of rt* त्वर् 526.

त्वरमाणा *nom. sin. f.* hastening, running quickly.

त्वरमाणो *nom. sin. m. of* त्वरमाण *m. f. n.* hastening.

त्वरमाणोपचक्रमे *for* त्वरमाणा उपचक्रमे *by* 32. *See both words.*

त्वरान्वितः *nom. sin. m.* in haste, quick, *lit.* possessed of haste; (त्वरा *cr.* haste, *and* अन्वित possessed of.)

त्वरिता *nom. sin. f. of* त्वरित *m. f. n.* hurrying, hastening, quick, swift; (*properly past p. p. of rt* त्वर्.)

त्वरिताः *nom. pl. m. of* त्वरित *m. f. n.* hurrying, hastening, quick, swift.

त्वरितो *for* त्वरितस् *nom. sin. m. of* त्वरित *m. f. n.* hurrying, hastening, quick.

त्वर्यमाणो *nom. sin. m. of* त्वर्यमाण *m. f. n.* being urged; *pres. p. of* त्वर् *in pass.* 528.

त्वा thee; *acc. sin. of* त्वत् thou, 219.

त्वां thee; *acc. sin. of* त्वत् thou, 219.

त्वाभिगम्याहं *for* त्वा अभिगम्य अहं *by* 31.

त्वाम् thee; *acc. sin. of* त्वत् thou, 219.

द.

द (*at the end of compounds*) *denotes* giving, causing, a giver; (*agt. of rt* दा.)

दंष्ट्रिभ्यः *abl. pl. of* दंष्ट्रिन् *m.* an animal having tusks, tusked, a boar, &c., *6th cl.* 159.

दक्षाम् *acc. sin. of* दक्ष *m. f. n.* upright, *1st cl.* 105.

दक्षिणापथं *acc. sin. of* दक्षिणापथ *m.* the Southern region, the Southern road or direction; (*from* दक्षिणा the South, *and* पथ a road.) दक्षिण 'the South' is properly that which is on the right hand. The Southern region means here the land to the South of the Narmadá or Nerbudda river. The word Dakshin is now corrupted into Deccan.

दक्षिणापथः *nom. sin. See last.*

दक्षिणावताम् *gen. pl. of* दक्षिणावत् *m. f. n.* having gifts, accompanied by presents or fees to Bráhmans; (*from* दक्षिणा a present to a Bráhman, *and* वत् possessed of.)

दक्षिणे *ind.* towards the South, 716.

दण्डधारणं *nom. sin. of* दण्डधारण *n.* punishment.

दण्डभयात् Tat. or Dep. comp. 743; दण्ड *cr.* rod, भयात् *abl. sin. of* भय *n.* fear, *1st cl.* 104. *See note under* यमः.

दण्डिभिः *ins. pl. of* दण्डिन् *m.* a warder, a door-keeper, *6th cl.* 159.

दण्ड्यस् *nom. sin. m.* to be punished, punishable; *fut. pass. p. of rt* दण्ड् 571.

दत्तं *nom. sin. n. of* दत्त *m. f. n.* given; *past p. p. of rt* दा 533. *a.*

दत्ता *nom. sin. f. of* दत्त *m. f. n.* given, 533. *a.*

दत्त्वा having given; *past ind. p. of rt* दा 556.

ददर्श he or she saw; *3d sin. perf. of rt* दृश् 364, 604.

ददर्शाथ *for* ददर्श अथ *by* 31.

ददर्शाद्भुतदर्शनान् *for* ददर्श अद्भुतदर्शनान् *by* 31.

ददर्शाश्रममण्डलम् *for* ददर्श आश्रममण्डलम् *by* 31.

ददुः they gave; *3d pl. perf. of rt* दा 663, 373.

ददृशुः *for* ददृशुस् they saw. *See next.*

ददृशुर् *for* ददृशुस् they saw, they beheld; *3d pl. 2d pret. of rt* दृश् 604.

ददृशे he or she saw; *3d sin. perf. átm. of rt* दृश् 364, 604.

ददौ he gave; *3d sin. perf. of rt* दा 663, 373.

दधुः they applied, they placed; *3d pl. perf. of rt* धा 373, 664. मनो दधुः they applied their minds, they entertained the idea, they resolved.

दन्तिभिः *ins. pl. of* दन्तिन् *m.* an elephant, 159.

दन्तैः *ins. pl. of* दन्त *m.* a tusk, a tooth, *1st cl.* 103.

दमं *acc. sin. of* दम *m.* Dama, brother of Damayantí, *1st cl.* 103.

दमः *nom. sin. of* दम *m.* temperance, self-restraint, *1st cl.* 103.

दमनं *acc. sin. of* दमन *m.* Damana, brother of Damayantí, *1st cl.* 103.

दमनः *for* दमनस् *nom. sin. m.* Damana.

दमनो *for* दमनस् *nom. sin. of* दमन *m.* Damana.

दमयन्ति *voc. sin. of* दमयन्ती, *q. v.*

दमयन्ती *f.* Damayantí, daughter of Bhíma and wife of Nala, 1*st cl.* 106.

दमयन्तीं *acc. sin. of* दमयन्ती.

दमयन्तीसकाशे TAT. OR DEP. COMP. 743; दमयन्ती *cr.* Damayantí, सकाशे *loc. of* सकाश, *used adverbially,* in the presence of.

दमयन्तीसखीगणात् TAT. OR DEP. COMP. 745; दमयन्ती *cr.* Damayantí, सखी *cr.* friend, गणात् *abl. sin. of* गण *m.* troop, company.

दमयन्त्यनवद्याङ्गी *for* दमयन्ती अनवद्याङ्गी *by* 34.

दमयन्त्यर्थं for the sake of Damayantí; (*comp. of* दमयन्ती *and* अर्थं, *see* 760. *d*, 791.)

दमयन्त्यर्थे *ind.* for the sake of Damayantí, in search of Damayantí; (*comp. of* दमयन्ती *and* अर्थे 731.)

दमयन्त्या *ins. sin. of* दमयन्ती, *q. v.*

दमयन्त्या *for* दमयन्त्यास् *gen. sin. of* दमयन्ती, *q. v.*

दमयन्त्यां *loc. sin. of* दमयन्ती, *q. v.*

दमयन्त्याः *gen. sin. of* दमयन्ती, *q. v.*

दमयन्त्याम् *loc. sin. of* दमयन्ती, *q. v.*

दमयन्त्यास् *gen. sin. f. of* दमयन्ती, *q. v.*

दमयन्त्येकवस्त्राथ *for* दमयन्ती एकवस्त्रा अथ *by* 34 *and* 31.

दमयन्त्यै *dat. sin.* to Damayantí.

दमशौचसमन्वितैः TAT. OR DEP. COMP. 740; दम *cr.* self-command, शौच *cr.* purity, समन्वितैः *ins. pl. of* समन्वित *m. f. n.* endowed with.

दयां *acc. sin. of* दया *f.* compassion, pity.

दयितं *acc. sin. m. of* दयित *m. f. n.* beloved, dear, cherished.

दयितः *nom. sin. m. of* दयित *m. f. n.* beloved.

दयितान् *acc. pl. m. of* दयित *m. f. n.* beloved, dear.

दरीश् *acc. pl. of* दरी *f.* a glen, 1*st cl.* 106.

दर्शनलालसाम् *acc. sin. f.* longing to see, ardently desirous of beholding; (*comp. of* दर्शन *cr.* seeing, *and* लालसा *f.* earnest longing, ardent desire, 761, 108.)

दर्शय shew thou; 2*d sin. imp. of rt* दृश् *in caus.* 604, 704.

दर्शयात्मानं *for* दर्शय आत्मानं *by* 31.

दर्शयितासि thou shalt shew; 2*d sin.* 1*st fut. of rt* दृश् *in caus.* 704.

दर्शयित्वा having shewed, having exhibited; *past ind. p. of rt* दृश् *in caus.* 558.

दश *acc. pl. of* दशन् ten, 204.

दशभिर् *ins. pl. of* दशन् ten, 204.

दशमः *nom. sin. m. of* दशम *m. f. n.* tenth, 209.

दशमे *loc. sin. n. of* दशम *m. f. n.* tenth, 209.

दशार्णाधिपतेः TAT. OR DEP. COMP. 743; दशार्ण *cr.* the country of Daśárṇa, अधिपतेः *gen. sin. of* अधिपति *m.* a sovereign, 121.

दशार्णेषु *loc. pl. m. of* दशार्ण (*declined in pl.*) in Daśárṇa, a country lying on the S. E. of the Vindhya mountains, in central Hindústán. It is mentioned in the Megha-dúta (verse 24), and its capital is there said to be Vidiśa. According to Professor Wilson, it may possibly correspond with the modern district Ćhattís-garh, as this place is so named, from its containing a number of forts (*ćhattís* 'thirty-six'), and Daśárṇa is derived from *daśa* 'ten' and *ṛiṇa* (*arṇa*) 'a stronghold.'

दष्टस्य *gen. sin. m. of* दष्ट *m. f. n.* bitten; *past p. p. of rt* दंश् 539.

दहति he or it burns; 3*d sin. pres. of rt* दह् 1*st cl.* 610.

दह्यते he is burnt; 3*d sin. pres. of rt* दह् *in pass.* 463.

दह्यन्तम् *acc. sin. m. of* दह्यत् *m. f. n.* burning; *pres. p. par. of rt* दह् 4*th cl.* 524.

दह्यमानः being consumed, being burnt; *pres. p. of rt* दह् *in pass.* 528.

दह्यमानस्य *gen. sin. m. of* दह्यमान *m. f. n.* being consumed.

दह्यमाना *nom. sin. f. of* दह्यमान *m. f. n.* being consumed, being burnt, being tormented.

दह्यमानाम् *acc. sin. f. of* दह्यमान *m. f. n.* being parched.

दह्यमानो *for* दह्यमानस् *nom. sin. m.* being consumed, being burnt.

दाक्ष्यं *nom. sin. of* दाक्ष्य *n.* cleverness, 1*st cl.* 104.

दाता *nom. sin. m. of* दातृ *m. f. n.* liberal, generous, a giver.

दाता he will give; 3*d sin.* 1*st fut. of rt* दा 663.

दानं *nom. sin. of* दान *n.* liberality, 1*st cl.* 104.

दान्तं *acc. sin. of* दान्त *m.* Dánta, brother of Damayantí, 1*st cl.* 103.

दारकौ two children; *nom. or acc. du. of* दारक *m.* a child, 1*st cl.* 103.

दारुणः *nom. sin. m. of* दारुण *m. f. n.* dreadful, grievous.

दारुणतरं *acc. sin. m. of* दारुणतर *m. f. n.* more dreadful, more terrible, 191.

दारुणाकृतिः Bah. or Rel. comp. 766; दारुण *cr.* terrible, dreadful, आकृतिः *nom. sin. m. from* आकृति *f.* form, 119.

दारुणाम् *acc. sin. f. of* दारुण *m. f. n.* fearful, terrible.

दारुणे *loc. sin. m. or n. of* दारुण *m. f. n.* terrible, fearful, 1*st cl.* 187.

दारुणो *nom. sin. m. of* दारुण *m. f. n.* terrible.

दारैः *ins. pl. of* दार (*always in m. pl.*) a wife, 103.

दारैस् *ins. pl. of* दार *m. pl.* a wife.

दावं *acc. sin. of* दाव *m.* a forest-fire.

दावविवर्जितम् Tat. or Dep. comp. 740; दाव *cr.* fire, विवर्जितम् *acc. sin. m.* free from, *lit.* abandoned by.

दासत्वम् *acc. sin. of* दासत्व *n.* slavery.

दासीनां *gen. pl. of* दासी *f.* a slave, a female-servant, 1*st cl.* 106.

दास्यामि I will give; 1*st sin.* 2*d fut. of rt* दा.

दिग्वाससम् *acc. sin. m. of* दिग्वासस् *m. f. n.* naked, (*lit.* having space or sky for vesture; *from* दिश् (43. *e*) a quarter of the sky, *and* वासस् a garment, raiment.)

दिदृक्षवः *nom. pl. of* दिदृक्षुः *m. f. n.* desirous of seeing, 3*d cl.* 111; *an adj. formed from the des. form of rt* दृश्, *see* 500. *c. and* 82. VII.

दिदृक्षुर् *nom. sin. m. of* दिदृक्षु *m. f. n.* desirous of seeing; *des. adj. from rt* दृश् 500. *c*, 82. VII.

दिवं *acc. sin. of* दिव् *f.* heaven; *see* 180. *b.*

दिवा *ind.* by day, 714.

दिवानिशम् *acc. sin. n. or ind.* day and night, Dvan. or Agg. comp., *see* 753.

दिवारात्रम् *ind.* day and night, 753.

दिवि *loc. sin. of* दिव् *f.* the sky, heaven, 8*th cl.* 180. *b.*

दिविस्पृग्भिर् *ins. pl. of* दिविस्पृश् *m. f. n.* touching the sky; (*comp. of* दिवि, *see last, and* स्पृश् *m. f. n.* touching, 8*th cl.* 181.)

दिवौकसः *nom. pl. of* दिवौकस् *m.* a deity, a celestial, an inhabitant of heaven, (*lit.* one whose dwelling is in heaven; *from* दिव *cr.* heaven, *and* ओकस् a habitation, 33, 762.)

दिव्यं *acc. sin. n. of* दिव्य *m. f. n.* divine, celestial.

दिव्यकाननदर्शनम् in aspect like to a celestial grove, Bah. or Rel. comp. 761; दिव्य *cr.* divine, कानन *cr.* a grove, दर्शनम् *acc. sin. of* दर्शन *n.* aspect.

दिव्यदर्शनविश्रुत O thou that art known by thy divine aspect, Complex comp. 771; दिव्य *cr.* divine, दर्शन *cr.* aspect, विश्रुत *voc. sin. of* विश्रुत *m. f. n.* celebrated, well-known, 1*st cl.* 103.

दिव्यमानुषं *nom. sin. n.* divine or human; (*comp. of* दिव्य divine, *and* मानुष human.)

दिव्याश् *acc. pl. f. of* दिव्य *m. f. n.* celestial, divine, 1*st cl.* 105, 187.

दिशः *gen. sin. of* दिश् *f.* a region, quarter, point of the compass, 8*th cl.* 181.

दिशः *acc. pl. of* दिश् *f.* a quarter of the sky, region, 181.

दिशम् *acc. sin. of* दिश् *f.* a region, 8*th cl.* 181.

दिशो *acc. pl. of* दिश् *f.* a quarter.

दिष्टं *acc. sin. n. of* दिष्ट *m. f. n.* pointed out; *past p. p. of rt* दिश् 539.

दिष्ट्या *ind.* How fortunate! Mayest thou be fortunate! Hail to thee! I congratulate thee. *An exclamation used in congratulating another on any piece of good fortune.*

दीन *m. f. n.* dejected, miserable, 1*st cl.* 187.

दीनम् *acc. sin. m. of* दीन *m. f. n.* miserable.

दीनमानसः BAH. OR REL. COMP. 761; दीन *cr.* miserable, मानसः *nom. sin. m.* the mind.

दीना *nom. sin. f. of* दीन *m. f. n.* miserable.

दीना *for* दीनास् *nom. pl. m. of* दीन miserable.

दीनां *acc. sin. f. of* दीन *m. f. n.* miserable.

दीप्ताम् *acc. sin. f. of* दीप्त *m. f. n.* glowing, blazing, kindled.

दीर्घकालम् for a long period; (*comp. of* दीर्घ long, *and* कालम् *acc. sin. of* काल *m.* time, *see* 821.)

दीर्घबाहुर् *for* दीर्घबाहुस् BAH. OR REL. COMP. 761; दीर्घ *cr.* long, बाहुर् *nom. sin. of* बाहु *m.* an arm.

दीर्घस्य *gen. sin. m. of* दीर्घ *m. f. n.* long.

दीर्यते he or it is rent or torn; 3*d sin. pres. of rt* दॄ *in pass.* 468.

दीव्य play thou; 2*d sin. imp. of rt* दिव् to play, 4*th cl.* 275.

दीव्यतः *gen. sin. m. of* दीव्यत् *m. f. n.* playing; *pres. p. of rt* दिव् 4*th cl.* 524, 275.

दीव्यमानम् *acc. sin. m. of* दीव्यमान *m. f. n.* playing, gambling; *pres. p. átm. of rt* दिव् 4*th cl.* 275, 526.

दीव्याव let us two play, let both of us play; 1*st du. imp. of rt* दिव् 4*th cl.* 275.

दीव्यावेत्यब्रवीद् *for* दीव्याव इति अब्रवीद् *by* 32, 34.

दुःखं *nom. or acc. sin. of* दुःख *n.* sorrow, affliction.

दुःखं *acc. sin., used adverbially,* painfully, sorrowfully, 713.

दुःखतरं *nom. sin. n. of* दुःखतर *m. f. n.* more painful, more grievous.

दुःखतरम् *acc. sin. of* दुःखतर *n.* more grievous (thing), greater sorrow or suffering.

दुःखपरीतात्मा COMPLEX COMP. 771; दुःख *cr.* sorrow, anguish, परीत *cr.* pervaded, affected by, आत्मा *nom. sin. m.* the soul, 147.

दुःखशोकसमन्विता COMPLEX COMP. 770; दुःख *cr.* pain, शोक *cr.* sorrow, समन्विता *nom. sin. f. of* समन्वित *m. f. n.* possessed of, filled with.

दुःखस्य *gen. sin. of* दुःख *n.* sorrow, affliction.

दुःखात् *abl. sin. of* दुःख *n.* pain.

दुःखाद् *abl. sin. of* दुःख *n.* pain, suffering, 1*st cl.* 104.

दुःखार्ता *nom. sin. f. of* दुःखार्त *m. f. n.* afflicted, pained; (*comp. of* दुःख pain, *and* आर्त 542.)

दुःखार्ता *for* दुःखार्तास् *nom. pl. of* दुःखार्त *m. f. n.* afflicted.

दुःखार्ताम् *acc. sin. f. of* दुःखार्त afflicted.

दुःखार्तो *nom. sin. m. of* दुःखार्त afflicted with pain, suffering misery; (*from* दुःख *cr.* misery, *and* आर्त pained, 542.)

दुःखितः *nom. sin. m. of* दुःखित *m. f. n.* afflicted; *past p. p. of rt* दुःख् 538.

दुःखितया *ins. sin. f. of* दुःखित *m. f. n.* afflicted, pained.

दुःखितस्य *gen. sin. m. of* दुःखित *m. f. n.* afflicted, 1*st cl.* 103.

दुःखितस्याभवत् *for* दुःखितस्य अभवत् *by* 31.

दुःखिता *nom. sin. f. of* दुःखित *m. f. n.* afflicted.

दुःखितां *acc. sin. f. of* दुःखित *m. f. n.* afflicted.

दुःखितो *for* दुःखितस् *nom. sin. m.* afflicted.

दुःखेन *ins. sin. of* दुःख *n.* sorrow, pain, 1*st cl.* 104.

दुःसहो *nom. sin. m.* difficult to be borne, irresistible; (*comp. of* दुर् 726. *d*, 71. *a*, *and* सह *m. f. n.* bearable.)

दुर्गम् *acc. sin. n. of* दुर्ग *m. f. n.* difficult of access, pathless.

दुर्धर्षां *acc. sin. f. of* दुर्धर्ष *m. f. n.* difficult of approach, not to be violated; (*from* दुर् 726. *d, and* धर्ष.)

दुष्करं *acc. sin. n.* difficult or painful act.

दुष्करं *nom. sin. n. of* दुष्कर *m. f. n.* painful, difficult, bad.

दुष्कृतं *nom. sin. n.* sin, crime, evil action; (*comp. of* दुर् 726. *d, and* कृत, *q. v.*)

दुष्टं *acc. sin. m. of* दुष्ट *m. f. n.* wicked.

दुष्टभावेन BAH. OR REL. COMP. 766; दुष्ट *cr.* wicked, depraved, भावेन *ins. sin. of* भाव *m.* nature, state, 1*st cl.* 103.

दुष्टासु *loc. pl. f. of* दुष्ट *m. f. n.* corrupted.

दुहितरम् *acc. sin. of* दुहितृ *f.* a daughter, 4*th cl.* 128.

दुहिता *nom. sin. of* दुहितृ *f* a daughter.

दुहितुस् *gen. sin. of* दुहितृ *f.* a daughter.

दुहितृ *f.* a daughter, 4*th cl.* 129.

दुहित्रर्थे *ind.* for the sake of (his) daughter; (*comp. of* दुहितृ a daughter, *and* अर्थे 760. *d*, 791, 34.)

दूत *for* दूतस् *nom. sin. m.* a messenger.

दूताश् *for* दूतास् *nom. pl. of* दूत *m.* a messenger.

दूती *nom. sin. f.* a female-messenger.

दूतीम् *acc. sin. of* दूती *f.* a female-messenger.

दूतो *for* दूतस् *nom. sin. of* दूत *m.* a messenger, an ambassador, 1*st cl.* 103.

दूरे *ind.* far off, at a distance, 716.

दृढं *ind.* excessively, very.

दृढव्रतः BAH. OR REL. COMP. 766; दृढ *cr.* strict, firm, faithful, व्रतः *nom. sin. from* व्रत *m. n.* a vow.

दृश्य to be seen, worthy to be seen; *fut. pass. p. of rt* दृश् 573. *b.*

दृश्यते he or she is seen; 3*d sin. pres. pass. of rt* दृश् 604, 463.

दृश्यन्ते they are seen; 3*d pl. pres. pass. of rt* दृश्.

दृश्यसे thou art seen; 2*d sin. pres. of rt* दृश् *in pass.* 463.

दृश्यैः *ins. pl. of* दृश्य to be seen, *q. v.*

दृष्टं *nom. sin. n. of* दृष्ट *m. f. n.* seen; *past p. p. of rt* दृश्.

दृष्टः *nom. sin. m. of* दृष्ट *m. f. n.* seen.

दृष्टपूर्वः *nom. sin. m.* seen before. *See next.*

दृष्टपूर्वस् seen before; *nom. sin. m. of* दृष्टपूर्व; दृष्ट *cr.* seen, पूर्वस् *nom. sin. m. of* पूर्व before, 1*st cl.* 103.

दृष्टपूर्वा *nom. sin. f.* seen before.

दृष्टवती *nom. sin. f. of* दृष्टवत् *m. f. n.* who has seen; *past act. p. of rt* दृश् 553.

दृष्टवन्तो who have seen; *nom. pl. m. of* दृष्टवत्. *See next.*

दृष्टवान् who has seen, (he saw;) *nom. sin. m. of* दृष्टवत् *past act. p. with sense of past tense*, 553, 897.

दृष्टस् *nom. sin. m. of* दृष्ट *m. f. n.* seen; *past p. p. of rt* दृश्.

दृष्टा *nom. sin. f. of* दृष्ट *m. f. n.* seen.

दृष्टास् *nom. pl. f. of* दृष्ट *m. f. n.* seen.

दृष्टिर् *for* दृष्टिस् *nom. sin. of* दृष्टि *f.* sight, eye-sight, 2*d cl.* 112.

दृष्टो *nom. sin. m. of* दृष्ट *m. f. n.* seen, observed; *past p. p. of rt* दृश् 604, 539.

दृष्ट्वा having seen, having beheld; *past ind. p. of rt* दृश् to see, 556, 604.

दृष्ट्वाशोकतरुं *for* दृष्ट्वा अशोकतरुं *by* 31.

दृष्ट्वेमां *for* दृष्ट्वा इमां *by* 32.

दृष्ट्वैव *for* दृष्ट्वा एव *by* 33.

देदीप्यमानां *acc. sin. f. of* देदीप्यमान *m. f. n.* shining brightly or intensely, *see* 507. *a.*

देयं *nom. sin. n. of* देय *m. f. n.* to be given.

देयो *nom. sin. m. of* देय *m. f. n.* to be given; *fut. pass. p. of rt* दा 571. *a.*

देव *m.* a god, 1*st cl.* 103.

देव *voc. sin. of* देव *m.* a god, 1*st cl.* 103.

देवं *acc. sin. of* देव *m.* a god.

देवगन्धर्वमानुषोरगराक्षसान् DVAN. OR AGG.

COMP. 748; देव *cr.* a god; गन्धर्व *cr.* a Gandharba or celestial musician, *see note under* गन्धर्वो; मानुष *cr.* a man; उरग *cr.* a serpent, *see under* नाग; राक्षसान् *acc. pl. of* राक्षस *m.* a demon, *1st cl.* 103, *see under* राक्षसी.

देवता *nom. sin. f.* a deity, a goddess.

देवताः *nom. or acc. pl. of* देवता *f.* a god, a deity, 105.

देवतानां *gen. pl. of* देवता *f.* a deity, *1st cl.* 105.

देवताभ्यर्चनपरो TAT. OR DEP. COMP. 745; देवता *cr.* a deity, अभ्यर्चन *cr.* worship, परो *nom. sin. of* पर *m. f. n.* devoted to.

देवतायतनानि *nom. pl. n. of* देवतायतन *n.* a temple; (*comp. of* देवता a deity, *and* आयतन *n.* an abode.)

देवदुन्दुभयो TAT. OR DEP. COMP. 743; देव *cr.* gods, दुन्दुभयो *nom. pl. of* दुन्दुभि *m.* a drum.

देवदूतम् TAT. OR DEP. COMP. 743; देव *cr.* a god, दूतम् *acc. sin. of* दूत *m.* a messenger, *1st cl.* 103.

देवने *loc. sin. of* देवन *n.* play, gaming, gambling, playing (with dice), *1st cl.* 104.

देवनेन *ins. sin. of* देवन *n.* playing, gambling.

देवपतिर् *for* देवपतिस् TAT. OR DEP. COMP. 743; देव *cr.* a god, पतिर् *nom. sin. of* पति *m.* a lord, *2d cl.* 110.

देवराजसमद्युतिः equal in glory to the king of the gods, ANOM. COMP. 777; देव *cr.* a god, राज *for* राजन् *cr.* a king, 57, सम *cr.* equal, द्युतिः *nom. sin. m. from* द्युति *f.* brightness.

देवराजस्य TAT. OR DEP. COMP. 743; देव *cr.* a god, राजस्य *for* राज्ञः (*by* 778 *and* 151) *gen. sin. of* राजन् a king.

देवराड् *nom. sin. of* देवराज् *m.* the king of the gods, Indra; (*comp. of* देव a god, *and* राज् a king, 176. *e.*)

देवरूपिणीम् *acc. sin. f.* having a divine form; (*comp. of* देव *cr.* god, *and* रूपिन् *m. f. n.* having a form, *see* 85. VI.)

देवलिङ्गानि TAT. OR DEP. COMP. 743; देव *cr.* a god, लिङ्गानि *acc. pl. of* लिङ्ग *n.* a mark, characteristic, *1st cl.* 104.

देवसन्निधौ TAT. OR DEP. COMP. 743; देव *cr.* a god, सन्निधौ *loc. sin. of* सन्निधि *f.* presence, *2d cl.* 112.

देवा *for* देवास् *nom. pl. of* देव a god.

देवाः *for* देवास् *nom. pl. of* देव a god.

देवान् *acc. pl. of* देव *m.* a god.

देवानां *gen. pl. of* देव *m.* a god.

देवाश् *nom. pl. of* देव *m.* a god.

देवास् *nom. pl. of* देव *m.* a god.

देवि *voc. sin. of* देवी *f.* a queen, *1st cl.* 106.

देवी *nom. sin. f.* a goddess, a queen, *1st cl.* 106.

देवीं *acc. sin. of* देवी *f.* a queen.

देवेन *ins. sin. of* देव *m.* play, sport, gambling, *1st cl.* 103.

देवेभ्यः *dat. pl. of* देव *m.* a god.

देवेभ्यो *for* देवेभ्यस् *dat. pl. of* देव *m.* a god.

देवेषु *loc. pl. of* देव *m.* a god.

देवैः *ins. pl. of* देव *m.* a god.

देवैर् *for* देवैस् *ins. pl. of* देव *m.* a god.

देवैस् *ins. pl. of* देव *m.* a god.

देशं *acc. sin. of* देश *m.* a region, a place.

देशकालज्ञा knowing the (proper) place and time, COMPLEX COMP. 770; (*from* देश *cr.* place, काल *cr.* time, ज्ञा *nom. sin. f. of* ज्ञ *m. f. n.* knowing, *see* 580.)

देशात् *abl. sin. of* देश *m.* a country.

देशातिथयो TAT. OR DEP. COMP. 743; देश *cr.* a country, अतिथयो *nom. pl. of* अतिथि *m.* a guest, 110.

देशो *nom. sin. of* देश *m.* a country, *1st cl.* 103.

देहं *acc. sin. of* देह *m. n.* the body.

देहस्य *gen. sin. of* देह *m. n.* the body, *1st cl.* 103, 104.

देहस्यास्य *for* देहस्य अस्य *by* 31.

देहा *for* देहास् *nom. pl. of* देह *m.* the body.

देहि give thou; *2d sin. imp. of rt* दा.

देहिनो *for* देहिनस् *gen. sin. of* देहिन् *m.* the embodied soul, the spirit.

देही *nom. sin. of* देहिन् *m.* the soul.

देहे *loc. sin. of* देह *m. n.* the body, 1*st cl.* 103, 104.

दैत्यदानवमर्दनं an epithet of the god Indra; दैत्य a Daitya or demon, दानव a Dánava, a demon or giant, मर्दनं *acc. sin. of* मर्दन *m.* the destroyer, (*lit.* the crusher, *agt. from rt* मृद् 582. *c.*) The Daityas and Dánavas, like the Titans, were a kind of demon or giant who waged perpetual war with the gods. *See note under* अमृतोपमां.

दैवतपरः *nom. sin.* a worshipper of the gods; (*comp. of* दैवत *cr.* a god, *and* परः *m.* devoted to.)

दैवदोषाद् TAT. OR DEP. COMP. 743; दैव *cr.* destiny, fate, दोषाद् *abl. sin. of* दोष *m.* fault.

दैवमानुषं *nom. sin. n.* divine or human; (*comp. of* दैव divine, *and* मानुष human, *see* 765.)

दैवात् *abl. sin. of* दैव *n.* fate, fortune, 1*st cl.* 103.

दैवेन *ins. sin. of* दैव *n.* fate, destiny; *or ins. sin. of* दैव *m. f. n.* divine.

दैवेनाक्रम्य *for* दैवेन आक्रम्य *by* 31.

दोला *nom. sin. f.* a swing, 1*st cl.* 105.

दोलेव *for* दोला इव *by* 32.

दोषं *acc. sin. of* दोष *m.* fault, crime.

दोषतः *for* दोषतस् *ind.* of a fault, of evil intentions; (*from* दोष *with affix* तस्, *see* 719.)

दोषश् *nom. sin. m.* fault, crime, sin.

दोषेण *ins. sin. of* दोष *m.* fault, crime.

दोषैर् *ins. pl. of* दोष *m.* a crime, fault.

दोषो *for* दोषस् *nom. sin. of* दोष *m.* fault, blame, 1*st cl.* 103.

दौत्येन *ins. sin. of* दौत्य *n.* a message, a mission, embassy.

दौत्येनागत्य *for* दौत्येन आगत्य *by* 31.

द्युतिं *acc. sin. of* द्युति *f.* brilliancy, beauty.

द्यूतम् *nom. sin. of* द्यूत *n.* game, gaming.

द्यूते *loc. sin. of* द्यूत *m. n.* game, play, gambling, gaming with dice, 1*st cl.* 103, 104.

द्रक्ष्यसि thou shalt see; 2*d sin.* 2*d fut. of rt* दृश् 604.

द्रक्ष्यसे thou shalt or wilt see; 2*d sin.* 2*d fut. átm. of rt* दृश्.

द्रक्ष्यामि I shall or will see; 1*st sin.* 2*d fut. of rt* दृश् 604.

द्रविणं *nom. sin. n.* property.

द्रविणेन *ins. sin. of* द्रविण *n.* property, wealth.

द्रव्यं *nom. sin. of* द्रव्य *n.* property, 1*st cl.* 104.

द्रष्टा he shall or will see, he will visit; 3*d sin.* 1*st fut. of rt* दृश् 604.

द्रष्टुं to see; *inf. of rt* दृश् 604, 459.

द्रुतं *ind.* quickly.

द्रुमः *nom. sin. of* द्रुम *m.* a tree.

द्रुमम् *acc. sin. of* द्रुम *m.* a tree.

द्रोणं *acc. sin. of* द्रोण *m.* Droṇa, name of a Bráhman, who was the instructor of both Kurus and Páṇḍavas in the art of war.

द्वयोर् *gen. and loc. of* द्वि two, 201.

द्वादशः *nom. sin. m.* twelfth, 210.

द्वादशे *loc. sin. m. of* द्वादश *m. f. n.* twelfth, 210.

द्वापरं *acc. sin. of* द्वापर *m.* the third Age of the world personified as a deity, 1*st cl.* 103.

द्वापरेण *ins. sin.* *See last.*

द्वारि *loc. sin. of* द्वार् *f.* a door, a gate, 8*th cl.* 180.

द्वाविंशतितमः *nom. sin. m.* the twentieth, 211.

द्विजः *nom. sin. m.* a Bráhman or twice-born man; *see note under* द्विजसत्तमः.

द्विजनिषेवितां TAT. OR DEP. COMP. 740; द्विज *cr.* a bird, निषेवितां *acc. sin. f. of* निषेवित *m. f. n.* resorted to, inhabited by.

द्विजसत्तमः *nom. sin. m.* best of Bráhmans, best of the twice-born. The first three classes or castes (see note under विशाम्पते) are called Dvija or twice-born. The first birth is from the natural mother, the second from the ligation of the sacrificial cord. (Manu II. 169.) This cord, called *Yajňopavíta*, was made of three strings of cotton (Manu II. 44), and suspended over the left shoulder of men of the first three classes at various ages, in token of their second or spiritual birth.

द्विजसत्तमम् *acc. sin. m.* best of the twice-born; (*from* द्विज *cr.* a twice-born man, *and* सत्तम best, *see* 743. *b.*)

द्विजसत्तमाः O best of Bráhmans; *voc. pl. m.*

द्विजात् *abl. sin. of* द्विज *m.* a Bráhman.

द्विजातयः *nom. pl. of* द्विजाति *m.* a Bráhman, 2*d cl.* 110.

द्विजातिजनवत्सलः a friend to the Bráhman race, 745; द्विजाति *cr.* twice-born, a Bráhman, जन *cr.* a person, वत्सल fond of, friendly to.

द्विजान् *acc. pl. of* द्विज *m.* a bird, (twice-born, first in the shell and then from it.)

द्विजान् *acc. pl. of* द्विज *m.* a Bráhman.

द्विजोत्तमम् *acc. sin. m.* best of Bráhmans.

द्विजोत्तमाः *voc. pl. m.* O best of Bráhmans.

द्वितीयं *acc. sin. m. of* द्वितीय *m. f. n.* second, 208.

द्वितीयं *ind.* a second time, 713.

द्वितीयः *for* द्वितीयस् *nom. sin. of* द्वितीय *m. f. n.* second, 208.

द्वितीयो *for* द्वितीयस् *nom. sin. m. of* द्वितीय *m. f. n.* second.

द्विधा *ind.* in two ways, in two parts, in two directions, 723.

द्विधेव *for* द्विधा इव *by* 32.

द्विपदां *gen. pl. of* द्विपाद् *m.* a man, a biped, 5*th cl. Observe—*द्विपाद् *becomes* द्विपद् *in acc. pl. and other vowel cases; see* 145.

द्विषताम् *gen. pl. of* द्विषत् *m.* an enemy, 5*th cl.* 136. *As a present participle this word means* hating, *see* 657.

द्वे *acc. du. f. of* द्वि two, 201.

द्वैरथेन *ins. sin. of* द्वैरथ *n.* single combat in chariots.

द्वौ *nom. du. of* द्वि two.

ध.

धनं *acc. sin. of* धन *n.* wealth, money.

धनानि *acc. pl. of* धन *n.* wealth, property, riches, 1*st cl.* 104.

धनुः *for* धनुस् *nom. sin. n.* a bow.

धनेन *ins. sin. of* धन *n.* wealth.

धन्विनां *gen. pl. of* धन्विन् *m.* an archer, a bow-man, 6*th cl.* 159.

धयानां *for* हयानां (50) *gen. pl. of* हय a horse.

धरणीतले on the surface of the earth; (*from* धरणी *cr.* earth, *and* तले *loc. sin. of* तल *n.* surface, 743.)

धरिष्यन्ति they shall continue, they shall remain; 3*d pl.* 2*d fut. of rt* धृ 1*st cl.* 393. *c.*

धर्म *for* धर्मस् *nom. sin. m.* duty.

धर्मं *acc. sin. of* धर्म *m.* virtue, justice.

धर्मज्ञ *voc. sin. m. of* धर्मज्ञ *m. f. n.* knowing (one's) duty; (*comp. of* धर्म *cr.* duty, *and* ज्ञ 688, 580.)

धर्मज्ञः *nom. sin. m.* a knower of duty.

धर्मज्ञस्य *gen. sin. of* धर्मज्ञ *m. f. n.* knowing (one's) duty.

धर्मज्ञाः *nom. pl. m. of* धर्मज्ञ *m. f. n.* knowing (their) duty, righteous.

धर्मज्ञो *nom. sin. of* धर्मज्ञ *m. f. n.* knowing (one's) duty, virtuous.

धर्मतः *for* धर्मतस् *ind.* justly, religiously, righteously, 719. *b.*

धर्मभृतां *gen. pl. of* धर्मभृत् *m.* a maintainer of justice; (*comp. of* धर्म *cr.* justice, *and* भृत् *agt. of rt* भृ to maintain, 84, I.)

धर्मवत्सल *voc. sin.* O thou that lovest virtue; (*comp. of* धर्म *cr. and* वत्सल *m. f. n.* fond.)

धर्मविच् *for* धर्मविद् *m.* one who knows his duties, 5*th cl.* 137, *see* 49; (*comp. of* धर्म *and* विद् 84, I.)

धर्मवित् Tat. or Dep. comp. 743; धर्म *cr.* duty, वित् *nom. sin. m. of* विद् knowing, 5*th cl.* 137.

धर्मस् *nom. sin. m.* duty.

धर्मात्मा *nom. sin. m. of* धर्मात्मन् *m. f. n.* virtuous, pious, pious-minded; (*comp. of* धर्म virtue, piety, *and* आत्मन् soul, 147.)

धर्मात्मानं *acc. sin. m. See last.*

धर्मान् *acc. pl. of* धर्म *m.* duty, *1st cl.* 103.

धर्मार्थदर्शिनः TAT. OR DEP. COMP. 745; धर्म *cr.* justice, duty, अर्थ *cr.* object, wealth, interest, दर्शिनः *gen. sin. m. of* दर्शिन् regarding, looking to, *6th cl.* 159.

धर्मे *loc. sin. of* धर्म *m.* law, usage, duty, virtue.

धर्मेण *ins. sin. of* धर्म *m.* right, justice, virtue, *1st cl.* 103.

धर्मेणासि *for* धर्मेण असि *by* 31.

धर्मेषु *loc. pl. of* धर्म *m.* virtue, duty, *1st cl.* 103.

धर्मो *for* धर्मस् *nom. sin. of* धर्म *m.* duty.

धर्म्यं *acc. sin. m.* lawful, consistent with duty.

धर्म्याद् *abl. sin. n. of* धर्म्य lawful, just, consistent with duty.

धर्षयितुम् to insult, *or, with pass. sense,* to be insulted, to be ill-treated; *inf. of rt* धृष् *10th cl.* 459, 869.

धर्षिताः *nom. pl. m. or f. of* धर्षित *m. f. n.* smitten, overcome, violated; *past p. p. of rt* धृष् 538.

धर्षितास् *nom. pl. m. or f. of* धर्षित ill-treated, smitten, overcome, violated.

धात्रा *ins. sin. of* धातृ *m.* the Creator, *4th cl.* 127.

धात्रीम् *acc. sin. of* धात्री *f.* a nurse, *1st cl.* 106.

धारयति he supports; *3d sin. pres. of rt* धृ *10th cl.* 285.

धारयतीं *acc. sin. f. of* धारयत् *m. f. n.* maintaining, supporting; *pres. p. of rt* धृ *10th cl.* 524, 285.

धारयन्ति they support, they maintain; *3d pl. pres. of rt* धृ *10th cl.* 285.

धारयामास he restrained; *3d sin. perf. of rt* धृ 285, 385. *a.*

धारयितुं to bear, to support, to hold; *inf. of rt* धृ *10th cl.* 285.

धावत run ye; *2d pl. imp. of rt* धाव् *1st cl.* 261.

धावताधुना *for* धावत अधुना *by* 31.

धावति he or she runs; *3d sin. pres. of rt* धाव् *1st cl.* 261.

धावन्तो *nom. pl. m. of* धावत् *m. f. n.* running; *pres. p. par. of rt* धाव् *1st cl.* 524.

धास्यामि I will cause, I will make, I will place; *1st sin. 2d fut. of rt* धा 664.

धि *for* हि for, *by* 50.

धिरण्यसदृशच्छदान् BAH. OR REL. COMP. 761; धिरण्य *for* हिरण्य (50) *cr.* gold, सदृश *cr.* like, resembling, छदान् *acc. pl. of* छद *m.* a wing, *1st cl.* 103; *see* 51. *a.*

धीमतः *gen. sin. m. of* धीमत् *m. f. n.* wise.

धीमान् *nom. sin. m. of* धीमत् *m. f. n.* wise, intelligent, *lit.* possessed of understanding, *5th cl.* 140.

धीरं *acc. sin. m. or n. of* धीर *m. f. n.* wise, sensible, grave, sedate, sober.

धीरस् *nom. sin. m.* a wise man, a sensible man.

धूमजालेन TAT. OR DEP. COMP. 740; धूम *cr.* mist, cloud, smoke, जालेन *ins. sin. of* जाल *m.* a multitude, a mass, film.

धूयमानो *nom. sin. m. of* धूयमान *m. f. n.* being agitated, being fanned; *pres. p. of rt* धू *in pass.* 528.

धृतम् *for* हृतम् taken, seized, *by* 50.

धृतिर् *nom. sin. of* धृति *f.* constancy, *2d cl.* 112.

धैर्यं *nom. sin. of* धैर्य *n.* firmness, strength.

ध्यात्वा having pondered, having reflected; *past ind. p. of rt* ध्यै 536, 556.

ध्यानतत्पराम् *acc. sin. f.* lost in thought; (*comp. of* ध्यान reflection, meditation, *and* तत्पर engaged in, intent on.)

ध्यानपरा lost in meditation, TAT. OR DEP. COMP. 744; ध्यान *cr.* meditation, परा *nom. sin. f. of* पर *m. f. n.* principally engaged in, devoted to, *1st cl.* 187.

ध्रियते it is fixed, it is held; *3d sin. pres. of rt* धृ *in pass.* 463.

ध्रियसे thou livest, thou survivest; *2d sin. pres. of rt* धृ *in pass.* (*The pass. of* धृ to hold *is thus used, i. e.* to be held in life.)

ध्रुवं *nom. sin. n. or acc. sin. m. or n. of* ध्रुव *m. f. n.* certain, 187.

ध्रुवम् *ind.* certainly, assuredly, 713.

ध्रुवाणि *nom. pl. n. of* ध्रुव *m. f. n.* perpetual, continual, constant.

ध्रुवो *nom. sin. m. of* ध्रुव *m. f. n.* certain, inevitable.

न.

न *ind.* not, no, nor, neither.

नः us, to us, *for* अस्मान् *or* अस्मभ्यं *acc. or dat. pl. of* मत्, (*nom.* अहं.)

नक्तं *ind.* by night, 713. *b.*

नक्षत्राणि *nom. pl. n. of* नक्षत्र *n.* a constellation, a star, *1st cl.* 104.

नग *m.* a tree, a mountain.

नगरं *acc. sin. of* नगर *n.* a city, town.

नगरसम्मितम् *acc. sin. m.* equal to a town; (*comp. of* नगर *cr.* a town, *and* सम्मित *m. f. n.* of equal measure or extent.)

नगराभ्यासे in the neighbourhood of the city; (*from* नगर *cr. and* अभ्यासे *ind.* near, 731.)

नगरीं *acc. sin. of* नगरी *f.* a city.

नगरे *loc. sin. of* नगर *n.* a city.

नगा *for* नगास् *nom. pl. of* नग *m.* a tree.

नगाग्राद् TAT. OR DEP. COMP. 743; नग *cr.* a mountain, अग्राद् *abl. sin. of* अग्र *n.* summit, top.

नगान् *acc. pl. of* नग *m.* a tree.

नग्नम् *acc. sin. m. of* नग्न *m. f. n.* naked.

नचिराद् *ind.* in no long time, in a short time, soon; (*comp. of* न not, *and* चिराद् 715.)

नदतो *gen. sin. m. of* नदत् *m. f. n.* sounding, thundering; *pres. p. of rt* नद् 524.

नदी *nom. sin. f.* a river.

नदीं *acc. sin. of* नदी *f.* a river.

नदीः *acc. pl. of* नदी *f.* a river, *1st cl.* 106.

नदीम् *acc. sin. of* नदी *f.* a river, *1st cl.* 106.

नदीश् *acc. pl. of* नदी *f.* a river, *1st cl.* 106.

नद्धान् *acc. pl. m. of* नद्ध *m. f. n.* furnished, provided with; *past p. p. of rt* नह् 556.

नद्याः *gen. sin. of* नदी *f.* a river.

ननु whether? *particle of interrogation*, 717. *b.*

नन्दन *voc. sin. of* नन्दन *m.* a son.

नन्दने *loc. sin. of* नन्दन *n.* the paradise or elysium of Indra, *see note under* इन्द्रलोकम्.

नभसि *loc. sin. of* नभस् *n.* the sky, the atmosphere, *7th cl.* 164.

नभस्तलात् *abl. sin. of* नभस्तल the sky, the lower sky; (*from* नभस् sky, *and* तल *n.* lower surface.)

नमस् *ind.* salutation; नमस् तेऽस्तु Hail to thee!

नमस्कारम् *acc. sin. of* नमस्कार *m.* homage, salutation, *1st cl.* 103.

नमस्कृत्य having saluted; *past ind. p. of* नमस्कृ.

नर *m.* a man, *1st cl.* 103.

नरः *nom. sin. of* नर *m.* a man.

नरकाय *dat. sin. of* नरक *m. n.* hell, the place of torment.

नरके *loc. sin. of* नरक *m. n.* hell, the infernal regions, *1st cl.* 103.

नरवरः *nom. sin. m.* an excellent or illustrious man; (*comp. of* नर *cr.* a man, *and* वर best.)

नरवरोत्तमम् *acc. sin. m.* the best of excellent men; (*comp. of* नर *cr.* a man, वर *cr.* excellent, उत्तमम् *acc. sin. of* उत्तम *m. f. n.* best, 743. *b.*)

नरवाहिना *ins. sin. n. of* नरवाहिन् *m. f. n.* carried by men; (*comp. of* नर a man, *and* वाहिन् a bearer.)

नरवीरस्य *gen. sin. of* नरवीर *m.* a hero, a heroic man, a hero of a man.

नरव्याघ्र KARM. OR DES. COMP. 758; नर *cr.* a man, व्याघ्र *voc. sin. of* व्याघ्र *m.* a tiger, *1st cl.* 103, (*i. e.* O chief of men, *see next.*)

नरशार्दूलो KARM. OR DES. COMP. 758; नर *cr.* a man, शार्दूलो *nom. sin. of* शार्दूल *m.* a tiger, (*i. e.* most illustrious of men.) The names of animals denoting superiority are often placed at the end of compounds; so पुरुषसिंहः a man-lion, नरर्षभः a man-bull.

नरश्रेष्ठ O best of men, TAT. OR DEP. COMP.

743; नर cr. a man, श्रेष्ठ *voc. sin. of* श्रेष्ठ *m. f. n.* best, 1*st cl.* 103.

नरस्य *gen. sin. of* नर *m.* a man.

नरस्यार्तस्य *for* नरस्य आर्तस्य *by* 31.

नराणाम् *gen. pl. of* नर *m.* a man.

नराधिप *voc. sin. m.* O lord of men.

नराधिपः *nom. sin. m.* lord of men; (*comp. of* नर a man, *and* अधिप *m.* a lord.)

नराधिपम् *acc. sin. m.* lord of men.

नराधिपैः Tat. or Dep. comp. 743; नर *cr.* a man, अधिपैः *ins. pl. of* अधिप *m.* a lord, 1*st cl.* 103.

नरेन्द्रस्य *gen. sin. of* नरेन्द्र *m.* chief of men.

नरेभ्यश् *abl. pl. of* नर *m.* a man.

नरेश्वर Tat. or Dep. comp. 743; नर *cr.* a man, ईश्वर *voc. sin. of* ईश्वर *m.* a lord, 1*st cl.* 103.

नरेश्वरे Tat. or Dep. comp. 743; नर *cr.* man, ईश्वरे *loc. sin. of* ईश्वर *m.* lord, 1*st cl.* 103. नर + ईश्वर = नरेश्वर *by* 32; *see, with reference to the locative case,* 819. *a.*

नरेषु *loc. pl. of* नर, *q. v.*

नरो *nom. sin. m.* a man.

नरोत्तम O best of men, *voc. sin.*; (*from* नर *cr.* a man, *and* उत्तम *m. f. n.* best, 743. *b.*)

नरोत्तमः *nom. sin. m.* most excellent of men.

नल *m.* NALA, king of Nishadha, 1*st cl.* 103.

नल *voc. sin. of* नल *m.* Nala.

नलं *acc. sin. of* नल Nala.

नलः *for* नलस् *nom. sin. of* नल Nala.

नलदर्शनकाङ्क्षया Tat. or Dep. comp. 745; नल *cr.* Nala, दर्शन *cr.* seeing, looking for, काङ्क्षया *ins. sin. of* काङ्क्षा *f.* desire.

नलनामानं *acc. sin. m.* named Nala, *see* 154.

नलपत्नी Tat. or Dep. comp. 743; नल *cr.* Nala, पत्नी *f.* the wife.

नलमार्गणे Tat. or Dep. comp. 743; नल *cr.* Nala, मार्गणे *loc. sin. of* मार्गण *n.* searching for.

नलवाजिषु Tat. or Dep. comp. 743; नल *cr.* Nala, वाजिषु *loc. pl. of* वाजिन् *m.* a horse, 159.

नलश् *for* नलस् *nom. sin. of* नल Nala.

नलशङ्कया Tat. or Dep. comp. 743; नल *cr.* Nala, शङ्कया *ins. sin. of* शङ्का *f.* suspicion.

नलशासनं *acc. sin. n.* *See next.*

नलशासनात् (as if) at the command of Nala, Tat. or Dep. comp. 743; नल *cr.* Nala, शासनात् *abl. sin. of* शासन *n.* command, 1*st cl.* 104.

नलसन्निधौ Tat. or Dep. comp. 743; नल Nala, सन्निधौ *loc. sin. of* सन्निधि *f.* presence.

नलसारथिः Tat. or Dep. comp. 743; नल *cr.* Nala, सारथिः *nom. sin. of* सारथि *m.* a charioteer.

नलसिद्धस्य Tat. or Dep. comp. 740; नल *cr.* Nala, सिद्धस्य *gen. sin. of* सिद्ध *m. f. n.* prepared, dressed.

नलस्याक्षेषु *for* नलस्य अक्षेषु *by* 31.

नलस्यानयने *for* नलस्य आनयने *by* 31.

नलस्यामित्रघातिनः *for* नलस्य अमित्रघातिनः *by* 31.

नलस्याराधने *for* नलस्य आराधने *by* 31.

नलस्यार्थाय *for* नलस्य अर्थाय *by* 31.

नलस्येष्टाम् *for* नलस्य इष्टाम् *by* 32.

नलामात्येषु Tat. or Dep. comp. 743; नल *cr.* Nala, अमात्येषु *loc. pl. of* अमात्य *m.* a minister, 1*st cl.* 103; *see* 861.

नलाय *dat. sin. of* नल *m.* Nala.

नलायाष्टौ *for* नलाय अष्टौ *by* 31.

नलाश्वास् Tat. or Dep. comp. 743; नल *cr.* Nala, अश्वास् *nom. pl. m.* horses. With reference to Book XXI. 3, it should be borne in mind that the horses of Nala had been before conducted to king Bhíma's city Vidarbha, by Nala's charioteer Várshṇeya.

नले *loc. sin. of* नल Nala.

नलेत्युच्चैः *for* नल इति उच्चैः *by* 32, 34.

नलो *for* नलस् *nom. sin. of* नल Nala.

नलोपाख्यानं Tat. or Dep. comp. 743; नल *cr.* Nala, उपाख्यानं *nom. sin. of* उपा-

ख्यान *n.* a tale, story, 1*st cl.* 104. अ + उ = ओ *by* 32.

नलोपाख्याने *loc. sin. of* नलोपाख्यानं, *q. v.*

नवमः *nom. sin. of* नवम *m. f. n.* ninth, 209.

नवां *acc. sin. f. of* नव *m. f. n.* new, young.

नवानि *acc. sin. n. of* नव *m. f. n.* new.

नश्यते he or it is destroyed or lost; 3*d sin. pres. of rt* नश् 4*th cl.* 463.

नष्टम् *nom. sin. n. of* नष्ट *m. f. n.* lost, forgotten; *past p. p. of rt* नश् 539.

नष्टरूपो BAH. OR REL. COMP. 767; नष्ट *cr.* destroyed, lost, रूपो *nom. sin. m. from* रूप *n.* form, 108.

नष्टसंज्ञा BAH. OR REL. COMP. 767; नष्ट *cr.* lost, perished, संज्ञा *nom. sin. f.* consciousness, mind, thought.

नष्टा *for* नष्टास् *nom. pl. of* नष्ट *m. f. n.* destroyed; *past p. p. of rt* नश् 539.

नष्टात्मा BAH. OR REL. COMP. 766; नष्ट *cr.* lost, deprived of, आत्मा *nom. sin. of* आत्मन् *m.* soul, mind, sense.

नष्टे *loc. sin. of* नष्ट *m. f. n.* destroyed, lost.

नाकाले *for* न अकाले *by* 31.

नाग *m.* a serpent, a demigod with a human face and the tail of a serpent. These fabulous beings are said to have sprung from Kadrú, the wife of Kaśyapa, and to have been created to people Pátála or the regions below the earth. The chief of these creatures is sometimes called S'esha or Ananta and Vásuki. The word नाग also means 'an elephant.'

नागं *acc. sin. of* नाग *m.* a serpent. *See last.*

नागः *nom. sin. m.* a serpent. *See* नाग.

नागराजं TAT. OR DEP. COMP. 743; नाग *cr.* a serpent, राजं *acc. sin.* king, *see* 151.

नागराजस् TAT. OR DEP. COMP. 743; नाग *cr.* a serpent, राजस् *nom. sin.* a king, 151.

नागराजस्य *gen. sin. m.* of the king of the serpents. *See last.*

नागराजानं *acc. sin.* the king of the serpents; नाग *cr.* a serpent, राजानं *acc. sin. of* राजन् *m.* a king, 6*th cl.* 149.

नागानां *gen. pl. of* नाग *m.* an elephant.

नागे *loc. sin. of* नाग *m.* a serpent.

नागेन्द्रो TAT. OR DEP. COMP. 743; नाग *cr.* a serpent, इन्द्रो *nom. sin. m.* chief.

नागैर् *ins. pl. of* नाग *m.* a serpent.

नातिचराम्यहम् *for* न अतिचरामि अहम् *by* 31 *and* 34.

नातिस्वस्येव *for* न अतिस्वस्या इव, *q. q. v. v.*

नात्मानं *for* न आत्मानं *by* 31.

नात्र *for* न अत्र *by* 31.

नाथ *voc. sin. of* नाथ *m.* a lord, guardian, husband, 1*st cl.* 103.

नादम् *acc. sin. of* नाद *m.* sound.

नादयन् *nom. sin. m. of* नादयत् *m. f. n.* causing to resound; *pres. p. of rt* नद् *in caus.* 527.

नादान् *acc. pl. of* नाद *m.* a cry.

नाद्य *for* न अद्य *by* 31.

नानाधातुशतैर् COMPLEX COMP. 770; नाना *ind.* various, धातु *cr.* a mineral, शतैर् *ins. pl. of* शत *n.* a hundred, *see* 206.

नानाधातुसमाकीर्णं TAT. OR DEP. COMP. 740; नाना *ind.* various, धातु *cr.* mineral, समाकीर्णं *acc. sin. m. of* समाकीर्ण *m. f. n.* filled with; *past p. p. of rt* कॄ *with* सम् *and* आ, 531.

नानापक्षिगणाकीर्णम् TAT. OR DEP. COMP. 745; नाना *ind.* various, पक्षि *for* पक्षिन् *cr.* (57) a bird, गण *cr.* a flock, आकीर्णम् *acc. sin. n. of* आकीर्ण *m. f. n.* filled with; *past p. p. of rt* कॄ *with* आ, 534.

नानापक्षिनिषेवितम् TAT. OR DEP. COMP. 740; नाना *cr.* various, पक्षि *cr.* birds, निषेवितम् *acc. sin. n.* resorted to, frequented by.

नानामृगगणैर् by flocks of various animals; (*comp. of* नाना *ind.* various, मृग *cr.* an animal, गणैर् *ins. pl. of* गण *m.* a flock.)

नानुधावसि *for* न अनुधावसि *by* 31.

नानुबभाति *for* न अनुबभाति *by* 31.

नान्यः *for* न अन्यः *by* 31.

नाप्यवारयत् *for* न अपि अवारयत् *by* 31 *and* 34.

नाप्राप्तकालो *for* न अप्राप्तकालो *by* 31.

नाबिभ्यत् *for* न अबिभ्यत् *by* 31.

नाभिचराम्यहं *for* न अभिचरामि अहं *by* 31 *and* 34.

नाभिनन्दति *for* न अभिनन्दति *by* 31.

नाभ्यजानात् *for* न अभ्यजानात् *by* 31 *and* 47.

नाभ्यभाषत *for* न अभ्यभाषत *by* 31.

नाम *ind.* by name, certainly, indeed.

नामतः *for* नामतस् *ind.* by name, 719.

नामसु *loc. pl. of* नामन् *n.* a name, *6th cl.* 152.

नामारिमर्दनं *for* नाम अरिमर्दनं *by* 31.

नामारिहा *for* नाम अरिहा *by* 31.

नामाहम् *for* नाम अहम् *by* 31.

नाम्यतां let it be bent, let it be drawn (as a bow); *3d sin. imp. of rt* नम् *in caus. pass.* 496.

नायम् *for* न अयम् *by* 31.

नारद *for* नारदस् *nom. sin. of* नारद Nárada. *See next.*

नारदः *nom. sin. of* नारद *m.* Nárada, usually regarded as one of the ten Ṛishis or Prajápatis first created by Brahmá, and called his sons. He is described as a friend of the god Kṛishṇa, as a celebrated lawgiver, and as the inventor of the víṇá or lute. Nárada is mentioned in Manu I. 34, 35, as one of the 'ten lords of created beings, eminent in holiness.' In the Hindú plays Nárada usually acts as a kind of messenger of the gods. See Vikramorvaśí end of Act V, and Śakuntalá end of Act VI. He is constantly employed in giving good counsel. He is by some considered to belong to the order of Devarshis, and by others to the Brahmarshis; see note under ब्रह्मर्षिभ्यश्.

नारदस्य *gen. sin. of* नारद. *See last.*

नारी *nom. sin. f.* a woman, *1st cl.* 106.

नारीणां *gen. pl. of* नारी a woman.

नारीरत्नं *acc. sin.* an excellent woman, Karm. or Des. comp. 758; नारी *cr.* a woman, रत्नं *acc. sin. of* रत्न a jewel, a gem.

नारीवाक्यानि Tat. or Dep. comp. 743; नारी *cr.* a woman, a wife, वाक्यानि *acc. pl. of* वाक्य *n.* a word.

नार्या *for* नार्यास् *gen. sin. of* नारी *f.* a woman, 106.

नाशयिष्यति he will remove or destroy, he will cause to perish; *3d sin. 2d fut. of rt* नश् *in caus.* 481, 620.

नाशयिष्यामि I will cause to perish or remove; *1st sin. 2d fut. of rt* नश् *in caus.*

नाश्रयेत् *for* न आश्रयेत् *by* 31.

नाश्वासयसि *for* न आश्वासयसि *by* 31.

नाश्वासयस्यद्य *for* न आश्वासयसि अद्य *by* 31 *and* 34.

नासं *for* न आसं *by* 31.

नास्ति *for* न अस्ति *by* 31.

नाहम् *for* न अहम् *by* 31.

नाहर्तुं *for* न आहर्तुं *by* 31.

नाहुषः *nom. sin. of* नाहुष *m.* descendant of Nahusha, *mentioned in* Manu VII. 41.

नि *prep.* in, within, into; on, upon.

निः *for* निर् *when followed by* श *or* स 71.

निःशब्दस्तिमिते Bah. or Rel. form of Dvan. or Agg. comp. 765; निःशब्द *cr.* noiseless, स्तिमिते *loc. sin. m. of* स्तिमित *m. f. n.* still, motionless. *This compound agrees with* अर्धरात्रसमये.

निःश्वस्य sighing; *past ind. p. of rt* श्वस् to breathe, *with* निर् out, 559.

निःश्वासपरमा constantly addicted to sighing, Tat. or Dep. comp. 744; निःश्वास *cr.* sighing, परमा *nom. sin. f. of* परम *m. f. n.* principally engaged in.

निःसंशयं *ind.* certainly, without doubt, 713.

निःसृतः *nom. sin. m. of* निःसृत *m. f. n.* came out, passed out; *past p. p. of rt* सृ *with* निर्, 896.

निकुञ्जान् *acc. pl. of* निकुञ्ज *m.* an arbour.

निकृतस् *nom. sin. m. of* निकृत *m. f. n.* afflicted, injured, wronged.

निकृता *nom. sin. f. of* **निकृत.** *See last.*

निकृतिप्रज्ञैर् *for* **निकृतिप्रज्ञैस्** by (men) versed in dishonesty or well acquainted with vice; (*comp. of* **निकृति** *cr.* wickedness, *and* **प्रज्ञैर्** *ins. pl. m. of* **प्रज्ञ** *m. f. n.* wise, learned.)

निकृतो *nom. sin. m. of* **निकृत** *m. f. n.* afflicted, injured; *past p. p. of rt* **कृ** *with* **नि,** 532.

निक्षिप्य having given in charge, having entrusted or deposited in a place of safety; *past ind. p. of rt* **क्षिप्** *with* **नि,** 559.

निक्षेपो *nom. sin. of* **निक्षेप** *m.* a pledge, something deposited as a compensation.

निगृह्णीष्व hold thou in, check thou; *2d sin. imp. átm. of rt* **ग्रह्** *with* **नि,** *9th cl.* 699.

निगृह्य having restrained; *past ind. p. of rt* **ग्रह्** *with* **नि,** *see* 565.

नितम्बांश् *for* **नितम्बान्** *acc. pl. of* **नितम्ब** *m.* the side or protuberant flank of a mountain, a precipice, *1st cl.* 103.

नित्यं *ind.* constantly, continually, always.

नित्यं *acc. sin. m. of* **नित्य** *m. f. n.* constant.

नित्यः *nom. sin. m. of* **नित्य** *m. f. n.* eternal, perpetual, constant.

नित्यजातं *acc. sin. m.* constantly born; (*comp. of* **नित्य** *and* **जात,** *q. v.*)

नित्यशो *for* **नित्यशस्** *ind.* constantly, perpetually, 725.

नित्यस्य *gen. sin. m. of* **नित्य** *m. f. n.* eternal.

निद्रया *ins. sin. of* **निद्रा** *f.* sleep, *1st cl.* 105.

निद्रयापहृता *for* **निद्रया अपहृता** *by* 31.

निद्रान्धा *for* **निद्रान्धास्** TAT. OR DEP. COMP. 740; **निद्रा** *cr.* sleep, **अन्धास्** *nom. pl. of* **अन्ध** *m. f. n.* blind.

निधनं *acc. sin. of* **निधन** *m.* death, *1st cl.* 103.

निन्दन्तस् *nom. pl. m. of* **निन्दत्** *m. f. n.* blaming, censuring, speaking slightingly of.

निपतिते *loc. sin. m. of* **निपतित** *m. f. n.* fallen; *past p. p. of rt* **पत्** *with* **नि,** 538.

निपेतुर् *for* **निपेतुस्** they fell down; *3d pl. 2d pret. of rt* **पत्** *with* **नि.** *See next.*

निपेतुस् they alighted; *3d pl. perf. of rt* **पत्** *with prep.* **नि,** 375. *a.*

निबद्धां *acc. sin. f. of* **निबद्ध** *m. f. n.* bound, impeded, obscured; *past p. p. of rt* **बन्ध्** *with* **नि,** 539.

निबोध know thou, understand thou, learn thou, attend thou; *2d sin. imp. of rt* **बुध्** *with* **नि,** *1st cl.* 261. *This verb seems only used in the imp. when* **नि** *is prefixed.*

निबोधास्मान् *for* **निबोध अस्मान्** *by* 31.

निबोधेदं *for* **निबोध इदं** *by* 32.

निभृतो *nom. sin. m. of* **निभृत** *m. f. n.* concealed, hidden, secret.

निमित्तं *acc. sin. of* **निमित्त** *n.* a sign, token, omen, prodigy.

निमित्तानि *acc. pl. of* **निमित्त** *n.* an omen, a sign of some future event (such as a quivering sensation or throbbing of the skin in the eyelid, arm, &c.)

निमेषेण *ins. sin. of* **निमेष** *m.* winking or twinkling of the eye, *1st cl.* 103.

नियतं *ind.* certainly, inevitably, constantly.

नियतैः *ins. pl. of* **नियत** *m. f. n.* self-restrained, self-denying.

नियोक्ष्ये I will enjoin; *1st sin. 2d fut. átm. of rt* **युज्** *with* **नि,** 670.

नियोगाद् *abl. sin. of* **नियोग** *m.* injunction, command, order, 103.

निर् *prep.* out, forth, without, deprived of.

निरनुक्रोशः *nom. sin. m.* without pity, merciless; (*comp. of* **निर्** 726. *e, and* **अनुक्रोश** pity.)

निरपायो *nom. sin. of* **निरपाय** *m. f. n.* free from harm or evil, unharmed; (**निर्** *prefixed to* **अपाय** 726. *e.*)

निरुद्विग्नमनाः BAH. OR REL. COMP. 767; **निरुद्विग्न** *cr.* undisturbed, **मनाः** *nom. sin. f. from* **मनस्** *n.* the mind, *see* 164. *a.*

निर्जने *loc. sin. n. of* **निर्जन** *m. f. n.* lonely, uninhabited, unfrequented by men; (*from* **निर्** 726. *e, and* **जन** *m.* a man.)

निर्जितः *nom. sin. m. of* **निर्जित** *m. f. n.* subdued; *past p. p. of rt* **जि** *with* **निर्,** 532.

निर्जितश् *nom. sin. m. of* निर्जित *m. f. n.* conquered, beaten; *past p. p. of rt* जि *with* निर्, 532.

निर्जितारिगणः COMPLEX REL. COMP. 771; निर्जित *cr.* one who has conquered, अरि *cr.* an enemy, गणः *nom. sin. of* गण *m.* a collection, number, host.

निर्जितो *for* निर्जितस् *nom. sin. m.* conquered. *See* निर्जितः.

निर्झरांश् *for* निर्झरान् (53) *acc. pl. of* निर्झर *m.* a cascade, waterfall, 1*st cl.* 103.

निर्नाथता *nom. sin. f.* the state of being without a guardian, widowhood.

निर्मलस्वादुसलिलम् COMPLEX COMP. 771; निर्मल *cr.* clear, free from dirt, 726. *e*, स्वादु *cr.* sweet, सलिलं *acc. sin. n. from* सलिल *n.* water.

निर्विचेष्टम् *acc. sin. m. of* निर्विचेष्ट *m. f. n.* unresisting; (*from* निर् 726. *e*, *and* विचेष्टा effort, exertion.)

निर्विशेषाकृतीन् BAH. OR REL. COMP. 766; निर्विशेष *cr.* without difference, precisely alike, आकृतीन् *acc. pl. m. from* आकृति *f.* form, 2*d cl.* 119.

निर्वृता *for* निर्वृतास् *nom. pl. m. of* निर्वृत *m. f. n.* happy, at ease.

निर्वृतिः *nom. sin. f.* happiness, gladness.

निवत्स्यति he shall dwell or inhabit; 3*d sin.* 2*d fut. of rt* वस् *with* नि, 413, 607.

निवर्तितुं to turn back; *inf. of rt* वृत् *with* नि.

निवस्य having put on (as a garment); *past ind. p. of rt* वस् 2*d cl. with* नि, 559.

निवारणे *loc. sin. of* निवारण *n.* prevention, 1*st cl.* 104; *see* 828.

निवारयितुम् to restrain; *inf. of rt* वृ *in caus. with* नि, 459, 481.

निवासयेः thou shouldest put on, put thou on; 2*d sin. pot. of rt* वस् *in caus. with* नि, 481.

निवृत्तः *nom. sin. m. of* निवृत्त *m. f. n.* ended, finished; *past p. p. of rt* वृत् *with* नि, 539.

निवृत्तहृदयः with relenting heart, BAH. OR REL. COMP. 766; निवृत्त *cr.* turned back, हृदयः *nom. sin. m. from* हृदय *n.* heart, 1*st cl.* 108.

निवेदय tell thou, inform thou; 2*d sin. imp. of rt* विद् *in caus. with* नि, 481, (*governing genitive case by* 859. *a.*)

निवेद्यतां let it be announced or made known; 3*d sin. imp. of rt* विद् *in caus. pass. with* नि, 496, 583.

निवेशनम् *acc. sin. of* निवेशन *n.* a house, dwelling.

निवेशने *loc. sin. of* निवेशन *n.* a house, an abode.

निवेशाय *dat. sin. of* निवेश *m.* entering; *see* 811.

निश् *prep. for* निर् *when followed by* च 71. *b*.

निशम्य having perceived, having heard, having observed; *past ind. p. of rt* शम् *with* नि, 559.

निशश्वास he or she sighed; 3*d sin. perf. of rt* श्वस् to breathe, *with* नि, 364.

निशां *acc. sin. of* निशा *f.* the night.

निशाकरः *nom. sin. m.* the moon; (*from* निशा night, *and* कर the maker.)

निशाकाले TAT. OR DEP. COMP. 743; निशा *cr.* night, काले *loc. sin. of* काल *m.* time.

निशायां *loc. sin. of* निशा *f.* the night.

निशास् *acc. pl. of* निशा *f.* the night, 1*st cl.* 105.

निशितेन *ins. sin. n. of* निशित *m. f. n.* sharp, sharpened.

निश्चक्राम he went out; 3*d sin. perf. of rt* क्रम् to step, *with* निर् (71. *b*), *see* 364.

निश्चयम् *acc. sin. of* निश्चय *m.* certainty, resolution, resolve, determination.

निश्चितं *ind.* certainly, plainly, distinctly.

निश्चिता *nom. sin. f. of* निश्चित *m. f. n.* fixed, settled.

निश्चित्य having decided; *past ind. p. of rt* चि *with* निर्, 560.

निश्वस्य *for* निःश्वस्य sighing, *q. v.*

निषध *m. declined in pl.* निषधास् *nom.* Nishadha, a country in the S. E. division of India, ruled over by Nala.

निषधवंशस्य *gen. sin. m.* of the race of Nishadha; (*comp. of* **निषध** *cr. and* **वंश** *m.* a race, 743.)

निषधाधिपः TAT. OR DEP. COMP. 743; **निषध** *cr.* Nishadha, the country ruled over by Nala, **अधिपः** *nom. sin. m.* a lord.

निषधाधिपतिर् *for* **निषधाधिपतिस्** TAT. OR DEP. COMP. 743; **निषध** *cr.* Nishadha, **अधिपतिर्** *nom. sin. of* **अधिपति** *m.* a lord, *2d cl.* 110.

निषधाधिपतेर् *for* **निषधाधिपतेस्** *gen. sin.* of the lord of Nishadha.

निषधाधिपतेश् *for* **निषधाधिपतेस्** *gen. sin.* of the lord of Nishadha.

निषधाधिपे *loc. sin. m.* in the lord of Nishadha.

निषधान् *acc. pl. of* **निषध** *m.* Nishadha.

निषधानां *gen. pl. of* **निषध** *m.* Nishadha.

निषधेश्वर *voc. sin. m.* O lord of Nishadha; (*comp. of* **निषध** *and* **ईश्वर** *m.* a lord.)

निषधेषु *loc. pl. of* **निषध** *m.* Nishadha.

निषसाद he sank down; *3d sin. perf. of rt* **सद्** (70) *with* **नि**, 364, 599. *a.*

निहतोष्ट्राश् BAH. OR REL. COMP. 767; **निहत** *cr.* killed, **उष्ट्राश्** *nom. pl. of* **उष्ट्र** *m.* a camel.

निहत्य having slain; *past ind. p. of rt* **हन्** *with* **नि**, 560.

नीतौ *nom. du. m. of* **नीत** *m. f. n.* taken, conducted.

नीलाभ्रसंवृताम् COMPLEX COMP. 771; **नील** *cr.* black, dark, **अभ्र** *cr.* clouds, **संवृताम्** *acc. sin. of* **संवृत** *m. f. n.* obscured, concealed.

नु *ind.* what? *a particle of interrogation,* 717. *b.*

नूनं *ind.* assuredly, certainly, in all probability, 717.

नृप *m.* a king, *1st cl.* 103.

नृप *voc. sin. of* **नृप** *m.* a king.

नृपं *acc. sin. of* **नृप** *m.* a king.

नृपः *nom. sin. of* **नृप** *m.* a king.

नृपति *m.* a king, *2d cl.* 110, 121.

नृपतिः *nom. sin. of* **नृपति** *m.* a king.

नृपतिम् *acc. sin. of* **नृपति** *m.* a king, *2d cl.* 110.

नृपतिर् *for* **नृपतिस्** *nom. sin. of* **नृपति** *m.* a king.

नृपतिशासनात् TAT. OR DEP. COMP. 743; **नृपति** *cr.* a king, **शासनात्** *abl. sin. of* **शासन** *n.* an order, decree.

नृपते O king; *voc. sin. of* **नृपति** *m.* a king.

नृपतेः *gen. sin. of* **नृपति** *m.* a king.

नृपश्रेष्ठो *nom. sin. m.* the best of kings; *see* 743. *b.*

नृपसुता TAT. OR DEP. COMP. 743; **नृप** *cr.* a king, **सुता** *nom. sin. f.* a daughter.

नृपस्नुषां TAT. OR DEP. COMP. 743; **नृप** *cr.* a king, **स्नुषां** *acc. sin. of* **स्नुषा** *f.* a daughter-in-law.

नृपाः *for* **नृपास्** *nom. pl. of* **नृप** *m.* a king.

नृपात्मजा TAT. OR DEP. COMP. 743; **नृप** *cr.* a king, **आत्मजा** *nom. sin. f.* a daughter.

नृपैः *ins. pl. of* **नृप** *m.* a king.

नृशंस *voc. sin. m. of* **नृशंस** *m. f. n.* cruel.

नृशंसं *acc. sin. n. of* **नृशंस** *m. f. n.* cruel, wicked; *in* Book XIX. 5 an unholy act. A second marriage in a woman is an unlawful act. (Compare Manu V. 160, 161.) 'A virtuous wife ascends to heaven, though she have no child, if after the decease of her lord she devotes herself to pious austerity; but a widow who, from a wish to bear children, slights her deceased husband by marrying again, brings disgrace on herself here below, and shall be excluded from the seat of her lord.'

नृणां *gen. pl. of* **नृ** *m.* a man, *4th cl.* 128. *b.*

नेता *nom. sin. of* **नेतृ** *m.* a leader, *4th cl.* 127.

नेता he shall lead; *3d sin. 1st fut. of rt* **नी** 590. *a.*

नेत्राभ्यां *ins. or abl. du. of* **नेत्र** *n.* the eye, *1st cl.* 104; (*formed from rt* **नी** to lead, *by* 80. VII.)

नेदुर् they sounded; 3d pl. impf. of rt नद् 375. a.

नैकत for न एकत by 33.

नैकदुःखदाम् acc. sin. f. the causer of many sorrows; (comp. of नैक cr. many, see नैकान्, दुःख cr. sorrow, and दाम् acc. sin. f. of द m. f. n. giver, 580.)

नैकवर्णैर् Bah. or Rel. comp. 767; नैक cr. many, various (न not, एक one, 33), वर्णैर् ins. pl. of वर्ण m. colour, 1st cl. 103.

नैकांश् for नैकान् (q. v.) by 53.

नैकान् acc. pl. of नैक m. f. n. various, many; (comp. of न not, and एक one, 33.)

नैकाश् acc. pl. f., 1st cl. 105. See last.

नैनं for न एनं by 33.

नैपुनेषु loc. pl. of नैपुन n. skill, anything which requires skill, a delicate matter, 104.

नैराश्यात् abl. sin. of नैराश्य n. despair.

नैव for न एव by 33.

नैवं for न एवं by 33.

नैषध m. a name of Nala, as king of Nishadha, 1st cl. 103; see also 80. XXXV.

नैषध voc. sin. m. O Nala.

नैषधं acc. sin. of नैषध m. Nala.

नैषधस्य gen. sin. of नैषध m. Nala.

नैषधस्याहं for नैषधस्य अहं by 31.

नैषधाः nom. pl. the people of Nishadha.

नैषधाद् abl. sin. of नैषध m. Nala.

नैषधानां gen. pl. of नैषधाः pl. the people of Nishadha.

नैषधान्वेषणे Tat. or Dep. comp. 743; नैषध cr. Nala, अन्वेषणे loc. sin. of अन्वेषण n. seeking, searching for, see 863.

नैषधाय dat. sin. of नैषध Nala.

नैषधे loc. sin. of नैषध m. Nala.

नैषधेन ins. sin. of नैषध m. Nala.

नो acc., dat. or gen. pl. us, to us, of us; same as अस्मान्, अस्मभ्यं, अस्माकं, (from nom. अहं I, 218.)

नोत्तरं for न उत्तरं by 32.

नोत्सहे for न उत्सहे by 32.

नोद्विजस्यमरप्रभे for न उद्विजसि अमरप्रभे by 32 and 34.

नौ us two, to us two, of us two; same as आवां, आवाभ्यां, आवयोस्, (from nom. अहं 218.)

न्यग्रोधैश् ins. pl. of न्यग्रोध m. the Indian fig-tree, 1st cl. 103.

न्ययच्छत् he restrained; 3d sin. impf. of rt यम् with नि, 1st cl. 270.

न्यवर्तत was dwelling on, was occupied in; 3d sin. impf. átm. of rt वृत् with नि, 1st cl. 598.

न्यवसत् he dwelt; 3d sin. impf. of rt वस् with नि, 1st cl. 607.

न्यवसद् for न्यवसत् he dwelt. See last.

न्यवेदयत् he or she recounted or related or represented; 3d sin. impf. of rt विद् to know, in caus. with prep. नि, 479, 861.

न्यवेदयद् he or she announced. See last.

न्याय्यं acc. sin. n. of न्याय्य m. f. n. just, proper, 1st cl. 187.

प.

पक्षिणं acc. sin. of पक्षिन् m. a bird.

पक्षिन् m. a bird, (lit. having a paksha or wing,) 6th cl. 159.

पञ्च five; nom. or acc. pl. of पञ्चन् 204.

पञ्चदशः nom. sin. the fifteenth, 210.

पञ्चमः nom. sin. of पञ्चम m. f. n. fifth, 209.

पञ्चविंशतितमः nom. sin. the twenty-fifth, 211.

पञ्चशीर्षा Bah. or Rel. comp. 768; पञ्च for पञ्चन् five (57), शीर्षा for शीर्षास् nom. pl. m. from शीर्ष n. a head, 1st cl. 108.

पञ्चाशद्भिर् ins. of पञ्चाशत् fifty.

पञ्चोनं nom. sin. n. of पञ्चोन m. f. n. minus five, less by five; (comp. of पञ्च five, and ऊन less.)

पटं acc. sin. of पट m. a garment.

पटस् nom. sin. m. a garment.

पटे loc. sin. of पट m. a garment.

पणः *nom. sin. of* **पण** *m.* a stake at play, *1st cl.* 103.

पणकालम् TAT. OR DEP. COMP. 743; **पण** *cr.* playing with dice, **कालम्** *acc. sin. of* **काल** *m.* time, *1st cl.* 103.

पणावः we will play, let us lay down (our) stakes; *1st du. pres.* (*used for imperative*) *of rt* **पण्** *1st cl.* 261.

पणावहे we two will play, let us two stake; *1st du. pres. átm.* (*used for imperative*) *of rt* **पण्** *1st cl.* 261. (*In* Book XXVI. 6 *this verb is joined with the gen. du.* **प्राणयोश्** we will play for our lives, let us stake our all.)

पणितो *nom. sin. of* **पणित** *m. f. n.* staked, played for; *past p. p. of rt* **पण्** 538.

पणेन *ins. sin. of* **पण** *m.* a stake, a wager, a game.

पण्डिताः *nom. pl. of* **पण्डित** *m. f. n.* learned, wise; a pundit, a scholar.

पततां *gen. pl. of* **पतत्** *m. f. n.* falling; *pres. p. par. of rt* **पत्** to fall, 524.

पततां let him fall; *3d sin. imp. átm. of rt* **पत्** *1st cl.* 261.

पतति he or she falls down; *3d sin. pres. of rt* **पत्** *1st cl.* 261.

पतत्रिभिर् *ins. pl. of* **पतत्रिन्** *m.* a bird, *6th cl.* 159.

पतन्ति they fall; *3d pl. pres. of rt* **पत्** *1st cl.* 261.

पताकाध्वजमालिनम् BAH. OR REL. COMP. 765; **पताका** *cr.* a flag, **ध्वज** *cr.* a banner, **मालिनम्** *acc. sin. m. of* **मालिन्** *m. f. n.* having garlands, 159. *In this compound* **मालिनम्** *agrees with* **नगरम्**, *which must be considered as masculine.*

पतिं *acc. sin. of* **पति** *m.* a husband, 121.

पतिता *nom. sin. f. of* **पतित** *m. f. n.* fallen; *past p. p. of rt* **पत्** to fall, 538.

पतिता *for* **पतितास्** *nom. pl. m. of* **पतित** *m. f. n.* fallen; *past p. p. of rt* **पत्** 538. *At* Book XII. 14 **पतिता** *must be translated* they fell; *see* 896.

पतितानि *nom. pl. n. of* **पतित** *m. f. n.* fallen.

पतितान्यपि *for* **पतितानि अपि** *by* 34.

पतित्वे *loc. sin. of* **पतित्व** *n.* the state of a husband, the state of wedlock, *1st cl.* 104; **देवं पतित्वे वरयस्व** choose the god for thy husband.

पतिदर्शनलालसाम् BAH. OR REL. COMP. 761; **पति** *cr.* husband, **दर्शन** *cr.* seeing, **लालसाम्** *acc. sin. of* **लालसा** longing desire.

पतिना *ins. sin. of* **पति** *m.* a husband, 121. *This word when it stands alone is generally declined like* **सखि** (120), *but in* p. 114, l. 19, *it follows* **अग्नि**.

पतिम् *acc. sin. of* **पति** *m.* a husband.

पतिर् *for* **पतिस्** *nom. sin. of* **पति** *m.* a husband.

पतिराज्यविनाकृता COMPLEX COMP. 771; **पति** *cr.* a lord, a husband, **राज्य** *cr.* a kingdom, **विनाकृता** *nom. sin. f. of* **विनाकृत** *m. f. n.* deprived of.

पतिलालसा BAH. OR REL. COMP. 761; **पति** *cr.* a husband, **लालसा** *f.* longing, eager desire.

पतिव्रता *nom. sin. f.* a woman faithful to her husband; (*from* **पति** *cr.* a husband, *and* **व्रत** a vow.)

पतिव्रताम् *acc. sin. f. of* **पतिव्रता**. *See last.*

पतिशोकाकुलां TAT. OR DEP. COMP. 745; **पति** *cr.* lord, husband, **शोक** *cr.* sorrow, **आकुलां** *acc. sin. f. of* **आकुल** *m. f. n.* agitated, disturbed.

पत्नी *nom. sin. f.* a wife.

पत्राणां *gen. pl. of* **पत्र** *n.* a leaf.

पत्राहारैस् *ins. pl.* feeding on leaves; **पत्र** *cr.* leaf, **आहारैस्** *ins. pl. of* **आहार** *m.* food, 761.

पथि *loc. sin. of* **पथिन्** *m.* a road, a way; *see* 162.

पदम् *acc. sin. of* **पद** *n.* a step, a foot.

पदातिजनसङ्कुलाः TAT. OR DEP. COMP. 740;

पदाति *cr.* a foot-man, a pedestrian, जन *cr.* a person, a man, सङ्कुलाः *nom. pl. of* सङ्कुल *m. f. n.* mingled, confused.

पदातिभिः *ins. pl. of* पदाति *m.* a foot-soldier, a foot-man.

पदाद् *for* पदात् *abl. sin. of* पद *n.* a step, a foot.

पदानि *acc. pl. of* पद *n.* a footstep, 1*st cl.* 104.

पदे *loc. sin. of* पद *n.* a step.

पद्भ्यां *ins. pl. of* पद् *m.* a foot, 5*th cl.* 138.

पद्मकामलकप्लक्षकदम्बोडुम्बरावृतं COMPLEX COMP. 771; पद्मक *cr.* a plant, the lotus, *see next;* आमलक *cr.* a plant (*Emblic myrobalan*); प्लक्ष *cr.* a kind of fig-tree; कदम्ब *cr.* the kadamba-tree (*Nauclea kadamba*); उडुम्बर *cr.* the uḍumbara, a kind of fig-tree, *see note under* शाल &c.; आवृतं *acc. sin. n. of* आवृत *m. f. n.* filled with.

पद्मनिभेक्षणम् BAH. OR REL. COMP. 761; पद्म *cr.* a lotus, निभ *cr.* like, ईक्षणम् *acc. sin. m. from* ईक्षण *n.* the eye. The lotus is as favourite a subject of allusion and comparison with Hindú poets as the rose is with Persian. Its varieties, blue, white, and red, are numerous, and bear some resemblance to our water-lily.

पद्मनिभेक्षणा BAH. OR REL. COMP. 761; पद्म *cr.* a lotus, निभ *cr.* like, resembling, ईक्षणा *nom. sin. f. from* ईक्षण *n.* the eye, 108.

पद्मसङ्काशो ANOM. COMP. 777; पद्म *cr.* a lotus, सङ्काशो *nom. sin. m.* like.

पद्मसौगन्धिकम् TAT. OR DEP. COMP. 740; पद्म *cr.* lotuses, सौगन्धिकम् *acc. sin. n. of* सौगन्धिक *m. f. n.* fragrant.

पद्मिनीम् *acc. sin. of* पद्मिनी *f.* a lotus-pool.

पद्मिन्याः *gen. sin. of* पद्मिनी *f.* a lotus-pool, a lotus-lake, 1*st cl.* 106.

पन्था *for* पन्थास् *nom. sin. of* पथिन् *m.* a road, 162.

पन्थाः *nom. sin. of* पथिन् *m.* a road.

पन्थानं *acc. sin. of* पथिन् *m.* a road.

पन्थानो *nom. pl. of* पथिन् *m.* a road, 6*th cl.* 162.

पन्नगः *nom. sin. m.* a serpent, a snake.

पपात he or it fell; 3*d sin. perf. of rt* पत् 364.

पप्रच्छ he or she asked; 3*d sin. perf. of rt* प्रच्छ् 381.

पप्रच्छानामयं *for* पप्रच्छ अनामयं *by* 31.

पप्रच्छुस् they asked, they enquired; 3*d pl. perf. of rt* प्रच्छ् 381.

पयोष्णी *f.* Payoshṇí, a river that rises in the Vindhya mountains. It is mentioned in the Brahmáṇḍa-Puráṇa.

पर *m. f. n.* great, excessive, best, chief, highest; other, another, an enemy.

परं *nom. sin. n. or acc. sin. m. or n. of* पर, *q. v.*

परकृतं *acc. sin. m.* done by another, committed by another; (*comp. of* पर another, *and* कृत done, 740.)

परन्तप *voc. sin. m.* O harasser of thy foes; (पर an enemy, तप who torments.)

परन्तपः *nom. sin. m. See last.*

परपुरञ्जयः conqueror of the cities of his enemies; (*comp. of* पर *cr.* an enemy, पुरं *acc. sin. of* पुर *n.* a city, जयः *nom. sin. m.* who conquers, *see* 739. *c.*)

परम् *nom. or acc. sin. n. or acc. sin. m. of* पर chief, highest, great, *q. v.*

परमं *acc. sin. m. or n. of* परम *m. f. n.* high, greatest, highest, 1*st cl.* 187.

परमदारुणा *nom. sin. f.* very dreadful; (*comp. of* परम *cr.* highest, most, *and* दारुण, *q. v.*)

परमदुःखितः *nom. sin. m.* deeply afflicted; (*comp. of* परम excessive, *and* दुःखित pained.)

परममन्युमान् deeply distressed; (*comp. of* परम *cr.* excessive, मन्यु *cr.* anguish, distress, wrath, -मान् *nom. sin. of the possessive affix* मत् 140, 84.VI.)

परमया *ins. sin. f. of* परम *m. f. n.* excessive, highest.

परमशोभनम् *acc. sin. m.* very glorious. *See next.*

परमशोभनाम् very brilliant, very beautiful;

(*comp. of* परम high, very, शोभनां *acc. sin. f. of* शोभन *m. f. n.* bright, beautiful.)

परमसंहृष्टा *nom. sin. f.* exceedingly rejoiced; (*comp. of* परम *cr.* very much, *and* संहृष्ट pleased, *past p. p. of rt* हृष् *with* सं.)

परमा *nom. sin. f. of* परम *m. f. n.* highest, excellent.

परमां *acc. sin. f. of* परम *m. f. n.* highest, superior, excellent, 1*st cl.* 187.

परमाङ्गना *nom. sin. f.* an excellent or noble woman. *See next.*

परमाङ्गनाः KARM. OR DES. COMP. 755; परम *cr.* best, excellent, अङ्गनाः *nom. pl. of* अङ्गना *f.* a woman, 1*st cl.* 105.

परमो *nom. sin. m. of* परम highest.

परया *ins. sin. f. of* पर *m. f. n.* great, excessive,

परवीरहा *nom. sin. m.* the slayer of the warriors (champions) of the enemy; (*comp. of* पर *cr.* an enemy, वीर *cr.* a warrior, हा *nom. sin. of* हन् *m.* a killer, 157. *b.*)

परव्यूहविनाशनम् TAT. OR DEP. COMP. 745; पर *cr.* an enemy, व्यूह *cr.* array, ranks, विनाशनम् *acc. sin. of* विनाशन *m.* a destroyer.

परस्परतः *ind.* mutually, 719. *b.*

परस्परसुखैषिणौ TAT. OR DEP. COMP. 745; परस्पर *cr.* one another, सुख *cr.* happiness, एषिणौ *nom. du. m. of* एषिन् *m. f. n.* desiring, seeking, 159, *agt. of rt* इष् 582. *a.*

परस्परहतास् TAT. OR DEP. COMP. 740; परस्पर *cr.* one another, हतास् *nom. pl. of* हत *m. f. n.* killed, *past p. p. of rt* हन् 545.

परस्वम् *acc. sin. n.* another's property; (*comp. of* पर another, *and* स्व *n.* that which is one's own, 232.)

परा *prep.* back, backward; over.

परां *acc. sin. f. of* पर *m. f. n.* highest.

पराजयः *nom. sin. m.* defeat. *In* Book XIII. 34 *this word is used in the sense of* turning away from, desertion, *and governs an ablative case.*

पराजितः *nom. sin. m. of* पराजित *m. f. n.* conquered.

परार्थम् for the sake of another; (*comp. of* पर *cr.* another, *and* अर्थं, *see* 760. *d.*)

परार्थे for the sake of others; (*comp. of* पर another, *and* अर्थे 731.)

परासुर् *for* परासुस् *nom. sin. m. of* परासु *m. f. n.* dead, expired; (*from* पर away, remote, *and* असु *m.* breath.)

परि *prep.* round, about; entirely.

परिगम्य having gone round; *past ind. p. of rt* गम् *with* परि, 602.

परिग्लानस्य *gen. sin. of* परिग्लान *m. f. n.* exhausted, languid; *past p. p. of rt* ग्लै to be weary, *with* परि, 536.

परिघोपमाः ANOM. COMP. 777, 32; परिघ *cr.* an iron-bar, an iron-club or mace, उपमाः *nom. pl. of* उपम *m. f. n.* like, resembling, 1*st cl.* 103. *So in* S'akuntalá, Act II, नगरपरिघप्रांशुबाहुर् having an arm long as the bar of a city-gate.

परिचर्यां *acc. sin. f. of* परिचर्या *f.* service, attendance upon, devotion, veneration.

परिचारकैः *ins. pl. of* परिचारक *m.* an attendant.

परिचारिकाम् *acc. sin. of* परिचारिका *f.* an attendant, servant, waiting-maid.

परिच्छिद्य having cut off; *past ind. p. of rt* छिद् *with* परि, 559.

परिच्युतो *nom. sin. m. of* परिच्युत *m. f. n.* ruined, lost; *past p. p. of rt* च्यु 532.

परिशिक्षा *nom. sin. f.* perfect skill or conversancy.

परित्यक्ता *nom. sin. f. of* परित्यक्त *m. f. n.* deserted, abandoned; *past p. p. of rt* त्यज् *with* परि, 539.

परित्यागो *nom. sin. of* परित्याग *m.* desertion, abandonment.

परिदह्यते is burnt up, is inflamed; 3*d sin. pres. of rt* दह् *in pass. with* परि.

परिदेवना *nom. sin. f.* lamentation.

परिदेवितम् *acc. sin. of* परिदेवित *n.* complaint, lamentation, 1*st cl.* 104.

परिधानेन *ins. sin. of* परिधान *n.* a lower garment, an under garment.

परिधावन् *for* परिधावन् (52) *nom. sin. m. of* परिधावत् *m. f. n.* running or roaming about; *pres. p. of rt* धाव् *with* परि, 524.

परिध्वंसम् *acc. sin. of* परिध्वंस *m.* disaster, distress, ruin.

परिपप्रच्छ he asked, he enquired; 3*d sin. perf. of rt* प्रच्छ् to ask, *with* परि, 631.

परिपालयन् *nom. sin. m. of* परिपालयत् *m. f. n.* protecting, governing; *pres. p. par. of rt* पाल् *with* परि, 524.

परिप्रेप्सोः *gen. sin. m. of* परिप्रेप्सुः *m. f. n.* desirous of obtaining; (*des. adj. formed from* आप् *with* प्र *and* परि, *see* 82. VII, 503.)

परिप्लुता *nom. sin. f. of* परिप्लुत *m. f. n.* overwhelmed; *past p. p. of rt* प्लु *with* परि, 532.

परिभ्रष्टसुखेन Bah. or Rel. comp. 767; परिभ्रष्ट *cr.* fallen, deprived of, सुखेन *ins. sin. m. from* सुख *n.* joy, pleasure, 104.

परिवत्सरान् *acc. pl. of* परिवत्सर *m.* a year.

परिवारिता *nom. sin. f. of* परिवारित *m. f. n.* surrounded, encircled; *past p. p. of rt* वृ *in caus. with* परि.

परिवृता *nom. sin. f. of* परिवृत *m. f. n.* surrounded.

परिवृतागच्छत् *for* परिवृता अगच्छत् *by* 31.

परिशङ्कितुम् to suspect; *inf. of rt* शङ्क् *with* परि, 459.

परिशुष्यति he or it dries up or is dried up; 3*d sin. pres. of rt* शुष् *with* परि, 4*th cl.*

परिश्रान्ते *loc. sin. m. of* परिश्रान्त *m. f. n.* wearied; *past p. p. of rt* श्रम् 546.

परिषोडशैः *ins. of* परिषोडश *m.* sixteen complete, exactly sixteen. (*Used at* Book XXVI. 2 *for* षोडशन्.)

परिष्वज्य having embraced or clasped; *past ind. p. of rt* स्वञ्ज् *with* परि, 559.

परिसङ्घुष्टान् *acc. pl. m. of* परिसङ्घुष्ट *m. f. n.* resonant on all sides; *past p. p. of rt* घुष् *with* सं *and* परि, 539.

परिस्रवन् *for* परिस्रवत् *acc. sin. n.* flowing down; *pres. p. of rt* स्रु *with* परि, 524.

परिहासो *nom. sin. of* परिहास *m.* joke, sport.

परिहीनस् *nom. sin. m. of* परिहीन *m. f. n.* deprived of, destitute of, (*governing abl.*)

परीक्षां *acc. sin. f. of* परीक्षा *f.* trial, examination.

परीक्षितो *nom. sin. m. of* परीक्षित *m. f. n.* tried, examined; *past p. p. of rt* ईक्ष् *with* परि, 538.

परीता *nom. sin. f. of* परीत *m. f. n.* affected by.

परेण *ins. sin. m. or n. of* पर *m. f. n.* great, highest; best, excellent; another, other, 238. *a.*

परेण *ind.* beyond, above, over.

परेणापकृते *for* परेण अपकृते *by* 31.

परो *nom. sin. m. of* पर *m. f. n.* highest, greatest.

परोक्षं *acc. sin. n. of* परोक्ष *m. f. n.* beyond or out of sight, imperceptible, invisible.

परोक्षता *nom. sin. f.* imperceptibleness, the state of being unperceived or unknown.

पर्णादं *acc. sin. of* पर्णाद *m.* Parṇáda, name of a Bráhman.

पर्णादवचनं Tat. or Dep. comp. 743; पर्णाद *cr.* Parṇáda, वचनं *acc. sin. n.* speech, words.

पर्णादस्य *gen. sin. of* पर्णाद *m.* Parṇáda.

पर्णादो *nom. sin. m.* Parṇáda, name of a Bráhman.

पर्णानि *nom. pl. of* पर्ण *n.* a leaf, 104.

पर्णाहारैस् *ins. pl.* feeding on leaves, पर्ण *cr.* leaf, आहारैस् *ins. pl. of* आहार *m.* food, 761.

पर्यचरत् he went round; 3*d sin. impf. of rt* चर् to go, *with* परि, 1*st cl.* 261.

पर्यचिन्तयत् he reflected, he thought about; 3*d sin. impf. of rt* चिन्त् *with* परि, 10*th cl.* 283, 641.

पर्यदेवयत् he or she bewailed or lamented; 3*d sin. impf. of rt* देव् *with* परि, 10*th cl.* 283.

पर्यधावत he or she ran about; 3*d sin. impf. átm. of rt* धाव् *with* परि, 1*st cl.* 261.

पर्यपतन् they fell, they stooped down; *3d pl. impf. of rt* **पत्** *with* **परि**, *1st cl.* 261.

पर्यपृच्छत् he or she enquired about; *3d sin. impf. of rt* **प्रच्छ्** *6th cl. with* **परि**, 631.

पर्याप्तः *nom. sin. m. of* **पर्याप्त** *m. f. n.* sufficient.

पर्युपासच् *for* **पर्युपासत्** he or she attended upon, waited on; *3d sin. impf. of rt* **आस्** *with* **उप** *and* **परि**, *2d cl.* 317. *a. This verb is properly of the átmane-pada only.*

पर्युषितं *acc. sin. n. of* **पर्युषित** *m. f. n.* stale, profitless, flat, idle, low.

पर्वतम् *acc. sin. of* **पर्वत** *m.* a mountain.

पर्वतराड् *for* **पर्वतराट्** (41) TAT. OR DEP. COMP. 743; **पर्वत** *cr.* a mountain, **राट्** *nom. sin. of* **राज्** *m.* a king, *8th cl.* 176. *e.*

पर्वतश् *nom. sin. of* **पर्वत** *m.* Parvata, one of the ten Ṛishis or sages, a friend and rival of Nárada; *see note under* **नारदः**.

पर्वतश्रेष्ठ *voc. sin. m.* O best of mountains, 743. *b.*

पर्वतस्य *gen. sin. of* **पर्वत** *m.* a mountain, *1st cl.* 103.

पर्वतस्याथवा *for* **पर्वतस्य अथवा** *by* 31.

पर्वतांश् *for* **पर्वतान्** *acc. pl. of* **पर्वत** *m.* a mountain.

पर्वतान् *acc. pl. of* **पर्वत** *m.* a mountain.

पल्लवापीडितं *acc. sin. m.* loaded with buds, TAT. OR DEP. COMP. 740; **पल्लव** *cr.* a bud, *and* **आपीडित** *m. f. n.* laden, oppressed.

पल्वलानि *acc. pl. of* **पल्वल** *n.* a pool, *1st cl.* 104.

पवनः *nom. sin. m.* wind, breeze.

पश्चाद् *ind.* afterwards, hereafter, 715.

पश्चिमाम् *acc. sin. f. of* **पश्चिम** *m. f. n.* western, evening; **पश्चिमा वेला** the evening time, the close of day.

पश्यतस् *gen. sin. m. of* **पश्यत्** *m. f. n.* seeing, looking on; *pres. p. of rt* **दृश्** 524.

पश्यताम् of them looking; *gen. pl. m. of* **पश्यत्** *m. f. n., pres. p. par. of rt* **दृश्** to see, 524.

पश्यति he sees; *3d sin. pres. of rt* **दृश्** 604.

पश्यन्ति they see; *3d pl. pres. of rt* **दृश्** *1st cl.* 604.

पश्यामस् we see; *1st pl. pres. of rt* **दृश्** *1st cl.* 604.

पश्यामि I see, I experience or feel; *1st sin. pres. of rt* **दृश्** *1st cl.* 604.

पश्याम्यस्मिन् *for* **पश्यामि अस्मिन्** *by* 34.

पश्येथास् thou mayest see; *2d sin. pot. átm. of rt* **दृश्** 604.

पश्येम we may see, we should see; *1st pl. pot. of rt* **दृश्** *1st cl.* 604.

पश्येयं I may see; *1st sin. pot. of rt* **दृश्** *1st cl.* 604.

पांशुगुण्ठितः TAT. OR DEP. COMP. 740; **पांशु** *cr.* dust, **गुण्ठितः** *nom. sin. of* **गुण्ठित** *m. f. n.* covered; *past p. p. of rt* **गुण्ठ्** 538.

पांशुध्वस्तशिरोरुहा BAH. OR REL. COMP. 761; **पांशु** *cr.* dust, **ध्वस्त** destroyed, spoilt, injured, fallen, **शिरोरुहा** *nom. sin. f. from* **शिरोरुह** *m.* the hair of the head.

पांशुभिश् *ins. pl. of* **पांशु** *m.* dirt, dust, *3d cl.* 110.

पाटयामास he clove asunder; *3d sin. perf. of rt* **पट्** *in caus.* 481, 385. *a.*

पाणिं *acc. sin. of* **पाणि** *m.* the hand.

पाणिभ्यां *ins. du. of* **पाणि** *m.* the hand, 110.

पाण्डव O son of Páṇḍu; *voc. sin. of* **पाण्डव** *m.*

पाण्डुवर्णा BAH. OR REL. COMP. 766; **पाण्डु** *cr.* pale, **वर्णा** *nom. sin. f. from* **वर्ण** *m.* colour, hue, complexion, *1st cl.* 108.

पातकं *acc. sin. n.* sin, crime.

पादधावनम् TAT. OR DEP. COMP. 743; **पाद** *cr.* feet, **धावनम्** *acc. sin. n.* washing.

पादयोः *gen. du. of* **पाद** *m.* a foot, *1st cl.* 103.

पादरजसा TAT. OR DEP. COMP. 743; **पाद** *cr.* a foot, **रजसा** *ins. sin. of* **रजस्** *n.* dust, *7th cl.* 164.

पादाव् *for* **पादौ** (37) *acc. du. of* **पाद** *m.* a foot.

पानीयार्थं for the sake of water, *see* 760. *d*, 791.

पापं *nom. or acc. sin. of* **पाप** *n.* sin, crime.

पापः *nom. sin. m. of* **पाप** *m. f. n.* wicked, evil.

पापकृतं *nom. sin. n.* evil deed, bad action; (*comp. of* **पाप** *and* **कृत**, *q. q. v. v.*)

पापबुद्धिना BAH. OR REL. COMP. 761; पाप *cr.* wicked, sinful, बुद्धिना *ins. sin. m. from* बुद्धि *f.* the mind, 119.

पापमतिः BAH. OR REL. COMP. 766; पाप *cr.* sinful, depraved, मतिः *nom. sin. m. from* मति *f.* the mind, *see* 119.

पापस् *nom. sin. m. of* पाप *m. f. n.* wicked.

पापां *acc. sin. f. of* पाप *m. f. n.* wicked, sinful.

पापाद् *abl. sin. of* पाप *n.* sin.

पापो *nom. sin. m. of* पाप *m. f. n.* evil, wicked.

पारं *acc. sin. of* पार *m.* the opposite side, the further bank or shore, the end.

पारग. *See* वेदपारगैः.

पारिषदः *nom. sin. m.* a spectator, a person present at an assembly.

पार्थ *voc. sin.* O Arjuna. (Pártha is a name of Arjuna, as one of the three sons of Pṛithá.)

पार्थिव *voc. sin. of* पार्थिव *m.* a king.

पार्थिवं *acc. sin. of* पार्थिव *m.* a king, *1st cl.* 103.

पार्थिवः *nom. sin. of* पार्थिव *m.* a king.

पार्थिवनन्दिनी TAT. OR DEP. COMP. 743; पार्थिव *cr.* a king, नन्दिनी *nom. sin. f.* a daughter, (*lit.* giver of joy.)

पार्थिवर्षभ *voc. sin. m.* O most illustrious of kings! *See* पुरुषर्षभ *and* 758.

पार्थिवश्रेष्ठः TAT. OR DEP. COMP. 743. *b;* पार्थिव *cr.* a king, श्रेष्ठः *nom. sin. m. of* श्रेष्ठ *m. f. n.* best, most excellent.

पार्थिवसुतां TAT. OR DEP. COMP. 743; पार्थिव *cr.* a king, सुतां *acc. sin. of* सुता *f.* a daughter, *1st cl.* 105.

पार्थिवाः *for* पार्थिवास् *nom. pl. of* पार्थिव, *q.v.*

पार्थिवात्मजाम् TAT. OR DEP. COMP. 743; पार्थिव *cr.* a king, *and* आत्मजाम् *acc. sin. f. of* आत्मजा a daughter, own daughter.

पार्थिवानां *gen. pl. of* पार्थिव *m.* a king.

पार्थिवाश् *nom. pl. of* पार्थिव *m.* a king, *1st cl.* 103.

पार्थिवेन्द्रेषु *loc. pl.*, KARM. OR DES. COMP. 758; पार्थिव *cr.* king, इन्द्रेषु *loc. pl. of* इन्द्र *m.* chief, *1st cl.* 103.

पावकः *nom. sin. m.* fire.

पाशवम् *nom. sin. n. of* पाशव *m. f. n.* belonging to animals or beasts; (*from* पशु an animal, *see* 80. XII.)

पार्श्वोपपार्श्वयोः DVAN. OR AGG. COMP. 752; पार्श्व *cr.* the side, the ribs, the flank, उपपार्श्वयोः *loc. du. of* उपपार्श्व the other flank, (? the false or short rib, the lesser ribs.)

पितरं *acc. sin. of* पितृ *m.* a father, *4th cl.* 128.

पितरः *nom. pl. of* पितृ *m.* a father.

पितरञ्चोभौ *for* पितरं च उभौ *by* 60 *and* 32.

पितरो *for* पितरस् *nom. pl. of* पितृ *m.* a father.

पिता *nom. sin. of* पितृ *m.* a father, 128.

पितामहाः *nom. pl. of* पितामह *m.* a grandfather.

पितामहान् *acc. pl. of* पितामह *m.* a grandfather.

पितुः *abl. sin. of* पितृ *m.* a father, 128.

पितुर् *gen. sin. of* पितृ *m.* a father, 128.

पितुस् *gen. sin. of* पितृ *m.* a father, 128.

पितॄन् *acc. pl. of* पितृ *m.* a father.

पित्रा *ins. sin. of* पितृ *m.* a father.

पिप्लुं *acc. sin. of* पिप्लु *m.* a mole, freckle.

पिप्लुना *ins. sin. of* पिप्लु *m.* a mole, freckle.

पिप्लुप्रच्छादनम् *acc. sin. n.* covering the mole; (*comp. of* पिप्लु a mole or freckle, *and* प्रच्छादन covering, *agt. of rt* छद् *with* प्र, 582. *c.*)

पिप्लुर् *nom. sin. of* पिप्लु *m.* a freckle, mole in the skin.

पिप्लुस् *nom. sin. of* पिप्लु *m.* a mark, freckle.

पिशाची *nom. sin. f.* a spirit, a female imp. *See next.*

पिशाचोरगराक्षसान् DVAN. OR AGG. COMP. 748; पिशाच *cr.* an imp, an elf, a sprite, उरग *cr.* a serpent, राक्षसान् *acc. pl. of* राक्षस an evil spirit, *see note under* राक्षसी. The Piśáća is a kind of evil spirit, mentioned several times by Manu, (see I. 37, 43; V. 50; XII. 44.) He is classed with Rákshasas and Yakshas, who are described as eating flesh-meat and unclean food.

पीडा *nom. sin. f.* pain, suffering.

पीड्यमानः *nom. sin. m. of* **पीड्यमान** *m. f. n.* being afflicted; *pres. p. pass. of rt* **पीड्** 528.

पीड्यमानस् *nom. sin. of* **पीड्यमान** *m. f. n.* being pained, being afflicted.

पीनश्रोणिपयोधराम् COMPLEX COMP. 771; **पीन** swelling, full, round, **श्रोणि** *cr.* the hip, **पयोधराम्** *acc. sin. f. from* **पयोधर** *m.* the breast of a woman; *see* 108.

पीना *for* **पीनास्** *nom. pl. m. of* **पीन** *m. f. n.* muscular, robust, 1*st cl.* 103; (*past p. p. of rt* **प्याय्** *or* **प्यै** 547.)

पुण्यं *acc. sin. of* **पुण्य** *m. f. n.* sacred, holy, pure.

पुण्यकृत् *nom. sin. m.* acting piously, virtuous; (*comp. of* **पुण्य** *cr.* pure, holy, *and* **कृत्** *m.* a doer, 84, 1.)

पुण्यजला BAH. OR REL. COMP. 766; **पुण्य** *cr.* pure, **जला** *nom. sin. f. from* **जल** *n.* water.

पुण्यश्लोक *for* **पुण्यश्लोकस्** *nom. sin. m.* Puṇyaśloka, a name of Nala. This name means properly 'celebrated in sacred song,' and is applied to other kings celebrated in Hindú poetry, as, for example, to Yudhishṭhira.

पुण्यश्लोक *voc. sin. m.* O Nala! *See last.*

पुण्यश्लोकं *acc. sin. of* **पुण्यश्लोक** *m.* Nala.

पुण्यश्लोकदिदृक्षया TAT. OR DEP. COMP. 743; **पुण्यश्लोक** *cr.* Puṇyaśloka, a name of Nala, **दिदृक्षया** *ins. sin. of* **दिदृक्षा** *f.* desire of seeing, *a noun formed from the desiderative of* **दृश्** 500. *c.*

पुण्यश्लोकपराङ्मुखान् TAT. OR DEP. COMP. 742; **पुण्यश्लोक** *cr.* Nala, **पराङ्मुखान्** *acc. pl. m. of* **पराङ्मुख** *m. f. n.* averse to, having the face averted, 1*st cl.* 103.

पुण्यश्लोकस्य *gen. sin. of* **पुण्यश्लोक** *m.* Puṇyaśloka.

पुण्यश्लोकेति *for* **पुण्यश्लोक इति** *by* 32.

पुण्यां *acc. sin. f. of* **पुण्य** *m. f. n.* pure, bright, 1*st cl.* 103.

पुण्याहवाचने TAT. OR DEP. COMP. 743; **पुण्याह** *cr.* a holyday, **वाचने** *loc. sin. of* **वाचन** *n.* declaration, proclamation; 'on the declaration of a holyday.'

पुण्ये *loc. sin. of* **पुण्य** *m. f. n.* pure, 1*st cl.* 187.

पुत्र *m.* a son. This word is properly written **पुत्त्र**, and is said to mean 'deliverer from hell.' Since the son delivers (**त्रायते**) his father from the hell called **पुत्**, he was therefore named **पुत्त्र** by Brahmá. (Manu IX. 138.) This accounts for the extreme desire entertained by the Hindús for male offspring. Thus Bhíma, like Daśaratha in the Rámáyaṇa, and many others, performed the holiest acts for the sake of obtaining a son. The son alone by the offering of the funeral libation (*śráddha*) is supposed to procure rest for the departed spirit of the father.

पुत्रं *acc. sin. of* **पुत्र** *m.* a son.

पुत्रनिवेशने TAT. OR DEP. COMP. 743; **पुत्र** *cr.* son, **निवेशने** *loc. sin. of* **निवेशन** *n.* habitation, abode.

पुत्रयोः *gen. du. of* **पुत्र** *m.* a son, a child.

पुत्रवत् *ind.* like a son, as a son; (*from* **पुत्र** a son, *affix* **वत्** 724.)

पुत्रस्य *gen. sin. of* **पुत्र** *m.* a son.

पुत्रान् *acc. pl. of* **पुत्र** *m.* a son.

पुत्रास् *nom. pl. of* **पुत्र** *m.* a son.

पुत्रिणीं *acc. sin. of* **पुत्रिणी** *f.* one who has borne male children.

पुत्रौ *acc. du. m. of* **पुत्र** *m.* a son, a child.

पुनः *for* **पुनर्** *ind.* again.

पुनः पुनः *for* **पुनःपुनर्** *ind.* again and again.

पुनर् *ind.* again.

पुनरागमनं *nom. sin. n.* coming back again, returning; (*comp. of* **पुनर्** again, *and* **आगमन** coming.)

पुनर्लाभान् *for* **पुनर्लाभात्** (47) *abl. sin. of* **पुनर्लाभ** *m.* recovery, obtaining again; (*comp. of* **पुनर्** again, *and* **लाभ** acquisition.)

पुनश् *for* पुनर् *ind.* again.

पुमांसं *acc. sin. of* पुंस् *m.* a man, *7th cl.* 169.

पुमान् *nom. sin. of* पुंस् *m.* a man, a male; *see* 169.

पुरम् *acc. sin. of* पुर *n.* a city.

पुरराष्ट्राणि DVAN. OR AGG. COMP. 748; पुर *cr.* a city, राष्ट्राणि *nom. pl. of* राष्ट्र *n.* a kingdom, a country, *1st cl.* 104.

पुरवासिनः *nom. pl. m. of* पुरवासिन् *m.* a citizen, a dweller in the city; (*comp. of* पुर *cr. and* वासिन्, *q. q. v. v.*)

पुरा *ind.* before, formerly, 714.

पुराणि *acc. pl. of* पुर *n.* a city.

पुराणो *nom. sin. m. of* पुराण *m. f. n.* ancient, existing of old.

पुरातनम् *acc. sin. n. of* पुरातन *m. f. n.* old, former.

पुराद् *abl. sin. of* पुर *n.* a city.

पुरीं *acc. sin. of* पुरी *f.* a city.

पुरुष *m.* a man, *1st cl.* 103.

पुरुषं *acc. sin. of* पुरुष *m.* a man.

पुरुषः *nom. sin. of* पुरुष *m.* a man.

पुरुषर्षभ *voc. sin. m.* O excellent man! (*comp. of* पुरुष a man, *and* ऋषभ a bull, *used in comp. to denote* eminent, *see* 758.)

पुरुषर्षभम् *acc. sin. m. See last.*

पुरुषव्याघ्र *voc. sin. m.* O excellent man! *See* पुरुषव्याघ्रैर्.

पुरुषव्याघ्रस् *nom. sin. m.* an excellent man. *See* पुरुषव्याघ्रैर्.

पुरुषव्याघ्रे *loc. sin. m. See next.*

पुरुषव्याघ्रैर् KARM. OR DES. COMP. 758; पुरुष *cr.* a man, व्याघ्रैर् *ins. pl. of* व्याघ्र a tiger; (*used in comp. to denote* excellent, eminent;) *see* 758.

पुरुषशार्दूलम् *acc. sin. m.* chief of men; (*lit.* tiger of men;) *see* 758.

पुरुषा *for* पुरुषास् *nom. pl. m. of* पुरुष *m.* a man.

पुरुषान् *acc. pl. of* पुरुष *m.* a man.

पुरुषैर् *for* पुरुषैस् *ins. pl. of* पुरुष *m.* a man, a servant, *1st cl.* 103.

पुरुषो *for* पुरुषस् *nom. sin. m.* a man, a servant.

पुरे *loc. sin. of* पुर *n.* a city, *1st cl.* 104.

पुरेव *for* पुरा इव *by* 32.

पुरोक्ताम् *acc. sin. f. of* पुरोक्त *m. f. n.* formerly spoken; (*comp. of* पुरा formerly, *and* उक्त spoken, *q. v.*)

पुरोगमाः *nom. sin. pl. of* पुरोगम *m. f. n.* going before, travelling in front; (*comp. of* पुरस् in front, 64, *and* गम going.)

पुरोत्तमम् *acc. sin. n.* the best of cities, the mighty city; (*comp. of* पुर *cr.* city, *and* उत्तम, *see* 743. *b.*)

पुलिनद्वीपशोभितां COMPLEX COMP. 771; पुलिन *cr.* sandbanks, shoals, द्वीप *cr.* islands, शोभितां *acc. sin. f. of* शोभित *m. f. n.* adorned, beautiful.

पुष्करम् *acc. sin. of* पुष्कर *m. See next.*

पुष्करस्य *gen. sin. of* पुष्कर *m.* Pushkara, name of a king, the brother of Nala, *1st cl.* 103.

पुष्करस्याक्षाः *for* पुष्करस्य अक्षाः *by* 31.

पुष्करेणैवम् *for* पुष्करेण एवं *by* 33.

पुष्कलम् *acc. sin. n. of* पुष्कल *m. f. n.* much, great.

पुष्पभङ्गः *nom. sin. m.* a festoon of flowers; (पुष्प a flower, भङ्ग a bend.)

पुष्पवृष्टिः TAT. OR DEP. COMP. 743; पुष्प *cr.* flowers, वृष्टिः *nom. sin. f.* a shower. The showering of flowers by some unseen heavenly beings on the head of the 'happy pair' on every auspicious occasion is a favourite device in the machinery of Hindú epics. So in Raghu-vanśa II. 60 no sooner has king Dilípa offered himself to die for the sacred cow of his Bráhmanical preceptor, than a shower of flowers falls on him. Sítá's innocence was similarly attested.

पुष्पाणि *nom. or acc. pl. of* पुष्प *n.* a flower, 104.

पुष्पितं *acc. sin. m. of* **पुष्पित** *m. f. n.* blooming, flowering, flowery, in flower.

पूजया *ins. sin. of* **पूजा** *f.* honour, worship.

पूजयामास he or she worshipped; *3d sin. perf. of rt* **पूज्** *10th cl.* 385. *a.*

पूजयित्वा having honoured; *past ind. p. of rt* **पूज्** *10th cl.* 558.

पूजयिष्यति he will honour; *3d sin. 2d fut. of rt* **पूज्** *10th cl.* 491.

पूजा *nom. sin. f.* worship, honour, homage.

पूजां *acc. sin. of* **पूजा** *f.* worship, homage.

पूजार्हाव् *for* **पूजार्हौ** (37) *acc. du. of* **पूजार्ह** *m. f. n.* worthy of honour.

पूजितः *nom. sin. m.* honoured. *See next.*

पूजिताः *nom. pl. m. of* **पूजित** *m. f. n.* honoured, *past p. p. of rt* **पूज्** 538.

पूजितो *nom. sin. m. of* **पूजित** *m. f. n.* honoured; worshipped; *past p. p. of rt* **पूज्** 538.

पूरयन्तो filling; *nom. pl. m. of* **पूरयत्** *pres. p. of rt* **पृ** *10th cl.* 640, 524.

पूरयन् *for* **पूरयन्** (52) *nom. sin. m. of* **पूरयत्** *m. f. n.* filling; *pres. p. of rt* **पृ** *10th cl.* 285, 524.

पूर्णचन्द्रनिभां Anom. comp. 777; **पूर्ण** *cr.* full, **चन्द्र** *cr.* moon, **निभां** *acc. sin. f. of* **निभ** *m. f. n.* like, resembling.

पूर्णचन्द्रनिभाननाम् Complex comp. 771; **पूर्ण** *cr.* full, **चन्द्र** *cr.* moon, **निभ** *cr.* like, **आननाम्** *acc. sin. f. from* **आनन** *n.* the face, the countenance; *see* 108.

पूर्णचन्द्रप्रभाम् Complex comp. 770; **पूर्ण** *cr.* full, **चन्द्र** *cr.* moon, **प्रभाम्** *acc. sin. f. of* **प्रभा** *f.* lustre.

पूर्णा *for* **पूर्णास्** *nom. pl. m. of* **पूर्ण** *m. f. n.* full, filled.

पूर्णेन्दुवदनो Bah. or Rel. comp. 761; **पूर्ण** *cr.* full, **इन्दु** *cr.* moon, **वदनो** *nom. sin. m. from* **वदन** *n.* the face.

पूर्वं *ind.* formerly, before, at first.

पूर्वदृष्टस् *nom. sin. m.* before seen; (*comp. of* **पूर्वं** before, *and* **दृष्ट**, *q. v.*)

पृच्छन्त्या *for* **पृच्छन्त्यास्** *gen. sin. f. of* **पृच्छत्** *m. f. n.* asking, enquiring; *pres. p. of rt* **प्रच्छ्** 631, 524.

पृच्छामि I ask; *1st sin. pres. of rt* **प्रच्छ्** *6th cl.* 631; *see* 873.

पृच्छेथाः thou mayest ask, ask thou; *2d sin. pot. átm. of rt* **प्रच्छ्** *6th cl.* 631.

पृच्छ्यमाना *nom. sin. f. of* **पृच्छ्यमान** *m. f. n.* being asked; *pres. p. pass. of rt* **प्रच्छ्** 472, 631.

पृथिवी *f.* the earth, *1st cl.* 106.

पृथिवीं *acc. sin. of* **पृथिवी** *f.* the earth.

पृथिवीक्षितः *nom. pl. of* **पृथिवीक्षित्** *m.* an 'earth-possessor,' a king, *5th cl.* 136; (**पृथिवी** the earth, **क्षित्** a possessor.)

पृथिवीपतिः *nom. sin. m.* lord of the earth, a king; (**पृथिवी** the earth, **पति** a lord.)

पृथिवीपतिम् *acc. sin. m.* lord of the earth.

पृथिवीपते *voc. sin. of* **पृथिवीपति** *m.* lord of the earth, *2d cl.* 110, 121, 743.

पृथिवीपालः *nom. sin. m.* protector of the earth, a king. *See next.*

पृथिवीपालाः *nom. pl. m.* protectors of the earth. *See next.*

पृथिवीपालास् Tat. or Dep. comp. 743; **पृथिवी** *cr.* the earth, **पालास्** *nom. pl. of* **पाल** *m.* a protector, *1st cl.* 103.

पृथिवीम् *acc. sin. of* **पृथिवी** *f.* the earth.

पृथिव्यां *loc. sin. of* **पृथिवी** *f.* the earth.

पृथुचार्वञ्चितेक्षणः Complex comp. 771; **पृथु** *cr.* wide, large, **चार्व्** *for* **चारु** (34) *cr.* beautiful, **अञ्चित** *cr.* curved, bent, **ईक्षणः** *nom. sin. m. from* **ईक्षण** *n.* the eye, *1st cl.* 108.

पृथुप्रोथान् Bah. or Rel. comp. 761; **पृथु** *cr.* broad, wide, **प्रोथान्** *acc. pl. of* **प्रोथ** *m.* the nose or nostril (of a horse).

पृथुलोचन Bah. or Rel. comp. 766; **पृथु** *cr.* broad, large, **लोचन** *voc. sin. from* **लोचन** *n.* the eye.

पृथुश्रीर् *for* **पृथुश्रीस्** Bah. or Rel. comp.

766; पृथु *cr.* great, wide, श्रीर् *nom. sin. of* श्री *f.* prosperity, fortune, 123.

पृष्टः *nom. sin. m. of* पृष्ट *m. f. n.* asked; *past p. p. of rt* प्रच्छ् 544.

पृष्ट्वा having asked; *past ind. p. of rt* प्रच्छ् 556.

पृष्ठतो *ind. for* पृष्ठतस् (64) behind, from behind, *see* 719. *b.*

पौत्राः *nom. pl. of* पौत्र *m.* grandson, son's son.

पौत्रान् *acc. pl. of* पौत्र *m.* a grandson.

पौरजनाः *nom. pl. of* पौरजन *m.* a citizen.

पौरजनो *nom. sin. of* पौरजन *m.* a citizen.

पौरजानपदाश् Dvan. or Agg. comp. 748; पौर *cr.* a citizen, जानपदाश् *nom. pl. of* जानपद *m.* an inhabitant of the country, country-person, rustic, country-folk.

पौरा *for* पौरास् *nom. pl. of* पौर *m.* a citizen.

पौरांश्च *for* पौरान् च *by* 53.

पौराणाम् *gen. pl. of* पौर *m.* a citizen.

पौरान् *acc. pl. of* पौर *m.* a citizen.

पौर्णमासीम् *acc. sin. of* पौर्णमासी *f.* day of full moon.

प्र *prep.* before, forward, onward, on, forth.

प्रकल्पितः *nom. sin. m. of* प्रकल्पित *m. f. n.* fitted, arranged, placed.

प्रकारैर् *for* प्रकारैस् *ins. pl. of* प्रकार *m.* kind, manner, 1st *cl.* 103.

प्रकाशतां *acc. sin. of* प्रकाशता *f.* glory, brightness.

प्रकुरुष्व turn thou, fix thou; 2d *sin. imp. átm. of rt* कृ *with* प्र, 683.

प्रकृतयः *for* प्रकृतयस् ministers and citizens; *nom. pl. of* प्रकृति *f.* any requisite of regal administration.

प्रकृतयो *for* प्रकृतयस् *nom. pl.* ministers and citizens, 2d *cl.* 112. *See last.*

प्रकृष्टम् *acc. sin. m. of* प्रकृष्ट *m. f. n.* extended, drawn out, long (as a road).

प्रकोपाद् *abl. sin. of* प्रकोप *m.* anger, 1st *cl.* 103.

प्रक्षालनं *nom. sin. n.* washing, cleaning.

प्रक्षालनार्थाय for the sake of washing; (*comp. of* प्रक्षालन washing, *and* अर्थाय *dat. sin.* for the sake of.)

प्रक्षाल्य having washed, having cleansed; having rinsed (the mouth); *past ind. p. of rt* क्षल् *with* प्र, 10th *cl.* 559. Washing the mouth after food (XXIII. 23), which Damayantí in the height of her emotion does not forget, is a duty strictly enjoined in the Indian law. See Manu V. 145: 'Having slumbered, having sneezed, having eaten, having spitten, having told untruths, having drunk water, and going to read sacred books, let him, though pure, wash his mouth.'

प्रक्ष्यामि I will ask; 1st *sin.* 2d *fut. of rt* प्रच्छ् 631.

प्रख्यायमानेन *ins. sin. n. of* प्रख्यायमान *m. f. n.* being celebrated, being talked about, spoken about; *pres. p. of* ख्या *in pass. with* प्र, 528, 465. *a.*

प्रचिनुहि gather thou; 2d *sin. imp. of rt* चि to collect, *with* प्र, 5th *cl.* 583.

प्रचुक्रुशुः they cried out; 3d *pl. perf. of rt* क्रुश् 364.

प्रच्छन्ना *for* प्रच्छन्नास् *nom. pl. m. of* प्रच्छन्न *m. f. n.* concealed, disguised; *past p. p. of rt* छद् *with* प्र, 540.

प्रच्छन्नाश् *nom. pl. m.* disguised. *See last.*

प्रच्युतो *nom. sin. of* प्रच्युत *m. f. n.* banished, expelled, fallen, degraded; *past p. p. of rt* च्यु *with* प्र, 532.

प्रजज्वाल he or she blazed or kindled; 3d *sin. perf. of rt* ज्वल् *with* प्र, 364.

प्रजज्वालेव *for* प्रजज्वाल इव *by* 32.

प्रजा *for* प्रजास् *acc. pl. of* प्रजा *f.* people, subjects, 1st *cl.* 105.

प्रजाकामः *for* प्रजाकामस् desirous of offspring, Bah. or Rel. comp. 762; प्रजा *cr.* offspring, कामः *nom. sin. of* काम *m.* desire, 1st *cl.* 103.

प्रजाकामस् *nom. sin. m.* desirous of offspring.

प्रजार्थे for the sake of offspring, Adv. comp. 791. *See note under* पुत्र.

प्रज्वलितस् *nom. sin. m. of* प्रज्वलित *m. f. n.* blazed forth; *past p. p. of rt* ज्वल् *with* प्र, 538, 896.

प्रणमे I salute, I bow before; *1st sin. pres. átm. of rt* **नम्** *with* **प्र**, *1st cl.* 261, 58.

प्रणम्य having bowed before; *past ind. p. of rt* **नम्** *with* **प्र.**

प्रणयम् *acc. sin. of* **प्रणय** *m.* affection, love, favour, *1st cl.* 103.

प्रणयस्व shew thou affection, give thy affection, bestow thy love; *2d sin. imp. átm. of rt* **नी** *with* **प्र**, *1st cl.* 590. *a*, 58.

प्रणश्यन्ति they perish, they are destroyed; *3d pl. pres. of rt* **नश्** *with* **प्र**, *4th cl.* 58.

प्रणष्टं *nom. sin. n. of* **प्रणष्ट** *m. f. n.* lost; *past p. p. of rt* **नश्** *with* **प्र**, 539.

प्रणेदुर् they called out, they uttered cries; *3d pl. perf. of rt* **नद्** *with* **प्र**, 375. *a.*

प्रतस्थे he or she set out, proceeded or went onward; *3d sin. perf. átm. of rt* **स्था** *with* **प्र**, 364, 587.

प्रति *ind.* toward, to; with regard to, about, concerning, 729, 730. *c. In these senses generally a* postposition. *As a preposition it means* against, back, back again.

प्रतिगृह्य having received; *past ind. p. of rt* **ग्रह्** *with* **प्रति**, 565.

प्रतिजग्मुर् they returned or went back; *3d pl. perf. of rt* **गम्** *with* **प्रति**, 602.

प्रतिजग्राह he received or took in return; *3d sin. perf. of rt* **ग्रह्** *with* **प्रति**, 699.

प्रतिजानामि I assent to, I agree to; *1st sin. pres. of rt* **ज्ञा** *with* **प्रति**, *9th cl.* 688.

प्रतिज्ञाय having promised; *past ind. p. of rt* **ज्ञा** *with* **प्रति**, 559.

प्रतिपत्कलुषस्य ANOM. COMP. 777; **प्रतिपद्** the first day of the moon's increase, **कलुषस्य** *gen. sin. of* **कलुष** *m. f. n.* opaque, dark.

प्रतिपत्कलुषस्येन्दोर् *for* **प्रतिपत्कलुषस्य इन्दोर्** *by* 32.

प्रतिपत्स्यसे thou wilt recover, thou wilt be restored to; *2d sin. 2d fut. átm. of rt* **पद्** *with* **प्रति**, 405.

प्रतिपद्यस्व gain thou, win thou; *2d sin. imp. of rt* **पद्** *with* **प्रति**, *4th cl.* 272.

प्रतिपद्येत he may find out, he may ascertain; *3d sin. pot. átm. of rt* **पद्** *with* **प्रति**, *4th cl.* 272.

प्रतिपश्यामि I behold, I look upon; *1st sin. pres. of rt* **दृश्** *with* **प्रति**, *1st cl.* 604.

प्रतिपाणः *nom. sin. m.* a counter-game, a counter-stake.

प्रतिपाणाय *dat. sin.* for a counter-game, for a counter-stake. *See last.*

प्रतिपाणो *nom. sin. of* **प्रतिपाण** *m.* a stake, a counter-stake, a thing staked against another thing, *1st cl.* 103.

प्रतिबन्धेन *ins. sin. of* **प्रतिबन्ध** *m.* hindrance, impediment (for a hindrance).

प्रतिब्रूयाद् he may answer, he may reply to; *3d sin. pot. of rt* **ब्रू** *with* **प्रति**, *2d cl.* 649.

प्रतिभयं *acc. sin. n. of* **प्रतिभय** *m. f. n.* fearful, terrible.

प्रतिभाषसे thou dost answer or speak in reply; *2d sin. pres. átm. of rt* **भाष्** *with* **प्रति**, *1st cl.* 261.

प्रतियोत्स्यामि I shall fight against; *1st sin. 2d fut. of rt* **युध्** *with* **प्रति.**

प्रतिवचस् *nom. sin. n.* an answer, *7th cl.* 164.

प्रतिवचो *for* **प्रतिवचस्** *acc. sin. of* **प्रतिवचस्** *n.* an answer.

प्रतिवाक्यं *acc. sin. of* **प्रतिवाक्य** *n.* an answer.

प्रतिवाक्ये *loc. sin. of* **प्रतिवाक्य** *n.* an answer.

प्रतिश्रयः *nom. sin. m.* abode, dwelling.

प्रतिश्रुत्य having promised; *past ind. p. of rt* **श्रु** *with* **प्रति**, 560.

प्रतिष्ठितः *nom. sin. m. of* **प्रतिष्ठित** *m. f. n.* famous, celebrated.

प्रतीक्षस्व wait thou; *2d sin. imp. átm. of rt* **ईक्ष्** *with* **प्रति**, 605.

प्रतीक्षे I expect, I wait for, I look toward; *1st sin. pres. átm. of rt* **ईक्ष्** *with* **प्रति.**

प्रत्यक्षं *ind.* in the sight of, visibly, 713.

प्रत्यक्षदर्शनं the power of perceiving the (godhead) present (in the sacrifice), TAT. OR DEP. COMP. 743; **प्रत्यक्ष** *cr.* visible, present to the eye, **दर्शनं** *nom. sin. of* **दर्शन** *n.* perception, seeing, *1st cl.* 104.

प्रत्यनन्दत he attended, he gave heed to, he

saluted; (*in* Book XXIV. 44) he fondled; *3d sin. impf. átm. of rt* नन्द् *with* प्रति, *1st cl.* 261.

प्रत्यभाषत he or she answered or addressed, he spoke to; *3d sin. impf. átm. of rt* भाष् *with* प्रति, *1st cl.* 261.

प्रत्यवेदयत् he declared, he made known; *3d sin. impf. of rt* विद् *in caus. with* प्रति, 481.

प्रत्यवेदयन् they announced; *3d pl. impf.*

प्रत्याख्याता *for* प्रत्याख्यातास् *nom. pl. m. of* प्रत्याख्यात *m. f. n.* rejected, refused; *past p. p. of rt* ख्या *with* आ *and* प्रति, 532.

प्रत्याख्यासि thou rejectest, thou refusest; *2d sin. pres. of rt* ख्या *with* आ *and* प्रति, *2d cl.* 307.

प्रत्याख्यास्यसि thou wilt refuse, thou shalt reject; *2d sin. 2d fut. of rt* ख्या *with* आ *and* प्रति.

प्रत्याह he answered; *3d sin. perf. of defective rt* अह् *with* प्रति, 384. *b.*

प्रत्याहरन्ती *nom. sin. f. of* प्रत्याहरत् uttering; *pres. p. par. of rt* हृ *with* आ *and* प्रति, 34, 524.

प्रत्याहृत्य having recovered or taken back; *past ind. p. of rt* हृ *with* आ *and* प्रति, 560.

प्रत्युवाच he or she answered; *3d sin. perf. of rt* वच् *with* प्रति (34), *see* 375. *c.*

प्रत्युवाचाथ *for* प्रत्युवाच अथ *by* 31.

प्रत्यूचुस् they answered; *3d pl. perf. of rt* वच् *with* प्रति, 375. *c*, 650.

प्रत्येत्य having returned; *past ind. p. of rt* इ *with* आ *and* प्रति, 560.

प्रथम *m. f. n.* first, 208.

प्रथमं *ind.* at first.

प्रददौ he gave; *3d sin. perf. of rt* दा *with* प्र, 373.

प्रदध्यौ he thought; *3d sin. perf. of rt* ध्यै *with* प्र, 374, 595. *b.*

प्रदातव्यः *nom. sin. m. of* प्रदातव्य *m. f. n.* to be given, to be granted; *fut. pass. p. of rt* दा *with* प्र, 569.

प्रदाय having given, having given away; *past ind. p. of rt* दा *with* प्र, 559, 663.

प्रदायास्य *for* प्रदाय अस्य *by* 31.

प्रदिशन्तु let them show, let them point out; *3d pl. imp. of rt* दिश् *with* प्र, *6th cl.* 583.

प्रदीप्ता *nom. sin. f. of* प्रदीप्त *m. f. n.* set on fire, inflamed; *past p. p. of rt* दीप् *with* प्र.

प्रदीप्तेव *for* प्रदीप्ता इव *by* 32.

प्रदुद्रुवुः they ran away, they fled; *3d pl. perf. of rt* द्रु 592, 368.

प्रदुष्यन्ति they are corrupted; *3d pl. pres. of rt* दुष् *with* प्र, *4th cl.*

प्रदेशितो *nom. sin. m. of* प्रदेशित *m. f. n.* urged, directed; *past p. p. of rt* दिश् *in caus. with* प्र, 549.

प्रद्रुते *loc. sin. m. of* प्रद्रुत *m. f. n.* fled, having fled; *past p. p. of rt* द्रु *with* प्र, 532, 896.

प्रधर्षयितुम् to force, to violate; *inf. of rt* धृष् *10th cl. with* प्र, 459.

प्रधावथ ye do run away; *2d pl. pres. of rt* धाव् *with* प्र, *1st cl.* 261.

प्रपन्नं *acc. sin. m. or n. of* प्रपन्न. *See next.*

प्रपन्ना *nom. sin. f. of* प्रपन्न *m. f. n.* taken refuge with, gone towards, arrived at; *past p. p. of rt* पद् *with* प्र, 540.

प्रपन्नास्मि *for* प्रपन्ना अस्मि *by* 31.

प्रपन्नो *nom. sin. m. of* प्रपन्न *m. f. n.* gone towards, depending on (as a refuge).

प्रपश्यद्भिर् *ins. pl. of* प्रपश्यत् *m. f. n.* looking, foreseeing; *pres. p. of rt* दृश् *with* प्र.

प्रपश्यन्ति they see, they discover; *3d pl. pres. of rt* दृश् *with* प्र, 604.

प्रपश्यामि I see, I foresee; *1st sin. pres. of rt* दृश् *with* प्र.

प्रभया *ins. sin. of* प्रभा *f.* splendour, brightness, beauty.

प्रभां *acc. sin. of* प्रभा *f.* light, lustre.

प्रभावेन *ins. sin. of* प्रभाव *m.* power.

प्रभाषितम् *acc. sin. n. of* प्रभाषित *m. f. n.* spoken, uttered; *past p. p. of rt* भाष् *with* प्र, 538.

प्रभाषेयं I may speak to, I may converse with; *1st sin. pot. of rt* भाष् *with* प्र, *1st cl.* 261.

प्रभु *m.* a lord, a master, a king, *3d cl.* 111.

प्रभुं *acc. sin. of* **प्रभु** *m.* a lord, noble.

प्रभुः *nom. sin. of* **प्रभु** *m.* a lord, noble, illustrious, 3*d cl.* 111.

प्रभूतयवसेन्धनम् Complex comp. 771; **प्रभूत** *cr.* abundant, abounding in, **यवस** *cr.* meadow-grass, fresh grass, **इन्धनम्** *acc. sin. n. of* **इन्धन** *n.* wood (for fuel).

प्रभो O king, O lord; *voc. sin. of* **प्रभु**.

प्रमत्तस्य *gen. sin. of* **प्रमत्त** *m.f.n.* not observing, not noticing, inattentive, careless.

प्रमदावने in the private pleasure-grounds, Tat. or Dep. comp. 743; **प्रमदा** *cr.* a woman, **वने** *loc. sin. of* **वन** *n.* a grove, a garden, 1*st cl.* 103. *This word properly denotes* a garden set apart for the females of the palace.

प्रमाणं *nom. sin. of* **प्रमाण** *n.* authority, proof; an authority, a judge, 1*st cl.* 104; *the nom. sin. n. is often used in apposition to a masculine or feminine noun in the plural.* **प्रमाणं भवन्तस्** your honours are the authority, *i. e.* it is yours to decide.

प्रमाणात् *abl. sin. of* **प्रमाण** *n.* proof.

प्रमुखे *ind.* in front, opposite.

प्रमुञ्चन्तः *nom. pl. of* **प्रमुञ्चत्** *m.f.n.* uttering, emitting; *pres. p. par. of rt* **मुच्** *with* **प्र**, 6*th cl.* 524.

प्रमृष्टमणिकुण्डलाः Complex comp. 771; **प्रमृष्ट** *cr.* polished, rubbed, bright, **मणि** *cr.* a gem, a jewel, **कुण्डलाः** *nom. pl. from* **कुण्डल** *n.* an earring, 1*st cl.* 108.

प्रयतः *nom. sin. m. of* **प्रयत** *m. f. n.* dutiful, pious, self-restrained.

प्रयतन्तु let them strive; 3*d pl. imp. of rt* **यत्** *with* **प्र**, 1*st cl.* 261. *This root is more commonly used in átmane-pada.*

प्रयत्तव्यम् *nom. sin. n. of* **प्रयत्तव्य** *m. f. n.* to be endeavoured; *fut. pass. p. of rt* **यत्** *with* **प्र**, 569. *Observe*—**प्रयतितव्य** *would be the usual form.*

प्रययौ he set out for, he departed, he proceeded; 3*d sin. perf. of rt* **या** *with* **प्र**.

प्रयाणे *loc. sin. of* **प्रयाण** *n.* the crupper (?) or the hind part or haunch of a horse or other animal.

प्रयाते *loc. sin. m. of* **प्रयात** *m. f. n.* gone towards, advanced, advancing; *past p. p. of rt* **या** *with* **प्र**, 532, 896. *a.*

प्रयुज्य having performed; *past ind. p. of rt* **युज्** *with* **प्र**, 559.

प्रयोजनम् *nom. sin. n.* object, occasion, business.

प्ररुरोद he wept, he burst into tears; 3*d sin. perf. of rt* **रुद्** *with* **प्र**, 364.

प्रलभ्या *for* **प्रलभ्यास्** *nom. pl. m. of* **प्रलभ्य** *m. f. n.* to be deceived; *fut. pass. p. of rt* **लभ्** *with* **प्र**, 569.

प्रलब्धो *nom. sin. m. of* **प्रलब्ध** *m.f.n.* deceived; *past p. p. of rt* **लभ्** *with* **प्र**, 539.

प्रलापानि *acc. pl. n. from* **प्रलाप** a lamentation.

प्रवदस्व speak thou; 2*d sin. imp. átm. of rt* **वद्** *with* **प्र**.

प्रवर्ततां let it proceed; 3*d sin. pres. átm. of rt* **वृत्** *with* **प्र**, 1*st cl.* 598.

प्रवर्तसे thou dost act; 2*d sin. pres. átm. of rt* **वृत्** *with* **प्र**, 1*st cl.* 598.

प्रविवेश he or she entered; 3*d sin. perf. of rt* **विश्** *with* **प्र**, 364.

प्रविशन्तं *acc. sin. m. of* **प्रविशत्** *m. f. n.* entering; *pres. p. par. of rt* **विश्** *with* **प्र**, 524.

प्रविशन्तीं *acc. sin. f. of* **प्रविशत्** *m. f. n.* entering; *pres. p. par. of rt* **विश्** *with* **प्र**, 524.

प्रविशामि I enter; (*in* Book XXI. 10) I throw myself into; 1*st sin. pres. of rt* **विश्** *with* **प्र**, 6*th cl.* 278.

प्रविश्य having entered; *past ind. p. of rt* **विश्** *with* **प्र**, 559.

प्रविष्टः *nom. sin. of* **प्रविष्ट** entered, (*with the sense in* Book IV. 25 *of* I entered, 896.)

प्रविष्टा *nom. sin. f. of* **प्रविष्ट** *m.f.n.* entered; *past p. p. of rt* **विश्** *with* **प्र**, 539, 896.

प्रविष्टो *for* **प्रविष्टस्** *nom. sin. m. of* **प्रविष्ट** *m. f. n.* entered.

प्रवेक्ष्यसि thou shalt enter; *2d sin. 2d fut. of rt* **विश्** *with* **प्र**, 411.

प्रवेक्ष्यसीति *for* **प्रवेक्ष्यसि इति** *by* 31.

प्रवेक्ष्यामि I shall or will enter; *1st sin. 2d fut. of rt* **विश्** *with* **प्र**, 411.

प्रवेशयामास he or she caused to enter; *3d sin. 2d pret. of rt* **विश्** *in caus. with* **प्र**, 490.

प्रवेश्यताम् let him be caused to enter, let him be introduced; *3d sin. pres. of rt* **विश्** *in caus. pass. with* **प्र**, 496.

प्रवेष्टुं to enter; *inf. of rt* **विश्** *with* **प्र**, 459.

प्रशंसद्भिर् *ins. pl. of* **प्रशंसत्** *m. f. n.* praising; *pres. p. par. of rt* **शंस्** *with* **प्र**, 524.

प्रशशंसुः *for* **प्रशशंसुस्** they praised; *3d pl. perf. of rt* **शंस्** *with* **प्र** to praise, 364.

प्रशशंसुस् they praised. *See last.*

प्रशाखिकाः *nom. pl. of* **प्रशाखिका** *f.* a small branch or twig.

प्रशान्ते *loc. sin. m. of* **प्रशान्त** *m. f. n.* tranquillised, made quiet; *past p. p. of rt* **शम्** 546.

प्रशासतम् *acc. sin. m. of* **प्रशासत्** *m. f. n.* governing, ruling; *pres. p. par. of rt* **शास्** *with* **प्र**, *see* 141. *a.*

प्रशासिता *nom. sin. of* **प्रशासितृ** *m.* a ruler, *4th cl.* 127.

प्रष्टव्यो *nom. sin. m.* to be asked, to be consulted; *fut. pass. p. of rt* **प्रच्छ्** 569, 631.

प्रसङ्गो *nom. sin. m.* attachment for, fondness for; (*governing the loc. sin.*)

प्रसन्नसलिलां BAH. OR REL. COMP. 766; **प्रसन्न** *cr.* clear, **सलिलां** *acc. sin. f. from* **सलिल** *n.* water.

प्रसन्नो *for* **प्रसन्नस्** *nom. sin. of* **प्रसन्न** *m. f. n.* graciously disposed, propitious, pleased; *past p. p. of rt* **सद्** *with* **प्र**, 540.

प्रसादं *acc. sin. of* **प्रसाद** *m.* favour, kindness.

प्रसीदतु let him be favourable; *3d sin. imp. of rt* **सद्** *with* **प्र**, *1st cl.* 599. *a.*

प्रस्थापयामास he or she despatched, he or she sent; *3d sin. 2d pret. of rt* **स्था** *in caus. with* **प्र**.

प्रस्थाप्य having despatched; *past ind. p. of rt* **स्था** *in caus. with* **प्र**, 566.

प्रस्थितं *acc. sin. m. of* **प्रस्थित** *m. f. n.* proceeding onward; *past p. p. of rt* **स्था** *with* **प्र**, 587, 896. *a.*

प्रस्थिता *for* **प्रस्थितास्** *nom. pl. m. of* **प्रस्थित** *m. f. n.* set out, setting out.

प्रस्थिताः *nom. pl. m. of* **प्रस्थित** *m. f. n.* setting out, departing; **प्रस्थिताः स्म** we are about to set out; *see* **स्म** *for* **स्मस्**.

प्रस्थितो *nom. sin. m. of* **प्रस्थित** *m. f. n.* set out, departed.

प्रहसन् *nom. sin. m. of* **प्रहसत्** *m. f. n.* laughing, smiling; *pres. p. of rt* **हस्** *with* **प्र**, 524.

प्रहसन्ति they mock, they laugh at; *3d pl. pres. of rt* **हस्** *with* **प्र**, *1st cl.* 261.

प्रहसन्न् *for* **प्रहसन्** (*q. v.*) *nom. sin. m. of* **प्रहसत्** *m. f. n.* smiling, *see* 52.

प्रहस्य having smiled or laughed; *past ind. p. of rt* **हस्** *with* **प्र**, 559.

प्रहस्येन्द्रो *for* **प्रहस्य इन्द्रो** *by* 32.

प्रहास्यति he or it shall cease, he or it shall depart; *3d sin. 2d fut. of rt* **हा** *with* **प्र**, 665.

प्रहृष्टः *nom. sin. m. of* **प्रहृष्ट** *m. f. n.* joyful, rejoiced.

प्रहृष्टमनसः BAH. OR REL. COMP. 766; **प्रहृष्ट** *cr.* rejoiced, **मनसः** *nom. pl. m. from* **मनस्** *n.* the mind, *7th cl.* 163.

प्रहृष्टात्मा BAH. OR REL. COMP. 767; **प्रहृष्ट** *cr.* rejoiced, **आत्मा** *nom. sin. m.* mind, 146.

प्रहृष्टेन *ins. sin. of* **प्रहृष्ट** *m. f. n.* delighted, pleased, rejoiced; *past p. p. of rt* **हृष्** *with* **प्र**, 539.

प्रहृष्टेनान्तरात्मना *for* **प्रहृष्टेन अन्तरात्मना** *by* 31.

प्राक्रोशद् *for* **प्राक्रोशत्** he or she called out to, she shrieked out; *3d sin. 1st pret. of rt* **क्रुश्** *with* **प्र**, *1st cl.* 261.

प्राज्ञः *nom. sin. m. of* **प्राज्ञ** *m. f. n.* wise, intelligent.

प्राज्ञायत he was known; *3d sin. 1st pret. of rt* **ज्ञा** *in pass. with* **प्र**.

प्राञ्जलयः *nom. pl. of* प्राञ्जलि *m. f. n.* joining the hands respectfully.

प्राञ्जलिर् *for* प्राञ्जलिस् *nom. sin. m. or f. of* प्राञ्जलि *m. f. n.* joining the hands reverentially, *2d cl.* 110.

प्राणयात्रां *acc. sin. of* प्राणयात्रा *f.* support of life, subsistence; (*comp. of* प्राण breath, *and* यात्रा support.)

प्राणयोश् *gen. or loc. du. of* प्राण *m.* life, (*in this sense often used in the plural.*)

प्राणा *for* प्राणास् *nom. pl. of* प्राण *m.* breath, *1st cl.* 103.

प्राणांश् *for* प्राणान् *acc. pl. of* प्राण *m.* breath, life.

प्राणान् *acc. pl. of* प्राण *m.* breath. (*The plural* प्राणास् *may be used to denote* life.)

प्राणेन *ins. sin. of* प्राण *m.* life, breath.

प्राणेश्वरम् TAT. OR DEP. COMP. 743; प्राण *cr.* life, ईश्वरम् *acc. sin. m.* lord.

प्रातिष्ठत् he proceeded, he travelled on; *3d sin. impf. of rt* स्था *with* प्र, 587.

प्रातिष्ठद् *for* प्रातिष्ठत्. *See last.*

प्रादात् he or she gave; *3d sin. aor. of rt* दा *with* प्र, *see* 438.

प्रादाद् *for* प्रादात् he gave; *3d sin. aor.*

प्राद्रवद् *for* प्राद्रवत् he or she ran towards, he or she fled or ran away; *3d sin. impf. of rt* द्रु *with* प्र, *1st cl.* 592.

प्राद्रवन् *for* प्राद्रवत् (47) he ran on, he ran away. *See last.*

प्राप he or she obtained; *3d sin. perf. of rt* आप् *with* प्र, 364. *a.*

प्राप्त *m. f. n.* reached, obtained, gained; *past p. p. of rt* आप् *with* प्र, 681.

प्राप्तं *acc. sin. m. of* प्राप्त *m. f. n.* arrived.

प्राप्तकालम् *acc. sin. m.* the time arrived, the time come; *or, as a* BAH. COMP., who or what has reached his or its time; (*comp. of* प्राप्त *cr.* arrived, *and* कालम् *acc. sin. of* काल *m.* time, *1st cl.* 103.)

प्राप्तकालम् *ind.* opportunely, choosing the right time. *See last.*

प्राप्तयौवनाम् BAH. OR REL. COMP. 766; प्राप्त *cr.* reached, attained, यौवनां *acc. sin. f. from* यौवन *n.* youth, bloom, *1st cl.* 108.

प्राप्तवती *nom. sin. f. of* प्राप्तवत् *m. f. n.* obtained, incurred; *past act. p. of rt* आप् *with* प्र, 553. प्राप्तवती असि thou hast incurred, *see* 897.

प्राप्तवत्यसि *for* प्राप्तवती असि *by* 34.

प्राप्तवत्यहम् *for* प्राप्तवती अहम् *by* 34.

प्राप्तव्यं *nom. sin. n. of* प्राप्तव्य *m. f. n.* to be possessed, to be obtained; *fut. pass. p. of rt* आप् *with* प्र, 569.

प्राप्ता *nom. sin. f. of* प्राप्त *m. f. n.* reached, arrived at.

प्राप्ता *for* प्राप्तास् *nom. pl. m. of* प्राप्त *m. f. n.* arrived.

प्राप्तुम् to obtain; *inf. of rt* आप् *with* प्र, 459, 681.

प्राप्ते *loc. sin. of* प्राप्त *m. f. n.* obtained, arrived; *past p. p. of rt* आप् *with* प्र, 539.

प्राप्तो *nom. sin. m. of* प्राप्त *m. f. n.* reached, arrived, obtained.

प्राप्नोति he or she obtains or possesses; *3d sin. pres. of rt* आप् *with* प्र, 681.

प्राप्य having obtained, having reached; *past ind. p. of rt* आप् *with* प्र, 559.

प्राप्स्यति he or she will obtain or incur; *3d sin. 2d fut. of rt* आप् *with* प्र, 681.

प्राप्स्यत्यनुव्रता *for* प्राप्स्यति अनुव्रता *by* 34.

प्राप्स्यसि thou wilt obtain; *2d sin. 2d fut.*

प्रायाद् he went, he proceeded; *3d sin. impf. of rt* या *with* प्र, *2d cl.* 644.

प्रार्थयन्तो *nom. pl. m. of* प्रार्थयत् *m. f. n.* asking for, seeking, soliciting, wooing; *pres. p. par. of rt* अर्थ् *with* प्र, *10th cl.* 642, 141.

प्रार्थयेद् he may demand; *3d sin. pot. of rt* अर्थ् *with* प्र, *10th cl.* 283.

प्रार्थितं *nom. sin. n. of* प्रार्थित *m. f. n.* desired, sought, required; *past p. p. of rt* अर्थ् *with* प्र, 538.

प्रावर्तत he or it proceeded, he or it went on; 3*d sin. impf. of rt* वृत् *with* प्र.

प्राविशत् he entered; 3*d sin. impf. of rt* विश् *with* प्र, 6*th cl.* 278.

प्राविशद् *for* प्राविशत् he entered. *See last.*

प्रावृणोद् he put on, he covered (himself); 3*d sin. impf. of rt* वृ *with* प्र, 5*th cl.* 675.

प्राश्य having tasted; *past ind. p. of rt* अश् to eat, *with* प्र, 559.

प्रासादगता *nom. sin. f.* gone to (the roof of) the palace; (*comp. of* प्रासाद *cr.* palace, *and* गत gone, 545; *see also* 739. *a.*)

प्रासादगतापश्यद् *for* प्रासादगता अपश्यद् *by* 31.

प्रासादतलम् TAT. OR DEP. COMP. 743; प्रासाद *cr.* palace, तलम् *acc. sin. of* तल *n.* surface. *In this compound* तल *denotes* the flat-terraced roof.

प्रासादस्था *nom. sin. f.* standing on the palace; (*comp. of* प्रासाद a palace, *and* स्थ staying, 580. *b.*)

प्रासादस्थाश् *nom. pl. m. or f.* standing on the palace; (*comp. of* प्रासाद *cr.* palace, *and* स्थ staying, 580. *b.*)

प्रास्थापयद् he or she sent or despatched, he dismissed; 3*d sin. impf. of rt* स्था *in caus. with* प्र, 483.

प्रास्रवद् he or it flowed; 3*d sin. impf. of rt* स्रु *with* प्र, 1*st cl.* 261.

प्रिय *voc. sin. m. of* प्रिय *m. f. n.* dear, kind.

प्रियं a kindness, a favour; *acc. sin. n. of* प्रिय *m. f. n.* kind, favourable, dear.

प्रियं *acc. sin. m. or n. of* प्रिय *m. f. n.* dear, agreeable.

प्रियकारिणी *nom. sin. f. of* प्रियकारिन् *m. f. n.* doing what is pleasing, acting kindly; (*from* प्रिय dear, *and* कारिन्, 159.)

प्रियदर्शन BAH. OR REL. COMP. 766; प्रिय *cr.* pleasant, दर्शन *voc. sin. m. from* दर्शन *n.* aspect, 108.

प्रियविनाकृतम् TAT. OR DEP. COMP. 740; प्रिय *cr.* dear, beloved, विनाकृतम् *nom. sin. n.* abandoned, deserted.

प्रिया *nom. sin. f.* dear one, beloved one.

प्रियां *acc. sin. f. of* प्रिय *m. f. n.* dear, beloved.

प्रियालतालखर्जूरहरीतकीविभीतकैः DVAN. OR AGG. COMP. 748; प्रियाल *cr.* the Priyála, a tree commonly called Piyál (*Buchanania latifolia*), ताल *cr.* the palmyra or palm-tree, खर्जूर *cr.* the date-tree, हरीतकी *cr.* yellow myrobalan (*Terminalia chebula*), विभीतकैः *ins. pl. of* विभीतक *m.* beleric myrobalan (*Terminalia belerica*).

प्रियास्तीत्यब्रवीः *for* प्रिया अस्ति इति अब्रवीः *by* 31 *and* 34.

प्रियैर् *ins. pl. m. of* प्रिय *m. f. n.* dear, cherished.

प्रीतः *nom. sin. m. of* प्रीत *m. f. n.* pleased, satisfied.

प्रीतिः *nom. sin. of* प्रीति *f.* joy, pleasure, 2*d cl.* 112.

प्रीतिम् *acc. sin. of* प्रीति *f.* happiness, joy.

प्रीतिर् *for* प्रीतिस् *nom. sin. f.* pleasure, delight.

प्रीतिस् *nom. sin. of* प्रीति *f.* joy, pleasure.

प्रीतेन *ins. sin. m. of* प्रीत *m. f. n.* pleased.

प्रीतो *nom. sin. m. of* प्रीत *m. f. n.* pleased.

प्रीतौ *nom. du. m. of* प्रीत *m. f. n.* pleased, delighted; *past p. p. of rt* प्री 532.

प्रीत्या *ins. sin. of* प्रीति *f.* joy, pleasure.

प्रीयमाणः *nom. sin. of* प्रीयमाण *m. f. n.* being pleased; *pres. p. pass. of rt* प्री 528.

प्रेक्षमाणायाः *gen. sin. of* प्रेक्षमाण *m. f. n.* looking on; *pres. p. átm. of rt* ईक्ष् *with* प्र, 526.

प्रेक्ष्य having observed; *past ind. p. of rt* ईक्ष् *with* प्र, 559.

प्रेषयामास he or she sent; 3*d sin. perf. of rt* इष् *in caus. with* प्र, 385.

प्रेषयितुम् to send; *inf. of rt* इष् *in caus. with* प्र, 481, 459.

प्रेषितं *nom. sin. n. of* प्रेषित *m. f. n.* sent; *past p. p. of rt* इष् *with* प्र, 538.

प्रेषितः *nom. sin. of* प्रेषित *m. f. n.* sent.

प्रेष्यतां *acc. sin. of* प्रेष्यता *f.* servitude.

प्रेष्याः *nom. pl. of* प्रेष्य *m.* a messenger, servant.

प्रोक्ता *nom. sin. f. of* प्रोक्त *m. f. n.* addressed; *past p. p. of rt* वच् *with* प्र, 543.

प्रोद्घुष्टां *acc. sin. f. of* प्रोद्घुष्ट *m. f. n.* resonant, resounding.

फ.

फलं *nom. sin. n.* fruit, consequence, result.

फलपुष्पोपशोभिताः COMPLEX COMP. 771; फल *cr.* fruits, पुष्प *cr.* flowers, उपशोभिताः *nom. pl. m. of* उपशोभित *m. f. n.* adorned.

फलमूलानि DVAN. OR AGG. COMP. 748; फल *cr.* fruit, मूलानि *acc. pl. of* मूल *n.* a root, 1st *cl.* 104.

फलमूलाशनाम् *acc. sin. f.* feeding on fruits and roots; (*comp. of* फल *cr.* fruits, मूल *cr.* roots, *and* अशन eating, an eater.)

फलवन्तं *acc. sin. m. of* फलवत् *m. f. n.* bearing fruit, frugiferous, covered with fruit, 140.

फलसहस्रे *nom. du. n.* two thousand fruits; (*comp. of* फल fruit, *and* सहस्र a thousand, 206.)

फलानि *nom. pl. of* फल *n.* fruit, 104.

ब.

बणिजः *acc. pl. of* बणिज् *m.* a merchant, a trader, 8*th cl.* 176.

बणिजो *for* बणिजस् *nom. pl. of* बणिज् *m.* a merchant.

बध्यतां *acc. sin. of* बध्यता *f.* destruction, fitness to be killed, 1*st cl.* 105.

बध्यश् *nom. sin. m. of* बध्य *m. f. n.* to be killed, worthy of death, to be put to death; *fut. pass. p. of rt* बध् 571.

बन्धुजनः *nom. sin. m.* kinsfolk, relations.

बन्धुजनेन *ins. sin. of* बन्धुजन *m.* kinsfolk; (*comp. of* बन्धु a kinsman, a relative, *and* जन a person.)

बन्धुवर्गाश् *nom. pl. of* बन्धुवर्ग *m.* the whole body of (one's) relations; (*comp. of* बन्धु a kinsman, *and* वर्ग a class, tribe.)

बन्धून् *acc. pl. of* बन्धु *m.* a relation, kinsman.

बभूव he or she was or became; 3*d sin.* 2*d pret. of rt* भू 585.

बल *n.* an army, a force, 1*st cl.* 104.

बलं *acc. sin. of* बल *n.* power.

बलवृत्रनिषूदन COMPLEX COMP. 770; बल *cr.* name of a demon, वृत्र *cr.* name of another demon, निषूदन *voc. sin. of* निषूदन *m.* a slayer, a killer, 1*st cl.* 103, 582. *c.* *See next.*

बलवृत्रहा a name of Indra, as the destroyer of two demons called Bala and Vṛitra; (COMPLEX COMP. 770; बल *cr.* name of a demon, वृत्र name of another demon, हा *nom. sin. of* हन् *m.* a slayer, 6*th cl.* 157.)

बलिन् *m. f. n.* strong, powerful, 6*th cl.* 159.

बली *nom. sin. m. of* बलिन् *m. f. n.* strong, mighty, 6*th cl.* 159.

बलेन *ins. sin. of* बल *n.* an army.

बलैर् *for* बलैस् *ins. pl. of* बल, *q.v.*

बहवः *nom. pl. m. of* बहु *m. f. n.* many.

बहवो *for* बहवस् *nom. pl. of* बहु *m. f. n.* many.

बहु *nom. sin. n. of* बहु *m. f. n.* much.

बहु *ind.* much, exceedingly, 713.

बहुकल्याण *voc. sin. m.* O most noble; (*comp. of* बहु *cr.* much, *and* कल्याण noble.)

बहुतिथे *loc. sin. m. or n. of* बहुतिथ *m. f. n.* many, much.

बहुधा *ind.* in many ways, much, 723.

बहुपुष्पफलोपेतं COMPLEX COMP. 771; बहु *cr.* many, पुष्प *cr.* flowers, फल *cr.* fruits, उपेतं *acc. sin. n. of* उपेत *m. f. n.* possessed of, having.

बह्वबद्धप्रलापिनः COMPLEX COMP. 770; बहु *cr.* much, अबद्ध unmeaning, foolish, प्रलापिनः *gen. sin. m. of* प्रलापिन् *m. f. n.*

talking, speaking, *agt. of* लप् *with* प्र, 582. *a.*

बहुभिर् *for* बहुभिस् *ins. pl. m. of* बहु *m. f. n.* many, 3*d cl.* 110.

बहुमता *nom. sin. f.* much loved; (*comp. of* बहु much, *and* मत *m. f. n.* esteemed, loved, 545.)

बहुमतो *for* बहुमतस् *nom. sin. m.* much esteemed, much valued.

बहुमूलफलान्विताः COMPLEX COMP. 771; बहु *cr.* many, मूल *cr.* a root, फल *cr.* a fruit, अन्विताः *nom. pl. of* अन्वित *m. f. n.* provided with, furnished with.

बहुला *for* बहुलास् *acc. pl. f. of* बहुल many, *see* 821.

बहुलाः *nom. pl. m. of* बहुल *m. f. n.* many.

बहुविधैः *ins. pl. m. of* बहुविध *m. f. n.* of various kinds, of many sorts, 1*st cl.* 103.

बहुव्यालनिषेविते COMPLEX COMP. 771; बहु *cr.* many, व्याल *cr.* a snake (*also* a wild beast), निषेविते *loc. sin. of* निषेवित *m. f. n.* infested by, inhabited by; *past p. p. of rt* सेव् *with* नि, 70, 538.

बहुश *for* बहुशस् *ind.* very much.

बहुशः *for* बहुशस् *ind.* often, frequently.

बहुशो *for* बहुशस् *ind.* much, exceedingly, 725.

बहून् *acc. pl. m. of* बहु *m. f. n.* many, 3*d cl.* 110.

बान्धवान् *acc. pl. of* बान्धव *m.* a relation, a kinsman.

बालकं *acc. sin. of* बालक *m.* a son, a child, 1*st cl.* 103.

बालकौ *nom. du. m. of* बालक *m. f. n.* young.

बालभावे *loc. sin. of* बालभाव *m.* state of childhood, childhood; (*comp. of* बाल a child, *and* भाव state.)

बाला *nom. sin. of* बाला *f.* a girl, a maiden, 1*st cl.* 105.

बाला *nom. sin. f. of* बाल *m. f. n.* young.

बाला *for* बालास् *nom. pl. of* बाल *m.* a youth, a child.

बाल्याद् *abl. sin. of* बाल्य *n.* childhood, infancy.

बाहवः *nom. pl. of* बाहु *m.* an arm, 3*d cl.* 110.

बाह्वोर् *gen. du. of* बाहु *m.* an arm, 3*d cl.* 110.

बिभर्षि thou bearest or wearest, thou possessest; 2*d sin. pres. of rt* भृ 3*d cl.* 332, 583.

बुद्धिं *acc. sin. of* बुद्धि *f.* the mind, intellect, 2*d cl.* 112; बुद्धिं प्रकुरुष्व turn thy mind or thy thoughts, make up thy mind.

बुद्धिः *nom. sin. f.* the mind; बुद्धिं कृ to set the mind on, to direct the mind towards anything.

बुद्धिपूर्वाणि *nom. pl. n.* preceded by intention, intentionally, designedly; (*comp. of* बुद्धि mind, intention, *and* पूर्व preceded by, 777. *d.*)

बुद्धिर् *for* बुद्धिस् *nom. sin. f.* mind, 2*d cl.* 112.

बुद्धिसम्मितैः TAT. OR DEP. COMP. 743; बुद्धि *cr.* understanding, सम्मितैः *ins. pl. m. of* सम्मित *m. f. n.* corresponding to, conformable to, of equal measure with.

बुद्ध्या *ins. sin. of* बुद्धि *f.* mind, 2*d cl.* 112.

बुद्ध्याय *for* बुद्ध्या अय *by* 31.

बुद्ध्वा having become awake, having awaked; *past ind. p. of rt* बुध्.

बुध्यसे thou knowest; 2*d sin. pres. átm. of rt* बुध् 4*th cl.* 614.

बुध्येत he or she may know; 3*d sin. pot. átm. of rt* बुध् 4*th cl.* 614.

बुध्येथास् thou mayest know or learn, know thou; 2*d sin. pot. átm. of rt* बुध् 4*th cl.* 614.

बुबुधे he or she awoke; 3*d sin. perf. átm. of rt* बुध् 614.

ब्रवीमि I say, I tell; 1*st sin. pres. of rt* ब्रू 2*d cl.* 649.

ब्रह्मण्यः *nom. sin. m. of* ब्रह्मण्य *m. f. n.* religious, pious.

ब्रह्मण्यो *for* ब्रह्मण्यस् *nom. sin. m. of* ब्रह्मण्य *m. f. n.* religious, pious, 1*st cl.* 103.

ब्रह्मर्षिभ्यश् *abl. pl. of* ब्रह्मर्षि *m.* a Brahmarshi, a divine or Brahmanical saint, 2*d cl.* 110. According to the Vishṇu Puráṇa there are three kinds of Ṛishis or saints: 1.

Brahmarshis or saints who are sons of Brahmá, and dwell in his sphere, such as Maríći, Atri, Vaśishṭha, &c.; 2. Devarshis or semi-divine saints, dwelling in the sphere of the gods; 3. Rájarshis or royal saints, such as Viśvámitra and others who were kings and men of the second class, but who gained the rank of Ṛishi by the practice of austerities. Four other classes of Ṛishis are enumerated in the Amarakosha, viz. 1. Maharshis, great saints; 2. Paramarshis, most excellent saints; 3. Káṇḍarshis, saints who teach a particular Káṇḍa or section of the Vedas; 4. S'rutarshis or inspired saints.

ब्रह्मर्षिर् *for* ब्रह्मर्षिस् *nom. sin. of* ब्रह्मर्षि *m.* a divine saint.

ब्राह्मणस् *nom. sin. m.* a Bráhman or man of the first class; *see note under* विशाम्पते.

ब्राह्मणा *for* ब्राह्मणास् *nom. pl. of* ब्राह्मण *m.* a Bráhman.

ब्राह्मणांश् *for* ब्राह्मणान् (53) *acc. pl. of* ब्राह्मण *m.* a Bráhman.

ब्राह्मणाः *nom. pl. of* ब्राह्मण *m.* a Bráhman.

ब्राह्मणान् *acc. pl. of* ब्राह्मण *m.* a Bráhman.

ब्राह्मणाश् *for* ब्राह्मणास् *nom. pl. of* ब्राह्मण *m.* a Bráhman.

ब्राह्मणास् *nom. pl. of* ब्राह्मण *m.* a Bráhman.

ब्राह्मणेन *ins. sin. of* ब्राह्मण *m.* a Bráhman.

ब्राह्मणैर् *ins. pl. of* ब्राह्मण *m.* a Bráhman.

ब्राह्मणो *nom. sin. of* ब्राह्मण *m.* a Bráhman.

ब्रुवति *loc. sin. m. of* ब्रुवत् *m. f. n.* speaking; *pres. p. of rt* ब्रू 524, 649.

ब्रुवतो *acc. pl. m. of* ब्रुवत् *m. f. n.* saying; *pres. p. of rt* ब्रू.

ब्रुवन् *nom. sin. m. of* ब्रुवत् *m. f. n.* saying; *pres. p. of rt* ब्रू.

ब्रुवन्तं *acc. sin. m. of* ब्रुवत् *m. f. n.* saying; speaking; *pres. p. par. of rt* ब्रू 649, 524.

ब्रुवन्त्यास् *gen. sin. f. of* ब्रुवत् *m. f. n.* speaking, saying. *The more usual feminine would be* ब्रुवती, *see* 141. *c.*

ब्रुवाणस् *nom. sin. m. of* ब्रुवाण *m. f. n.* speaking; *pres. p. átm. of rt* ब्रू 526.

ब्रुवाणान् *acc. pl. m. of* ब्रुवाण *m. f. n.* speaking; *pres. p. átm. of rt* ब्रू 526.

ब्रूयात् he may say; *3d sin. pot. of rt* ब्रू. *See* 649.

ब्रूयाश् *for* ब्रूयास् say thou, thou mayest say; *2d sin. pot. of rt* ब्रू *2d cl.* 649.

ब्रूयास्त may ye speak, speak ye; *2d pl. benedictive of rt* ब्रू 442.

ब्रूहि tell thou, say, speak; *2d sin. imp. of rt* ब्रू *2d cl.* 649.

भ.

भक्ता *nom. sin. f. of* भक्त *m. f. n.* devoted to, attached to, faithful.

भक्ताहम् *for* भक्ता अहम् *by* 31.

भक्तिं *acc. sin. of* भक्ति *f.* devotion, *2d cl.* 112.

भक्षयति he devours; *3d sin. pres. of rt* भक्ष् *10th cl.* 643. *b. In* Book XII. 20 *the present may have a future sense,* he will devour; *see* 873.

भक्षयत्येष *for* भक्षयति एष *by* 34.

भक्ष्यो *for* भक्ष्यस् *nom. sin. of* भक्ष्य *m. f. n.* to be eaten, eatable.

भगवंस् *for* भगवन् *voc. sin. of* भगवत् *m. f. n.* venerable, holy, 53.

भगवताम् *gen. pl. of* भगवत् *m. f. n.* reverend, venerable.

भगवन् *for* भगवन् *voc. sin. of* भगवत् *m. f. n.* venerable, holy, 52.

भगिनीम् *acc. sin. of* भगिनी *f.* a sister.

भगिन्या *for* भगिन्यास् *gen. sin. of* भगिनी *f.* a sister.

भजमानाम् *acc. sin. f. of* भजमान *m. f. n.* courting, waiting on; *pres. p. átm. of rt* भज् 526.

भजसि thou honourest; *2d sin. pres. of rt* भज् *1st cl.* 261.

भद्रं *ind.* good, well, health. *Exclam.* भद्रं ते May it be well with thee! Health to thee! Hail! Good luck!

भद्रे O good lady! *voc. sin. f. of* भद्र *m. f. n.* good, 1*st cl.* 105.

भयं *nom. sin. n.* fear, danger, cause of fear.

भयकर्तारं TAT. OR DEP. COMP. 743; भय *cr.* fear, कर्तारं *acc. sin. of* कर्तृ *m.* a causer, 4*th cl.* 127.

भयङ्करी *nom. sin. f. of* भयङ्कर *m. f. n.* causing fear, formidable, frightful; (*comp. of* भय fear, *and* कर causing, 739. *c.*)

भयविह्वला TAT. OR DEP. COMP. 740; भय *cr.* fear, विह्वला *nom. sin. f.* agitated.

भयशोकसमाविष्टा COMPLEX COMP. 771; भय *cr.* fear, शोक *cr.* sorrow, समाविष्टा *nom. sin. f. of* समाविष्ट *m. f. n.* affected by, filled with.

भयसन्त्रस्तमानसा COMPLEX COMP. 771; भय *cr.* fear, सन्त्रस्त *cr.* terrified, scared, मानसा *nom. sin. f. from* मानस *n.* the mind, 108.

भयात् *abl. sin. of* भय *n.* fear.

भयाद् *abl. sin. of* भय *n.* fear.

भयाबाधं *acc. sin. m.* undisturbed by fear, unexposed to danger; (*comp. of* भय *cr.* fear, *and* अबाध undisturbed, 726, 740.)

भयार्तं *acc. sin. m. of* भयार्त *m. f. n.* frightened, terrified; (*comp. of* भय fear, *and* आर्त afflicted, 542.)

भरतश्रेष्ठ *voc. sin. m.* O best of the descendants of Bharata; *see note under* भारत.

भरस्व support thou, maintain thou, take thou into (thy) service; 2*d sin. imp. átm. of rt* भृ 1*st cl.* 261.

भर्तव्या *nom. sin. f. of* भर्तव्य *m. f. n.* to be supported; *fut. pass. p. of rt* भृ 569.

भर्ता *nom. sin. of* भर्तृ *m.* a husband, 4*th cl.* 127.

भर्तारं *acc. sin. of* भर्तृ *m.* a husband, 4*th cl.* 127.

भर्तुः *gen. or abl. sin. of* भर्तृ *m.* a husband.

भर्तुर् *gen. or abl. sin. of* भर्तृ *m.* a husband.

भर्तृदर्शनकांक्षया TAT. OR DEP. COMP. 745; भर्तृ *cr.* husband, दर्शन *cr.* seeing, कांक्षया *ins. sin. of* कांक्षा *f.* desire.

भर्तृदर्शनलालसाम् BAH. OR REL. COMP. 761; भर्तृ *cr.* husband, दर्शन *cr.* seeing, sight, लालसां *acc. sin. f. of* लालसा *f.* longing, eager desire.

भर्तृभिश् *ins. pl. of* भर्तृ *m.* a husband.

भर्तृराज्यापहरणं TAT. OR DEP. COMP. 745; भर्तृ *cr.* a husband, राज्य *cr.* kingdom, अपहरणं *nom. sin. n.* seizure, taking away.

भर्तृव्यसनपीडिता TAT. OR DEP. COMP. 745; भर्तृ *cr.* a husband, व्यसन *cr.* calamity, पीडिता *nom. sin. f.* pained, afflicted, grieved.

भर्तृशोकपरा TAT. OR DEP. COMP. 745; भर्तृ *cr.* husband, शोक *cr.* grief, परा *nom. sin. f. of* पर absorbed, wholly engrossed.

भर्तृशोकपरीताङ्गी COMPLEX COMP. 771; भर्तृ *cr.* a husband, शोक *cr.* grief, परीत *cr.* affected by, अङ्गी *nom. sin. f. from* अङ्ग *n.* a limb, 1*st cl.* 108.

भर्तृशोकाभिपीडिता TAT. OR DEP. COMP. 745; भर्तृ *cr.* a husband, शोक *cr.* sorrow, अभिपीडिता *nom. sin. f. of* अभिपीडित *m. f. n.* afflicted; *past p. p. of rt* पीड् *with* अभि, 538.

भर्तृहीनाम् *acc. sin. f.* deserted by her husband, TAT. OR DEP. COMP. 740; भर्तृ *cr.* a husband, हीनाम् *acc. sin. f. of* हीन *m. f. n.* abandoned, quitted.

भर्त्रा *ins. sin. of* भर्तृ *m.* a husband.

भव be thou, become thou; 2*d sin. imp. of rt* भू 585.

भवतः of you, of your highness; *gen. sin. of* भवत् 233.

भवताम् *gen. pl. of* भवत् you, your honour, 233.

भवती *nom. sin. f.* your ladyship, her ladyship.

भवतु let (her) be; 3*d sin. imp. of rt* भू 585.

भवत्सु *loc. pl. of* भवत् *pron.* you, your honour, 233.

भवद्भिर् *for* भवद्भिस् by you, by your honours; *ins. pl. of* भवत् 233.

भवनं *acc. sin. of* भवन *n.* a mansion, a palace, a residence, 1*st cl.* 104.

भवन्तः *for* **भवन्तस्** your honours; *nom. pl. of* **भवत्** *m.*, 233.

भवन्तस् your honours; *nom. pl. of* **भवत्** *m.*, 233.

भवान् *nom. sin. of* **भवत्** *m.* your honour, your highness; *honorific pronoun*, 233.

भवाशोक *for* **भव अशोक** *by* 31.

भवितव्यं it is to be; *nom. sin. n. of* **भवितव्य** *fut. pass. p. of rt* **भू** 569, *see* 902. *a.*

भविता he, she or it will be or become; 3*d sin.* 1*st fut. of rt* **भू** 585.

भवितासि thou wilt be; 2*d sin.* 1*st fut. of rt* **भू** 585.

भवितास्येक *for* **भवितासि एकस्** *by* 34 *and* 66.

भवितेति *for* **भविता इति** *by* 32.

भविष्यति he will be, there will be; 3*d sin.* 2*d fut. of rt* **भू** 585.

भविष्यसि thou wilt be; 2*d sin.* 2*d fut. of rt* **भू**.

भविष्यामः we shall be; 1*st pl.* 2*d fut. of rt* **भू**.

भविष्यामि I shall exist, I shall or will be; 1*st sin.* 2*d fut. of rt* **भू** 585. In Book XXIV. 14 Damayantí uses the word **भविष्यामि** with reference to what Nala had said at Book V. 32.

भविष्याम्यद्याहम् *for* **भविष्यामि अद्य अहम्** *by* 34 *and* 31.

भवेज् *for* **भवेत्** he or she may be, may there be, 48.

भवेत् he or she may be, may there be; 3*d sin. pot. of rt* **भू** 585.

भवेत्तु *for* **भवेत् तु**, *q. q. v. v.*

भवेथा *for* **भवेथास्** thou mayest become, thou shouldest become; 2*d sin. pot. átm. of rt* **भू** 1*st cl.* 586.

भवेद् *for* **भवेत्** he or she may be, may there be.

भवेन् *for* **भवेत्** he may be, may there be, 47.

भवेयुर् *for* **भवेयुस्** they may be; 3*d pl. pot. of rt* **भू** 585.

भागधेयं *nom. sin. of* **भागधेय** *n.* destiny, fortune, 1*st cl.* 104.

भाङ्गासुरिं *acc. sin. of* **भाङ्गासुरि** *m.* the son of Bhangásura.

भाङ्गासुरिनृपाज्ञया TAT. OR DEP. COMP. 745; **भाङ्गासुरि** *cr.* the son of Bhangásura, **नृप** *cr.* a king, **आज्ञया** *ins. sin. of* **आज्ञा** *f.* order, command.

भाङ्गासुरिर् *for* **भाङ्गासुरिस्** *nom. sin. of* **भाङ्गासुरि** *m.* the son of Bhangásura, *see* 81. VI.

भाति he, she or it shines; 3*d sin. pres. of rt* **भा** 2*d cl.* 307.

भारत *voc. sin. of* **भारत** *m.* a descendant of king Bharata, a name applied to Yudhishṭhira, to whom the story of Nala is related by the sage Vṛihadaśva. Bharata was the son of Dushyanta and Śakuntalá. His empire extended over a great part of India, whence India is called Bhárata-varsha.

भारतीं *acc. sin. f. of* **भारती** *f.* speech.

भार्यया *ins. sin. of* **भार्या** *f.* a wife, 1*st cl.* 105.

भार्या *f.* a wife, 1*st cl.* 105.

भार्याम् *acc. sin. of* **भार्या** *f.* a wife, 1*st cl.* 105.

भार्यासमं ANOM. COMP. 777; **भार्या** *cr.* a wife, **समं** *nom. sin. n. of* **सम** *m. f. n.* equal to.

भार्येयं *for* **भार्या इयं** *by* 32.

भावं *acc. sin. of* **भाव** *m.* state, property, 1*st cl.* 103.

भावः *nom. sin. of* **भाव** *m.* mind, soul.

भाविनि O lady! O noble lady! *voc. sin. of* **भाविनी** *f.*, 1*st cl.* 106.

भाविनी *nom. sin. f.* a lady, a noble lady.

भाविनी *nom. sin. f. of* **भाविन्** *m. f. n.* illustrious.

भावो *for* **भावस्** *nom. sin. of* **भाव** *m.* existence.

भाषसे thou speakest; 2*d sin. pres. átm.*

भाष्यमाणो *nom. sin. m. of* **भाष्यमाण** *m. f. n.* being addressed; *pres. p. of rt* **भाष्** to speak, *in pass.* 528.

भासि thou shinest; 2*d sin. pres. of rt* **भा** 2*d cl.* 307.

भिषजाम् *gen. pl. of* भिषज् *m.* a physician, *8th cl.* 176.

भीतः *nom. sin. of* भीत *m. f. n.* terrified, alarmed.

भीता *nom. sin. f. of* भीत *m. f. n.* terrified; *past p. p. of rt* भी 532.

भीतां *acc. sin. f. of* भीत *m. f. n.* terrified, alarmed.

भीताः *nom. pl. m. of* भीत *m. f. n.* terrified, alarmed.

भीतो *for* भीतस् *nom. sin. m. of* भीत *m. f. n.* terrified, alarmed.

भीम *m.* BHÍMA, a proper name; *m. f. n.* terrible, terrific.

भीमः *for* भीमस् *nom. sin. of* भीम *m.* Bhíma.

भीमनन्दिनीम् TAT. OR DEP. COMP. 743; भीम *cr.* Bhíma, नन्दिनीम् *acc. sin. of* नन्दिनी *f.* a daughter.

भीमपराक्रमः *nom. sin. m. See next.*

भीमपराक्रमम् BAH. OR REL. COMP. 761; भीम *cr.* terrible, formidable, पराक्रमम् *acc. sin. m.* valour, might.

भीमपराक्रमान् *acc. pl. See last.*

भीमपुत्रिकाम् TAT. OR DEP. COMP. 743; भीम *cr.* Bhíma, पुत्रिकाम् *acc. sin. of* पुत्रिका *f.* a daughter, a favourite daughter.

भीमरूपांश् *for* भीमरूपान् (53) BAH. OR REL. COMP. 766; भीम *cr.* terrific, terrible, रूपान् *acc. pl. m. from* रूप *n.* form, *1st cl.* 108.

भीमवचनाद् TAT. OR DEP. COMP. 743; भीम *cr.* Bhíma, वचनाद् *for* वचनात् *abl. sin. of* वचन *n.* order, command.

भीमशासनात् TAT. OR DEP. COMP. 743; भीम *cr.* Bhíma, शासनात् *abl. sin. of* शासन *n.* order, summons, invitation, *1st cl.* 104.

भीमसुता *nom. sin. f.* the daughter of Bhíma, *i. e.* Damayantí.

भीमस्य *gen. sin. of* भीम *m.* Bhíma, *q. v.*

भीमान् *acc. pl. m. of* भीम *m. f. n.* terrible.

भीमाय *dat. sin. of* भीम *m.* Bhíma, *q. v.*

भीमे *loc. sin. of* भीम *m.* Bhíma, *q. v.*

भीमो *for* भीमस् *nom. sin. of* भीम *m.* Bhíma, *q. v.*

भीरु O timid one; *voc. sin. of* भीरु *f.* (125) *from* भीरु *m. f. n.* timid.

भीष्मं *acc. sin. m.* Bhíshma, great-uncle to Duryodhana, and leader of the Kuru army.

भुंक्ष्व enjoy thou; *2d sin. imp. átm. of rt* भुज् *7th cl.* 346, 668. *a.*

भुजगं *acc. sin. of* भुजग *m.* a snake, a serpent.

भुजङ्गं *acc. sin. of* भुजङ्ग *m.* a serpent.

भुजिष्यां *acc. sin. of* भुजिष्या *f.* a slave-girl, a maid-servant, a hand-maid.

भुञ्जीय I should eat, I should enjoy; *1st sin. pot. átm. of rt* भुज् *7th cl.*

भुञ्जीयां I may eat; *1st sin. pot. of rt* भुज् *7th cl.* 668. *a.*

भुवनं *acc. sin. of* भुवन *n.* the world.

भुवि *loc. sin. of* भू *f.* the earth, the ground, 125. *a.*

भूतग्रामाः TAT. OR DEP. COMP. 743; भूत *n.* a living being, a spirit, ग्रामाः *nom. pl. of* ग्राम *m.* a multitude, a collection.

भूतले *loc. sin. of* भूतल *n.* the ground, the earth, *1st cl.* 104; (*lit.* the surface of the earth, *from* भू *cr.* the earth, *and* तल *n.* surface, 743.)

भूतसाक्षी TAT. OR DEP. COMP. 743; भूत *cr.* a being, a spirit, साक्षी *nom. sin. of* साक्षिन् *m.* a witness, 159. With reference to Book XXIV. 32, compare the law of ordeal mentioned Asiatic Researches, vol. i. p. 402: 'On the trial by fire, let both hands of the accused be rubbed with rice in the husk, and well examined; then let seven leaves of the Aśvattha (the religious fig-tree) be placed on them, and bound with seven threads, saying these words; Thou, O fire, pervadest all beings; O cause of purity, who givest evidence of virtue and of sin, declare the truth in this my hand.'

भूतस्य *gen. sin. of* भूत *m. n.* a living being, a spirit, *1st cl.* 103.

भूतानि *nom. or acc. pl. of* भूत *n.* a being, a human being, a creature, a spirit.

भूत्वा having been, having become; *past ind. p. of rt* भू 585.

भूमाव् *for* भूमौ *loc. sin. of* भूमि *f.* the earth.

भूमिं *acc. sin. of* भूमि *f.* land, region.

भूमिप *voc. sin.* O king.

भूमिपते O king! *lit.* O lord of the earth! (भूमि *cr.* the earth, पते *voc. of* पति lord, 121, 743.)

भूमिष्ठो *for* भूमिष्ठस् *nom. sin. m. of* भूमिष्ठ *m. f. n.* standing on the ground; (*comp. of* भूमि *cr.* the ground, *and* ष्ठ (*for* स्थ *by* 70) *m. f. n.* standing, 580, 744.)

भूमौ *loc. sin. of* भूमि *f.* the ground, *2d cl.* 112.

भूय *for* भूयस् *ind.* again, again and again.

भूयः *for* भूयस् *ind.* again.

भूयस् *ind.* again, still more, more and more.

भूयो *for* भूयस् *ind.* again, still more, further on.

भूरिदक्षिणैः Bah. or Rel. comp. 766; भूरि *cr.* many, abundant, दक्षिणैः *ins. pl. m. from* दक्षिणा *f.* a gift, *1st cl.* 108.

भूषणं *nom. sin. n.* an ornament.

भूषणानि *acc. pl. of* भूषण *n.* an ornament, *1st cl.* 104.

भूषणैर् *for* भूषणैस् *ins. pl. of* भूषण *n.* an ornament, *1st cl.* 104.

भृतिम् *acc. sin. of* भृति *f.* hire, wages, *2d cl.* 112.

भृशं *ind.* exceedingly, very much, 713.

भृशदारुणम् *acc. sin. n.* very terrible; (*comp. of* भृश *cr.* exceedingly, *and* दारुण *m. f. n.* terrible.)

भृशदुःखिता *nom. sin. f.* very much afflicted; (*comp. of* भृश exceedingly, *and* दुःखित pained.)

भृशपीडितः *nom. sin. m.* very much afflicted; (*comp. of* भृश excessively, *and* पीडित pained.)

भेषजं *nom. sin. of* भेषज *n.* a medicine, a remedy.

भैक्ष्यम् *acc. sin. n.* mendicity, beggary, begging.

भैमि *voc. sin. f. of* भैमी *f.* Damayantí, *1st cl.* 106.

भैमी *nom. sin. f.* daughter of Bhíma, *i. e.* Damayantí.

भैमीं *acc. sin. of* भैमी *f.* Damayantí.

भैम्या *ins. sin. of* भैमी *f.* Damayantí.

भैर् *for* भैषीर् *2d sin. aor. of rt* भी *3d cl.* 666; मा भैर् fear not, *see* 889.

भो भो *interj.* Ho! Hark! Listen!

भोक्तुं to eat, to suffer, to possess; *inf. of rt* भुज् 459.

भोक्ष्यसे thou shalt enjoy, thou shalt possess; *2d sin. 2d fut. átm. of rt* भुज्.

भोगवतीम् *acc. sin. of* भोगवती *f.* the capital of the Nágas or serpents in the subterranean world, *1st cl.* 106.

भोगाः *nom. pl. m.* enjoyments. *See next.*

भोगान् *acc. pl. of* भोग *m.* enjoyment, that which is enjoyed, a feast, a banquet.

भोगैर् *ins. pl. of* भोग *m.* enjoyment.

भोजनीयम् *nom. sin. n.* food.

भोजने *loc. sin. of* भोजन *n.* food; (*in* Book XXII. 12 the dressing of food.)

भ्रंशयिष्यामि I will cause to fall; *1st sin. 2d fut. of rt* भ्रंश् *in caus.* 481.

भ्रमति he wanders, he or it whirls or turns round; *3d sin. pres. of rt* भ्रम् *1st cl.* 261.

भ्रमन्ति they wander about; *3d pl. pres. of rt* भ्रम् *1st cl.* 261.

भ्रष्टं *acc. sin. n. of* भ्रष्ट *m. f. n.* fallen; *past p. p. of rt* भ्रंश् 544.

भ्रष्टः *nom. sin. m. of* भ्रष्ट *m. f. n.* fallen.

भ्रष्टराज्यं Bah. or Rel. comp. 767; भ्रष्ट *cr.* fallen from, deprived of, राज्यं *acc. sin. m. from* राज्य *n.* a kingdom.

भ्रष्टा *nom. sin. f. of* भ्रष्ट *m. f. n.* fallen, separated from; *past p. p. of rt* भ्रंश् 544.

भ्राजमान *for* भ्राजमानस् *nom. sin. of* भ्राजमान *m. f. n.* shining; *pres. p. átm. of rt* भ्राज् 526.

भ्राजमानं *acc. sin. of* **भ्राजमान** *m. f. n.* shining; *pres. p. átm. from rt* **भ्राज्** *1st cl.* 526.

भ्राजमानो *for* **भ्राजमानस्** *nom. sin. m. of* **भ्राजमान** *m. f. n.* shining, brilliant; *pres. p. átm. of rt* **भ्राज्** 526.

भ्रातरं *acc. sin. of* **भ्रातृ** *m.* a brother.

भ्रातरश् *nom. pl. of* **भ्रातृ** *m.* a brother.

भ्राता *nom. sin. of* **भ्रातृ** *m.* a brother, *4th cl.* 127.

भ्रातुर् *for* **भ्रातुस्** of a brother. *See next.*

भ्रातुस् *gen. sin. of* **भ्रातृ** *m.* a brother, *4th cl.* 128.

भ्रातॄन् *acc. pl. of* **भ्रातृ** *m.* a brother.

भ्रात्रा *ins. sin. of* **भ्रातृ** *m.* a brother.

भ्रुवोर् *gen. du. of* **भ्रू** *f.* an eye-brow, 125. *a.*

म.

मंस्यति he or she will think of; *3d sin. 2d fut. par. of rt* **मन्** *4th cl.* 617. *This verb is properly conjugated in the átmane-pada.*

मंस्यन्ते they will imagine; *3d pl. 2d fut. átm. of rt* **मन्** to think, to suppose.

मघवन् *voc. sin. of* **मघवन्**. *See next.*

मघवा *nom. sin. of* **मघवन्** a name of Indra, 155.

मघवान् *nom. sin. of* **मघवन्** a name of Indra. *Note, that the nom. of this noun is either* **मघवा** *or* **मघवान्**. *In the latter case it is declined like a noun in* **वत्**.

मङ्गलेन *ins. sin. of* **मङ्गल** *n.* good fortune.

मङ्गलेनाशु *for* **मङ्गलेन आशु** *by* 31.

मच्छरीरे *loc. sin. n.* in my body; (*from* **मत्** 218, *and* **शरीर** body, 49, 743.)

मज्जेद् let him sink, he may be plunged, *6th cl.* 633.

मणिभद्रः *nom. sin. m.* Maṇi-bhadra, the king of the Yakshas, the tutelary deity of travellers and merchants, probably another name for Kuvera the god of wealth.

मणिभद्रो *nom. sin. m.* Maṇi-bhadra.

मण्डनार्हाम् *acc. sin. f.* worthy of ornaments; (*comp. of* **मण्डन** an ornament, *and* **अर्ह** worthy.)

मतं *nom. sin. n. of* **मत** *m. f. n.* approved; *past p. p. of rt* **मन्** 545.

मतिं *acc. sin. of* **मति** *f.* an intention, design, 112.

मतिः *nom. sin. f.* purpose, determination.

मतिभेदो *nom. sin. m.* difference of opinion; (*comp. of* **मति** *cr.* opinion, *and* **भेद** difference, 743.)

मतिर् *for* **मतिस्** *nom. sin. m.* opinion.

मत्कृतात् *abl. sin. m.* made (uttered) by me; (*comp. of* **मत्** 218, *and* **कृत** made.)

मत्कृते on my account; (*from* **मत्** 218, *and* **कृते** for the sake of, 731.)

मत्तवारणविक्रमः BAH. OR REL. COMP. 761; **मत्त** *cr.* mad, **वारण** *cr.* an elephant, **विक्रमः** *nom. sin. m.* strength, might.

मत्तो *for* **मत्तस्** *ind.* from me; (**मत्** 218, *with affix* **तस्** 719.)

मत्प्रसादान् *for* **मत्प्रसादात्** *abl. sin.* through the favour of me, through my favour.

मत्प्रसूतम् TAT. OR DEP. COMP. 742; **मत्** from me, 218, **प्रसूतम्** *nom. sin. n. of* **प्रसूत** *m. f. n.* produced.

मत्वा having considered, having imagined; *past ind. p. of rt* **मन्**.

मत्सकाशे in my presence; (*comp. of* **मत्** 218, *and* **सकाशे**, *see* 716.)

मत्समः *nom. sin. m.* equal to me; (*comp. of* **मत्** 218, *and* **सम** equal.)

मत्समक्षं in the presence of me, in my sight; (*comp. of* **मत्** *and* **समक्षं** *see* 731.)

मत्समो *nom. sin. m.* like to me, equal to me; (*comp. of* **मत्** 218, *and* **सम** *m. f. n.* equal.)

मदप्रस्रवणाविलाम् TAT. OR DEP. COMP. 745; **मद** *cr.* the juice that flows from an elephant's temples (when in rut), **प्रस्रवण** *cr.* oozing, trickling, **आविलाम्** *acc. sin. f. of* **आविल** *m. f. n.* turbid. On each side of the elephant's temples there is an aperture about the size of a pin's head, whence in the season of rut a juice exudes, which is called *mada* or *dána*. Whilst it flows the elephant is called *matta*, and at other times *nirmada*. The fragrance of this fluid is frequently alluded to in Hindú poetry. See Wilson's Megha-dúta, l. 132. 'Its scent is compared to the odour of the sweetest flowers, and is supposed to deceive and attract the bees.'

मदीयेन *ins. sin. of* मदीय *m. f. n.* my, mine, 231.

मदोत्कटाः *nom. pl. m.* furious with passion or heat; (*comp. of* मद *cr.* passion, *and* उत्कट furious.)

मद्गृहे *loc. sin.* in my house; (*comp. of* मत् 218, *and* गृह *q. v.*)

मद्भक्ता devoted to me; (*from* मद् 218, *and* भक्ता *nom. sin. f. of* भक्त *m. f. n.* devoted.)

मद्भक्तेयम् *for* मद्भक्ता इयं *by* 32.

मद्भाग्यसङ्क्षयात् TAT. OR DEP. COMP. 745; मद् *for* मत् *cr.* my, 218, भाग्य *cr.* fortune, संक्षयात् *abl. sin. of* संक्षय *m.* destruction, ruin, decay, decline, consumption.

मद्वचः *acc. sin. n.* my words; (*comp. of* मत् 218, *and* वचस् *n.* speech, *7th cl.* 164.)

मद्विहीना *nom. sin. f.* separated from me; (*from* मद् 218, *and* विहीना *nom. sin. f. of* विहीन *m. f. n.*)

मधुरभाषिणीं *acc. sin. f.* sweetly speaking; (*from* मधुर *cr.* sweet, *and* भाषिणीं *acc. sin. f. of* भाषिन् speaking, 582. *a.*)

मधुरां *acc. sin. f. of* मधुर *m. f. n.* sweet, *1st cl.* 187.

मधुसूदनः *nom. sin. m.* slayer of (the demon) Madhu, a name of Vishṇu.

मध्यं *acc. sin. of* मध्य *n.* the middle, the midst.

मध्यमकक्षायां KARM. OR DES. COMP. 755; मध्यम *cr.* middle, कक्षायां *loc. sin. of* कक्षा *f.* an enclosure, court-yard.

मध्ये *ind.* in the midst, in the middle, 716.

मनः *for* मनस् *nom. or acc. sin. n.* the mind, heart, 164.

मनस् *n.* the mind, the heart, *7th cl.* 164.

मनसस् *gen. sin. of* मनस् *n.* the mind, 164.

मनसा *ins. sin. of* मनस् *n.* mind, thought; (मनसाऽपि even in thought.)

मनसापि *for* मनसा अपि *by* 31.

मनांसि *acc. pl. of* मनस् *n.* the mind, *7th cl.* 164.

मनुः *nom. sin. of* मनु *m.* name of a great legislator, the holy, mythological ancestor of the Hindús, *3d cl.* 110. In the Indian version of the Deluge, Manu is the survivor of the human race, and the second ancestor of mankind. The first Manu is named Svayambhuva or Sváyambhuva, sprung from Brahmá the self-existing. From him came six descendants or other Manus, each giving birth to a race of his own. The Hindús firmly believe their great code of laws to have been promulgated in the beginning of time by Manu, whom they consider not only the oldest, but the noblest of legislators.

मनुजव्याघ्र *voc. sin.* O most illustrious of men! *see* 758.

मनुजा *for* मनुजास् *nom. pl. of* मनुज *m.* a man.

मनुजाः *nom. pl. of* मनुज *m.* a man.

मनुजात्मजे TAT. OR DEP. COMP. 743; मनुज *cr.* a man, आत्मजे *voc. sin. of* आत्मजा *f.* a daughter, *1st cl.* 105.

मनुजाधिप *voc. sin. m.* O king of men; (*comp. of* मनुज *cr.* a man, *and* अधिप *q. v.*)

मनुजाधिपतेः TAT. OR DEP. COMP. 743; मनुज *cr.* a man, अधिपतेः *gen. sin. of* अधिपति *m.* a sovereign, *2d cl.* 110.

मनुजेन्द्राणां TAT. OR DEP. COMP. 743; मनुज *cr.* a man, इन्द्राणां *gen. pl. of* इन्द्र *m.* chief, *1st cl.* 103.

मनुष्यं *acc. sin. of* मनुष्य *m.* a man, *1st cl.* 103.

मनुष्याणां *gen. pl. of* मनुष्य *m.* a man.

मनुष्येन्द्र *voc. sin. m.* O chief of men; (*comp. of* मनुष्य a man, *and* इन्द्र chief.)

मनो *for* मनस् *nom. or acc. sin. of* मनस् *n.* the mind, *7th cl.* 164.

मनोजवान् swift as thought; (*comp. of* मनस् *for* मनो *cr.* mind, thought, जवान् *acc. pl. of* जव *m.* speed, 761.)

मनोभिस् *ins. pl. of* मनस् *n.* the mind, the heart, *7th cl.* 164.

मनोविशुद्धिम् TAT. OR DEP. COMP. 743; मनस् *for* मनो *cr.* mind, विशुद्धिम् *acc. sin. of* विशुद्धि *f.* purity, 2*d cl.* 112.

मनोहरैः *ins. pl. n. of* मनोहर *m. f. n.* charming, pleasant; (*lit.* mind-captivating, *from* मनस् 164, *and* हर *noun of agency of rt* हृ 580.)

मनोहारि *acc. sin. n.* enchanting the soul; (*comp. of* मनो *for* मनस् *cr.* the mind, *and* हारि *acc. sin. n. from* हारिन् *m. f. n.* a seizer, captivating, *agt. of rt* हृ 582. *a.*)

मन्त्रिणः *nom. pl. of* मन्त्रिन् *m.* a minister, 6*th cl.* 159.

मन्त्रिभिः *ins. pl. of* मन्त्रिन् *m.* a minister, a counsellor of state, 6*th cl.* 159.

मन्द *for* मन्दस् *nom. sin. m.* foolish, vile, wicked.

मन्दं *ind.* slightly, little; slightingly, disparagingly, 713.

मन्दप्रज्ञस्य BAH. OR REL. COMP. 761; मन्द *cr.* dull, stupid, प्रज्ञस्य *gen. sin. of* प्रज्ञ *m. from* प्रज्ञा *f.* understanding, 108.

मन्दप्रज्ञेन BAH. OR REL. COMP. 761; मन्द *cr.* foolish, dull, प्रज्ञेन *ins. sin. m. from* प्रज्ञा *f.* understanding, 108.

मन्दभाग्याद् KARM. OR DES. COMP. 755; मन्द *cr.* evil, bad, भाग्याद् *for* भाग्यात् *abl. sin. of* भाग्य *n.* fate, luck.

मन्दस्य *gen. sin. m. of* मन्द *m. f. n.* wicked, good for nothing.

मन्दात्मा BAH. OR REL. COMP. 761; मन्द *cr.* foolish, wicked, आत्मा *nom. sin. of* आत्मन् mind, soul, 6*th cl.* 147.

मन्दो *for* मन्दस् *nom. sin. m.* foolish, wicked.

मन्मथं *acc. sin. of* मन्मथ *m.* love, 1*st cl.* 103; *see note under* कन्दर्प.

मन्मथस्य *gen. sin. of* मन्मथ *m.* the god of love, 1*st cl.* 103; *see last.*

मन्यते he imagines, he thinks; 3*d sin. pres. átm. of rt* मन् 4*th cl.*

मन्यसे thou thinkest, thou thinkest of, thou thinkest (fit); 2*d sin. pres. átm. of rt* मन् 4*th cl.* 684, 617.

मन्युना *ins. sin. of* मन्यु *m.* grief, sorrow, anger, 3*d cl.* 110.

मन्युपरीतेन TAT. OR DEP. COMP. 740; मन्यु *cr.* anger, परीतेन *ins. sin. of* परीत *m. f. n.* filled with, affected by.

मन्ये I believe, I think, I imagine; 1*st sin. pres. átm. of rt* मन् 4*th cl.* 617.

मम of me; *gen. sin. of* मत् *or* अस्मत्, *q. v.*

ममर्दुः they crushed, they trampled down; 3*d pl. perf. of rt* मृद्; *but* ममृदुः *is the usual form, see* 364.

ममाचक्ष्व *for* मम आचक्ष्व *by* 31.

ममाद्यायं *for* मम अद्य अयं *by* 31.

ममान्तिकम् *for* मम अन्तिकम् *by* 31.

ममापि *for* मम अपि *by* 31.

ममाभीक्ष्णम् *for* मम अभीक्ष्णम् *by* 31.

ममास्ति *for* मम अस्ति *by* 31.

ममृदे he rubbed, he bruised or crushed; 3*d sin. perf. átm. of rt* मृद् 364.

ममैष *for* मम एष *by* 33.

ममोपरि *for* मम उपरि *by* 32.

मरणं *nom. sin. of* मरण *n.* death.

मरणाद् *abl. sin. of* मरण *n.* death.

मर्त्यं *acc. sin. of* मर्त्य *m.* a mortal.

मर्त्यानाम् *gen. pl. of* मर्त्य *m.* a mortal, 103.

मर्त्यो *for* मर्त्यस् *nom. sin. of* मर्त्य *m.* a mortal, 1*st cl.* 103.

मया by me; *ins. sin. of* अस्मत् 218.

मयासकृत् *for* मया असकृत् *by* 31.

मयि in me; *loc. sin. of* अस्मत् 218. *At* Books XIII. 65, XV. 7, *it denotes* with me or at my house.

मलं *acc. sin. of* मल *n.* dust, dirt.

मलदिग्धाङ्गीम् COMPLEX COMP. 771; मल *cr.* mire, dust, दिग्ध *cr.* smeared, defiled, अङ्गीम् *acc. sin. f. from* अङ्ग *n.* a limb, the body, 108.

मलपङ्कानुलिप्ताङ्गीम् COMPLEX COMP. 771; मल *cr.* dirt, पङ्क *cr.* mud, mire, अनुलिप्त *cr.* besmeared, अङ्गीम् *acc. sin. of* अङ्गी *f. from* अङ्ग *n.* a limb, 108.

मलपङ्किनी *nom. sin. f.* covered with dust and mire; (*from* **मल** *cr.* dirt, *and* **पङ्किन्** muddy, 159.)

मलिनः *nom. sin. m. of* **मलिन** *m. f. n.* dirty, covered with dirt.

मलिना *nom. sin. f.* dirty, covered with mud and dust.

मलिनां *acc. sin. f. of* **मलिन** *m. f. n.* dirty, dusty, tarnished, (the lustre of whose beauty was tarnished,) *lit.* dirty.

मलेन *ins. sin. of* **मल** *n.* dirt, dust, want of brightness.

महत् *m. f. n.* great, 5*th cl.* 142.

महत् *nom. or acc. sin. n. of* **महत्** *m. f. n.* great, 142.

महतः *gen. sin. m. or n. of* **महत्** *m. f. n.* great.

महता *ins. sin. m. or n. of* **महत्** *m. f. n.* great.

महति *loc. sin. m. or n. of* **महत्** *m. f. n.* great.

महती *nom. sin. f. of* **महत्** *m. f. n.* great.

महत्या *ins. sin. f. of* **महत्** *m. f. n.* great.

महद् *for* **महत्** *nom. or acc. sin. n. of* **महत्** great.

महदध्वानम् *acc. sin. m.* a long journey; (*comp. of* **महद्**, *anomalously used for* **महा** 778, *and* **अध्वन्** a road.)

महर्षिभिस् by the great sages, (Karm. or Des. comp. 755; **महा** *cr.* great, *for* **महत्** *by* 778, **ऋषिभिस्** *ins. pl. of* **ऋषि** *m.* a sage, 2*d cl.* 110; **आ + ऋ = अर्** *by* 32.)

महर्षिर् *for* **महर्षिस्** *nom. sin. m.* the great sage. *See last.*

महर्षीणाम् *gen. pl. of* **महर्षि** *m.* a great sage or saint; (*from* **महा** *for* **महत्** 778, *and* **ऋषि** *m.* a sage, 32.)

महाकायः Karm. or Des. comp. 755; **महा** *for* **महत्** (778) *cr.* great, **कायः** *nom. sin. of* **काय** *m.* body.

महाघोरे *loc. sin. n. of* **महाघोर** *m. f. n.* very terrible; (*comp. of* **महा** 778, *and* **घोर** terrible.)

महाजवान् Bah. or Rel. comp. 761; **महा** great, 778, **जवान्** *acc. pl. of* **जव** *m.* speed, velocity, fleetness.

महातपाः Bah. or Rel. comp. 761; **महा** *for* **महत्** *cr.* great, 778, **तपाः** *nom. sin. m. from* **तपस्** *n.* penance, devotion, 164. *a.*

महातेजाः *nom. sin. m. of* **महातेजस्** *m. f. n.* of great glory, very glorious, 7*th cl.* 164. *a*, 778.

महात्मन् *m. f. n.* high-minded, magnanimous, (Bah. or Rel. comp. 766; **महा** *for* **महत्** *cr.* great, 778, **आत्मन्** mind, soul, 6*th cl.* 147.)

महात्मनः *gen. sin. of* **महात्मन्** *m. f. n.* magnanimous, great-minded, 6*th cl.* 147.

महात्मना *ins. sin. of* **महात्मन्** *m. f. n.* noble-minded.

महात्मनां *gen. pl. of* **महात्मन्** *m. f. n.* great-minded, 6*th cl.* 147.

महात्मानं *acc. sin. of* **महात्मन्** *m. f. n.* high-minded.

महात्मानश् *nom. pl. m. of* **महात्मन्** *m. f. n.* high-minded.

महात्मानौ *nom. du. m. of* **महात्मन्** high-minded.

महाद्युतिः Bah. or Rel. comp. 761; **महा** *for* **महत्** great, 778, *and* **द्युतिः** *nom. sin. m. from* **द्युति** *f.* lustre, glory.

महाद्युते *voc. sin.* O most illustrious. *See last.*

महान् *nom. sin. m. of* **महत्** great, *q. v.*

महानसाच् *for* **महानसात्** *abl. sin. of* **महानस** *m. n.* a kitchen.

महानुभावान् *acc. pl. m. of* **महानुभाव** *m. f. n.* magnanimous; (*comp. of* **महा** *for* **महत्** great, *and* **अनुभाव** disposition.)

महान्तं *acc. sin. m. of* **महत्** *m. f. n.* great.

महाप्राज्ञौ very wise, Bah. or Rel. comp. 766; **महा** *for* **महत्** *cr.* great, 778, **प्राज्ञौ** *nom. du. of* **प्राज्ञ** *m.* a wise man, 1*st cl.* 103.

महाबलः *nom. sin. m.* of great strength, very powerful, 778.

महाबाहुः strong-armed, Bah. or Rel. comp. 766; **महा** *for* **महत्** *cr.* great, 778, **बाहुः** *nom. sin. of* **बाहु** *m.* an arm, 3*d cl.* 110.

महाबाहो *voc. sin. m.* O long-armed, O strong-armed, O valiant one. *See last.*

महाबुद्धे *voc. sin. m.* O great-minded one; (*comp. of* **महा** great, 778, *and* **बुद्धि** mind, reason, intellect, 119, 761.)

महाभागस् *nom. sin. m.* greatly blessed, gifted, or endowed. *See next.*

महाभागा *nom. sin. f. of* **महाभाग** *m. f. n.* highly fortunate, greatly blessed, of exalted virtue; (*from* **महा** *for* **महत्** great, 778, *and* **भाग** portion.)

महाभागाः *voc. pl. m.* O greatly blessed!

महाभागे *voc. sin. f.* O greatly blessed!

महाभागैः *ins. pl. m. of* **महाभाग** *m. f. n.* highly blessed.

महाभागो *for* **महाभागस्** *nom. sin. m.* greatly blessed.

महाभुज *voc. sin. m.* O mighty armed; (*comp. of* **महा** great, 778, *and* **भुज** the arm, 766.)

महामते *voc. sin. m. or f.* O high-minded one; (*comp. of* **महा** great, 778, *and* **मति** the mind, 119.)

महामनाः *nom. sin. m. or f. of* **महामनस्** *m. f. n.* high-minded; (*comp. of* **महा** *for* **महत्** great, 778, *and* **मनस्** the mind, *see* 164. *a.*)

महायशाः *nom. sin. m. of* **महायशस्** *m. f. n.* of great renown, very glorious; (*comp. of* **महा** great, 778, *and* **यशस्** fame, 164. *a.*)

महारण्ये in the vast forest, (Karm. or Des. comp. 755; **महा** *for* **महत्** *cr.* great, 778, **अरण्ये** *loc. sin. of* **अरण्य** *n.* a forest, 1*st cl.* 104.)

महारथः *nom. sin. of* **महारथ** *m.* a great warrior; (*lit.* one who fights in a large car, *comp. of* **महा** *for* **महत्** 778, *and* **रथ** *m.* a chariot.) (The size of the chariot was anciently regulated by the rank of the warrior.)

महारथाः *nom. pl. m.* great warriors. *See last.*

महाराज *voc. sin. m.* O great king, (Karm. or Des. comp. 755; **महा** *for* **महत्** *cr.* great, 778, **राज** *for* **राजन्** *voc. sin. of* **राजन्** a king, 6*th cl.* 151.)

महाराजः *nom. sin. m.* a great king.

महाराजम् *acc. sin. of* **महाराज** *m.* a great king. *See last.*

महाराजेति *for* **महाराज इति** *by* 32.

महावने *loc. sin.* in the great forest; (*comp. of* **महा** 778, *and* **वन** *n.* a wood.)

महावीर *voc. sin. m.* O great hero; (*comp. of* **महा** 778, *and* **वीर** *m.* a hero.)

महावीर्यस् Bah. or Rel. comp. 761; **महा** great, 778, **वीर्यस्** *nom. sin. m. from* **वीर्य** *n.* valour, heroism.

महाव्रतौ very devotional, great devotees, (Bah. or Rel. comp. 766; **महा** *for* **महत्** *cr.* great, 778, **व्रतौ** *nom. du. m. from* **व्रत** *n.* a religious vow, 1*st cl.* 104.)

महाशैल *voc. sin.* O great mountain, (Karm. or Des. comp. 755; **महा** *for* **महत्** great, 778, **शैल** *voc. sin. of* **शैल** *m.* a mountain, 1*st cl.* 103.)

महाशैलः *nom. sin. m.* great mountain. *See last.*

महासार्थं *acc. sin. m.* a great caravan; (*comp. of* **महा** 778, *and* **सार्थ** *m.* a caravan.)

महासार्थे *loc. sin. m.* in a great caravan. *See last.*

महासिंहाः Karm. or Des. comp. 755; **महा** *for* **महत्** *cr.* great, **सिंहाः** *nom. pl. of* **सिंह** *m.* a lion, 1*st cl.* 103.

महास्वनम् *acc. sin. m.* loud-sounding; (*comp. of* **महा** great, 778, *and* **स्वन** sound, 766.)

महाहनुः Bah. or Rel. comp. 761; **महा** *for* **महत्** great, 778, **हनुः** *nom. sin. m. of* **हनु** *m.* the jaw.

महाहनून् *acc. pl. m.* *See last.*

महिषांश् *for* **महिषान्** *acc. pl. of* **महिष** *m.* a buffalo, 1*st cl.* 103.

महिषीम् *acc. sin. of* **महिषी** *f.* a queen, 1*st cl.* 106.

महिष्या *ins. sin. of* **महिषी** *f.* a queen royal.

महीं *acc. sin. of* **मही** *f.* the earth.

महीकृते *ind.* for the sake of the earth; (**मही** the earth, *and* **कृते** on account, 731, 791.)

महीक्षितः *nom. pl. of* **महीक्षित्** *m.* a king, a sovereign, 5*th cl.* 136.

महीक्षितां *gen. pl. of* **महीक्षित्** *m.* a king.

महीतले *loc. sin. of* **महीतल** *n.* the surface of the ground, the ground; (*comp. of* **मही** *cr.* the earth, *and* **तल** *n.* surface, 743.)

महीधर *voc. sin. of* महीधर *m.* a mountain, 1*st cl.* 103.

महीपतिः *for* महीपतिस् *nom. sin. m.* a king, (TAT. OR DEP. COMP. 744; मही *cr.* the earth, पतिः *nom. sin. of* पति a lord.)

महीपते *voc. sin. m.* O king! *see* 121.

महीपतेः *gen. sin. m.* of a king, *see* 121.

महीपाल *m.* a king, *lit.* earth-protector; (*from* मही the earth, *and* पाल a guardian.)

महीपालं *acc. sin. of* महीपाल *m.* guardian of the earth.

महीपालः *nom. sin. m.* a king, earth-protector.

महीपालान् *acc. pl. of* महीपाल *m.* guardian of the earth.

महीपालो *nom. sin. m.* a king, earth-protector.

महीभृतः *gen. sin. of* महीभृत् *m.* a mountain.

महीम् *acc. sin. of* मही *f.* the earth.

महेन्द्रं *acc. sin. of* महेन्द्र *m.* the great chief; (*comp. of* महा 778, *and* इन्द्र 32, 755;) a name applied to the god Indra.

महेन्द्राद्याः *nom. pl. m.* of whom the great Indra is the first, (BAH. OR REL. COMP. 764. *b;* महेन्द्र *cr.* the great Indra, आद्याः *nom. pl. m. of* आद्य *m. f. n.* first, 1*st cl.* 103.)

महेश्वराः *nom. pl. m.* great lords, (KARM. OR DES. COMP. 755; महा *for* महत् great, 778, ईश्वराः *nom. pl. of* ईश्वर lord, 1*st cl.* 103.)

महोत्सवे *loc. sin. of* महोत्सव *m.* a great festival; (*comp. of* महा 778, *and* उत्सव a festival.)

महौजसः *nom. pl. m. of* महौजस् *m. f. n.* of great might, very mighty; (*comp. of* महा great, *and* ओजस् power, strength, 776.)

मा me; *acc. sin. from nom.* अहं I, 218.

मा *negative, dissuasive or prohibitive particle,* not, do not; *often used with the* 3*d pret., the augment being dropped, as* मा शुचः do not grieve, *see* 889, 717. *a.*

मां me; *acc. sin. from nom.* अहं I, 218.

मांसं *nom. or acc. sin. of* मांस *n.* meat, flesh.

माचिरं *ind.* without delay, quickly; (*from* मा *prohib.* not, *and* चिर long.)

मातः *for* मातर् *voc. sin.* O mother!

मातर् O mother! *voc. sin. of* मातृ 129.

मातरं *acc. sin. of* मातृ *f.* a mother, 129.

मातलिर् *for* मातलिस् *nom. sin. m.* Mátali, the charioteer of Indra; *compare* S'akuntalá Act VII, *and* Raghu-vanśa XII. 86.

माता *nom. sin. of* मातृ *f.* a mother, 129.

मातुः *for* मातुस् *gen. sin. of* मातृ *f.* a mother.

मातुर् *for* मातुस् *gen. sin. of* मातृ *f.* a mother, 129.

मातुलाः *nom. pl. of* मातुल *m.* a maternal uncle.

मातुलान् *acc. pl. of* मातुल *m.* a maternal uncle.

मातृष्वसा TAT. OR DEP. COMP. 743, maternal aunt; मातृ *cr.* a mother, ष्वसा *for* स्वसा (70) *nom. sin. of* स्वसृ *f.* a sister, 129. *a.*

मात्रा *ins. sin. of* मातृ *f.* a mother, 129.

मानद O giver of honour; *voc. sin. m. of* मानद *m. f. n.;* (*comp. of* मान honour, *and* द who gives, 580.)

मानयसि thou regardest, thou respectest; 2*d sin. pres. of rt* मन् 10*th cl.* 283.

मानुष *m.* a man, a human being, 1*st cl.* 103.

मानुषं *acc. sin. of* मानुष *m.* a man, 1*st cl.* 103.

मानुषं *nom. sin. n. of* मानुष *m. f. n.* human.

मानुषः *nom. sin. m.* a man.

मानुषाः *nom. pl. of* मानुष *m.* a man.

मानुषी *nom. sin. f.* a woman, a female mortal.

मानुषी *nom. sin. f. of* मानुष *m. f. n.* human.

मानुषीं *acc. sin. of* मानुषी *f.* a woman.

मानुषीं *acc. sin. f. of* मानुष *m. f. n.* human.

मानुषेषु *loc. pl. of* मानुष *m.* a man, mankind.

मानुष्यं *acc. sin. n. of* मानुष्य *m. f. n.* human.

माम् me; *acc. sin. from nom. sin.* अहं.

माया *nom. sin. f.* magic, sorcery, witchcraft.

मारिष *voc. sin. of* मारिष *m.* a venerable or excellent person.

मारुतः *nom. sin. m.* the wind.

मार्गं *acc. sin. of* मार्ग *m.* a path, a road.

मार्गणे *loc. sin. of* मार्गण *n.* searching for.

मार्गमाणा *nom. sin. f. of* मार्गमाण *m. f. n.* seeking for; *pres. p. âtm. of rt* मार्ग् 526.

मार्गा *for* मार्गास् *nom. pl. of* मार्ग *m.* a path, a road, a way.

मार्गाणां *gen. pl. of* मार्ग *m.* a path, a road.

मार्गामि I seek; *1st sin. pres. of rt* मार्ग् *1st cl.* 261.

मार्गाम्यपराजितम् *for* मार्गामि अपराजितम् *by* 34.

मासं *acc. sin. of* मास *m.* a month, (for a month, 821.)

मासान् *acc. pl. of* मास *m.* a month, *see* 821.

मास्म *prohibitive particle* (मा स्म), *used with the 3d preterite, after rejection of the augment, and equivalent to* do not.

मित्रं *nom. sin. of* मित्र *n.* a friend, *1st cl.* 104.

मित्रद्रोहे *loc. sin. m.* in the injury of a friend; (मित्र *cr.* a friend, द्रोह *m.* injury.)

मिथुनं *acc. sin. of* मिथुन *n.* a couple, a pair, a brace; a pair of children, twins, a pair of gifts, &c., *1st cl.* 104.

मिथ्या *ind.* falsely, untruly, 717. *e.*

मिष्टकर्ता Tat. or Dep. comp. 743; मिष्ट *cr.* a sweetmeat, a dainty, कर्ता *nom. sin. m. of* कर्तृ *m.* a maker, 127. (*Lit.* a maker of dainties, a skilful cook.)

मुक्तः *nom. sin. m. of* मुक्त *m. f. n.* released, emitted, sent forth; *past p. p. of rt* मुच् 628, 539.

मुक्तकेशीम् Bah. or Rel. comp. 767; मुक्त *cr.* dishevelled, loose, केशीम् *acc. sin. f. from* केश hair, 108.

मुखं *nom. or acc. sin. of* मुख *n.* the mouth, the face, the countenance.

मुखतः *for* मुखतस् *ind.* in the face, in the mouth, from the mouth; (मुख *with affix* तस्, 719.)

मुखात् *abl. sin. of* मुख *n.* the mouth, the face.

मुखानि *nom. n. of* मुख *n.* the face, the countenance, *1st cl.* 104.

मुख्यशः *ind.* principally, 725. *In* Book VIII. 21 *it is used for* मुख्येषु *loc. pl. of* मुख्य principal.

मुख्यानि *nom. or acc. pl. n. of* मुख्य *m. f. n.* excellent, *1st cl.* 104, 187.

मुख्यैर् *ins. pl. of* मुख्य *m. f. n.* chief, excellent.

मुञ्चतु let him let go, let him set free, let him allow to depart, let him release; *3d sin. imp. of rt* मुच् *6th cl.* 281, 628.

मुदं *acc. sin. of* मुद् *f.* joy.

मुदा *ins. sin. of* मुद् *f.* joy, delight.

मुदिताः *nom. pl. m. or f. of* मुदित *m. f. n.* rejoiced, delighted.

मुदितो *nom. sin. m. of* मुदित *m. f. n.* rejoiced, joyful; *past p. p. of rt* मुद् 538.

मुदितौ *nom. du. m. of* मुदित *m. f. n.* joyful, happy.

मुनिभिः *ins. pl. of* मुनि *m.* a saint, a hermit, *2d cl.* 110.

मुमुदे he rejoiced, he was delighted; *3d sin. perf. âtm. of rt* मुद् 364.

मुष्टिभिः *ins. pl. of* मुष्टि *m.* the fist, *2d cl.* 110.

मुष्णन्ती *nom. sin. f. of* मुष्णत् stealing, captivating; *pres. p. of rt* मुष् *9th cl.* 524.

मुहुः *for* मुहुस् *ind.* repeatedly, again and again.

मुहुर् *for* मुहुस् *ind.* repeatedly.

मुहूर्तं *acc. sin. m.* for a moment, for a short time, 821. मुहूर्त *is properly* a space of forty-eight minutes.

मुह्यति he is troubled, bewildered, or perplexed; *3d sin. pres. of rt* मुह् *4th cl.* 612.

मूढ O fool; *voc. sin. of* मूढ *m.* a fool.

मूढेन *ins. sin. m. of* मूढ *m. f. n.* foolish.

मूढो *for* मूढस् *nom. sin. m. of* मूढ *m. f. n.* foolish, *1st cl.* 103.

मूत्रं *acc. sin. of* मूत्र *n.* urine, *1st cl.* 104.

मूर्तिमान् *nom. sin. m. of* मूर्तिमत् *m. f. n.* corporeal, possessing a material form, incarnate, *5th cl.* 140.

मूर्त्या *ins. sin. of* मूर्ति *f.* form, figure, image, *2d cl.* 112.

मूर्ध्नि *loc. sin. of* मूर्धन् *m.* the head, *6th cl.* 149, 150.

मृगजीवनः *nom. sin. m.* one who lives by hunting, a hunter; (*from* मृग an animal, a wild beast, game, *and* जीवन living.)

मृगद्विजान् DVAN. OR AGG. COMP. 748; मृग *cr.* an animal, a wild beast, द्विजान् *acc. pl. of* द्विज *m.* a bird, *1st cl.* 103.

मृगपक्षिणः DVAN. OR AGG. COMP. 748; मृग *cr.* an animal, पक्षिणः *acc. pl. of* पक्षिन् *m.* a bird, *6th cl.* 159, 58.

मृगपक्षिषु DVAN. OR AGG. COMP. 748; मृग *cr.* an animal, पक्षिषु *loc. pl. of* पक्षिन् *m.* a bird, *6th cl.* 159.

मृगयध्वं seek ye, hunt ye for, search ye out; *2d pl. imp. átm. of rt* मृग् *10th cl.* 283.

मृगयसे thou dost seek, thou searchest for; *2d sin. pres. átm. of rt* मृग् *10th cl.* 283.

मृगयाणेन *ins. sin. m. of* मृगयाण *m. f. n.* searching for; *pres. p. átm. of rt* मृग् *1st cl.*

मृगयितुं to search for; *inf. of rt* मृग् *10th cl.* 459.

मृगयिष्यन्ति they shall search for, they shall seek; *3d pl. 2d fut. of rt* मृग् *10th cl.* 491.

मृगराट् TAT. OR DEP. COMP. 743; मृग *cr.* a beast, राट् *nom. sin. of* राज् *m.* a king, a monarch, *8th cl.* 176. *e.*

मृगव्याधम् *acc. sin. m.* See *next.*

मृगव्याधो TAT. OR DEP. COMP. 743; मृग *cr.* an animal, wild beast, व्याधो *nom. sin. of* व्याध *m.* a hunter.

मृगव्यालनिषेविते COMPLEX COMP. 771; मृग *cr.* an animal, a wild beast, व्याल *cr.* a serpent, निषेविते *loc. sin. n. of* निषेवित *m. f. n.* infested, haunted by; *past p. p. of rt* सेव् *with* नि (70), 538.

मृगशावाक्षि *voc. sin. of* मृगशावाक्षी having eyes like those of a young deer or fawn; (*from* मृगशाव *cr.* a young deer, *and* अक्ष *substituted for* अक्षि the eye, *see* 778.)

मृगश्रेष्ठ *voc. sin.* O best of beasts, O chief of animals, TAT. OR DEP. COMP. 743. *b;* मृग *cr.* a beast, श्रेष्ठ *voc. sin. of* श्रेष्ठ *m. f. n.* best.

मृगाणाम् *gen. pl. of* मृग *m.* a beast, *1st cl.* 103.

मृगेन्द्र O king, monarch, or chief of beasts.

मृगेन्द्रेह *for* मृगेन्द्र + इह *by* 32.

मृणालीम् *acc. sin. of* मृणाली *f.* a fibre of the stalk of a lotus, a lotus-stalk.

मृतं *acc. sin. m. of* मृत *m. f. n.* dead, dying; *past p. p. of rt* मृ.

मृतस्य *gen. sin. n. of* मृत *m. f. n.* dead.

मृत्युं *acc. sin. of* मृत्यु *m.* death.

मृत्युर् *for* मृत्युस् *nom. sin. of* मृत्यु *m.* death, *3d cl.* 110.

मृदिता *nom. sin. f. of* मृदित *m. f. n.* trampled on, crushed; *past p. p. of rt* मृद् 538.

मृदुपूर्वं *ind.* blandly, softly, coaxingly, *see* 792.

मृदुपूर्वया commencing softly; (*from* मृदु *cr.* soft, mild, *and* पूर्वया *ins. sin. f. of* पूर्व *m. f. n.* first, preceding; *see* 777. *d. and* 792.)

मृद्यमानानि *nom. sin. n. of* मृद्यमान *m. f. n.* being crushed, being bruised; *pres. p. pass. of rt* मृद् 528.

मृधे *loc. sin. n. of* मृध *n.* war, battle.

मृष्टसलिलाम् BAH. OR REL. COMP. 766; मृष्ट *cr.* clean, bright, pure, सलिलाम् *acc. sin. f. from* सलिल *n.* water, *1st cl.* 108.

मे to me, of me; *dat. or gen. sin. of* मत् *or* अस्मत्, *q. v.*

मेघनाद *for* मेघनादे *loc. sin.* at the sound of rain; (*from* मेघ a cloud, *and* नाद sound.) The Indian peacock is very restless at the approach of the rains, in which it is observed to take delight. Its circular movements are a frequent subject of allusion with Hindú poets, and are often by them compared to dancing; thus S'akuntalá Act IV, 'The peacock on the lawn ceases its dance.' Megha-dúta (l. 215): 'Pleased on each terrace, dancing with delight, The friendly peacock hails thy grateful flight.' Málati-Mádhava (p. 108): 'As pleased the peafowl hail the bow of heaven,' &c. Compare also Raghu-vaṇśa XIV. 69.

मेघनिर्घोषो BAH. OR REL. COMP. 761; मेघ *cr.* a cloud, निर्घोषो *nom. sin. m.* sound; 'sounding like a thunder-cloud.'

मेघस्य *gen. sin. of* मेघ *m.* a cloud.

मेदिनीं *acc. sin. of* मेदिनी *f.* the earth.

मेदिन्याम् *loc. sin. of* मेदिनी *f.* the earth, 1*st cl.* 106.

मेने he or she thought; 3*d sin. perf. átm. of rt* मन् 375. *a,* 617.

मोक्षयित्वा having released; *past ind. p. of rt* मोक्ष् 10*th cl.* 559.

मोक्ष्यसि thou shalt be liberated; 2*d sin.* 2*d fut. of rt* मुच् *in pass.* 628, 463. *The parasmai-pada terminations are here used in the passive verb, see* 461. *e. note.*

मोचयित्वा having loosed, having unharnessed; *past ind. p. of rt* मुच् *in caus.* 549.

मोदस्व rejoice thou, take thou pleasure; 2*d sin. imp. átm. of rt* मुद् 1*st cl.* 261.

मोहयन् *nom. sin. m. of* मोहयत् *m. f. n.* bewildering, depriving of sense, stupefying; *pres. p. of rt* मुह् *in caus.* 527.

मोहितः *nom. sin. m. of* मोहित *m. f. n.* infatuated; *past p. p. of rt* मुह् *in caus.* 612, 549.

मोहिता *nom. sin. f. of* मोहित *m. f. n.* bewildered, stupefied, infatuated.

म्रियते he, she or it dies; 3*d sin. pres. átm. of rt* मृ 6*th cl.* 626.

म्लानस्रग् BAH. OR REL. COMP. 761; म्लान *cr.* drooping, faded, स्रग् *nom. sin. of* स्रज् *f.* a garland, a chaplet, 8*th cl.* 176.

म्लेच्छतस्करसेवितम् COMPLEX COMP. 771; म्लेच्छ *cr.* a wild man, a barbarian, तस्कर *cr.* a robber, सेवितम् *acc. sin. n. of* सेवित *m. f. n.* infested by; *past p. p. of rt* सेव् 538.

य.

य *for* यस् who; *nom. sin. m. of* यत् *m. f. n.,* 226.

यं *acc. sin. m. of* यत् *m. f. n.* who, which, 226.

यक्षराड् *nom. sin. m.* the king of the Yakshas; (*comp. of* यक्ष *cr.* a Yaksha, *and* राड् *for* राट् (41) *nom. sin. of* राज् *m.,* 8*th cl.* 176.*e.*) The Yaksha was a kind of demi-god, attendant on Kuvera, the god of wealth, and employed by him in the care of his gardens &c. situated on mount Kailása. The Yakshas were supposed to be much courted by the Apsarasas or nymphs of Indra's heaven, but that they had wives of their own is clear from the Megha-dúta. Their name is said to be derived from *yaksh* 'to worship,' either because they worship Kuvera, or are themselves worshipped by men.

यक्षाधिपः TAT. OR DEP. COMP. 743; यक्ष *cr.* a Yaksha, a kind of demi-god, *see last,* अधिपः *nom. sin.* a lord, a sovereign.

यक्षी *nom. sin. f.* a Yakshí, the wife of a Yaksha. *See last.*

यक्षेषु *loc. pl. of* यक्ष *m.* a Yaksha. *See last.*

यक्षो *nom. sin. of* यक्ष *m.* a Yaksha, 1*st cl.* 103. *See last.*

यच् *for* यत् *nom. sin. n.* what.

यच्छतु let him curb, let him guide; 3*d sin. imp. of rt* यम् 1*st cl.* 270.

यजमानश् *for* यजमानस् *nom. sin. of* यजमान *m. f. n.* sacrificing; *pres. p. átm. of rt* यज् 597. (*It means sometimes* a master.)

यज्ञे *loc. sin. of* यज्ञ *m.* sacrifice, 1*st cl.* 103.

यज्ञेषु *loc. pl. of* यज्ञ *m.* a sacrifice, 1*st cl.* 103.

यज्ञैर् *for* यज्ञैस् *ins. pl. of* यज्ञ *m.* a sacrifice.

यत् *pron. m. f. n.* who, which, what, 226.

यत् *acc. sin. n. of* यत् who, which, what, 226.

यत् *ind.* since, because, inasmuch as, that, 713. *a.*

यत strive thou, make effort; 2*d sin. imp. of rt* यत् 1*st cl.* 261. *The more usual form is* यतस्व, *this root being generally in the átmane-pada.*

यतः *for* यतस् as, because, since.

यतध्वं strive ye, take pains, make ye effort; *2d pl. imp. átm. of rt* यत् *1st cl.* 261.

यतस् *ind.* as, in the same way as, because.

यतिष्ये I will strive; *1st sin. 2d fut. átm. of rt* यत् 415. *b.*

यत्कृते *ind.* on whose account, by reason of whom; (*comp. of* यत् 526, *and* कृते on account of, 791, 917.)

यत्न *m.* effort, exertion, pains, trouble.

यत्नं *acc. sin. of* यत्न *m.* effort.

यत्र *ind.* where, wherever, because, since, wherefore, that.

यत्रसायम्प्रतिश्रयाम् *acc. sin. f.* having (my) dwelling wherever evening (falls); यत्र where, सायम् evening, प्रतिश्रयाम् *acc. sin. f. from* प्रतिश्रय *m.* a dwelling, 108.

यथा *ind.* so that, that, as, so as, 721.

यथाकामं *ind.* according to will, according to pleasure, at pleasure; (*from* यथा as, *and* काम desire, 760.)

यथागतं as they came, ADV. COMP. 760; यथा *ind.* as, गतं *acc. sin. n. of* गत gone, went, *see* 760.

यथातत्त्वम् *ind.* according to the truth; (*comp. of* यथा as, *and* तत्त्व truth, *see* 760.)

यथातथं *ind.* truly, circumstantially; (*in* Book XXI. 25) for such a purpose.

यथातथं *acc. sin. n.* narrative, circumstantial account. *This compound may also be regarded as indeclinable* (*from* यथा *and* तथा 721), circumstantially.

यथातथा *ind.* in any way, any how.

यथात्थ *for* यथा आत्थ *by* 31.

यथान्यायं according to truth, justice, fitness or propriety, justly, fitly; (*from* यथा as, *and* न्याय justice, fitness, *see* 760.)

यथायं *for* यथा अयं *by* 31.

यथार्हं *ind.* worthily, properly, suitably; (*comp. of* यथा as, *and* अर्ह worthy, 760.)

यथावच् *for* यथावत् (48) *ind.* truly, exactly, rightly.

यथावत् *ind.* according to usage, suitably, fitly.

यथावन् *for* यथावत् *ind.* justly, according to rule.

यथाविधि *ind.* according to rule, fitly, *see* 760.

यथावृत्तं *ind.* as (it) happened, as took place, circumstantially; (*from* यथा as, *and* वृत्त happened, occurred, took place, 760.)

यथाश्रद्धं *ind.* according to faith, in all faith, in all fidelity; (*comp. of* यथा as, *and* श्रद्धा *f.* faith, *see* 760.)

यथासङ्गम् *ind.* at the moment of contact, at the moment of (his) approach, opportunely; (*from* यथा as, *and* सङ्ग contact, meeting, 760.)

यथासत्यम् *ind.* according to the truth, truthfully, *see* 760.

यथासुखं *ind.* happily, conveniently, pleasantly; (*from* यथा as, *and* सुख pleasure, 760.)

यथाहम् *for* यथा अहम् *by* 31.

यथेच्छसि *for* यथा इच्छसि *by* 32.

यथेदं *for* यथा इदं *by* 32.

यथेयं *for* यथा इयं *by* 32.

यथेरितम् *for* यथा ईरितम् *by* 32.

यथैव *for* यथा एव *by* 33.

यथोक्तं ADV. COMP. 760; as said, as spoken, according to what was said, according to request; (*comp. of* यथा as, *and* उक्त said.)

यथोक्तानि *nom. pl. n. of* यथोक्त *m. f. n.* as said.

यथोत्साहं *ind.* with as great effort as possible, 760; (*from* यथा as, *and* उत्साह effort.)

यद् *ind.* that, inasmuch as, 713.

यदा *ind.* when, as soon as.

यदि *ind.* if, 727. *e.*

यदिवा *ind.* whether, whether or no, 728. *b.*

यदिवाप्यर्थकामः *for* यदिवा अपि अर्थकामः *by* 31, 34.

यदृच्छया *ind.* spontaneously; (*ins. sin. of* यदृच्छा.)

यद्यपि *ind.* although, if even.

यद्यबुद्ध्यापि *for* यदि अबुद्ध्या अपि *by* 34, 31.

यद्यस्यस्मिन् *for* यदि असि अस्मिन् *by* 34.

यन् *for* यत् (47) that, 920. *b*.

यन्ता *nom. sin. of* यन्तृ *m.* a driver, a charioteer.

यमः *nom. sin. of* यम *m.* Yama, the god of justice, presiding over the different Narakas or hells, son of Súrya, the sun, regent of the south and of the lower world. He is the judge of departed souls (corresponding to the Greek god Pluto or Minos), and as such is identified with death. His abode is in the infernal city of Yama-pur, whither the Hindús believe that a departed soul repairs, and receiving a just sentence from Yama, ascends to Svarga or descends to Naraka, or assumes on earth the form of some animal according to its deserts. As god of punishment, Yama is represented bearing a cord or noose (पाश) as well as a दण्ड or rod.

यमस् *nom. sin. of* यम *m.* Yama, 1*st cl.* 103. *See last.*

यमो *nom. sin. of* यम *m.* Yama, the god of death. *See last.*

यया by which; *ins. sin. f. of* यत् 226.

ययातिर् *for* ययातिस् *nom. sin. of* ययाति *m.* Yayáti, a celebrated king of India, fifth of the Lunar race, 2*d cl.* 110.

ययुः they went; 3*d pl. perf. of rt* या 644.

ययुर् *for* ययुस् they went; 3*d pl. perf. of rt* या 373.

ययैतज् *for* यया एतत् *by* 33 *and* 48. *a*.

ययौ he went; 3*d sin. perf. of rt* या 644.

यश् *for* यस् who; *nom. sin. of* यत् 226.

यशः *for* यशस् *acc. n. of* यशस् glory, fame.

यशस् *n.* glory, fame, 7*th cl.* 164.

यशसा *ins. sin. of* यशस् *n.* fame, fair fame, good character, virtue, 7*th cl.* 164.

यशस्विनि O illustrious lady! *voc. sin. f. of* यशस्विन् *m. f. n.* famous, 159.

यशस्विनी *nom. sin. f.* noble, illustrious; (*from* यशस् fame, *and affix* विन् 85. IX.)

यश्चैवं *for* यस् च एवं *by* 62 *and* 33.

यष्टा *nom. sin. of* यष्टृ *m.* a sacrificer, 4*th cl.* 127.

यस्मिन् *loc. sin. of* यत् *m. f. n.* who, which, what, 226.

यस्य of whom; *gen. sin. of* यत् *m. f. n.*, 226.

यस्याभिशापाद् *for* यस्य अभिशापाद् *by* 31.

यस्याहं *for* यस्य अहं *by* 31.

या who; *nom. sin. f.*

यां *acc. sin. f. of* यत् *m. f. n.* who, which, 226.

याचते *dat. sin. m. of* याचत् *m. f. n.* asking, soliciting; *pres. p. of rt* याच् to ask, 524.

यातं *acc. sin. m. of* यात *m. f. n.* gone, going; *past p. p. of rt* या 532, 896. *a*.

याति he, she or it goes; 3*d sin. of rt* या 2*d cl.* 317, 644.

यातु let him go, let it pass; 3*d sin. imp. of rt* या to go, 2*d cl.* 644.

यातुं to go; *inf. of rt* या 459.

याते *loc. sin. m. of* यात *m. f. n.* gone; *past p. p. of rt* या to go, 532, 644.

यातो *nom. sin. m. of* यात *m. f. n.* arrived at, restored to; *past p. p. of rt* या to go, 532.

यात्येताम् *for* याति एताम् *by* 34.

यात्वा having gone; *past ind. p. of rt* या 556.

यान् *acc. pl. m. of* यत् *m. f. n.* who, which, 226.

यानं *acc. sin. of* यान *n.* a vehicle, a carriage.

यानयुग्यस्य of (or about) his yoked chariot; (*comp. of* यान *cr.* a vehicle, a carriage, *and* युग्यस्य *gen. sin. of* युग्य *m. f. n.* capable of being yoked.)

यानि *nom. pl. n. of* यत् who, which, 226.

यानेन *ins. sin. of* यान *n.* a vehicle.

यान्ति they go to; 3*d pl. pres. of rt* या 2*d cl.* 644.

यान्तो *nom. pl. m. of* यात् *m. f. n.* going; *pres. p. par. of rt* या, *see* 524.

याम् *acc. sin. f. of* यत् *m. f. n.* who, which, 226.

यावच् *for* यावत् as long as.

यावत् *ind.* as long as, as much as, whilst.

याश् *nom. pl. f. of* यत् *m. f. n.* who, which, what, 226.

यास् *nom. pl. f. of* यत् *m. f. n.* who, which, 226.

यासावद्य *for* **या असौ अद्य** *by* 31 *and* 37.

यास्यति he, she or it will go; *3d sin. 2d fut. of rt* **या** 644.

यास्यसि thou wilt go; *2d sin. 2d fut. of rt* **या** 644.

यास्यामि I will go; *1st sin. 2d fut. of rt* **या**.

याहि go thou; *2d sin. imp. of rt* **या** 2d cl. 644.

युक्तं *nom. sin. n. or acc. sin. m. of* **युक्त** *m. f. n.* fit, fitting; yoked, joined; endowed with, possessed of.

युक्तः *nom. sin. m. of* **युक्त** *m. f. n.* endowed with, possessed of, invested with, skilled, practised, clever; *past p. p. of rt* **युज्** 539.

युक्तास् *nom. sin. m. of* **युक्त** *m. f. n.* possessed of, endowed with.

युक्ताः *nom. pl. m. of* **युक्त** *m. f. n.* possessed of, endowed with.

युज्यस्व be thou prepared, prepare thyself, gird thyself; *2d sin. imp. of rt* **युज्** *in pass.*

युतं *acc. sin. n. of* **युत** *m. f. n.* possessed of, filled with; *past p. p. of rt* **यु** 532.

युता *nom. sin. f. of* **युत** *m. f. n.* endowed with, possessed of; *past p. p. of rt* **यु** 532.

युद्धं *acc. sin. of* **युद्ध** *n.* war, battle.

युद्धद्यूतम् *nom. sin. n.* the game of war or single combat; (*comp. of* **युद्ध** battle, *and* **द्यूत** game.)

युद्धाच् *for* **युद्धात्** *abl. sin. of* **युद्ध** *n.* war.

युद्धाय *dat. sin. of* **युद्ध** *n.* battle.

युद्धे *loc. sin. of* **युद्ध** *n.* war, battle.

युधिष्ठिर *voc. sin. m.* O Yudhishṭhira! Yudhishṭhira was the elder of the five Páṇḍu princes, and leader in the great war between them and the Kurus. It is to him that the sage Vṛihadaśva relates the story of Nala. (In the Mahá-bhárata he is commonly designated **राजा**.)

युध्यस्व fight thou; *2d sin. imp. átm. of rt* **युध्** *4th cl.*

युयुत्सुं *acc. sin. m. of* **युयुत्सु** *m. f. n.* desirous of fighting, pugnacious; (*adj. formed from the des. of* **युध्**.)

युवस्थविरबालाश् DVAN. OR AGG. COMP. 748; **युव** *for* **युवन्** (57) *cr.* young men, **स्थविर** *cr.* old men, **बालाश्** *nom. pl. of* **बाल** *m.* a child, a boy, *1st cl.* 103.

युष्मत् *pron.* thou, you, 219.

यूथभ्रष्टाम् TAT. OR DEP. COMP. 742; **यूथ** *cr.* a herd, a flock, **भ्रष्टाम्** *acc. sin. f. of* **भ्रष्ट** *m. f. n.* strayed, wandered.

यूथशो *for* **यूथशस्** *ind.* in herds, in flocks, in troops; (*from* **यूथ** a herd, *affix* **शस्** 725.)

यूयं you; *nom. pl. of* **युष्मत्** 220.

ये who; *nom. pl. m. of* **यत्**.

येन by whom, by which, by what reason, because, since; *ins. sin. m. or n. of* **यत्**.

येन केन *ins. sin. m.* by any whatsoever; (*rel. pron. joined to the interrogative*, 226, 227.)

येषां of whom; *gen. pl. m. of* **यत्**.

योक्ष्यसे thou wilt be joined, thou shalt or wilt become possessed of; *2d sin. 2d fut. of rt* **युज्** *in pass., see* 702.

योक्ष्ये I will unite, I will join; *1st sin. 2d fut. átm. of rt* **युज्** 670.

योगं *acc. sin. of* **योग** *m.* occupation, employment.

योजनं *acc. sin. of* **योजन** *n.* a yojana, a measure of distance equivalent to nine miles, or (according to some) five miles, 823.

योजनशतं *acc. sin. n.* a hundred yojanas; (*comp. of* **योजन** a yojana, or about five miles, *and* **शत** a hundred, 206.)

योजय yoke thou, harness thou; *2d sin. imp. of rt* **युज्** *in caus.* 481.

योजयामास he yoked, he put to; *3d sin. 2d pret. of rt* **युज्** *in caus.* 490.

योजयामि I (will) yoke or will harness; *1st sin. pres. of rt* **युज्** *in caus.* 481.

योजयित्वा having yoked; *past ind. p. of rt* **युज्** *10th cl.* 558; *see also page* 248.

योत्स्य *for* **योत्स्ये** (36) I will fight; *1st sin. 2d fut. átm. of rt* **युध्**.

योद्धा *nom. sin. of* **योद्धृ** *m.* a fighter, a warrior, a combatant, *4th cl.* 127.

योषिद्रत्नम् *nom. sin. n.* a jewel of a woman, *i. e.* a most excellent woman; (*comp. of* योषित् *f.* a woman, *and* रत्न *n.* a gem.)

यौवनं *nom. sin. n.* youth, manhood, the bloom or prime of youth.

र.

रंस्यते he shall take pleasure or enjoy himself; 3*d sin.* 2*d fut. átm. of rt* रम् 410, 433.

रंस्यसे thou shalt enjoy thyself, thou shalt take thy pleasure; 2*d sin.* 2*d fut. átm. of rt* रम् 410, 433.

रक्तान्ताभ्यां *abl. du. n. of* रक्तान्त *m. f. n.* having red corners; (*from* रक्त red, *and* अन्त an extremity, 766.)

रक्ष defend thou; 2*d sin. imp. of rt* रक्ष् 1*st cl.* 261.

रक्षणीया *nom. sin. f. of* रक्षणीय *m. f. n.* to be protected; *fut. pass. p. of rt* रक्ष् 570.

रक्षन्तु let them preserve; 3*d pl. imp. of rt* रक्ष् 1*st cl.* 261.

रक्षा *nom. sin. f.* preservation, deliverance.

रक्षिणश् *nom. pl. of* रक्षिन् *m.* a guardian, 159.

रक्षिता *nom. sin. m. of* रक्षितृ *m. f. n.* a protector, a guardian, 4*th cl.* 127.

रक्ष्यमाणा *nom. sin. f. of* रक्ष्यमाण *m. f. n.* being guarded; *pres. p. of rt* रक्ष् *in pass.* 528.

रङ्गम् *acc. sin. of* रङ्ग *m.* an arena, stage.

रजःस्वेदसमन्वितः Tat. or Dep. comp. 740; रजस् *for* रजः *cr.* dust, स्वेद *cr.* perspiration, समन्वितः *nom. sin. m. of* समन्वित *m. f. n.* possessed of, possessing.

रजनीं *acc. sin. of* रजनी *f.* the night.

रज्जुम् *acc. sin. of* रज्जु *f.* a rope, a cord; hanging, 3*d cl.* 112. It is to be noted with reference to Book IV. 4, that hanging was not considered by the Hindús an undignified mode of self-destruction. See Hindú Theatre II. 237 and 299.

रणविशारदम् *acc. sin. m.* skilled in war; (*comp. of* रण *cr.* war, *and* विशारद *m. f. n.* learned, skilled, 744.)

रणाद् *for* रणात् *abl. sin. of* रण *m. n.* battle.

रणे *loc. sin. of* रण *m. n.* war, battle.

रतं *acc. sin. of* रत *m. f. n.* devoted to, delighting in; *past p. p. of rt* रम् 545.

रति *f.* enjoyment, pleasure, 2*d cl.* 112.

रतिं *acc. sin. of* रति enjoyment, pleasure.

रतीम् *acc. sin. of* रती *f.* Ratí, the wife of Kámadeva or Manmatha (god of love).

रत्नं *nom. sin. of* रत्न *n.* a jewel, a gem.

रत्नकोषनिचयैः Complex comp. 770; रत्न *cr.* jewels, कोष *cr.* treasure, gold or silver, निचयैः *ins. pl. of* निचय *m.* a heap.

रत्नगर्भगृहोचिताम् Anom. comp. 777; रत्नगर्भ *cr.* filled with jewels, गृह *cr.* a house, उचिताम् *acc. sin. f. of* उचित *m. f. n.* fit for, worthy of, suited to.

रत्नभूतां *acc. sin. f. of* रत्नभूत *m. f. n.* one who is a gem or jewel; (*comp. of* रत्न a gem, *and* भूत *past p. p. of rt* भू 531.)

रत्नराशिर् *for* रत्नराशिस् Tat. or Dep. comp. 743; रत्न *cr.* jewels, राशिर् *nom. sin. m.* a heap, a quantity, a collection.

रथं *acc. sin. of* रथ *m.* a chariot.

रथघोषं Tat. or Dep. comp. 743; रथ *cr.* a chariot, घोषं *acc. sin. of* घोष *m.* sound, rumbling or rattling noise.

रथघोषेण *ins. sin. m.* *See last.* The scene at the commencement of Book XXI reminds us of the watchman reporting the rapid approach of Jehu, 'the driving is like the driving of Jehu, the son of Nimshi, for he driveth furiously.'

रथनिर्घोषं Tat. or Dep. comp. 743; रथ *cr.* a chariot, निर्घोषं *acc. sin. of* निर्घोष *m.* sound, rattling.

रथनिर्घोषः *nom. sin. m.* *See last.*

रथनिर्घोषो *for* रथनिर्घोषस् *nom. sin. m.* the rattling of the chariot.

रथनिस्वनः Tat. or Dep. comp. 743; रथ *cr.* a chariot, निस्वनः *nom. sin. m.* a sound.

रथम् *acc. sin. of* रथ *m.* a chariot.

रथवरं an excellent chariot; (*comp. of* रथ

cr. chariot, *and* वर *acc. sin. of* वर *m. f. n*. excellent, choice, best.)

रथवाहकः *nom. sin. m.* a charioteer, the driver of a chariot; (*from* रथ *cr*. chariot, *and* वाहकः one who conveys.)

रथशालाम् TAT. OR DEP. COMP. 743, a coach-house; रथ *cr*. a chariot, शालाम् *acc. sin. of* शाला *f*. a house.

रथात् *abl. sin. of* रथ *m*. a chariot.

रथिनम् *acc. sin. of* रथिन् *m*. a warrior who is borne in a chariot, a charioteer.

रथे *loc. sin. of* रथ *m*. a chariot.

रथेन *ins. sin. of* रथ *m*. a chariot.

रथोत्तमं *acc. sin. m.* the best of chariots, 743. *b*.

रथोत्तमात् TAT. OR DEP. COMP. 743. *b*; रथ *cr*. chariot, उत्तमात् *abl. sin. of* उत्तम *m. f. n.* best.

रथोपस्थ *for* रथोपस्थे *loc. sin.* on the charioteer's seat (lower than the main body of the car).

रथोपस्थाद् *abl. sin. of* रथोपस्थ *m*. the charioteer's seat for driving, driving-box.

रथोपस्थे *loc. sin. m.* on the charioteer's seat; (*from* रथ a chariot, *and* उपस्थ a seat.)

रमणीयेषु *loc. pl. of* रमणीय *m. f. n.* pleasant, agreeable, 1*st cl.* 103.

रम्यं *acc. sin. m. or n. of* रम्य *m. f. n.* pleasant, delightful, charming.

रम्या *nom. sin. f. of* रम्य *m. f. n.* pleasant.

रम्यां *acc. sin. f. of* रम्य *m. f. n.* pleasant.

रम्यान् *acc. pl. m. of* रम्य *m. f. n.* pleasant.

ररक्ष he governed, he protected; 3*d sin. perf. of rt* रक्ष् 364.

रराज he or she shone; 3*d sin. perf. of rt* राज् 364.

रविं *acc. sin. of* रवि *m*. the sun, 2*d cl.* 110.

रविसोमसमप्रभः COMPLEX COMP. 771; रवि *cr*. the sun, सोम *cr*. the moon, सम *cr*. equal to, प्रभ *nom. sin. m. from* प्रभा *f*. light, lustre, glory, 1*st cl.* 108.

रश्मिभिश् *ins. pl. of* रश्मि *m*. a rein.

रश्मीन् *acc. pl. of* रश्मि *m*. a rein, 110.

रहिता *nom. sin. f. of* रहित *m. f. n.* deprived of, separated from, (*governing instrumental case*); *past p. p. of rt* रह्.

रहिता *for* रहितास् *nom. pl. f. of* रहित *m. f. n.* abandoned, deserted; *past p. p. of* रह् 538.

रहो *for* रहस् *ind.* secretly, in private.

राक्षसी *nom. sin. f.* a Rákshasí or female Rákshasa, a fairy. The Rákshasa is a spirit or demon who appears to be of various descriptions. As a kind of Titan, or enemy of the gods, he assumes a gigantic superhuman form, after the manner of Rávaṇa and others. He is sometimes represented as the guardian (रक्षकः) of the treasure of Kuvera, the god of wealth; and sometimes as a cannibal imp or goblin, haunting cemeteries, devouring human beings, impeding sacrifices, and disturbing religious people in their devotions. In this last character the Rákshasas appear to have waged continual war with men, as the Daityas or Dánavas did with the gods.

रागं *acc. sin. of* राग *m*. affection, love.

रागो *for* रागस् *nom. sin. m.* passion, 1*st cl.* 103.

राजंस् *for* राजन् O king; *voc. sin., q. v.*

राजते shines; 3*d sin. pres. átm. of rt* राज् 1*st cl.* 261.

राजन् O king; *voc. sin. of* राजन् *m*. a king, 149. In the Mahá-bhárata राजन् in the vocative is often applied to Yudhishṭhira, the eldest of the Páṇḍu princes, to whom the sage Vṛihadaśva relates the story of Nala.

राजन्न् O king; *voc. sin. for* राजन् *by* 52.

राजपुत्रं *acc. sin. m. of* राजपुत्र *m*. a prince, a king's son.

राजपुत्राश् *nom. pl. of* राजपुत्र *m*. a king's son, a prince; (*from* राज *for* राजन् a king, 57. *b*, *and* पुत्राश् *nom. pl. of* पुत्र *m*. a son, 743.)

राजपुत्रीं *acc. sin. of* राजपुत्री *f*. a princess, a king's daughter; (*comp. of* राज *for* राजन् a king, 57. *b*, *and* पुत्री *f*. a daughter.)

राजप्रेष्यैर् TAT. OR DEP. COMP. 743; राज *for* राजन् (57. *b*) a king, प्रेष्यैर् *ins. pl. of* प्रेष्य *m.* a servant, messenger.

राजभक्तिपुरस्कृतः TAT. OR DEP. COMP. 740; राज *for* राजन् (57. *b*) *cr.* king, भक्ति *cr.* devotion to, loyalty, पुरस्कृत preceded by, placed in front, adorned.

राजभार्यां TAT. OR DEP. COMP. 743; राज *for* राजन् *cr.* a king, 57, भार्यां *acc. sin. of* भार्या *f.* a wife, 1*st cl.* 105.

राजमाता *nom. sin. f.* the royal mother, the mother of the king, queen-mother; (*comp. of* राज *for* राजन् *cr.* a king, 57, *and* माता *nom. sin. of* मातृ 129, 743.)

राजमातुर् *gen. sin. f.* of the royal mother. *See last.*

राजमातेदम् *for* राजमाता इदम् *by* 32.

राजमार्गाः *nom. pl. m.* the royal roads or streets; (*from* राज *for* राजन् a king, 57, *and* मार्ग *m.* a road.)

राजर्षभस्य *gen. sin. of* राजर्षभ *m.* the chief of kings, *see* 758.

राजवेश्मनः TAT. OR DEP. COMP. 743; राज *for* राजन् (57) *cr.* the king, वेश्मनः *gen. sin. of* वेश्मन् *n.* a house, a dwelling, 6*th cl.* 152.

राजवेश्मनि *loc. sin. n.* in the palace of the king. *See last.*

राजशार्दूल *voc. sin. m.* O great king; (*lit.* O tiger of a king, *from* राज *for* राजन् 57. *b*, *and* शार्दूल a tiger, *see* 758.)

राजसमितिं TAT. OR DEP. COMP. 743; राज *for* राजन् (57) *cr.* a king, समितिं *acc. sin. of* समिति *f.* assembly, congress, 2*d cl.* 112.

राजसु among kings; *loc. pl. m. of* राजन् *m.* a king, 148.

राजसूयाश्वमेधानां DVAN. OR AGG. COMP. 748; राजसूय *cr.* a royal sacrifice, performed only by a universal monarch, अश्वमेधानां *gen. pl. of* अश्वमेध the Aśvamedha or horse-sacrifice, *see note under* अश्वमेधेन. Great sacrifices were performed by kings in celebration of auspicious events, especially after marriage, in the hope of securing issue, when largesses (दक्षिणा) were distributed to the Bráhmans and officiating priests.

राजा *nom. sin. of* राजन् *m.* a king, 148.

राजानं *acc. sin. of* राजन् *m.* a king, 148.

राजानः *nom. pl. of* राजन् *m.* a king.

राजानो *for* राजानस् *nom. pl. m.* kings, 148.

राजापसद *voc. sin.* O fallen king, O degraded king; (*comp. of* राज *for* राजन् a king, 57. *b*, *and* अपसद *m.* an outcast.)

राजेन्द्र *voc. sin. m.* O chief of kings; (*comp. of* राज *for* राजन् 57. *b*, 148, *and* इन्द्र chief.)

राजेन्द्रो *nom. sin. m.* chief of kings.

राज्ञः *gen. sin. of* राजन् *m.* a king, 148.

राज्ञश् *gen. sin. of* राजन् *m.* a king, 148.

राज्ञस् *gen. sin. of* राजन् *m.* a king, 148.

राज्ञा *ins. sin. of* राजन् *m.* a king, 148.

राज्ञां *gen. pl. of* राजन् *m.* a king.

राज्ञि *voc. sin. of* राज्ञी *f.* a queen.

राज्ञी *nom. sin. f.* a queen.

राज्ञे *dat. sin. of* राजन् *m.* a king, 148.

राज्ञो *for* राज्ञस् *gen. sin. m.* of a king.

राज्यं *nom. or acc. sin. of* राज्य *n.* a kingdom.

राज्यपरिभ्रष्टः TAT. OR DEP. COMP. 742; राज्य *cr.* kingdom, परिभ्रष्टः *nom. sin. m.* fallen from, deprived of; *past p. p. of rt* भ्रंश् 544. *a*.

राज्यान् (*for* राज्यात् *by* 47) *abl. sin. of* राज्यं *n.* a kingdom, 1*st cl.* 104.

राज्यापहरणं TAT. OR DEP. COMP. 743; राज्य *cr.* kingdom, अपहरणं *acc. sin. of* अपहरण *n.* taking away, deprivation.

राज्येन *ins. sin. of* राज्य *n.* a kingdom.

रात्रिं *acc. sin. of* रात्रि *f.* the night.

रात्रिर् *nom. sin. of* रात्रि *f.* the night.

राहुग्रस्तनिशाकराम् BAH. OR REL. COMP. 761; राहु *cr.* Ráhu, a demon with the tail of a dragon, who was translated to the stellar sphere, and became the author of eclipses by occasionally swallowing the sun and moon; ग्रस्त *cr.* seized, swallowed; निशाकराम् *acc. sin. f. from* निशाकर *m.* the moon, 108. The origin of the hostility of Ráhu to the sun and moon is this. When the gods were drinking the amṛita (see note under अमृतोपमां) produced at the churning of the ocean, Ráhu, a demon, assumed the form of a god, and began to drink also, when the sun and moon, in friendship to the gods, revealed the deceit. His head was then cut off by Vishṇu, but being immortal by having tasted the amṛit, the head and tail retained their separate existence, and were transferred to the sky. The head became the cause of eclipses by its animosity to the sun and moon, and the tail became Ketu or the descending node. Compare Málati-Mádhava (p. 115, Wilson): '—and now thou fall'st a prey to death, like the full moon to Ráhu's jaws consigned.'

रिपुनिपातिनम् Tat. or Dep. comp. 743; रिपु *cr.* an enemy, निपातिनम् *acc. sin. m. of* निपातिन् *m. f. n.* causing to fall, a destroyer, *agt. of rt* पत् *in caus.* 582. *a.*

रुचिरानना Bah. or Rel. comp. 766; रुचिर *cr.* beautiful, sweet, आनना *nom. sin. f. from* आनन *n.* face, *1st cl.* 108.

रुचिरापाङ्गीं having beautiful eyes, (*lit.* the outer corners of whose eyes were beautiful,) Bah. or Rel. comp. 766; रुचिर *cr.* beautiful, अपाङ्गीं *acc. sin. f. from* अपाङ्ग *n.* the outer corner of the eye, *1st cl.* 108.

रुदती *nom. sin. f. of* रुदत् *m. f. n.* weeping, crying; *pres. p. par. of rt* रुद् 524, 141. *c.*

रुदतीं *acc. sin. f. of* रुदत् *m. f. n.* weeping; *pres. p. par. of rt* रुद् 524, *see also* 141. *c.*

रुदत्यथ *for* रुदती अथ *by* 34.

रुदन्तीं *acc. sin. f. of* रुदत् *m. f. n.* weeping; *pres. p. par. of rt* रुद् 524. *The more usual form is* रुदतीं.

रुदन्त्याः *gen. sin. f. of* रुदत् *m. f. n.* weeping; *pres. p. par. of rt* रुद् 524.

रुदन्त्यौ *nom. du. f. of* रुदत् *m. f. n.* weeping, 524.

रुदिते he or she weeps; *3d sin. pres. átm.* (*more usually par.*) *of rt* रुद् *2d cl.* 653.

रुदित्वा having wept; *past ind. p. of rt* रुद् 556.

रुद्रा *for* रुद्रास् *nom. pl. of* रुद्र *m.* a Rudra, one of a group of semi-divine beings, (eight in number,) usually regarded as manifestations of S'iva, but in the earlier ages of Hindú mythology connected with the worship of Váyu or the wind. The eight Rudras are thus enumerated in the Vishṇu Puráṇa (p. 58),—Rudra, Bhava, Sarva, Is'ána, Pas'upati, Bhíma, Ugra, Mahádeva, most of which are merely other names for S'iva. 'Brahmá assigned to them as their respective stations, the sun, water, earth, air, fire, ether, the ministering Bráhman, and the moon.' These are their types or representatives in this world. See the opening verse of S'akuntalá. In other places the Rudras are described as eleven in number, and as children of Kas'yapa and Surabhi.

रुरोद he or she wept; *3d sin. perf. of rt* रुद् 364, 653.

रुषान्विता *nom. sin. f.* filled with anger, full of wrath; (*from* रुषा *cr.* anger, rage, *and* अन्वित *m. f. n.* possessed with.)

रूप *n.* form, figure, beauty, *1st cl.* 104.

रूपं *nom. or acc. sin. of* रूप *n.* form.

रूपतः *for* रूपतस् *ind.* in form; (*from* रूप *with affix* तस्.)

रूपमात्रवियोजितः Tat. or Dep. comp. 740; रूप *cr.* form, मात्र merely, only, वियोजितः *nom. sin. m.* deprived of, separated from.

रूपवती *nom. sin. f. of* रूपवत् *m. f. n.* beautiful, endowed with (a beautiful) form, *1st cl.* 105; *see* 140. *b.*

रूपवान् *nom. sin. m. of* रूपवत् *m. f. n.* possessed of (a beautiful) form, 140.

रूपसम्पदा Tat. or Dep. comp. 743; रूप *cr.* form, figure, सम्पदा *ins. sin. of* सम्पद् *f.* perfection, excellence, *5th cl.* 136.

रूपसम्पन्ना Tat. or Dep. comp. 740; **रूप** *cr.* beauty, **सम्पन्ना** *nom. sin. f. of* **सम्पन्न** *m. f. n.* endowed with, *past p. p. of rt* **पद्** *with prep.* **सम्**, 540.

रूपे *loc. sin. of* **रूप** *n.* form.

रूपेण *ins. sin. of* **रूप** *n.* form, shape, beauty.

रूपेणाप्रतिमाम् *for* **रूपेण अप्रतिमाम्** *by* 31.

रूपेणाप्रतिमेन *for* **रूपेण अप्रतिमेन** *by* 31.

रूपौदार्यगुणोपेताम् Complex comp. 771; **रूप** *cr.* beauty, **औदार्य** *cr.* generosity, **गुण** *cr.* quality, **उपेताम्** *acc. sin. f. of* **उपेत** *m. f. n.* endowed with.

रेमे he enjoyed bliss, he took pleasure; *3d sin. perf. átm. of rt* **रम्**, *see* 375. *a.*

रोदिति he or she weeps; *3d sin. pres. of rt* **रुद्** *2d cl.* 322.

रोदिमि I weep for, I sorrow for; *1st sin. pres.*

रोमहर्षश् *nom. sin. m.* erection of the hair of the body, either from a thrill of horror or delight; (**रोम** hair, *and* **हर्ष** *q. v.*)

रोषताम्राक्षस् Bah. or Rel. comp. 766; **रोष** *cr.* anger, **ताम्र** *cr.* red, coppery, **अक्षस्** *nom. sin. of* **अक्ष** *m. for* **अक्षि** the eye, *see* 778.

रोहिणी *nom. sin. f.* the fourth Lunar asterism personified as the moon's favourite wife, the moon being always a male deity in Hindú mythology.

रौद्रो *for* **रौद्रस्** *nom. sin. of* **रौद्र** *m. f. n.* fierce, ferocious.

ल.

लक्षणैर् *for* **लक्षणैस्** *ins. pl. of* **लक्षण** *n.* a mark, a spot, a characteristic.

लक्षणैश् *ins. pl. of* **लक्षण** *n.* a mark, indication.

लक्षय observe thou, take note of; *2d sin. imp. of rt* **लक्ष्** *10th cl.* 283.

लक्षयन्ती *nom. sin. f. of* **लक्षयत्** *m. f. n.* observing; *pres. p. of rt* **लक्ष्** *10th cl.* 524.

लक्षयित्वा having observed or noticed; *past ind. p. of rt* **लक्ष्** *10th cl.* 558.

लक्षये I observe, I see; *1st sin. pres. átm. of rt* **लक्ष्** *10th cl.* 283.

लक्षितं *nom. sin. n. of* **लक्षित** *m. f. n.* observed, perceived; *past p. p. of rt* **लक्ष्** 538.

लक्षितः *nom. sin. m. of* **लक्षित** *m. f. n.* seen, observed.

लक्षिता *nom. sin. f. of* **लक्षित** *m. f. n.* perceived.

लक्षितेयं *for* **लक्षिता इयं** *by* 32.

लक्षितो *for* **लक्षितस्** *nom. sin. m. of* **लक्षित** *m. f. n.* seen, perceived; *past p. p. of rt* **लक्ष्**.

लक्ष्म्या *ins. sin. of* **लक्ष्मी** *f.* fortune, the goddess of fortune, 124; *see note under* **श्री**.

लक्ष्यते he or it is perceived or seen; *3d sin. pres. of rt* **लक्ष्** *in pass.* 463.

लघुश् *nom. sin. m. of* **लघु** *m. f. n.* light, of little weight, 187.

लज्जां *acc. sin. of* **लज्जा** *f.* shame, modesty.

लज्जावत्यो *nom. pl. of* **लज्जावती** *f.* bashful, filled with shame, *1st cl.* 106, *see* 140.

लब्धवान् *nom. sin. m. of* **लब्धवत्** *m. f. n.* he obtained; *past act. p. of rt* **लभ्** 553.

लब्ध्वा having received, having obtained, having regained; *past ind. p. of rt* **लभ्** 556.

लभन्ते they receive, they take, they undertake (?); *3d pl. pres. átm. of* **लभ्**.

ललाटे *loc. sin. of* **ललाट** *n.* the forehead.

लाघवं *nom. or acc. sin. n.* lightness, contempt, disrespect.

लाभाय *dat. sin. of* **लाभ** *m.* gain, *see* 811.

लिङ्गधारणे Tat. or Dep. comp. 743; **लिङ्ग** *cr.* mark, badge, characteristic, **धारणे** *loc. sin. of* **धारण** *n.* bearing, holding, possessing, wearing, *1st cl.* 104.

लिङ्गानि *nom. or acc. pl. of* **लिङ्ग** *n.* a sign, a mark, characteristic, attribute, *1st cl.* 104.

लुब्धको *nom. sin. of* **लुब्धक** *m.* a hunter.

लेखा *nom. sin. f.* a streak, a line, a digit (of the moon).

लेभे he recovered; *3d sin. perf. átm. of rt* **लभ्** 375. *a.*

लोक *m.* the world, people, mankind, *1st cl.* 103.

लोककान्ताम् *acc. sin. f.* loved by the world, dear to all mankind; (*comp. of* लोक *cr.* the world, *and* कान्त beloved.)

लोककृताम् *gen. pl. of* लोककृत् *m.* creator of the world or worlds; (*comp. of* लोक the world, *and* कृत् 580.)

लोकपाल *m.* guardian of the world, 1*st cl.* 103; (*comp. of* लोक the world, *and* पाल guardian, 743.) The guardians of the world are the eight deities next below the Hindú Triad. They are, 1. Indra; 2. Agni or fire; 3. Súrya, the sun; 4. Ćandra, the moon; 5. Pavana, the wind; 6. Yama, the god of justice and lord of the infernal regions; 7. Varuṇa, the god of water; and 8. Kuvera, the god of wealth. In the Nala only four are introduced, viz. Indra, Agni, Varuṇa, and Yama. See Hindú Theatre I. 219.

लोकपालसमे Anom. comp. 777; लोकपाल *cr., see last,* समे *loc. sin. m. of* सम *m. f. n.* like, resembling, 1*st cl.* 187.

लोकपाला *for* लोकपालास् *nom. pl. m.* guardians of the world. *See* लोकपाल.

लोकपालाः *nom. pl. m.* guardians of the world.

लोकपालानां *gen. pl. m.* of the guardians of the world.

लोकपालाश् *nom. pl. m.* guardians of the world.

लोकपालास् *nom. pl. m.* guardians of the world.

लोकपालेषु *loc. pl. of* लोकपाल, *q. v.*

लोकस्य *gen. sin. of* लोक *m.* the world.

लोकान् *acc. pl. of* लोक *m.* the world.

लोके *loc. sin. of* लोक *m.* the world.

लोकेषु *loc. pl. of* लोक *m.* the world.

लोको *for* लोकस् *nom. sin. of* लोक *m.* the world.

लोचने *nom. du. of* लोचन *n.* the eye.

लोभाच् *for* लोभात् *abl. sin. of* लोभ *m.* eager desire.

लोभोपहतचेतसः *nom. pl. m.* having minds perverted by covetousness; (लोभ, उपहत, चेतस्, Bah. or Rel. comp. 767.)

लोष्टभिः *ins. pl. of* लोष्टन् *m. n.* a clod, lump of earth, 6*th cl.* 147.

व.

वंशभोज्यं *nom. sin. n.* to be possessed by a family, hereditary; (*comp. of* वंश *cr.* a family, *and* भोज्य to be enjoyed, 740.)

वः *for* वस् (*same as* युष्मान् *or* युष्माकं) you, of you; *acc. or gen. pl. of* त्वत् 219.

वक्तव्यं *nom. sin. n. of* वक्तव्य *m. f. n.* to be said, to be spoken; *fut. pass. p. of rt* वच् 569.

वक्तुं to speak, to say; *inf. of rt* वच् 459, 650.

वक्त्रं *acc. sin. of* वक्त्र *n.* the face, the mouth.

वक्षसि *loc. sin. of* वक्षस् *n.* the breast.

वक्ष्यन्ति they will bear, they will carry; 3*d pl.* 2*d fut. of rt* वह् 414.

वक्ष्यसि thou shalt say; 2*d sin.* 2*d fut. of rt* वच्.

वचः *for* वचस् *nom. or acc. sin. of* वचस् *n.* speech, word, 7*th cl.* 164.

वचनं *nom. or acc. sin. of* वचन *n.* word, speech, 1*st cl.* 104.

वचनाद् *for* वचनात् *abl. sin. of* वचन *n.* order, injunction, 1*st cl.* 104.

वचने *loc. sin. of* वचन *n.* a word, 1*st cl.* 104.

वचस् *nom. or acc. sin. of* वचस् *n.* speech, 7*th cl.* 164.

वचो *for* वचस् *nom. or acc. sin. of* वचस् *n.* speech.

वत *interj.* Ah! Oh! Alas!

वत्स्यसि thou shalt dwell; 2*d sin.* 2*d fut. of rt* वस् 607.

वत्स्यामि I will dwell; 1*st sin.* 2*d fut. of rt* वस् 607, 304. *a.*

वत्स्याम्यहमसंशयं *for* वत्स्यामि अहम् असंशयं *by* 34.

वद say thou, tell thou; 2*d sin. imp. of rt* वद् 1*st cl.* 599.

वदति he speaks, he describes; 3*d sin. pres. of rt* वद्.

वदरीविल्वसञ्छन्नं Complex comp. 771; वदरी *cr.* the jujube, a kind of tree or plant,

विल्व *cr.* the vilva or bel-tree, **सञ्छन्नं** *acc. sin. n. of* **सञ्छन्न** *m. f. n.* covered, concealed; *past p. p. of rt* **छद्** *with* **सं**, 540.

वदस्व speak thou; *2d sin. imp. átm. of rt* **वद्** *1st cl.* 599.

वदिष्यन्ति they will speak; *3d pl. 2d fut. of rt* **वद्**.

वदेद् *for* **वदेत्** he or she may speak; *3d sin. pot. of rt* **वद्** *1st cl.* 599.

वन *for* **वने** *loc. sin. of* **वन** *n.* a wood, *see* 36.

वनं *nom. or acc. sin. of* **वन** *n.* a wood.

वनगजान् KARM. OR DES. COMP. 755; **वन** *cr.* a wood, a forest, **गजान्** *acc. pl. of* **गज** *m.* an elephant.

वनगुल्मांश् *for* **वनगुल्मान्** (53) TAT. OR DEP. COMP. 743; **वन** *cr.* the forest, **गुल्मान्** *acc. pl. of* **गुल्म** *m.* a bush, a shrub.

वनपन्नगान् TAT. OR DEP. COMP. 743; **वन** *cr.* wood, **पन्नगान्** *acc. pl. of* **पन्नग** *m.* a snake, *1st cl.* 103.

वनस्थया *ins. sin. f. of* **वनस्थ** *m. f. n.* staying in the wood, a forester; (*from* **वन** *cr.* a wood, *and* **स्थ** staying, 580. *b.*)

वनस्थास्य *for* **वनस्थ अस्य** *by* 31.

वनानि *acc. pl. of* **वन** *n.* a wood.

वनान्तरे TAT. OR DEP. COMP. 743; **वन** *cr.* wood, **अन्तरे** *loc. sin. of* **अन्तर** *n.* midst, middle space, other, *1st cl.* 104.

वने *loc. sin. of* **वन** *n.* a wood.

वनेषु *loc. pl. of* **वन** *n.* a wood, *1st cl.* 104.

वनेषूपवनेषु *for* **वनेषु उपवनेषु** *by* 31.

वनोद्भवैः *ins. pl. of* **वनोद्भव** *m.* that which is produced in a forest, a tree, bough, bush, &c.; (*comp. of* **वन**, *q. v.*, *and* **उद्भव** produced.)

वपुः *nom. or acc. sin. of* **वपुस्** *n.* body, form, 165. *a.*

वपुर्मलसमाचितम् TAT. OR DEP. COMP. 745; **वपुस्** *cr.* the body, 65, **मल** *cr.* dirt, **समाचितम्** *nom. sin. n.* covered over.

वपुषा *ins. sin. of* **वपुस्** *n.* form, body, figure, *7th cl.* 165. *a.*

वयं we; *nom. pl. of* **अस्मत्**, *q. v.*

वयः *for* **वयस्** *nom. sin. n.* age.

वयःप्रमाणं TAT. OR DEP. COMP. 743; **वयः** *cr.* age, **प्रमाणं** *nom. sin. n.* measure, quantity, length, proof.

वयस् *nom. sin. n.* age, period of life, 164.

वयसा *ins. sin. of* **वयस्** *n.* age, time of life, *7th cl.* 164.

वयसि *loc. sin. of* **वयस्** *n.* age, period of life.

वरं *acc. sin. of* **वर** *m.* a boon, a gift, *1st cl.* 103.

वरः *nom. sin. m. of* **वर** *m. f. n.* best, most excellent, *1st cl.* 103, *see* 187.

वरनारीणां KARM. OR DES. COMP. 755; **वर** *cr.* best, most excellent, **नारीणाम्** *gen. pl. of* **नारी** *f.* a woman, *1st cl.* 106.

वरय choose thou; *2d sin. imp. par. of rt* **वृ** *in caus. with sense of the simple verb*, 675.

वरयस्व choose thou; *2d sin. imp. átm. of rt* **वृ** *in caus. with sense of the simple verb*, 675; *there is also a root* **वर्** *10th cl.*

वरयामास he or she chose; *3d sin. perf. of rt* **वृ** *10th cl.* 283.

वरयिष्यति he or she will choose; *3d sin. 2d fut. of rt* **वृ** *10th cl.* 283.

वरयिष्यामि I will choose; *1st sin. 2d fut. par. of rt* **वृ**, *see* 283.

वरयिष्ये I will choose; *1st sin. 2d fut. átm. of rt* **वृ** *10th cl.* 283.

वरयेत् she would choose; *3d sin. par. of rt* **वृ** *10th cl.* 283.

वरयेद् *for* **वरयेत्** he or she may choose.

वरवर्णिनि O excellent lady; *voc. sin. of* **वरवर्णिनी** *f.* an excellent or beautiful woman, *1st cl.* 106.

वरवर्णिनी *nom. sin. f.* an excellent woman; (**वर** best, *and* **वर्ण** class, caste, colour, *with affix* **इन्**.)

वरवर्णिनीं *acc. sin. f.* an excellent or lovely woman.

वरस्त्रियः *nom. pl. f.* excellent women; (*comp. of* **वर** excellent, *and* **स्त्री** 123. *b.*)

वराङ्गना KARM. OR DES. COMP. 755; **वर**

cr. excellent, best, अङ्गना *nom. sin. f.* a woman, *see* 743. *b.*

वराङ्गनाः *nom. pl. f.* best of women, 743. *b.*

वरान् *acc. pl. of* वर *m.* a blessing, a gift, a boon, 1*st cl.* 103.

वरारोहा *nom. sin. f.* an elegant or graceful woman; (*comp. of* वर excellent, *and* आरोह waist or hip.)

वरारोहां *acc. sin. of* वरारोहा *f.* a beautiful woman.

वराहांश् *for* वराहान् *acc. pl. of* वराह *m.* a hog, a boar, 1*st cl.* 103.

वरिष्यति he or she will choose; 3*d sin.* 2*d fut. of rt* वृ 398.

वरुणं *acc. sin. of* वरुण Varuṇa. *See next.*

वरुणो *for* वरुणस् *nom. sin. of* वरुण *m.* Varuṇa, the god of the waters. In the later mythology he is a kind of Hindú Neptune. He is regent of the west, and lord of punishment, in which latter capacity he resembles Yama, and, like him, holds a snaky cord or noose with which he binds incorrigible offenders under the water. His váhana or vehicle is the fabulous fish called Makara.

वर्चस्विनी *nom. sin. f. of* वर्चस्विन् *m. f. n.* bright, brilliant, 6*th cl.* 159.

वर्जितं *nom. sin. n. of* वर्जित *m. f. n.* deprived of, destitute of, (*governing instrumental case.*)

वर्जितॉंल् *for* वर्जितान् (*by* 56) *acc. pl. m. of* वर्जित *m. f. n.* free from, destitute of, void of.

वर्ण्यमानेषु *loc. pl. of* वर्ण्यमान being extolled, being described; *pres. p. pass. of rt* वर्ण् 528.

वर्ततां let it abide, let it remain, let it proceed; 3*d sin. imp. átm. of rt* वृत् 1*st cl.* 598.

वर्तते he lives or exists, he abides; 3*d sin. pres. átm. of rt* वृत् 1*st cl.* 598.

वर्तमाने *loc. sin. m. of* वर्तमान *m. f. n.* existing, taking place, going on, extant; *pres. p. átm. of rt* वृत् 598.

वर्तयन् *nom. sin. m. of* वर्तयत् *m. f. n.* supporting existence; *pres. p. par. of rt* वृत् *in caus.* 598, 525.

वर्तयामास he lived, he passed (his days); 3*d sin. perf. of rt* वृत् *in caus.* 490.

वर्धयसि thou dost increase, thou augmentest; 2*d sin. pres. of rt* वृध् *in caus.* 481.

वर्धयस्यमरोपम *for* वर्धयसि अमरोपम *by* 34.

वर्षायुतं *acc. sin. n.* for ten thousand years; (*comp. of* वर्ष a year, *and* अयुत *n.* ten thousand.)

वर्षे *loc. sin. of* वर्ष *m. n.* year, 1*st cl.* 103.

वल्कलाजिनसंवीतैर् COMPLEX COMP. 771; वल्कल *cr.* bark, अजिन *cr.* a skin, a hide, संवीतैर् *ins. pl. of* संवीत *m. f. n.* clothed.

ववन्दे he or she saluted; 3*d sin. perf. átm. of rt* वन्द् 364.

ववृधे it increased, he increased; 3*d sin. perf. átm. of rt* वृध् 364.

ववौ he or it blew; 3*d sin. perf. of rt* वा 373.

वशं *acc. sin. of* वश *m.* power, influence.

वशवर्तिनः *acc. pl. m. of* वशवर्तिन् *m. f. n.* obedient, submissive to authority, acting in obedience to (another's) will; (*from* वश will, authority, *and* वर्तिन् behaving, being, abiding in.)

वशिष्ठभृग्वत्रिसमैस् like to Vaśishṭha, Bhṛigu, and Atri, COMPLEX COMP. 771; वशिष्ठ *cr.* Vaśishṭha, भृग्व् *for* भृगु (34) *cr.* Bhṛigu, अत्रि *cr.* Atri, समैस् *ins. pl. m. of* सम *m. f. n.* equal to, like. Vaśishṭha, Bhṛigu, and Atri are three of the great saints or sages called Prajápatis or Brahmádikas, that is, mind-born sons of Brahmá. They belong to the highest order of saints, and are also called Brahmarshis. They are variously described as seven, nine, ten, and even twenty-one in number. See Vishṇu Puráṇa, p. 49.

वस् of you; *gen. pl.* (= युष्माकं) 219.

वस dwell thou; 2*d sin. imp. of rt* वस् 1*st cl.* 607.

वसतस् they two dwell; 3*d du. pres. of rt* वस् 1*st cl.* 607.

वसति he or she dwells; *3d sin. pres. of rt* वस्.

वसती *nom. sin. f. of* वसत् *m. f. n.* dwelling; *pres. p. of rt* वस् 524.

वसतो *gen. sin. of* वसत् *m. f. n.* dwelling, residing; *pres. p. of rt* वस्.

वसत्यनर्हस् *for* वसति अनर्हस् *by* 34.

वसवो *nom. pl. of* वसु *m.* a Vasu, a name of eight semi-divine beings, personifications of natural phenomena, whose names are variously enumerated. In the Vishṇu Puráṇa (p. 120, Wilson) they are thus given: 1. Ápa, water, or according to others Ahar, day; 2. Dhruva, the Pole-star; 3. Soma, the moon; 4. Dava, fire; 5. Anila, the wind; 6. Anala or Pávaka, fire; 7. Pratyúsha, dawn; 8. Prabhása, light. They are represented as always attendant on their leader Fire, and in their relationship to this deity and to the worship of the Sun and Light, seem to belong to the Vedic period of Hindú mythology.

वसस्व dwell thou; *2d sin. imp. átm. of rt* वस् *1st cl.* 607.

वसु *nom. or acc. sin. n.* wealth, property, substance, *3d cl.* 114.

वसुधां *acc. sin. of* वसुधा *f.* the earth, *1st cl.* 105.

वसुधाधिप O lord of the earth; (*from* वसुधा the earth, *and* अधिप *m.* a lord.)

वसुधाधिपं *acc. sin. m.* sovereign of the earth.

वसुधाधिपः *nom. sin. m.* lord of the earth.

वसुन्धरा *nom. sin. f.* the earth.

वसुन्धरां *acc. sin. of* वसुन्धरा *f.* the earth.

वसुसम्पूर्णां TAT. OR DEP. COMP. 740; वसु *cr.* wealth, सम्पूर्णां *acc. sin. f. of* सम्पूर्ण *m. f. n.* filled with, *1st cl.* 105.

वसूनि *acc. pl. of* वसु *n.* wealth, substance, *3d cl.* 114.

वसेतां *irregularly for* अवसेतां they two dwelt; *3d du. impf. átm. of rt* वस्. वसेतां *may also be the 3d du. pot. par.*

वस्तुं to dwell; *inf. of rt* वस् 607, 459.

वस्त्रं *acc. sin. n. of* वस्त्र *n.* a garment.

वस्त्रान्ते TAT. OR DEP. COMP. 743; वस्त्र *cr.* garment, अन्ते *loc. sin. of* अन्त *n.* end, *1st cl.* 104.

वस्त्रार्धं *acc. sin. n.* the half of a garment; (*comp. of* वस्त्र *cr.* a garment, *and* अर्ध *n.* half.)

वस्त्रार्धप्रावृताम् TAT. OR DEP. COMP. 745; वस्त्र *cr.* garment, अर्ध *cr.* half, प्रावृताम् *acc. sin. f. of* प्रावृत *m. f. n.* covered.

वस्त्रार्धसंवीता TAT. OR DEP. COMP. 745; वस्त्र *cr.* garment, अर्ध *cr.* half, संवीता *nom. sin. f. of* संवीत *m. f. n.* clothed.

वस्त्रार्धसंवृता TAT. OR DEP. COMP. 745; वस्त्र *cr.* a garment, अर्ध *cr.* half, संवृता *nom. sin. f. of* संवृत *m. f. n.* clothed.

वस्त्रार्धस्य of half (her) garment; (*from* वस्त्र *cr., q. v., and* अर्धस्य *gen. sin. of* अर्ध *n.* half, 743.)

वस्त्रार्धस्यावकर्तनं *for* वस्त्रार्धस्य अवकर्तनं *by* 31.

वस्त्रार्धेन *ins. sin. n. See* वस्त्रार्धं.

वस्त्रार्धेनाभिसंवृता *for* वस्त्रार्धेन अभिसंवृता *by* 31.

वस्त्रावकर्तेन TAT. OR DEP. COMP. 743; वस्त्र *cr.* a garment, अवकर्तेन *ins. sin. of* अवकर्त *m.* a part cut off, a strip, a fragment.

वहति he or it flows or is borne onwards; *3d sin. pres. of rt* वह् *1st cl.* 261.

वहतो *acc. pl. m. of* वहत् *m. f. n.* bearing, conveying; *pres. p. of rt* वह् 524.

वा *ind.* or, 728.

वाक्यं *acc. sin. of* वाक्य *n.* speech, words, *1st cl.* 104.

वाक्यानि *acc. pl. of* वाक्य *n.* speech, words.

वाक्ये *loc. sin. of* वाक्य *n.* speech, words.

वाक्येन *ins. sin. of* वाक्य *n.* speech, words.

वाग्भिर् *ins. pl. of* वाच् *f.* a word, 176.

वाग्मी *nom. sin. m. of* वाग्मिन् *m. f. n.* eloquent, *6th cl.* 159.

वाच् *f.* speech, a word, words, *8th cl.* 176.

वाचं *acc. sin. of* वाच् *f.* a speech, a word.

वाचा *ins. sin. of* वाच् *f.* speech, a word, 176.

वाचो *for* वाचस् *acc. pl. of* वाच् *f.* speech.

वाजिनाम् *gen. pl. of* वाजिन् *m.* a horse, 159.

वाञ्छति he wishes, he desires; 3*d sin. pres. of rt* वाञ्छ् 1*st cl.* 261.

वाञ्छसि thou desirest, thou wishest; 2*d sin. pres. of rt* वाञ्छ्.

वाढं *ind.* very well; (*particle of assent.*)

वातजवैर् *ins. pl. m.* fleet as the wind; (*comp. of* वात *cr.* the wind, जवैर् *ins. pl. of* जव fleet.)

वातरंहसः BAH. OR REL. COMP. 761; वात *cr.* the wind, रंहसः *acc. pl. m. from* रंहस् *n.* speed, velocity, 164. *a.*

वाथ *for* वा अथ *by* 31.

वान्यत्र *for* वा अन्यत्र *by* 31.

वापीश् *acc. pl. of* वापी *f.* a pool, 1*st cl.* 106.

वामलोचना BAH. OR REL. COMP. 766; वाम *cr.* beautiful, लोचना *nom. sin. f. from* लोचन *n.* an eye.

वायुना *ins. sin. of* वायु *m.* the wind, 110.

वायुभक्षैश् *for* वायुभक्षैस् *ins. pl. of* वायुभक्ष *m. f. n.* living on air; (*comp. of* वायु *cr.* air, *and* भक्षैश् *ins. pl. of* भक्ष feeding on.)

वायुर् *for* वायुस् *nom. sin. of* वायु *m.* the wind, the air, 3*d cl.* 110.

वायौ *loc. sin. of* वायु *m.* the wind, 110.

वारणाः *nom. pl. of* वारण *m.* an elephant.

वारयित्वा having driven off, having expelled, having prohibited; *past ind. p. of rt* वृ *in caus.* 558.

वारि *nom. sin. n.* water, tears, 2*d cl.* 114.

वारिणा *ins. sin. of* वारि *n.* water, moisture, tears.

वार्ष्णेय *voc. sin. m.* O Várshṇeya! O descendant of Vṛishṇi! name of Nala's charioteer, *also* a name of Kṛishṇa. (Vṛishṇi, son of Madhu, of the family of Yadu, was the ancestor of Kṛishṇa.)

वार्ष्णेयं *acc. sin. m.* Várshṇeya, Nala's charioteer.

वार्ष्णेयजीवलौ *nom. du. m.* Várshṇeya and Jívala, DVAN. OR AGG. COMP. 751.

वार्ष्णेयश् *nom. sin. m.* Várshṇeya.

वार्ष्णेयसहिते TAT. OR DEP. COMP. 740; वार्ष्णेय *cr.* Várshṇeya, सहिते *loc. sin. of* सहित *m. f. n.* accompanied by.

वार्ष्णेयसारथिः BAH. OR REL. COMP. 761; वार्ष्णेय *cr.* Várshṇeya, सारथिः *nom. sin. n.* a charioteer.

वार्ष्णेये *loc. sin. of* वार्ष्णेय *m.* Várshṇeya.

वार्ष्णेयेन *ins. sin. of* वार्ष्णेय *m.* Várshṇeya.

वार्ष्णेयो *for* वार्ष्णेयस् *nom. sin. m.* Várshṇeya.

वाशतीम् *acc. sin. f. of* वाशत् *m. f. n.* screaming, crying; *pres. p. of rt* वाश् 1*st cl.* 524. *This root more usually belongs to the* 4*th cl.*

वाष्पं *acc. sin. of* वाष्प *m.* tears.

वाष्पकलया TAT. OR DEP. COMP. 740; वाष्प *cr.* tears, suppressed tears, कलया *ins. sin. f. of* कल *m. f. n.* low in tone, 1*st cl.* 105.

वाष्पसन्दिग्धया TAT. OR DEP. COMP. 740; वाष्प *cr.* tears, suppressed tears, सन्दिग्धया *ins. sin. f. of* सन्दिग्ध *m. f. n.* doubtful, indistinct.

वाष्पाकुलां TAT. OR DEP. COMP. 740; वाष्प *cr.* tears, moisture of the eye, आकुलां *acc. sin. f. of* आकुल *m. f. n.* confused, 1*st cl.* 105.

वाष्पेण *ins. sin. of* वाष्प *m.* tears, (*only used in the singular.*)

वाष्पेणापिहिता *for* वाष्पेण अपिहिता *by* 31.

वासश् *for* वासस् (62) *acc. sin. of* वासस् *n.* a garment, 7*th cl.* 164.

वाससश् *for* वाससस् of the garment; *gen. sin. of* वासस् *n.* a garment.

वाससा *ins. sin. of* वासस् *n.* a garment, vest.

वाससां *gen. pl. of* वासस् *n.* a garment.

वाससाच्छन्नः *for* वाससा आच्छन्नः *by* 31.

वाससो *for* वाससस् *gen. sin. of* वासस् *n.* a garment, dress, 7*th cl.* 164.

वासांसि *acc. pl. of* वासस् *n.* clothes, a garment, 164.

वासो *for* वासस् *nom. sin. of* वास *m.* dwelling, abode.

वासो *for* वासस् *acc. sin. n.* a garment.

वासोयुगं *acc. sin. n.* a pair of garments; (*comp. of* वासो *for* वासस् *n.* a garment, *and* युग a pair, a couple, 743.) The dress of a Hindú consists of two pieces of cloth, one, the lower garment, fastened round the waist, and one, the upper garment, thrown loosely and gracefully over the shoulders.

वाहने *loc. sin. of* वाहन *n.* the act of driving (horses &c.); *lit.* causing to carry or draw.

वाहिना *ins. sin. of* वाहिन् *m.* a vehicle, a chariot, 6*th cl.* 159.

वाहुक *voc. sin. of* वाहुक *m.* Váhuka, name of a charioteer.

वाहुकं *acc. sin. m.* Váhuka. *See last.*

वाहुकच्छद्मिनं *acc. sin. m.* in the disguise of Váhuka; (*from* वाहुक Váhuka, *and* छद्मिन् *m. f. n.* possessed of a disguise, 159.)

वाहुकरूपिणम् *acc. sin. m.* in the form of Váhuka; (*comp. of* वाहुक, *and* रूपिन् having a form, 85. VI, 159.)

वाहुकस्य *gen. sin. of* वाहुक *m.* Váhuka.

वाहुके *loc. sin. of* वाहुक *m.* Váhuka.

वाहुकेन *ins. sin. of* वाहुक *m.* Váhuka.

वाहुको *for* वाहुकस् *nom. sin. m.* Váhuka.

वाह्यतः *for* वाह्यतस् (63) *ind.* outside, out-of-doors, 719. *b.*

वि *prep. implying* disjunction, distinction, dispersion, &c.

विंशतितमः *nom. sin. m.* twentieth, 211.

विकटो *nom. sin. of* विकट *m. f. n.* without a mat (to rest on); (*from* वि 726. *e, and* कट *m.* a mat made of grass or straw.)

विकम्पितुम् to hesitate, to shrink, to waver; *inf. of rt* कम्प् *with* वि.

विकर्तेयं I may cut off; 1*st sin. pot. of rt* कृत् *with* वि, *here used as a verb of the* 1*st cl.*, *but properly of the* 6*th cl.*, *see* 281.

विकारं *acc. sin. of* विकार *m.* emotion, feeling.

विकृतं *acc. sin. m. of* विकृत *m. f. n.* changed in form, deformed; *past p. p. of rt* कृ *with* वि, 532.

विकृताकारा Bah. or Rel. comp. 767; विकृत *cr.* distorted, mis-shaped, आकारा *nom. sin. f. from* आकार *m.* form, shape.

विकृतो *for* विकृतस् *nom. sin. m. of* विकृत *m. f. n.* deformed.

विकोषं *acc. sin. m. of* विकोष *m. f. n.* unsheathed; (*from* वि 726. *e, and* कोष *m.* a sheath, a scabbard.)

विक्रान्त *voc. sin. m. of* विक्रान्त *m. f. n.* valiant.

विक्रान्तः *nom. sin. of* विक्रान्त *m. f. n.* valiant, brave.

विख्यातां *acc. sin. f. of* विख्यात *m. f. n.* called, named, known as; *past p. p. of rt* ख्या *with* वि, 530.

विख्यातो *for* विख्यातस् *nom. sin. of* विख्यात *m. f. n.* celebrated.

विगणयन् *nom. sin. m. of* विगणयत् *m. f. n.* weighing, pondering, thinking on; *pres. p. of rt* गण् *with* वि, 10*th cl.* 525.

विगतज्वरम् Bah. or Rel. comp. 767; विगत *cr.* freed from, ज्वरम् *acc. sin. of* ज्वर *m.* trouble, feverishness, distress of mind.

विगतसङ्कल्पा *for* विगतसङ्कल्पास् Bah. or Rel. comp. 767; विगत *cr.* devoid of, सङ्कल्पास् *nom. pl. of* सङ्कल्प *m.* purpose, resolution, design, 1*st cl.* 103.

विघ्नं *acc. sin. of* विघ्न *m.* an obstacle, a difficulty.

विघ्नकर्तॄणाम् *gen. pl. of* विघ्नकर्ता *m.* the causer of obstacles; (*comp. of* विघ्न *cr.* an obstacle, *and* कर्तृ a doer, 4*th cl.* 127.) The deity Gaṇeśa is worshipped at the commencement of all undertakings as both creating and removing obstacles.

विचरतां of them roaming or flying about; *gen. pl. m. of* विचरत्. *See* विचरत्.

विचरति he or she roams about; 3*d sin. pres. of rt* चर् *with* वि, 1*st cl.* 261.

विचरत्येका *for* विचरति एका *by* 34.

विचरन् *nom. sin. m. of* विचरत् *m. f. n.* roaming about; *pres. p. par. of rt* चर् *with* वि, 524.

विचरामि I wander about; *1st sin. pres. of rt* चर् *with* वि, *1st cl.* 261.

विचरामीह *for* विचरामि इह *by* 31.

विचरितं *acc. sin. of* विचरित *n.* wandering, roaming.

विचलितुम् to move; *inf. of rt* चल् *with* वि, 459.

विचारणा *nom. sin. f.* doubt, hesitation.

विचार्य having deliberated, having considered, having debated; *past ind. p. of rt* चर् *in caus. with* वि, 566.

विचित्रमाल्याभरणैर् *for* विचित्रमाल्याभरणैस् COMPLEX COMP. 771; विचित्र *cr.* variegated, माल्य *cr.* garland, आभरणैर् *ins. pl. of* आभरण *n.* an ornament, *1st cl.* 103.

विचिन्त्य having reflected, having thought; *past ind. p. of rt* चिन्त् *with* वि, *10th cl.* 566.

विचिन्वानो *for* विचिन्वानस् *nom. sin. m. of* विचिन्वान *m. f. n.* seeking for, searching through; *pres. p. átm. of rt* चि *with* वि, *5th cl.* 524.

विचेष्टितम् *acc. sin. of* विचेष्टित *n.* action, act, conduct.

विच्युतिः *nom. sin. f.* severance, separation.

विजने *loc. sin. m. or n. of* विजन *m. f. n.* lonely, deserted; (*from* वि 726. *e, and* जन a person.)

विजने *loc. sin. n.* in private, in a private place, in the desert.

विजयं *acc. sin. of* विजय *m.* victory.

विजहार he rambled, he roamed; *3d sin. perf. of rt* हृ *with* वि, 593.

विजहारामरोपमः *for* विजहार अमरोपमः *by* 31.

विजानीत know ye; *2d pl. imp. of rt* ज्ञा *9th cl. with* वि, 688.

विजानीहि know thou; *2d sin. imp. of rt* ज्ञा *9th cl. with* वि.

विजितः *nom. sin. m. of* विजित *m. f. n.* conquered; *past p. p. of rt* जि *with* वि, 532.

विज्ञाते *loc. sin. m. of* विज्ञात *m. f. n.* known; *past p. p. of rt* ज्ञा *with* वि, 532.

विज्ञाय having known, having ascertained; *past ind. p. of rt* ज्ञा *with* वि, 559.

विज्ञेयौ *nom. du. m. of* विज्ञेय *m. f. n.* to be perceived; *fut. pass. p. of rt* ज्ञा *with* वि, 571. *a.*

वितरसि thou dost grant; *2d sin. pres. See next.*

वितरामि I bestow, I grant; *1st sin. pres. of rt* तॄ *with* वि, *1st cl.* 261.

वितिमिराम् *acc. sin. f. of* वितिमिर *m. f. n.* devoid of gloom; (*comp. of* वि 726. *e, and* तिमिर darkness.)

वित्तं *nom. sin. n.* wealth, property.

वित्तवन्तम् *acc. sin. of* वित्तवत् *m. f. n.* possessed of riches, 140.

वित्रासितविहङ्गमाम् BAH. OR REL. COMP. 767; वित्रासित *cr.* frightened away, विहङ्गमाम् *acc. sin. f. from* विहङ्गम *m.* a bird.

विदर्भ *m., generally declined in pl.* विदर्भास *nom.* Vidarbha, a district and city to the S. W. of Bengal, also called Kuṇḍina. It is supposed to be the same as the modern Berár or Nágpúr. Some take Vidarbha as the name of the country and Kuṇḍina as its capital. Mention is made of both Vidarbha and its capital Kuṇḍina in the Málatí-Mádhava (Act I) as follows: विदर्भराजमन्त्रिणा देवरातेन माधवं पुत्रम् आन्वीक्षिकीश्रवणाय कुण्डिनपुराद् इमां पद्मावतीं प्रहिणवता सुविहितं 'It has been well done by Devaráta, the minister of the king of Vidarbha, (in) sending his son Mádhava from the city of Kuṇḍina to this Padmávatí to study logic.' According to Prof. H. H. Wilson, Kuṇḍina corresponds to the modern district of Kondavir.

विदर्भतनया TAT. OR DEP. COMP. 743; विदर्भ *cr.* Vidarbha, तनया *nom. sin. f.* daughter.

विदर्भनगरीं TAT. OR DEP. COMP. 743; विदर्भ

cr. Vidarbha, नगरीं *acc. sin. of* नगरी *f.* a city, *1st cl.* 106.

विदर्भपतये *dat. sin. of* विदर्भपति *m.* lord of Vidarbha; (*comp. of* विदर्भ *and* पति lord, 121.)

विदर्भराजतनयां TAT. OR. DEP. COMP. 743; विदर्भ *cr.* Vidarbha, राज *for* राजन् *cr.* king, 57, तनयां *acc. sin. of* तनया *f.* a daughter.

विदर्भराजस् TAT. OR DEP. COMP. 743; विदर्भ *cr.* Vidarbha, राजस् *nom. sin. m. for* राजा a king, *by* 151.

विदर्भराजाधिपतिः *for* विदर्भराजा अधिपति *by* 31.

विदर्भराजो *for* विदर्भराजस् *nom. sin. m.* king of Vidarbha.

विदर्भराज्ञो TAT. OR DEP. COMP. 743; विदर्भ *cr.* Vidarbha, राज्ञो *for* राज्ञस् *gen. sin. of* राजन् 148.

विदर्भराड् *nom. sin. m.* king of Vidarbha; (*comp. of* विदर्भ *and* राड् *for* राट् 41, *nom. sin. of* राज् *m.*, *8th cl.* 176. *e.*)

विदर्भसरसस् TAT. OR DEP. COMP. 743; विदर्भ *cr.* Vidarbha, सरसस् *abl. sin. of* सरस् *n.* a lake, *7th cl.* 164.

विदर्भस्य *gen. sin. of* विदर्भ *m.* Vidarbha.

विदर्भां *acc. sin. of* विदर्भा *f.* the city of Vidarbha.

विदर्भांस् *for* विदर्भान् *acc. pl. of* विदर्भ Vidarbha.

विदर्भाणां *gen. pl. of* विदर्भ *m.* Vidarbha.

विदर्भाधिपतिः *nom. sin. m.* the sovereign of Vidarbha.

विदर्भाधिपतेर् *for* विदर्भाधिपतेस् *gen. sin. m.* of the lord of Vidarbha; (*comp. of* विदर्भ *and* अधिपति *m.* lord, sovereign.)

विदर्भाधिपनन्दिनी TAT. OR DEP. COMP. 745; विदर्भ *cr.* Vidarbha, अधिप *cr.* king, नन्दिनी *f.* a daughter.

विदर्भान् *acc. pl. of* विदर्भ *m.* Vidarbha.

विदर्भाभिमुखो *nom. sin. m.* having his face towards Vidarbha, facing Vidarbha; (*comp. of* विदर्भ Vidarbha, *and* अभिमुख 761.)

विदर्भेषु *loc. pl. of* विदर्भ *m.* Vidarbha.

विदितं *nom. sin. n. of* विदित *m. f. n.* known; *past p. p. of rt* विद् 538.

विदिता *nom. sin. f. of* विदित *m. f. n.* known.

विदित्वा having known, knowing; *past ind. p. of rt* विद्.

विद्धि know thou; *2d sin. imp. of rt* विद् *2d cl.* 308, 583.

विद्ध्यक्षहृदयज्ञं *for* विद्धि अक्ष° *by* 34.

विद्मः we know; *1st pl. pres. of rt* विद् *2d cl.*

विद्यते he or it exists, there exists or is found; *3d sin. pres. of rt* विद् *6th cl. in pass.* 463.

विद्या *nom. sin. f.* science.

विद्यां *acc. sin. of* विद्या *f.* science, knowledge, skill.

विद्यां I may know; *1st sin. pot. of rt* विद् *2d cl.* 583.

विद्युत् *nom. sin. f.* lightning, *5th cl.* 136. Beautiful women are often compared in Hindú poetry to lightning, which, as the forerunner of the rainy season, is regarded as an object of desire and admiration.

विद्युद् *for* विद्युत् *nom. sin. f.* lightning.

विद्युर् *for* विद्युस् they may know, they may recognise; *3d pl. pot. of rt* विद् *2d cl.* 583.

विद्योतयति he or she causes to shine, he or she illuminates; *3d sin. pres. of rt* द्युत् *in caus. with* वि, 481.

विद्रवन्ति they run away, they fly; *3d pl. pres. of rt* द्रु *with* वि, *1st cl.* 502.

विद्वान् *nom. sin. m. of* विद्वस् *m. f. n.* wise, prudent, 168. *e.*

विद्वेषणेन *ins. sin. of* विद्वेषण *n.* enmity, *1st cl.* 104.

विधत्स्व do thou ordain, do thou act; *2d sin. imp. átm. of rt* धा *3d cl. with* वि, 664.

विधिदृष्टेन TAT. OR DEP. COMP. 740; विधि *cr.* rule, दृष्टेन *ins. sin. n. of* दृष्ट *m. f. n.* seen, prescribed, approved.

विधिना *ins. sin. of* विधि *m.* manner, mode, action, 110.

विधिर् *nom. sin. of* विधि *m.* fate, destiny, fated event, rule.

विधिवच् *for* विधिवत् *ind.* according to rule, 48, 724. *a.*

विधिवद् *for* विधिवत् *ind.* according to rule.

विधीयतां let it be managed, let it be done; 3*d sin. imp. pass. of rt* धा *with* वि, 465.

विधेः *gen. sin. of* विधि *m.* fate, destiny, 2*d cl.* 110.

विध्वस्तपर्णकमलां COMPLEX COMP. 771; विध्वस्त fallen off, पर्ण leaf, कमलां *acc. sin. f. from* कमल *n.* a lotus.

विनंक्ष्यामि I shall perish; 1*st sin.* 2*d fut. of rt* नश् *with* वि, 415. *k.*

विनमते he bows himself; 3*d sin. pres. átm. of rt* नम् *with* वि, 1*st cl.* 261.

विनयावनता *nom. sin. f.* modestly bending or bowing low with modesty; (*comp. of* विनय *cr.* modesty, *and* अवनत bent, 740.)

विनशेद् he may perish; 3*d sin. pot. of rt* नश् *here* 1*st cl., but properly* 4*th cl.* 620. विनश्येद् *would be more usual.*

विनष्टा *nom. sin. f. of* विनष्ट *m. f. n.* lost; *past p. p. of rt* नश् 539.

विना *ind.* without, (*governing ins.* 731, 917.)

विनाशं *acc. sin. m. of* विनाश *m.* destruction.

विनिःश्वस्य having sighed; *past ind. p. of rt* श्वस् *with* निर् *and* वि, 559.

विनिःसृतः *nom. sin. m. of* विनिःसृत *m. f. n.* come out, issued forth; *past p. p. of rt* सृ *with* निर् *and* वि, 896.

विनिक्षिप्य having given in charge, having delivered over; *past ind. p. of rt* क्षिप् *with* नि *and* वि, 559.

विनिर्दिष्टं *nom. sin. n. of* विनिर्दिष्ट *m. f. n.* pointed out; *past p. p. of rt* दिश् *with* निर् *and* वि, 539.

विनिर्मितः *nom. sin. m. of* विनिर्मित *m. f. n.* formed, made; *past p. p. of rt* मा *with* निर् *and* वि, 533.

विनिर्मुक्ताः *nom. pl. m. of* विनिर्मुक्त *m. f. n.* escaped, set free; *past p. p. of rt* मुच् *with* निर् *and* वि, 539.

विनिष्क्रम्य having gone forth from; *past ind. p. of rt* क्रम् *with* निर् *and* वि, 559.

विनिश्चित्य having deliberated, having weighed; *past ind. p. of rt* चि *with* निर् *and* वि (71. *b*), *see* 560.

विनिश्वस्य having sighed; *past ind. p. of rt* श्वस् *with* नि *and* वि, 559.

विनिहतं *nom. sin. n. of* विनिहत *m. f. n.* destroyed, slain; *past p. p. of rt* हन् *with* नि *and* वि, 545.

विनीतैः *ins. pl. m. of* विनीत *m. f. n.* submissive, well-conducted.

विन्दति he incurs; he or she finds or meets with; he perceives or discovers; 3*d sin. pres. of rt* विद् 6*th cl.* 281.

विन्दामि I find; 1*st sin. pres. of rt* विद् 6*th cl.* 281.

विन्दे I find; 1*st sin. pres. átm. of rt* विद् 6*th cl.* 281.

विन्देत she may find; 3*d sin. pot. átm. of rt* विद् 6*th cl.* 281.

विन्देतापि *for* विन्देत अपि *by* 31.

विन्ध्यो *for* विन्ध्यस् *nom. sin. of* विन्ध्य *m.* the Vindhya mountain, a chain which divides Hindústán from the Dekhan or South country. These mountains, sometimes called Bindh, hold an important position both in the mythology and geography of India. According to some authorities they are called Bindhya, because they appear to obstruct the progress of the sun. The course of the Nerbudda (Narmadá) river falls in with the direction of the principal range; but the mountainous tract called Bindhya spreads much more widely, meeting the Ganges in several places to the North, whilst the Godavarí is held to be its Southern limit.

विन्यस्य having laid, having placed; *past ind. p. of rt* अस् *with* वि *and* नि, 559.

विपरीतं *nom. sin. n. of* **विपरीत** *m.f.n.* adverse, reverse, contrary.

विपरीतानि *acc. pl. n.* adverse, unfavourable.

विपरीतास् *nom. pl. m. of* **विपरीत** adverse.

विपर्ययः *nom. sin. of* **विपर्यय** *m.* contrariety, difference.

विपर्ययश् *nom. sin. of* **विपर्यय** *m.* the contrary, the reverse.

विपिने *loc. sin. of* **विपिन** *n.* a wood, a forest.

विपुलश्रोणि Bah. or Rel. comp. 766; **विपुल** *cr.* large, **श्रोणि** *voc. sin. of* **श्रोणी** *f.* the hip, 106; (O lady with swelling hips! O round-limbed!)

विपुले *loc. sin. m. of* **विपुल** *m. f. n.* large, vast, 1*st cl.* 187.

विप्र O Bráhman! *voc. sin. of* **विप्र** *m.* a Bráhman.

विप्रयुक्तः *nom. sin. m.* separated; *past p. p. of rt* **युज्** *with* **प्र** *and* **वि**, 539.

विप्रसमागमम् Tat. or Dep. comp. 743; **विप्र** *cr.* a Bráhman, **समागमम्** *acc. sin. of* **समागम** *m.* concourse.

विप्रा *for* **विप्रास्** *nom. pl. of* **विप्र** *m.* a Bráhman.

विप्रा *for* **विप्रास्** O Bráhmans! *voc. pl. of* **विप्र** *m.* a Bráhman.

विप्रियं *acc. sin. of* **विप्रिय** *n.* offence, anything disagreeable; (*comp. of* **वि** 726. *e, and* **प्रिय** agreeable.)

विबुधा *for* **विबुधास्** O gods! *voc. pl. of* **विबुध** *m.* a god.

विबुधान् *acc. pl. of* **विबुध** *m.* a god.

विबुधास् *voc. pl. of* **विबुध** *m.* a god, 1*st cl.* 103.

विबुधेश्वराः O lords of the immortals! Tat. or Dep. comp. 743; **विबुध** *cr.* a god, an immortal, **ईश्वराः** *voc. pl. of* **ईश्वर** *m.* a lord, 1*st cl.* 103, *see* 32.

विब्रुवन्तु let them speak out; 3*d pl. imp. of rt* **ब्रू** *with* **वि**, 649.

विभावसो *gen. sin. of* **विभावसु** *m.* the sun.

विभीतकं *acc. sin. of* **विभीतक** *m.* the Vibhítaka-tree (*Beleric myrobalan*).

विभीतकश् *nom. sin. m.* the Vibhítaka-tree.

विभुः *for* **विभुस्** *nom. sin. of* **विभु** *m.* a lord, a master, 3*d cl.* 110.

विभूत्यर्थम् *ind.* through (his) omnipotence, for the sake of (displaying) his creative power; (*comp. of* **विभूति** superhuman power, *and* **अर्थं** 760. *d*, 791.)

विभो *voc. sin. of* **विभु** *m.* a lord, a master.

विभ्रमन् *nom. sin. m. of* **विभ्रमत्** *m. f. n.* wandering over; *pres. p. of rt* **भ्रम्** *with* **वि**, 524, (*governing acc.*)

विमनास् *nom. sin. m. of* **विमनस्** out of one's mind, out of one's senses; (*comp. of* **वि** 726. *e, and* **मनस्**, *see* 164. *a.*)

विमानानि *acc. pl. of* **विमान** *n.* a vehicle, a car; *usually* a self-moving aerial chariot of the gods.

विमुक्तं *acc. sin. m. or n. of* **विमुक्त** *m. f. n.* freed, released, free from; *past p. p. of rt* **मुच्** *with* **वि**, 539.

विमुक्तः *nom. sin. m. of* **विमुक्त** *m. f. n.* released, set free.

विमुच्य having released, having quitted; *past ind. p. of rt* **मुच्** *with* **वि**, 559.

विमुञ्चन्तो *for* **विमुञ्चन्तस्** *nom. pl. m. of* **विमुञ्चत्** *m. f. n.* uttering, emitting; *pres. p. par. of rt* **मुच्** *with* **वि**, 524.

विमृश्य having considered, having pondered; *past ind. p. of rt* **मृश्** *with* **वि**, 559.

विमोक्ष्यति he will release; 3*d sin.* 2*d fut. of rt* **मुच्** *with* **वि**, 628.

विमोचनात् *abl. sin. of* **विमोचन** *n.* liberation, setting free, 1*st cl.* 104; *see also* 814. *b.*

विमोचय do thou release; 2*d sin. imp. of rt* **मुच्** *with* **वि**, 10*th cl.* 283.

वियोगं *acc. sin. of* **वियोग** *m.* separation.

वियोगश् *for* **वियोगस्** *nom. sin. m.* separation.

विरजांसि *acc. pl. n. of* **विरजस्** *m. f. n.* free from dust, 7*th cl.* 164; (*comp. of* **वि** 726. *e, and* **रजस्** dust.)

विरहिता *nom. sin. f. of* **विरहित** *m. f. n.* deserted by, separated from; *past p. p. of rt* **रह्** *with* **वि**, 538.

विराजद्भिर् *ins. pl. of* **विराजत्** *m. f. n.* brilliant, splendid, shining, glittering; *pres. p. par. of rt* **राज्** *with* **वि**, 524.

विराजितम् *acc. sin. m. of* **विराजित** *m. f. n.* splendid, radiant.

विरूपो *nom. sin. m. of* **विरूप** *m. f. n.* deformed; (*comp. of* **वि** 726. *e, and* **रूप**.)

विलज्जमाना *nom. sin. f. of* **विलज्जमान** *m. f. n.* being modest; *pres. p. átm. of rt* **लज्ज्** *with* **वि**, 526.

विलपन्ती *nom. sin. f. of* **विलपत्** *m. f. n.* lamenting, wailing.

विलपन्तीं *acc. sin. f. of* **विलपत्** *m. f. n.* lamenting, mourning; *pres. p. of rt* **लप्** *with* **वि**, 524.

विलपमाना *nom. sin. f. of* **विलपमान** *m. f. n.* lamenting; *pres. p. átm. of rt* **लप्** *with* **वि**, 526.

विलपितम् *acc. sin. of* **विलपित** *n.* lamentation.

विलप्य lamenting, bewailing; *past ind. p. of rt* **लप्** *with* **वि**, 559.

विलम्बितुम् to delay; *inf. of rt* **लम्ब्** *with* **वि**, 1*st cl.* 261, *see* 459.

विललाप he or she lamented or uttered lamentations; 3*d sin. perf. of rt* **लप्** *with* **वि**, 364.

विललापाश्रुपूर्णाक्षी *for* **विललाप अश्रुपूर्णाक्षी** *by* 31.

विवरो *nom. sin. of* **विवर** *m.* expansion, widening, dilatation.

विवर्णवदना BAH. OR REL. COMP. 766; **विवर्ण** *cr.* colourless, pale, **वदना** *nom. sin. f. from* **वदन** *n.* face, 108.

विवर्णा *nom. sin. f.* pale, colourless.

विवर्णां *acc. sin. f. of* **विवर्ण** *m. f. n.* pale, colourless; (*comp. of* **वि** 726. *e, and* **वर्ण** colour.)

विवस्त्रं *acc. sin. m. of* **विवस्त्र** *m. f. n.* without clothes; (*from* **वि** 726. *e, and* **वस्त्र** *q. v.*)

विवस्त्रो *nom. sin. of* **विवस्त्र** *m. f. n.* unclothed, without a garment.

विवाससम् *acc. sin. m. of* **विवासस्** *m. f. n.* without clothes, 7*th cl.* 163; (*from* **वि** 726. *e, and* **वासस्**.)

विवासाद् *abl. sin. of* **विवास** *m.* banishment from home; (in consequence of her exile.)

विवाहं *acc. sin. of* **विवाह** *m.* marriage, 1*st cl.* 103.

विविधांश् *for* **विविधान्** *acc. pl. m.* various.

विविधान् *acc. pl. m. of* **विविध** *m. f. n.* various.

विविधेषु *loc. pl. n. of* **विविध** *m. f. n.* various, different, 1*st cl.* 103.

विविधैः *ins. pl. n. of* **विविध** *m. f. n.* various.

विविधैर् *ins. pl. m. of* **विविध** *m. f. n.* various.

विविधोपलभूषितम् COMPLEX COMP. 771; **विविध** *cr.* various, **उपल** *cr.* gem, jewel, **भूषितम्** *acc. sin. m. of* **भूषित** *m. f. n.* adorned.

विविशाते they two entered; 3*d du. perf. átm. of rt* **विश्** *with prep.* **वि**, 364.

विविशुर् *for* **विविशुस्** they entered; 3*d pl. perf. of rt* **विश्** *with* **वि**, 364.

विविशुस् they entered; 3*d pl. perf. of rt* **विश्** *with* **वि**, 364.

विवेश he or she entered; 3*d sin. perf. of rt* **विश्** *with* **वि**, 364.

विवेशाश्रमपदं *for* **विवेश आश्रमपदं** *by* 31.

विशङ्कां *acc. sin. of* **विशङ्का** *f.* suspicion, doubt.

विशस्य having cut in two, having cut open; *past ind. p. of rt* **शस्** *with* **वि**, 559.

विशाम्पतिः *nom. sin. m., lit.* lord of (many) men of the Vaiśya caste, *i. e.* either peasants or men engaged in trade. *See next.*

विशाम्पते O lord of men! *voc. sin. of* **विशाम्पति** TAT. OR DEP. COMP., *in which the case of the first member is retained, see* 743. *c*; **विशाम्** *gen. pl. of* **विश्** *m.* a man, especially one of the commercial or agricultural class, 181; **पते** *voc. sin. of* **पति** 121. According to the original constitutions of Hindú society, as described in Manu, the population was divided into four castes or classes: 1. Bráhmans or priests; 2. Kshatriyas or soldiers; 3. Vaiṡyas or working-men, such as peasants or agricultural labourers and men in trade; 4. S'údras or slaves.

विशारदम् *acc. sin. m. of* विशारद *m. f. n.* skilled, skilful.

विशालाक्षः *nom. sin. m.* large-eyed; (*comp. of* विशाल *cr.* large, *and* अक्ष *for* अक्षि 778.)

विशालाक्षीम् *acc. sin. f. See last.*

विशितेन *ins. sin. n. of* विशित *m. f. n.* sharp, sharpened, 1*st cl.* 104.

विशिष्ट *m. f. n.* illustrious, distinguished, excellent, 1*st cl.* 103.

विशिष्टाया *for* विशिष्टायास् *gen. sin. f. of* विशिष्ट illustrious.

विशिष्टेन *ins. sin. m. of* विशिष्ट illustrious, distinguished.

विशीर्णो *for* विशीर्णस् *nom. sin. m. of* विशीर्ण *m. f. n.* crushed, trampled on, broken; *past p. p. of rt* शॄ *with* वि, 534.

विशेषतः *for* विशेषतस् *ind.* excellently, especially, particularly, 719. *b. In* Book XV. 3 *it governs an instrumental case, and must be translated* more excellently than, *or* in an especial manner compared with (others), 830; (*formed from* विशेष *by affix* तस्.)

विशेषतो *for* विशेषतस् *ind.* especially, 719. *b.*

विशेषेण *ins. sin. of* विशेष, *used adverbially,* especially, particularly.

विशोका *nom. sin. f.* free from sorrow.

विशोकां *acc. sin. f. of* विशोक *m. f. n.* free from sorrow, without sorrow; (*comp. of* वि 726. *e, and* शोक *m.* sorrow.)

विश्रब्धं *acc. sin. m. of* विश्रब्ध *m. f. n.* confidential, faithful, trusty, 1*st cl.* 103.

विश्रान्तं *acc. sin. m. of* विश्रान्त *m. f. n.* rested.

विश्रान्ता *nom. sin. f. of* विश्रान्त *m. f. n.* rested, reposed; *past p. p. of rt* श्रम् *with* वि, 546.

विश्राम्यताम् let it be rested, let repose be taken; 3*d sin. imp. of rt* श्रम् *in pass. with* वि, 463.

विश्रुत *voc. sin. m. See* विश्रुतः.

विश्रुतः *nom. sin. m. of* विश्रुत *m. f. n.* celebrated, known; *past p. p. of rt* श्रु *with* वि, 532.

विश्रुता *nom. sin. f. of* विश्रुत *m. f. n.* celebrated, known.

विश्रुतां *acc. sin. f.* known, celebrated.

विषं *acc. sin. of* विष *n.* poison, bane.

विषनिमित्ता *nom. sin. f.* caused by the poison; (*comp. of* विष *n.* poison, *and* निमित्त cause, 761.)

विषमस्थः *nom. sin. of* विषमस्थ *m. f. n.* being in difficulty or misfortune; (*comp. of* विषम *cr.* difficulty, misfortune, *and* स्थ remaining, 580.)

विषमस्थस्य *gen. sin. m. of* विषमस्थ *m. f. n.* being in trouble. *See last.*

विषमस्थेन *ins. sin. m.* involved in calamity.

विषमे *loc. sin. of* विषम *n.* difficulty, trouble, calamity.

विषमेषु in rough places; *loc. pl. n. of* विषम *m. f. n.* rough, uneven; (*comp. of* वि 726. *e, and* सम even.)

विषविमुक्तात्मा Bah. or Rel. comp. 761; विष *cr.* poison, विमुक्त *cr.* released from, आत्मा *nom. sin. m. of* आत्मन् soul, 146.

विषीदन् *nom. sin. m. of* विषीदत् *m. f. n.* sorrowing, grieving; *pres. p. of rt* सद् to despond, *with* वि.

विषीदन्तम् *acc. sin. m. of* विषीदत् *m. f. n.* sorrowing, desponding; *pres. p. of rt* सद् *with* वि.

विषेण *ins. sin. of* विष *n.* poison.

विष्टभ्य having stopped, having made to stand still; *past ind. p. of rt* स्तम्भ् *with* वि, 70.

विष्ठितं *acc. sin. of* विष्ठित *m. f. n.* abiding, staying; *past p. p. of rt* स्था *with* वि, 70, 896. *a.*

विसर्जने *loc. sin. of* विसर्जन *n.* desertion.

विससृपुः they flew about, they fluttered hither and thither; 3*d pl. perf. of rt* सृप् *with prep.* वि, 364.

विसृज्य having let fall, having loosed or let go; *past ind. p. of rt* सृज् *with* वि.

विस्तरेण *ind.* at full length, 714.

विस्तरेणाभिधास्यामि *for* **विस्तरेण अभिधास्यामि** *by* 31.

विस्तीर्णां *acc. sin. f. of* **विस्तीर्ण** *m. f. n.* spread out; broad, wide.

विस्पष्टां *acc. sin. f. of* **विस्पष्ट** *m. f. n.* clear, distinct.

विस्मयं *acc. sin. of* **विस्मय** *m.* astonishment.

विस्मयान्विताः TAT. OR DEP. COMP. 740; **विस्मय** *cr.* wonder, admiration, **अन्विताः** *nom. pl. of* **अन्वित** *m. f. n.* possessed of.

विस्मयाविष्टो TAT. OR DEP. COMP. 740; **विस्मय** *cr.* astonishment, wonder, **आविष्टो** *for* **आविष्टस्** *nom. sin.* affected by, filled with.

विस्मयो *for* **विस्मयस्** *nom. sin. of* **विस्मय** *m.* admiration, wonder, astonishment.

विस्मितस् *nom. sin. m. of* **विस्मित** *m. f. n.* astonished; *past p. p. of rt* **स्मि** *with* **वि**, 532.

विस्मिता *nom. sin. f. of* **विस्मित** *m. f. n.* astonished, surprised.

विस्मिता *for* **विस्मितास्** *nom. pl. of* **विस्मित** *m. f. n.* surprised, astonished, dismayed; *past p. p. of rt* **स्मि** *with* **वि**, 530.

विस्मिताननः BAH. OR REL. COMP. 767; **विस्मित** *cr.* astonished, surprised, **आननः** *nom. sin. m. from* **आनन** *n.* face, 108.

विस्मिताश् *nom. pl. f. of* **विस्मित** *m. f. n.* astonished.

विस्मितैर् *ins. pl. of* **विस्मित** *m. f. n.* surprised, astonished; *past p. p. of rt* **स्मि** *with* **वि**, 532.

विहगैर् *ins. pl. of* **विहग** *m.* a bird.

विहङ्गैर् by birds; *ins. pl. of* **विहङ्ग** *m.* a bird.

विहरंश् *for* **विहरन्** *nom. sin. of* **विहरत्** *m. f. n.* roaming, sauntering about, taking pleasure; *pres. p. par. of rt* **हृ** *with* **वि**, 593.

विहातुम् to abandon; *inf. of rt* **हा** *with* **वि**, 459, 665.

विहाय having abandoned; *past ind. p. of rt* **हा** *with* **वि**.

विहायसा *ind.* in the sky, aloft, 714.

विहितश् *nom. sin. m. of* **विहित** *m. f. n.* planned, devised; *past p. p. of rt* **धा** *with* **वि**, 533. *a.*

विहिता *nom. sin. f. of* **विहित** *m. f. n.* performed, enacted, committed.

विहितो *for* **विहितस्** *nom. sin. m. of* **विहित** *m. f. n.* appointed, destined, decreed; *past p. p. of rt* **धा** *with* **वि**, 533. *a.*

विहीनौ *nom. du. m. of* **विहीन** *m. f. n.* deprived of, separated from.

विह्वलं *acc. sin. m. of* **विह्वल** *m. f. n.* agitated.

विह्वला *nom. sin. f. of* **विह्वल** *m. f. n.* agitated (with grief).

विह्वलां *acc. sin. f. of* **विह्वल** *m. f. n.* disturbed, agitated.

वीक्षितुम् to see, to be seen; *inf. of rt* **ईक्ष्** *with* **वि**, 459, 869.

वीतशोक *voc. sin. m.* O Víta-śoka! *lit.* O free from sorrow; another name for the Aśoka-tree, 1st *cl.* 103.

वीर *voc. sin. of* **वीर** *m.* a hero.

वीरं *acc. sin. of* **वीर** *m.* a hero, 1st *cl.* 103.

वीरः *nom. sin. of* **वीर** *m.* a hero, heroic.

वीरप्रजायिनि *voc. sin. f.* O mother of heroes! (*comp. of* **वीर**, *q. v., and* **प्रजायिनी** *f.* a mother, one who brings forth, gives birth.)

वीरबाहोर् *for* **वीरबाहोस्** *gen. sin. of* **वीरबाहु** name of a prince.

वीरश् *nom. sin. m.* a hero, heroic.

वीरसेन *for* **वीरसेनस्** *nom. sin. m.* Vírasena.

वीरसेननृपस्नुषा TAT. OR DEP. COMP. 745; **वीरसेन** *cr.* Vírasena, **नृप** *cr.* a king, **स्नुषा** *nom. sin. f.* a daughter-in-law.

वीरसेनसुतप्रिया *nom. sin. f.* beloved by the son of Vírasena, TAT. OR DEP. COMP. 745; **वीरसेन** *cr.* Vírasena, **सुत** *cr.* a son, **प्रिया** *nom. sin. f. of* **प्रिय** *m. f. n.* beloved, dear.

वीरसेनसुतो TAT. OR DEP. COMP. 743; **वीरसेन** *cr.* Vírasena, **सुतो** *for* **सुतस्** *nom. sin. of* **सुत** *m.* a son.

वीरस्य *gen. sin. of* **वीर** *m.* a hero.

वीराः *for* **वीरास्** O heroes! *voc. pl. of* **वीर** *m.* a hero.

वीरे *loc. sin. of* **वीर** *m.* a hero.

वीरेण *ins. sin. of* **वीर** *m.* a hero, heroic.

वीरो *for* **वीरस्** *nom. sin. m.* a hero, heroic.

वीर्यसत्त्ववतो *gen. sin. m. of* **वीर्यसत्त्ववत्** *m.f.n.* possessed of valour and worth; (*comp. of* **वीर्य** *cr.* valour, **सत्त्व** *cr.* strength, worth, **वत्** *affix*, 84. VII, 140.)

वीर्यसम्पन्नः TAT. OR DEP. COMP. 740; **वीर्य** *cr.* valour, **सम्पन्नः** *nom. sin. of* **सम्पन्न** *m. f. n.* endowed with.

वृक्षमूलेषु TAT. OR DEP. COMP. 743; **वृक्ष** *cr.* a tree, **मूलेषु** *loc. pl. of* **मूल** *n.* a root, 1*st cl.* 105.

वृक्षे *loc. sin. of* **वृक्ष** *m.* a tree.

वृक्षेषु *loc. pl. of* **वृक्ष** *m.* a tree, 1*st cl.* 103.

वृक्षेष्वारुह्य *for* **वृक्षेषु आरुह्य** *by* 34.

वृणीते he or she chooses; 3*d sin. pres. átm. of rt* **वृ** 9*th cl.* 675 *note.*

वृणे I choose; 1*st sin. pres. átm. of rt* **वृ** 9*th cl.* 675 *note.*

वृतं *acc. sin. m. of* **वृत** *m. f. n.* surrounded; *past p. p. of rt* **वृ** 675.

वृतः *nom. sin. of* **वृत** *m.f.n.* elected, selected, chosen; *past p. p. of rt* **वृ** 675.

वृतस् *nom. sin. m.* chosen, elected.

वृतां *acc. sin. f. of* **वृत** *m. f. n.* covered, overspread, surrounded; *past p. p. of rt* **वृ** 675.

वृते *loc. sin. m. of* **वृत** *m.f.n.* chosen, elected; *past p. p. of rt* **वृ** 675.

वृतो *for* **वृतस्** *nom. sin. m. of* **वृत** *m. f. n.* chosen; *past p. p. of rt* **वृ** 675.

वृत्तान्तं *acc. sin. of* **वृत्तान्त** *m.* tidings, news, 1*st cl.* 103.

वृद्धानाम् *gen. pl. of* **वृद्ध** *m.* an old man, a sage.

वृद्धानुशासनम् TAT. OR DEP. COMP. 743; **वृद्ध** *cr.* an old man, a seer, **अनुशासनम्** *nom. sin. n.* precept.

वृषेण *ins. sin. of* **वृष** *m.* *See* **वृषो**.

वृषेणेति *for* **वृषेण इति** *by* 32.

वृषो *for* **वृषस्** *nom. sin. of* **वृष** *m.* a bull, 1*st cl.* 103; *used in* Book VII. 6 as the name of the principal die in a game with dice.

वृहत्सेनां *acc. sin. of* **वृहत्सेना** *f.* Vṛihatsená, the name of Damayantí's nurse.

वृहत्सेने *voc. sin. f.* *See last.*

वृहदश्व *for* **वृहदश्वस्** *nom. sin. of* **वृहदश्व** *m.* Vṛihadaśva, the name of the sage who relates the story of Nala to Yudhishṭhira.

वेगः *nom. sin. m.* onset, impetus.

वेगतः (*by* 63. *a*) *for* **वेगतस्** *ind.* quickly, speedily; (*from* **वेग** *with affix* **तस्**, 719.)

वेगेन *ins. sin. of* **वेग** *m.* impetuosity, 1*st cl.* 103.

वेतनं *nom. sin. n.* wages, hire, salary, pay.

वेतसैर् *for* **वेतसैस्** *ins. pl. of* **वेतस** *m.* a cane, a ratan, 1*st cl.* 103.

वेत्ति he knows; 3*d sin. pres. of rt* **विद्**.

वेत्थ thou knowest, thou mayest know; 2*d sin. of a contracted perf.* (*used for pres.*) *of rt* **विद्**, *see* 308. *a.*

वेत्स्यामि I shall know; 1*st sin.* 2*d fut. of rt* **विद्** 404.

वेद he knows, he comprehends; 3*d sin. of a contracted form of the perf. of rt* **विद्** *used as a present, see* 308. *a.*

वेदपारगैः *ins. pl. m. of* **वेदपारग** *m. f. n.* thoroughly conversant with the Vedas; (*comp. of* **वेद** *and* **पारग**, *q. v.*)

वेदविच् *for* **वेदविद्** *by* 49. *See next.*

वेदविद् *nom. sin. m.* knowing the Vedas, *see note under* **वेदाः**; (*comp. of* **वेद** *cr.* the Veda, *and* **विद्** *m.* a knower, 137.)

वेदवेदाङ्गपारगः *nom. sin. m.* well-read in the Vedas and Vedángas, *see next*; (*comp. of* **वेद** *cr.* the Vedas, *see next*; **वेदाङ्ग** the Vedángas or sciences subordinate to the Vedas, such as grammar, prosody, pronunciation, etymology, &c., *see note under* **साङ्गोपाङ्गाः**; **पारगः** *nom. sin. of* **पारग** *m. f. n.* well-versed in, *lit.* going right through, going to **पार**, the opposite side.)

वेदाः *nom. pl. of* वेद *m.* the Veda or sacred scripture of the Hindús, 1*st cl.* 103. The four Vedas are the Ṛig-veda, the Yajur-veda, the Sáma-veda, and the Atharva-veda. Of these the Ṛig-veda is the oldest. It consists of metrical hymns or prayers termed súktas or mantras, each stanza of which is called a *ṛić*, addressed to the gods of the elements, and especially to *Indra*, god of the atmosphere, and *Agni*, fire. The composition of the principal mantras of the Ṛig-veda is supposed to have taken place about thirteen or fourteen centuries B. C.

वेदाक्षनैपुणं *for* वेद अक्षनैपुणं *by* 31.

वेदान् *acc. pl. of* वेद *m.* the Veda or sacred writings of the Hindús.

वेदितुम् to know; *inf. of rt* विद् 459.

वेपथुश् *nom. sin. m.* tremor, trembling.

वेपमानः *nom. sin. of* वेपमान *m. f. n.* trembling; *pres. p. átm. of rt* वेप् 526.

वेपमाना *nom. sin. f. of* वेपमान *m. f. n.* trembling; *pres. p. átm. of rt* वेप् 526.

वेपमानां *acc. sin. f. of* वेपमान *m. f. n.* trembling.

वेपमानेदम् *for* वेपमाना इदम् *by* 32.

वेपमानो *for* वेपमानस् *nom. sin. m. of* वेपमान *m. f. n.* trembling; *pres. p. átm. of rt* वेप् 526.

वेलाम् *acc. sin. of* वेला *f.* time.

वेश्म *nom. or acc. sin. of* वेश्मन् *n.* a house, a dwelling, 153.

वेश्मनि *loc. sin. of* वेश्मन् *n.* a house, 153.

वेश्मानि *acc. pl. n. of* वेश्मन् *n.* a house, a dwelling, 153.

वै *ind.* indeed, truly. *Often a mere expletive.*

वैक्लव्यम् *acc. sin. of* वैक्लव्य *n.* agitation of mind.

वैदर्भि *voc. sin. of* वैदर्भी O daughter of the king of Vidarbha! *i. e.* Damayantí.

वैदर्भी *nom. sin. f.* Damayantí, daughter of the sovereign of Vidarbha.

वैदर्भीं *acc. sin. of* वैदर्भी *f.* Damayantí, 1*st cl.* 106.

वैदर्भीजननी *nom. sin. f.* the mother of Damayantí (*see* जननी).

वैदर्भीत्येव *for* वैदर्भि इति एव *by* 32, 34.

वैदर्भ्या *ins. sin. of* वैदर्भी *f.* Damayantí.

वैदर्भ्या *for* वैदर्भ्यास् *gen. sin. of* वैदर्भी *f.* Damayantí.

वैदर्भ्यां *loc. sin. of* वैदर्भी *f.* Damayantí.

वैदर्भ्याः *gen. sin. of* वैदर्भी *f.* Damayantí, 1*st cl.* 106.

वैशसं *acc. sin. of* वैशस *n.* slaughter, destruction.

वैश्रवणः *nom. sin. m.* Vaiśravaṇa, a name of Kuvera, the god of wealth, (so called from his father विश्रवस्.)

वैषम्यं *acc. sin. of* वैषम्य *n.* calamity, misfortune, evil condition.

वो *for* वस् you, for you, to you, of you; *acc., dat. or gen. pl. from* युष्मद्, *q. v.*

व्यक्तं *ind.* plainly, evidently, certainly, 713.

व्यथते he or it grieves or suffers pain; 3*d sin. pres. of rt* व्यथ् 1*st cl.* 261.

व्यथयन्ति they afflict, they pain; 3*d pl. pres. of rt* व्यथ् 10*th cl.*

व्यथितं *nom. sin. n. of* व्यथित *m. f. n.* agitated; *past p. p. of rt* व्यथ् 538.

व्यथिताः *nom. pl. m. of* व्यथित *m. f. n.* disturbed, troubled.

व्यदीर्यत he or it was torn asunder; 3*d sin. impf. átm. of rt* दॄ *in pass. with* वि, 468.

व्यदीर्यतेव *for* व्यदीर्यत इव *by* 32.

व्यपनीय having laid aside, having put away; *past ind. p. of rt* नी to lead, *with* अप *and* वि, 559.

व्यपाकर्षद् he removed; 3*d sin. impf. of rt* कृष् *with* अप *and* वि, 606.

व्यभ्रे *loc. sin. n. of* व्यभ्र *m. f. n.* cloudless; (*from* वि 726. *e, and* अभ्र *q. v.*)

व्ययुज्यत he was separated; 3*d sin. impf. of rt* युज् *in pass. with* वि, 702.

व्यरोचत he or it shone forth or appeared; 3*d sin. impf. átm. of rt* रुच् *with* वि, 261.

व्यवर्धत he or it grew stronger or increased; *3d sin. impf. átm. of rt* वृध् *with* वि, *1st cl.* 261.

व्यवसायेन *ins. sin. of* **व्यवसाय** *m.* effort, exertion.

व्यवसिता *for* **व्यवसितास्** *nom. pl. m. of* **व्यवसित** *m. f. n.* resolved, determined.

व्यसनं *acc. sin. of* **व्यसन** *n.* calamity, misfortune. This word is especially applied to a king's neglect of his duty for the pleasures of the chase, gambling, &c.

व्यसनान्विताम् *acc. sin. f.* involved in calamity; **व्यसन** *cr.* calamity, misfortune, **अन्विताम्** *acc. sin. of* **अन्वित** *m. f. n.* possessed of, *1st cl.* 104.

व्यसनाप्लुतम् TAT. OR DEP. COMP. 740; **व्यसन** *cr.* calamity, **आप्लुतम्** *acc. sin. m.* overwhelmed with.

व्यसनिनं *acc. sin. m. of* **व्यसनिन्** *m. f. n.* afflicted, fallen into calamity, 159.

व्यसनेन *ins. sin. of* **व्यसन** *n.* calamity.

व्यसनेनार्दितं *for* **व्यसनेन अर्दितं** *by* 31.

व्यसर्जयत् he left, he lost, he dismissed; *3d sin. impf. of rt* सृज् *in caus. with* वि, 481.

व्यसुः *nom. sin. m. of* **व्यसु** *m. f. n.* lifeless; (*from* वि 726. *e, and* **असु** *m.* breath.)

व्याकुलाम् *acc. sin. f. of* **व्याकुल** *m. f. n.* agitated.

व्याघ्रैर् *ins. pl. of* **व्याघ्र** *m.* a tiger, *1st cl.* 103.

व्याजहार he uttered; *3d sin. perf. of rt* हृ *with prep.* आ *and* वि, 593.

व्यात्तास्यो BAH. OR REL. COMP. 766; **व्यात्त** *cr.* open, **आस्यो** *for* **आस्यस्** *nom. sin. m. from* **आस्य** *n.* mouth, 108.

व्याधः *nom. sin. m.* a hunter, *1st cl.* 103.

व्याहरसे thou dost talk jestingly, thou dost rail; *2d sin. pres. átm. of rt* हृ *with* आ *and* वि, 593.

व्याहरिष्यसि thou wilt talk jestingly, thou wilt rail; *2d sin. 2d fut. of rt* हृ *with* आ *and* वि, 593.

व्याहर्तुम् to utter, to say; *inf. of rt* हृ *with* आ *and* वि, 459, 593.

व्युषितो *for* **व्युषितस्** *nom. sin. m. of* **व्युषित** *m. f. n.* lodged, (having lodged, 896); *past p. p. of rt* वस् *with* वि, 607.

व्युष्टा *nom. sin. f. of* **व्युष्ट** *m. f. n.* lodged, having lodged; *past p. p. of rt* वस् *with* वि. N. B. *The regular past passive participle of this root is* उषित, *see* 607, 543.

व्यूढोरस्क *voc. sin. m.* O broad-chested one! 766; (*from* **व्यूढ** *cr.* broad, *and* **उरस्** *n.* the breast, *with affix* क, *see* 80. LVI.)

व्योम्नि *loc. sin. of* **व्योमन्** *n.* sky, heaven, *6th cl.* 152.

व्रज go thou, depart thou; *2d sin. imp. of rt* व्रज् *1st cl.* 261.

व्रजामात्यान् *for* **व्रज आमात्यान्** *by* 31.

व्रजामि I go; *1st sin. pres. of rt* व्रज्.

व्रजाम्येनम् *for* **व्रजामि एनम्** *by* 34.

व्रजेत् he or it may go; *3d sin. pot. of rt* व्रज् *1st cl.* 261.

व्रजेद् he or she may go; *3d sin. pot. of rt* व्रज्.

व्रतम् *nom. sin. of* **व्रत** *n.* a vow.

व्रीडिता *nom. sin. f. of* **व्रीडित** *m. f. n.* ashamed; *past p. p. of rt* व्रीड् 538.

व्रीडिता *for* **व्रीडितास्** *nom. pl. of* **व्रीडित** *m. f. n.* ashamed.

श.

शंस tell thou; *2d sin. imp. of rt* शंस्.

शंसत tell ye; *2d pl. imp. of rt* शंस् *1st cl.* 261.

शंसति he tells, he relates, he announces; *3d sin. pres. of rt* शंस् *1st cl.* 261.

शंससि thou declarest, thou makest known; *2d sin. pres. of rt* शंस् *1st cl.* 261.

शकुना *for* **शकुनास्** *nom. pl. of* **शकुन** *m.* a bird.

शकुनानाम् *gen. pl. of* **शकुन** *n.* an omen.

शकुनैर् *ins. pl. of* **शकुन** *m.* a bird.

शक्तो *for* **शक्तस्** *nom. sin. of* **शक्त** *m. f. n.* able, capable; *past p. p. of rt* शक् 679, 539.

शक्नुवन्ति they are able; *3d pl. pres. of rt* शक् *5th cl.* 679.

शक्नोमि I am able; *1st sin. pres. of rt* शक् *5th cl.* 679.

शक्यते he or it is able; *3d sin. pres. of rt* शक् *in pass.* 679 *note*, 869.

शक्यसे thou art able; *2d sin. pres. átm. of rt* शक् *4th cl.* 679 *note*, 869.

शक्या *nom. sin. f. of* शक्य *m. f. n.* able; *fut. pass. p. of rt* शक् 573.

शक्याव् *for* शक्यौ *nom. du. m. of* शक्य *m. f. n.* able.

शक्र *m.* a name of Indra, *1st cl.* 103.

शक्रं *acc. sin. of* शक्र *m.* Indra.

शक्रः *nom. sin. of* शक्र *m.* S'akra, a name of Indra, *1st cl.* 103.

शक्रेण *ins. sin. of* शक्र *m.* Indra.

शक्रो *for* शक्रस् *nom. sin. of* शक्र *m.* Indra.

शङ्कमाना *nom. sin. f. of* शङ्कमान *m. f. n.* suspecting, fearing; *pres. p. átm. of rt* शङ्क् 526.

शङ्कसे thou dost fear, thou dost doubt; *2d sin. pres. átm. of rt* शङ्क् *1st cl.* 261.

शङ्का *nom. sin. f.* doubt, suspicion.

शङ्के I suspect, I fancy; *1st sin. pres. átm. of rt* शङ्क् *1st cl.* 261.

शङ्केत he might suspect; *3d sin. pot. átm. of rt* शङ्क् *1st cl.* 261.

शचीपतिः Tat. or Dep. comp. 743; शची *cr.* S'aćí, wife of Indra, पतिः *nom. sin. of* पति *m.* a husband, *2d cl.* 121.

शच्या *ins. sin. of* शची *f.* the wife of Indra, *1st cl.* 106.

शच्येव *for* शच्या इव *by* 32.

शत *n.* a hundred, 206, 835. *c.*

शतं *nom. or acc. sin. n.* a hundred, 206, 835. *b.*

शतक्रतुम् *acc. sin. of* शतक्रतु *m.* Indra; (*from* शत a hundred, *and* क्रतु a sacrifice; 'lord of a hundred sacrifices.')

शतपत्त्रायतेक्षणाम् Bah. or Rel. comp. 761; शतपत्त्र *cr.* a lotus, आयत *cr.* long, ईक्षणाम् *acc. sin. f. from* ईक्षण *n.* the eye.

शतयोजनयायिभिः Complex comp. 771; शत *cr.* a hundred, योजन *cr.* a yojana, यायिभिः *ins. pl. of* यायिन् *m. f. n.* going, travelling, 159.

शतशो *for* शतशस् (64) *ind.* by hundreds; (शत 206, *with affix* शस् 725.)

शताः *nom. pl. of* शत *m.* a hundred; *used in* Book XV. 6 *for* शतानि, *as denoting* a hundred suvarṇas or gold coins. शतं शताः *may be translated* ten thousand gold coins.

शत्रुकर्षण *voc. sin. m.* O destroyer of (thy) foes; (*comp. of* शत्रु *cr.* an enemy, *and* कर्षण one who tears.)

शत्रुघ्न *voc. sin.* O killer of your enemies! (*comp. of* शत्रु *cr.* an enemy, *and* घ्न a killer, *from rt* हन् 580. *b.*)

शत्रुतो *for* शत्रुतस् from an enemy, *for* शत्रोस् *abl. of* शत्रु, *see affix* तस् 719. *a.*

शनकै *for* शनकैस् *ind.* slowly, by degrees.

शनकैर् *for* शनकैस् *ind.* slowly.

शनकैस् *ind.* slowly, softly, gently, *for* शनैस् 714.

शनैः *for* शनैस् *ind.* by degrees, 714.

शपेन् (*for* शपेत् *by* 47) let him or he should curse; *3d sin. pot. of rt* शप् *1st cl.* 261.

शप्तुं to curse; *inf. of rt* शप् 459.

शप्तो *for* शप्तस् *nom. sin. m. of* शप्त *m. f. n.* cursed; *past p. p. of rt* शप् 539.

शप्स्यसे thou wilt curse; *2d sin. 2d fut. átm. of rt* शप् 408.

शब्दं *acc. sin. of* शब्द *m.* sound, cry.

शब्दः *nom. sin. of* शब्द *m.* sound.

शब्दो *for* शब्दस् *nom. sin. of* शब्द *m.* a sound.

शम *for* शमस् *nom. sin. of* शम *m.* calmness of mind, tranquillity, equanimity.

शयानं *acc. sin. m. of* शयान *m. f. n.* lying down; *pres. p. átm. of rt* शी 646, 526. *a.*

शय्यासनभोगेषु Dvan. or Agg. comp. 749; शय्या *cr.* a bed, a couch, lying down, आसन *cr.* a seat, sitting down, भोगेषु *loc. pl. of* भोग *m.* a meal, eating, *1st cl.* 103.

शरणं *acc. sin. of* **शरण** *n.* a refuge, one who acts as a protection or defence; *also* taking refuge.

शरणार्थिनः *nom. pl. m. of* **शरणार्थिन्** *m. f. n.* seeking a refuge, seeking for protection; (*comp. of* **शरण** *cr.* refuge, *and* **अर्थिन्** seeking, *6th cl.* 159.)

शरणार्थिनी *nom. sin. f.* seeking a refuge.

शरण्य *voc. sin. m. of* **शरण्य** *m. f. n.* that which or who affords refuge or protection, *1st cl.* 103.

शरदः *acc. pl. of* **शरद्** *f.* a year, (*properly* autumn.)

शरदां *gen. pl. of* **शरद्** *f.* autumn.

शरीराणि *acc. pl. of* **शरीर** *n.* the body.

शरीरान् *for* **शरीरात्** (47) *abl. sin. of* **शरीर** *n.* the body.

शरीरान्तकरो *for* **शरीरान्तकरस्** TAT. OR DEP. COMP. 743; **शरीर** *cr.* the body, **अन्तकरस्** *nom. sin. of* **अन्तकर** *m.* the destroyer.

शरीरिणः *gen. sin. of* **शरीरिन्** *m.* the (embodied) spirit.

शरीरे *loc. sin. of* **शरीर** *n.* the body.

शशाप he or she cursed; *3d sin. perf. of rt* **शप्** 364. The terrific power of a curse, according to Indian ideas, is well illustrated by Southey's 'Curse of Keháma,' and by 'The Death of Yajña-datta' in the Rámáyaṇa, translated into English verse by the late Dean Milman.

शशापैनं *for* **शशाप एनं** *by* 33.

शशास he ruled, he governed; *3d sin. perf. of rt* **शास्** 658.

शशिनः *gen. sin. of* **शशिन्** *m.* the moon, *6th cl.* 159.

शशिनो *for* **शशिनस्** *gen. sin. of* **शशिन्** *m.* the moon, *6th cl.* 159.

शश्वज् *for* **शश्वत्** (48) *ind.* always, perpetually.

शस्त्र *n.* a weapon, (*lit.* the instrument of hurting, *from rt* **शस्** 80. XX), *1st cl.* 104.

शस्त्रपाणयः *nom. pl. m.* armed, having weapons in (their) hands; (**शस्त्र** a weapon, **पाणि** a hand; BAH. OR REL. COMP. 767.)

शस्त्राणि *nom. pl. of* **शस्त्र** *n.* a weapon.

शस्त्रेण *ins. sin. of* **शस्त्र** *n.* a weapon, an arrow, *1st cl.* 104.

शाखयोः *loc. du. of* **शाखा** *f.* a branch, 105.

शाखामृगगणायुतम् TAT. OR DEP. COMP. 745; **शाखामृग** *cr.* a monkey, **गण** *cr.* a troop, **आयुतम्** *acc. sin. n. of* **आयुत** *m. f. n.* filled with, possessed of.

शाखायाः *gen. sin. of* **शाखा** *f.* a branch, 105.

शाखे *acc. du. of* **शाखा** *f.* a branch, 105.

शातयामास he cut, he clove, he severed; *3d sin. perf. of rt* **शद्** *in caus.*

शातयित्वा having cut down, having cloven, having severed; *past ind. p. of rt* **शद्** *in caus.* 558.

शातयिष्ये I will cut down or off, I will cleave, I will tear; *1st sin. 2d fut. átm. of rt* **शद्** *in caus.* 481.

शान्तज्वरा BAH. OR REL. COMP. 767; **शान्त** *cr.* allayed, alleviated, assuaged, **ज्वरा** *nom. sin. f. from* **ज्वर** *m.* fever, pain, suffering, 108.

शान्तिस् *nom. sin. of* **शान्ति** *f.* settlement of difference, satisfaction.

शापाग्निः TAT. OR DEP. COMP. 743; **शाप** *cr.* curse, **अग्निः** *nom. sin. m.* fire, 110.

शापान् *or* **शापाद्** *for* **शापात्** *abl. sin. of* **शाप** (47) *m.* a curse, *1st cl.* 103.

शापेन *ins. sin. of* **शाप** *m.* a curse.

शारदी *nom. sin. f. of* **शारद** *m. f. n.* autumnal.

शार्दूलमृगसेवितम् COMPLEX COMP. 771; **शार्दूल** *cr.* a tiger, **मृग** *cr.* a deer, **सेवितम्** *acc. sin. n. of* **सेवित** *m. f. n.* infested by, resorted to, inhabited.

शार्दूलो *for* **शार्दूलस्** *nom. sin. of* **शार्दूल** *m.* a tiger.

शालवेणुधवाश्वत्थतिन्दुकेङ्गुदकिंशुकैः DVAN. OR AGG. COMP. 748; **शाल** *cr.* the S'ála-tree, **वेणु** *cr.* a bambu, **धव** *cr.* Dhava, a kind of tree, **अश्वत्थ** *cr.* the holy fig-tree,

तिन्दुक Tinduka, a kind of ebony-tree, इङ्गुद Inguda, a kind of tree or plant, किंशुकैः *ins. pl. of* किंशुक *m.* the Kinśuka-tree, 1*st cl.* 103. The S'ál-tree is the *Shorea-robusta,* which yields a resinous exudation; the Dhava is the *Grislea tomentosa;* the Aśvattha is the *Ficus religiosa* or holy fig-tree, also called Pippala. There are two other celebrated fig-trees in India, the *Ficus glomerata,* called Uḍumbara in this list, and the *Ficus Indica,* called Nyagrodha or Vaṭa, or in English the Banyan-tree. The Ingudí, commonly called Ingua or Jiyaputa, is a tree from the fruit of which necklaces of a supposed prolific efficacy were made (Jíva-putraka). In the Raghu-vanśa (XIV. 81) there is an allusion to the fruit being used by hermits to supply oil, and in the S'akuntalá (Act II) to its furnishing them with ointment. The Kinśuka is the *Butea frondosa,* a tree bearing beautiful red blossoms.

शालास्थाश् *nom. pl. m.* standing in the stables; (*comp. of* शाला a stable, *and* स्थ staying, 580.)

शालिहोत्रो *for* शालिहोत्रस् *nom. sin. m.* S'áli-hotra, name of a personage skilled in horses.

शाश्वताः *nom. pl. m. of* शाश्वत *m. f. n.* eternal.

शाश्वतो *for* शाश्वतस् *nom. sin. m. of* शाश्वत *m. f. n.* everlasting.

शासनं *nom. sin. n.* a precept, a maxim.

शासनात् *abl. sin. of* शासन *n.* order, command, decree, 104.

शास्त्रतः *for* शास्त्रतस् *ind.* according to rule, (*lit.* according to the S'astras; *from* शास्त्र *and affix* तस् 719.)

शिखरैश् *ins. pl. of* शिखर *m. n.* a peak, 1*st cl.* 103.

शिखिनः *nom. pl. of* शिखिन् *m.* a peacock, 159.

शिखिनस् *nom. pl. of* शिखिन् *m.* a peacock, 159.

शिरस् *acc. sin. of* शिरस् *n.* the head, 164.

शिलातलं TAT. OR DEP. COMP. 743; शिला *cr.* a rock, तलम् *acc. sin. of* तल *n.* surface.

शिलोच्चयम् *acc. sin. of* शिलोच्चय *m.* a mountain, 1*st cl.* 103.

शिल्पानि *nom. pl. of* शिल्प *n.* an art, craft.

शिवः *nom. sin. m. of* शिव *m. f. n.* auspicious, propitious, safe.

शिष्टा *nom. sin. f. of* शिष्ट *m. f. n.* left; *past p. p. of rt* शिष् 672, 539.

शिष्यस् *nom. sin. m.* a disciple, scholar, pupil.

शीघ्रं *ind.* quickly.

शीघ्रयाने KARM. OR DES. COMP. 755; शीघ्र *cr.* rapid, याने *loc. sin. of* यान *n.* motion, going, driving, 1*st cl.* 104.

शीघ्रयानेषु *loc. pl. n. See last.*

शीघ्रा *for* शीघ्रास् *nom. pl. m. of* शीघ्र *m. f. n.* fast, rapid, fleet.

शीतांशुना *ins. sin. of* शीतांशु *m.* the moon; (*from* शीत cold, *and* अंशु a ray, beam.)

शीर्णानां *gen. pl. of* शीर्ण *m. f. n.* broken off; *past p. p. of rt* शॄ 534.

शीलनिधिः TAT. OR DEP. COMP. 743; शील *cr.* virtue, निधिः *nom. sin. m.* treasure.

शीलवान् *nom. sin. of* शीलवत् *m. f. n.* of a good disposition, amiable, 5*th cl.* 140.

शुचः *for* अशुचः 2*d sin. aor. of rt* शुच् to grieve, *see* 889.

शुचिर् *for* शुचिस् *nom. sin. of* शुचि *m.* S'ući, the name of the captain of the caravan.

शुचिस्मिता smiling serenely or sweetly, BAH. OR REL. COMP. 761; शुचि *cr.* serene or white (showing the teeth), स्मिता *nom. sin. f. from* स्मित *n.* a smile, 108, *or from* स्मित *past p. p. of rt* स्मि 896. *b.*

शुचिस्मिताम् *acc. sin. f.* smiling sweetly.

शुचिस्मिते *voc. sin. f.* O sweetly smiling (maiden)!

शुच्युपचारो BAH. OR REL. COMP. 766; शुचि *cr.* holy, pure, उपचारो *for* उपचारस् *nom. sin. m. from* उपचार practise, action, usage.

शुद्धान् *acc. pl. m. of* **शुद्ध** *m. f. n.* correct, faultless, pure.

शुध्यते is cleared (from blame &c.), is acquitted; *3d sin. pres. pass. of rt* **शुध्** 463.

शुभ *m. f. n.* beautiful, happy, good, *1st cl.* 187.

शुभा *nom. sin. f. of* **शुभ** *m. f. n.* good, beautiful.

शुभां *acc. sin. f. of* **शुभ** *m. f. n.* beautiful, auspicious, happy.

शुभानना BAH. OR REL. COMP. 766; **शुभ** *cr.* beautiful, **आनना** *nom. sin. f. from* **आनन** *n.* face.

शुभे *loc. sin. of* **शुभ** *m. f. n.* auspicious, *1st cl.* 187.

शुभे *voc. sin. f. of* **शुभ** *m. f. n.* beautiful.

शुभ्रेण *ins. sin. m. of* **शुभ्र** *m. f. n.* bright, splendid.

शुश्राव he or she heard; *3d sin. perf. of rt* **श्रु** 369.

शुश्रुवुः they heard; *3d pl. perf. of rt* **श्रु** 369, 676.

शुश्रुवुस् they heard; *3d pl. perf. of rt* **श्रु**.

शुष्कस्रोतां BAH. OR REL. COMP. 761; **शुष्क** *cr.* dried up, **स्रोतां** *acc. sin. of* **स्रोता** *f. substituted for* **स्रोतस्** *n.* a stream.

शून्यं *acc. sin. n. of* **शून्य** *m. f. n.* deserted, desert, lonely, empty, void, hollow.

शून्ये *loc. sin. n. of* **शून्य** *m. f. n.* deserted, lonely.

शूर *m.* a hero, *1st cl.* 103.

शूरः *for* **शूरस्** (63) *nom. of* **शूर** *m.* a hero.

शूरा *for* **शूरास्** (66. *a*) *nom. pl. of* **शूर** *m.* a hero.

शृङ्गशतैर् *ins. pl.* with (thy) hundred peaks, or with hundreds of peaks; **शृङ्ग** *cr.* a peak, **शतैर्** *for* **शतैस्** *ins. pl. from* **शत** *n.* a hundred, 743. *a.*

शृङ्गाणां *gen. pl. of* **शृङ्ग** *n.* a peak, a crag.

शृङ्गैर् *for* **शृङ्गैस्** *ins. pl. of* **शृङ्ग** *n.* the peak of a mountain, a horn.

शृणु Hear! Listen! *2d sin. imp. of rt* **श्रु** *5th cl.* 676.

शृणुत hear ye; *2d pl. imp. of rt* **श्रु** *5th cl.* 676.

शृणोति he hears; *3d sin. pres. of rt* **श्रु** *5th cl.* 676.

शृण्वतोः of (those) two hearing; *gen. du. of* **शृण्वत्** *pres. p. par. of rt* **श्रु** to hear, *5th cl.* 676, *see* 524.

शेते he or she sleeps or lies down; *3d sin. pres. âtm. of rt* **शी** *2d cl.* 315, *see* 646.

शेषे *ind.* as to the rest, in regard to what remains; (*loc. sin. of* **शेष** *m.* remainder, *used adverbially.*)

शोकं *acc. sin. of* **शोक** *m.* sorrow, *1st cl.* 103.

शोककर्षिता TAT. OR DEP. COMP. 740; **शोक** *cr.* sorrow, **कर्षिता** *nom. sin. f. of* **कर्षित** *m. f. n.* harassed, *past p. p. of rt* **कृष्**.

शोककर्षिताम् *acc. sin. f. See last.*

शोकजं *nom. sin. n. of* **शोकज** *m. f. n.* produced by sorrow, *lit.* sorrow-born; (*from* **शोक** grief, *and* **ज** 580. *b.*)

शोकजेन *ins. sin. n. of* **शोकज** caused or produced by grief; (*comp. of* **शोक** *and* **ज** 580.)

शोकजेनाथ *for* **शोकजेन अथ** *by* 31.

शोकदुःखसमन्विता COMPLEX COMP. 771; **शोक** *cr.* sorrow, **दुःख** *cr.* pain, **समन्विता** *nom. sin. f. of* **समन्वित** *m. f. n.* affected by.

शोकदुःखाभ्याम् DVAN. OR AGG. COMP. 752; **शोक** *cr.* sorrow, **दुःखाभ्याम्** *ins. du. of* **दुःख** *n.* pain, grief.

शोकनाशन TAT. OR DEP. COMP. 743; **शोक** *cr.* sorrow, *and* **नाशन** *voc. sin. of* **नाशन** *m.* remover, destroyer, *agt. of rt* **नश्** 582. *c.*

शोकनाशनम् *acc. sin. m. See last.*

शोकपरायणा *nom. sin. f.* given up to grief; (*comp. of* **शोक** *cr.* sorrow, *and* **परायण** wholly addicted to.)

शोकपरिप्लुतः TAT. OR DEP. COMP. 740; **शोक** *cr.* sorrow, **परिप्लुतः** *nom. sin. m.* overwhelmed.

शोकविनाशिनीम् TAT. OR DEP. COMP. 743; **शोक** *cr.* sorrow, **विनाशिनीम्** *acc. sin. f. of* **विनाशिन्** *m. f. n.* destroying, removing, *agt. from rt* **नश्** *with* **वि**, 582, *6th cl.* 159.

शोकविवर्धन TAT. OR DEP. COMP. 743; **शोक** *cr.* sorrow, **विवर्धन** *voc. sin. of* **विवर्धन**

m. one who increases, *from rt* वृध् *with* वि, 582. *c.*

शोकविवर्धनः *nom. sin. m.* *See last.*

शोकसंविग्नमानसः *nom. sin. m.* having his heart distracted with grief; (शोक sorrow, संविग्न agitated, मानस mind, *see* 771.)

शोकसन्तप्ता TAT. OR DEP. COMP. 740; शोक *cr.* sorrow, सन्तप्ता *nom. sin. f. of* सन्तप्त *m.f.n.* burned, inflamed, consumed, *past p. p. of rt* तप् *with* सं, 539.

शोकात् *abl. sin. of* शोक *m.* sorrow.

शोकार्ता *nom. sin. f. of* शोकार्त *m.f.n.* afflicted with grief; (*comp. of* शोक *cr.* sorrow, *and* आर्त pained, 542.)

शोकार्ताम् *acc. sin. f.* afflicted, grieved.

शोकार्तौ *nom. du. m.* afflicted.

शोके *loc. sin. of* शोक *m.* sorrow.

शोकेन *ins. sin. of* शोक *m.* grief, anguish.

शोकेनावसीदति *for* शोकेन अवसीदति *by* 31.

शोकोन्मथितचित्तात्मा COMPLEX COMP. 771; शोक *cr.* sorrow, उन्मथित *cr.* agitated, चित्त *cr.* mind, thought, आत्मा *nom. sin. of* आत्मन् *m.* soul, 146.

शोकोपहतचेतना BAH. OR REL. COMP. 761; शोक *cr.* sorrow, उपहत *cr.* affected, चेतना *f.* mind, soul.

शोचति he or she sorrows for or grieves for; *3d sin. pres. of rt* शुच् *1st cl.* 261.

शोचन् grieving for, lamenting; *nom. sin. m. of* शोचत् *m.f.n.; pres. p. of rt* शुच् 524.

शोचन्तीं *acc. sin. f. of* शोचत् *m.f.n.* grieving, sorrowing; *pres. p. par. of rt* शुच् 524.

शोचन्ते they grieve for, they mourn over; *3d pl. pres. átm. of rt* शुच् *1st cl.* 261.

शोचन्त्या *ins. sin. f. of* शोचत् *m.f.n.* grieving, sorrowing; *pres. p. of rt* शुच् 141. *b*, 524.

शोचसे thou dost bewail, thou grievest for; *2d sin. pres. átm. of rt* शुच् *1st cl.* 261.

शोचामि I grieve, I sorrow for; *1st sin. pres. of rt* शुच् *1st cl.* 261.

शोचाम्यहम् *for* शोचामि अहम् *by* 34.

शोचितुम् to mourn, to lament; *inf. of rt* शुच्.

शोधयामास he or she cleared or wiped away; *3d sin. perf. of rt* शुध् *in caus.* 385. *a.*

शोभते he or she shines; *3d sin. pres. átm. of rt* शुभ् *1st cl.* 261.

शोभने O beautiful one! *voc. sin. of* शोभना *f. of* शोभन *m.f.n.* beautiful, *1st cl.* 105.

शोभन्ते they look beautiful, they shine; *3d pl. pres. átm. of rt* शुभ् *1st cl.* 261.

शोभमाना *nom. sin. f. of* शोभमान *m. f. n.* being beautiful, shining; *pres. p. átm. of rt* शुभ् 526.

शोषयति he or it dries; *3d sin. pres. of rt* शुष् *in caus.* 481.

शौचं *nom. or acc. sin. of* शौच *n.* purity, purification, cleansing, *1st cl.* 104.

श्यामः *nom. sin. of* श्याम *m.f.n.* black, *1st cl.* 187.

श्यामा *nom. sin. f. of* श्याम *m.f. n.* dark.

श्यामां *acc. sin. f. of* श्याम *m. f. n.* dark.

श्यामायाः *gen. sin. f. of* श्याम *m.f. n.* dark.

श्यालाः *nom. pl. of* श्याल *m.* a wife's brother, brother-in-law.

श्रमं *acc. sin. of* श्रम *m.* fatigue, weariness.

श्रमकर्षितः TAT. OR DEP. COMP. 740; श्रम *cr.* fatigue, toil, कर्षितः *nom. sin. of* कर्षित *m. f. n.* worn out.

श्रममोहिताम् TAT. OR DEP. COMP. 740; श्रम *cr.* fatigue, मोहिताम् *acc. sin. f. of* मोहित *m.f.n.* bewildered, paralysed, stupefied.

श्रान्तः *nom. sin. m. of* श्रान्त *m.f.n.* wearied; *past p. p. of rt* श्रम् 546.

श्रान्तस्य *gen. sin. of* श्रान्त *m. f. n.* wearied, fatigued; *past p. p. of rt* श्रम् 546.

श्रान्ता *nom. sin. f. of* श्रान्त *m. f. n.* wearied; *past p. p. of rt* श्रम् 546.

श्रावयाञ्चक्रिरे they caused to be heard, they proclaimed; *3d pl. perf. átm. of rt* श्रु *in caus.* 490.

श्रावितश् *nom. sin. m. of* श्रावित *m.f. n.* made to hear; *past p. p. of rt* श्रु *in caus.* 549.

श्रियं *acc. sin. of* श्री *f.* the goddess of

fortune or beauty, prosperity, 123. *See below.*

श्रिया *ins. sin. of* श्री *f.* beauty, fortune, happiness, 123.

श्री *f.* beauty, prosperity; a name of the goddess of beauty and abundance, also called Lakshmí. She is the wife of Vishṇu, and was produced at the churning of the ocean; *see note under* अमृतोपमां.

श्रीभगवान् *nom. sin. m. of* श्रीभगवत् Kṛishṇa.

श्रीमतीं *acc. sin. f. of* श्रीमत् *m. f. n.* fortunate, happy, 140.

श्रीमन्तं *acc. sin. m. of* श्रीमत् fortunate.

श्रीमांश् *for* श्रीमान् *nom. sin. m. of* श्रीमत् *m. f. n.* fortunate, illustrious, 5*th cl.* 140.

श्रीमान् *nom. sin. m. of* श्रीमत् *m. f. n.* prosperous, fortunate, 5*th cl.* 140.

श्रीर् *for* श्रीस् *nom. sin. f.* the goddess of fortune or beauty.

श्रुत *m. f. n.* heard; *past p. p. of rt* श्रु 676.

श्रुतं *nom. sin. n. of* श्रुत *m. f. n.* heard.

श्रुतः *nom. sin. m. of* श्रुत *m. f. n.* heard, called; *past p. p. of rt* श्रु 532.

श्रुता *nom. sin. f. of* श्रुत *m. f. n.* heard.

श्रुतानि *acc. pl. n. of* श्रुत *m. f. n.* heard, heard of; *past p. p. of rt* श्रु to hear, 532.

श्रुतो *for* श्रुतस् *nom. sin. m. of* श्रुत heard.

श्रुत्वा having heard; *past. ind. p. of rt* श्रु.

श्रुत्वारण्ये *for* श्रुत्वा अरण्ये *by* 31.

श्रेयः *nom. sin. n. of* श्रेयस् *m. f. n.* better, preferable; *irreg. comparative of* प्रशस्य good, excellent, *see* 194, 167.

श्रेयस् *acc. sin. of* श्रेयस् *n.* felicity, eternal happiness, 7*th cl.* 164.

श्रेयसा *ins. sin. of* श्रेयस् *n.* eternal happiness, happiness, a state of felicity, 7*th cl.* 164.

श्रेयो *for* श्रेयस् *nom. sin. n. of* श्रेयस् *m. f. n.* better, preferable, 164.

श्रेयो *for* श्रेयस् *acc. sin. of* श्रेयस् *n.* felicity, eternal happiness, welfare, prosperity.

श्रेष्ठं *acc. sin. m. of* श्रेष्ठ *m. f. n.* best.

श्रेष्ठः *for* श्रेष्ठस् *nom. sin. m. of* श्रेष्ठ *m. f. n.* best, most eminent, 1*st cl.* 103.

श्रोतुं to hear; *inf. of rt* श्रु 459.

श्रोष्यामि I shall hear; 1*st sin.* 2*d. fut. of rt* श्रु 676.

श्लक्ष्णया *ins. sin. f. of* श्लक्ष्ण *m. f. n.* smooth, bland, soft, gentle.

श्लोकम् *acc. sin. of* श्लोक *m.* a verse, a couplet.

श्व *for* श्वस् *ind.* to-morrow.

श्वशुराः *nom. pl. of* श्वशुर *m.* a father-in-law.

श्वशुरान् *acc. pl. of* श्वशुर *m.* a father-in-law.

श्वशुरो *for* श्वशुरस् *nom. sin. of* श्वशुर *m.* a father-in-law.

श्वापदसेविते TAT. OR DEP. COMP. 740; श्वापद *cr.* a beast of prey, सेविते *loc. sin. n. of* सेवित *m. f. n.* infested by, frequented by.

श्वापदाचरिते TAT. OR DEP. COMP. 740; श्वापद *cr.* a beast of prey, आचरिते *loc. sin. n. of* आचरित *m. f. n.* infested, overrun.

श्वोभूते *loc. sin.* on its being to-morrow, at to-morrow's dawn; (*comp. of* श्वस् to-morrow, *and* भूत been, appeared.)

ष.

षट्शतैश् *ins. of* षट्शत *m.* six hundred, 103; (*comp. of* षष् six, 43. *f, and* शत a hundred, 206. *The latter word, when used by itself, is declined in the singular.*)

षष्ठः *nom. sin. m. of* षष्ठ sixth, 209.

षोडशः *nom. sin. m.* sixteenth, 210.

स.

स *a contraction of* सह with, *which often appears at the beginning of adverbial and of relative compounds.*

स *for* सस् (*by* 67) he, that; *nom. sin. m. of* तत् *m. f. n.* he, she, it, 220.

सं *prep.* with, together, altogether.

संयच्छ restrain thou; 2*d sin. imp. of rt* यम् *with* सं, 270.

संयताहारैर् BAH. OR REL. COMP. 767; संयत

cr. restrained, strict, temperate, आहारैर् *ins. pl. of* आहार *m.* food, 1*st cl.* 103.

संयतेन्द्रियः BAH. OR REL. COMP. 767; संयत *cr.* restrained, इन्द्रियः *nom. sin. m. from* इन्द्रिय *n.* an organ of sense, 1*st cl.* 108.

संयतेन्द्रियैः *ins. pl. m. See last.*

संरब्धाः *nom. pl. m. of* संरब्ध *m. f. n.* agitated.

संरम्भो *for* संरम्भस् *nom. sin. m.* anger, fury.

संरुध्य having obstructed, having blocked up; *past ind. p. of rt* रुध् *with* सम्, 559.

संविग्ना *nom. sin. f. of* संविग्न *m. f. n.* distracted, agitated, terrified.

संविधीयताम् let it be arranged or managed, let it be decided; 3*d sin. imp. of* धा *in pass. with* वि *and* सं, 465.

संवीता *nom. sin. f. of* संवीत *m. f. n.* clothed, clad, covered; *past p. p. of rt* व्ये *with* सं, 535.

संवृता *nom. sin. f. of* संवृत *m. f. n.* covered; *past p. p. of rt* वृ *with* सं.

संवृतां *acc. sin. f. of* संवृत *m. f. n.* covered.

संवृतैर् *for* संवृतैस् *ins. pl. of* संवृत *m. f. n.* filled with, surrounded or pervaded by.

संवृतो *for* संवृतस् *nom. sin. of* संवृत *m. f. n.* covered; *past p. p. of rt* वृ *with* सं, 532.

संवृत्तः *nom. sin. m. of* संवृत्त *m. f. n.* become, (*in* Book XX. 41 became, *see* 896;) *past p. p. of rt* वृत् *with* सं, 539.

संवृत्तो *for* संवृत्तस् *nom. sin. m.* become.

संवेद्यो *for* संवेद्यस् *nom. sin. m.* to be made known; *fut. pass. p. of rt* विद् *in caus. with* सं, 571, (*governing loc. by* 861.)

संशयः *nom. sin. of* संशय *m.* uncertainty, doubt.

संशयस् *nom. sin. m.* doubt.

संश्रुत्य having heard, having promised; *past ind. p. of rt* श्रु *with* सं, 560, 676.

संसक्तवदनाश्वासा BAH. OR REL. COMP. 767; संसक्त *cr.* adhering to, sticking, वदन *cr.* mouth, आश्वासा *nom. sin. f. from* आश्वास *m.* breath, 108. *Lit.* with breath adhering to (her) mouth, *i.e.* with suppressed breath.

संसुप्तम् *acc. sin. m. of* संसुप्त *m. f. n.* asleep, sleeping, sound asleep, fast asleep. *See* सुप्त.

संस्पृश्य having touched; *past ind. p. of rt* स्पृश् *with* सं, 559.

संस्मर्तव्यस् to be remembered, to be thought upon; *fut. pass. p. of rt* स्मृ *with* सं, 594, 569.

संस्मृत्य having called to mind; *past ind. p. of rt* स्मृ *with* सं, 560.

संहर्तुं to restrain; *inf. of rt* हृ *with* सं, 459, 593.

सकातराः *voc. pl. m. of* सकातर *m. f. n.* cowardly, dastardly.

सकाशं *ind.* into the presence of, near, 731.

सक्ता *nom. sin. f. of* सक्त *m. f. n.* fixed, intent; *past p. p. of rt* सञ्ज् to adhere, 597. *a.*

सक्ताभूत् *for* सक्ता अभूत् *by* 31, 47.

सखा *nom. sin. of* सखि *m.* a friend, 120.

सखायं *acc. sin. of* सखि *m.* a friend, *see* 120.

सखी *nom. sin. f.* a female friend, 1*st cl.* 106.

सखींस् *for* सखीन् *acc. pl. of* सखि *m.* a friend.

सखीगणसमावृतां TAT. OR DEP. COMP. 745; सखी *cr.* a female friend, गण *cr.* a company, समावृताम् *acc. sin. f. of* समावृत *m. f. n.* surrounded by, 1*st cl.* 103; (*past p. p. of rt* वृ *with* आ *and* सम्, 531.)

सखीगणावृता TAT. OR DEP. COMP. 745; सखी *cr.* a female friend, गण *cr.* a crowd, a number, आवृता *nom. sin. f. of* आवृत *m. f. n.* surrounded, *past p. p. of rt* वृ *with* आ, 675.

सखीजनं *acc. sin. m.* a female friend, a number of female friends.

सखीजनः *nom. sin. m.* a female friend, a number or company of female friends.

सखीनां *gen. pl. of* सखी *f.* a female friend, 1*st cl.* 106.

सखीभिः *ins. pl. of* सखी *f.* a female friend.

सखीमध्ये TAT. OR DEP. COMP. 743; सखी *cr.* a friend, मध्ये *loc. sin. of* मध्य *n.* the middle, midst, 1*st cl.* 104.

सख्यश् *for* सख्यस् *nom. pl. of* सखी *f.* a female friend, 1*st cl.* 106.

सख्यस् *nom. pl. of* सखी *f.* a female friend.

सगणाः with companies of attendants, BAH. OR REL. COMP. 769; स *for* सह with, गणाः *nom. pl. m. from* गण *m.* a company, a troop, a host, 1*st cl.* 103.

सङ्कटे *loc. sin. of* सङ्कट *n.* a narrow passage.

सङ्करो *for* सङ्करस् *nom. sin. m.* confusion, mixture of caste or tribe, proceeding from indiscriminate intercourse.

सङ्कल्पं *acc. sin. of* सङ्कल्प *m.* resolution, resolve, plan, 1*st cl.* 103.

सङ्कीर्त्यमानेषु being proclaimed, being celebrated; *loc. pl. of* सङ्कीर्त्यमान *m. f. n., pres. pass. p. of rt* कृत् *with* सं, 528.

संक्षिप्य having compressed; *past ind. p. of rt* क्षिप् *with* सं, 559, 635.

संख्यातुम् to calculate, to enumerate; *inf. of rt* ख्या *with* सं, 459.

संख्याने *loc. sin. of* संख्यान *n.* numbering, numeration, arithmetic.

संख्याय having counted, having numbered; *past ind. p. of rt* ख्या *with* सं, 559.

संख्यास्यामि I will number or count; 1*st sin.* 2*d fut. of rt* ख्या *with* सं, 394.

संख्ये *loc. sin. of* संख्य *n.* battle, war.

सङ्गच्छ be thou united, unite thyself; 2*d sin. imp. of rt* गम् *with* सं, 1*st cl.* 602.

सङ्गत्या by chance, haply; *ins. sin. of* सङ्गति.

सङ्गत्येह *for* सङ्गत्या इह *by* 32.

सङ्गमो *for* सङ्गमस् *nom. sin. of* सङ्गम *m.* union.

सङ्गम्य having come together, having become united; *past ind. p. of rt* गम् *with* सं, 559.

सङ्गृहीतेषु *loc. pl. m. of* सङ्गृहीत *m. f. n.* restrained, curbed.

सङ्ग्रामं *acc. sin. of* सङ्ग्राम *m.* war, battle.

सङ्ग्रामजिद् *nom. sin. m.* a conqueror in battle; (*comp. of* सङ्ग्राम *cr.* war, *and* जित् a conqueror, victorious, 84. III.)

सङ्ग्रामेषु *loc. pl. of* सङ्ग्राम *m.* war, battle, 1*st cl.* 103.

सञ्चारं *acc. sin. of* सञ्चार *m.* a passage, way, entrance, doorway.

सञ्चिन्तयन्ती thinking; *nom. sin. f. of* सञ्चिन्तयत् *m. f. n., pres. p. of rt* चिन्त् 10*th cl.* 524.

सञ्चेष्टमानस्य *gen. sin. m. of* सञ्चेष्टमान *m. f. n.* acting; *pres. p. átm. of rt* चेष्ट् *with* सं, 526.

संचोदयामास he urged on; 3*d sin. perf. of rt* चुद् *with* सं, 10*th cl.* 385.

सञ्जय *voc. sin. m.* Sañjaya, the name of the charioteer of king Dhṛita-ráshṭra.

सञ्जीव live thou; 2*d sin. imp. of rt* जीव् *with* सं, 603.

सतः *gen. sin. of* सत् *m. f. n.* existing, being; *pres. p. of rt* अस्.

सततं *ind.* always, ever, perpetually, 713.

सतस् *gen. sin. m. of* सत् *m. f. n.* being; *pres. p. of rt* अस् 524.

सति *loc. sin. m. of* सत् *m. f. n.* being; *pres. p. of rt* अस्, *see* 840.

सती *nom. sin. f.* a virtuous woman.

सती *nom. sin. f. of* सत् *m. f. n.* being; *pres. p. of rt* अस् 2*d cl.* 524.

सत्कारं *acc. sin. of* सत्कार *m.* hospitality, 1*st cl.* 103.

सत्काराहों *for* सत्काराहेस् worthy of hospitable treatment; (*from* सत्कार, *q. v., and* अर्हस् *nom. sin. m. of* अर्ह *m. f. n.* worthy.)

सत्कारेण *ins. sin. of* सत्कार *m.* hospitable treatment, hospitality, 1*st cl.* 103.

सत्कृतः *nom. sin. m. of* सत्कृत *m. f. n.* honoured, hospitably treated.

सत्कृता *nom. sin. f. of* सत्कृत *m. f. n.* well-treated.

सत्कृतो *for* सत्कृतस् *nom. sin. m. of* सत्कृत *m. f. n.* honoured, treated with hospitality.

सत्कृत्य having honoured, having treated courteously, having entertained hospitably; *past ind. p. from* सत्कृ 560.

सत्यं *nom. or acc. sin. of* सत्य *n.* truth, troth, an oath.

सत्यदर्शिनः *gen. sin. m. or nom. pl. m. of* सत्यदर्शिन् *m. f. n.* foreseeing the truth, truth-discerning; (*comp. of* सत्य *cr.* the truth, *and* दर्शिन् *agt.* one who sees, 582. *a.*)

सत्यधर्मपरायणः COMPLEX COMP. 771; सत्य *cr.* truth, धर्म *cr.* virtue, परायणः *nom. sin. m. of* परायण *m. f. n.* devoted, attached to.

सत्यनामा BAH. OR REL. COMP. 766; सत्य *cr.* true, नामा *nom. sin. m. from* नामन् *n.* a name, *6th cl., see* 154.

सत्यपराक्रमः *nom. sin. m.* truly brave, (BAH. OR REL. COMP. 766; सत्य *cr.* true, पराक्रम *m.* valour.)

सत्यवाग् *nom. sin. m. of* सत्यवाच् *m. f. n.* truthful, speaking the truth; (*comp. of* सत्य true, *and* वाच् 176, 766.)

सत्यवादी TAT. OR DEP. COMP. 743; सत्य *cr.* truth, वादी *nom. sin. m. of* वादिन् *m. f. n.* a speaker, 582. *a.*

सत्यवान् *nom. sin. m. of* सत्यवत् *m. f. n.* truthful, *5th cl.* 140.

सत्यविक्रमं BAH. OR REL. COMP. 766; सत्य *cr.* true, विक्रमम् *acc. sin. of* विक्रम *m.* valour.

सत्यविक्रमः *nom. sin. m. See last.*

सत्यव्रतो *for* सत्यव्रतस् *nom. sin. of* सत्यव्रत *m. f. n.* strict in the observance of duty, true to a promise or vow, faithful, (BAH. OR REL. COMP. 766; *from* सत्य true, *and* व्रत a religious duty, promise, vow.)

सत्यसन्ध *voc. sin. m.* O thou that art true to thy engagements! BAH. OR REL. COMP. 766; (सत्य *cr.* true, सन्धा *f.* agreement.)

सत्यसन्धो *nom. sin. m. See last.*

सत्याः *acc. pl. f. of* सत्य *m. f. n.* true, *1st cl.* 105.

सत्येन *ins. sin. of* सत्य *n.* truth, *1st cl.* 104.

सत्यो *for* सत्यस् *nom. pl. of* सती *f.* a virtuous woman, 106.

सदश्वांश् *for* सदश्वान् (53) *acc. pl. m.* good horses; (*comp. of* सत् good, *and* अश्व.)

सदा *ind.* always, ever, continually, 722.

सदागतिः *m.* the wind, the air; (*from* सदा always, *and* गति motion.)

सदारो *for* सदारस् *nom. sin. m.* along with (thy) wife; (*comp. of* स *for* सह *and* दार a wife, *see* 769.)

सदृश *m. f. n.* like, similar, resembling.

सदृशं *acc. sin. m. of* सदृश *m. f. n.* like.

सदृशी *nom. sin. f. of* सदृश *m. f. n.* like.

सदृशो *for* सदृशस् *nom. sin. m. of* सदृश, *q. v.*

सनातनः *nom. sin. m. of* सनातन *m. f. n.* eternal.

सनातनाः *nom. pl. m. of* सनातन *m. f. n.* eternal.

सन्त्रस्ता *nom. sin. f. of* सन्त्रस्त *m. f. n.* terrified, affrighted; *past p. p. of rt* त्रस् *with* सं, 539.

सन्दिदेश he charged, he enjoined; *3d sin. perf. of rt* दिश् *with* सं, 364.

सन्दिश्य having instructed, having pointed out; *past ind. p. of rt* दिश् *with* सं, 559.

सन्देहाद् *for* सन्देहात् *abl. sin. of* सन्देह *m.* doubt, *1st cl.* 103.

सन्ध्याम् *acc. sin. of* सन्ध्या *f.* morning and evening devotions, *1st cl.* 105. There are properly three daily devotional services performed by pious men, termed *Sandhyás*, either from the word *Sandhi* 'junction,' because they take place at 'the joinings' of the day, as it were, that is, at dawn, noon, and twilight; or, as the term is otherwise derived, from *sam* 'with' and *dhyai* 'to meditate religiously.'

सन्निधौ *loc. sin. of* सन्निधि *f.* presence, *2d cl.* 112.

सन्निपातिताः *nom. pl. m. of* सन्निपातित *m. f. n.* assembled, collected together; *past p. p. of rt* पत् *in caus. with* सं *and* नि, 549.

सन्निमन्त्रयामास he invited; *3d sin. perf. of rt* मन्त्र् *with prep.* सं *and* नि, *10th cl.* 385. *a.*

सन्न्यासस् *nom. sin. m.* a stake, that which is laid down as a wager, a deposit.

सपत्नानाम् *gen. pl. of* सपत्न *m.* an enemy.

सपरीवारो *for* सपरीवारस् *nom. sin. m.* along with (thy) retinue, with thy family and dependants; (*comp. of* स *for* सह *and* परीवार *or* परिवार retinue, 769.)

सपुत्रायां *loc. sin. f.* accompanied by (her)

children, along with (her) children; (*comp. of* स *for* सह with, *and* पुत्र a son, 769.)

सप्तदशः *nom. sin. m.* seventeenth, 210.

सप्तमः *nom. sin. m. of* सप्तम *m. f. n.* seventh, 209.

सफलं *acc. sin. n. of* सफल *m. f. n.* fruitful, 1*st cl.* 103, *see* 769.

सभां *acc. sin. of* सभा *f.* an assembly, a meeting; a house, a cabin, a cottage, 1*st cl.* 105.

सभामध्ये in the middle of the cottage, in the cottage; (*from* सभा *cr., q. v., and* मध्ये *loc. sin. of* मध्य *n.* the midst, 743.)

सभार्याय with his wife; *dat. sin. m. of* सभार्य BAH. OR REL. COMP., *see* 769.

सभार्ये BAH. OR REL. COMP. 769; स *for* सह with, along with, भार्ये *loc. sin. m. from* भार्या *f.* a wife, 1*st cl.* 108.

सभोद्देशे in the neighbourhood or precincts of the cottage; (*from* सभा *cr., and* उद्देशे *loc. sin. of* उद्देश *m.* spot, 743.)

सम् *prep.* with, together, altogether. *Observe* —सं, सङ्, *and* सम् *are forms assumed according to the nature of the following consonant.*

सम *m. f. n.* equal, similar, 1*st cl.* 103, *see* 187.

समङ्गलैः *ins. pl. m. of* समङ्गल *m. f. n.* auspicious.

समचिन्तयत् he reflected; 3*d sin. impf. of rt* चिन्त् *with* सम्, 10*th cl.* 641.

समतिक्रम्य having passed by; *past ind. p. of rt* क्रम् *with* अति *and* सम्, 559.

समतिक्रान्ता *nom. sin. f. of* समतिक्रान्त *m. f. n.* excelled, surpassed, (has surpassed, surpasses, 896, 896. *a*;) *past p. p. of rt* क्रम् *with* अति *and* सम्, 546.

समतिक्रान्ते *loc. sin. m. of* समतिक्रान्त *m. f. n.* passed onwards, gone beyond; *past p. p. of rt* क्रम् *with* अति *and* सम्, 546.

समतिक्रान्तो *for* समतिक्रान्तस् *nom. sin. m.* passed beyond, gone beyond; *past p. p. of rt* क्रम् *with* अति *and* सम्, 546.

समधिश्रित्य having gone forth, having advanced; *past ind. p. of rt* श्रि *with* अधि *and* सम्, 560.

समनुज्ञाते *loc. sin. of* समनुज्ञात *m. f. n.* permitted, permitted to depart; *past p. p. of rt* ज्ञा *with* अनु *and* सं, 532.

समनुज्ञातो *for* समनुज्ञातस् *nom. sin. m.* permitted to depart. *See last.*

समनुप्राप्तो *for* समनुप्राप्तस् *nom. sin. m. of* समनुप्राप्त *m. f. n.* obtained, assumed; *past p. p. of rt* आप् *with* प्र, अनु, *and* सम्, 539.

समनुव्रतां *acc. sin. of* समनुव्रता *f.* entirely devoted (as a wife to a husband); *governing accusative case.*

समनुशास्ति he rules; 3*d sin. pres. of rt* शास् *with* अनु *and* सम्, 2*d cl.* 658.

समन्ताद् *for* समन्तात् (45) *ind.* all around, on all sides, 715.

समपूजयत् he honoured; 3*d sin. impf. of rt* पूज् *with* सं, 10*th cl.* 283.

समभिक्रम्य having approached; *past ind. p. of rt* क्रम् *with* अभि *and* सम्, 559.

समभिज्ञाय having recognised; *past ind. p. of rt* ज्ञा *with* अभि *and* सम्, 559.

समयं *acc. sin. of* समय *m.* a compact, an agreement, 1*st cl.* 103.

समयेन on condition or conditionally; *ins. sin. of* समय *m.* a condition, agreement.

समयेनोत्सहे *for* समयेन उत्सहे *by* 32.

समरुद्गणौ with the company of the Maruts, BAH. OR REL. COMP. 769; स *for* सह *ind.*, मरुद् *cr.* Marut, a personification of the wind, गणौ *nom. du. m. from* गण *m.* a troop, a class, a company. The Maruts are the forty-nine winds personified. In the Vishṇu Puráṇa (p. 151) they are described as the children of Diti, by Kaśyapa, or rather as the child, divided by Indra into forty-nine portions, and afterwards addressed by him in the words *má rodíḥ* 'weep not,' whence the name *Marud.*

समर्थांस् *for* समर्थान् *by* 53. *See next.*

समर्थान् *acc. pl. of* समर्थ *m. f. n.* powerful.

समर्थो *for* समर्थस् *nom. sin. m. of* समर्थ *m. f. n.* able.

समलङ्कृतं *nom. sin. n. of* समलङ्कृत *m. f. n.* adorned; *past p. p. of rt* कृ *with* अलम् *and* सम्, 682, 787. *a.*

समलङ्कृता *nom. sin. f. of* समलङ्कृत *m. f. n.* adorned.

समवाप्तकामा BAH. OR REL. COMP. 767; समवाप्त *cr.* obtained, gained, कामा *nom. sin. f. from* काम *m.* wish, desire.

समवेतान् *acc. pl. m. of* समवेत *m. f. n.* assembled.

समस्तलोकस्य KARM. OR DES. COMP. 755; समस्त *cr.* all, the whole, लोकस्य *gen. sin. of* लोक *m.* the world.

समाकुलं *acc. sin. m. or n. of* समाकुल *m. f. n.* crowded, filled with.

समागतं *acc. sin. m. of* समागत *m. f. n.* arrived.

समागताः *nom. pl. of* समागत *m. f. n.* united, joined together; *past p. p. of rt* गम् *with* आ *and* सम्, 545.

समागतान् *acc. pl. of* समागत *m. f. n.* assembled, come together, congregated.

समागमं *acc. sin. of* समागम *m.* assembling, coming together, assembly, 1*st cl.* 103.

समागमात् *abl. sin. of* समागम *m.* union.

समागम्य having approached, having come to meet, having gone to meet; *past ind. p. of rt* गम् *with* आ *and* सम्, 559.

समादधत् he held out; *irregular form for* समादधात्; 3*d sin. impf. of rt* धा *with* आ *and* सम्, 664.

समादाय having taken; *past ind. p. of rt* दा *with* आ *and* सम्, 559.

समादायैहि *for* समादाय एहि *by* 33.

समादिष्टं *acc. sin. m. of* समादिष्ट *m. f. n.* pointed out; *past p. p. of rt* दिश् *with* आ *and* सम्, 539.

समादिष्टा *nom. sin. f. of* समादिष्ट *m. f. n.* commanded, ordered.

समाद्रवन्त they rushed on to the attack; 3*d pl. impf. átm. of rt* द्रु *with* आ *and* सम्, 261, 592.

समानीता *nom. sin. f. of* समानीत *m. f. n.* brought, conducted; *past p. p. of rt* नी *with* आ *and* सम्, 532.

समानेतुं to bring, to conduct; *inf. of rt* नी *with* आ *and* सम्, 459.

समाप्लुताभ्यां *ins. du. n. of* समाप्लुत *m. f. n.* moistened, overflowing with moisture; *past p. p. of rt* प्लु *with* आ *and* सम्, 530.

समायान्ति they are arrived, they are come; 3*d pl. pres. of rt* या *with* आ *and* सम्, 317, 644.

समायुक्तं *acc. sin. m. of* समायुक्त *m. f. n.* joined to, united with; *past p. p. of rt* युज् *with* आ *and* सम्, 539.

समारोहत् he ascended; 3*d sin. impf. of rt* रुह् *with* आ *and* सम्, 1*st cl.* 261.

समाविशत् he entered; 3*d sin. impf. of rt* विश् *with* आ *and* सम्, 6*th cl.* 278.

समाविश्य having entered; *past ind. p. of rt* विश् *with* आ *and* सम्, 559.

समावृणोत् he covered; 3*d sin. impf. of rt* वृ *with* आ *and* सम्, 5*th cl.* 675.

समावृता *nom. sin. f. of* समावृत *m. f. n.* protected, guarded; *past p. p. of rt* वृ *with* आ *and* सम्, 532.

समाश्वसत् he or she revived or took courage, (*lit.* he or she took breath;) 3*d sin. impf. of rt* श्वस् *with* आ *and* सम्, 322. *a.*

समाश्वसिहि take thou courage, cheer up! 2*d sin. imp. of rt* श्वस् *with* आ *and* सम्, 322. *a.*

समाश्वासयत he consoled, he comforted; 3*d sin. impf. átm. of rt* श्वस् *in caus. with* आ *and* सम्, 481.

समाश्वासयितुम् to console; *inf. of rt* श्वस् *in caus. with* आ *and* सम्, 459.

समाश्वास्य having cheered, having encouraged or refreshed, having fondled or caressed; *past ind. p. of rt* श्वस् *with* आ *and* सम्.

समास् *nom. pl. m. of* सम the same, equal.

समासाद्य having met with, having obtained; *past ind. p. of rt* सद् *in caus. with* आ *and* सम्, 566.

समास्थिताः *nom. sin. m. of* समास्थित *m. f. n.* having recourse to, practising; *past p. p. of rt* स्था *with* आ *and* सम्, 533, 896. *a.*

समाहितं *nom. sin. n. of* **समाहित** *m. f. n.* placed, imposed, composed; *past p. p. of rt* **धा** *with* **आ** *and* **सम्**, 533.

समाहितः *nom. sin. of* **समाहित** *m. f. n.* having the mind fixed or intent, intent upon.

समाहिता *nom. sin. f. of* **समाहित** *m. f. n.* composed in mien.

समाहृष्यन्त they rejoiced; *3d pl. impf. âtm. of rt* **हृष्** *with* **आ** *and* **सम्**, *4th cl.* 272.

समाह्वानं *acc. sin. of* **समाह्वान** *n.* a challenge.

समीक्ष्य having perceived, having observed, having beheld, having examined; *ind. p. of rt* **ईक्ष्** *with prep.* **सम्**, 605, 564.

समीप *m. f. n.* near, contiguous, at hand.

समीपं *ind.* near to, into the presence of, (*governing genitive case*, 713, 731.)

समीपस्था *nom. sin. f.* standing near, adjacent; (*from* **समीप** near, *and* **स्थ** staying, 580. *b.*)

समीपे *ind.* in the presence of, in the neighbourhood of; (*loc. sin. of* **समीप** 716.)

समुत्पत्य having flown upwards, having flown away; *ind. p. of rt* **पत्** *with* **उत्** *and* **सम्**, 564.

समुत्पन्नः *nom. sin. m.* excited, produced; *past p. p. of rt* **पद्** *with* **उत्** *and* **सम्**, 540.

समुत्पेतुर् they leaped up or sprang; *3d pl. perf. of rt* **पत्** *with* **उत्** *and* **सम्**, 375. *a.*

समुत्पेतुस् they jumped up; *3d pl. perf. See last.*

समुद्यम्य having restrained, having curbed; *past ind. p. of rt* **यम्** *with* **उत्** *and* **सम्**, 559.

समुद्रगा *nom. sin. f. of* **समुद्रग** *m. f. n.* flowing towards the ocean; (*from* **समुद्र** the sea, *and* **ग** going, 580. *b.*)

समुपदिश्यते is pointed out; *3d sin. pres. of rt* **दिश्** *in pass. with* **उप** *and* **सम्**, 463, 583.

समुपस्थितं *acc. sin. m. or n. of* **समुपस्थित** *m. f. n.* assembled, standing near together; arrived, happened, overtaken. *See next.*

समुपस्थिताः (are) present together, (have) approached together; *nom. pl. m. of* **समुपस्थित** *m. f. n., past p. p. of rt* **स्था** *with* **उप** *and* **सम्**, 533.

समुपाजग्मुर् they came together, collected together; *3d pl. perf. of rt* **गम्** *with* **आ**, **उप**, *and* **सम्**, 376.

समुपाद्रवन् they ran after, they pursued; *3d pl. impf. of rt* **द्रु** (*1st cl.* 592) *with prep.* **उप** *and* **सं**.

समुपाधावद् (she) ran after, (she) ran towards; *3d sin. impf. of rt* **धाव्** (*1st cl.* 261) *with prep.* **उप** *and* **सं**.

समुपेतं *acc. sin. m. or n. of* **समुपेत** *m. f. n.* come near to, approached, resorted to, visited.

समृद्धं *nom. sin. m. or n. of* **समृद्ध** *m. f. n.* wealthy, flourishing.

समृद्धः *nom. sin. m. of* **समृद्ध** *m. f. n.* rich, affluent, opulent, prosperous.

समृद्धो *for* **समृद्धस्** *nom. sin. of* **समृद्ध** *m. f. n.* prosperous, happy.

समे *acc. du. n. of* **सम** *m. f. n.* equal, the same.

समेतो *for* **समेतस्** *nom. sin. m. of* **समेत** *m. f. n.* united to, come together, joined; *past p. p. of rt* **इ** *with* **आ** *and* **सम्**, 532.

समेत्य having come together, having had a meeting, having met; *past ind. p. of rt* **इ** *with* **आ** *and* **सम्**, 645, 560.

समेष्यसि thou shalt meet, thou shalt be united with; *2d sin. 2d fut. of rt* **इ** *with* **सम्**, 645.

समेष्यामि I shall meet; *1st sin. 2d fut. of rt* **इ** *with* **सम्**, 645.

सम्पतन्तीं *acc. sin. f. of* **सम्पतत्** *m. f. n.* flitting, going backwards and forwards; *pres. p. of rt* **पत्** *with* **सं**, 524.

सम्पतन् *for* **सम्पतन्** *nom. sin. m. of* **सम्पतत्** *m. f. n.* alighting, arriving; *pres. p. of rt* **पत्** *with* **सं**, 524.

सम्पन्ने *loc. sin. n. of* **सम्पन्न** *m. f. n.* completed, achieved; *past p. p. of rt* **पद्** *with* **सं**, 540.

सम्पूर्णाम् *acc. sin. f. of* **सम्पूर्ण** *m. f. n.* full.

सम्प्रणष्टे *loc. sin. m. of* **सम्प्रणष्ट** *m. f. n.*

vanished, disappeared; *past p. p. of rt* नश् *with* प्र *and* सम्, 539.

सम्प्रवृत्ते *loc. sin. m. of* सम्प्रवृत्त *m.f.n.* passed, gone by; *past p. p. of rt* वृत् *with* प्र *and* सम्, 539.

सम्प्रहृष्टतनूरुहाः BAH. OR REL. COMP. 767; सम्प्रहृष्ट *cr.* erect, erected (as when thrilling with pleasure), तनूरुह *m.* the hair of the body.

सम्प्रहृष्टस्य *gen. sin. m. of* सम्प्रहृष्ट *m.f.n.* rejoiced, joyful; *past p. p. of rt* हृष् *with* प्र *and* सम्.

सम्प्राप्तं *acc. sin. m. of* सम्प्राप्त *m.f.n.* reached, arrived at. *See next.*

सम्प्राप्ता *nom. sin. f. of* सम्प्राप्त *m. f. n.* obtained, arrived at; *past p. p. of rt* आप् *with* प्र *and* सं, 539.

सम्प्राप्ते *loc. sin. of* सम्प्राप्त *m. f. n.* arrived.

सम्प्राप्तो *for* सम्प्राप्तस् *nom. sin.* obtained, met with.

सम्प्रेक्ष्य having seen, having observed; *past ind. p. of rt* ईक्ष् *with* प्र *and* सं.

सम्बन्धिनस् *nom. pl. of* सम्बन्धिन् *m.* a relation.

सम्बन्धी *nom. sin. of* सम्बन्धिन् *m.* a kinsman, relative, connexion, 159.

सम्भारं *acc. sin. of* सम्भार *m.* collection of goods, goods and chattels.

सम्भावनीयस् *nom. sin. m.* (*agreeing with* स्वयंवर *m.* a bridal, *understood*) to be honoured with the presence (of any one); *fut. pass. p. of rt* भू *in caus. with* सं.

सम्भावितस्य *gen. sin. m. of* सम्भावित *m.f.n.* honoured, honourable.

सम्भ्रान्ताः *nom. pl. m. or f. of* सम्भ्रान्त *m.f.n.* bewildered, agitated; *past p. p. of rt* भ्रम् *with* सं, 546.

सम्मते *loc. sin. of* सम्मत *n.* assent, consent, approval; 'with the consent.'

सम्यक् *ind.* fitly, properly, entirely, truly.

सम्यक्कर्तुं to make true; *inf. of* सम्यक्कृ; (*from* सम्यक् *and rt* कृ.)

सम्यग् *for* सम्यक् (41) *ind.* wholly, altogether, in a friendly manner, well, 713.

सम्यग्गोप्ता *nom. sin. m.* a good protector, a true guardian; (*from* सम्यक् *and* गोप्तृ.)

सम्यग्वृत्तः altogether relying, well-abiding; (*comp. of* सम्यक् *ind.* altogether, *and* वृत्त *m. f. n.* fixed, abiding.)

सरांसि *acc. pl. of* सरस् *n.* a lake, a pool, *7th cl.* 164.

सराष्ट्राणि *acc. pl. n.* with the kingdoms; (*comp. of* स *for* सह with, *and* राष्ट्र *n.* a kingdom, *see* 769.)

सरितस् *acc. pl. of* सरित् *f.* a river, *5th cl.* 136.

सरितो *for* सरितस् *acc. pl. See last.*

सरिद्भिः *ins. pl. of* सरित् *f.* a river, 136.

सर्गः *nom. sin. of* सर्ग *m.* a chapter, a section.

सर्व *m.f.n.* all, every, 237.

सर्वं *nom. or acc. sin. n. or acc. sin. m. of* सर्व all.

सर्वः *nom. sin. m. of* सर्व *m. f. n.* all.

सर्वकामैः KARM. OR DES. COMP. 755; सर्व *cr.* all, कामैः *ins. pl. of* काम *m.* wish, desire, want.

सर्वगतं *nom. or acc. sin. n. of* सर्वगत *m.f.n.* universally diffused, all-pervading, (TAT. OR DEP. COMP. 739; सर्व all, *and* गत gone.)

सर्वगतः *nom. sin. m.* going everywhere, all-pervading; (सर्व, गत.)

सर्वगात्रेभ्यो KARM. OR DES. COMP. 755; सर्व *cr.* all, गात्रेभ्यो *for* गात्रेभ्यस् *abl. pl. of* गात्र *n.* a limb, *1st cl.* 104.

सर्वगुणैर् *for* सर्वगुणैस् KARM. OR DES. COMP. 755; सर्व *cr.* all, गुणैर् *ins. pl. of* गुण *m.* quality, excellence.

सर्वगुणोपेतं COMPLEX COMP. 771; सर्व *cr.* all, गुण virtue, good quality, उपेतं *acc. sin. m. of* उपेत *m.f.n.* endowed with.

सर्वज्ञो *for* सर्वज्ञस् *nom. sin. m. of* सर्वज्ञ *m.f.n.* all-knowing, omniscient; (*comp. of* सर्व all, *and* ज्ञ knowing, 580. *b.*)

सर्वतः *for* सर्वतस् *ind.* in every direction.

सर्वतो *for* सर्वतस् *ind.* in every direction.

सर्वतोदिशं *acc. sin.* to every quarter, in every direction; (*comp. of* सर्वतो *for* सर्वतस् *ind.* 64, every way, *and* दिशम् *acc. sin. of* दिश् *f.* a quarter, 181.)

सर्वतोदिशः *acc. pl.* in all directions. *See last.*

सर्वतोभद्रम् *acc. sin. n.* everywhere auspicious; (*comp. of* सर्वतस् 64, on every side, *and* भद्र *m. f. n.* good.)

सर्वत्र *ind.* everywhere, in every place.

सर्वत्रेति *for* सर्वत्र इति *by* 32.

सर्वथा *ind.* by all means, at all, in every way, in every respect, altogether, 721.

सर्वदुःखेषु KARM. OR DES. COMP. 755; सर्व *cr.* all, दुःखेषु *loc. pl. of* दुःख *n.* grief, pain, sorrow.

सर्वदेवानां KARM. OR DES. COMP. 755; सर्व *cr.* all, देवानां *gen. pl. of* देव *m.* a god, 1*st cl.* 103.

सर्वपापेभ्यः KARM. OR DES. COMP. 755; सर्व *cr.* all, पापेभ्यः *abl. pl. of* पाप *n.* sin, 1*st cl.* 104.

सर्वभूतानाम् KARM. OR DES. COMP. 755; सर्व *cr.* all, भूतानाम् *gen. pl. of* भूत *n.* a created being.

सर्वम् *nom. or acc. sin. n. or acc. sin. m. of* सर्व *m. f. n.* all, every.

सर्वयोषितः KARM. OR DES. COMP. 755; सर्व *cr.* all, योषितः *acc. pl. of* योषित् *f.* a woman, 136.

सर्वरत्नसमन्वितम् COMPLEX COMP. 771; सर्व *cr.* all, रत्न *cr.* gems, jewels, समन्वितम् *acc. sin. m. of* समन्वित *m. f. n.* possessed of.

सर्वराष्ट्रेषु KARM. OR DES. COMP. 755; सर्व *cr.* all, राष्ट्रेषु *loc. pl. of* राष्ट्र *n.* a kingdom, 104.

सर्वलोकभयङ्करम् COMPLEX COMP. 771; सर्व *cr.* all, लोक *cr.* the world, भयङ्करम् *acc. sin. n.* causing fear, formidable, *see* 739. *c.*

सर्वशः *for* सर्वशस् *ind.* altogether, entirely, wholly, on all sides, 725.

सर्वशस् *ind.* entirely, altogether, one and all, 725.

सर्वसम्भारं *acc. sin. m.* all (thy) goods; (*comp. of* सर्व all, *and* सम्भार *q. v.*)

सर्वा *for* सर्वास् *nom. or acc. pl. f. of* सर्व all.

सर्वां *acc. sin. f. of* सर्व *m. f. n.* all, every.

सर्वाः *nom. or acc. pl. f. of* सर्व *m. f. n.* all.

सर्वाणि *nom. or acc. pl. n. of* सर्व all.

सर्वान् *acc. pl. m. of* सर्व *m. f. n.* all.

सर्वानवद्याङ्ग O thou of altogether faultless form! (BAH. OR REL. COMP. 761; सर्व *cr.* all, अनवद्य *cr.* faultless, not to be found fault with, अङ्ग *voc. sin. m. from* अङ्ग *n.* body, limb, member, 1*st cl.* 108.)

सर्वानवद्याङ्गि *voc. sin. f.* O faultless in every limb; (सर्व *cr.* all, अनवद्य *cr.* faultless, not to be spoken against, अङ्गि *voc. sin. of* अङ्गी *f. from* अङ्ग *n.* a limb, 771, 106.)

सर्वाभरणभूषिता COMPLEX COMP. 771; सर्व *cr.* all, आभरण *cr.* ornament, भूषिता *nom. sin. f. of* भूषित *m. f. n.* adorned, *past p. p. of rt* भूष् 538.

सर्वार्थकुशलाम् COMPLEX COMP. 771; सर्व *cr.* all, अर्थ *cr.* business, affair, कुशलाम् *acc. sin. f. of* कुशल *m. f. n.* skilful, 1*st cl.* 105.

सर्वे *nom. pl. m. of* सर्व *m. f. n.* all.

सर्वेभ्यः *dat. or abl. pl. m. or n. of* सर्व *m. f. n.* all.

सर्वेषाम् *gen. pl. of* सर्व *m. f. n.* all.

सर्वै *for* सर्वैस् *ins. pl. of* सर्व all, 65. *a.*

सर्वैर् *for* सर्वैस् *ins. pl. of* सर्व *m. f. n.* all.

सर्वैस् *ins. pl. of* सर्व *m. f. n.* all.

सलिलेन *ins. sin. of* सलिल *n.* water, 1*st cl.* 104.

सवाससि *loc. sin. m. of* सवासस् *m. f. n.* having a garment, clothed, *see* 769.

सवितुस् *gen. sin. of* सवितृ *m.* the sun, 127, (towards the sun.)

सविदिशो *for* सविदिशस् *acc. pl. f.* with the intermediate quarters, 769; (*comp. of* स *for* सह with, 778, *and* विदिश् *f.* an intermediate point of the compass.)

सविस्तराः *nom. pl. m.* with the details, in detail, '*in extenso;*' (*comp. of* स *for* सह + विस्तर detail, extension, *see* 769.)

सविहङ्गाभिः BAH. OR REL. COMP. 769; स *for* सह with, विहङ्गाभिः *ins. pl. f. from* विहङ्ग *m.* a bird, *1st cl.* 105.

सशरं *acc. sin. m.* with (its) arrow; (स *for* सह with, *and* शर an arrow.)

सशाल्मलैः BAH. OR REL. COMP. 769; स *for* सह with, 778, *and* शाल्मलैः *ins. pl. of* शाल्मल *m.* the silk-cotton tree (*Bombax heptaphyllum*).

सस्वजे he embraced; *3d sin. perf. of rt* स्वञ्ज् 364.

सह *ind.* (*governing instrumental case*) with, along with. *Often contracted into* स.

सहजः *nom. sin. m. of* सहज *m. f. n.* born with one, produced at birth, congenital, natural; (*from* सह with, *and* ज 580. *b.*)

सहवार्ष्णेयजीवलः *nom. sin. m.* along with Várshṇeya and Jívala. *In these and similar compounds* सह *is generally contracted into* स, *see* 769.

सहवार्ष्णेयवाहुकं BAH. OR REL. COMP. 769; सह *for the contracted form* स with, वार्ष्णेय Várshṇeya, वाहुकं *acc. sin. m.* Váhuka.

सहवार्ष्णेयसारथिः *nom. sin. m.* along with the charioteer Várshṇeya; (*comp. of* सह, *anomalously used for the contracted form* स with, वार्ष्णेय, *and* सारथि, 769.)

सहवाहनाः with their vehicles, BAH. OR REL. COMP. 769; सह with, वाहनाः *nom. pl. m. from* वाहन *n.* a vehicle.

सहसा *ind.* quickly, suddenly, 714.

सहसाभ्यागताम् *for* सहसा अभ्यागताम् *by* 31.

सहस्रं *acc. sin. of* सहस्र *n.* a thousand; *governing genitive case, see* 206, 835. *c.*

सहागम्य *for* सह आगम्य *by* 31.

सहायेन *ins. sin. of* सहाय *m.* a companion, *1st cl.* 103.

सहितः *nom. sin. m. of* सहित *m. f. n.* accompanied by.

सहितां *acc. sin. f. of* सहित *m. f. n.* associated, accompanied.

सहिताः *nom. pl. m. of* सहित *m. f. n.* associated together, united, joined.

सहिताव् (*by* 37) *for* सहितौ *nom. du. m. of* सहित *m. f. n.* associated together, in each other's company.

सहितो *for* सहितस् *nom. sin. m. of* सहित *m. f. n.* accompanied by, together with; assisted.

सहितौ *nom. sin. du. m. of* सहित *m. f. n.* united, joined together.

सहैकान्ते *for* सह एकान्ते *by* 33.

सा she; *nom. sin. f. of* तत्, *q. v.*

साक्षाद् *for* साक्षात् *ind.* before the eyes, in sight, in presence, openly, in public.

साक्षिणो *for* साक्षिणस् *nom. pl. of* साक्षिन् *m.* a witness, 159.

साक्षिवत् *ind.* like a witness; (*comp. of* साक्षि *for* साक्षिन् a witness, 57, *and* वत् 724.)

सागरङ्गमां *acc. sin. f.* flowing to the ocean; (*comp. of* सागरं *acc. sin. of* सागर *m.* the ocean, *and* गमां *acc. f. of* गम *m. f. n.* going, 580. *a*; *see* 739. *c.*)

साग्निकाः accompanied by Agni, BAH. OR REL. COMP. 769; स *for* सह with, अग्निकाः *nom. pl. m. of* अग्निक *for* अग्नि fire, *see* 769. *a.*

साग्निहोत्राश्रमास् BAH. OR REL. COMP. 769; स *for* सह with, अग्निहोत्र *cr.* a sacred fire, आश्रमास् *nom. pl. m. of* आश्रम *m.* a hermitage.

साङ्गोपाङ्गाः *nom. pl. m.* along with the Angas and Upángas, *i. e.* the sciences and secondary sciences subordinate to the Vedas; the Angas are usually called Vedángas. Six are enumerated, viz. 1. Pronunciation, शिक्षा; 2. Guide to the performance of sacrifices, कल्पः; 3. Grammar, व्याकरणं; 4. Metre, छन्दस्; 5. Astronomical calendar, ज्योतिषं; 6. Explanation of difficult words, etymology, निरुक्तं. (*Comp. of* स + अङ्ग + उपाङ्ग, *see* 769.)

साचिराद् *for* **सा अचिरात्** *by* 31, 45.

साद्योपतिष्ठति *for* **सा अद्य उपतिष्ठति** *by* 31, 32.

साधु *interj.* Well done! Bravo! Well! Come on!

साधुवृत्तश् *nom. sin. of* **साधुवृत्त** *m. f. n.* virtuous in conduct; (*comp. of* **साधु** good, *and* **वृत्त** practice, 766.)

साध्वी *nom. sin. f. of* **साधु** *m. f. n.* good, virtuous, 187.

सानुक्रोशो *for* **सानुक्रोशस्** *nom. sin. m.* compassionate, merciful; (*comp. of* **स** *for* **सह** with, *and* **अनुक्रोश** pity, 769.)

सान्त्वयन् *nom. sin. m. of* **सान्त्वयत्** *m. f. n.* flattering, coaxing, conciliating; *pres. p. of rt* **सान्त्व्** 10*th cl.* 524, 141. *In* Book VIII. 12 *the nominative masculine is used irregularly for the feminine* **सान्त्वयन्ती.**

सान्त्वयामास he flattered, he soothed, he encouraged or cheered; 3*d sin. perf. of rt* **सान्त्व्** 10*th cl.* 385. *a.*

सान्त्वयित्वा having consoled; *past ind. p. of rt* **सान्त्व्** 10*th cl.* 558.

सान्त्वितो *for* **सान्त्वितस्** *nom. sin. of* **सान्त्वित** *m. f. n.* consoled, comforted.

सापत्या *nom. sin. f.* having children, having offspring; (*comp. of* **स** *for* **सह** with, *and* **अपत्य** offspring, 769.)

सापश्यद् *for* **सा अपश्यद्** *by* 31.

साब्रवीत् *for* **सा अब्रवीत्** *by* 31.

साब्रवीद् *for* **सा अब्रवीद्** *by* 31.

साभिकामां *acc. sin. f. of* **साभिकाम** *m. f. n.* loving; (*from* **स** *and* **अभिकाम** love.)

साभिवाद्य *for* **सा अभिवाद्य** *by* 31.

सामर्थ्यं *acc. sin. of* **सामर्थ्य** *n.* power, prowess.

सामात्यप्रमुखा *for* **सामात्यप्रमुखास्** *nom. pl. m.* with the chief ministers; (*comp. of* **स** *for* **सह** with, **अमात्य** a minister, *and* **प्रमुख** chief, principal, 769.)

सामान्यम् *nom. sin. n. of* **सामान्य** *m. f. n.* common, general.

सायं *ind.* in the evening.

सायाह्ने *loc. sin. of* **सायाह्न** *m.* the evening, 716.

सारथिः *nom. sin. m.* a charioteer.

सारथे *voc. sin. of* **सारथि** *m.* a charioteer.

सारथ्ये *loc. sin. of* **सारथ्य** *n.* the office of a charioteer.

सारथ्येन *ins. sin. of* **सारथ्य** *n.* the office of a charioteer, 1*st cl.* 104.

सार्थं *acc. sin. of* **सार्थ** *m.* a caravan.

सार्थः *nom. sin. m.* a caravan.

सार्थघ्नीं *acc. sin. of* **सार्थघ्नी** *f.* a destroyer of a caravan.

सार्थजान् *acc. pl. m. of* **सार्थज** *m. f. n.* reared in the caravan; (*comp. of* **सार्थ** *q. v., and* **ज** 580. *b.*)

सार्थमण्डलम् TAT. OR DEP. COMP. 743; **सार्थ** *cr.* caravan, **मण्डलम्** *nom. sin. n.* circle, assembled body.

सार्थवाहं *acc. sin. of* **सार्थवाह** *m.* the leader or commander of a caravan.

सार्थवाहः *nom. sin. m.* a leader of a caravan.

सार्थवाहवचस् *acc. sin. n.* the words of the captain of the caravan; *see* **सार्थवाह** *and* **वचस्** 743.

सार्थवाहस्य *gen. sin. m.* of the leader of a caravan.

सार्थस्य *gen. sin. of* **सार्थ** *m.* a caravan.

सार्थात् *abl. sin. of* **सार्थ** *m.* a caravan.

सार्थिकाः *nom. pl. of* **सार्थिक** *m.* a merchant, a trader, a travelling merchant.

सार्थे *loc. sin. of* **सार्थ** *m.* a caravan.

सार्थेन *ins. sin. of* **सार्थ** *m.* a caravan.

सार्धं *ind.* with, along with, in company with, 731.

साशोकवृक्षं *for* **सा अशोकवृक्षं** *by* 31.

साहं *for* **सा अहं** I myself, *see* 220. *a.*

साहाय्यं *acc. sin. of* **साहाय्य** *n.* assistance, help.

सिंहद्वीपिरुरुव्याघ्रमहिषर्क्षगणैर् COMPLEX COMP. 770; **सिंह** *cr.* a lion, **द्वीपि** *for* **द्वीपिन्** (57) *cr.* a panther, **रुरु** *cr.* a deer, **व्याघ्र** *cr.* a tiger, **महिष** *cr.* a buffalo, **ऋक्ष**

cr. a bear, गणैर् *ins. pl. of* गण *m.* a troop, a herd, a multitude, *1st cl.* 103.

सिंहविक्रान्तो *nom. sin. m.* valiant as the lion; (सिंह *cr.* a lion, *and* विक्रान्त valiant.)

सिंहव्याघ्रनिषेविते COMPLEX COMP. 771; सिंह *cr.* a lion, व्याघ्र *cr.* a tiger, निषेविते *loc. sin. of* निषेवित *m. f. n.* infested by, inhabited by, frequented by, *past p. p. of rt* सेव् *with* नि, 70.

सिंहशार्दूलमातङ्गवराहर्क्षमृगायुतम् COMPLEX COMP. 771; सिंह *cr.* a lion, शार्दूल *cr.* a tiger, मातङ्ग *cr.* an elephant, वराह *cr.* a boar, ऋक्ष *cr.* a bear, मृग *cr.* a deer, आयुतम् *acc. sin. m. of* आयुत *m. f. n.* frequented by, *past p. p. of rt* यु *with* आ, 532. *Note*—वराह + ऋक्ष *becomes* वराहर्क्ष *by* 32.

सिक्ताः *nom. pl. m. of* सिक्त *m. f. n.* watered, sprinkled; *past p. p. of rt* सिच् 539.

सिन्धुजान् *acc. pl. m.* bred or reared in Sindh; (*comp. of* सिन्धु the country along the Indus, *and* ज 580.) Sindhu is the Indian name of the river Indus or of the country along its banks, now called Sindh.

सीदति he sinks, he pines away; *3d sin. pres. of rt* सद् *1st cl.* 270, *see* 599. *a.*

सीदन्ति they sink, they give way, they quail; *3d pl. pres. of rt* सद्.

सीदन्त्यङ्गानि *for* सीदन्ति अङ्गानि *by* 34.

सु *a prefix meaning* good, well, very, 726. *f.*

सुकुचा *nom. sin. f.* having beautiful breasts, *1st cl.* 105, *see* 726. *f.*

सुकुमारतनुत्वचं having very soft and delicate skin, COMPLEX COMP. 771; सुकुमार *cr.* very soft, 726. *f*, तनु *cr.* delicate, त्वचं *acc. sin. of* त्वच् *f.* skin.

सुकुमाराङ्गीं BAH. OR REL. COMP. 766; सुकुमार *cr.* very delicate, 726. *f*, अङ्गीं *acc. sin. f. from* अङ्ग *n.* a limb, *1st cl.* 108.

सुकुमारानवद्याङ्गीम् COMPLEX COMP. 771; सुकुमार *cr.* very delicate, 726. *f*, अनवद्य *cr.* irreproachable, faultless, blameless, अङ्गीम् *acc. sin. f. from* अङ्ग *n.* a limb, member, *see* 108.

सुकुमारी *nom. sin. f.* very tender, very delicate; (*from* सु very, 726. *f, and* कुमारी *f. of* कुमार young.)

सुकुमारीं *acc. sin. f. of* सुकुमार *m. f. n.* very delicate.

सुकेशान्तानि *nom. pl. n. of* सुकेशान्त *m. f. n.* having beautiful locks of hair or ringlets; (*comp. of* सु good, 726. *f*, केश hair, *and* अन्त *m.* the end.)

सुकेशी *nom. sin. f.* having beautiful hair, *1st cl.* 106, *see* 726. *f.*

सुखं *acc. sin. of* सुख *n.* happiness, bliss.

सुखं *ind.* happily, joyfully, pleasantly, 713. *b.*

सुखतरो *for* सुखतरस् *nom. sin. m.* more pleasant; *comparative degree of* सुख, *q.v.*, 191.

सुखदुःखे *acc. du. n.* pleasure and pain; (DVAN. OR AGG. COMP. 752.)

सुखात् *abl. sin. m. or n. of* सुख *m. f. n.* pleasant, happy.

सुखानि *nom. or acc. pl. of* सुख *n.* pleasure.

सुखार्हां *acc. sin. f. of* सुखार्ह *m. f. n.* deserving of happiness; (*comp. of* सुख joy, *and* अर्ह worthy of.)

सुखास्पर्शं *acc. sin. n.* pleasant to the touch, thrilling; (*from* सुख pleasant, *and* आस्पर्श touch.)

सुखिनः *nom. pl. m. of* सुखिन् *m. f. n.* happy.

सुखी *nom. sin. m. of* सुखिन् *m. f. n.* happy.

सुखोपविष्ट *nom. sin. m.* pleasantly seated; (*comp. of* सुख pleasant, *and* उपविष्ट.)

सुखोषितं *acc. sin. m.* comfortably lodged; (*comp. of* सुख pleasant, *and* उषित lodged, *past p. p. of rt* वस् 607.)

सुगन्धीनि *nom. pl. n. of* सुगन्धिन् *m. f. n.* fragrant; (*from* सु good, 726. *f*, गन्ध odour, smell, *affix* इन् 159.)

सुचिरं *nom. sin. n. of* सुचिर *m. f. n.* very long; (*comp. of* सु 726. *f, and* चिर long while.)

सुचिरं *ind.* for a very long time.

सुजाताङ्गीं BAH. OR REL. COMP. 767; सुजात *cr.* well-formed, अङ्गीं *acc. sin. f. from* अङ्ग *n.* a limb, 108.

सुतं *acc. sin. of* सुत *m.* a son, 1*st cl.* 103.

सुता *f.* a daughter, 1*st cl.* 105.

सुतां *acc. sin. of* सुता *f.* a daughter.

सुते *nom. du. of* सुता *f.* a daughter, 1*st cl.* 105.

सुतेयं *for* सुता इयं *by* 32.

सुतो *for* सुतस् *nom. sin. m.* a son.

सुतौ *acc. du. of* सुत *m.* a child.

सुदाम्नश् *gen. sin. of* सुदामन् *m.* Sudáman, name of a king, 153, 154.

सुदारुणम् *acc. sin. n.* very terrible; (*comp. of* सु 726.*f, and* दारुण *q. v.*)

सुदुःखं *ind.* very sorrowfully, in great pain.

सुदुःखितः *nom. sin. m. of* सुदुःखित *m. f. n.* very grieved; (*comp. of* सु 726.*f, and* दुःखित grieved, afflicted.)

सुदुःखिता *nom. sin. f.* greatly afflicted.

सुदुर्बुद्धे O very foolish! *voc. sin. m. of* सुदुर्बुद्धि *m. f. n.*, 2*d cl.* 110; (*from* सु 726.*f*, दुर् 726. *d, and* बुद्धि mind.)

सुदुष्करम् *nom. sin. n. of* सुदुष्कर *m. f. n.* very difficult to be done; (*comp. of* सु 726.*f*, दुर् 726. *d*, 72, *and* कर doing.)

सुदेव *voc. sin. of* सुदेव *m.* name of a Bráhman.

सुदेवं *acc. sin. m.* Sudeva.

सुदेवस्य *gen. sin. m.* of Sudeva.

सुदेवेन *ins. sin. m.* by Sudeva.

सुदेवो *for* सुदेवस् *nom. sin. m.* Sudeva, name of a Bráhman.

सुद्विजानना Bah. or Rel. comp. 761; सु *ind.* good, beautiful, 726. *f*, द्विज *cr.* a tooth, आनना *nom. sin. f. from* आनन *n.* a mouth, 1*st cl.* 108.

सुनन्दा *nom. sin. f.* Sunandá, name of a woman.

सुनन्दां *acc. sin. of* सुनन्दा *f.* Sunandá, name of a woman.

सुनन्दासहितां *acc. sin. f.* in company with Sunandá; (*comp. of* सुनन्दा *and* सहित accompanied by.)

सुनन्दे *voc. sin. f.* O Sunandá! *See* सुनन्दा.

सुनासाक्षिभ्रुवाणि Bah. or Rel. comp. 765; सु good, well, well-formed, 726.*f*, नासा *cr.* the nose, अक्षि *cr.* the eye, भ्रुवाणि *nom. pl. n. from* भ्रू *f.* the eyebrow, *see* 125. *a. b.*

सुन्दर *m. f. n.* beautiful, lovely, 1*st cl.* 187.

सुन्दरी *nom. sin. f. of* सुन्दर beautiful, 106.

सुपरिश्रान्तवाहास् Bah. or Rel. comp. 767; सुपरिश्रान्त *cr.* very wearied, 726.*f*, वाहास् *nom. pl. of* वाह *m.* a horse, a bearer.

सुपुष्पैर् *ins. pl. m. of* सुपुष्प *m. f. n.* having beautiful flowers; (*comp. of* सु 726.*f, and* पुष्प *n.* a flower.)

सुपूजितौ *nom. du. m. of* सुपूजित *m. f. n.* much honoured, 1*st cl.* 103; (*comp. of* सु 726.*f, and* पूजित *past p. p. from rt* पूज्.)

सुप्तां *acc. sin. f. of* सुप्त *m. f. n.* asleep, sleeping.

सुप्तायां *loc. sin. f.* (*see* 840) *of* सुप्त *m. f. n.* asleep, sleeping; *past p. p. of rt* स्वप् 543.

सुप्ते *loc. sin. m. of* सुप्त *m. f. n.* asleep.

सुप्रतिष्ठा *nom. sin. f. of* सुप्रतिष्ठ *m. f. n.* very glorious, very celebrated; (*comp. of* सु 726.*f, and* प्रतिष्ठा *f.* fame, renown.)

सुप्रीता *for* सुप्रीतास् *nom. pl. f. of* सुप्रीत *m. f. n.* well-pleased, 1*st cl.* 105, *see* 726.*f.*

सुबहून् *acc. pl. m. of* सुबहु *m. f. n.* very numerous; (*comp. of* सु 726. *f, and* बहु many, 3*d cl.* 187.)

सुबाहोः *gen. sin. of* सुबाहु *m.* Subáhu, the king of Ćedi.

सुभाषिताम् *acc. sin. f. of* सुभाषित *m. f. n.* speaking well, eloquent; (*comp. of* सु 726.*f, and* भाषित *n.* speech.)

सुभ्रूः *nom. sin. f.* having beautiful eyebrows, 125. *b.*

सुमध्यमा *nom. sin. f.* slender-waisted. *See next.*

सुमध्यमे O slender-waisted! *voc. sin. of* सुमध्यमा *f.* a woman with a beautiful or slender waist; (*from* सु good, 726.*f, and* मध्यम the middle;) 1*st cl.* 105.

सुमहत् *acc. sin. n. of* सुमहत् *m. f. n.* very

great, very important; (*comp. of* सु very, 726.*f, and* महत् great, 142.)

सुमहद्द् *for* सुमहत् *nom. sin. n.* very great.

सुमहांश् *for* सुमहान् *nom. sin. m. of* सुमहत् very great; (*comp. of* सु 726.*f, and* महत् *q. v.*)

सुमहाकक्षं the very great gate, the large court-yard, KARM. OR DES. COMP. 755; सु very, 726.*f*, महा *for* महत् great, 778, कक्षं *acc. sin. of* कक्ष *m.* a gate, an enclosure.

सुमहान् *nom. sin. m. of* सुमहत् *m. f. n.* very large, very great.

सुमहामनाः *nom. sin. m.* very high-minded; (*comp. of* सु 726.*f, and* महामनस् *q. v.*)

सुमृष्टपुष्पाढ्या BAH. OR REL. COMP. 767; सु well, 726. *f*, मृष्ट clean, bright, washed, पुष्प *cr.* a flower, आढ्या *for* आढ्यास् *nom. pl. m. of* आढ्य abounding, filled with.

सुर *m.* a god, an inhabitant of heaven, 1*st cl.* 103.

सुरक्षितं *nom. sin. n. of* सुरक्षित *m. f. n.* well-guarded; (*comp. of* सु well, 726.*f, and* रक्षित *past p. p. of rt* रक्ष् 538.)

सुरक्षितः *nom. sin. m.* well-preserved.

सुरक्षितानि *acc. pl. n. of* सुरक्षित *m. f. n.* well-guarded.

सुरभिस्रग्धराः COMPLEX COMP. 770; सुरभि *cr.* fragrant, स्रग् *for* स्रज् *cr.* a garland (43. *d*), धराः *nom. pl. of* धर *m. f. n.* wearing, bearing, holding, 1*st cl.* 103.

सुरसत्तमैः TAT. OR DEP. COMP. 743; सुर *cr.* a god, सत्तमैः *ins. pl. of* सत्तम best, 1*st cl.* 103, *see* 191.

सुरसुतोपमौ ANOM. COMP. 777; सुर *cr.* a god, सुत *cr.* a child, a son, उपमौ *acc. du. m. of* उपम *m. f. n.* like, resembling.

सुराः *nom. pl. of* सुर *m.* a god.

सुराङ्गना *nom. sin. f.* a celestial nymph, a divine female; (*comp. of* सुर *cr.* a god, *and* अङ्गना *f.* a woman.)

सुराणां *gen. pl. of* सुर *m.* a god, a deity.

सुरोत्तमाः O best of the gods! TAT. OR DEP. COMP. 743. *b*; सुर *cr.* a god, उत्तमाः *voc. pl. m. of* उत्तम *m. f. n.* best, 1*st cl.* 103.

सुरोत्तमान् *acc. pl. m.* best of the gods.

सुलोचनां *acc. sin. f. of* सुलोचन *m. f. n.* having beautiful eyes, fine-eyed, 726.*f*.

सुवर्चसं *acc. sin. m. of* सुवर्चस् *m. f. n.* very bright, very glorious; (*comp. of* सु *ind.* very, *and* वर्चस् *n.* light, glory, 7*th cl.* 164. *a.*)

सुवर्णस्य *gen. sin. of* सुवर्ण *n.* gold, 1*st cl.* 104.

सुविपुलां *acc. sin. f. of* सुविपुल *m. f. n.* very great; (*from* सु very, 726.*f, and* विपुल.)

सुविहिता *nom. sin. f. of* सुविहित *m. f. n.* well-supplied; (*comp. of* सु 726.*f, and* विहित furnished, fixed.)

सुविहितैः *ins. pl. of* सुविहित *m. f. n.* well-appointed, well-furnished, well-arranged.

सुशान्ततोयां BAH. OR REL. COMP. 767; सुशान्त *cr.* very placid, very calm, 726.*f*, तोयां *acc. sin. f. from* तोय *n.* water.

सुशीतलं *acc. sin. n.* very cool; (*comp. of* सु 726.*f, and* शीतल *m. f. n.* cool.)

सुश्रोणि *voc. sin. of* सुश्रोणी *f.* a woman who has beautiful hips; (*from* सु 726.*f, and* श्रोणी a hip; 'O slender-waisted one!')

सुश्रोणी *nom. sin. f.* having beautiful swelling hips or loins.

सुश्लक्ष्णाः *nom. pl. m. of* सुश्लक्ष्ण *m. f. n.* very smooth, 1*st cl.* 103, *see* 726.*f*.

सुष्वाप he slept; 3*d sin. perf. of rt* स्वप् 655.

सुसंरब्धस् *nom. sin. m.* greatly enraged or incensed; (*comp. of* सु 726.*f, and* संरब्ध *q. v.*)

सुसदृशं *nom. sin. n. of* सुसदृश *m. f. n.* very like; (*comp. of* सु 726.*f, and* सदृश like; *governing genitive case, see* 827. *b.*)

सुसमाहितः *nom. sin. of* सुसमाहित *m. f. n.* very intent, *i. e.* having the mind anxiously fixed on an object; (*comp. of* सु *ind.* very, *and* समाहित *past p. p. of rt* धा *with* आ *and* सम्, 533. *a.*)

सुसिद्धार्थो *for* सुसिद्धार्थस् *nom. sin. m.* one whose object is completely effected; (*from* सु well, 726.*f*, सिद्ध *cr.* accomplished, अर्थ object, 767.) *In* Book XXIV. 51, 'completely supplied with.'

सुस्निग्धगम्भीरां very soft and deep-toned; सुस्निग्ध *cr.* very soft, very kind, 726.*f*, गम्भीरां *acc. sin. f. of* गम्भीर *m. f. n.* deep, deep-toned.

सुस्वरम् *ind.* in a loud, sonorous voice; (*comp. of* सु 726.*f*, *and* स्वर voice, 713.)

सुहृच्छोकविवर्धनः TAT. OR DEP. COMP. 745; सुहृच् *for* सुहृद् (49) *cr.* a friend, छोक *for* शोक (49) *cr.* grief, विवर्धनः *nom. sin. m. of* विवर्धन *m. f. n.* making great, augmenting, making to increase, 582. *c.*

सुहृत्त्यागं TAT. OR DEP. COMP. 743; सुहृत् *cr.* a friend, त्यागं *acc. sin. of* त्याग *m.* desertion.

सुहृत्स्वजनवाक्यानि COMPLEX COMP. 770; सुहृत् *for* सुहृद् (46) *cr.* a friend, स्वजन *cr.* kindred, वाक्यानि *nom. pl. of* वाक्य *n.* a word, 1*st cl.* 104.

सुहृदः *acc. pl. of* सुहृद् *m.* a friend, 138.

सुहृदश् *acc. pl. of* सुहृद् *m.* a friend.

सुहृदां *gen. pl. of* सुहृद् *m.* a friend, 138.

सुहृद्वाक्यम् TAT. OR DEP. COMP. 743; सुहृद् *cr.* a friend, वाक्यम् *acc. sin. of* वाक्य *n.* a speech, a word, 1*st cl.* 104.

सूचितः *nom. sin. of* सूचित *m. f. n.* revealed; indicated; *past p. p. of rt* सूच् 538.

सूचिता *nom. sin. f. of* सूचित *m. f. n.* indicated, revealed.

सूत *for* सूतस् *nom. sin. of* सूत *m.* a charioteer. The सूत or charioteer in Hindú poetry is always one of the great officers of state, corresponding, in a manner, to the English 'Master of the Horse.'

सूत *voc. sin. m.* O charioteer!

सूतं *acc. sin. of* सूत *m.* a charioteer.

सूतत्वे *loc. sin. of* सूतत्व *n.* the business of a charioteer.

सूतपुत्रं TAT. OR DEP. COMP. 743; सूत *cr.* a charioteer, पुत्रं *acc. sin. of* पुत्र *m.* a son.

सूतस् *nom. sin. m.* a charioteer.

सूतो *for* सूतस् *nom. sin. m.* a charioteer.

सूर्यं *acc. sin. of* सूर्य *m.* the sun.

सूर्योदये *loc. sin.* at sunrise; (*from* सूर्य the sun, *and* उदय *m.* rise.)

सृत्वा having approached; *past ind. p. of rt* सृ 556.

सेनया *ins. sin. of* सेना *f.* an army, a host.

सेनयोर् *gen. du. of* सेना *f.* an army.

सेयम् *or* सेयं *for* सा इयम् *by* 32, she the same; *see* 221. *a.*

सैरन्ध्री *or* सैरिन्ध्री *nom. sin. f.* a handmaiden, attendant, workwoman, needlewoman.

सैरन्ध्रीं *acc. sin. of* सैरन्ध्री *f.* a handmaiden.

सैवं *for* सा एवं *by* 33.

सोचिता *for* सा उचिता *q. q. v. v.*

सोढुम् to bear, to endure; *inf. of rt* सह् 459.

सोमपो *for* सोमपस् *nom. sin. of* सोमप *m.* one who drinks the juice of the Soma-plant or *Asclepias acida* (at a sacrifice). The offering and drinking the juice of this plant was an important part of all Vedic sacrifices. Professor H. H. Wilson (Introduction to the Ṛig-veda, p. xxxvi) says, 'The great importance attached to the juice of this plant is a singular part of the ancient Hindú ritual. Almost the whole of the Sáma-veda is devoted to its eulogy, and this is no doubt little more than a repetition of the Soma-maṇḍala of the Ṛić. The only explanation of which it is susceptible is the delight which the discovery of the exhilarating properties of the fermented juice of the plant must have excited in simple minds on first becoming acquainted with its effects.' The veneration of the Soma-plant does not appear to have been connected with any worship of the moon or planets, which are not, like the sun, objects of special adoration in the Veda. The Soma is mentioned in the following passages of Manu: III. 85, 158, 180, 197, 257; V. 96; VII. 7; IX. 129; X. 88; XI. 7, 12. All the ancestors of the Bráhmans are *Soma-pas* 'moon-plant drinkers.'

सौदामिनी *f.* a name of lightning, *1st cl.* 106. *See note under* **विद्युत्.**

सौभाग्येन *ins. sin. of* **सौभाग्य** *n.* good fortune, *1st cl.* 104.

सौहार्दं *nom. sin. n.* friendship.

सौहृदेन *ins. sin. of* **सौहृद** *n.* affection, love, *1st cl.* 104.

सौहृदेनावकृष्यते *for* **सौहृदेन अवकृष्यते** *by* 31.

स्कन्धदेशे on the shoulders, TAT. OR DEP. COMP. 743; **स्कन्ध** *cr.* the shoulder, *and* **देशे** *loc. sin. of* **देश** *m.* region, part.

स्तब्धलोचनान् BAH. OR REL. COMP. 766; **स्तब्ध** *cr.* rigid, motionless, **लोचनान्** *acc. pl. m. from* **लोचन** *n.* an eye, *1st cl.* 108. The gods are supposed by the Hindús to be exempt from the necessity of winking their eyes. Hence a deity is called *Animisha* 'one whose eyes do not twinkle.' There are other marks which distinguish divine from mortal bodies. They cast no shadow, they are exempt from perspiration, they remain unsoiled by dust, they float on the earth without touching it, and the garlands they wear stand erect, the flowers remaining unwithered.

स्त्रियं *acc. sin. of* **स्त्री** *f.* a woman, 123. *b.*

स्त्री *f.* a woman, a female, 123. *b.*

स्त्रीमन्त्रं TAT. OR DEP. COMP. 743; **स्त्री** *cr.* a woman, **मन्त्रं** *acc. sin. of* **मन्त्र** *m.* counsel, plot, stratagem.

स्त्रीषु *loc. pl. of* **स्त्री** *f.* a woman.

स्त्रीस्वभावश् TAT. OR DEP. COMP. 743; **स्त्री** *cr.* a woman, **स्वभावश्** *nom. sin. m.* nature, disposition.

स्थ (*at the end of compounds*) *denotes* staying, abiding, being, existing; (*agt. of rt* **स्था**, *see* 580.)

स्थविरेभ्यः *abl. pl. m. of* **स्थविर** *m. f. n.* old, an elder, *1st cl.* 187.

स्थविरैर् *for* **स्थविरैस्** *ins. pl. m. of* **स्थविर** *m. f. n.* old, *1st cl.* 103.

स्थाणुर् *for* **स्थाणुस्** *nom. sin. m. of* **स्थाणु** *m. f. n.* steadfast, firm.

स्थापयामास he placed, he fixed; *3d sin. perf. of rt* **स्था** *in caus.*

स्थापयित्वा having made to stand, having drawn up (as a chariot); *past ind. p. of rt* **स्था** *in caus.*

स्थावर *for* **स्थावरस्** *nom. sin. m.* a fixed or immovable object.

स्थितं *acc. sin. m. or n. of* **स्थित** *m. f. n.* standing; *past p. p. of rt* **स्था** 533, 587, 896. *a.*

स्थिता *nom. sin. f. of* **स्थित** *m. f. n.* standing.

स्थितां *acc. sin. f. of* **स्थित** *m. f. n.* standing, 896. *a.*

स्थिताः *nom. pl. f. of* **स्थित** *m. f. n.* standing.

स्थितान् *acc. pl. of* **स्थित** *m. f. n.* standing; *past p. p. of rt* **स्था** 533, *see also* 896. *a.*

स्थितिं *acc. sin. of* **स्थिति** *f.* steadfastness.

स्थित्या *ins. sin. of* **स्थिति** *f.* constancy, *2d cl.* 112.

स्नुषां *acc. sin. of* **स्नुषा** *f.* a daughter-in-law, *1st cl.* 105.

स्पृशेयं I may touch, let me touch; *1st sin. pot. of rt* **स्पृश्** *6th cl.*

स्पृष्टस् *nom. sin. m. of* **स्पृष्ट** *m. f. n.* touched or influenced by; *past p. p. of rt* **स्पृश्** 539.

स्फीतो *for* **स्फीतस्** *nom. sin. m. of* **स्फीत** *m. f. n.* great, bulky; (*in* Book XXIV. 37 *it may mean* in all its fulness, in all its integrity.)

स्म *ind. A redundant particle which often gives a past signification to the present tense.*

स्म *for* **स्मस्** we are; *1st pl. pres. of rt* **अस्** 584. *In* **स्मेह** *the dropping of* **स्** *is a violation of the rules of Sandhi, and a poetic license peculiar to the Mahá-bhárata.*

स्मयन् *nom. sin. m. of* **स्मयत्** *m. f. n.* smiling; *pres. p. of rt* **स्मि** 524.

स्मयमानं *acc. sin. of* **स्मयमान** *m. f. n.* smiling; *pres. p. átm. of rt* **स्मि** 526, 591.

स्मरंस् *for* **स्मरन्** (53) calling to mind, recollecting; *pres. p. of rt* **स्मृ** 524.

स्मरन्ती *nom. sin. f. of* **स्मरत्** *m. f. n.* calling to mind, thinking of; *pres. p. of rt* **स्मृ** 524.

स्मरन्त्या *for* **स्मरन्त्यास्** *gen. sin. f. of* **स्मरत्** *m. f. n.* remembering.

स्मरामि I remember, I call to mind; *1st sin. pres. of rt* **स्मृ** *1st cl.* 594.

स्मराम्यशुभं *for* **स्मरामि अशुभं** *by* 34.

स्मर्तुम् to call to mind, to remember; *inf. of rt* **स्मृ** 459.

स्मितपूर्वा smiling first, ANOM. COMP. 777; **स्मित** *cr.* smiling, 896. *a*, **पूर्वा** *nom. sin. f. of* **पूर्व** *m. f. n.* first, before, *1st cl.* 103.

स्मितपूर्वाभिभाषिणी *for* **स्मितपूर्वा अभिभाषिणी** *by* 31.

स्मेत्यथाब्रुवन् *for* **स्म इति अथ अब्रुवन्** *by* 32, 34, 31. *The* **स्** *of* **स्मस्** *is irregularly dropped. See* **स्म**.

स्मेह *for* **स्म इह** *by* 32. *See* **स्म**.

स्यन्दतां *gen. pl. of* **स्यन्दत्** *m. f. n.* moving on, rushing on; *pres. p. par. of rt* **स्यन्द्** 524.

स्यन्दनं *acc. sin. of* **स्यन्दन** *m.* a chariot, *1st cl.* 103.

स्यन्दनैश् *ins. pl. of* **स्यन्दन** *m.* the Syandana, a kind of tree (*Dalbergia Ougeinensis*), *1st cl.* 103.

स्याज् *for* **स्यात्** he or it may be; *3d sin. pot. of* **अस्** 48.

स्याद् he or it may be; *3d sin. pot. of rt* **अस्**.

स्यान् *for* **स्यात्** he or it may be; *3d sin. pot. of rt* **अस्**.

स्याम we may be; *1st pl. pot. of rt* **अस्**.

स्रंसते it falls, it slips; *3d sin. pres. of rt* **स्रंस्** *1st cl.*

स्रजं *acc. sin. of* **स्रज्** *f.* a garland.

स्रजश् *acc. pl. of* **स्रज्** *f.* a garland, *8th cl.* 176.

स्रजश्चोत्तमगन्धाढ्याः *for* **स्रजश् च उत्तमगन्धाढ्याः**, *q. q. v. v.*

स्रजस् *acc. pl. of* **स्रज्** *f.* a garland.

स्व *m. f. n.* own, his own, her own, my own, &c., 232. *b.*

स्वं *acc. sin. m. or n. of* **स्व** *m. f. n.* own, 232. *b.*

स्वकं *acc. sin. m. n. of* **स्वक** *m. f. n.* own, one's own, his own, (*same as* **स्व** 232. *b.*)

स्वकां *acc. sin. f. of* **स्वक** *m. f. n.* own.

स्वकान् *acc. pl. m. of* **स्वक** *m. f. n.* own, *for* **स्व** 232. *b.*

स्वगृहे *loc. sin. n.* in (one's) own house; (*comp. of* **स्व** 232. *b, and* **गृह** *n.* a house.)

स्वजनं *acc. sin. of* **स्वजन** *m.* own kindred, own people.

स्वजनाच् *for* **स्वजनात्** (48) *abl. sin. of* **स्वजन** *m.* a kinsman; (*comp. of* **स्व** own, *and* **जन** man, *q. v.*)

स्वजनावृतः *nom. sin. m.* accompanied by his own people; (*comp. of* **स्वजन** own people, kindred, **आवृत** surrounded, attended, 740.)

स्वञ्चैव *for* **स्वं च एव** *by* 60 *and* 33.

स्वधर्मं *acc. sin. m.* own duty; (*from* **स्व** 232. *b, and* **धर्म** duty.)

स्वधर्माचरणेषु in (your) own duties and actions; in the practising of (your) own duties; (*comp. of* **स्वधर्म** *cr.* own duty, **आचरणेषु** *loc. pl. of* **आचरण** *n.* conduct.)

स्वधीता *for* **स्वधीतास्** *nom. pl. of* **स्वधीत** well read; (*comp. of* **सु** 726. *f, and* **अधीत** 311.)

स्वनः *nom. sin. m.* sound.

स्वपामि I sleep; *1st sin. pres. of rt* **स्वप्**. *This root is properly conjugated like* **रुद्** *2d cl.* 322. *a, making its present* **स्वपिमि**, **स्वपिषि**, &c., *see* 655.

स्वपुरं *acc. sin. n.* to his own city; (*comp. of* **स्व** own, 232. *b, and* **पुर** *n.* a city.)

स्वप्नो *for* **स्वप्नस्** *nom. sin. of* **स्वप्न** *m.* a dream.

स्वबान्धवान् *acc. pl. m.* (our) own relations; (**स्व** own, *and* **बान्धव** a relative.)

स्वयं *ind.* self, himself, she herself, I myself; of one's own accord, of one's self.

स्वयंवर *m.* the public choice of a husband by a princess from a number of suitors assembled for the purpose; (*comp. of* **स्वयं** of one's self, 713. *b*, *and* **वर** selecting.) In former times the princesses of India appear to have enjoyed this singular privilege. In Manu, Book III, ver. 27 &c., eight different forms of marriage are mentioned, but the **स्वयंवर** is not one of them. In the 9th Book, ver. 9, there is an allusion to it, but it is doubtful whether this has reference to any but the commercial and servile classes. 'Three years let a damsel wait though she be marriageable. After that time let *her choose for herself* a bridegroom of equal rank.' In Kálidása's celebrated poem, called Raghu-vanśa, there is a beautiful description of the Svayamvara of Indumatí, sister of the king of Vidarbha, in which she chooses Aja, the son of Raghu, out of a large assemblage of royal suitors, In the Mahá-bhárata we have an account of the Svayamvara of Draupadí, the daughter of Drupada king of Pańćála, and afterwards the common wife of the five Páṇḍu princes.

स्वयंवरं *acc. sin. of* **स्वयंवर**, *q. v.*

स्वयंवरः *nom. sin. of* **स्वयंवर** a bridal ceremony in which the bride chooses her own husband.

स्वयंवरकथां Tat. or Dep. comp. 743; **स्वयंवर** *cr.* a Svayamvara, **कथां** *acc. sin. of* **कथा** *f.* talk, declaration.

स्वयंवरकृते *ind.* for the Svayamvara; (*comp. of* **स्वयंवर** *q. v., and* **कृते** for the sake of, on account of, 731, 917.)

स्वयंवरे *loc. sin. of* **स्वयंवर**, *q. v.*

स्वयंवरो *for* **स्वयंवरस्** *nom. sin. m. See* **स्वयंवर.**

स्वयम् *ind.* self, himself, herself; of one's self, of one's own accord.

स्वरूपं *acc. sin. n.* thy own form; (*comp. of* **स्व** own, 232. *b*, *and* **रूप** form.)

स्वरूपधारिणं *acc. sin. m.* having his own form; (*comp. of* **स्व** *cr.* own, **रूप** *cr.* form, *and* **धारिन्** possessing, *6th cl.* 159.)

स्वरूपिणं *acc. sin. m.* having his own form; (*from* **स्व** own, 232. *b*, *and* **रूपिन्** possessed of form, 159.)

स्वर्गं *acc. sin. of* **स्वर्ग** *m.* heaven.

स्वर्गमार्गदिदृक्षुभिः Tat. or Dep. comp. 745; **स्वर्ग** *cr.* heaven, **मार्ग** *cr.* road, **दिदृक्षुभिः** *ins. pl. of* **दिदृक्षु** *m. f. n.* desirous of seeing, *from rt* **दृश्** *in des.* 82. VII, 502. *a*, 604.

स्वलङ्कृतः *nom. sin. m.* well adorned; (*comp. of* **सु** 726. *f*, *and* **अलङ्कृत** adorned, 787. *a.*)

स्वलङ्कृताः *nom. pl. m.* well adorned. *See last.*

स्वलङ्कृतैः *ins. pl. n. of* **स्वलङ्कृत** *m. f. n.* beautifully adorned; (*comp. of* **सु** well, 726. *f*, 34, *and* **अलङ्कृत** *past p. p. of rt* **कृ** *with* **अलं**, 787. *a.*)

स्वल्पं *acc. sin. m. of* **स्वल्प** *m. f. n.* very little; (*comp. of* **सु** very, 726. *f*, 34, *and* **अल्प** small.)

स्वसितायतलोचना having beautiful black and long eyes, Complex comp. 771; **सु** *ind.* very, 726. *f*, **असित** *cr.* black, **आयत** *cr.* long or large, **लोचना** *nom. sin. f. from* **लोचन** *n.* the eye.

स्वसुतौ *acc. du. m.* his own children; (*comp. of* **स्व** own, 232. *b*, *and* **सुत** *m.* a child, 103.)

स्वस्ति *ind.* welfare, benediction.

स्वस्थ *m. f. n.* in health, *lit.* self-staying; (*from* **स्व** one's own, 232. *b*, **स्थ** staying, 580. *b*;) **न स्वस्था बभूव** she was not *herself*.

स्वस्था *nom. sin. f. of* **स्वस्थ** in health.

स्वां *acc. sin. f. of* **स्व** *m. f. n.* own.

स्वागतं *nom. sin. n.* salutation, welcome; (*from* **सु** well, 726. *f*, *and* **आगत** *m. f. n.* come.)

स्वानि *acc. pl. n. of* **स्व** *m. f. n.* own, 232. *b*.

स्वामिन् *voc. sin. of* स्वामिन् *m.* a master, *6th cl.* 159.

स्वार्थम् own cause, (my) own cause; *acc. sin. of* स्वार्थ *m., 1st cl.* 103; (*comp. of* स्व own, 232. *b, and* अर्थ an object.)

स्वेन *ins. sin. of* स्व own, 232. *b.*

स्वैर् *for* स्वैस् *ins. pl. m. of* स्व own.

स्वैरवृत्ता *nom. sin. f.* following her own inclinations; (*from* स्वैर self-willed, *and* वृत्त practice.)

स्वैरेषु *loc. pl. n. of* स्वैर *m. f. n.* free, unrestrained.

स्वोरसि *loc. sin. n.* on (his or her) own breast; (*comp. of* स्व own, 232. *b, and* उरस् *n.* breast, 164.)

ह.

ह *ind.* indeed, *an expletive.*

हंस *m.* a kind of wild goose of a white colour with golden wings, something between a swan and a flamingo. It must be a graceful bird, as the bearing, gait, and even voice of a beautiful woman is often compared by Hindú poets to that of a hansa. It serves the god Brahmá as a vehicle, and hence the hansa-náda or cry of this bird has a sacred character, just as the cry of the swan with the Greeks.

हंसं *acc. sin. of* हंस *m.* a swan.

हंसस्य *gen. sin. of* हंस *m.* a swan.

हंसा *for* हंसास् *nom. pl. of* हंस *m.* a swan.

हंसाः *for* हंसास् *nom. pl. of* हंस *m.* a swan, goose.

हंसान् *acc. pl. of* हंस *m.* a swan.

हंसानां *gen. pl. of* हंस *m.* a swan.

हंसेन *ins. sin. of* हंस *m.* a swan.

हंसैः *ins. pl. of* हंस *m.* a swan.

हतं *acc. sin. m. of* हत *m. f. n.* killed, slain.

हतकराटकं Bah. or Rel. comp. 767; हत *cr.* destroyed, removed, कराटकं *nom. sin. n. from* कराटक *m.* a thorn, a foe, 108.

हतशिष्टजनास् *nom. pl.* the men left or remaining out of the slain.

हतशिष्टा *for* हतशिष्टास् *nom. pl. m.* those left or remaining out of the slain; (*comp. of* हत *cr.* killed, *and* शिष्ट left, remained.)

हतशिष्टैः *ins. pl. m. of* हतशिष्ट left or remaining out of the slain.

हतशेषैः *ins. pl. m. of* हतशेष left or remaining out of the killed, escaped; (*comp. of* हत *cr.* killed, *and* शेष remainder.)

हता *nom. sin. f. of* हत *m. f. n.* killed, slain; *past p. p. of rt* हन् 545: हतास्मि I am lost, I am undone.

हता *for* हतास् *nom. pl. of* हत *m. f. n.* killed.

हतो *for* हतस् *nom. sin. m. of* हत *m. f. n.* killed, slain.

हत्वा having slain; *past ind. p. of rt* हन्.

हन्तव्यो *for* हन्तव्यस् *nom. sin. of* हन्तव्य *m. f. n.* to be killed; *fut. pass. p. of rt* हन् 654.

हन्ता *nom. sin. m. of* हन्तृ *m.* a killer, *4th cl.* 127.

हन्ति he or it kills; *3d sin. pres. of rt* हन् to kill, *2d cl.*

हन्तुं to slay; *inf. of rt* हन्.

हन्यते he or it is killed; *3d sin. pres. of rt* हन् to kill, *in pass.*

हन्यात् let him slay, he may kill; *3d sin. pot. of rt* हन् 654.

हन्याम we would kill; *1st pl. pot. of rt* हन् *2d cl.*

हन्युस् they should slay; *3d pl. pot. of rt* हन् *2d cl.*

हयकोविद *voc. sin. m.* O skilled in horses! (*comp. of* हय *cr.* horses, *and* कोविद skilful.)

हयज्ञताम् *acc. sin. of* हयज्ञता *f.* knowledge of horses; (*abstract noun from* हयज्ञ skilled in horses, *see* 80. LXII.)

हयज्ञस्य *gen. sin. of* हयज्ञ *m.* one skilled in horses.

हयज्ञानं Tat. or Dep. comp. 743; हय *cr.* horses, ज्ञानं *nom. sin. n.* knowledge, skill.

हयज्ञानस्य TAT. OR DEP. COMP. 743; हय *cr.* horses, ज्ञानस्य *gen. sin. of* ज्ञान *n.* knowledge.

हयतत्त्वज्ञ TAT. OR DEP. COMP. 745; हय *cr.* a horse, तत्त्व *cr.* nature, truth, ज्ञ *voc. sin. m. of* ज्ञ a knower, 580. *b.*

हयतत्त्वज्ञः *nom. sin. m. See last.*

हयनिर्घोषम् TAT. OR DEP. COMP. 743; हय *cr.* a horse, निर्घोषम् *acc. sin. of* निर्घोष *m.* sound, noise.

हयसङ्ग्रहणं TAT. OR DEP. COMP. 743; हय *cr.* a horse, सङ्ग्रहण *n.* restraining, curbing, checking.

हयसङ्ग्रहणे *loc. sin. See last.*

हया *for* हयास् *nom. pl. of* हय *m.* a horse.

हयांस् *for* हयान् (53) *acc. pl. of* हय *m.* a horse, 1*st cl.* 103.

हयाः *nom. pl. of* हय *m.* a horse.

हयान् *acc. pl. of* हय *m.* a horse.

हयाश् *for* हयास् *nom. pl. of* हय *m.* a horse.

हयैः *ins. pl. of* हय *m.* a horse.

हयैर् *for* हयैस् *ins. pl. of* हय *m.* a horse.

हयैश् *for* हयैस् *ins. pl. of* हय *m.* a horse.

हयोत्तमाः *nom. pl. m.* best of horses; (*comp. of* हय *cr.* a horse, *and* उत्तम *m. f. n.* best, 743. *b.*)

हयोत्तमान् *acc. pl. m.* the best of horses, the noblest of horses.

हरिणीम् *acc. sin. of* हरिणी *f.* a female deer, a doe, 106.

हर्षजः *nom. sin. m.* arising from joy; (*comp. of* हर्ष joy, *and* ज produced, 580. *b.*)

हर्षविवर्धनः TAT. OR DEP. COMP. 743; हर्ष *cr.* joy, विवर्धनः *nom. sin. m. of* विवर्धन *m. f. n.* increasing, an increaser, *from rt* वृध् *with* वि, 582. *c.*

हर्षविवृद्धसत्त्वा COMPLEX COMP. 771; हर्ष joy, विवृद्ध increased, सत्त्वा *nom. sin. f. from* सत्त्व *n.* vigour, energy.

हव्यवाहनः *nom. sin. m.* fire; (*from* हव्य an oblation, *and* वाहन what carries.)

हस्त *m.* the hand, the proboscis or trunk of an elephant.

हस्तात् *abl. sin. of* हस्त *m.* the hand.

हस्ताभ्याम् *ins. du. of* हस्त *m.* the hand.

हस्तिभिः *ins. pl. of* हस्तिन् *m.* an elephant.

हस्तियूथं TAT. OR DEP. COMP. 743; हस्ति *for* हस्तिन् (57) *cr.* an elephant, यूथम् *nom. sin. n.* a herd. The mischief caused by the trampling of rushing elephants is a frequent subject of description in Hindú poetry; compare the end of Act I of the S'akuntalá and Book V. 43–49 of the Raghu-vanśa.

हस्तियूथेन *ins. sin. n. See last.*

हस्तिहस्तपरामृष्टां TAT. OR DEP. COMP. 745; हस्ति *for* हस्तिन् (57) *cr.* an elephant, हस्त *cr.* the trunk of an elephant, परामृष्टां *acc. sin. f. of* परामृष्ट *m. f. n.* touched, struck, ruffled, chafed.

हस्त्यश्वरथघोषेण COMPLEX COMP. 770; हस्त्य् (*by* 34) *for* हस्ति (*by* 57. *b*) *for* हस्तिन् *cr.* an elephant, अश्व *cr.* a horse, रथ *cr.* a chariot, घोषेण *ins. sin. of* घोष *m.* noise, rattle, roar, 1*st cl.* 103.

हस्त्यश्वरथसङ्कुलम् COMPLEX COMP. 771; हस्ति *cr.* elephants (34), अश्व *cr.* horses, रथ *cr.* chariots, सङ्कुलम् *acc. sin. m. of* सङ्कुल *m. f. n.* crowded, filled, choked up.

हा *interj.* Alas! Ah! Oh! 732.

हाहाकारम् *acc. sin. of* हाहाकार *m.* lamentation, cries for help; (*comp. of* हाहा interjection of pain, *and* कार making.)

हाहाभूतम् *nom. sin. n. of* हाहाभूत *m. f. n.* making lamentations; (*comp. of* हाहा Alas! *and* भूत become, being.)

हि *ind.* for, because, 727. *d.*

हितं *acc. sin. n. of* हित *m. f. n.* beneficial, for the good of, 1*st cl.* 103.

हितां *acc. sin. f. of* हित *m. f. n.* friendly, salutary, 1*st cl.* 104.

हित्वा having abandoned; *past ind. p. of rt* हा 557.

हिरण्यस्य *gen. sin. of* हिरण्य *n.* gold, bullion, plate, *1st cl.* 104.

हीनं *acc. sin. m. of* हीन *m. f. n.* deprived of; *governing instrumental case*, 825.

हीनां *acc. sin. f. of* हीन *m. f. n.* deprived of, separated from.

हीनैः *ins. pl. n. of* हीन *m. f. n.* bad, inferior.

हीनो *for* हीनस् *nom. sin. n.* *See* हीनां.

हुताशं *acc. sin. of* हुताश *m.* a name of the god Agni or fire, (*lit.* eater of the burnt-offering.)

हुताशनं *acc. sin. of* हुताशन *m.* fire. *See next.*

हुताशनः *nom. sin. of* हुताशन Hutáśana, a form of the god of fire; (*comp. of* हुत a burnt-offering, *and* अशनः *nom. sin.* eater, 743.)

हृच्छयं *acc. sin. of* हृच्छय *m.* love.

हृच्छयः *nom. sin. of* हृच्छय *m.* love, *1st cl.* 103; (*comp. of* हृद् the heart, *and* शय who lies or reclines, *see* 49.)

हृच्छयपीडिताः TAT. OR DEP. COMP. 740; हृच्छय *cr.* love, पीडिताः *nom. pl. m. of* पीडित *m. f. n.* tormented, suffering pain, *1st cl.* 103.

हृच्छयवर्धन TAT. OR DEP. COMP. 743; हृच्छय *cr.* love, वर्धन *voc. sin. m. of* वर्धन *m. f. n.* increaser, *1st cl.* 103.

हृच्छयाविष्टचेतना COMPLEX COMP. 771; हृच्छय *cr.* love, passion, आविष्ट *cr.* affected by, penetrated by, चेतना *nom. sin. f. of* चेतना *f.* the heart, *1st cl.* 108.

हृतं *nom. sin. n. of* हृत *m. f. n.* taken, carried away; *past p. p. of rt* हृ, 539, 593.

हृतद्रव्यं BAH. OR REL. COMP. 766; हृत *cr.* taken away, robbed, द्रव्यं *acc. sin. m. from* द्रव्य *n.* property, 108.

हृतराज्यं *acc. sin. m. of* हृतराज्य *m. f. n.* deprived of his kingdom, BAH. OR REL. COMP. 766; हृत *cr.* taken, राज्यं *acc. sin. m. from* राज्य *n.* kingdom, *1st cl.* 108.

हृतराज्ये *loc. sin. m. or n.* *See last.*

हृतराज्यो *for* हृतराज्यस् *nom. sin. m.* *See* हृतराज्यं.

हृतवाससः BAH. OR REL. COMP. 767; हृत *cr.* taken away, carried off, वाससः *gen. sin. m. from* वासस् *n.* dress, 164. *a.*

हृतसर्वस्वम् BAH. OR REL. COMP. 761; हृत *cr.* deprived of, robbed of, सर्वे *cr.* all, स्वं *acc. sin. of* स्व *n.* own property, *1st cl.* 104.

हृतां *acc. sin. f. of* हृत *m. f. n.* seized, taken, overcome.

हृद् *n.* the heart, the mind, *5th cl.* 139.

हृदयं *nom. or acc. sin. of* हृदय *n.* the heart; knowledge.

हृदयस्य *gen. sin. of* हृदय *n.* the heart.

हृदये *loc. sin. of* हृदय *n.* the heart.

हृदयेन *ins. sin. of* हृदय *n.* the heart.

हृदा *ins. sin. of* हृद् *n.* the heart, the mind.

हृदि *loc. sin. of* हृद् *n.* the heart, *5th cl.* 139.

हृद्यं *acc. sin. m. of* हृद्य *m. f. n.* pleasant, agreeable, captivating the heart.

हृद्याः *nom. pl. m. of* हृद्य *m. f. n.* pleasant, agreeable.

हृषितस्रग्रजोहीनान् COMPLEX COMP., *see* 771. *a*; हृषित *cr.* standing erect, not drooping, स्रज् *for* स्रग् (*by* 43. *d*) *cr.* a garland, रजो *for* रजस् (*by* 64) *cr.* dust, हीनान् *acc. pl. m. of* हीन *m. f. n.* free from, *past p. p. of rt* हा 533. *b.*

हृषितानि *nom. sin. n. of* हृषित *m. f. n.* erect and fresh looking (applied to flowers just gathered).

हृष्टः *nom. sin. m. of* हृष्ट *m. f. n.* rejoiced.

हृष्टसङ्कल्पौ BAH. OR REL. COMP. 767; हृष्ट *cr.* pleased, rejoiced, सङ्कल्पौ *nom. du. m. of* सङ्कल्प *m.* mind, soul.

हृष्टा *nom. sin. f. of* हृष्ट *m. f. n.* joyful, pleased.

हृष्टा *for* हृष्टास् *nom. pl. m. of* हृष्ट *m. f. n.* rejoiced, joyful; *past p. p. of rt* हृष् 539.

हृष्टे *loc. sin. of* हृष्ट *m. f. n.* rejoiced, pleased.

हृष्ट्वा being delighted; *ind. p. of rt* हृष् to be pleased, 556.

हेति *for* हा इति *by* 32.

हेतुभिर् *ins. pl. of* हेतुः *m.* a cause, a reason, an argument.

हेतोः *ind.* for the sake of; *governing genitive case or preceded by the crude stem.*

ह्यदेवं *for* हि अदेवं *by* 34.

ह्यनुरक्तैव *for* हि अनुरक्ता एव *by* 34 *and* 33.

ह्यन्नपानपरिच्छदां *for* हि अन्नपा° *by* 34.

ह्युन्मत्तदर्शना *for* हि उन्मत्तदर्शना *by* 34.

ह्रदिनीं *acc. sin. of* ह्रदिनी *f.* a river (either as feeding a lake (ह्रद) or flowing out of one.)

ह्रदे *loc. sin. of* ह्रद *m.* a lake, 1*st cl.* 103.

ह्रस्वं *acc. sin. m. of* ह्रस्व *m. f. n.* low (as a doorway, passage), short, dwarfish.

ह्रस्वबाहुकः BAH. OR REL. COMP. 766; ह्रस्व *cr.* short, बाहुकः *nom. sin. m.* an arm; (*from* बाहु *with* क *added,* 80. LVI.)

ह्रीता *nom. sin. f. of* ह्रीत *m. f. n.* ashamed.